The Blackwell Encyclopedia of Sociology

P9-CNB-968

11 D0004915

Volume XI

Index

Edited by

George Ritzer

Blackwell
Publishing

© 2007 by Blackwell Publishing Ltd

BLACKWELL PUBLISHING
350 Main Street, Malden, MA 02148-5020, USA
9600 Garsington Road, Oxford OX4 2DQ, UK
550 Swanston Street, Carlton, Victoria 3053, Australia

First published 2007 by Blackwell Publishing Ltd

1   2007

Library of Congress Cataloging-in-Publication Data

Blackwell encyclopedia of sociology, the / edited by George Ritzer.
  p. cm.
Includes bibliographical references and index.
ISBN 1-4051-2433-4 (hardback : alk. paper) 1. Sociology—Encyclopedias. I. Ritzer, George.

HM425.B53 2007
301.03—dc22

2006004167

ISBN-13: 978-1-4051-2433-1 (hardback : alk. paper)

A catalogue record for this title is available from the British Library.

Set in 9.5/11pt Ehrhardt
by Spi Publisher Services, Pondicherry, India
Printed in Singapore
by COS Printers Pte Ltd

For further information on
Blackwell Publishing, visit our website:
www.blackwellpublishing.com

Contents

About the Editor and Managing Editors   vii

Advisory Editors   ix

Contributors   xv

Acknowledgments   lxi

Introduction   lxiii

Timeline   lxxi

Lexicon   xciii

Volume I: A–B   1

Volume II: C   383

Volume III: D–E   967

Volume IV: F–HE   1553

Volume V: HE–LE   2067

Volume VI: LE–M   2583

Volume VII: N–P   3141

Volume VIII: Q–SE   3725

Volume IX: SE–ST   4233

Volume X: ST–Z   4773

Select Bibliography   5319

Selected Websites   5331

Index   5333

Index

Entries in bold indicate a main section on a particular subject in the text.
Page spans for Volumes 1–10 are indicated by footnotes.

Abbott, A. 445–8, 2077, 3121, 3249, 3661, 3663
Abbott, E. 444
Abbott, G. 131
Abdinsky, H. 1233
Abegglen, J. C. 2436
Abelard, Peter 598, 1087
Abels, G. 1488–91, 1906–9
Abercrombie, N. 1638
Abernathy, W. J. 2740
Ablett, P. 406–7
abolitionism 1–2, 3744
  death penalty 1, 976–7
  and feminism 2618
  slavery 1, 2618
Aborigines
  biosociological theories 3186
  cultural tourism 921
  religion 3633
  self-identification 1457
  and symbolic classification 4906–7
abortion as a social problem 3–4, 558, 1610–11, 3206
  among teenagers 1728
  anti-abortion agendas 1984
  conservatism and 680
  criminalization 1610, 1611
  and disability 1907, 3206
  Ellis and 1365
  and eugenics 1489, 1490
  and euthanasia 1497
  and family sociology 1617
  and fertility control 1609, 2707
  late-term abortion 3
  legalization 1675
  medical profession crusade against 3652–3
  parental notification laws 2620
  and partisan politics 2234
  and patriarchy, struggle against 3378
  restrictions on 1676
  sex-selective 1029, 1158, 2302, 3535
  socio-demographic trends 4

  unsafe abortion 2314
  unwanted abortion 3207
  see also pro-choice and pro-life movements
Abraham 2449
Abrahamson, E. 2715, 2721, 2729, 2730
Abrams, E. 3175
Abramson, L. Y. 2568
absence cultures 5
absenteeism 4–7, 1769, 2291, 2750
  medical models 5
  social construction of 6
  withdrawal model 4–5
absolute monarchies 680, 2623
absolute negativity 1147, 1149
absolutism 1436, 5011
absolutization of markets 2775
absorptive capacity 2478
abstract universals 1147
abstraction 1079
Abu-Lughod, L. 289, 290, 3344
abuse
  athletic abuse 4666
  see also child abuse; domestic violence
academic achievement *see* educational attainment
academic capitalism 4069
academic community 617
academic dependency 400
academic imperialism 399, 400
academy
  black women 306, 3119
  radicalization of 1121
  sexism 272, 1670
accentuation principle 76
accidents, alcohol-involved 115
accommodation 7–9
  and assimilation 8
  definition 2945
Acconci, V. 2834
accountability
  and auditing 213
  and axial civilizations 521

accountability (*cont'd*)
  and bureaucrats 379
  charter schools 4036–7
  and crime 2820
  and fieldwork research 1445–6
  health care delivery systems 2709
  medical 2246
  and regulatory trends 2929
  see also social accountability and governance
accountancy 354, 355
  new accounting history 2732
accountancy firms 1387, 2720
  capital accumulation strategies 3664
  commercialization 2665–6
  and management consultancy 2720
accounts 9–11
  empirical validity 13, 14
  restorative accounts 10–11
  and rule breaking 10
  typologies 13
accounts, deviant 12–14
acculturation 14–16
  Anglo-conformity model 137
  and assimilation 192–3
  and creolization 817
  definition 2945
  and the ethnic economy 1460
  ideational acculturation 15
  indigenous communities 340
  and language 817
  material acculturation 15
  second-language acquisition 281–2
  and tourism 1994
  see also accommodation; assimilation;
    integration
acid rain 1417
ACID Test 356
Acker, J. 1892, 1893, 1894
Ackroyd, S. 2716, 3306–7
Acquaviva, S. 3976–7
acquired immunodeficiency syndrome *see*
    AIDS, sociology of
action 16
  and agency 60–1
  Arendt on 169, 173
  Blumer on 319–20
  joint activity 320
  logical/non-logical distinction 3361
  and role-taking 319
  theory of reasoned action 200
Action for Children's Television (ACT) 695
action frame of reference 3366

action inquiry 18
action mobilization 1781
action research 16–20, 2617
  and ethics in fieldwork 1444
  formative research 17
  and gerontology 1933
  Kent and 1933
  Lewin and 2617
  methodological approaches 18
  and operations management 3270
  participatory 16
  summative research 17
action science 18
action system 1319
action-structure loops 4918–19
active entertainment 2598
active interviewing 2410
activism 577
  AIDS activism 1166, 1211
  anti-abortion activism 1490, 3093
  anti-nuclear activism 139, 1166, 1273, 1431,
    1679, 1806, 2387, 3087, 3193, 3551
  and asceticism 188
  black activism 129
  black feminist activism 124, 306–8
  class-based 781
  community media activism 626, 627,
    628, 629
  consumer activism 697, 2894
  disability activism 480, 481, 482
  and documentaries 1211–12
  ecological activism 1166, 2387
  environmental activism 1273, 1429
  Internet activism 780
  Islamic activism 781
  lesbian feminist activism 2603
  peace activism 1166
  political activism 957
  tactical repertoires of contention 779–82
  transnational activism 782
  see also civil rights activism; collective action;
    direct action; feminism, first, second, and
    third waves; social movements; and
    specific movements
activist mothering 1679, 2848
activities of daily living (ADLs) 2546
activity theory 98, 2478
actor-network theory 20–1, 21–3, 2904,
    2905, 3182–3
  and aging 1928
  and auteurism 219
  and bibliometrics 4121

central network positions 3183
and documentary analysis 1215
and economic sociology 1321
and interaction 2364
and intervention processes 3618–19
and management innovation 2740–1
and network exchange theory 3003
and network production 2905
and organizational communication 3296
PIEM four-step model 2741
and power-dependence theory 3599–600
and profit expectations 3183
and social construction of science 4096
and social science 4071–2
and sociology of scientific knowledge 219,
    2364, 4098–9
and spatial relationships 4634
and weak tie networks 2743
actor-network theory, actants
and affect control theory 35, 36, 38
and expectation states theory 1524
and impression formation 2273
and materiality 2846
social identities 2224
actor–observer difference 206–7
ACTUP (AIDS Coalition ot Unleash Power)
    1835, 1837, 4199
Acuña, R. 2549
acupuncture 631, 632, 2079, 2080
Adam, B. D. 2154–7
Adam, Kanya 162–5
Adams, C. 1289
Adams, D. 2892
Adams, G. 1797
Adams, K. 2633
Adams, M. 1202–6, 2307–10
Adams, R. 1787–8, 1795–9, 3504–7
Adams St.Pierre, E. 5296–8
adaptation 292, 1809, 3367
and deviance 1102–3
immigrant children 1270–1
see also conformity
adaptive structuration theory 3295
Addams, Jane 23–6, 273, 1145, 1941, 2618,
    2838, 3193, 3363, 4542
and cultural feminism 902
feminist sociology 1670
Hull-House studies 444, 446
pragmatism 3610, 3611
addiction and dependency 26–7
disease model 118, 1817
gambling 1111, 1817

online sexual addiction 966
see also alcoholism and alcohol abuse; drugs,
    drug abuse, and drug policy
additive bilingualism 282–3
adjacency pairs 792
Adler, F. 1694, 1857
Adler, M. 2679
Adler, Patricia A. 320, 1129, 2207–10
Adler, Peter 320, 2207–10
administrative law 2554
adolescence, adolescents
adolescent culture 1327
and crime 48
and developmental theory 1071
extra-familial relationships 1548
extracurricular activities 154–7
fertility 1725–9
friendships 1799–800
and gender identity 1547
and generational change 1901
life course perspective 2636
parenting 1603
status hierarchies 1547
see also friendships of adolescence; juvenile
    delinquency
adolescents, *see also* juvenile delinquency
adoption
adopted grandchildren 2017
awareness contexts 235
gay and lesbian parents 2608
transracial 1198, 3732
Adorno, Theodor W. 27–30
and the authoritarian personality 28, 220
and Benjamin 268
and capitalism 518, 2815, 2817
and collective action 577
and consumption 741
cultural critique 610, 1754, 2648, 2881
culture industry thesis 416, 942,
    944, 2824
and the Frankfurt School 865, 874, 875, 897,
    1569, 2881
and Hegelian dialectics 1149
and Horkheimer 2163, 2164, 2165
and jazz 913, 2124
and mass culture 2822, 2824, 2882, 3482
negative dialectics 2815
neo-Marxism 869, 1638
and radio sociology 3780
and sport 2235, 2236
adrenaline response 1866, 1867
adultery *see* infidelity and marital affairs

adulthood
  and developmental theory 1071
  transitions to 2636
advance directive (living will) 973
advanced reproductive technologies (ARTs)
    2322, 2323
Adventist movement 2439
advertising 30–4, 2825
  brand promotion 357, 358
  and commodity fetishism 758
  and consumption 683, 737, 740, 741
  and consumption and the body 709
  and credit cards 816
  and culture jamming 945
  and desire 420
  and digital capitalism 1162
  drug advertising 1233
  and experiential consumption 716–17
  feminist studies 1849
  gender advertisements 1850
  and gender norms 2986
  and generic terms 1914–15
  history of 30–1
  manipulative advertising 1440
  and masculinity/femininity 1849, 1850
  mass advertising 2874–5
  misleading 826
  and multimedia 3111
  political campaigns 33
  and popular culture 3482
  semiotics 32, 300, 703, 758
  sports advertising 2920
  subliminal messages 32
  television advertising 1233
  therapeutic role 741
  and visual consumption 771–2
  and youth culture 774, 775
aerobic activity 1878, 2598
aesthetic norms 323
aesthetic relativism 3814
aesthetic vangardism 758
aesthetics 34–5
  aesthetic assessments 178
  aesthetics of use 2762
  and art worlds 178
  and arts-based research 2971–2, 2973
  and consumer culture 3554–5
  corporate aesthetics 3555
  and cultural capital 891
  digital 1163–4
  "highbrow" 891
  multimedia 3110

  and paradigm theory 3355
  and visual culture 770
  see also art; literature; music; taste,
    sociology of
Aetherius Society 3204
affect control theory 35–8
  and emotions 1380, 1383, 1386
  impression formation 2270, 2272
  impression management 13, 2215, 2221, 2433
affective arousal 1379
affective-expressive elements of culture 325
affective reaction principle 36
affiliation 315, 1311
affinity cards 815
affirmative action 39–42, 1676, 2955,
    4737–8, 5261
  and black urban regime 311
  college and university policies 39–40,
    2956, 3756
  enforcement 39
  gendered 4204
  and institutional racism 3766
  opposition to 3750
  paternalism 3372
  and reparations 3877
  see also equality of opportunity
**affirmative action for majority groups
    42–5**
**affirmative action (race and ethnic
    quotas) 45–8**, 1198
Afghanistan
  civil wars 1473
  cultural imperialism 907
  migration 1044
  mortality 1029
  purdah 3723
  US attacks on 3175
Africa
  AIDS epidemic 106, 4210–11
  colonialism 602, 603
  community media 626, 627, 628, 629
  decolonization 340
  female genital mutilation 1653–7
  female poverty 1724
  fertility levels 1725, 1726–7, 1738
  infertility 2321
  life expectancies 3097
  medical sociology 2935
  mortality 1726, 2314, 3097, 3099
  multiracial feminism 3118
  sexual cultures 4209–12
  see also specific countries

African Americans *see* black Americans

African Charter on Human and Peoples' Rights 2184

African National Congress (ANC) 43, 163, 164, 165, 660

African Traditional Religion (ATR) 1980

Afrikaners 162

agape love 2671

Agar, M. 1371–4

Age of Aquarius 3190, 3191

age and crime 48–9, 842
  see also juvenile delinquency

Age Discrimination in Employment Act 1967 (US) 105

age identity 49–52
  gender differences 50
  subjective age identification 50, 51

age, period, and cohort effects 52–6, 74
  age–period–cohort conundrum 52, 53
  and late-life economic outcomes 3255

age prejudice and discrimination 56–60, 1182

age pyramids 1030

age-specific fertility rate (ASFR) 1039, 1587, 1742

age stratification principle 74

age transition 1036

age/sex composition 1028

Agel, J. 2692

agency (and intention) 60–2
  and actor-network theory 22
  civilizational perspective 528, 530
  constructivist agency 62
  and liberty 2041
  material agency 2846
  and organization theory 3327
  and practice theory 3608
  Thomas theorem 991
  see also structure and agency

agency–structure debate 871, 872
  and disability 1170
  and micro–macro questions 2999

agenda setting 63–4
  media 2877, 3635

agent-based modeling 639, 640

ageographical cities 1642

aggravated assault 2278

aggregates 2029

aggression 64–7
  aggressive masculinity 2093
  alcohol-related 115
  biological perspective 65

bullying 4013
  discriminatory aggression 1183
  displaced aggression 4774
  game-play aggression 5210
  and hormonal activity 293
  hostile aggression 64
  instrumental aggression 64
  modeling 65
  in schools 843
  and social learning theory 4439
  in sport 4292
  and violence among athletes 2093
  see also violent crime; war

aggressors 64–5

Agigian, A. 4827–9

AGIL system 1322, 1317, 1318

aging, *see* entries below and *see also* elderly; gerontology; life course

aging, demography of 67–71, 285–6, 1028
  biological aging 285, 1927
  cultural diversity of aging 898–901
  fertility and mortality declines 1028
  and grandparenthood 2017–18
  longevity, social aspects of 2668–9
  old-age mortality 2095, 2098
  see also retirement

aging and health policy 71–3
  caregiving 401, 402
  and cultural diversity 899

aging and the life course, theories of 73–7, 1934, 2630–1, 2634, 2635, 2637
  and adult education 1330–1
  and generational change 1902
  life stage model 1927
  lived experience 337
  rural aging 3961–2
  status passages 4760

aging, longitudinal studies 77–9, 2635, 2637
  and income inequality 3256

aging, mental health, and well-being 79–84
  autonomy 337
  friendships 1787–8, 1796, 1931, 3905
  isolation and institutionalization 1842
  physical aging 1927
  rural aging 3962
  self-reported health (SRH) 2085
  work performance, 103, 104, 105

aging research 93

aging and social policy 84–8
  caregiving 401
  cost of public support 1739, 1740

aging and social policy (*cont'd*)
  and pensions 86–7
  work performance and 103
aging and social support 88–93
  elder care 1349–51
  entitlement programs 2367, 2368
  formal care services 91
  and friendship 1787–8, 1796, 1931, 3905
  informal support 90–1
  oldest old 2668
aging, sociology of 93–101, 1935
  age and migration patterns 3017
  cultural diversity of aging 898–901
  and death and dying 972–5
  disability 481
  double standard 1842, 1929
  and fashion consumption 719
  feminist studies 1841
  and gender 1840–3
  intergenerational conflict 2367
  late-life economic outcomes 3254–6
  longitudinal studies 77–9
  mental health and well-being 79–83
  old age dependency rates 1740
  online support 101–2
  political economy of 1929
  and poverty 1718, 1719, 1720, 1721,
    1722, 1842
  psychological aging processes 1927
  and spirituality 4642, 4643
aging and technology 101–3
aging and work performance 103–6
agism 56–9
Agnew, R. 2818, 2819, 4779–82, 4781–2
Agramonte, R. 2948
agrarian communism 614, 615
  agrarian societies 293, 701, 706, 4822–3
  feudalism 2311, 2627
  marketization 3085
  marriage and kinship 2324
  sexual permissiveness 4248
  social structures 1199, 2629
  see also rural sociology
agrarian theism 3870
agribusiness 625, 1040, 3032
agricultural biotechnology 1908
agricultural labor 3248
agriculture
  evolution 2141
  Green Revolution 3439
  and hybridity 2189
  overcropping 3527

  political power 625
  semi-domestication (plants) 4178–9
  subsistence agriculture 2766
  see also rural sociology
Agrippa, Cornelio 2697
agrotourism 921
Aguirre, A. 5138–41
Aguirre Beltrán, G. 340, 341, 342, 343
ahimsa 1782
Ahmiddya 3203
Aichorn, A. 837
Aid to Families with Dependent Children
    (AFDC) 1617, 1884
AIDS activism 1166, 1211
AIDS, sociology of 106–11, 1984
  community responses 2606, 2608, 3995–6
  demographic dimensions 2137–9
  economic impact 107
  gay/AIDS conflation 711
  HIV prevention 107–8
  human rights approach 108–9
  and medical sociology 2935
  Moral Right responses 2606
  mother-to-child transmission 2137
  research 2160, 2161, 2162
  and safer sex 3987–9
  sex panic 4199–200
  stigma 109, 711
  triangulation analysis 778
  and women 333, 2309, 2319, 2398, 3535–6
  see also HIV/AIDS
air pollution 1418, 1419, 1421, 1424, 3533
Airaudi, O. 3191
Airken, I. 1210
airports 706
Aix School 2714
Ajrouch, K. J. 3828–9
Akbar, Emperor 2131
Akçura, Y. 2000, 2001
Ake, C. 2838
Akers, R. 848–9, 1857, 1858
Akiba, T. 2498
al-Biruni 111–14
al-Din al-Afghani, Sayyid Jamal 1492
al-Jazeera 2879
al-Qaeda 2801, 3383, 3469, 3470
Alarcón, N. 2550
Alasuutari, Pertti 208–12
Alatas, S. F. 111–14, 399–400, 1491–4,
    2458–62, 3938–41, 3989–90
Alatas, S. H. 399–400, 1492
Alba, R. 191–6, 2257

Albania
  forced atheization 198
  Orthodox Church 3345
Albertus Magnus 1352
Albini, J. 833
Albrecht, G. 482
Albright, J. M. 3572–6
Alcatraz Island, Native American occupation
  of 2283
Alchina, A. A. 3327
Alcoff, L. 3562
alcohol
  and casual leisure 2599
  and health lifestyles 2060, 2061
  laddish drinking culture 4259
alcohol and crime 114–16, 2663
alcohol production and consumption 820
Alcoholics Anonymous 1111
alcoholism and alcohol abuse 114, **116–19,**
  1104, 1143, 2599
  and absenteeism 5
  Bateson on 247–8
  binge drinking 118
  and deviance 1078, 1107, 1111, 1112
  and deviance in sport 1134
  and disease prevalence 1184
  and divorce 1207, 1208
  and drug use 1233
  and ethnicity 2078
  gender-related 117
  and homelessness 2149
  media portrayal 1109
  medicalization of 1112, 1542
  school students 1548
  and socially disorganized communities 1102
  stigma 583
  and suicide 4882
  and traditional family structure 1589
  underage drinking 114
Alderson, A. S. 3182
Aldrich, H. 1460
Alexander the Great 418, 642
Alexander, J. 1257, 1812, 3578
Alexander, M. J. 1704
Alexandre, R. 1382–4
Alexandrian Library 2896
Alford index 551
Alford, R. 551
Alger, J. 2177
Alger, S. 2177
Algeria 2040
  decolonization 985

French conquest of 2686
  revolution 3907
algorithms 640
Ali-Baba corporations 47
Aliberti, D. 1718–25
alienation 119–21
  advertising, effects of 33
  alienated memory 592
  and situational improprieties 1997–8
  and anomie 145
  Baudrillard and 703
  and blasé/neurasthenic personalities 312
  of the body 711
  and capitalism 614–15, 874
  collective efficacy and crime and 585
  and collective memory 588
  and commodification 610, 757
  and consumption 703
  and critical theory 876
  and everyday life 1502
  Feuerbach and 1748
  and industrialization 1839
  of labor 119, 874, 929, 1200, 1502, 2580,
    2750, 2752, 2807, 2816
  and McDonaldization 2690
  Marxist critique 119, 874, 929, 1200, 1502,
    2580, 2807, 2816, 5158
  of myth 262
  and popular culture 3482
  and poverty 951
  in the public sphere 3719–20
  and reification 3845
  and shame 3007
  Shariati and 4295, 4296
  and situationism 4336
  and social movements, emergence of 954
Alihan, M. 443
alimony awards 1721
Allam, K. F. 2424–8
Allan, G. 1618–21, 1792, 1792–5, 2168–70,
  2469–71, 2770–2, 2791–4
Allan, S. 3180–2, 3703–7
Allardyce, G. 1644
Allen, F. A. 969–70
Allen, P. 677
Allen, V. 2291
Allende, Salvador 1565, 2575
alliances 121–3, 2744
  anti-war and peace movements 161
  defining 121
  oral/written 121–2
  organizational 355

alliances (*cont'd*)
 and outsourcing 3352
 strategic 355
alliances (racial/ethnic) 123–5
Allinson, C. W. 378–80
Allison, D. 2610
Allmendinger, J. 5092–6
allocentrism 598
allopathic medicine 2245
allostatic load 2074
Allport, F. 3700, 3701
Allport, G. 199–200, 2339, 2566, 3614, 3778
Almeida, P. 781
Alter, N. 3990–2
altercasting 2214, 2215
alternate-forms reliability 3850
alternative dispute resolution (ADR) 2562–3
alternative medicine *see* complementary and
 alternative medicine
Altheide, D. L. 1107–10, 1651
Althusser, Louis 125–7, 1774, 2212, 2648
 and base/superstructure metaphor 245
 and commodity relations 610
 ideology, theory of 126, 2110, 2815, 2877
 Marxism 125–6, 298, 299, 914, 2815, 3598
 and mass media 2877
 materialist analysis 2838
 and structural functionalism 1810
Alton, D. 3087
altruism
 Comte and 655
 empathy–altruism hypothesis 3681
 ethnic groups 294
 genetic transmission 3680
 and gift giving 1939
 and individualism 1940
 positive deviance 3543
 and the professions 3663
 and prosocial behavior 3678, 3679, 3681
 reciprocal altruism 292, 3227, 3229
 Spencer and 655
 and suicidal inclinations 3008
 and volunteering 3681
Alvarez, S. 1685, 1688
Alvesson, M. 2721, 3665, 3830–4
Alwin, D. F. 77–9
Alzheimer's disease 234
amateurism 4657, 4667
 see also sport, amateur
Amazonism 2857
Ambedkar, B. R. 3612
ambivalence 127–8, 4988

Amenta, E. 4466–70
America Creed 128–9
American Anthropological Association 322,
 2348–9
American Association for the Advancement of
 Science (AAAS) 4089
American Association for Public Opinion
 Research 2564
American Association of University
 Professors 2171
American Bill of Rights 2183
American Civil War 2830, 4168
 technological innovation 3038
American Community Survey (ACS) 1014
American Constitution 174, 2623
American Declaration of Independence 2183
American Dilemma, An (**Gunnar Myrdal**)
 128–30, 2444, 2466
American Dream 704, 706, 821, 1120, 1570
 and false consciousness 1570
American Economic Association 130
American Family Federation 886
American Federation of Labor (AFL)
 2519, 2520
American Holistic Medical Association 631
American Holistic Nurses' Association 631
American Indian Movement 587, 2283
American Journal of Sociology (*AJS*) 130, 131, 443
American Medical Association (AMA) 3652
American Political Science Association 130
American Psychological Association 644
 intelligence report 265
American Revolution 170, 182, 407, 1067,
 1324, 1652, 3915
 and individualism 2706
 and intellectual freedom 3468
 and liberalism 2622–3
 and nationalism 3145
American Social Science Association (ASSA)
 1670
American Sociological Association (ASA)
 130–4, 270, 318, 443, 644, 699, 4602
 African American membership 131
 Marxist Sociology Section 2838
 Medical Sociology Section 2934
American Sociological Review (*ASR*) 131, 443
American Sociological Society (ASS) 1670
American Sugar Refining Company 827
American Supreme Court 174
American War of Independence 3038
Americanization 137, 739, 991, 1962
 and cultural homogenization 2888, 3158

films and 1753, 2874
and global culture 1965, 1970
and grobalization 2023
and immigration 2257, 2260
and language immersion programs 2260
and the Olympics 3264
see also melting pot
Americans for Generational Equity (AGE) 57
Amersfoort, H. van 2255–8
Amin, S. 1060, 2838, 3179
Amino, Y. 1402, 3059, 3220
Amir, Y. 1814
Amish
   marginality by choice 2764
   and patriarchal authority 2302
Amnesty International 976–7, 2156, 3259
   funding 3212
   organizational form 3259
   resource mobilization 3067
AMOS software program 2975
amphetamines 1236, 1238
Amsterdam Treaty of the European
   Union 1869
amusement parks 704, 765, 766
Anabaptism 3409
anal sex 2702, 3542
analogue data 1159, 1160
analysis of covariance 1534
analysis of variance 1535
analytic induction 134–5, 3167, 3168
analytic labor 3565
analytical realism 3366
anarchism 136–7, 3259
   and collective trauma 597
   Debord and 980–1
   détournement 980–1
   and direct action 1165
   and global justice movement 1948
   Goldman and 2004–5, 2006, 2007
   Internet and 734
   and terrorism 4970
anatamo-politics of the body 323, 337, 338
anatomy 335
ancestor worship 3629, 3870
ancien régime 680
Anderson, B. 618, 628, 1353, 1467, 1468,
   1993, 2248, 2900, 2901, 3059, 3139,
   3147, 3148, 3149, 3156
Anderson, Elijah 715
Anderson, Eric 638–9
Anderson, K. B. 1146–50, 2685–8
Anderson, N. 714, 1129, 1554, 2147–8

Anderson, Perry 2135, 3178
Anderson, Peter B. 4117–19
Anderson, R. 2105, 2987
andragogy 4565
Andrews, C. 4596–8
Andrews, D. L. 4702–4
Andrews, E. B. 2170
Andrews, F. 625
Andrews, O. A. 2948
androgyny 301–2, 902
   and cultural feminism 902
andronormativity 2612
Angel, R. 2241–5
angels 582
Anglican Church 408, 1054, 1981, 3689, 3690
Anglo-conformity 137–8
   and assimilation 195, 2945
Angola
   decolonization 985
   electoral processes 1952
   revolution 3907
   UN intervention 1952
Angrist, J. 3028
Angry Brigade 981
anhedonia 2568
animal abuse 2177
animal behavior 1508
animal ecology 2418
animal experiments 2567–8
animal–human interaction *see* human–
   non-human interaction
Animal Liberation Front 139
animal populations 3590
animal racing 1820
animal-related occupations 2178
animal rights movements 138–41, 1273,
   2178, 3821
   and anthrozoology 150, 151, 2177
   and direct action 1166
animal sacrifice 3981, 3984, 4011
animal welfarism 138
animism 141–2, 608
   pre-animism 142
Annales School 142–4, 446, 517, 2446–7
   Braudel and 360, 2426
   and comparative historical sociology 2135
   and historical demography 1046
   historical studies 143
   and religious issues 2426
anomia 2544–5
anomie 144–6, 516, 3465
   and alienation 145

anomie (*cont'd*)
  anomie model of family conflict 1582
  and authoritarianism 221
  and collective action 575
  and collective memory 592
  and collective trauma 597
  and deviance 1081, 1102, 1119–20
  Durkheim and 144, 145, 516, 593, 595, 1102,
    1199, 1200, 1261, 3124, 3230
  Germani and 1922
  and health-related subcultures 2073, 2074
  Merton and 117, 144–5, 597, 809, 1102,
    1103, 3589
  and modernity 3124, 3230
  and social disintegration 1922
  and social movements, emergence of 954
  and sport 1134
  see also alienation
anonymity, for research participants
  1443, 1444
anonymous sex 2160
anorexia nervosa 326, 336–7, 722
  and family theory 1632
ANOVA (analysis of variance) 146–7, 2119,
  2542, 2975
  ANCOVA (analysis of covariance) 147, 2119
  and the general linear model 1898
  multivariate ANOVA (MANOVA)
    147, 2119
Anselm 1087
Anthony, S. B. 1673, 2308, 2618
anthropocentrism 3632
  science fiction critique of 3495
anthropological evolutionism 2697
anthropological linguistics 2535, 2536
anthropology 4073
  American anthropology 938
  animism 141
  applied anthropology 1482, 2986
  Boas and 321–2
  and body techniques 326, 327, 336
  and brands and branding 359
  cognitive anthropology 1372
  and commodity relations 610
  cultural anthropology 610, 2362
  and cultural geography 1299
  Darwinian 292
  and deconstruction 988
  ecological anthropology 2250
  economic anthropology 1306
  emic/etic approaches 1371, 1372, 2539
  ethnographic work 327

  and gift giving 1940
  hermeneutic method 322
  and human–animal relations 151
  and imperialism 340
  indigenista model 339
  and kinship 2469
  life histories 288, 289
  Margaret Mead and 2865–7
  Marxist 341, 342
  medical anthropology 630
  Mexican anthropology 339–43
  of myth 3136, 3137
  Olympic anthropology 3264
  philosophical anthropology 324
  political role 341
  professionalization 322
  qualitative research, imperialist 2982–3
  and religion 3519
  social anthropology 1689, 1690, 3582
  structural-historical anthropology 4008, 4009
  structuralist anthropology 365, 2539
  synchronic and nomothetic revolution 2705
  and totemism 5019–20
  visual anthropology 3407
  "with commitment" 341
  see also ethnography; ethnomethodology
anthropology, cultural and social: early
  history 147–50
  Durkheim and 1251
  photography, use of 247
  Radcliffe-Brown and 3772
anthroposemiotics 2537
anthrozoology 150–2, 2177, 3500–3
anti-abortion activism 1490, 3093
anti-Americanism 1966
anti-branding movement 359
anti-capitalist movements 981, 1949
anti-Catholic attitudes 1325
anti-colonialism 1273, 3460
  and nationalist movements 1468, 3147
  revolutionary movements 3907
anti-communism 2838, 3195
anti-consumerist social movements 685, 743,
  1851, 2549–50
anti-Defamation League 153
anti-essentialism
anti-feminist movements 1873
anti-globalization 729, 1062, 1273, 1969, 1977,
  1991, 3217
  and feminist activism 1679
  and gender 1874
  and logos 730

and moral entrepreneurship 3087
value system 1993
anti-globalization movements
anarchist resonances 136
anti-Semitism 160
consumer choice and 352
and documentaries 1211
and ecological problems 1282
see also global justice movement
anti-homosexuality *see* homophobia
anti-imperialism 164
anti-militarist activism 1273
anti-multiculturalism 3108
anti-neoliberalism 1977
anti-nepotism 1880
anti-nuclear activism 139, 1166, 1273, 1431,
1679, 1806, 3551
and the Internet 2387
and moral entrepreneurship 3087
and the new left 3193
anti-reductionism 1417, 1418
anti-retroviral therapy (ART) 107, 110
anti-Semitism (religion) 152–4, 159, 2453
anti-Semitism (social change) 154–60,
1089, 3767, 3768
and authoritarianism 1805–6
and collective memory 593
and collective trauma 595
and Durkheim 1253
economic anti-Semitism 152, 154, 156–8
pogroms 3426–8
political anti-Semitism 152, 154, 158–9, 160
racial anti-Semitism 152, 154, 155–6,
159–60
anti-slavery movement 1, 2618
anti-statism 1069
anti-tax revolts 2034
anti-technology attitudes 687
anti-terrorism 1297, 4897
and information technology 2334, 2335
anti-trust laws and institutions 625, 934, 1309,
2356, 2557, 4731
anti-trust violations 826, 850
anti-urbanism 1550
anti-war and peace movements 161
investigative poetics 2420–3
peace and reconciliation processes 3380–3
personal is political concept 3401
student movements 4865
Antichrist 3048
anticlericalism 2530, 2532
antifoundationalism 3609

antinomianism 522
antiretrovirals 2139
antisocial behavior 832, 2455
personality traits and 838
antisocial personality disorder 449, 823, 848,
1081, 1623
Antonio, R. J. 876, 2805–15, 3213–17
anxiety disorder 2243, 3852
see also depression and distress
Anzaldúa, G. 2398, 2549, 3728
apartheid and Nelson Mandela
162–5, 3744
collective memory and 593
and racial divisions of labor 1463
and racial/ethnic conflict 660
sport resistance 4700
apartheid schools 370
apathy 1008
aphasia 3187
apocalypticism 3049, 3190, 3702
Appadurai, Arjun
and commodity relations 610–11, 742
and the global cultural economy 1963
and global cultural flows 1990, 1994, 2888
apperception 2432, 2434
Applebaum, R. 3184
Appleby, S. R. 1814
applied social psychology 4517–20
applied sociology *see* ethics, fieldwork;
observation, participant and non-
participant; participatory action research
appreciative enquiry 18
Apter, D. 3065
Apter, E. 1746
Aquinas, Thomas 1447, 2833, 4116
Aquino, A. 4011
Arabandi, B. 3479–80
Arabic language 282
Araujo, Eddie "Gwen" 1829
Arber, S. 1929
arbitrary liberty 2041
arcades 165–6
Benjamin and 269
Paris 1763
Archer, Margaret 872, 1640
The Archers 3499
architecture
elitism 2124
new urban architecture 5149
postmodern 3553, 3556, 3570, 3573
Arditi, J. 2484
Arena, J. 310–12

Arendt, Hannah 166–75, 3034, 3886
  and Benjamin 268
  biography 166–7
  and bureaucracy 168
  and fascism 1645
  and legitimacy 229
  and power 3597
  and the public sphere 2906, 3718–19, 3721
  and totalitarianism 167, 168, 169, 175, 1645
Arensberg, C. 1575, 1576, 1577, 1579
Arentino, Pietro 3540
Argentina
  authoritarian regimes 222, 223, 224
  charismatic movement 440
  colonialism 411
  and federalism 1652
  feminist activism 1685, 1688
  fertility levels 1730
  human rights activism 5061
  immigration 1457
  Jewish community 2453
  medical sociology 2935
  neopopulism 413
  Peronism 411
  transition processes 1924
Argyle, M. 2362
Argyris, C. 982, 2513
Arianism 3345
Ariès, P. 460, 1269, 4123
aristocracy 679, 2311
Aristotle
  and causality 653
  and communism 613
  and the elite nature of science 3222
  and emotions 1374
  and empiricism 1397
  and ethics 1447
  and genre 1914
  and happiness 33
  and householding 1385
  and justice 857, 1447
  and materialism 2836
  Organon 4116
  and the polis 2990
  and political sociology 3458, 3463, 3465
  political typology 3257
  Rhetoric 3674
Arkoun, M. 2427
Arluke, A. 2176, 2177, 2178
Armenia
  Armenian holocaust 1451
  diaspora 1151

  Orthodox Church 3346
  premodern nation 3151
arms industry 3037
arm's-length subcontracting 3352, 3354
Armstrong, A. 1440
Armstrong, E. 2159, 4440–3
Armstrong, G. 1751, 1767–9
Armstrong, J. 3151, 3157
army, armed forces *see* militarism; military
    sociology; war
Arnason, J. 3069
Arnett, R. 309
Arnheim, R. 3780
Arnold, Matthew 912, 918
Aron, Raymond 175–7
Aronowitz, S. 1570, 2678–81
Aronson, E. 561, 562
Aronson, P. 1247–9, 3920–1
arousal theory 562, 823–4
  dissonance-induced arousal 563
arranged marriages 2671, 4214
Arrestee Drug Abuse Monitoring Program
    (ADAM) 1235
Arrighi, G. 2268
Arrigo, B. A. 665–8
Arrow, K. 1760, 3326
Arruñada, B. 1315
arson 2278, 3675
art 178–9
  Benjamin and 268, 517
  Buddhist 373
  capitalism and 517
  commodification of 517
  and cultural capital 891
  and cultural production 952
  and cultural sociology 923
  and genre 1914
  high art 1753, 1754
  Lévis-Strauss and 366
  marginal art 2761–3
  and political expression 779
  popular art 2762
  and pornography 894
  postmodern 3556, 3570
  receptivity to 383
  reproducibility 268
  social construction 330
  sport as art 4535–6
art film tradition 1753
art music 3128
art worlds 177–80
  and collective memory 592

and cultural production 952
and music 3128
and visual culture 770, 771
art/science dichotomy 2981
arthritis 2242, 2246
Arthur Andersen accounting firm 827
Arthur, M. B. 3288
Arthur, M. M. L. 1366–8, 3092–3, 3732–4,
    3765–7, 4474–5
Articles of Confederation 1652
articulated arrangements 2926–7
artificial insemination 1907
artificial intelligence 640
artificial social intelligence 639
artificial societies 634
artistic tastes 347
artists 178
    and gentrification 1919
arts-based research 2971–4
arts tourism 919, 920
Aruga, K. 2239–40
Aryan Brotherhood 2049
Aryans 1489, 3767, 3768
'*asabiyya* **180–5**, 2459–60
asceticism 185–9, 4136
    ascetic Protestantism 2699
    and charismatic leadership 433
    monasticism 3689
Asch, Solomon 189
Asch experiments 189–91
    and authority and conformity 226, 227,
        3034, 3701
ascription 1335
Aseltine, E. 3211–12
asexual reproduction 556
Ashkenazic Jews 2450
Asia
    Buddhism 371
    economic growth 3199
    female migration 1716
    fertility levels 1738, 1739
    financial meltdowns 1075, 3324
    new middle classes 3198–201
    sexual cultures 4213–17
    social change 4374–9
    teenage fertility 1726, 1727
    Tiger economies 1296
    urban way of life (East Asia) 5143–5
    women and information technology 5262–4
    see also specific countries
Asian Americans
    businesses 1454

cultural heterogeneity 901
culture and patriarchy 1218
education 1158
ethnic enclaves 1452, 1453, 1454
exogamy 1405
interracial marriage 1405, 2394
residential segregation 3888, 3889
see also Chinese Americans; Japanese
    Americans; Korean Americans;
    Vietnamese Americans
"Asian values" 1075
Asimov, Isaac 3495
aspiration, linguistic 1371
aspiration theory 81
    and career advancement 1341
    and educational attainment 1337
    see also expectations and aspirations
Asquith, P. 2249–52, 3627
assassinations 779, 780, 835
Assassins 2800
assault
    in the workplace 3305
    see also sexual violence and rape; violent
        crime
assembly line work 363, 2710–11, 2746, 2828
asset specificity 3352
assimilation 191–6, 260
    and accommodation 8
    and acculturation 192–3
    American Dilemma, An (Gunnar Myrdal) 128
    and American pluralism 3421, 3422
    Anglo-conformity model 137, 2945
    behavioral assimilation 2944
    Chicago School research 194
    cultural assimilation 1458, 2944
    definition 2945
    and ethnic cleansing 1451
    and the ethnic economy 1460
    and ethnic enclaves 1455
    ethnic groups 1457, 1458, 1461
    ethnocentric bias 194
    and homogenization 3143
    immigrant assimilation 191–6, 1969, 2257,
        2258, 3011, 3025, 3446, 3479, 4816
    and imperialism 1393
    indigenous peoples 341, 2279, 2281
    Jews 2452
    "magic crucible" view 3364
    marital 2394
    middleman minorities 3010
    multidimensionality 192
    negative assimilation 3759

assimilation (*cont'd*)
  Park and 192, 3025, 3363–4
  and political machines 3446
  and racial/ethnic boundaries 345
  refugees 3837
  segmented assimilation 195, 196, 278,
    2254, 3479
  socioeconomic assimilation 193
  spatial assimilation 193, 3889
  structural assimilation 193, 1458
  and Thomas theorem 991
  see also acculturation; Americanization;
    melting pot
association 2031
Association for the Advancement of Women 1670
Association of American Universities (AAU)
  2012
Association of Black Sociologists 133, 1244
Association for Humanist Sociology 132
Association for the Sociology of Religion 133
associational ties 1401–2
Assyrians 1451
astrology 261, 1140
astronomy 275, 1485, 2699, 4116
asylum seekers 2256, 3011, 3835, 3837
  and immigration policy 2262
asylums 1169, 2694
  see also mental disorder
asynchronisms 1922, 1924
Atalay, Z. 3808–10
atavism 822, 1101, 1118
  and Nazism 875
Atchley, R. C. 4641–3
Atchley, Robert C. 4641–3
atheism 196–9
  and eclipse of the sacred 3977
  humanist 197
  methodological 197
  moral 197
  ontological 197
  scientistic 197
Athens, ancient 2990
Athens, L. 2861–4, 3166–70
athletic identity 2221–3, 4709
athletic mascots, Native American 2283, 4683–4
athletics *see* sport
Atkinson, J. 2514
Atkinson, M. 5208–11
Atkinson, R. 1643
Atkinson, T.-G. 2602, 3774
Atlanta Sociological Laboratory 604
Atlee, Clement 2141

ATM-related crime 1105
Atran, S. 2801
Attac 1978–9
attachment theory 221, 2674
attention deficit hyperactivity disorder
  (ADHD) 1113
attention economy 353, 770
Attias-Donfut, C. 2633
attitudes and behavior 199–202
  and activism 577
  adaptations 293
  adaptive benefits 292
  and attraction 202
  and built environment 375
  and chaos and complexity theories 432
  collective 320
  correspondence inference theory 205
  and decision-making 983
  dissonance theory 562–5
  field theory 2616
  gender differences 292
  generative mechanisms 292
  and hormonal activity 292–3
  and identity 2225
  police 3432
  political 3444
  proximate causation 292, 293
  situational 201
  socioeconomic behaviors 625
  theory of reasoned action 200
  ultimate causation 292
  youth 773
  see also behaviorism; norms; prejudice;
    psychological social psychology; public
    opinion; specific types of behavior
Attlee, Clement 2141, 3039
attraction 202–4
  familiarity 202
  homogamy 203
  and interpersonal relationships 2391
  and mate selection 2391
  and passionate love 2672
  physical attractiveness 203–4, 3701–2
  proximity 202–3
  reciprocity 203
  similarity 203
attribution equations 37
Attribution Style Questionnaire (ASQ) 2568–9
attribution theory 205–8
  and emotions and economy 1388
  internal attribution 205
  and learned helplessness 2568–9

and love 2672–3
  measuring attributions 2568–9
  and reification 3844
Atwood, Margaret 3495
Auburn Penitentiary 802, 3640–1
audience ethnography 210–11
audiences 208–12
  active audience concept 2877
  art worlds 179
  and celebrity culture 416
  and deviance 1076–7
  and encoding/decoding 1403–4, 2882
  fan/spectator dichotomy 760
  and fandom 1640
  mass audiences 2875, 2882
  and popular culture 1108
  and ratings 3793
  reality TV 3491
  reception studies 3816–17
  ritual audience 753–4
  science fiction 3497
  soap operas 2823, 3499
  and texts 300
  youth audience 774
  see also fans and fan culture
audiocassettes 3132
audit culture 2929
audit trails 3643
auditing 212–13
  metaevaluation 213
  performance auditing 212
  program auditing 212–13
Auf der Heide, L. 4437–40
Augustine of Hippo 188, 4180
Ault, J. 2987
Aum Shinrikyo 886, 3047
Aunger, R. 1449–50
Auschwitz 2142
Austin, J. 1181
Australia
  Aboriginal religion 3633
  anti-nuclear activism 1273
  anti-trafficking campaigns 1984
  beach holidays 3484, 3485
  bilingual education 279
  child custody and child support 453, 454
  citizenship 497
  class voting 551
  colonialism 603
  complementary and alternative medicine
    630, 631, 632, 2068
  consumer culture 743

cultural elite 1361
cultural tourism 921
diasporic experience in 2886
and discriminatory aggression 1183
divorce 452
enterprise bargaining 1417
environmental movements 1431
fantasy cities 1641
and federalism 1652, 1653
gender poverty ratios 1723
health care system 2055
higher education 602
immigration 661, 1198, 1457, 1460, 2260,
  2263, 3028
immigration policy 1198, 3022
indigenous peoples 2280
internal migration 3017
labor–management relations 2512
laborism 2526
lone parenthood 2663, 2664
multiculturalism 1938, 3106
multiracial feminism 3118
neoliberalism 3176
nonmarital births 1587
public broadcasting 3703, 3707
totemism 5020
transnational corporations 1944
unions 2511
welfare capitalism 392
Austria
  birth rates 1015
  cohabitation 566
  and federalism 1652
  industrial democracy 2750
  retirement policies 3902
  social security system 2055
  vocational training systems 1399
Austrian Struggle 2038
Austrin, T. 2902–6
Austro-Marxism 344
authenticity
  catalytic authenticity 215
  cultural authenticity 763
  educative autheticity 214–15
  ontological authenticity 214
  and performance ethnography 3394
  staged authenticity 763
  tactical authenticity 215–16
authenticity criteria 213–16
  fairess and balance 214
author/auteur 216–20
  author-function 217

author/auteur (*cont'd*)
  Barthes on 216, 219, 244
  "death of the author" 1914, 4974
  Derrida on 217–18, 219
  and digital texts 1159, 1164
  Enlightenment notions 730
  and film 1753, 1755, 1756
  and film studies 218
  Foucault on 216–17, 219
  and genre 1916
  Romantic notions 730
  signature effects 217–18, 219
  structuralism and 219, 2402
authoritarian personality 220–2
  adherence to cultural conventions 220
  aggression toward outgroups 220
  attachment theory and 221
  and collective action 577
  deference to authorities 220
  and fascism 220–1
  intolerance of ambiguity 5293
  and Nazism 220
  and prejudice 3614
  sadomasochistic 875, 877
authoritarian state 297, 2576
  and genocide 1911
authoritarianism 222–5
  Adorno and 28, 220
  authoritarian regimes 224
  bureaucratic authoritarianism 222, 224–5
  caudillismo 224
  and civil society 512
  and critical theory 876
  and democracy 223, 225
  and developmentalism 1074
  F scale 1806
  Frankfurt School and 865
  Fromm and 1805–6
  and Latin American sociology 224, 225, 1926
  and masculinity 1891
  mentality 223
  Nazi 1569
  school discipline 4021
  and totalitarianism 222, 223
authority
  authoritative parenting 3224
  bureaucratic 377, 434, 2565
  charismatic 226, 230, 434, 435, 3442,
    3597, 3806
  colonialist 1471
  and conformity 226
  and conservatism 679

  corporate 228
  and ethnic/nationalist movements 1471
  federated authority 1471
  legitimate 227, 230, 2585
  macro-level authority 228
  and managerial agency 2747
  organizational 2387
  patriarchal 2858
  political 229, 3459
  rational-legal 226, 230, 3311, 3442, 3464, 3597
  religious 228, 679
  resistance to 227
  scientific 1541–3
  status and 227–8
  textual 2643
  traditional 226, 230, 3597, 3806
  Utrecht studies 227
  and validity 2585
  Weber and 2585
  see also leadership; legitimacy; patriarchy;
    power
authority and conformity 225–9
  Asch experiments 189–91, 227
  globalization and 228
  Milgram experiments 226–7, 3034–7,
    3230–1, 3701
authority and legitimacy 229–30
authorship *see* author/auteur
autism
  infantile 258
  "refrigerator mother" theory 1573
autobiography *see* life history
autocratic regimes and civil society 594
autoethnography 230–2, 1480, 3141
  and human–animal interaction 2178
  and life history 2642
  performative texts 231
  and reflexivity 3833
autoimmune diseases, and gender 1865
automation 1200, 2689
  McLuhan and 2692
  Marx and 2811
automobile accident fatalities 2152
automobile seatbelt use 2061
autonomization of secular subsystems 4141, 4143
autonomy
  and aging 337
  autonomy protection 4080
  and capitalism 516
  charter schools 4035
  and disability 337, 480
  and divorce 1207

ethnic 660
and ethnonationalism 1487
European cities 493
feminist 1687
health care implications 2056
and human rights 2183
indigenous peoples 341, 342, 343
and the Internet 2386
Kantian moral autonomy 654, 2187
of legal practice 2583
occupational 4162
professional 2075, 2929
and professional dominance in medicine
    3657, 3658
and the public sphere 1862
scientific 4109
social 407
and social responsibility 2759
state action 663
and wealth 2311
women 1854, 2620
women's loss of, in marriage 2619, 2768
workers 407, 429
youth culture 774
autopoiesis 232–3
autopoietic social systems theory 2675–7
Luhmann and 233
autoproduction of culture 953
autoregressive latent trajectory model
    (ALT) 2544
autoregressive moving average (ARIMA)
    models 5008
autoscthonous peoples 342
avant-garde culture 2821
Avellar, S. 1209
Averson, R. 1755
Avison, W. R. 4843–5
avoidance learning 3753–4
Avolio, B. J. 2566
Avruch, K. 2059, 5085–7
awareness contexts 233–5
closed awareness 233
and grounded theory 234
mutual-pretense awareness 233, 234
open awareness 233, 234
suspicion awareness 232
Axelrod, R. 640
axiology 2968, 2969
of disinterest 3235
and mixed methods research 2979
and naturalistic enquiry 3161, 3163
quantitative research paradigm 2978

axis of evil 3175
Ayabe, T. 1402
Ayurveda medicine 631
Aznar, Jose Maria 3469
AZT 2137
Aztec sacrifices 1939
Azzi, C. 1315

ba **237–9**, 2240
categories 237
and group organization 2240
Baba'u'llah 3048
Babbage, C. 3436–7
Babès, L. 2427
Babeuf, G. 614
baby boomers 74, 1030, 1043, 2573
and adult education 1331
aging 95, 102
and the body beautiful 325
demographic diversity 3901
and family/household structure 1586
health care service utilization 2070
income trajectories in later life 3256
retirement 3902
and young adult living arrangements 2572
baby bulge 1036
baby busters 1331
Babylonia, protoscience 2140
babysitting 725
Bacharach, S. B. 3601
Bachelard, G. 22
Bachhofen, J. J. 2858
Bachman, R. 1219
Bachnik, J. 4935–8
Bachofen, J. J. 1595, 3670
Bacon, Francis 260, 2286, 3573, 4070, 4116
Bacon, Roger 3636–7
Bacon-Smith, C. 1638
Badahdah, A. M. 205–8, 598
Baecker, D. 2676
Baer, H. A. 629–33
Baffinland 321
Bagdikian, B. H. 2895–9
Bagehot, W. 3669
Bagemihl, B. 638
Baha'i religion 1982, 3048, 3203
Bahr, S. 1206–10
Bahrain, male/female median earnings
    ratios 1724
Bailey, A. 3190
Bailey, A. J. 1606, 1607, 1608
Bain, A. 3609

Bain, R. 2176
Bainbridge, W. S. 639–45, 885, 886, 2146, 3633
Baird, John Logie 2875
Bairner, A. 500–2, 1636–7, 3158–61
Baker, E. 509, 2621, 3194
Baker, T. 2735
Baker, W. 1321
Bakhtin, M. and the carnivalesque 417, 5046
Bakker, J. I. (Hans) 991–2, 1293–4, 1352,
    1447–50, 1553–4, 2533–9, 2857–9,
    2963–4, 2967–71, 4011–12, 4107–8,
    4116–17, 4321–3
Bakunin, M. 136, 1165
    and anarchism 136, 1165
    and atheism 197
balance theory 214, 3701
    and attraction 203
    and friendships 795, 796
Balch, E. G. 131
Baldwin, J. M. 799
Bale, J. 4717–19
Bales, R. F. 1524, 2027, 2031, 2361
Bali 2986
Balibar, E. 3139
balkanization 239–40, 3107
Balkars 1451
Balkin, S. 2341
Ballard, J. G. 3496
ballet 327, 336, 582
ballparks 768
ballroom 1223–5
Bambara, T. C. 308, 3119
Bambuti Pygmies 3870
Bamyeh, M. A. 1970
Banaji, M. R. 3188
bandits 414
Bandung conference (1955) 603–4
Bandura, A. 4437–9
bandwagon effects 2730
Banfield, E. 3592
Bangkok 2991, 3623
Bangladesh 3020, 4167
    child health disparities 1157
    consumer movements 697
    family planning programs 1738–9
    microcredit programs 1158
    public housing 3710
banking capital 1395
banking industry 872, 1189
    consumer banks 729
    credit 393
    and credit cards 815

deregulation 1453
ethnic 1454
and financial sociology 1760
Jewish bankers 157, 160
recruitment practices 1890
bankruptcy 241–2
    credit cards and 817
Banks, I. M. 3497
Banks, M. 1477
Bannister, Roger 4712
Banque Générale 2022
Banton, M. 1183
baptism in the Holy Spirit 441
Baptist Church 1051, 1053, 1054, 1056,
    3689, 3692
bar mitzvahs 2452
Barak, G. 668
Baran, P. 1395, 2267, 2838, 3039, 3178,
    3179, 3437
Barbalet, J. 497–500, 1374–7, 1384, 1650,
    2794–6, 3676–8
barbarism 529, 531
    civilized barbarism 531
    and Nazism 875
Barber, B. 1994
Barbie 726
barbiturates 1235, 1238
Bardot, Brigitte 254
Bardy, David 4812–15
bargaining and negotiation studies 1267
bargaining theory 2443, 3601
Barings Bank 3566
Barkan, S. E. 4471–4
Barker, C. 297–301
Barker, E. 3201–26
Barker, M. 1640
Barker, V. 1657
Barley, S. R. 2723
Barnard, C. 2713, 2714, 2747
Barnard, H. 4041
Barnard College 2488
Barner, L. 1920–6
Barnes, B. 786
Barnes, T. J. 1299
Barnett, Ida B. Wells 306, 307, 2838
Barone, T. 2971–4
Barr, M. 3496
Barr, R. 3273
Barragan, R. 2948
Barrett, M. 2843
Barro, R. 1317, 1332
barter communities 745

Barth, F. 345, 915, 1457, 1475
Barthes, Roland 242–4, 2648, 2691
    and advertising 758
    on auteurism 216, 219, 244
    biography 242
    and commodity fetishization 757
    film theory 1755
    and genre 1916
    and intertextuality 3581
    and literary poststructuralism 3581
    Marxism 298
    and myth 3137
    Mythologies 242, 243, 244
    and photography 771
    and popular culture 2882
    semiotics 758, 3581, 3583, 4182
Bartholomew, G. 284
Bartkowski, J. P. 152–4, 250–1
Bartky, S. 1850
Bartley, T. 4440–3
Bartolomé, L. I. 281–3
base and superstructure 244–6, 299, 942
    economic reductionism 299
    Marxist theory 299, 539, 839, 932, 1307,
        1318, 2227, 2648, 2812, 2815, 3880
baseball 4714
    and gambling 1819–20
    and identity 2222
    and idioculture 2237
basho 237
basketball 4645
    and gambling 1820
    and globalization 2236
    and identity 2222
    media coverage 2918
    women's basketball 2918
Basque nationalism 1430, 1470
Bass, B. M. 2566
Bastian, A. 321, 1486
Bastide, R. 2190
bat mitzvahs 2452
Bataille, Georges 246–7, 3569
    and gift exchange 1940
    and redistribution thesis 1939
    and taboo 246, 5045
Bateson, Gregory 247–50, 2865–6, 3387
    communication theory 249
    and deviance 1136
    ethnography 2986
    and framing theory 248, 1778
    and social interaction 2362
Bateson, M. 2867

Batson, D. 3681
battered women
    domestic violence shelters 3775
    safety 1711–12
    see also domestic abuse
battle fatigue 2694
    see also post-traumatic stress disorder
Battle, J. 2944–6
Baubérot, J. 2529–33
Bauchspies, W. K. 2981–6, 4074–6
Baudelaire, Charles 268, 757
    and *flânerie* 1762
    and modernity 3068
Baudrillard, Jean 683, 3879
    and alienation 703
    and commodification 610, 711
    and consumption 702–3, 704, 707, 741, 758,
        2835, 2883, 3569
    and corporate culture 3567
    floating signifier effect 709, 711, 3574
    and hyperreality 2194, 2195–6, 2925–6
    implosion theory 2268–9, 2692
    mass culture/mass society thesis 2824
    and mediation 2926
    political economy theory 610
    postmodernism 685, 929, 3496, 3552, 3570,
        3573, 3574
    poststructuralism 3581
    and science fiction 3496
    semiotics 758, 2835, 3569, 3581
    simulation theory 3879, 3881–2, 4330,
        4332, 4333
    and symbolic exchange 4909
Bauer, B. 1748, 2806, 2807
Bauman, Zygmunt 344, 406, 3552
    and flawed consumers 699–700
    and consumer culture 420, 748, 2193
    and "dream of community" 1578
    and fantasy cities 1643
    and genocide and modernity 1911
    and glocalization 1994
    and the Holocaust 2142, 3571
    and individual choice 2062
    and intimacy 2413
    and nation 1476
    and postmodern sexualities 3568
    and postmodernism 3570–1
    and sociological ambivalence 127–8
Baumer, R. 1519–20
Baumgardener, J. 1677
Baur, N. 3120–3, 5176–9
Bavelas, A. 1513

Baxandall, R. 2615
Baxter, V. 4886–8
Bayard de Volo, L. 2214
Bayesian probability theory 2287
Bayesian statistics 2969
Bazin, A. 1916
BCE and CE 2449
beach 3484–6
Beach Boys 3493
Beale, F. 307, 308, 2621
Beamish, R. 244–6, 1150–1, 1515–16, 2098–9,
    2507–9, 3844–5, 4637–8, 4660–2, 5155,
    5167–8
Beamish, T. D. 1294–7
Bean, F. D. 2262–6, 3480
Beard, Mary Ritter 250–1
    and women's civilizing influence 251
Beatles 1361, 3131–2, 3493, 3509
beatniks 809
Beattie, J. H. M. 2698
beauty
    conformity to beauty ideals 1850
    gendered beauty standards 2603
    racial perceptions of 3765
beauty industries
    and entrepreneurship 712
    see also cosmetic products
beauty pageants 3774
Beauvoir, Simone de 251–5, 1674, 3052
    and agism 57, 253–4
    and the female body 332
    and gender construction 326, 1663
    The Second Sex 250, 252, 253, 326,
        332, 336
Bebel, A. 2841
bebop music 797
Beccaria, Cesare 255–6, 857, 976, 1105,
    1118, 3799
    deterrence theory 256, 1065, 1066, 3799
Beck, Ulrich 1174, 1576, 1577
    and elective affinities 3075
    and family theory 1633–4
    and genetic engineering 1906
    and reflexive modernization 3070,
        3829–30, 3926
    and the risk society 2084, 2285, 3466
Beck Anxiety Inventory (BAI) 3852
Beck-Gernsheim, E. 1578, 1633–4
Becker, G. 1734, 1760, 2415, 3800
Becker, Howard 2362, 2472
    church–sect theory 4137
    and cults 885

and deviance 1087, 1123, 1125, 1136,
    1137, 1143, 2207, 2208, 2501, 2502,
    2505, 2976, 2977
and jazz 3488
and master status 2832
and medical student socialization 2930, 2934
and moral entrepreneurship 3086, 3087
and mysticism 885
and photography 770
social learning theory 3505
and sociology of art 178, 1146
symbolic interactionism 320
and visual sociology 2986
Becker, M. 2105
Becker, R. 4734–7
Beckfield, J. 3182
Beckford, J. A. 484, 2438
Beckham, David 325, 4670, 4716
Bedborough, G. 1365
Bedouin society 289–90, 2459, 2460
Beeghley, L. 2151–2
Beere, C. A. 1868
Befu, H. 1286–9, 3219
beggars and itinerants 2147, 2149, 2766
behavior *see* animal behavior; attitudes and
    behavior; behaviorism; health behavior;
    illness behavior; norms; psychological social
    psychology; specific types of behavior
behavior modification techniques 257–8
behavior-status theory 1525–6
behavior therapy 258
behavioral ecology 291, 292, 1508
behavioral economics 1387
behavioral genetics 635
behavioral-prediction equations 37
behavioral predispositions 293
behavioral psychology 2145, 2146
behavioral theory of the firm 3281, 3282, 3329
behaviorism 256–8, 4542–3
    and empiricism 1434
    and hermeneutics 1481
    individualistic behaviorism 3056
    learned helplessness 67, 2567–70
    Mead and 3055–6
    psychological behaviorism 3056
    purposive 257
    radical 257
    Skinner and 257
    social behaviorism 3055–6
    and social learning theory 4437
    see also attitudes and behavior; attribution
        theory

Beichner, D. 3787–9
Beilharz, P. 2526–7, 3492–4, 3503–4, 3507
Beirne, P. 2177
Bekhterev, V. I. 3672
Belafonte, Harry 3135
Belarus 3039
   Jewish population 2453
Belgium
   and accommodation 8
   Catholicism 2530
   centralized control 1488
   cohabitation 566
   democracy 1001
   and ethnonationalism 1488
   and federalism 1652
   immigration policies 3020
   laicism 2531–2, 4145, 4146
   new religious movements 3205
   social security system 2055
   technology assessment 689
   teenage motherhood 1728
   wealth inequalities 2312
   World War I atrocities 1886
belief 258–62
   alienation 262
   anthropology of 424
   collective 259
   and collective memory 589
   and collective trauma 594, 595
   contested 288
   defining 258
   deviant beliefs 1140–1
   and dissonance theory 562
   faith/belief dichotomy 258
   false belief 992
   groundlessness 260
   institutionalization of 198
   legitimating 230
   magical belief 517
   metaphysical beliefs 3355
   modernity and 260, 261
   religious belief 258, 475, 1256–7, 1317, 1476,
      3858, 3866
   social construction 1141
   socially shared 260
   status beliefs 4758
   and subjectivism 198, 541
   unstable beliefs 562
   see also attitudes and behavior; non-belief
belief systems
   ideological 2756
   utopian 2756

Belk, R. W. 737–46, 742
Bell, A. 2159
bell curve 262–3
   and norms 3231
Bell Curve, The **(Herrnstein and Murray)**
   263–5, 4115
Bell, Daniel 325, 1760, 2231, 2327, 2328–9,
   2334, 2650, 2823, 3051, 3172, 3466, 3550
Bell, David 961–5, 4254–6
Bell McKenzie, K. 1771–4
Bell-Scott, Patricia 308
Bellah, R. 506, 1261, 1582, 1811, 2285, 2803,
   3633, 3937, 3978–9
Bellamy, E. 3495
Bello, A. 1565
Belmont Report 2346, 2348
Belorussia, ethnic cleansing 1451
Bem, D. 562
Ben-David, J. 4070
Ben-Rafael, E. 4370–4
Ben-Yehuda, N. 1087, 1090, 3088, 3089, 3090
Ben-Ze'ev, A. 965
benchmarking 3396
Bendix, R. 547, 549, 1921, 2133, 2134,
   2795, 3061
Benedict, R. 238, 909, 1083, 2865, 2867, 3749
benefit and victimized zones 265–7, 4526
Benford, R. 3067
Bengel, J. A. 3408
Benglis, L. 2834
Bengston, V. L. 2380–2
Benhabib, S. 3560
Benjamin, J. 1806, 3696
Benjamin, Walter 267–70, 2539, 3127
   and Adorno 27
   and arcades 165–6
   art and capitalism 517
   and collective memory 591, 592
   and consumer culture 592, 741
   and *flânerie* 1762, 2650
   and the Frankfurt School 865, 2881
   and high art 1753–4
   and mechanical reproduction 1753, 1754
   and media technologies 943
   and modernity 268, 3068
   photography and visual culture 3406
Benmayor, R. 2550
Bennett, G. 1348
Bennett, T. 2103, 5253–4
Bensman, J. 1376
Benson, M. L. 12–14
Benson, S. 743

Benston, M. 2841
Bentham, Jeremy 857, 1105, 1118
   and deterrence theory 1065, 1066, 3799
   and liberalism 2622
   panoptics 1177, 1776, 2565, 4896
   utilitarianism 2441
Bentley, A. F. 3811
Bentley, G. 1224
Benton, T. 1419, 1420
benzodiazepines 1235
Berard, T. J. 4872–7
Berberoglu, B. 2838
Berbers 1838, 2459
Berea College v. *Kentucky* 368
bereavement 974–5
   see also death and dying; widowhood
Berends, M. 4721–5
Berezin, M. 1644–7, 3576–7
Berger, J. 990, 1524–8, 2856
Berger, M. T. 2397
Berger, Michele 3117–20
Berger, P. 686, 1087–8, 1141, 1436, 1520, 1582,
     1812, 2345, 2484, 2529, 2587, 3403, 3867,
     3874, 3975, 4094
Berghe, P. L. van den 3156
Bergman, T. O. 1352
Bergson, H. 1286, 2003, 2040, 2047, 3124, 3859
Berk, R. A. 789, 790
Berking, H. 1939, 1940
Berkman, A. 136, 2005, 2006, 2007
Berkman, L. F. 2073
Berlant, L. 2413
Berle, A. A. 3055
Berlin Doctors Club 2806
Berlin, Isaiah 2624, 3155
Berlin Olympics (1936) 4682
Berlin Wall 2749, 3042, 3157, 3203, 3648
Berman, E. 1315
Bermeo, N. 1647
Bernal, H. 414
Bernal, J. D. 4066, 4110, 4119
Bernard, Jessie 270–3, 1670
   biography 270–1
   on marriage 2301
   and patriarchal relations 3378
Bernard, L. L. 270–1, 272, 273
Bernard, M. 2668–9
Bernard, P. 4364–70
Bernard, T. J. 668
Bernardi, B. 3869–71
Bernardi, F. 674–6, 5054–7
Berners Lee, T. 3110

Bernstein, B. 2655
Bernstein, E. 245, 2679, 2685
   historical materialism 350–1
Bernstein, M. 2215
Berque, J. 2427
Berry, Chuck 3492
Berscheid, E. 2672
Berson, G. 2604
Berstein, B. 2117
Bertelsmann 2898
Besant, A. 3190
Best, A. L. 724–7
Best, J. 979, 1087, 1089, 1091, 1100
best practice 2480, 2720, 2929
Best, S. 2269
beta thalassemia 1907
Bethune Cookman Institute 397
Bethune, M. M. 307
Bettelheim, B. 1572–3
Bettez, S. 3117–20
Bevan, P. 2628
Beveridge, W. H. 2625
Beyer, P. 1980–3, 3861
Bezdek, W. 2029–33
Bhabha, H. 2886, 2984, 3576
Bhagavad Gita 2130
Bharatiya Janata party 1982
Bhaskar, R. 871, 2109
Bhavnani, K. K. 3344
Bhutan 1458
Biafra 240
Bialik, C. N. 3427
Bianchi, A. J. 4172–5
bias 2925
   actor–observer difference 206–7
   biases in attribution 206
   and case study methods 1890
   in communication 3672, 3778
   confirmation bias 2270
   correspondence bias 206
   gender bias 1843–5
   mobilization of bias 3472
   and naturalistic enquiry 3163
   self-serving bias 207, 2271
   in student selection 2956
   see also classism; ethnocentrism;
     homophobia; prejudice; racism; sexism
Biblarz, T. J. 2380–2
Bible
   accounts of madness 2694
   biblical hermeneutics 2107–8, 3690, 4322
   Old Testament punishments 3521–2

and Protestantism 3689
vernacular translations 3636
Bible Students 2439
biblical sciences 3409
bibliometrics 4120, 4121
Bicchieri, C. 3229, 3232
bicultural education 278
Biddlecom, A. E. 1609–12
Bidermann, J. 2340
Bienenstock, E. J. 1514
Bierman, A. 262–3
Biernacki, R. 933, 934, 1308, 3607–9
bifurcated consciousness, line of fault
    274–5, 3960
Big Bang 642
big box stores 1058–9, 4311
"big government" 2296
Big Science and collective research 275–7
Biggart, N. W. 1294–7, 1296
Biggs, L. 630
bikers 329
bilateralism 1691
bilingual, multicultural education
    277–81
    English, acquisition of 277, 278
    immigrants 2261
    maintenance programs 283
    strong forms 277, 278, 280
    transitional 283
    weak forms 277, 280
bilingualism 281–3
    additive bilingualism 282–3
    balanced bilinguals 282
    elite bilingualism 282
    folk bilingualism 282
    individual 281
    limited 277
    proficiency variations 282
    semilingualism 282
    societal 281, 282
    stable bilingual societies 282
    subtractive 283
    transitory bilingual societies 282
biliteracy 277
Billings, J. S. 2932
Bills, D. B. 39–42, 367–70, 1328–31, 1333–6,
    1784–5, 3250, 4029–32
Bils, M. 1332
bin Laden, Osama 1637, 2801
binary codes 2675–6
Binet, A. 1745, 1746
binge drinking 118

Binkley, S. 34–5, 755–60, 809–10, 999–1000,
    2646–51, 3141–2, 5010–11
Binnie, J. 1983–6
bio queens 1223
bio-politics 181–2, 324, 337, 338
bio-power 1178, 1776
biodemography 283–7
    biodemographic interactions 1584
    biodemographical models 1743
    biological demography 283, 284–5
    biomedical demography 283, 286–7
biodiversity, reduction of 1281, 1418,
    1419, 3533
bioethics 2174
biographical time 73
biography 73, **287–91**
    and biracialism 295
    collaborative 289
    coming out narratives 606
    cultural 290
    and documentary analysis 1215
    and the life course 2632
    and life history 2642
    mass market 289
    see also life history; social movements,
      biographical consequences of
biological demography 283, 284–5
biological determinism 969, 1366
biological evolutionary theory 1504
biological fitness of the population 594
biological gerontology 284–5
biological psychiatry 2951
biological reductionism 4197
biological relativism 908
biology
    biosociological theories 291–5
    evolutionary biology 291, 292, 294
    neurobiology 291
    society and biology 4583–5
    sociobiology 291, 292
biomass 1424
biomedical demography 283, 286–7
biomedical gerontology 1927
biomedicalization 1113
biomedicine 284, 337, 2081
    biomedical research 1442, 1443, 2172
    and complementary and alternative medicine
      630, 632
    and disability 1700
    gender biases 1683–4
    and lesbianism 2612
    research ethics 2349

biomedicine (*cont'd*)
  and social epidemiology 4403
  and sport 1241
biometric identification 3643
Bion, W. R. 3443
biopolitics 1908, 4584–5
biopower 2711, 3884
biosocial criminology 822–5
  evolutionary neuroandrogenic (ENA)
    theory 824
  evolutionary theory 823
  neurologically specific theories 823–4
biosociological theories 291–5
  and crime 822–5
  and genealogy 1897
  and neurosociology 3186, 3187
biotech industries 337
biotechnology 689, 691, 3930
biovalues 2172
biphobia 304
biracialism 295–7, 1405
  biracial coalitions 124
  biracial identity 296
  once drop rule 3265–6
  see also interracial unions; segregation
Birch, M. 2659
Bird, C. 2934
Birdwhistell, R. 1995, 2362–3
Birmingham, Alabama 781
Birmingham School 297–301
  counterculture studies 809
  and cultural criminology 893
  cultural studies 744, 913–14, 2648,
    2882, 3482
  culturalism and structuralism 298
  feminist studies 301
  film theory 1755
  and hegemony concept 2101
  and masculinity and consumption 736
  media studies 2882
  neo-Gramscian Marxism 298–9, 2103
  and reception theory 210
  and social identity construction 746
  subcultural studies 53–4, 912, 4871, 4874
birth control 101, 1047
  abortion as 3
  coitus interruptus 4277
  Goldman and 2005
  Malthus and 2707, 2708
  "natural method" 4143
  see also contraception; family planning
birth interval analysis 1744

birth rates
  Crude Birth Rate (CBR) 1014, 1015, 1016,
    1039
  and fertility 1014
  and gender 1156
  and industrialization 2295–6
bisexuality 301–5, 2160
  bisexual identity 303, 304
  and collective identity 588
  Freudian theory 302
  and polyamory 3477
  psychoanalytic feminist perspective 3697
  self-identification 2162
  self-reporting 1129
  stigmatization 639
  see also friendships of gay, lesbian, and
    bisexual people
Bismarckism 411, 413
bitmap images 1163, 1164
Bittner, E. 1137
black Americans
  and accommodation 8
  adolescent fertility 1728
  American Dilemma, An (Gunnar Myrdal)
    128–30
  anti-Semitism 153
  and assimilation 193–4, 195, 3106–7
  Black Nationalism 4188
  black urban regime 310–12
  black youth, and dual marginality 2764–5
  businesses 708
  cohabitation 566, 1208
  consumption 706–9, 766, 1851
  and criminal justice system 804
  criminality 3734, 3735
  criminalization 1664
  and division of household labor 1204
  domestic violence 1219
  and drag subculture 1224, 1225
  education 605, 1325, 1327, 1330, 2013
  educational attainment 1335
  educational segregation 3753
  and elder care 2381
  employment 2305–7, 2711, 3968
  exogamy 1405
  fatherhood 1603, 1626
  and fertility 2018
  folk medicine 631
  franchise 370, 507, 510
  genetic conditions 2080
  and the ghetto 1936, 1937
  graduate education 2013

grandparenting 1842, 2020
health care-seeking behavior 2069
and homelessness 2149
housing segregation 316–18, 2419, 3708
hypersegregation 2196, 2197, 2198
incarceration 3642, 3733, 3736, 3738,
    3739, 3766
ingroup association 795
internal migration 3028
and kindergarten 2463
life expectancy 394, 2078, 3761
literacy levels 2654
and marital quality 2774
marriage 566, 1734, 2415
middle class 311, 707, 708, 709, 2306, 3747
morbidity and mortality 3757, 4150
and nest-leaving 2572
nonmarital births 1721, 1735
parental involvement in education 3358
patriarchal authority 2302
poverty 1613, 1627, 1719, 1842, 2625–6,
    3255–6, 3650
and the racial hierarchy 3761
rates of pay 1844
religiosity 4642
residential segregation 2196, 2197, 2306,
    3888, 3889–90, 3898–9
and school dropout 1230
school segregation 367–70
and sport 2222
stereotyping 1664, 1665, 1879, 2122, 3650
style 715, 719
unemployment 4030
urban migration 510
voting behavior 2233
workplace discrimination 41
youth culture 809
see also black women; Civil Rights
    Movement; segregation
black athleticism 2918, 4687–9, 4699–700
Black Bloc papers 981
Black Caucus 131
black church 1245
and Civil Rights Movement 509, 587
Black Death 4092–3
black feminist thought 305–10, 309,
    1155, 1672, 1673, 1675–6, 1677, 1711,
    2395, 2621
distinctive elements 305–6
and ethic of care 1438
and exclusion 2847
and intersectionality 2395, 2397, 2842, 2859

lesbian feminist critique 2604, 2605, 2621
maternal politics 2847
and multiracial feminism 3118
outsider-within concept 3350–1
personal is political 3400
and racialized gender 3764
and social movements 1873
and standpoint theory 1712
Black Mass 4010
Black Nationalism 4188
black political leaders 311
    see also black urban regime
Black Power 2467, 3106, 3548
Black Report on Inequalities in Health 2086,
    2087
Black Sox Scandal 1919 1133, 1819–20
Black Studies Associations 1244
black urban regime 310–12
interracial coalitions 124
pro-business agenda 311–12
black women
    black matriarchy 3266
    businesswomen 708
    clubs and organizations 307
    consciousness-raising 677
    and consumption 1851
    labor force participation 993
    and social movements 1873
    women of color feminism 2621, 3117–20
    see also black feminist thought
blackness
    demarcations of 3265–6
    stereotypes 3737
    see also one drop rule
Blackpool Pleasure Beach 3484
Blackwell, E. 2932
Blair, Tony 2527, 3471
blaming 2561–2
Blank, G. 721–4
blasé/neurasthenic personalities 312–13
Blasko, Z. 911
Blatt, J. 4113–15
Blau, Peter 313–16, 795, 2960
    and educational attainment 1334, 1336
    and exchange theory 2361
    and intergenerational mobility 2276–7, 3062
    macro-structural theory 795, 796
    and occupational scaffolding 3249
    and organizational structure 3313
    and status attainment 2629, 4753, 4754
    and stratification 1334
Blauner, R. 603

Blaxter, M. 2062
Bleaney, M. 1332
Blee, Kathleen M. 3767–71
blended families 695
    and family sociology 1617
    and family theory 1632
blessings, religious 3521
blind persons 1194
Bloch, M., and Annales School 142, 143, 144,
    2047, 2135
Block, M. 3131
blockades 780, 1165, 1887
blockbusting 316–18
    and the concentric zone model 1278
    and invasion-succession 2419
blocking 1534
blogging 777, 1164, 1445, 2905
blood donation 1939, 3681
blood feuds 2140
Blood, R. 2770–1
blood sports 1819, 1820
Bloom, A. 1807, 3214
Bloom, L. R. 1703
Bloom, P. 698
Bloor, B. 786
Bloor, D. 4071
Bloyve, D. 1751
Blücher, H. 166
blue-collar sector 1344
    displacement 1917
    workers' movements 2829
    see also working class
blues 3492
Bluestone, B. 994
Blumenbach, J. F. 4114
Blumenfeld, K. 167
Blumer, Herbert George 318–21, 447, 1227
    and attitudes and behavior 201
    and collective action 2961
    collective selection 719, 720
    and crowd sociology 880
    and fashion 719, 4932–3
    and industrialization and social change 2962
    and mesostructure 2961
    race relations theory 3741–2
    and racial prejudice 3615
    and the self 2217
    and social problems theory 1097, 1098
    symbolic interactionism 1087, 1130, 1436,
        1812, 1996, 2214, 2362, 2997, 4909–10
BMW 352
BMX 4655

Boas, Frank 321–3, 4115
    cultural anthropology 149, 1083, 2866
    and cultural relativism 909
    and scientific racism 4115
Boatca, M. 1067–70
Bobo's 810
Boddy, W. 2905
bodhisattva 371, 3854–5
bodily capital 1850
Bodin, J. 613
body
    alienation 711
    anatamo-politics of 324, 337, 338
    asceticism 188
    bio-politics of 324, 337, 338
    the body beautiful 325
    body politic 807, 808
    body techniques 326, 336
    coding/decoding 327, 337
    and consumption 709–11
    cultural representation 328, 336
    cultural text analysis of 330
    cybersexuality 966
    and disciplinary techniques 1177
    discipline and surveillance 332, 334,
        337, 338
    dominated body 710–11
    expressive and erotic body 325–6, 710, 711
    and female criminality 1694
    feminine body 736
    feminist theories of 336
    fetishization 711
    gendered body 331, 7336
    governmentality 324, 325, 332
    and identity 2219
    lesbian body 2612
    and the lifeworld 2652
    lived body concept 326–7, 334, 335, 336
    masculine body 736
    medicalized 338
    mind–body dualism 327, 335, 337
    naturalist/materialist views 332
    othered bodies 711
    ownership rights 337
    playful body 326
    political economy of the 2711, 2713
    postmodern body 326
    productive body 325
    queering 330
    reflexive self-fashioning 711
    representation of social organization 326, 335
    sacralization of 741

self-surveillance 711, 1113
site of contestable meaning 711
social construction 326, 335, 337
sociology of the body 335–8
spectacularization of 759
sport and the body 4658–60
symbolic capital 327, 336
symbolic interactionism and 325, 336
training 325
virtual body 966
body, abominations of the 323–4
and stigma 583, 1094
body art 328
body and cultural sociology 324–8
beach theory 3485
civilizing process and 530
Foucault and 324
body image 336, 1516
anxiety over 2084
and disability 1697
and exercise/fitness 1516
and feminism 1677
body imaging 3376
body language 347
body maintenance 709, 710
body modification 324, 328–30, 2827
see also cosmetic surgery
body parts 337
loss of 335
body piercing 324, 329, 330
body play 330
body searches 1870
body and sexuality 330–4
cybersexualities 965–6
and disability 1698
discursive analysis 331, 332
and feminist disability studies 1697
gendered patterns 333, 1845–8
materialist analysis 331
naturalistic accounts 331
non-dualistic account 1847
social construction 332
sociobiological explanations 331
body shape, ideal 722
Body Shop 1441
body and society 335–8
body and cultural sociology 324–8
cloning and 556–9
disability as a social problem 1168–70
bodybuilding 1878
bodywork 631, 632, 710
and self-identity 710

Boer, C. de 3711–15
Boerema, A. 4721–5
Bogardus, E. 3344, 4398
Bogdan, R. 3950
Bögenhold, D. 2827–9
Boggs, G. L. 308
Bogue, D. 132
bogus stranger paradigm 2391
Böhm-Bawerk, E. 1304
Böhme, G. 1757
Boli, J. 1967, 1990, 1992
Bolivia
bilingual education 278
child labor 460
economy 411
ethnic conflicts 3318
indigenous movements 2279
Bollen, K. A. 1001, 1002, 2544
Bollier, D. 732
Bollywood 2874
Bologna declaration 1973
Bolshevism 680, 2006–7
film propaganda 1753
Jews and 158–9
see also Russian Revolutions
bombings 779, 780
Bommier, A. 1904
Bon, M. 2159
Bonacich, E. 664, 1460, 1463, 2838, 3009, 3012, 3184
Bonacich, P. 1514
Bonald, L. de 2837
bonanza economics 3511
Bonaparte, Louis 412, 2809, 2810
Bonapartism 411, 412, 413
bondage and discipline (B&D) 330
see also sadomasochism
Bondi, L. 1919
bonding
collective bonding 1839
and deviance 1081
male sexual bonding 2155
pair bonding 2672
same-sex bonding 2155, 2156
social bonding 1253, 1254
bonesetters 2079
Bonfil Batalla, Guillermo 339–43
Bongaarts, J. 1731, 1737–41
Bonger, W. 840
Bonhoeffer, D. 198
Bonilla, R. G. 2948
bonsai 2762

Bonstead-Bruns, M. 5284–7
Bontemps, A. 2444
Bookchin, Murray 136
books 3635, 3637
    book publishing 944
    see also print media
Boolean logic 4117
Boolean operators 645
boom and bust cycle 2022
Boon, V. 4877–8
Boorstin, D. 741
boosterism 2035
boot camps 803, 855
Booth, C. 1244, 2407, 2731–3
Booth, D. 3485
bootstrap methods 2974–6, 3878
booty capitalism 1075
border studies 345, 3926–32
"borderless world" 1956, 1960
borders 288
    border controls 2262, 2265, 3020
    and migration flows 2256
    open-border system 3020
    porosity 1952
    security 2334
    see also boundaries
Bordo, S. 326, 1697, 1850
Borges, G. 2550
Borges, Jorge Luis 1914
Bork, R. 3654
Boruch, R. F. 2403–6
Bose, C. E. 1852–6, 2382–4
Boserup, E. 1853, 2840, 3526
Bosma, H. A. 2221
Bosnia 584, 660, 661
    civil wars 1470
    genocide 1183
    peace process 3381
    shuttle diplomacy 3380
Bosserman, P. 2040–3
Boswell, G. 898–902
Boswell, J. 1828
botany 2699, 4116
Botha, P. W. 163
Botswana 106
    AIDs mortality 2137
    life expectancy 1864
Bott, E. 672–3, 2742, 2743, 3182
Bottenberg, M. van 1751
Bottero, W. 539–42, 545–7
Botticini, M. 1315
Bottomore, T. B. 334–5

Boucicaut, A. 1057
Boudin, L. 245
Bouffard, J. A. 3799–802
Boulle, P. 3495
boundaries
    class boundaries 662
    and collective identity 586
    community 714, 715
    and discourse 1179, 1181
    and endogamy 1404
    and family theory 1632
    and family therapy 1635
    and in-groups and out-groups 2338, 3128
    indigenous 2281
    and the Internet 2387
    kinship 2469
    moral 1114, 1115
    and music 3128
    nation-states 1469, 3012, 3151
    organizational 355, 2387
    sexual 345
    symbolic 4774
    territorial 1468
boundaries (racial/ethnic) 345–7, 346, 661,
        662, 1459, 1460, 1475, 3751
    and assimilation 195
    boundary crossing 195
    boundary making and maintenance 345, 346
    boundary shifting 195, 295
    and business ethics 1439
    changes 1474
    and ethnic, racial, and social movements
        1465
    and middleman minorities 3009
    and refugees 3838
    and self-determination 4167
boundary crossing 195
    mestizaje 2190
boundary objects 4548
boundary shifting 195, 295
boundary work, science/nonscience 4080–1
boundaryless careers 3288–9
bounded rationality 2748, 3282, 3287, 3313,
        3795–6, 3800, 3802
    satisficing model 3795
Bourdieu, Pierre 347–50, 871
    and aesthetics 34, 35, 591, 1361
    and art worlds 179
    and aspirations/expectations 1530
    and the body 327, 336
    class analysis 541, 723, 741, 2125, 2628, 2648
    and conspicuous consumption 685, 934, 1308

and cultural capital 383, 384, 887–9, 891, 1326, 1337, 1361, 2125, 2645
and cultural distinction 1189, 1190, 1639
and cultural reproduction 910
and culture and stratification 915
and education 2117
and fan cultures 1639, 1840
field theory 1322
and Foucault 1778
and gift exchange 3937
habitus/field 346, 347–8, 710, 742, 934, 1309, 2045, 2062, 2534, 2536, 2648, 2962, 3452, 3582, 3583
and hermeneutics 2109
and improvisation 2734
and life chances 2628
and lifestyle selection 2062
and multiple correspondence analysis (MCA) 2969
musicology 3135
and objectivism 3235
and phenomenology 2045
political party theory 3452
postmodernism 3582
and reproduction of elites 1362
and school curricula 1337
and social capital 4355, 4356, 4693
and social resources 2627
and social space 1189
and social stratification 2645
social theory 1170, 3135
and sport and class 4534, 4696, 4697
structure and agency 4863
and symbolic interaction 2045
symbolic power of naming 555
and taste 741, 1361, 2651, 4930, 4933–4
bourgeois status hierarchies and commodity relations 609
bourgeoisie
  bourgeois consciousness 2680
  bourgeois hegemony 2227
  and imagined communities 2249
  and moral solidity 2682
  tastes 1360
  see also middle class
bourgeoisie and proletariat 350–1
  and class conflict 538
  and fashion 718
  Marxist theory 534, 539
Bourne, R. 3193, 3213, 3216
Bowers, W. J. 977
Bowker, G. 20–1, 2362

Bowles, S. 1323, 2116
Bowser, B. P. 123–5
boxing 1819, 1821, 2918, 3472, 4699
Boy Scouts 1877
boycotts 706, 745, 780, 1874, 1948, 3008, 3009, 3010, 4688, 4700
Boyd, M. 3027
Boyd-Barrett, O. 2889
Boyle, J. 732
Boyle, Robert 4107
Bracero program 2263
bracketing 3402
Bradbury, T. N. 2774–5
Brady, I. 2422, 3424–6
Brah, A. 1154
Brahma Kumaris 3202
Brahmans 404, 405, 521, 1764, 2129
Brailsford, D. 1819
brain
  and aging 1927
  cognitive algorithms 293
  evolutionary perspective 3186
  hemispheric functioning theory 824
  infant brain development 1270
  and neurosociology 3185–9
brain drain 1040, 1344
brain imaging 2243–4
Brain, R. 1790
brainwashing
  and cults 886, 887, 3205
  in organizations 3339
  and resocialization 3892
Braithwaite, J. 543, 827, 2502, 2506, 3304
Brake, M. 2112
Branch Davidians 886, 3047
brand bullies 732
brand communities 359
brand culture 351–3
brand equity 352, 358
brand identity 351, 352, 354
brand image 351, 352
brand loyalty 775
brand management system 358
branded stores 4306–7
Branden, K. 1614–8
branding and organizational identity 353–7
  see also franchising
brands and branding 329, 357–60
  branded environment 730
  and children's consumer culture 694, 696, 740

brands and branding (*cont'd*)
  and consumer movements 698
  and consumption 683, 737, 738, 739,
    740, 743
  corporate brands 352
  and fantasy cities 1642
  genericide 731
  global brands 1956, 1957, 1961
  and politics 740
  urban branding 1455
Branford, V. 3123
Brannen, J. 457–9
Brant, B. 3119
Brantingham, P. 1427
Brass, Paul R. 3155
Braudel, Fernand 360–3, 5112
  and Annales School 143, 2135, 2426
  and consumer culture 743
Braungart, M. M. 1901
Braungart, R. G. 1901
Braverman, Harry 363–5
  deskilling thesis 2521–2, 2523
  and the labor process 3179, 5284–5
  materialist analysis 2838
Brazil 1566
  authoritarian regimes 223, 224
  charismatic movement 440, 441–2
  consumer movements 697, 698
  decolonization 985
  economy 1561
  and federalism 1652
  film industry 1753
  indigenous peoples 2279
  industrialization 2299
  interracial unions 3732
  Jewish community 2453
  literacy program 865
  medical sociology 2935
  multiracial feminism 3118
  peripheral state 1395
  racial categorization 2080
  retirement policies 3903
  sex tourism 4201
  television corporations 2890
breaching experiments 1484, 4387–8
breadwinner/homemaker model 1272, 1883,
    1884, 2309, 2416
  and family migration 1606
  and fatherhood 1649
break dancing 3486
breast cancer 2938, 3376
breastfeeding 2308, 2319

Brecht, Bertolt 268
Breckenridge, S. 444
Breen, R. 2368–73, 2369
Brelich, A. 2700
Brenner, N. 1917–20
Breslau, D. 4069–72
Bretton Woods Agreements 1567, 1951
Breuilly, J. 3150, 3155
Brewer, J. 744
Brewer, R. 2838
Brewer, T. W. 842–4
Briar, S. 846
bricolage 365–6, 2846, 3871
  and hybridity 2189
  and management improvisation 2734–5
  religious 4147
bride burnings 2303
bride buying 1158
bride-price 3534
bridging relationships 1802
Brint, S. 599–602, 622
Britain *see* United Kingdom
British Asians 2886
British Broadcasting Corporation (BBC) 628,
    2875–6, 2897, 3703, 3706, 3777–8
British cultural studies 242–3
British Documentary Movement 1210
British Household Panel Survey 810
British Sociological Association
    344, 366–7
  Medical Sociology Group 2934
Brito, M. 3537–9
Britton, D. 1894
broadband technology 2915, 3111
  and intellectual property issues 2358
Broderick, D. 3496
Brody, H. 1577
broken windows theory of crime 825–6,
    3432, 3716
  deductive approach 1397–8
  and fear of crime 2341
Bromley, D. G. 3089–92
Bronner, S. 743
Brooks, A. 937
Brooks, D. 1190
Brotton, J. 1966
Brown, N. 2175
Brown, R. 2616
Brown, R. M. 2604
Brown, S. E. 856–60, 1478–9, 2552–3, 3838–9
Brown, S. K. 2262–6
Brown, S. L. 2733

Brown v. Board of Education
  and affirmative action 39
  and political opportunities 3448
  and school desegregation **367–70**, 1326,
    2444, 3448, 3742, 3747, 4023–4
Browning, C. R. 1646, 2072–5
Brownmiller, S. 905, 2113, 3774, 3786, 4249
Brubaker, R. 1452, 1466, 1467, 1471
Bruce, S. 4091–3
Bruce, T. 2916–21
Brunch, C. 2113
Brundtland Report 1285
Bruno, Giordano 2697
Brunson, R. K. 1825–8
Brustein, W. I. 154–60, 1646
brute being 1521
Bryan, T. 1012–3
Bryant, A. 2026
Bryant, C. 1495–8, 2176
Bryman, A. 1187, 1187–8, 4950–1
Bryson, B. 890
BSkyB 2887
bubbles 2021–2
Buber, M. 624, 3673
Buchanan, I. 423–5
Buchanan, J. 3177
Buchmann, C. 4753–6
Büchs, M. 4489–90
Buckle, H. T. 3811
Buddha 2129
Buddhadharma 371, 373
Buddhism 370–4, 520, 521, 524, 752, 1980,
    2130, 3854–5, 3856
  American voluntarism 1055
  and asceticism 188
  atheism 2131
  and Confucianism 669, 671, 672
  en 1400–1
  fundamentalism 1813, 1816
  global activities 1982
  and homosexuality 4214
  and martyrdom 2799
  millenarianism 3047
  nonviolence 2130
  peacemaking 3384
  and popular religiosity 3518
  and self-help movements 1407
  and sexuality 4276, 4278
  theocracy 3094
  Zen Buddhism 750
Budig, M. 1882
Buechler, S. M. 3208–11, 4479–82

built environment **374–6**, 500–1
  exurbia 1549–50
  and gentrification 1917–20
  and nature and culture 946
  new urbanism 3211
Bukatman, S. 3496
Bukharin, N. 2015, 2686
Bulgaria
  ethnic cleansing
  nationalism 3145, 3347
  Orthodox Church 3345, 3346, 3347
  population exchange 1451
bulimia 337, 722
  and dissonance theory 564
  and family theory 1632
Bull, M. 746
bullet trains 266, 2126, 2127, 3476, 3477
bullfighting 3160
bullying 4013
Bumstead, H. 604
Bunch, C. 2603–4
Bunzel, D. 3805–8
Buonarroti, Filippo 614
Burawoy, M. 1807, 2041, 2043, 2229, 2523,
    2838, 3179
bureaucracy
  Arendt and 168
  authority and 377
  and biomedicine 631
  bureaucratic elite 1363
  bureaucratic inertia 3313
  bureaucratic nature of evil 3034, 3037
  bureaucratic organizations 1893
  bureaucratic vicious circle 2748
  bureaucratization of church life 439
  career structure 379
  Catholic Church 410
  characteristics 376
  and church 483
  coercive organizations 3316, 3317
  and colonialism 603
  Confucian 376
  and death and dying 973
  and democracy 1004, 1006
  economic bureaucracy 1074
  efficiency 2689, 3313, 3807
  and emotions 1390
  and everyday life 703, 2581
  and friendships 1798
  and health care 2709
  and the Holocaust 2143
  and ideal type 2201, 2202

bureaucracy (*cont'd*)
  and improvisation 2736
  industrial bureaucracy 3287
  and institutionalism 2355
  "iron cage" 3311, 3442
  and leadership 2565
  and McDonaldization 3567
  machine bureaucracies 3288
  managerial 2523
  and the nation-state system 2498
  and organization theory 3330
  and organizational learning 3330
  and organized crime 834
  parliamentary bureaucracy 2809
  professional bureaucracies 3288
  and rational legal authority 3807
  ritualism 3312–3
  and same-sex intimacy 1836
  and secondary groups 4131
  segmentalism 377
  and social movements 3259, 4441
  Weberian 313, 376, 377, 378, 379, 428, 437,
    664, 1176, 1441, 2202, 2355, 2747, 3281,
    3287, 3311–2, 3442, 3459, 3597, 3808–9,
    5230–1
bureaucracy and public sector
  governmentality 376–8
  bureaucratic authority 434
  and capitalism 397
  and disasters 1174
  performance measurement 3396–7, 3398
  and rationalization 3808–9
bureaucratic authoritarianism 222, 224–5
bureaucratic personality 378–80, 3807
  and capitalism 397
  coercive organizations 3316
  and organizational social structure 3323
bureaucratic rationality 3312
Bures, R. M. 498–500
Burgess, Ernest 2770
  and the central business district 422
  and the Chicago School 443, 714,
    1597, 3362–4
  and the concentric zone model 176–7, 1277,
    1918, 2991, 3944
  family sociology 1597–8, 1616
  Park-Burgess collaboration 3362–4
  and social change 445–7
  urban sociology 443, 444, 501, 1289
  see also Park, Robert E. and Burgess, Ernest W.
burglary 2278, 2555, 2556, 3959
  female offenders 4192

Burkam, D. T. 2462–5
Burke, Edmund 170, 679, 2837, 3071,
  3916, 5255
Burke, K. 354–5, 1179, 1226, 1227,
  1996, 2362
Burke, P. 2202–7, 2218, 2225, 3183
Burkert, W. 3984
Burkina Faso, female genital mutilation
  1654, 1656
Burn, S. M. 1854
burnout
  and caregiving 2546
  and marital life 2547
Burns, J. M. 2566
Burns, L. R. 2065–6
Burns, T. 1229, 2738, 3281, 4914–20
Burr, W. R. 1616
Burrows, R. 554–6
Bursik, R. J. 1825, 1826
Burstein, L. 3274
Burt, R. S. 1321, 3184
Burton, M. 2289–90, 2292
Burundi and Rwanda (Hutu, Tutsi) 380–2,
  661, 1183, 1451, 1909, 1910, 1912,
  3673, 3749
Bush administration
  and neoconservatism 3172, 3175
  post 9/11 3175
  and pro-life agenda 3654
  propaganda 3674
  Social Security policy 3256
  see also War on Terror
Bush, B. 415
Bush, George W. 876, 1404, 3602
Bush, J. 415
Bush, R. 2838
Bush, V. 2850, 2852, 3109–10, 3438, 4101
Busia, A. 309
business ethics 1439–42
business improvement districts (BIDs) 1642
business and industrial communication 3291
business and management schools 2725–8, 2750
Business Process Re-Engineering (BPR) 2715,
  2729, 3268
business-format franchising 1784
businesses
  in decentralized states 4731
  ethnic 768, 1452–6, 1460, 1461–2, 1464
  gay 768
  and middleman minorities 3008, 3009, 3010
  neighborhood and community businesses 715
  urban 714–15

youth-oriented 774
see also organizations; transnational
    corporations (TNCs)
busing 39, 48, 370, 1326
Buss, D. 1984
butch queens 1224
butch/femme culture 1658, 1835, 2603
Butler, J. 333, 1663, 1664, 1777, 1847, 1998,
    2114, 2155, 2611–72, 2612, 3570, 3581,
    3728, 4241, 4258
Butler, R. 3879–82
buyer beware principle 1386
Byrd, H. F. 2830, 2831
Byron, Lord 416
bystander intervention 1540, 3679, 3680
Bytheway, B. 56–60, 1927
Byzantine Church 3346
Byzantine Empire 3346

cacique 414
Cage, J. 3557
Cagney, K. A. 2072–5
Cahiers du cinema 1755
Cairnes, J. 1300, 1302, 1303
Calasanti, T. 1840–3
calculative agencies 936
Calder, R. 3458–63
Caldwell, J. C. 1042, 1740
calendar and clock time (CCT) 5001–2, 5004
calendars
    Christian (Gregorian) 2449
    Jewish 2449
Calhoun, C. 1391
Calhoun, T. 2501–54
Califia, P. 2605, 2610
California
    charter schools 4035
    economic geography 1298
    ethnic enclave 1454
caliphate 2425
call centers 365, 2327, 2383
call girls 1660, 1661
Callero, P. L. 4417–20
Callon, M. 20, 22, 23, 219, 786, 1310, 2364,
    4098, 4099
Calvinism 188, 750–1, 1319, 3692
    and asceticism 187, 1319
    and material wealth 707
    Reformations 3689
    religious legitimizion of work 3691
    theocracy 3094
Cambodia 1452

genocide 1909, 1910
    peace processes 3383
Campanella, T. 1175, 2697
Campbell, Alistair 3471
Campbell, Anne 1826
Campbell, Clive 3486
Campbell, Colin 684, 742, 751
Campbell, D. T. 2978
Campbell, J. L. 4730–4
Campbell, J. W. 3494
Campbell, K. E. 1797
Campbell, P. 698
Campbell Collaboration 2406
campesinos 3613
Camus, Albert 1229, 1520
Canada
    and accommodation 8
    aging and social policy 86
    bankruptcy law 241
    bilingual education 278–9
    bilingualism 281, 283
    centralized control 1488
    child custody and child support 453
    class voting 551
    colonialism 603
    complementary and alternative medicine
        630, 631, 632
    crime reporting system 1128
    cultural tourism 921
    demographic data collection 1012
    divorce 452
    drag queens and kings 1224
    elder care services 1350
    emigration 3020
    environmental movements 1431
    ethnic population 899
    eugenic sterilization laws 1489
    and federalism 1652
    female labor force participation 1204
    gay and lesbian self-identity 1129
    gender poverty ratios 1723
    immigration 661, 1198, 1457, 1460, 2260,
        2262, 3026, 3032
    immigration policy 3022
    indigenous peoples 2282
    internal migration 3017
    Jewish community 2453
    migration 1044, 2264
    multiculturalism 1938, 3106
    prostitution 1659
    public broadcasting 2897, 3707
    radical feminism 3775

Canada (*cont'd*)
  religiosity 1054
  school system 1324
  socioeconomic policies 392
  transnational corporations 1944
  wealth inequalities 2312
  welfare capitalism 392
cancer
  ethnic variations 2078, 2080
  and health behavior 2060
  and illness behavior 2241
  and social class variations 2088
cancer research 1757
cancer treatment 973
Candomblé 1980
Canguilhem, G. 335
Cannella, G. S. 867–70
Cannon, W. B. 1749
canon law 3348
canonization 3520–1
Canti, F. 1447
Cantril, H. 3778, 3779
Capa, R. 2988
capital: economic, cultural, and social 383–4
  and educational attainment 1228, 4030
capital
  banking capital 1395
  bodily capital 1850
  and child labor 456
  circulation of 388–9
  and cultural trauma coping resources 597
  definition 390
  economic 1321
  finance capital 1395
  formation 703
  globalization of 1943, 1959
  human capital 1321
  industrial capital 1395
  internationalization of 1061
  liberalization of 1959
  real estate capital 1919
  share capital 1945
  social capital 1321
  social relation of production 703
capital cities 494
  see also global/world cities
capital culture 517
capital deterritorialization 3566
capital flows, transnational 1454
capital punishment 385–8, 802, 974, 1178
  abolition 976–7

  Beccaria and 256
  and conservatism 680
  courts and 814
  death penalty as a social problem 976–8
  methods 385–6
  and race 386
  self-destruction thesis 394
  see also death penalty as a social problem
capital, secondary circuit of 388–9, 2581–2
capitalism 390–5
  academic capitalism 4069
  accumulation regime 3840
  and alienation 615, 874
  Althusser and 125–6
  anarcho-capitalism 136
  Anglo-American 1295
  anomie of memory 592
  and brands and branding 357
  Braudel and 361–2
  breakdown theory 245, 515, 538, 615, 1148, 3437
  and Calvinism 750
  capitalism–communism struggle 1945
  capitalist accumulation 350
  capitalist civiliation 517
  capitalist mode of production 350
  Castoriadis and 406
  center-periphery relationship 1068
  city as agent of 501
  and class struggle 663
  and colonialism 603, 2686
  and commodity relations 609, 610
  competitive capitalism 362
  conservative capitalism 680, 681
  consumer capitalism 761
  craft-based capitalism 2519
  and crime 840–1
  cycles of accumulation 1061
  and Darwinianism 1507
  dehumanizing effect 1310
  and democracy 1001
  and deskilling 363–4
  digital capitalism 1162
  disorganized capitalism 760
  dual systems approach 1711
  early capitalist society 1169
  and ecological exploitation 1291, 1292
  economic institutions 395–6
  and empire 1394
  and entrepreneurship 1412
  and environmental problems 1421
  and Eurocentrism 1491

and exchange relations 757
fiscal and social policies 393
Frankfurt School and 865
global capitalism 1991, 2842
globalizing capitalism 1944
Golden Age of Capitalism 1398–9
and grobalization 2023
hegemonic global capitalism 661
and imperialism 1394–5, 2686
industrial capitalism 392, 501, 534, 535, 537,
    718–19, 1200, 3840
and industrial relations 2287–8
information-era capitalism 518
informational capitalism 3180
laissez-faire capitalism
late capitalism 3179
and leisure 2589
Marxist critique 362, 390–1, 394, 515–16,
    607, 718, 873, 874, 1394, 1949, 2294,
    2518, 2808–19, 2810–11, 2817, 2925
and meritocracy 2955
and militarism 2686
and modernity 3069
and modernization theory 2808, 3072, 3073
monopoly capitalism 1394
and nationalism 517, 3144
neoliberal capitalism 136
networked capitalism 1295
and new social movement theory 3210
and patriarchy 1892
and politics 3451
post-Fordist 759, 1769–70
pre-industrial capitalism 3071
production-centered 761
Protestant 933, 1307
proto-capitalism 718
racial/ethnic conflict under 661
rational capitalism 1318–19, 2298, 3809–10
regulated capitalism 2233, 3840–2
reification 874
and religion and consumption 750
Smith on 362, 390, 515
social institutions 395–8
and sport 4660–2
and women's domestic liberation 2768
workings of 393
capitalism, social institutions of 395–8
    and labor market dualism 1250
    labor process and 1769
    private property 3677
    welfare state and 1769
    see also institutionalism

capitalist blow-outs 3591–2
capitalist imperialism 1394–5, 2268
capitalist space-economy 1298
capitalist triumphalism 1945
capitation 2066, 2709
Caplovitz 706–7
Capraro, R. M. 5006–9
captive mind 398–400
Caputo, R. K. 1331–3
car industry 739, 2741
car ownership 1424, 2479
carbon dioxide emissions 1283, 1285, 1419,
    1423, 1424, 1425
Carbonari 4132
Cárdenas, L. 413
Cárdenas, V. H. 2279
Cardenism 411
Cardindale, M. 2146–51
cardiovascular disease
    and ethnicity 2080
    and health behavior 2060, 2062
    social class variations 2088
Cardoso, Fernando Henrique 1565, 1566, 3538
care
    care relationships 458–9
    commodification of 403
    community-based care 1350
    concept of 457
    ethic of care 457, 458
    paid and unpaid 403
    racial/ethnic minority provision 403
    see also caregiving; carework; managed care
careers
    boundaryless careers 3288–9
    career development 3287
    careerism, and masculinity 1891
    concept 1142
    and cultural production 953
    deviant careers 1142–4
    occupational biographies 1142
    organizational careers 3286–9
    see also criminal careers; educational and
        occupational attainment; occupational
        mobility; occupations; work, sociology of
caregiver parity model 1272
caregiving 401–2
    caregiver distress process 2071
    and disabled children 1572, 1573
    economic issues 402
    emotional 401
    formal and informal caregivers 1349, 1350
    gendered nature of 91, 403, 1573

caregiving (*cont'd*)
  health risks of stress 94
  informational 401
  instrumental 401
  intergenerational exchanges 2380–1
  in later-life marriage 2546
  lived experiences 1697
  and mental health patients 998
  non-spousal caregiving 91
  racial/ethnic variations 402
  social networks 2071
  spousal 2546
  support services 2070–1
  see also childcare; elder care
Caren, N. 3455–8, 4466–70
carework 401, **402–4**
  earner–carer model 1271–2
  externalization 1717
  gendered 1849, 2301
  intersectionality 2849
  in lesbian and gay families 2608
  and maternalism 2849
  migrant workers 1717
  paid and unpaid care 2383
  see also childcare; elder care
Carey, J. R. 283–7
cargo cults 3047, 3049
Caribbean Association for Feminist Research
  and Action (CAFRA) 1855
Carley, K. M. 641
Carmichael, Stokely (later, Kwame Toure)
  1785
Carmines, E. G. 2232–5
Carmody, D. C. 1219–20
Carmody, M. 4280–3
Carnap, R. 3545, 3546–7
Carnegie Corporation 128
carnivalesque 417, 5046
Carpenter, E. 331
Carpenter, L. M. 4234–8
Carpignano, P. 2921
Carr, D. 972–5
Carrington, B. 4686–90
Carrington, C. 2161
Carroll, J. 3271–2
Carroll, J. B. 2359
Carroll, P. 947
carrying capacity concept 3532
Carson, R. 1281, 3532
Carspecken, P. 3822–5
carte de visite 3407
cartels 2558, 4133, 4714

Carter, C. 2351–2, 2710–19, 2729–31, 3662–5,
  4350–3
Carter, Jimmy 2420, 3173
Carter, M. J. 2223–6
Cartesian dualism 335, 1684, 4094, 4322
Cartesian rationalism 650, 1434, 2176
Cartwright, D. 560, 561
Casanova, J. 507
Case, C. 2177
case management 2066
case studies
  feminist case studies 2977
  and institutional review boards 2349
  see also life history
case study methods 2485, 2486, 2976–7
  and finalization in science 1758
  and grounded theory 2977
  organizational learning 3309
  single case studies 2976–7
Cashmore, E. 417–21, 797–8, 1818–21, 3507–10
casinos 704, 1187, 2124
  Native American 2283
Caso, A. 339, 340
Casper, L. M. 1583–9
Casper, M. J. 1696–701
Cassirer, E. 261, 262
caste: inequalities past and present 404–6
caste consciousness 342
caste system
  and division of labor 2129
  and Hinduism 2129, 2130
  and Sanskritization 4001
Castellanos, C. 441
Castells, Manuel
  and capitalism 748
  and collective consumption 748
  and globalization 1961
  and homosexuality 2159
  and the information society 518, 2327, 2329
  and information technology 2334
  materialist analysis 2838
  and the network society 1994, 2329, 2334,
    2902, 3180–2
  and new social movement theory 3209
  urban sociology 501, 3209, 5116, 5120
Castillo, A. 2550
Castles, S. 2252, 3011, 3836
Castoriadis, Cornelius 175, **406–7**, 2815
  and creative knowledge 3466
  and modernity 3069
castration, fear of 2528, 3697
Castro, Fidel 616, 2838, 3052, 3195

casualty aversion 3319
casuistry 2536
catalytic research 215
catapults 3037
categoric units 3000, 3001
categorical demography 5289
Cathars 3203
catharsis, sport as 4662–3
Catholic Pentecostalism 441
Catholic schools 571
Catholic Social Movement 410
Catholicism 407–11, 485, 671
   American Catholic Church 1053
   and American voluntarism 1055
   anti-abortion policy 3653
   and anti-Semitism 156
   and anticlericalism 2530
   and asceticism 187
   and birth control 4143
   Catholic faith 258
   Catholic schools 1325, 4054
   charismatic movement 441–2, 582
   and economics of religion 1316
   female activism 1874
   fundamentalism 1813
   global organizations and movements 1981
   and imperialism 1393
   Index Librorum Prohibitorum 490
   and laicization 4145–6
   membership 475
   moralpolitik 3094
   and national sentiment 2531
   organizational deviance 3304
   popular religiosity 3518–24
   and science, challenge of 3572–3
   sexual abuse scandals 4279
   trusteeism 1055
   see also Vatican
Catsambis, S. 3357–60
Cattell, R. B. 1558
Cattell's Structure of Intellect model 1557
Catterall, H. 3265
caudillismo 411–15
   authoritarianism and 224
Caughie, J. 2921
causal analysis 3122, 3700
   and attribution theory 206
   Comte and 653, 654
   social change and causal analysis 4364–70
causal attribution 206
   attribution-linked effects 206
   outcome-dependent effects 206

causal modeling 426, 4174
causal rationality 182–3
causal relationships 426, 1533
causal schemata 206
causality 1287
   and health and culture 2060
   Marx and 2813
   and naturalistic enquiry 3162
cause-of-death life tables 1024
Cayton, H. 445, 2444
Cazaux, G. 2177
CD-ROM interactive media 3109
Ceasaropapism 3346
Celebration 5148
celebratory direct action 1165–6
celebrity and celetoid 415–17
   achieved celebrity 415, 416
   ascribed celebrity 415–16
   celebrity managers and gurus 2719, 2730
   and the leisure class 2595
   and positive deviance 3543
   sports celebrities 4716–17
   stalking 4719
   structuralist accounts 416
   subcultural celebrities 1639
   subjectivist accounts 416
   see also reputation; sports heroes and
     celebrities
celebrity culture 417–21
   and infotainment 2337
celebrity endorsements 3895–6
celebrity ware 32
celibacy
   late-life 2540
   lesbians 2610
   religious 4277–8
cellular networks 2902, 3270, 4962
censorship 421–2, 2912
   of culture industries 953
   of pornography 3540
   print media 2912, 2913
   self-censorship 422
censuses 1011–12, 1040, 1046, 3016, 4127–8, 4746
centenarians 2668
center-periphery relationship, global 1068
Central African Republic, capitalist growth 390
Central Atlanta Progress (CAP) 311
central business district 422–3, 3944
   and the concentric zone model 1277–8
   erosion of 2992
   and the multinucleated metropolitan region
     3112, 3113, 3114, 3116

central business district (*cont'd*)
  and the multiple nuclei model 1280
  and the sector model 1279
  and segregation 2197
central economic planning 617
central limit theorem 263
centrally planned economies 391
  see also communism
Centre for Contemporary Cultural Studies
    (CCCS) *see* Birmingham School
Centre for Education in the Built Environment
    (CEBE) 375
cerebrovascular disease 1864
Certeau, Michel de 423–5, 3584
  and bricolage 365, 366
  and consumption 704, 3554
  and improvisation 2734
Césaire, A. 1396, 2984
Cesari, J. 2427
Cesarism 411, 412–13
Cetina, K. K. 3578–80
Cevdet, A. 2000
Cezanne 2581
Chadwick, Edwin 2087, 4523
Chadwick, J. 4762–5
Chafetz, J. 2837
Chagall, Marc 2040
Chagnon, N. A. 2458
chain migration 2253, 3012
Challenger space shuttle 836, 1174,
    3337, 3517
Chamard, S. 3957–60
Chambers, I. 914
Chambers, J. K. 4593–6
Chambliss, W. 668, 1096, 1097, 2502
Chan, A. 949
chance and probability 425–6
  convenience samples and 788
  probability sampling 3782
Chancer, L. 1850
Chandler, A. 2299, 2738, 2739, 2745, 3281
Chandra, K. 1470
Chaney, D. 2646
change
  and charisma 434
  conservative attitude toward 679
  evolutionary 431
  revolutionary 431
  social change 434
  symbolic change 956
change management 427–31
  defining 427

  drivers for change 427
  human responses to 428, 430
  and management consultants 2720
  types of 427
change programs 2720
Chanlat, J.-F. 2744–52
channeling 631
Chanver, L. 1677
Chao, A. 683
chaos 432–3
chaos theory 432–3
  and risk 1387
chaotic behavior, computer simulations 642–3
chaotic social processes 644
chaotic systems 633
Chapin, S. 684
Chaplin, B. 330–4
Chaplin, Charlie 1752, 1753
Charamz, K. 1495, 1496
charisma 433–7
  anti-economic character 437
  and *'asabiyya* 182
  and cults 886
  democratization of 436
  and deviance 3543
  and Pentecostalism 3690
  positive deviance 3543
  transmission of 435
charisma, routinization of 435–6, 437–8
  and Jehovah's Witnesses 2438
charismatic authority 226, 230
charismatic deflation 435, 436
charismatic leader 259, 433–6
  cults 3874
  Latin America 412, 413, 415
  and millenarianism 3049
  new religious movements 3203
  and popular culture 3510
  and populism 3537, 3538
  succession to 437
charismatic movement 439–42
  collective consciousness formation 582
  mysticism 188
charismatic renewal 436, 3205
Charles I of England 3468
Charles II of England 3468, 3470
Charles, Prince of Wales 754
Charles, M. 3246–7
Charles, Ray 3135
Charmaz, K. 479–83, 2023–7, 2362, 4157–60
Charnay, J.-P. 2427
Charon, R. 2247

Charrad, M. 958
Charren, P. 695
Chartier, R. 144
Chase, S. E. 1703, 2643, 2846–9
Chase-Dunn, C. 1060–2
chastity 4213–14
Chatterton, P. 1643
Chauncey, G. 2159
chauvinisms 2998
Chaves, M. 485
Cheal, D. 1630–4
cheating 13
    drugs/substance use 1240
    in sport 1132, 1240
Chechens 1451
Chechnya 2801
Checkland, P. 3268, 3269, 3270
Cheddadi, A. 2427
Chee-Beng, T. 668–72
chemistry 432, 653, 1757
    Comte and 653
Cheney, Dick 3175, 3602
Cheney, G. 3292
Cheng-Ho, Admiral 1392
Cherlin, A. 1623, 2772
Chernobyl disaster 499
Chesher, C. 3108–12
Chesney-Lind, M. 1856
Chesterton, G. K. 1055, 1857, 3672
Chew, S. C. 1424
Chezzi, S. 4399–403
Chicago
    concentric zone model 1277
    crime rates 2869
    ethnic enclaves 1454
    ghetto 1937
    homicide rates 2151
    Rustbelt city 3968
    and social worlds theory 4546–7
    urban ecology 1289
    urbanization 1424
Chicago School 442–5
    and the ASA 131–2
    assimilation research 192, 194, 3026
    and the case study model 1129, 1480
    and the central business district 422
    consumption studies 714–16
    crime studies 585, 1102, 1119
    decline of influence 443
    and dramaturgy 1227
    and ecological studies 1281
    economics 2777

ethnographic studies 2362
    and family sociology 1597
    and interpretive sociology 2968
    invasion–succession studies 2418
    migration studies 619, 3011
    neo-Chicagoans 1125, 2472
    Park-Burgess collaboration 3362–5
    and political culture 957
    research programs 442–5
    segregation studies 2196
    sexuality studies 2159
    and social control theory 844, 4387
    and social learning theory 847
    symbolic interactionism 2218, 2220
    unstructured interviewing 2407
    urban sociology 503, 619, 1277, 1597,
        3363–4, 5104, 5152
    women scholars 444
    see also individual scholars
Chicago School: social change 445–8
Chicago Urban League 2444
Chicago Women's Liberation Union 3773, 3774
chick flicks 1850
child abuse 403, 448–51, 457, 1597
    alcohol-related 115
    and the Catholic Church 4279
    chidlhood sexual abuse (CSA) 3386
    and child gender 66
    consequences 449
    cycle of 450
    defining 448–9
    and deviance 1107–8
    and domestic violence 449, 1220
    emotional abuse 449, 450
    and family conflict 1582
    and female criminality 1695
    and feminist criminology 1106
    gender bias 1857
    and later-life depression 100
    medicalization of 1542
    and moral panics 3090
    physical abuse 448–9, 450, 465
    satanist 1090, 4011
    and secrecy 4134
    sexual abuse 449
    social costs 450
    stigma neutralization 1094
    see also pedophilia
child allowances 725
child custody and child support
    451–5, 1624
    access–maintenance nexus 3225

child custody and child support (*cont'd*)
  balance theory 561
  and child well-being 1624
  custody access 1649
  and gender politics 3226
  informal parenting arrangements 3225
  joint parental responsibility 452–3
  non-resident parents 3225–6
  "tender years" doctrine 452
child development
  developmental theory 3680
  looking-glass self 2669–70
  psychosocial development 1071
  self, developing 3617
  see also game stage; play stage
child guidance field 1634
Child, J. 2714
child labor 455–6, 460, 738
  child athletes 4709
  child prostitution 3682–3, 4202
  child-centered perspective 456
  commodification 935
  defined 455
  globalization and 351
  household labor 1204
  human capital perspective 456
  legal regulation 1594
  removal from labor markets 1310
  social responsibility perspective 456
  and sport/leisure-wear industry 1986
  typology of 455
child marriage 4003, 4004
child mortality
  calculating 2318
  causes 2314
  definition 2313
  and high fertility rates 2314
  and HIV/AIDS 3099
  intervention programs 2316–17
  statistics 2314
  under-5 mortality rate 2313
  see also infant mortality
child neglect 449–50, 456
  see also child abuse
child pornography 960, 1659
  online 966
child poverty 450, 1591, 1614, 1622, 1624, 3587
  lone-parent families 1627
  racial differences 1628
child prostitution 3682–3, 4202
child socialization 1269
child support 1721

Child Survival Revolution 2316–17
child well-being 3224
  academic well-being 1621
  in cohabitation relationships 1624
  and divorce 1621
  and family structure 1621, 1622–3
  life course and intergenerational
    outcomes 1621
  and parental conflict 1623
  and parenting 1648
  in single-parent families 1621, 1623
  socioemotional well-being 1621
childbearing 333
  and stratified reproduction 4828
  cohabitation and 566, 568
  cost/difficulty 1732
  and female circumcision 1655
  and the life course 2631
  multiple births 2323
  out-of-wedlock 1043, 1586, 1613, 1621
  postponement 450, 1036, 1247, 1586, 1587,
    1589, 1729, 2018, 2020, 2322
  teenage 1621, 1622, 1725–9
  see also birth rates; infant, child, and
    maternal health and mortality; infant
    mortality; nonmarital childbearing
childcare 457–9
  accessibility 1649
  commodification 458
  cost/difficulty 1732
  custodial grandparents 95
  division of labor 457
  dual-earner couples 1248, 1692
  engagement 1649
  and family migration 1607
  gendered 452, 457, 1884, 2301
  as household labor 1203
  in lone-parent families 2666
  non-parental care 1602, 1849
  nurturing 1649
  paternal 452, 457
  in peer marriages 2303
  private childcare services 1849
  private sphere 457–8
  public sphere 458–9, 840
  responsibility 1649
  stepparents 1603
childhood 459–62
  authoritarian surveillance 465
  "childhood innocence" 462, 463, 464,
    465, 693
  cross-cultural view 460

definitions 463, 464
and enculturation 908
ghettoization of children 696
history of 460, 464
kindergarten 2462–5
new paradigm 459, 460–1
progress model 463
school dropout, predictors for 1232
social construction 459–60, 464
transition to adulthood 2570
welfare protectionism 466
see also child poverty
childhood sexuality 462–7
heterosexual presumption 463, 464, 465, 466
and sex education 4194
sexual innocence 3386
sexual minority children 466
childlessness
and family sociology 1616
involuntary 2320, 2322
and labor force participation 1883
varuable rates of 2018
see also infertility
childminding 457
see also childcare
childrearing 457
cross-cultural differences 1269
and cultural capital 892
and the Industrial Revolution 2296
middle-class 1326
and patriarchy 3378
working-class 1326
see also parenting
children
adult children in the parental home 2169
brand awareness 740
category "child" 455
childhood disabilities 1572–4
commodification of 1310
consumer culture 693–6, 738, 740
and conversation 790
definition 1585
emotional socialization
friendships 1801–2
in gay and lesbian families 2607–8
gender formation 3697
and gender identities
and HIV/AIDS 2137, 2139, 2319
human rights 455, 456, 2317
identity standards 2206
immigrant children 1270–1, 3741
language development 2654

and learned helplessness 2569
media literacy 2894
missing children 1108
"mixed-race" children 1405, 2394
"own children" 1585
physical punishment 1107
play 3413, 3414, 3416
psychosocial development 1071
self-control, development of 4164
shortness in 1111
social actors 461
social and economic benefits in developing
countries 1738
social value of 1042, 1043, 1156
socialization 1269, 1270, 1503, 1581, 1594,
1630, 1857, 2020, 2296, 4019, 4321, 4568,
4571–2, 4574–5
and sport 5308–11
stepchildren 4765, 4766–72
"tender years" doctrine 452
trafficking in female children 2317
see also adoption; friendships of children;
juvenile delinquency; stepchildren
children and divorce 467–71, 1592, 1616,
1617, 1621, 1623
behavior problems 1623
child custody and child support 451–4
mental health problems 1623
and non-resident parents 3223–6
and own marital problems 1623
triadic interaction 1266
see also child custody and child support
Chile 1565
authoritarian regimes 222, 223, 224, 2575
birth rates 1015
colonialism 411
diffusion of protest 3686
feminist activism 1685, 1686, 1688
medical sociology 2935
Pinochet regime 3177
revolution 3907
Chilton, R. 542–5, 2869–73, 3734–7
Chin, E. 706–9, 744
China
adolescent fertility 1725
axial civilization 520, 521
and balance of power 3043
Buddhism 371, 1982
censuses 1011
Chinese medicine 631
command economy 515
communism 391, 615, 672, 677

China (*cont'd*)
  complementary and alternative medicine
    630, 631, 632, 2068
  Confucianism 523, 668–72
  consciousness-raising 677
  consumer culture 744, 745
  consumer movements 697, 698
  cosmopolitan commodity culture 1985
  cultural imperialism 907
  cultural revolution 705, 2636
  death penalty 977
  demographic system 1047
  diaspora 1151
  differential treatment of children by sex
    1157–8
  economic modernization 672
  economic and political power 549
  economy 391, 3200–1
  and empire 1392
  environmental problems 1285
  family planning programs 1738
  fantasy cities 1641
  and federalism 1652
  film industry 1753
  Great Leap Forward 1158
  homosexuality in 4215
  industrialization 430, 704, 1407, 3201
  information technology 2335
  life expectancies 3097
  market socialism 2299
  medical sociology 2935
  middle class 3200
  migration 1044
  mortality 3099, 3100
  nuclear technology 3038
  oldest old 2669
  one-child policy 1158
  Overseas Chinese 2885
  population 1044
  protoscience 2140
  retirement policies 3903
  revolution 3907, 3909, 3912
  Rustbelt cities 3968
  sex ratios 1029
  Soviet influence 1295
  stem cell rseearch 2172
  T'aiping Rebellion 3048
  Taoism 670, 1766, 3855, 4924–30
  television corporations 2890
  urbanization 1407
  and women in development 1855
  working class 1410
  world holidays 740
China Pro-Democracy movement 511
Chinese Americans 196, 1454
  middleman minorities 3010
Chinese Exclusion Act 1882 137, 2262, 3746
Chinese medicine 631
Chipko movement 1274
Chirac, Jacques 1979
chiropractic 630, 631, 632
Chisholm, S. 2621
Chistman, H. 533
chivalry perspective 1856
Chivers, W. 2466
Cho, Y. 440
Chodorow, N. 904, 939, 1806, 3104, 3696,
    3697, 4571
Chomsky, Noam
  anarchist thought 136
  and grammatical and communicative
    competence 1180
  linguistics 2535, 2538, 3570, 3672
  propaganda model 3674
chonaikai 471–4
Chorbajian, L. 2625–6
chrematistics 1385
Chriss, J. J. 3182–5, 3227–9, 3819–22
Christ, O. 2542–6, 4517–21
Christ, W. G. 2891–5
Christakis, N. 974
Christaller, W. 2304
Christian devotion 1375
Christian fundamentalism 3541
Christian Identity 3768, 3771
Christian liturgy 488
Christian martyrs 2799, 2800
Christian Right 956, 2611
Christian Science *see* Church of Christ,
    Scientist
Christian theology 488
Christian–Jewish relationship *see* Christianity;
    Judaism
Christianity 474–9, 524, 672, 1980, 3855
  and capital punishment 976
  charismatic Christianity 439–42
  charismatic leadership 414
  civilization and 529
  early Christianity and communism 612
  early Christianity, as new religious
    movement 3203
  early deviant associations 1141
  and Hindu synthesis 2131
  and magic 2696

and medieval civilization, role played
  in 1981
millenarianism 3047, 3048, 3049
missionaries 408, 1055, 1982, 2131
and modernity 3068
muscular Christianity 2082, 2120, 4691
popular religiosity 3518–24
primitive Christianity 885
and purdah 3723
religious anti-Semitism 155, 159
theology 4974–5
violence 3215
see also Orthodoxy; specific denominations
Christmas 740
  consumption rituals 753, 754
  gift giving 753
  secularization 4146
  shopping rituals 752
Christopher, K. 1723
chronic fatigue syndrome 1112
chronic illness and disability 479–83
  age-related 1349
  alcoholism 116–18
  biodemography and 284
  child abuse, effects of 449
  and continuity of the self 337
  diability as a social problem 1168–70
  and health behavior 2051
  and the illness experience 2246
  and the illness narrative 2248
  and Internet medicine 2389
  mortality–morbidity–disability relation
    2095, 2097
  subordination of women and 326, 336
Chu, D. 825–6
Chua, A. 1991, 3742
Chua, P. 2754–6, 3343–5
church 483–9
  black church 509
  bureaucratization of church life 439
  church attendance 1317
  church–sect continuum 484, 884–5, 1052
  church–state relations 408–9, 506, 548, 1317,
    2532, 3346, 4053, 4141
  and consumption 713
  electronic church 4964
  membership decline 1053
  political authority 679
  primitive house church 1523
  see also individual faiths
Church of Christ, Scientist (Christian
  Science) 631

Church of England 1051
Church of Jesus Christ of Latter Day Saints
  (Mormons) 436, 886, 1055, 2302, 3048,
  3202, 3518, 4277
Church Ladies for Choice 1225
Church of Satan 4010–11
Church of Scientology 886, 3202, 3204,
  4117–18
Cialis 2541, 2542
cicatrization 329
Cicciolina 2337
Cicero, Marcus Tullius 3853, 3885
Cicourel, A. V. 2472, 3403
cinema
  and experiential consumption 716
  product placement 731
  and visual saturation 756
  see also film
Cinema Novo 1753
cinéma Vérité 1211
Cipriani, Roberto 3853–64
circumcision
  female 323
  Jewish 2452
  male 2429, 2452
Cisneros-Puebla, C. A. 3725–6
citation indexing 4120, 4121
citations and scientific indexing 489–93
cities in Europe 493–7, 503
  megalopolises 2943
citizens' movements 2657
citizenship 497–500
  civil rights 497, 498, 499
  and class inequality 2796
  and community media 628
  corporate citizenship 2189
  dual citizenship 1153
  flawed citizens 700
  green citizenship 499
  hybridity 2189
  and immigration policy 2262
  and language proficiency 2259
  legal requirements 497
  liberal democratic citizenship 4206
  Marshall and 497–8
  middle distance theory 2795
  and nationalism 1839
  political rights 497, 498, 499
  and postnationalism 3576
  rights and duties 497, 498, 499
  Roman citizenship 2990
  sexual citizenship 2163, 4205–8

citizenship (*cont'd*)
  social rights 457, 497, 499
  transnational 499
  universal criteria 2955
  women's citizenship rights 2793
citizenship schools 866
city 500–2
  ageographical cities 1642
  Fordist cities 3841–2
  industrial cities 765–7, 992, 1954, 2298
  and nature and culture 947
  new urbanism 3211
  post-industrial cities 767–9
  postmodern city 758
  Rustbelt cities 3968
  spatial dimension 502, 504
  sport and the city 4664–5
  urban consumption 765–9
  see also global/world cities; inequality and
    the city; metropolis; urban sociology;
    urban space, specific cities and types of
    city, e.g. edge cities
City Beautiful Movement 502
city planning/urban design 501, **502–4**
  built environment 374–6
  ecological perspective 503
  exurbia 1549–50
  Levittown 2614–15
  market factors 503
  new urbanism 3211
  political economy perspective 503
  smart growth policies 503–4
  see also suburbs; urban renewal and
    development
civic boosterism 501
civic consciousness 1486
civic entrepreneurship 2189
civic involvement, and earlier extracurricular
    activities 1548
civic loyalty 3142
civic nationalism 1486
civic scientific literacy 4103
civic spaces 4628
civil courts 814, 818
civil disobedience
  animal rights movement 139
  and contentious politics 780
  and direct action 1166
  peace activists 1166
  see also social movements
civil inattention 1997
civil law 582

and patriarchy 2302
  penalties 2553
civil liberties 1447
  and mental health patients 998
civil–military relations debate 3042
civil minimum 505–6
civil religion 506–7, 4142
  Confucianism 671
  and laicism 2532
  millenial civil religion 3047
  and sexual/gender ambivalence 4214
civil rights 497, 498, 499
  and fashion 719
  framing strategy 1781, 1836
  and gay and lesbian movement 1834, 1836,
    2610, 2611
  and global justice movements 1976
  and human rights 2184
Civil Rights Act 1964 370, 510, 4737
Civil Rights Act (Fair Housing Act) 1968
    316, 317
civil rights activism
  and direct action 1165
  and ethnic, racial, and nationalist movements
    1466
  and individualism 1207
Civil Rights Movement 507–12, 1812,
    2618–19, 2823, 3460
  affirmative action 39
  and African American consumption 706
  black feminist contributions 309
  Cold War and 510
  and critical pedagogy 866
  and cultural pluralism 1455
  and deinstitutionalization movement 995
  diffusion of protest 3686
  direct action 1166
  and feminism 1674, 1873
  and gender 1874
  and injustice accounts 11
  internal movement culture 587
  and the Internet 2387
  King and 2466–7
  and multicultural education 277
  and the new left 3193
  non-violent protest 3747
  and perfoming arts, support of 3135
  personal is political concept 3401
  and political opportunities 3448
  and political process theory 3456
  and racial conflict 660
  and racial interests 3733

radical feminism and 676
recruitment and mobilization 3067
rise of 508–10
and school desegregation 370
strategies 2618
civil service 2099
civil society 512–13, 4582
   autocratic regimes and 594
   and community 619
   and democratization 2578
   global civil society 513, 1959–60
   Hegel and 2099
   and ideological hegemony 2227–8
   and the Internet 2387
   and knowledge societies 2482
   nation-based versions 611
   and networks 2903–4
   and organic intellectuals 3482
   pluralism 3423
   and popular culture 3482
   post-communist 513
   and privacy 3646
   and the public realm 3720
   and social justice 3812–13
   and tolerance 5014
civil society organizations *see* voluntary
   organizations
civil wars
   and ethnic conflict 1467
   and ethnic diversity 1468
   and nationalist movements 1465
   and regime instability 1470
   and religious identities 1467
civilization
   culture and 929
   and Eurocentrism 1493
civilization and economy 514–19
civilizations 519–29
   axial civilizations 520, 522–3, 526
   capitalist civilization 517
   and the ecological view of history 1287, 1288
   elites and 520, 521–2
   and empire 1392, 1393
   matriarchal civilization 2858
   and mental evolution 2140
   sociogenesis of 1358
civilized barbarism 531
civilizing process 529–33
   Elias and 721–2, 1359–60, 1750–1
Cixous, H. 302
claims making, politics of 1090–1
   and environmental problems 1418

and ethnic, racial, and nationalist movements
   1467
and social movements 4468
and social problems 4502, 4503
claims-making activities 2473
Clair, J. M. 2067–72, 2081–3, 4533–7
Clair, R. P. 2983
Clammer, J. 744
Clarenbach, K. 1674
Clark, C. 1521
Clark, D. A. T. 2278–80
Clark, J. B. 1304, 1305, 1306, 2778
Clark, K. 369
Clark, M. C. 2641–4
Clark, Mamie 369
Clark, P. 2736–42, 3629–34, 5001–6
Clark, S. P. 866
Clark, T. 2125, 2721
Clark, W. 2282
Clarke, A. E. 2027, 2962, 4546–9
Clarke, J. 2589
clash of civilizations 1970, 1991, 1993, 2189, 3174
class 533–7
   and absenteeism 6
   Birmingham School studies 299, 300
   and black urban regime 311
   and the body 327
   Bottomore and 344
   boundaries 537
   Bourdieu and 541, 723, 741, 2125,
     2628, 2648
   and capitalism 2816
   citizenship and 498
   class cultures 342
   class identity 533, 541
   class imagery 545
   class loyalty 2796
   class-based activism 781
   class-based affirmative action policies 46, 47
   and conflict theory 663
   and consumer culture 685
   and crime rates 637
   and cultural capital 889
   and cultural reproduction 910
   and cultural sociology 926
   culturalist class analysis 541
   culturalist model 4806–8
   and cyberculture 963
   and discrimination 1182
   economic class 533
   and economic status 515
   and elder care 2381

class (*cont'd*)
  embodiment 710
  and emotions 1384
  and entrepreneurship 1412
  and eugenics 1489, 1490
  exploitation 538, 663, 840, 841, 1543,
    2816, 3678
  and fascism 1646
  and fashion 719
  and feminist standpoint theory 1711
  and friendships 795, 796, 1798
  and gender and consumption 1851
  and gentrification 1917, 1918
  habitus theory 336, 348, 2645
  and health inequalities 2086–91
  and health lifestyles 2062
  and health locus of control 2063
  and income 2628
  intersectionist approach 2852
  and intimate union formation and dissolution
    2415
  and juvenile delinquency 2455
  and language usage 2536
  and lifestyle 2645
  and literacy levels 2654
  Marshall and 2795
  Marxist theory 914
  and masculinities 735, 1891
  and materialist feminisms 2839
  and media hegemony 2103
  objective social class 534
  and older people 1929
  polarization 539, 553
  and political economy 1302
  post-communist societies 889
  and self-reported health (SRH) 2085
  and social mobility 3060
  solidarity 539
  and sport 4695–8
  structural model 4805–6
  subjective social class 534
  and visual culture 756
  weakening of class distinctions 756
class church *see* denomination
class conflict 537–9, 2796
  and generational conflict 1902
  Marxist perspective 3550
  in post-industrial society 3551–2
  and working-class exploitation 1544
class consciousness 342, 533, **539–42**, 1568
  class, perceptions of 545–7
  development 538

  and labor markets 2515
  Lukács and 2227
  Marcuse and 2228
  Marx and 2585
  objective 2227
  revolutionary 540, 2228, 2679, 2680
  subjective 2227
class and crime 542–5
  and neighborhood characteristics 3735–6
  white-collar crime 850–1
class mobility
  absolute mobility 2368, 2374
  Goldthorpe class schema 2373, 2374
  intergenerational 2373
class, perceptions of 545–7
  reference-group forces 546
class polarization crisis 1946
class reductionism 663
class, status, and power 547–51
  and political parties 3451
  Takata and 4922
class struggle 534, 537, 548, 663
  communism and 614
  Marxian theory 663, 3584, 3585
  see also life chances and resources
class and voting 551–4, 3451
classical economics, and markets 2776, 2778–9
classical experimental design (CED) 2967
classical liberalism 2624
classical test theory 3849, 3852
classicide 1452
classification 554–6
  and comparative research 2135
  and deviance 1137
  generic 1914
  as political tool 786
  racial 3741, 4114
  and sport 1172
classism
  and difference 1155
  and feminist activism 1677
  and occupational segregation 1890
classless society 537
Clausell, E. 639
Clausen, J. 2636
Clausewitz, C. von 3672, 5213
Clegg, H. 2290–1
Clegg, S. 376–8, 949, 2201–2, 2351–2,
  2710–19, 2729–31, 3314
clergy
  admission of women into 3691
  secularization 3690–1

clientalism 3463
Clifford, J. 2985
climate change 1418, 1419, 1423
clinical epidemiology 1434
clinical inquiry 18
Clinical Sociology Association 133
clinical trials 788, 1865, 2079
Clinton, Bill 417, 1835, 2337, 3186, 3603, 3654,
   3886, 4289
Clinton, C. 415
cliques 878, 1802
clitoridectomy 1654, 1655, 2399
cloning 337, **556–9**
   animal cloning 557
   ethical issues 1908
   therpaeutic/reproductive 557
closed shops 2515
closure in scientific debates 787
clothing styles
   Calvinist 751
   clothing norms, challenges to 1679
   and consumption 736
   dress reform activists 1673
   and ethnicity 715
   sport/leisure-wear industry 3441, 4701
   subversion/resistance and 766
Clough, P. 3334
Clough, S. 1683, 1713, 1714
Cloward, R. 781, 1166, 4781
club model of religion 1315
Club of Rome 1282, 3526
Clunas, C. 744
cluster analysis 643, 3121
cluster-randomized trials 2404
cluster sampling procedure 3782
Clynes, M. 3626
coactive power 2717
coaine 1238
Coakley, J. 760, 1133, 1241, 4576–80, 4643–53
Coale, A. 1035, 1041–2, 1743
Coalition of Labor Union Women 1675
coalitions 1356
   formation 293, 1266, 1353, 1369, 3184
   and networks 3184
   political coalition theory 3434
   political elites 3714–15
   see also exchange network theory; social
     movements; social network theory
Coase, R. 3326
coastal zone destruction 1423
Coates, C. C. 3042
Coates, R. 4336–9, 4612–15

Cobb, S. 2051
Cobbe, F. P. 2176
Coca-Cola 352, 358, 739, 914, 2883, 2887
Coca-Colanization 1962
cocaine 1233, 1234, 1235, 1238, 1660, 2149,
   3736, 3738
   women users 1856
Cochrane, A. 5119–21
Cochrane Collaboration 2406
Cockburn, C. 1890, 2516, 3320
Cockerham, W. C. 2051–2, 2061–3, 2932–6
Code Pink 1677
code-and-retrieve 647
code-based theory builders 647–8
codification
   analogic 248
   digital 248
   gestalt 248
Cody, S. 2301–4
coeducation 4055–6
   see also single-sex schools
coercion, and repression of social movements
   4476
coercive isomorphism 2351
coercive organizations 3310, 3315–19
coercive power 2717, 4462
   non-violent 4460–1
coercive relations 1356
   and power-dependence theory 3601
cogito ergo sum 2527
cognitive algorithms 293
cognitive anthropology 1372
cognitive appraisal process 1375
cognitive balance theory (Heider) 559–62,
   3701, 4612
   balancing operations 560–1
   and cognitive dissonance theory 561
   graph theoretic notion 560, 561
   partitioning 561
   and social psychology 3701
   and sociometry 4612
cognitive consistency theories 982
cognitive deviance 1140–1
cognitive dissonance theory (Festinger)
   562–5
   and balance theory 561
   and collective trauma 595
   and decision-making 982
   dissonance, reducing 564
   forced compliance paradigm 563
   hydraulic model of dissonance 564
   hypocrisy condition 563, 564

cognitive dissonance theory (Festinger)
  (*cont'd*)
  and Jehovah's Witnesses 2440
  and myth 3138
  post-decisional dissonance 563
  and religious movements 2438
  and social psychology 3702
cognitive economy 3356
cognitive empathy 3680
cognitive exhaustion 2569
cognitive and intrapersonal social psychology
    4508–9
cognitive map 257
cognitive neuroscience 635
  and Thomas theorem 992
cognitive processing, age-related changes in 104
cognitive psychology 281
  and decision-making 983
cognitive-rational components of culture 325
cognitive relativism 3814
cognitive revolution 257, 258
cognitive science 2083
cognitive skills differentials 2654
cognitive sociology 2757
cohabitation 565–9, 2570
  and child outcomes 1625
  and childrearing 1588, 1603, 1625
  dissolution of 1624
  duration 567
  and family conflict 1581
  and family demography 1587–8
  and family diversity 1589
  and family migration 1607
  and family sociology 1616
  and family structure 1620
  and family units 1575
  and fatherhood 1601, 1603
  and fertility decline 1043
  and households 2170
  increasing rates of 1585, 1587, 1735, 2792
  instability 1037
  and kinship 2471
  and LAT relationships 810, 811, 812
  and later divorce 1207
  and later marital dissolution 567
  and later marital quality 2774
  and later marriage 565, 567
  measures of 565, 1625
  nonmarital births 1622, 1736, 2793
  and partner similarities 2416
  postmarital cohabitation 1587
  racial differences 566, 567

  relationship disruption 567, 3224
  and religious preferences 1315
  replacing remarriage 1585
  social acceptance of 1622, 1735, 1736, 2417
  see also same-sex marriage/civil unions
Cohen, A. 477–8, 1137, 1578, 4873
Cohen, B. P. 990, 2856
Cohen, J. 1352, 1898, 2362
Cohen, L. 744, 1427, 3958–9
Cohen, M. A. 2575–80
Cohen, P. 914
Cohen, R. 817–18
Cohen, S. 1089, 3089, 4199
Cohen's kappa 3850
Cohn, N. 3047
Cohn, S. F. 4471–4
cohort fertility rates 1741
cold fusion theory 787
Cold War 1566, 2748, 3383, 3460
  balkanization 240
  and Civil Rights Movement 510
  and conservatism 681
  democracy, threat to 2803
  and the developmental state 1074
  drugs/substance use in sport 1240, 1241
  end of 3042
  and ethnic mobilization 1471
  and military sociology 3041
  and nationalism 2900
  propaganda 2879
  science, role of 785
  sovereignty violations 4625, 4626
  and weapons R&D 3039
Cold War dystopia 2760
Cole, A. L. 2641, 2642–3
Cole, E. R. 940
Cole, G. D. H. 3423, 3424
Cole, J. 2960
Cole, S. 2960
Colectivo Magin 1686
Coleman, James 569–74, 773, 2960, 3303
  and adolescent culture 1327, 1546, 1800
  economic sociology 1760, 3803–4
  and educational opportunity 3272
  and educational segregation 3753, 4050
  and exchange network theory 1512
  mathematical sociology 2855
  process model building 2856
  and rational choice theories 570, 572, 573
  and school climate 4016–17, 4018, 4356–7
  and social capital 572–3, 1326, 4355
Coleman, M. 4765–8, 4770–2

Colen, S. 4827
Coles, K. 1397–8
collective action 574–81
    attitudinal support 577
    and collective identity 780
    contentious politics approach 779–82
    and crowd behavior 880, 881, 883
    defining 575
    direct action 1164–7
    and emergent norm theory 575, 1366–7
    and emotions 1389–91
    and entrepreneurship 1412
    ethnic groups 1460
    free-rider problem 577, 587, 1823
    and group activities 2031
    and group identity 1467
    intentionality 780
    and mesostructure 2961–2
    mobilizing structures 578
    movement outcomes 579–80
    and nationalism 1466
    and political opportunities 3448
    and political process theory 576, 3456–7
    and rational choice theory 3232
    rationalist theory 577
    recruitment 576–8
    resource mobilization 576
    selective incentives 577
    sites of contestation 780
    social dilemmas 4392–4
    strain theories 575–6
    see also coalitions; riots; social movement
        organizations; social movements
collective action frames 1781, 1783, 3067
collective bargaining 2288, 2289, 2291, 2292,
        2510, 4739, 5100
    citizenship, instrument of 2509
    disintegrated bargaining 2511
    multi-employer bargaining 2511–12
    and unions 2515
collective cognition 4381
collective consciousness 581–3, 3007
    Durkheim and 581–2, 591, 923, 1966, 2474
    Gökalp and 2003
    and interpersonal contact 2474
    and nationality 2003
collective deviance 583–4
collective efficacy and crime 584–6
collective identity 294, **586–8**, 756, 780, 954,
        955, 956, 1152
    class interests 1836
    cultural identity 541

gay and lesbian movement 1836
    nation-state 2901
    and new social movement theory 3208
    and social movements 1390, 1874, 1949
collective interest 2031
collective memory 588–90, 959
    preliterate and traditional societies 590
    story-telling form 592
    urban memory 592
collective memory (social change) 590–3
collective mentality 261
collective rights 2185
collective selection 719, 720
collective trauma 593–8
    investigative poetics 2420–3
collectivism 598
    attribution theory and 207
    coercive organizations 3315–16
    collectivist ideologies 2624
    and emergent thinking 635
    voluntary organizations 3341
collectivities 2029
    and power 1079
college degrees 2123
    see also credentialism
colleges and universities 599–602
    academic deviance 1084–5
    academic science 4069
    admissions policies 39–40, 2956–7
    affirmative action policies 39–40,
        2956, 3756
    black college graduates 605
    captive mind concept 398–9
    college-for-all philosophy 622
    community colleges 620–3
    cooling out 621
    female students 1344, 1859
    friendship networks 1796, 1797, 1801, 3067
    German elite university model 621
    Humboldtian ideal 2012, 2013
    and institutional racism 3766
    interracial interaction 3756
    junior colleges 600
    medieval universities 599
    multiversities 600
    occupational success in 99
    professional schools 4045–8
    program and performance auditing 213
    and race/ethnicity 1343, 1344
    research universities 599–600, 2012
    and retirement communities 3904
    segregation 368

colleges and universities (*cont'd*)
   student social movements 3193–5, 4864–8
   tenure 601
Collier, J. 2986
Collier, M. 2986
Collins, H. 1531, 1532, 2287
Collins, J. 2402
Collins, K. M. T. 2979
Collins, P. H. 274, 305, 306, 309, 1438, 1668,
      1676, 1683, 1711, 1712, 1713, 1714, 1895,
      2395, 2396, 2397, 2838, 4997–8
   and maternal politics 2848
   and matrix of domination 2859, 3119, 3776
Collins, Randall 750, 1257, 2032, 2627
   and conflict theory 663, 3937–8
   and emotions 1376, 1379, 1384, 1390
   and financial sociology 1760
   and macro reality 2997
   outsider-within concept 3350–1
   and social change 4363–4
   and status attainment 1323
   and stratification 2837
Collinson, D. 1889, 1891
Colombia
   failed revolution 3910
   feminist activism 1688
   indigenous movements 2279
colonialism (neocolonialism) 602–4, 985–6
   and anti-Semitism 156
   and balkanization 239–40
   and bilingualism 281
   and biracialism 295
   and capitalism 2686
   captive mind concept 398–9
   and caste 405
   and civilization 529
   civilizing mission 1505, 2755
   colonial languages 2260–1
   conceptual and ideological bases 603
   and cultural formations of nature 947–8
   cyberspace 962
   and development 1852, 1853
   and dialectics 1149
   disintegration 1295
   and documentaries 1211
   and ecofeminism 1275
   economic effects 603
   and empire 1393, 1394
   and family systems 1595
   Fanon and 275, 1636
   and genocide 1910
   and geography 1297

   and the global sex trade 1984
   and imperialism 602–3
   and indigenous depopulation 2282
   and industrialization 2297
   internal colonialism 603, 1469
   and international division of labor 1068
   and the international economy 1944
   and interracial marriage 2394
   language policies 280
   Latin America 411
   and manifest destiny doctrine 2755
   medical colonization 1111
   and middleman minorities 3009, 3010
   and nationalist movements 1468
   and Orientalism 3343, 3990
   paternalist relations 3370
   and plural society 3420
   and political poetry 2422
   power relations 603
   and racial divisions of labor 1463
   and racial domination 603
   and racial/ethnic conflict 659
   Rizal and 3939–40
   and social anthropology 340
   and social evolution 1505
   and sport and politics 3473, 3547
   stereotyping of the colonized subject 1396
   and territorial boundaries 1468
   and traumatogenic change 595
   see also decolonization; imperialism
colonization 602
color-blind society 296
color blindness 1831
color line 604–5, 1938, 3732
   Blumer and 320
   changing nature of 3741
   Du Bois and 1245, 3746
   Frazier and 1785
   and interracial marriage 2394
color tax 316
colorblind racism 3615–16
Colton, J. 2007
Coltrane, J. 797
Columbia School 570
Colwell, S. 1751
Combahee River Collective 307, 1676, 2842, 3118
combat exposure, long-term effects of 99
combat soldiers 3041
Combined Statistical Areas (CSAs) 2995
Comfort, A. 2833, 3277
coming out/closets 605–7, 2159, 4239
   coming-out narratives 303

and friendships 1803
and the gay and lesbian movement 1834, 2611
command economies 515, 1384
command technology 3038
commemoration 592
  and collective memory 589
  commemorative symbolism 589
  negative 589
commercialization 610
  sport 3474–5
commitment ceremonies, and deviance 2208, 2209
commitment, relationship 2673–4, 3478
committed identities 2224, 2226
Committee to Save Public Schools 2831
Committees of the Mothers of the Disappeared 1697
committees, theory of 3434
commodification
  of art 517
  of bodily parts and processes 2172
  and the body 337
  of child labor 935
  of childcare 458
  of children 1310
  of culture 517, 740
  of everyday life 610, 703–6
  of fitness 482
  of football 4347–8, 4349
  of girls 725, 726
  of human relationships 515
  of knowledge 2716, 2726
  of labor 1201
  of medical care 481
  of the museum experience 3127
  of promises 1387
  of qualifications 2726
  of science 4069
  of sexuality 4242–4, 5033
  of slavery 706
  of social life 756, 758, 763, 1991
  of social space 703, 705
  of speech 4294
  of transgression 5046–7
  of women 711–12
  of youth 719
  see also commodities, commodity fetishism, and commodification
commodities, commodity fetishism, and commodification 607–12
  commodities as symbols 762

commodity life expectancy 702
commodity social value 609
  exchange-value 702–3, 756–7, 762, 1515
  and fashion 718
  fetishization of media symbols 2883
  Marxist critique of commodity fetishism 741, 756, 758, 864, 1745, 2679, 2811
  morphology of 758
  overproduction 3591
  and planned obsolesence 2582
  and reification 3845
  sign value 762
  spectacular consumption and 755
  use-value 261, 702, 703, 709, 757, 762, 1515
commodity chains 749, 1944
commodity exchange 742
commodity production 1403, 2679
common law of England 1092, 2183, 2454, 2552, 2554, 2555
common pool resources 3531
Commoner, B. 1420
Commons, J. R. 2510
commons dilemma 1282
Commons Movement 2898
Commonwealth Games 3474
communal democracy 3423
communal ethics 1441
communal living 3477
communal property 3677
communalism, norm of 3667
communication
  abstraction paradoxes 248
  adolescent 773
  bias 3672, 3778
  and collective identity 2901
  collective orientation 1576–7
  communicative legitimacy in the public sphere 2909
  and community media 628–9
  computer simulations 641
  computer-mediated 2386
  Cooley and 798, 799
  and cults 3873
  and decision-making 2713
  and diaspora 1152
  and diffusion of protest 3688
  and discourse 1179
  encoding/decoding model 2918
  ethnography of 1181
  and Frankfurt School 876
  gender differences 2301
  globalization 2385, 2387

communication (*cont'd*)
  hierarchical levels 248
  industrial communication 3291
  and interaction 2361
  Japanese patterns 3219
  and law framework 2561
  and management innovation 2739
  marketing communication 770
  metacommunication 248
  and migration 2257
  and nationalism 2900
  and non-human animals 2537
  nonverbal cues 248
  and organic society 581
  organizational communication 3290–8
  parent–child 799
  public relations 3469–70
  religious 486–8, 3873
  risk communication 3929, 3930
  and ritual 3935
  and social systems 2676
  symbolic 3228
  systems theory of 2676
  two-step theory of 2564, 2739
  see also public opinion
communication networks 3291
communication technology (CT) 3294–5
communication theory
  Bateson and 249, 2362
  Lazarsfeld and 208
  mass communication research (MCR)
    tradition 208
communicative action in the lifeworld 2652–3
communicative competence 1180
communicative genres 1916
communicative interaction 2033
communion sacrifice 3981
communism 535, **612–17**
  agrarian communism 613–14
  American communists 1140
  Arendt on 167
  capitalism–communism struggle 515, 1945
  and class struggle 614
  collapse of 160, 391, 1644, 1956
  "communist imperialism" 2267
  Comte and 652
  expansion 1295
  and fascism 1647
  forced atheization 198
  Goldman and 2007
  ideological enemy 681
  individualist critique 617

  Jews and 158–60
  Leninist 616
  Luxemburg and 2686
  modernization model 1925
  and modernization theory 3072
  political movement 612
  pre-socialist communism 614
  primitive communism 537
  revolutionary communism 617, 3047
  and science 4110
  social organization 612
  and social relations of science movement
    1542
  and socialism 614
  transition from 5047–50
  utopianism 2528
  and women's equality 1674
  and the working class 1201
  see also Marxism; Marxism-Leninism
Communist International 874
Communist League 2809
Communist Party of the Soviet Union (CPSU)
  1150, 1151
communitarian economy 1411
Communitarian Movement 885
communitarianism 1188
  and communism 614
  and fascism 1646
  and neoliberalism 3177
  utopianism 2528
communitas 754
community 617–20
  academic community 617
  Bernard on 272
  black American 707
  boundaries 714, 715
  businesses 715
  church as 485
  cohesion 619
  collapse of 594, 1577
  communities of attachment 1578
  communities of interest 535, 626, 628, 1578
  community organizing 5149–50
  community politics 618
  construction 1713
  corrosive community 1421
  and cultural studies 916
  definitions 1575
  and disasters 1421
  discourse community 1179
  "dream of community" 1578
  and emotional experience 1378

ethnic communities 1468, 1476
gated communities 619
Gemeinschaft 183, 500, 594, 598, 620, 661,
  1458, 1576, 2003, 2031, 3621, 3964, 4130
identity construction 916, 2213
imagined communities 618, 627, 1578,
  2248–9
initiatives 619
Internet communities 620, 1578, 5150
invisible colleges 4107–8
mixed communities 619
moral community 2699
and nationalism 3154
neighborhood communities 1575
and networks 673
occupational communities 617
online communities 962
place community 1578
political dimension 618
recruitment 618
revival of 628
rural sociology 3964
and self-actualization 702
shared interests 1146
and social capital 1326–7
state-sponsored community work 619
strong and weak ties 2903
as structure 1578
as symbol 1578
therapeutic community 1175, 1421
transnational communities 3836
unstable/disorganized communities
  1102, 1119
urban planning and 504, 5144
virtual communities 628
and weak-tie networks 2743, 2903
women and community life 1579
women's communities 2604
community action research 18
community cohesion 1576
community college 620–3
  and adult education 1329, 1330, 1331
  and race/ethnicity 1344
community corrosion 1175
community and economy 624–6
  and Latinidad consumer culture
    2549, 2550
  market exchange economy 3429
  and moral economy 3084–5
community forum function of print
  media 3635
community governance 864

community housing 997
community and media 626–9
  Deadhead community 3504, 3505, 3506
  diasporic media 2885–6
  electronic relationships 2921
  mediated interaction and
  and national identity 2901, 2902
  sociopolitical origins 627
  see also public broadcasting
community mental health centers 997
Community Mental Health Centers Act 1965
community policing 3431–2
community rankings 545
community service 803, 855
community treatment centers 995
community-based care 995, 996, 997, 998,
  1350
  and childhood disabilities 1573
  gendered 1579
commuter belts 1576
commuter marriages 810, 811
compact disc (CD) 3132–3
companion animals
  agency 62
  cross-species companionship 947
  human–non-human interaction 2175–8
companionate love 2672
company credos 3335–6
company unions 1416
comparable worth 1669, 4189, 4191
  see also sex-based wage gap and comparable
    worth
comparative advantage theorem 3595
comparative anatomy 302
comparative historical analysis 644, 2135
comparative historical sociology 2133–6
  classification 2135
  concept formation 2135
  measurement issues 2135
comparative method 653
comparative philology 2534
comparison, problem of 2201
compensation culture 2562
competition 531, 3944
  authentic competitiveness 1562
  competition against a standard 4644
  competition theory of racist
    movements 3769
  and conflict theory 662
  corporate competition 1309
  direct competition 4644
  imperfect competition 2776

competition (*cont'd*)
  and industry centralization 1314
  insulation from 1463
  and labor markets 1469
  parallel competition 4644
  perfect or pure competition 2776, 2777
  and race/ethnic movements 1469
competitive advantage 2513, 2524
  and organizational learning 3307
competitiveness axis 1560
**complementary and alternative medicine
  629–33**, 2389
  and health promotion 2080
  and health-care seeking patterns 2068, 2245
completeness theorem 561
complex organizations 4131
complexity and emergence 633–6
  and crowd behavior 883
  and system theories 4914
complexity theory 432–3
  and organizational communication 3296
compliance
  power and 229
  see also conformity and compliance
compositional theory of urbanism 636–8
Comprehensive Drug Abuse Prevention and
  Control Act 1972
compression of morbidity thesis 72–3
compulsory heterosexuality 638–9, 2113
  childhood 463, 464, 465, 466
computational ethnology 643
computational sociology 639–45
**computer-aided/mediated analysis
  645–50**
computer-assisted interviewing 1540
Computer-Assisted Qualitative Data Analysis
  (CAQDAS) 3725
computer games
  digital aesthetics 1163
  and fantasy cities 1643
  ratings 3793
computer models of human interaction 639
computer program languages 2536
computer simulations 640–3, 4105
  agent-based 642, 4105
  multi-agent simulations 641, 644
  and technology assessment 691
computer software
  and content analysis 777
  and innovation 2741
computer-supported cooperative work (CSCW)
  2364

computer technology
  architectural and incremental innovations
    2740–1
  and systems theory 634
Comstock, A. 2833, 3087
Comte, Auguste 650–6, 1242, 1258, 1301,
  1304, 1542, 1760, 2108, 2186
  and altruism 655, 3679
  and animism 141
  biography 650
  and communism 652
  Comtean sociology 650–1, 2587, 2784, 3465,
    3547, 3700–1, 4600, 4852
  and economic sociology 2442, 2780–1, 2784
  and fetishism 608, 651–2, 3629
  and industrial capitalism 3550
  law of three stages 651, 3670
  Martineau and 655, 2798
  positivism 651, 1506, 1818, 1901, 2186, 2836,
    3545, 4117
  and property rights 652
Conant, J. B. 3222
concentric zone model 176–7, 1277–9, 1918,
  2991, 3113, 3944
  and gentrification 1918
conceptual network builders 648
Concerned Women for America 1665
concomitant variables 1534
conditionalism 2439
conditionality 4989
condoms 1609, 1610, 1728
  HIV effects 2138
Condorcet, Marquis de 651, 652, 653, 1541,
  2706, 3071, 3669
  and expert knowledge/democracy conflict 1543
  and scientific progress 3669–70
Coney Island 766
confession, institution of 1315
confidence games 1388
confidence intervals 656–9, 4743–4
confidentiality 3644
  in research 1449
  see also trust
configuration theory 3282
confirmatory factor analysis (CFA) 1558, 4848
conflict of interest model of family
  conflict 1582
conflict, Israeli–Palestinian 4519
conflict (racial/ethnic) 659–62, 663, 664, 1471
  and accommodation 7–8
  affirmative action, effects of 46–7
  anti-essentialist perspective 3013

and anti-Semitism 154–60
and balkanization 239–40
boundaries and 346
civil wars 1467
and diversity 1198
immigrant–ethnic minority relations 661
inter-caste conflicts 405
pogroms 3426–8
predictors of 1467
and racial/ethnic consciousness 3742
and refugees 3837
urban 1454
conflict resolution
collectivism and 598
in schools 843
Conflict School 2038
conflict theory 2, 384, **662–5**, 4980
and absenteeism 5
benefit and victimized zones concept 265
Bernard on 272
and criminology 858
and deviance 118–19, 666, 1078,
1102, 1106
and division of labor 1199
and ecological problems 1282
and education 1323
and educational expansion 1971, 1972, 1974
and functionalism 662, 1809, 1812
and gender inequalities 2309–10
group conflict theory 667
and the hidden curriculum 2116–17
and illness 2059
in-groups and out-groups 2338–9
intergenerational conflict 2366–8
and labeling theory 2501, 2506
and majority/minority relations 2702
Marxist 662, 663, 2806
and materialist social analysis 2837
and the medical professions 2077
pluralist 666, 667
and property conflicts 2755
radical conflict perspectives 666, 667–8
Ratzenhofer and 3811
and retirement communities 3905
and ritual 3937–8
Simmel and 666, 4327
and slurs 4340
and social control 4388
and stratification 4798–9
Weberian 663
conflict theory and crime and delinquency
665–8

confluent love 2323–4
conformity
agents of 1079
Asch experiments 189–91, 226, 227
authority and conformity 225–9,
3034, 3701
collectivism and 598
and helping behaviors 3680
mechanisms influencing 227
Milgram experiments 226–7
and social control theory of crime 844
and sport 1134
and strain theory 4780
supraconformity 3543
to norms 1078–9, 3230
working class values 3076
Zimbardo experiments 227
see also compliance
Confucianism 523, **668–72**, 3855
and modernization 2499
and *moralpolitik* 3094, 3095, 3096
New Confucianism 669, 670
Confucius 669, 670, 3095
congregationalism 1053–5, 3692
trusteeism 1055
Congregationalist church 1051, 1053
Congress of Industrial Organizations (CIO)
2519
Congressional Black Caucus 1244
Congressional Union 1673
congruency effects 2273
conjugal roles and social networks 672–4
Conk, M. A. 3249
Conklin, J. 821
Conlon, B. 202–4, 2567–70
connaissance 1772, 1773
connectionism 258
connectivity 935, 1161
Connell, R. 1668, 1878, 2099, 2100, 2101
Conner, T. L. 1528
Connidis, I. A. 4314–15
Connolly, B. 2987
Connor, W. 1486–8, 2900, 3142–3,
3148, 3156–7
connotation 1403
connubium (who marries whom?) 674–6,
4821
and occupational scaling 3251
partner effects 4810–12
conoisseurship 1637
Conquergood, D. 3394
conquest hypothesis 2039

Conrad, F. 3130
Conrad, Joseph 1220
Conrad, P. 1110–14, 2174, 2934, 2935
conscientious objectors 1165
consciousness
    bifurcated consciousness 274–5
    black feminist consciousness 305, 309
    bourgeois consciousness 2680
    caste consciousness 342
    civic consciousness 1486
    class consciousness 342, 1568, 2680
    collective identity and 586
    and critical theory 874
    and cultural feminism 903
    diasporic consciousness 1153
    double consciousness 274–5
    ethnic consciousness 433
    false consciousness 1568–70
    gay consciousness 1985
    global consciousness 1957, 1960
    group consciousness 238
    and ideologies 877
    indigenous consciousness 2280
    legal consciousness 2561
    nationalist consciousness 3135, 3144
    oppositional consciousness 1713
    pure consciousness 3402
    race and ethnic consciousness 3611, 3740–2
    reification of 874
    self-consciousness 2098
    social being and 244
    and spatiality 2047, 2048
    subjugated and dominant consciousnesses
        275
    and temporality 2047
    worker consciousness 2746
consciousness raising 676–8, 1675
    black feminist 305, 307
    Dorothy Smith and 274
    and feminist pedagogy 1707
    and feminist standpoint theory 1711
    personal is political 3400
    and racism 129
    radical feminism 3774
    and rape culture 3784
    through music 3135–6
consensus 665, 2925
    and anti-pollution measures 968
    art worlds 179
    and attribution theory 205–6
    and benefit and victimized zones concept
        265, 266

and democracy 1006–7
    functionalist consensus paradigm 667
    high consensus deviance 1081
    and indigenous movements 2279
    and role theory 3953
    subcultural consensus 950
    and technology assessment 691
consensus conferences 691
consensus mobilization 1781, 3067
consensus theory, and the hidden curriculum
    2116, 2117
consequentialist explanations 1824
conservationism 1430
conservatism 678–81
    and authority 679
    and cultural issues 2234
    and educational attainment 1868
    and evolutionary theory 1504
    and female labor force participation 1868
    and fundamentalism 1868
    liberal conservatism 681
    liberal–conservative continuum 681, 2232
    and management theory 2749
    Mannheim and 2758
    moral conservatism 3683
    neoconservatism 681, 3174
    political economy 679
consistency
    and attribution theory 206
    and reliability 3848–9
Consolidated Metropolitan Statistical Areas
    (CMSAs) 2942, 2992, 2995, 5103
conspicuous consumption 681–6
    the body and 709
    and commodity relations 611
    and construction/reproduction of
        culture 682
    economic accounts 682
    and hyperconsumption/overconsumption
        2191–4
    and the leisure class 2595
    and lifestyle 2645
    public visibility 683
    and self-identity 710
    social orientation 683
    Veblen and 681–2, 684, 685, 701, 709, 718,
        721, 736, 741, 816, 934, 1189, 1190, 1308,
        1763, 1851, 2192, 2647, 4619
conspiracy 2555
Constant, B. 3539
Constantine, Emperor 3345, 3346
Constantinople 765

Constitution 1652
  and criminal law 2553
  and press freedom 2912
constitutive effect of culture 1307
construct validity 1557
constructed conditionality 4910–11
constructionism 686–7
  and agency 62
  and audience ethnography 211
  and authenticity criteria 214–15
  autopoieses and 233
  body and sexuality and 332
  constructionist epistemology 1435–6
  and critical realism 871
  and deviance 1076–9, 1086–91, 1105–6
  and disability studies 1700
  and disasters 1174–5
  and ecological problems 1283, 1422
  and emotions 1375, 1380
  essentialism and constructionism 1436–7
  and ethnography 1481
  and feminist epistemology 1683
  and gounded theory 2025–6
  individual/personal constructionism
    1086, 1087
  and norms 1079
  and organizational performance
    measurement 3397, 3398
  and phenomenological sociology 1087
  and positivism 1089, 1120
  and poststructuralism 1091
  and psychology and psychotherapy 1087
  and racial/ethnic boundaries 345
  and reflexivity 3831
  social constructionism 326, 1086, 1087,
    1088–9, 1091, 1681
  and social problems theory 1087
  stakeholder groups and 214–15
  and symbolic interaction 1087
  see also essentialism and constructionism
**(constructive) technology assessment
  687–93**
constructivism *see* constructionism
consumer activism 697, 2894
  and media literacy 2894
consumer banks 729
consumer culture 740, 741, 1963
  and academic interest in the body 325
  and advertising 32, 33
  and celebrity culture 420–1
  class patterning 685
  commodification of the world 738

conspicuous consumption and 682
  and consumer movements 699
  counterculture and 810
  and critical theory 876
  and the ecological crisis 1946
  and global consumption 1963, 2335
  and information technology 2335
  Latinadad and consumer culture 2548–51
  middle-class 2192
  neo-Marxist evaluation 744
  origins 743–4
  performative consumption 1639
  and self-creation 685
  and Situationism 981
  see also advertising; brands and branding;
    consumer culture, children's;
    consumption; consumption, mass
    consumption, and consumer culture;
    McDonaldization
consumer culture, children's 693–7
  flawed consumers 700
  girls' 724–7
consumer decision-making 983
consumer goods
  planned obsolescence 702
  sign value 741
  social meanings 684
  see also commodities, commodity fetishism,
    and commodification
consumer movements 697–9
  green/sustainable consumption 729
  seikatsusha 4152
consumer societies 702, 775
consumer spending patterns 683
consumers, flawed 699–701
Consumers International 697, 698
consumers' leagues 1058
Consumers Union 697, 698
consumption 701–5
  and advertising 31
  bureaucratic society of controlled
    consumption 703, 704
  and celebrity 416
  and celebrity culture 420–1
  the city and 501
  collective 702
  compensatory consumption 707
  and culture and economy 1308–9
  decoupling form production 733
  defining 701
  definitional issues 737–8
  democratization 738–9, 744, 756, 766

consumption (*cont'd*)
demonstration effect 399
and encoding/decoding 1403
ethnic consumption 768
and gender 735, 1848–51
global flows 744
globalization 2335
horizontal/vertical accounts 749
hybrid consumption 1187
immigrant consumption patterns 3029
individual 702
marginalization from 2766
and museums 3126
post-Fordist 762
posthuman consumption 745
postmodern 762
privatization 1849
second-hand exchange and consumption
    5218–19
and self-formation 717
self-therapy through 743
semiotic critique 758
and sexualities 42549
urban consumption 715
virtual consumption 745
see also hyperconsumption/
    overconsumption; McDonaldization
consumption, African Americans 706–9,
    766, 1851
consumption and the body 709–12
food and cultural consumption 721–3
girls 726
and smoking 4344
consumption, cathedrals of 712–13, 734–5,
    752, 766, 2883–4
and fantasy cities 1642
and hyperconsumption 2193
see also department stores; shopping malls
consumption celebrities 741
consumption and the Chicago tradition
    714–16
consumption communities 359
consumption, experiential 716–18
consumption, fashion and 718–21
consumption, food and cultural 721–4
supermarkets 4888–90
consumption, girls' culture and 724–7
consumption, green/sustainable 727–9
consumption and intellectual property
    729–32
consumption and the Internet 732–4
cyberculture 961–4

and intellectual property laws 731
consumption, landscapes of 734–5
cathedrals of consumption 712–3
and hyperconsumption 2193
consumption, masculinities and 735–7,
    1849–50
consumption, mass consumption, and
    consumer culture 737–46
and commodity relations 611
and credit cards 815–17
and Disneyization 1187–8
and *flânerie* 1762–3
flawed consumers 699–701
and globalization 1960–3
household consumption 609
implosion theory 2268–9
and the Internet 732–4
and lifestyle 2645
postmodern consumption 3552–5
programmed consumption 2582
women and 609
see also hyperconsumption/
    overconsumption; popular culture
consumption of music 746–8, 3129–34
consumption, provisioning and 748–50
flawed consumers 700
consumption, religion and 750–3
consumption rituals 753–4
shopping 752
consumption, spectacles of 755–60
and fantasy cities 1643
consumption of sport 760–1
in later life 2593
consumption, tourism and 761–4
beach holidays 3484–5
cultural tourism 919–21
retirement migration 3022
and rites of passage 3933
consumption, urban/city as
    consumerspace 765–9
and the department store 1056–9
fantasy cities 1641–3
consumption, visual 769–73
consumption, youth culture and 773–6
girls 724–7
hip-hop 3486–7
containment theory 846
content analysis 776–9
contention, tactical repertoires of 779–82
contentious politics 3457
contest mobility systems 5024
continental drift theory 787

contingency tables 2565
contingency theory
  and change management 429
  and institutionalism 2355
  and leadership 2566, 3443
  and management theory 2714, 2717, 2748
  organizational contingencies 3299–302, 3313, 3621
    positivistic tradition 429
    structural contingency theory 3281, 3299
continuous learning 2728
continuous quality management 2929
continuous time data 1018–19
continuous variables 1897
contraception 450, 558, 972, 2308, 3206
  adolescents 1728
  condoms 1609, 1610, 1728, 2138
  family planning programs 1738–9
  and family sociology 1617
  and fertility control 1609
  HIV effects 2138
  male contraception 4094
  misuse and failure 1737
  non-use of 1610
  the pill 1609, 1738, 2541, 2793
  sterilization 1609
  and women's health status 2319
contract state 4728
contracting out 378
  see also outsourcing
contradiction 125, 126, 1147, 4988
control balance desirability (CBD)
control balance theory 782–4
control rations 783
control systems theory, and crowd
  behavior 883
controversy studies 784–8
convenience foods 695
convenience sample 788–90
convergence 1160–1, 3701, 5103
  asymmetrical convergence 4069
  cultural 1991, 1992
  and cultural differences 1599
  health care delivery systems 2056–7
  social processes 642
conversation 790–1
  casual 790
  institutional 790
  sociable conversation 2598
  spatial organization 2363
  talk-in-interaction 2363
  turn-taking 789, 790, 2537

conversation analysis 791–4, 1181, 1213, 2032, 2535
  action 792
  and dramaturgy 1228
  and dyads/triads 1267
  and ethnomethodology 2032–3
  and interaction 2363
  intersubjectivity 792–3
  and the lifeworld 2653
  and management discourse 2723
  and microsociology 3005
  participant/non-participant observation 3238
  Sacks and 3971
  structure 792
  telephone talk 4961–2
  transcription 5036–7
Conversi, D. 4166–9
convivium (who is friends with whom?) 795–7
Coogan, Jackie 694
Cook, D. T. 693–7, 765–9
Cook, J. A. 1702
Cook, K. 1368–71, 3599, 5081–3
Cooke, T. J. 1607, 1608
Cooksey, E. 1725–9
Cookson, P. W. 1325
cool 797–8
  and jazz 3488, 3489
  Rat Pack 3516
Cooley, Charles Horton 798–801, 1130, 1996
  ASA president 130
  communication theory 798, 799
  and the development of the self 799, 2432
  and identity 2212, 2217
  and the looking-glass self 2208, 2669–70, 3007, 4157
  pragmatist sociology 430, 794, 798
  and primary groups 3620–1, 4130
  and reputation 3887
  and symbolic interaction 319, 847, 858, 1087
  sympathetic introspection 319
cooling out 621
Coombe, R. 730
Cooper, A. J. 306, 2621, 2838
Cooper, J. 562, 563
cooperation
  Arendt on 172, 173
  art worlds 179
  between strangers 641
  computer simulations 640
  and conversation 790

cooperation (*cont'd*)
cooperative game theory 1822
cooperative social behavior 292
ethnic groups 1460
and family/community 1576
and kin selection 293, 294
and norm of reciprocity 3227
organizational 355
Pareto efficient cooperation 1822
and prosocial behavior 3679
and rational choice theory 3232
and self-interest 640
and strategy ecology 293
work groups 2712
cooperative inquiry 18
cooperative movement, and collective
memory 591
cooperatives 729
Cope, V. 561
Copelton, D. A. 5273–5
Copernican revolution 1519, 3572
Copes, H. 3675–6
Coptic Christians 1655
copyright 729–30, 2357–8, 2898, 2912
and cultural production 953
digital copyright 1162
and file-sharing networks 3489
flexible digital copyright 1162
see also intellectual property
Corbin, J. 2025, 2026
core competencies
medical education 2931
organizational 3314, 3324
core and periphery 1395
Cornelius, H. 27, 2163–4
Corner, J. 1210
coronary heart disease 1864
and gender 1865–6, 1867
risk factors 1866
treatment decisions 3376–7
coronation ritual 3937
Coronation Street 3499
corporal punishment 450, 802
and conservatism 680
in schools 4022
corporate aesthetics 3555
corporate authority 228
corporate boards 1363
corporate branding 353, 355
corporate citizenship 2189
corporate colonization 3295
corporate communication 353

corporate competition 1309
corporate crime 816–18, 820, 840, 850, 851,
1106, 3738, 4132
corporate cultures 933, 1307, 2509, 2724,
2750, 3567
and economics 950
employee and company culture fit 950
and labor–management relations 2509
corporate deviance
and sport 1134–5
corporate disasters 1441
corporate elites 1004, 1008, 1010, 3714
corporate familism 2240
corporate finance 17577
corporate financial scandals 685
corporate governance 2751
corporate identity 353, 354, 355, 730
corporate image 353
corporate media 1108
corporate personality 353
corporate power, and democracy 1004
corporate property 3677
corporate reputation 353
corporate scandals 2751
corporate social responsibility 355, 2182
and ethics 1439
corporate sponsorship 2920
corporate units 3000, 3001
corporation associations 1401–2
corporation law 2559
corporations
capitalist ideology 945
and consumer behavior 684
and consumption 945
and critical pedagogy 866
environmental impacts 1284–5
industrial corporations 2299
interfirm networks 1313
organizational culture 934
see also organizations
corporatist state 4728
corporatization 3658
Corr, C. 1496
correctionalism 1136
corrections 801–3, 854–15
community-based corrections 803, 854,
855, 856
and courts 812–15
jails and prisons 803, 804, 854
parole 855
probation 854–5
see also prisons

correlation 805–7
  and regression 3839
correspondence analysis 3121
correspondence bias 206
correspondence inference theory 205
correspondence principle 2116
corroboration 1571
corroboree 2366
corrosive community 1421
corruption 807–9
  coercive organizations 3316
  corporate 1440, 3303–4
  financial scandals 1320, 3324, 3339, 3340
  and gambling 1819–20
  police 3431
  political 835
  see also white-collar crime
Corruption Perceptions Index (CPI) 808
Corsaro, W. A. 1269
Corteen, K. 462–7
corvée system 1543
Corwin, Z. B. 2345–51
Cory, D. W. 2158
Coser, L. 1809–10, 1812, 2338, 2960,
  3193, 3334
Coser, R. 2960, 3644
cosmetic products 683, 725, 1850
  and black women 1851
cosmetic surgery 325, 334, 1656
  and deviance 1113
  genital surgery 2399
  and hyperconsumption 611, 1850
Cosmides, L. 1509
cosmogonic mythologies 3138
cosmology
  Buddhist 371
  chaotic effects 642
cosmopolitanism 818
cost–benefit analysis
  crime and 837
  and regulatory trends 2929
  and technology assessment 691
Costa Rica
  life expectancy 390
  mortality decline 3100
  sex tourism 4201
Côte d'Ivoire 1727
Coté, P. 2440, 2441
Cothran, T. 131
cottage industry system 2294
Coubertin, P. de 3262, 4661
Couch, C. 1129, 1367, 2362

Coughlan, D. 3270
Coughlan, P. 3270
Coulange, F. de 3630
Couldry, N. 1639
Coulter, D. 630
Coulter, I. 630
Council of Chalcedon 258
Council on Contemporary Families 1617
counseling and coaching 1266, 1267, 2750
counter-cultural movements 597, 4872
Counter-Enlightenment 148, 678, 909
Counter-Reformation 3094
counterculture 809–10
  and conservatism 681
  hacker counterculture 1162
  and jazz 3488
  and sexual revolution 875
  youth counterculture 885
counterhegemony 2228
countermobilization 1781
counterproductivity 4294
countertransference 3694, 3695
coup d'état 594
Coupland, C. 2210–14
Coupland, D. 356, 3557
couples living apart together 810–12, 2169,
  2414, 2417
Cournot, A. 2776
Courpasson, D. 1004–11
courtesy stigma 1572, 1573
courtization 530
courts 812–15, 2962
  due process model 852
  federal and state courts 853
  judicial decisions 2554
  juvenile courts 855, 2454, 2505
  public awareness of 1109
  sentencing 853–4
  see also criminal justice system
courtship regimes 2682, 2683
covariation analysis 205
covenantal ethics 1444
Covington, H. C. 2440
"cow sociology" 363
Cox, L. 1392–7, 1950–3, 3143–52, 4549–54
Cox, O. 2838
Cox regression model 1019, 1020
"crack babies" 3087
craft workers 1200, 2518, 4805
  demise of 364
craft-based capitalism 2519
Crane, D. 177–80

craniometry 3731
Crapanzano, V. 289
Craske, N. 1685
Crawford, G. 760–1, 1639
creation science 1510
creationism 1508, 1510, 1595
creative class 1361, 3073
Creative Commons license 1162
creative destruction 1901, 1991, 3338, 3437
creative disequilibrium 4007
creative economy 1455, 1456
creative interviewing 2407, 2409
creative knowledge 3466
creative liberty 2041
creative resistance 2397
creative tourism 920
creativity, digital 1163
credentialism 1345, 4030, 4045
credibility 1388, 5083
credit 325, 393, 1189
    and consumption 702
    democratization of 815
    and entrepreneurship 1460
    and female poverty 1724
    and interest 1302
    microcredit programs 1158
    redlining 3825
credit and bank card fraud 960
credit cards 815–17, 1759, 1761, 2193
    collateralized cards 816
    and debt 1761
credit-rating agencies 1387
Crenshaw, E. M. 3528–30
Crenshaw, K. 308, 2395
creolization 817–18, 1992
    creole political elites 1923
    and hybridity 2190
Cressey, D. 818, 827, 3333
Cressey, P. G. 443, 447, 1129
Crick, F. 2171
cricket 1819, 4714
crime 818–22
    age and 818
    age, period, and cohort effects 52
    alcohol-related 114–16, 2663
    biological theories 2662
    and class 542–5, 850–1, 3735–6
    classification 2554–5
    clearance rates (US) 3676
    conflict theory 665–8
    corrections 801–4
    and corruption 807–8

crime–delinquency distinction 818
cybercrime 960–1
and dangerousness 969
defenses to criminal liability 2556
defining 542, 818–19, 821, 856, 1080
determinants 1426
and deviance 1080, 1092–4
deviance–crime distinction 1093
drug–crime relationship 1234–5
elements of 2555
epidemiology of 1094
etiology of 1094
fear of 2339–43, 2827, 3941
female crime rates 1857, 4192
female offenders 2663, 3676, 4191–3
and gender 2455
high-consensus crimes 1093, 1094
inductive approach 1397–8
life course theory of 830–2
low-consensus crimes 1093, 1094
measuring 820
and neighborhood poverty 1614
parties to 2555
political economy of 894
public order crime 3715–17
and race/ethnicity 3676
rational choice perspective 3799–882
recidivism 3818–19
and relativism 1092
reporting 821
routine activity theory 3957–9
school drop-out as predictor for 1229
self-reporting 542, 2454, 2455, 3735, 3818
slavery, impact of 3735
social disorganization theory 846, 848,
    4395–8
societal reaction to 819
statistics 2277–8
transnational crime 3317
types of 2555–6
urban crime 637
urban crime and violence 5107–9
see also age and crime; deviance; measuring
    crime; transgression; victimization;
    violent crime; types of crime, e.g.,
    property crime
crime, biosocial theories of 822–5
    psychological theories of crime 836–9
crime, broken windows theory of 825–6
crime, corporate 826–8, 3303–5
    see also crime, white-collar
crime, hot spots 828–9, 4397

crime, life course theory of 830–3
   and juvenile delinquency 2454, 2455
   self-control theory 4165
crime mapping 1427
crime news 1108
crime, organized 833–4
   organizational crime 3303–4
crime pattern theory 828
crime, political 835–6
crime prevention 256
   through environmental design 828
   see also police
crime, psychological theories of 836–9
crime, radical/Marxist theories of 839–42
   and peacemaking 3385
crime, schools and 842–4
   see also juvenile delinquency
crime, social control theory of 844–7, 2454
crime, social learning theory of 847–50,
   2454
crime, white-collar 850–1
Crimean Tatars 1451
criminal careers 76, 830–2, 1144
   age–crime curve 830–1
   career length 830
   chronic offenders 832
   frequency 830
   life-course-persistent offending 831
   neuropsychological deficits 831
   participation 830
   seriousness 830
   single-pathway model 831–2
   three-pathway model 831
Criminal Code 2553
criminal economy 1411
criminal justice system 851–6
   Beccaria and 256
   and criminology 1094
   due process tradition 256
   and ethnicity 2207
   juvenile justice 48–9, 855–6
   law enforcement 852–3
   Marxist theory 840
   racial disparities 3737–9
   women workers 1694, 1695
   see also corrections; courts
criminal law
   characteristics 2553
   consensus model 2
   objectives 2553
   penalties 2553, 2554
   sources 2553–4

criminal liability, defenses to 2556
criminology 856–60
   Bataille and 246–7
   Beccaria and 255
   biosocial perspective 822–5
   class and crime 542–5
   classical school of 857, 1426, 1427
   and conflict theory 665
   critical criminology 858
   cultural criminology 892–5
   and dangerousness 969–70
   and deconstruction 988
   defining 756
   and deviance 1081
   and deviant friendships 1799–800
   Durkheim and 249, 819, 1809
   environmental criminology 1426–7, 3958
   establishment criminology 3197
   and insecurity and fear of crime 2339–40
   interactionist model 893
   Lombroso and 2662–3
   Marxist 839–41, 2506
   "new criminology" 893
   and new left realism 3197
   peacemaking criminology 3384
   positivist criminology 857, 861, 1094, 1426,
      1427, 2506
   postmodern critique 858
   and prisons 1176
   rational choice perspective 3799–802
   self-control theory 846, 4163–6
   self-report studies 1144
   social disorganization theory 585
   and social support 4531–3
   see also cultural crimonology; feminist
      criminology
criminology research methods 861–4
   class and crime 542–5
   crime measures 2869–72
   and gangs 1826–7
Crimmins, E. 2097
crisis management 2734
crisis of representation 1482
Critcher, C. 2589
critical case sampling 3999
critical consciousness 866
critical discourse analysis 1181
   and management discourse 2723
Critical Legal Studies movement 2583–4
Critical Mass 981
critical pedagogy 399, 864–7
critical qualitative research 867–70

critical race theory 3610
   postcolonial methodology and 2982
critical realism 870–3
   and environmental problems 1419
   and humanity–nature relationship 3165
critical theory/Frankfurt School 869,
      873–7, 1434, 2806, 4982
   and Adorno 27
   aesthetic theory 34
   and capitalism 517–18, 943, 2838
   and commodity relations 610, 611, 757
   and critical pedagogy 864–5
   and cultural critique 897, 3810
   and cultural studies 897, 913, 915, 3810
   culture industry critique 942, 2881, 4329
   and dialectics 1149
   and epistemology 1435
   and false consciousness 1569
   and genre analysis 1914
   and Horkheimer 2163, 2165
   and identity 2220
   and ideology 2231
   and interpretive sociology 2968–9
   and lifeworld theory 2652
   Marx–Freud synthesis 2760, 2816, 3193
   mass culture critique 684
   and mass media 2877
   modernity critique 3720–1
   neo-Marxism 1805, 2810, 3178, 3179
   and organization theory 3285
   and organizational communication 3292
   and peacemaking 3385
   and postmodern consumption 3554
   and technology 687
criticalism 2968, 2969
Croatia 660, 1451
   separatism 4188
Croce, Benedetto 1644, 2015
Crompton, R. 1272
Cronin, A. 4263–8, 4554–5
crony capitalism 1075
Crook, T. 3777–81
Cros, H. 920
Crosnoe, R. 1799–801, 4016–19
Cross, G. 743
Cross, S. 626–9
cross-border finance and trading 1945
cross-classified data 1016
cross-culture analysis, and feminist
      research 1702
cross-cutting social circles 3075
cross-dressing 1223, 1224, 1226, 2599, 5037, 5038

cross-sectional studies 78, 97
cross-sex friendship 877–9
   children 1802
   and gender differences 1863
   and the hidden curriculum 2118
   and sexual activity 1804
cross-validation replicability analysis 3878
Crossan, M. 2733, 3309
Crossman, R. H. 1009
crossover, and hybridity 2190
Crow, G. 617–20, 1578
crowd behavior 880–4
   ad hoc gatherings 880
   assembling process 880
   coerced dispersals 881–2
   collectivities 2029–30
   dispersals 880, 881–92
   emergency dispersal 882
   emergent norm theory 1366–7
   and emotions 1390
   and football hooliganism 1767
   manipulation 3672
   political gatherings 880, 881
   religious gatherings 880, 881, 883
   routine dispersals 881
   sport gatherings 880, 881
   symbolic interaction perspective 3065
   violence 1466
   see also riots
crowd psychology 799, 3923
Crowder, K. 3014–19
Crowley, Aleister 4010
Crowley, G. J. 5128–32
Crozier, M. 2748, 3313
Crude Birth Rate (CBR) 1014, 1015, 1016,
      1039, 1742
cruise missiles 3040
Cruise, Tom 416
cruising 2162
Crump, J. 1549–51
Crusade for Voters 2831
Crusades 2453
cryonics 3047
Crystal, D. 2534
Crystal, S. 3254–7
Csicsery-Ronay, I. 3497
Csikszentmihalyi, M. 742, 743, 2590
Cuarandersmo/Cuarandersma 2079
Cuba 3055
   communism 391, 615
   cultural imperialism 907
   feminist activism 1686–7

sex tourism 4201
    and women in development 1855
Cuban revolution 340, 616, 1566, 3052, 3195,
    3909, 3912, 3913
Cubitt, S. 4331–4
Cult-Awareness Network 886
cultists 1638
cults
    anti-cult organizations 886
    audience cult 885
    and charisma 886, 4139
    client cult 885–6
    countercult movement 3205
    faith-based definitions 886
    and new religious movements 1141, 3202
    see also religious cults
cults: social psychological aspects 884–7
    and charisma 435
    religious worldviews 885
cultural anthropology 922, 929, 938
    Durkheim and 1251, 1259
    interviewing 2409
    visual methods 2986
cultural apprenticeship 3991
cultural assimilation 1458
cultural borrowing 14
cultural bourgeoisie 889
cultural capital 383–4, 596, 597, 710, 741, **887–91**
    Bourdieu and 383, 384, 887–9, 891, 1326,
        1337, 1361, 2125, 2645
    and distinction 1190
    and educational attainment 1335, 1337
    embodied form 888
    and ethnic products 1456
    fan cultural capital 1639, 1640
    highbrow/lowbrow 2125
    inherited 888
    and intertextuality 2402
    and life chances 2629
    and status 685
    subcultural capital 1639
    and symbolic capital 889
    and taste 710
cultural capital in schools 888, 889, **891–2**
    and cultural reproduction 911
    and educational attainment 1337, 4017
    and the hidden curriculum 2117
    and school climate 4017
cultural competence 899, 901
cultural conservatism 680
cultural criminology 892–6
cultural critique 896–8

self-reflexivity 897
cultural desirability 205
cultural determinism 322
cultural diasporas 1152
cultural differentialist analysis 1992
cultural diffusion 907
cultural disorganization 595–6
cultural disorientation 596
**cultural diversity and aging: ethnicity,
    minorities, and subcultures 898–902**
cultural division of labor 1464
cultural domination, and empire 1392
cultural elites 1190
cultural feminism 902–6, 3775
    cultural feminist critique 2603
    and psychoanalytic feminism 3696
cultural genocide 2755
cultural globalization 1990
cultural habituation 299
cultural hegemony 297, 3597
cultural homogeneity 2888
    and nationalism 2900, 3156
cultural imperialism 739, **906–8**, 2878, 2888
    and mass media 2878, 2888
    and nationalism 2900
    and television 2889
cultural industries 943
cultural lag 446, 2486, 2487
cultural meaning makers 737
cultural modernity 3069
cultural nationalism 3058
cultural omnivorousness 953
cultural philistinism 896
cultural pluralism 277, 322, 342, 1455, 3423
    and assimilation 2945, 3364
    and segregation 15
    Southeast Asia 4379
    and values 5171
cultural production 2767
cultural racism 3014
cultural relativism 908–10
    anthropology and 322, 1083
    Boas and 322, 1083
    and ethnocentrism 1478, 1479
    and human rights 909, 2183
    and postmodernism 910
    radical cultural relativism 909
cultural repertoire 955
cultural reproduction 383, **910–11**
    and conspicuous consumption 682
    Durkheimian tradition 910, 911
    Nietzschean critique 3215

cultural resistance 911–13
  and cool 797
cultural resonance 782
cultural resources 3896
cultural scenarios 4122
cultural scientific literacy 4103
cultural sociology 922, 923
  and death and dying 974
  and Durkheim 1259
cultural studies 913–18, 2649, 3817
  counterculture studies 809
  and critical qualitative research 869
  and cultural geography 1299
  and deconstruction 988
  interdisciplinarity 915
  and museum studies 3127
  organizational sociology 3324
  and popular culture 2910, 3482
  postmodernist ideas 3553
  poststructural methodology 3583
cultural studies, British 913–14, 918–19
  Birmingham School 297–301, 809
  and cultural critique 897
  as political project 297–8
cultural subordination 1469
cultural synchronization 2189
cultural tensions model of family conflict 1582
cultural tourism 919–21
  arts tourism 919, 920
  creative tourism 920
  heritage tourism 919, 920
  indigenous cultural tourism 921
  popular cultural tourism 921
  rural cultural toruism 921
  urban cultural tourism 920–1
cultural transmission 14
  crime rates 585
  and gangs 585
  and professors 3666
cultural trauma 595–6, 597
culturalism 298
culture 922–8
  anthropological definition 298
  autoproduction of 953
  and class 533
  cognitive category 931
  commodification of 517
  constitutive effect of 933
  definition issues 898, 910, 922, 938, 2123
  democratization 1753, 2758–9
  descriptive category 931
  deterministic models 951

elite culture 518
  embodied category 931
  genesis of 931
  and globalization 1964–70
  "high" culture 897, 913
  highbrow/lowbrow 518, 923, 2123–5
  idioculture 2237–8
  and imagined communities 2249
  mass culture 518
  postmodern culture 518, 3556–8
  production of 924
  reconceptualizations 924
  social catgeory 931
  and symbols 954, 955
  as theory of social structure 929
  see also corporate cultures; health and
    culture; Latinidad and consumer culture;
    political culture
culture audit 950
Culture Change 2729
culture: conceptual clarifications 928–32
culture, economy and 932–6
  culture war issues 2234
  and economic geography 1298
  markets 2786–7
culture and emotions 1374–7
culture, gender and 936–42
culture industries 416, 865, **942–5**, 953,
    3139, 3140
  American 897
  homogenization 2884
  and infotainment 2336–7
  and mass culture 2824
  and sport 2235
culture industry thesis 416, 942, 944, 2824
culture jamming 945–6
culture, nature and 946–8
culture, organizations and 948–51
culture of poverty 4, 288, **951–2**, 1612,
    1613, 1728
culture, production of 924, **952–4**
  artworks 177–80
  institutionalized 925
  and myth 3139
culture shock 918
culture, social movements and 954–7
  gender and social movements 1874–5
  and indigenous languages 2280
culture, the state and 957–9
culture-structure theories 926
culture war games metaphor 949
culture wars 2234

culture wars theory 2234, 4260, 4261–2
Culver, L. 851–6
Cumming, E. 1928
Cumming, G. 656–9
cumulative advantage/disadvantage, theory of
    99, 2860, 3222
    and late-life economic outcomes 3255
    see also Matthew effect
Cunha, M. P. 2734
cunnilingus *see* oral sex
Cunningham, S. 3673
Cunow, H. 245
Cuomo, C. 1275
curanderos 2348
curfew violations 855
Curra, J. 4585–90
Curran, P. J. 2544
Curran, S. R. 3530–3
currency devaluation 594
currency floats 2749
Current Population Survey (CPS) 566
curriculum, school 1326
    achieved curriculum 3271
    child-centric 1973
    cross-national similarities 1973
    curricular hierarchies 1339
    decentralized decision-making 2893
    design 2893
    enacted curriculum 3271
    and feminist pedagogy 1707
    and friendship formation 1800
    and graduate study 2012
    intended curriculum 3271
    manifest curriculum 3271
    organization 1338–9
    patriarchal assumptions 1706
    public schools 4051–2
    sex education 4194
    sexist biases 1706, 1708, 4943–4
    and social values 1337
    see also hidden curriculum
Currie, G. 3299–302
Curry, G. 1751
Curry, L. 901
Curtis, B. 3276–8
Curtis, C. 2144
Custer, L. 2772–5
Custer, R. L. 1817
customer rights 1440
customized production 1411
Cutler, S. J. 101–3
Cutright, P. 1001

cyber sex 3989
cyber shopping 2884
cyber squatting 731
cybercrime 960–1, 2915
cyberculture 961–5, 2386
    and cultural studies 916
    and the information society 2329, 2330
    and McLuhan 2693
    see also multimedia
cyberfeminism 962, 1678
cybernetic organism 3626
cybernetics 328, 1160, 2326
    Macy Conferences 247
    and structural functional theory 633
cyberporn 965
cyberqueer 965
cybersex 965–6, 1661–2
**cybersexualities and virtual sexuality 963,
    965–6**, 3569
    disembodiment 333
    online sexual interaction 2541
cyberspace 961, 962, 963, 964, 1984, 2334,
    4628–9
    and *flânerie* 1763
    and the information society 2334
    and the public realm 3720
cyberspace economy 1161
cyberstalking 960, 965
cyberterrorism 960
cyborg 966
cyborg sex 965, 3569
cyborgs 2190
Cyert, R. M. 3282
Cyprus 1451
    Orthodox Church 3345
cystic fibrosis 2173, 2940, 3376
Czech Republic, stratification system 889
Czechoslovakia, social security system 2055
Czolgosz, L. 2006

Dadaism 980, 2189, 4329, 4335
Daele, W. van den 1757
Daguerre, L. J. 3405
Dahl, R. A. 1004, 3442, 3460
Dahlgren, P. 2906–11
Dahms, H. 876
Dahrendorf, R. 344, 538, 547, 1811, 2338
daily life pollution 967–9
    high-speed transportation pollution 2126–7
    and local residents' movements 2658–9
    structural strains 4855–6
Dale, P. 3219–20

Dalits 405
Dall, C. H. 1670
Dalton, H. 2141
Dalton, M. 3336
Dalton, R. 2234
Daly, M. 904, 2603
dance 325–6, 327, 336
    break dancing 3486
    injury and accident 336
    and jazz 3489
Dandaneau, S. P. 2759–61, 3050–5, 3229–32,
    3948–51, 4487–9
dangerousness 969–70
    and disasters 1174
Daniel, E. V. 4179–87
Daniels, J. 777
Danish Technology Board 689–90, 691
Dannecker, M. 2159
Dant, T. 2835
Daoism 1980
    millenarianism 3047
Darby, J. 3380–4
Darley, J. 3679, 3680
Darnell, J. A. 2117
Darwin, Charles 244, 1199, 1488
    and ecology 1289
    evolutionary theory 292, 1504, 1507, 1510,
        1595, 1896
    and hermaphroditism 302
    and Malthus 2708
    and Marx 1506–7
Darwinian anthropology 292
Darwinianism 799, 1509
    and capitalism 1507
    see also Social Darwinism
Dash, J. M. 2984
data analysis
    and evaluation studies 1500–1
    qualitative data 1500–1
    and statistical techniques 1897
    see also analysis of covariance; analysis of
        variance; event history analysis
data collection techniques 1555
    and evaluation 1500
    log-linear models 2659–60
data fusion 643
data mining 643, 3725
data triangulation 5076, 5077
databases 2479, 2927, 2989, 3725
date rape 4252
dating regimes 2683
dating violence 1220

Daughters of Bilitis 1834
Davenport, C. B. 1489
David, M. 556–9
Davidson, A. 2014–16
Davidson, J. 1053
Davidson, K. 5251–3
Davies, S. 4014–15
Davis, A. 309, 2398, 2621
Davis, D. 744
Davis, F. 479, 720
Davis, Kingsley 970–2, 1811
    biography 971
    on family planning 971–2
    on fertility and public policy 971
    multiphasic response theory 3532
    on population explosion 1034, 1035
    and prostitution 3682
    on stratification and inequality 971
    and structural functionalism 1808–9
Davis, L. J. 3231
Davis, Mike 1174, 1642
Davis, Miles 797
Dawkins, R. 1507, 3815
Dawson, P. 427–31, 431
De Forest, L. 2874
De Gaulle, Charles 22
De Graaf, N. D. 1337
De Grazia, V. 1646
de Klerk, F. W. 163
De Knop, P. 5308–11
De Lauretis, T. 1657–8
De Martino, E. 2700
De Mille, J. 2858
De Soto, H. 1760, 2550
De Swaan, A. 2627
De Vall, W. 2159
De Ventos, R. 2902
Dean, H. 2765–6, 5235–8
Dean, J. J. 2152–4
death awareness movement 973
death certificates 1214
death and dying 972–5
    and awareness contexts 233–4
    and cultural diversity 901
    de Beauvoir and 254
    euthanasia 974, 1178, 1495–8
    participant observation 2934
    psychodynamic stage coping theory 234
    see also mortality; suicide
death penalty as a social problem 976–8,
    2234, 2556
death rates *see* mortality

death of the sociology of deviance?
    978–80
D'Eaubonne, F. 1273
debit cards 1759
Debord, Guy 980–1, 2580
    and commodity relations 757
    mass culture/mass society thesis 2824
    situationism 707, 980–1, 4329, 4335–6
    Situationist International 705, 755
    and spectacular consumption 755, 757–8,
        2882–3, 3567, 4329, 4704
debt
    bankruptcy 241
    credit card debt 816, 1761
    liquidation 241
    reorganization 241
    student debt 1761
debt bondage 603
debt relief 1978, 1979
debtors
    credit counseling 241
    socioeconomic categories 241
Debuyst, C. 969–70
Decade of the Woman 1687
Decade for Women 1853
decentering technique 2966
decentralization
    health care delivery systems 2056
    of industry 2817
    and metropolises 2990
    organizational 2387, 3398
    urban space 3114, 3115
decision-making 981–4
    Asch experiments 189–91
    and brain processes 3186
    centralized 780
    and communication 2713
    and community media 627
    consensus conferences 691
    consensus decision-making 4464
    consumer decision-making 983
    and contentious politics 780
    criminal 3800–1
    decision-value maximization 3233
    democratic 3195
    economic perspective 3800
    in environmental uncertainty 3301
    and ethics 1439
    in euthanasia 1495
    family and household decision-making 1584,
        1633, 2303, 3082, 3083
    group 982

    individual 982
    irresponsible, crime and 838
    in leadership groups 3444
    marital 2301
    and new left politics 3195
    organizational 3323
    in peer marriages 2303
    postmodern organizations 3564
    risk decisions 3927–8
    strategic decisions 4784–9
    subjective expected utility model 3800
    temporal nature 3928
    under risk and uncertainty 3601
    within marriage 2770, 2771
    see also game theory; money management in
        families; rational choice theory
decisional privacy 3644
decisive liberty 2041
Decker, S. H. 3941–2
Declaration of Barbados 342
Declaration of Helsinki 1442
Declaration on the Rights of Development
    2184
Declaration of the Rights of Man and of the
    Citizen 2183, 2530, 3145
decolonization 984–6, 984–6
    Africa 340
    and church establishment 408
    and dependency theory 2267, 2382
    and diaspora 3835–6
    of knowledge 399
    and modernization 2267
    and self-determination 4167
decommodification 739, 742, 2817
decomposition analysis 1015, 1016, 1017, 1744
deconcentration 3114
deconstruction 986–9
    and cultural criminology 893
    Derridean 1062–3, 1154, 1436
    and difference 1154
    and film 1755
    and hermeneutics 2107
    and intersexuality 2399
    and management discourse 2723
    of masculinity/femininity 1223
    and metatheory 2966
    and postmodern feminism 3559, 3560, 3562
    and psychoanalysis 3694
    of sexual identities 4266–7
    and strategic essentialism 4790
deductive reductionism 2998
deductive theorizing 1557

deductive theorizing (*cont'd*)
  analytic deduction 3167
  and attitudes and behavior 199
  and crime 1397–8
  enumerative deduction 3167
deductivism 1555, 2286, 2287
Deegan, M. J. 23–6, 1785–6, 2444
deep acting 1382
Deetz, S. 2723, 3294
defensive hate crimes 2049
deference 990
  and interaction order 2366
deficit hypothesis 3930
deficit model of family conflict 1581
deficit model of the public understanding of
  science 4100–1
defined-benefit plans 1840
definition of the situation 991–2
deflection 37
Deflem, M. 144–6, 2583–4
DeFleur, M. 848
DeForest, L. 3130
deforestation 728, 1285, 1418, 1423, 1425, 3527
DeFrain, J. 1583
Defrance, J. 4705–8
degeneration theory 1169, 5080
Degher, D. 2208
DeGrazia, V. 744
Deibert, G. 1065–7
deictics 4184
Deil-Amen, R. 620–3
deindustrialization 992–4
  and exercise/fitness 1517
  and fantasy cities 1643
  and gentrification 1918
  and homelessness 2149
  and the urban poor 3968
  and wealth inequalities 2313
deinstitutionalization 994–9, 1999, 3693
  and disability 1169
  of family life 1633
  of marriage 2772
  of mental health care 2505
  and Protestantism 3693
deism 652, 654
  American 173
DeKeseredy, W. S. 3196–8, 5107–9
Delacroix, J. 390–5
Delanty, G. 3068–71, 3721–2, 4598–669
DeLaverié, S. 1224
Deleuze, Gilles 999–1000, 1775, 2009
  and capital deterritorialization 3566
  and capitalist political economy 999–1000
  and desire 3574
  and economic geography 1299
  and essentialism 999
  and Guattari 2037, 3566, 3574
  and identity 1897
  and immanent difference 999
  postmodernism 999, 3552, 3573, 3574
  poststructuralism 999, 2333
  and rationalism 999
  and virtuality 4334
Delgado, R. 2549
Delhi 765
deliberative democracy 229, 1005, 3715
deliberative intelligence 1146
deligitimation 2586
delinquency 48–9
  age and 818
  androcentric perspective 1856
  anomie and 809
  Chicago School studies 443, 447
  child abuse and 449
  class–crime relationship 543
  differential association theory 48
  girls 724, 2819
  intelligence test score relation 2360
  and labeling 2504
  latent delinquency 837
  middle-class 543
  predictors 2119
  psychoanalytic theory 837
  school-aged youth 843
  self-reported 845
  and situational choice 846
  social bond theory 48
  and sport, positive effects of 2121
  strain theory 48
  structural-Marxist theory 841
  subcultural theory 48
  see also gangs; juvenile delinquency
Della Fave, L. R. 2585
Della Porta, Giambattista 2697
Delmar, R. 1685
Delphy, C. 2113, 2841
demagogues 3481
demand management 1388
demarcation, and falsification 1571
dementia, caregiving 403
Demeny, P. 1729
Demerath, N. 3975
demerol 1238
Deming, W. 2750

Demo, D. H. 1589–94
democracy 1000–4, 3463, 3465
  authoritarianism 223, 225
  characteristics 1000
  circularity of 1006
  civil disobedience 139
  communal democracy 3423
  competitive approach 1005
  conservative critique 679
  constitutional 1295
  and cultural sociology 923
  definitions 1004–5
  deliberative democracy 229, 1005, 3715
  democratic construction 2579
  democratic equality 1005
  democratic tradition 1004
  democratization of charisma 436
  digital democracy 1162
  direct democracy 3454
  and economic development 1001, 1002,
    1003, 1852
  egalitarianism 1007
  expert knowledge/democracy conflict 1543
  failure of 1006, 1911, 1912
  and feminist pragmatism 24
  formal democracies 1000, 1001
  and global politics 1951
  and globalization 1991
  Greek 407
  and human rights implementation 2185
  and income inequalities 2276
  and industrialization 2298, 2299, 2510
  and the information society 2330
  and the Internet 2387
  and leadership 2617
  liberal tradition 1004, 2623, 2624, 2757, 3076
  and marginalization 2766
  mass democracy 3453
  and the media 2906
  and modernization 3076
  and neoconservatism 3173
  neoliberal perspective 3177
  oligarchic drift 1006
  organizational democracy 3295
  participatory democracy 3258, 3259
  political democracy 1947, 2577, 3646
  political perspective 1004–5
  and positivism 3545
  predictors of 1001, 1002
  and Protestantism 3692
  representative democracy 407, 1428, 3311
  resources contributing to 1002

  restricted democracies 1000
  semiotic democracy 210
  and sport 4650–1
  stability 1009
  and structural functionalism 1810
  substantive democracies 1000
  third world countries 1001
  and tolerance 5012–13
  transition processes 1924
  transitions to 1470, 2576
  and traumatic change 595
  unrestricted democracies 1000
  see also citizenship
democracy and organizations 1004–11, 2996
  industrial relations 2287–93
  participatory democracy 3258, 3259, 4463–5
  social movements 3258–9
  workers' participation in management
    (WPM) 2752–4
democratic republicanism 2296
democratic socialism 2296
democratization of science 4088–91
Democrats 2233, 2234
Democrazia Cristiana party 188
**demographic data: censuses, registers,
    surveys 1011–14**, 4127–8
  and fertility transitions and measures 1741–2
  and internal migration 3015, 3016
demographic discontinuity 1902
Demographic and Health Surveys (DHS) 1014,
    1040, 3100
demographic principle 74
demographic quantum 1741
**demographic techniques, decomposition
    and standardization 1014–17**
**demographic techniques: event history
    methods 1017–21**
**demographic techniques: life-table
    methods 1021–5**
**demographic techniques, population
    projections and estimates 1025–8**
**demographic techniques, population
    pyramids and age/sex structure
    1028–30**
demographic techniques, time use 1030–3
demographic transition theory 972, **1033–8**
  and age structures 93–4
  aging, demography of 68
  classic theory 1041
  family demography and 2572
  first demographic transition 4123, 4124–5,
    4126

demographic transition theory (*cont'd*)
  growth patterns 1034
  and health care systems 2053
  historical demography and 1045
  and the Industrial Revolution 2295–6
  and internal migration 3015
  reformulations 1041–2
  see also population growth; second
    demographic transition
demography 1038–45
  biological demography 283, 284–6
  biomedical demography 283, 286–7
  developed and developing countries
    compared 1043
  formal demography 1038
  indigenous peoples 2282–3
  model systems 285, 286
  molecular demography 286
  and population management 338
  social demography 1038
  whole-animal phenomena 285
  see also second demographic transition
demography: historical 1045–8
  and the Industrial Revolution 2295–6
Demsetz, H. 3327
denationalization 1048–51, 3648
denaturalization 1700
Denisoff, R. S. 3134
Denmark
  births outside marriage 2663
  cohabitation 566, 1587
  complementary and alternative medicine 631
  democracy 1001
  demographic data collection 1012
  divorce rates 2664
  health care system 2055
  lone parenthood 2663, 2664, 2665
  marriage, delayed 1587
  technology assessment 689–90
  teenage motherhood 1728
Denney, R. 3917
Dennis, K. N. 14–16
Dennis, R. M. 7–9, 282, 1220–3, 1242–7,
  2763–5, 2829–31, 3876–7, 4187–9
Denny, R. 2691
denomination 1051–6, 4138
  American denominationalism 1052
  interdenominationalism 1052
  membership decline 1053
  and pluralism 1051
  Protestant dynamic 1052
  sect–demomination distinction 1315

  voluntarism 1054, 1055
  and women 1053
DeNora, T. 746–8
denotation 1403
density dependence theory 2353
dental services 266
Denton, N. A. 2196–9, 2306
Denzin, N. K. 134–5, 1390, 1448, 2362, 2448,
  2643, 2980, 2981, 5075–80
department store 740, 766, **1056–9**, 4305–6
  and children's consumer culture 693
  credit cards and 816
  cultural stimulus 743
  dream world 4306
  gender segregation 1850
  and the museum experience 3126
  and the shopping mall 1058
Depauw, K. P. 1171
dependency ratios 1029–30, 2367
dependency and world-systems theories
  390, 526, **1060–2**, 1068, 1069, 1472
  and capitalism 390, 517
  capitalist world-system 1069
  captive mind concept 398–9
  and decolonization 986, 2267
  and deindustrialization 994
  depoliticization 348, 349–50
  and development 1853
  and economic cycles 1263
  and economic development 1295, 1296
  and endogenous development 1407
  and family sociology 1599–600
  and globalizing processes 1950
  hegemonic cycle 2491
  and international gender division of labor
    2382
  and the Kondratieff cycle 2491
  and Latin America 1060, 1567
  and modernization theory 3072
  neo-Marxist world-system theory 1282
  and political economy of development 1069
  and political economy of science 3439
  and political sociology 3460
  and primate cities 3624
  structural perspective 1060
dependentistas 1060
depression and distress
  child abuse and 449
  demographic variables 82
  and health locus of control 2064
  incarceration and 838
  and lack of interpersonal relationships 2391

in later life 81, 82
and learned helplessness 2568, 2569
and physical illness 2242, 2243
post-partum depression 1112
social antecedents 81–2, 83
subordination of women and 326, 336
unipolar depressive disorders 1864
deprivation
  aspirational 4474
  decremental 4474
  progressive 4474
  see also social movements, relative
    deprivation and
deprofessionalization 2076
depth psychology 875, 1639, 1863
deregulation 355, 2513, 2521
  economic 2512
  industrial 2749
  markets 2887
  media 2914
  and welfare regimes 2513
derivations 3361
derivatives 3324
Dermott, E. 1647–50
Derné, S. 1786–7
Derrida, Jacques 125, 126, 869, **1062–4**, 1775
  auteur theory 217–18, 219
  and bricolage 365, 366
  deconstructionism 986–9, 1062–3, 1436,
    2661, 3552, 3581
  différance 3581
  and discourse, framing of 3673
  and economic geography 1299
  and genre 1916
  logocentrism 2660, 2661, 3111
  metaphysics of presence 2643
  postmodernism 3552, 3570, 3573
  poststructuralism 244, 3581
  and queer theory 2114
Des Pres, T. 2421
Desai, M. 5057–60
DeSanctis, G. 3295
Descartes, René 327, 798, 1397
  Cartesian dualism 335, 1684, 4094, 4322
  and ethics 1447
  inertia theory 4116
  and mediation 2924
  and modernism 3573
  rationalism 650, 1434, 2176
  and the subject 2527
  subject–object dichotomy 2534
descriptive discriminant analysis 1557

descriptive statistics 1064–5
  correlation and 805
  see also secondary data analysis
desensitization 257
desertification 1423
designer babies 558, 1490, 2172, 3207
desire
  capitalism and 990
  and commodities 4243
  democratization of 1057
  Freudian account 3698
  Lacan and 3698
  opposite-sex desire 4197
  and plastic sexuality 3412
  postmodern analysis 3574
  same-sex desire 3728, 4197
  and sex education programs 4195
  sexual desire 2612, 2613
  see also lust balance
deskilling thesis 363–4, 364–5, 366, 538,
  1200, 1959
  Braverman and 2521–2
  and the information society 2330
  management deskilling strategy 2523
desktop technologies 1162
DeSpelder, L. A. 1495
despotism 1006, 1007, 1010, 3073–4
destabilization 3831–2
determinism
  biological determinism 969, 1366, 1847, 1875
  Comte and 654–5
  and criminology 857, 969, 970
  economic 896, 897, 1293, 1955
  and ethnic and race relations 661
  and feminist epistemology 1682
  and freedom 2041
  genetic determinism 172
  geographical determinism 620
  institutional determinism 3283
  linguistic determinism 3280
  objectivist determinism 406
  overdeterminism 1896
  and positivism 1101
  psychological determinism 969
  scientific determinism 1287
  social determinism 734, 969
  technological determinism 734, 1160,
    2327, 2879
  underdeterminism 1896
deterrence studies 564
deterrence theory 1065–7
  Beccaria and 256, 1065, 1066, 3799

deterrence theory (*cont'd*)
  Bentham and 3799
  and the death penalty 977
  rational choice perspective 3799–802
détournement 980–1
deus ex machina 1387
Deutsch, K. W. 2899, 2900, 3065
DeVault, M. L. 274–5, 1703, 1849,
    2859, 3960–1
developing countries
  aging and social policy 84
  contraceptive use
  cultural imperialism 907
  and demography of aging 68–9
  economic restructuring 2382–3
  fertility behavior 1043
  and marginalization 2766
  population growth 3526
  school systems 1324
  structural adjustment programs (SAPs) 1724,
    2382–3
  transparency norms 5073
  see also dependency and world-systems
    theories; specific countries
development: political economy
    1067–70, 3435
development
  and democracy 1852
  dependency approach 1944
  endogenous development 1406–7
  global North 1852, 2382
  global South 1852, 1853, 2382
  and human rights 2184
  measuring 1852
  and populism 3538
  science and technology, role of 3439
  sport as tool for 3474
  state-centric view 1295, 1296
  survival issues 1852
  urban strategies 1854
  women in development (WID) perspective
    1852, 1853, 1854
  see also economic development; population
    and development
development agencies 808
Development Alternatives with Women for a
    New Era (DAWN) 1855
development gap, and industrialization 2297
development projects 1948
development scholarship 1294
developmental psychology 281
  captive mind concept 399, 400

and childhood 459
and friendship 1799
and generational change 1901
and helping behaviors 3680
moral development 3679
developmental stages 1070–3
developmental state 1073–5, 1296
  and endogenous development 1406
  and industrialization 2299
deviance 1075–82
  and absenteeism 5, 6
  and anomie 809, 3544
  Becker and 1087, 1123, 1125, 1136, 1137,
    1143, 2207, 2208, 2501, 2502, 2505,
    2976, 2977
  becoming a deviant 1124
  biological deviance theory 2952
  bodily abominations as 323
  and body modification 330
  and charisma 3543
  commitment ceremonies 2208
  and compositional theory of urbanism 636
  and conflict theory 666, 1078
  constructionist approach 1076–9
  control balance theory 782–4
  and cool 797
  and corruption 809
  and counterculture 809–10
  and crime 819
  criminalization 1097
  and criminology 1081, 1799–800
  death of the sociology of deviance? 978–80
  definitions 1100, 1116, 1117, 2207
  determining deviant behavior 2502–3
  deviance denial/acceptance 2209
  deviance–crime distinction 1093
  deviance–difference distinction 1126
  deviant accounts 12–14
  deviant careers 1142–4
  deviant emotions 1383
  deviant friendships 1799–800
  deviant identity 1124, 2207–10, 3505
  deviant mystique 1126, 1127, 1130
  and difference 1155
  and disability 1170, 1698, 1700
  doing deviance 1124
  drugs/substance use in sport 1240
  and entrepreneurship 1412
  essentialist perspective 2209
  and ethnocentrism 1478
  ethnomethodological definition 1077
  etiology of 1078, 1081

etymology and synonyms 1136
ex-deviants 3543
explanatory theories of 1076, 1079–82
female sex work as 1659–62
and football hooliganism 1767
functionalist perspective 3087
high consensus deviance 1081
homosexuality as 638
illness as 2059
interactionist theory 2506
Kitsuse and 2472
labeling perspective 858, 1078, 1124, 1125,
 2207–8, 2501–3, 2505, 2766, 2832,
 2951, 2952
and leadership 3543
leisure as 2593, 2596, 2598–9
and marginalization 2766
and medical sociology 2935
medicalization 2506, 2952, 2953
and mental disorder 2695
and moral entrepreneurship 3087
and moral panics 3089, 3091
mutual deviantization 584
negative deviance 3543, 3544
non-criminal 1100, 1104
and norms 1083, 1117
organizational deviance 3303–5
and personality disorders 846
and political power 1114
and popular culture 3482
positive deviance 2121, 2503, 2506,
 3542–4
primary deviance 1087, 1123, 1137, 2209,
 2501, 2505, 2507
and reintegrative shaming 2506
relativist perspective 1092, 2207
retrospective reinterpretation 2207
and rule creation 2505, 2506
secondary deviance 1087, 1123, 1137, 2209,
 2501, 2505, 2506, 2507
secret deviance 1117, 1124
self-destructive forms 2819
and self-fulfilling prophecy 2506
self-reported 1128
sexuality and 332
situational deviance 1078
social construction 1078, 2504, 2505
and social control 1095, 2951
and social learning theory 4439
societal deviance 1078, 1079
and sociocultural relativism 979, 4588–9
sociological theories 1081

and stigma 1127, 1140, 2504, 2505, 2506
structuralist perspective 2207
tertiary deviance 2209
and violent death 974
and welfare fraud 5240
see also sexual deviance; subcultures, deviant
deviance, absolutist definitions of 979,
 1082–4
deviance, academic 1084–6
deviance, constructionist perspectives
 1076–9, **1086–92**
deviance, crime and 1092–5
androcentric theories 1856–7
deviant accounts 12, 13
and gender 1856–8
and women 1857–8
deviance, criminalization of 1095–100
and marginalization 2766
deviance, explanatory theories of 1100–7
deviance, the media and 1107–10
and cultural criminology 893–4
deviance, medicalization of 1110–14
and alcoholism 117
and drug use 26
and gambling 1817
deviance, moral boundaries and 1114–16
deviance, normative definitions of
 1116–17, 1123, 2503, 3543
deviance, positivist theories of 1079–80,
 1081, 1100–1, **1117–21**, 2121, 2503, 2506,
 3542–4
deviance processing agencies 1121–3
deviance, reactivist definitions of 1083,
 1123–6, 2503, 3543
deviance, research methods 1126–31
ethnographic research 1129–30
respondent-derived quantitative data 1128–9
and stigma 1127
deviance, sport and 1131–5
corporate deviance 1134–5
drugs/substance use 1240, 1241
gambling 1818–21
deviance, theories of 1135–40
androcentive perspective 1856
and anomie 1102
and conflict theory 1102
constructionist theory 1076–9,
 1086–91, 1118
and dangerousness 970
and differential association 1102
explanatory theory 1079–81
and labeling theory 858, 1102

deviance, theories of (*cont'd*)
  and learning theory 1102
  positivist 1079–80, 1081, 1100–1, 1117–21
  and routine activity theory 1102
  and self-control theory 1102
  and social control theory 1102
  and social disorganization theory 1102
deviant beliefs/cognitive deviance 1140–2
  deviant accounts 12–14
deviant careers 1138, **1142–5**
  and inclusion/exclusion 2208
deviant identity careers 2207, 2209
Devil
  and madness 2694
  and magic 2696
devil worship 1117
devil's advocacy 5017
Devine, J. A. 374–6
devolution 8
devotional practices 3520–1, 3522
DeVries, D. 1698
Dewey, John 318, **1145–6**, 1996, 3193, 3194, 3363
  and Addams 24, 25
  and democracy 2807
  and double consciousness 1220
  and educational reform 1262
  and educational theory 864
  and instrumentalism 1145
  and Mead 2861, 2864
  and occupational psychosis 379
  and Orientalism 3344
  pragmatism 1145, 2431, 2670, 3051, 3610
  and the public sphere 2906, 2908, 3466–7
  and school discipline 4019–20
  and social change 446
DeYoung, M. 3086–9
Dezalay, Y. 1310, 2558
dharma 2128
diabetes 2078, 2080, 2246
dialectic 1146–50
  Gurvitch and 2042
  Lefebvre and 2580
  master–slave dialectic 1147
  and negativity 1149
  processes 2042
  Sartre and 4009
  and symbolic interaction 4911–12
dialectical materialism 268, 1148, **1150–1**
  and economic determinism 1293
  and elective affinity 1352

Diamond, L. 1001
Diamond, T. 2977
Diana, Princess of Wales 754
dianetics 4117, 4118
Diani, M. 4455–8
diaspora 1151–3
  and community media 628
  and cultural translation 2886
  diasporic identity 288
  and the ghetto 1937
  imperial diasporas 3835–6
  Islamic 2427
  Jewish 2450, 2453
  Latino/a 2548
  media and diaspora 2885–6
  metaphoric implications 1152
  and NGOs 1969
  religious institutions, role of 1981
  transnational diasporas 1152, 5065
  see also immigration; migration
diasporic consciousness 1153
Díaz, P. 412, 414, 2947
Dick, P. K. 3496
Dickens, Charles 1594, 3638, 3662
Dickens, P. 1419, 1420
Dickie-Clark, H. F. 2763
Dickinson, J. 2989–93
dictatorships 1006, 1852
  Latin America 1852, 1923, 2576
Diderot, D. 155, 1911
Dieguez, M. 2948
Diekmann, A. 1281–6
Diener, E. 626
diet 325, 336
  and disease prevalence 1184
  and health behavior 2051, 2060
  and health lifestyles 2061
diethylstilbestrol 1865
dieting 1850
Dietzgen, J. 1150
différance 987, 988, 1154, 3570, 3581
difference 259, 260, 1147, **1153–5**, 1992
  biological 332
  cultural 3422
  deconstructionist account 1154
  and deviance 1155
  deviance–difference distinction 1126
  and football 4346
  as identity 1154
  Lefebvre and 2581
  postmodern feminist perspective 3562
  Simmel and 4326

sport, and reproduction of difference 4291
  as subjectivity 1154
  taxonomies of racial difference 3731
difference feminism 251
difference principle 3812
differential association theory 845, 848, 849,
  4901–92
  and deviance 1081, 1102, 1103–4, 1133,
    1143, 4901–2
  and peer pressure 1799
differential reinforcement 849
**differential treatment of children by sex
  1155–9**
  and the hidden curriculum 2117, 2118
  sex-selective abortion 3535
differentiation
  and the church 485
  and the hidden curriculum 2118
  and organizations 314, 950, 3300
  social 315, 1359
  and urban ecology 1290
diffuse status characteristic 1525
diffusion theory 293
  and cultural differences 1599
  and democracy 1003
  and direct action 1167
  and hate crime laws 1099
  Malinowski and 2705
  and management innovation 2737, 2738
  Matthew effect 2860–1
  and sport 4711
DiFranco, A. 1677
Diggers (American activists) 1165
Diggers (English sect) 613–14, 3048
digital 1159–64, 2916
  analogue–digital distinction 1159
  and community media 628
  cyberculture 961–4
  and ethnography 1483
  and globalization 1956
  and media boundaries, abolition of 2914
  new media 2876
  and visual saturation 756
  see also information technology; multimedia
digital aesthetics 1163–4
digital capitalism 1162
digital copyright 1162
digital democracy 1162
digital divide 628, 733, 2330, 2334, 2387,
  2388, 2878
  and inequality 3182
  and telemedicine 2390

digital lifestyles 2880
digital media 1160–1
  characteristics 1160–1
  convergence 1160–1
  creativity 1163
  digital aesthetics 1163–4
  digital imaging tradition 1163
  interactivity 1160
  linearity 1164
digital music 3132–3
digital rights management 1162
diglossia 282
Dilaudid 1233
Dill, B. T. 308
Dillon, M. 3–4, 3864–9
Dilthey, Wilhelm 2861, 5187
  and Comte 654
  and hermeneutics 1901, 2108, 2231, 2535
  and the interpretive meta-paradigm 2968
  and reflexivity 3819
  and Simmel 4324
  and the sociology of knowledge 2474
Dilworth-Anderson, P. 898–902
DiMaggio, P. 891, 933, 1307, 2125, 2351,
  2714, 2739
Dingwall, R. 2560–4, 2937–41
Dinnerstein, D. 3696
Diocletian 3248, 3348
Diotallevi, L. 483–9
diplomacy
  shuttle diplomacy 3380, 3381
  sports diplomacy 3474
direct action 1164–7
  anarchist-inspired 136, 1165
  animal rights movement 138–9
  celebratory direct action 1165–6
  and diffusion 1167
  and global justice movement 1166, 1948
  moral witnessing 1166
  non-violent 1165–6
  religiously based 1166
  repression of 1167
  violent 1166
  see also activism; terrorism
Direct Action Network 1166
disability
  and aging 68, 72
  autonomy and mobility 337
  biologization of 2172
  bodily abominations 323, 324
  and caregiving 401, 403
  causes 1169

disability (*cont'd*)
  changes in disability 2096
  communities of attachment 1578
  defining 1168
  and depression 82
  disability activism 480, 482
  disability history 1169
  disablement framework 2095
  and discrimination 1182, 1907
  epidemiology of 1168
  and eugenics 2938
  and gender 1172, 1864, 2097
  and homelessness 2149
  and later life chronic illness 482
  life-table model 2095–6
  lived experience 337
  and low birthweight infants 1726
  medical model 337, 480
  mortality–morbidity–disability
    relation 2097
  personal narratives 481, 482
  phenomenological studies 337
  rehabilitation policy 1169
  social construction 337, 479, 1697
  statistics 1168
  welfare disability programs 995
  WHO classifications 1168
  see also chronic illness and disability
disability rights 1908, 2172
disability as a social problem 1168–71
  chidhood disabilities 1572–4
  and deviance 1117, 1170
  and euthanasia 1490
  feminist disability studies 1696–700
  labeling perspective 1170
  and marginalization 2766
  social model 337
  stigma 323, 324, 583, 1169–70, 1572, 3950
disability sport 1171–4
  elite sport 1172
  female athletes 1172
  as rehabilitation 1173
  social construction 3472
disasters 1174–6, 4092
  and emergent norm theory 1367
  and refugee movements 3834
disc jockeys 3131, 3486
disciplinary society 1176–9
  class issues 4111
  school discipline 4019–22
  see also coercive organizations;
    governmentality and control

discount stores 4306
discourse 1179–82
  colonial discourse 2981–2, 2984
  and communication 1179
  discursive language 2537
  and documentary analysis 1214
  formalist and functionalist paradigms 1180
  Foucault and 3583, 3884
  and identity theory 2213
  management discourse 2722–5
  metatheory discourse analysis 1179
  methodological perspectives 1181
  postcolonial discourse 2983, 2984
  postmodern 3582–3
  Sacks and 3971
  terministic screen 1180, 1181
discourse analysis 776, 925
  and feminist research 1702
  and hermeneutics 2107
  and microsociology 3005
  participant/non-participant observation 3238
discourse community 1179, 1180, 1181
discriminant analysis
discrimination 1182–4, 3748, 3749
  agism 56–9
  anti-discrimination law 4737–8
  avoidance learning 3753–4
  and the death penalty 977
  and disability 1172, 1907
  and divisions of labor 1463
  educational 3751
  ethnic/racial 1463, 1907, 2305
  feminist perspectives 1183
  and genetic information 1907
  and health 2078
  and housing 2420, 3733
  human rights perspective 1183, 2182
  and illness 2246
  and immigramts 3032
  institutionalized 2444, 3649
  and majorities 2702
  punishment for 3750
  religious 2440
  and restrictive covenants 3898
  in sport 3475, 4683
  in training opportunities 2516
  workplace diversity and 5290
  see also affirmative action; anti-Semitism;
    occupational segregation; race (racism);
    redlining; social exclusion; steering, racial
    real estate
discriminatory aggression 1183

discursive fields 1782–3
discursive opportunity structures 1782
discursive practices 1776
discursive processes of frame articulation 1782
discursive psychology 1181
disease 479
    causation 2082
    chronic degenerative diseases 3097
    as commodity 337
    and death and dying 972–5
    epidemics 3535
    and epidemiology 1433–4
    and ethnicity 2080
    gender differences 1864
    and genomics 2172
    and health care delivery systems 2054
    indeigenous depopulation 2282
    indigenous peoples, impact on 2281
    leading causes of disease burden 1864
    measurement of 1433
    mortality impacts 72, 3099
    prevalence 1433
    psychosomatic disease 1522
    sex-specific susceptibility 3535
    see also chronic illness and disability; sick role
disease management 2066
disease, social causation 1184–7
    fundamental causes 1184, 1185
    multifactorial causation 1185
    neighborhood hazards 2073
    proximate (lifestyle) causes 1184
    social epidemiology 4403–6
disembedding *see* distanciation and
    disembedding
disenchantment of the world 377, 4143
disengagement theory, and gerontology
    1927, 1929
disintegration 1922, 1923
disinterestedness, norm of 3667, 4110
Disney 713, 730, 732, 767, 1642, 2898
Disney, Walt 150, 1754
Disneyization 1187–8, 5142
    and commodification 1991
    and fantasy cities 1643
    structural 1187
    transferred 1187
Disneyland 759
    and *flânerie* 1762–3
    and hyperreality 2590
    simulacrum 3567
Disneyland Dads/Moms 3224
disorder and order maintenance 3715–16

disorientation 596
dispersion 1741
disposability 1923
dispositions, attribution theory 205
disruptive protest 579
dissenters 1051
dissonance theory
    attitudes and behavior 562–5
    see also cognitive dissonance theory
distance relationships 810, 811
distanciation and disembedding 1188–9
    and modernity 3070
    of social systems 2922
    time–space distanciation 1958, 2889,
        2922, 3070
distinction 1189–91
distinctiveness, and attribution theory 206
distortion 2925
distributive justice 6, **1191–7**, 2145
    and exchange relations 1369
    and group equilibrium 2145
    and moral economy 3084
    and multiculturalism 3107
    and social justice 4432–4
    utopian perspective 3233
    see also social justice, theories of
Ditton, J. 1138, 1651
divergence theory 5103
divergent social processes 642
diversity 1197–9
    cultural 1154, 1992, 2890, 3217
    cultural diversity of aging 898–901
    and difference 1153
    and ethnic/race relations 662
    homogenizing 1395
    and the Internet 2387
    and multiculturalism 899
    see also family diversity; melting pot;
        workplace diversity
diversity management 2750, 3296
divination 4926
Divine Light Mission 885
division of labor 1199–201
    Adam Smith on 515, 2288
    and alienation 664
    breadwinner/homemaker model 1883, 1884,
        2309, 2416
    and community–economy relation 624
    cultural division of labor 1464, 1469
    Durkheim and 1261, 1319, 2298, 2561,
        2969, 3229
    efficiency 2712

division of labor (*cont'd*)
  and environmental activism 1273
  ethnic and racial 1463–4
  forced division 1199, 1200, 2561
  and functionalism 1810
  and gender mainstreaming 1870
  gendered 1273, 1716, 1848, 1893, 2307,
    2486, 2516, 2619
  Hindu 2129
  and industrialization 1922, 2298
  and interdependent individuality 582
  international 1068, 2382–3, 3181
  mechanically organized societies 4616
  and middleman minorities 3009
  and modernization 3074
  new international division of labor
    (NIDL) 1715
  organically organized societies 4616
  in organizations 1893
  and science and technology 3436, 3437
  and social and moral fragmentation 2561
  sociobiological explanations 2309
  within social movements 1874
  see also ethnic and racial division of labor
divisions of household labor 1202–6
  biosociological theory 293
  childcare 457, 1203
  children's contributions 1204
  cohabitation and 568
  dual-earner couples 1248, 1844
  economic dependency theory 1205
  egalitarian ideology 1881
  and family structure 1620
  food preparation 722
  gendered 673, 1202–6, 1580–1, 1582, 1591,
    1620, 1633, 1669, 1840, 1859, 1881, 2112,
    2301, 2310, 2547–8, 2790–1, 3081
  and the heterosexual imaginary 2110
  industrialization, effects of 1594
  and later-life marriage 2547
  and marital power theory 2772
  and marital quality 2774
  and Marxist model of capitalism 2841
  men's housework participation 1204–5, 1206
  paternalist relations 3371
  patriarchal 1687, 3378
  in peer marriages 2303
  perceived fairness 1868
  psychoanalytic feminist perspective 3698
  racial and ethnic patterns 1204
  relative resource theories 1205
  ritual performance roles 753

  same-sex couples 2161, 2608
  second shift 1203, 1248, 1669, 1881, 2619–20
  separate spheres ideology 1205, 1849
  subcontracted services 1849
  time availability 1205
divorce 1206–10
  accounts 10
  adults, effects on 1208–9, 1592
  alimony awards 1721
  biosociological theory 293
  blended families 695
  child custody and child support 451–4
  children and divorce 467–71, 1592, 1616,
    1617, 1621, 1623
  conservatism and 680
  divorce adjustment 1208–9
  divorce rates 1206–7, 1586, 1616, 1617, 1620,
    2414, 2415, 2417, 2792, 2793
  and early childhood 1269
  economic consequences 1628, 1721
  elederly couples 2547
  and epidemiological method 1434
  and family conflict 1581, 1582
  and family decline 1617
  and family diversity 1589
  and family sociology 1037
  and family structure 3223
  and fatherhood 1649
  and friendship networks 1793
  genetic and biological contributions 470
  and grandparents 2019
  and individualism 1615
  and kinship 2471
  and labor force participation 1883
  and marital infidelity 2324, 2325
  no-fault divorce laws 1721
  and parent–child relationships 70
  parenting education courses 469
  positive implications 1625
  and poverty 1613, 1614
  and prior cohabitation 567
  risk factors 1207–8
  social acceptance of 1622
  standard of living post-divorce, gendered
    1628
  see also child custody and child support;
    lone-parent families; stepfamilies
Djibouti, female genital mutilation 1654
DNA 286, 556, 557, 1486, 2937, 2940
  double helix structure 2171, 3814
  mutability 2937
  patenting 2172

doable problems 4548
Doane, R. 735–7
Dobbelaere, K. 487, 4140, 4140–8
Dobbin, F. 933, 1308, 2354, 2356, 2557
doctoral studies 2012
documentary 1210–13
documentary analysis 1213–16
 circulation of documents 1215
 consumption of documents 1214–15
 production of documents 121
documentary method of interviewing 2407
docusoaps 3491
Dodd, N. 3078–81, 3079
Dodge, D. L. 3543, 3544
Doeringer, P. B. 2514
Doezema, K. 1984
dog racing 1820, 1821
dogmatism 897
Doi, T. 3218
doing gender 1216–19, 2820
 and accountability 2820
 cohabitation and 568
 culture and gender 936–41
 and hegemonic masculinity 2099
Dolnick, D. 1661
Domberger, S. 3353
Domei 1414
domestic economy 1594
domestic labor *see* divisions of household labor
domestic science 325
domestic service 3–29, 1600, 1669, 1716, 1849,
 1854, 3031
 and stratified reproduction 4827
 see also households
domestic sphere, privatization of 1578, 4627
domestic violence 65, **1219–20**, 2301,
 2302–3, 2309
 and abortion 4
 alcohol-related 115
 children and 449
 cohabitation relationships 1624
 and compulsory heterosexuality 639
 and discriminatory aggression 1183
 and divorce 1207
 economic costs 1219–20
 emotional/psychological abuse 1219
 and family theory 1632
 feminist criminology 1106
 gender bias 1844, 1856, 1857
 and the heterosexual imaginary 2110
 HIV-related 2139
 and inequalities in marriage 2302

 and infidelity 2324
 and learned helplessness 2569
 and male deviance 1856
 medicalization of 1111
 new left analysis 3197, 3198
 physical abuse 1219
 and post-war trauma 1887
 and poverty 1614
 power dynamics 1695
 sexual abuse 1219
 and stalking 1098
 toward pregnant women 2315
 and traditional family structure 1589
domestic violence shelters 3775
domesticity, cult of 1849
Domhoff, W. 2838
Dominelli, L. 4521–4
Dominican Republic
 male prostitution 1661
 sex tourism 4201
Donnelly, P. 2092, 2221, 2222, 4677–80,
 4708–10
Donoghue, E. 2613
donor insemination 3207
Donzelot, J. 1582
Doomsday Cult 3047
Dore, R. 1411
dormitory towns 1576
Dorst, J. 3125–8
Dos Santos, T. 1566
Dostoevsky, Fyodor 1220
dot.com crash 2022, 2751, 2876
double consciousness 1220–3
 Du Bois and 1220–3, 1245, 3369–70
 literary motif 1220
 and passing 3369–70
double dissimilar situations 1527
double hermeneutic 554
double jeopardy, sociological 1343
double loop learning model 3336
doubt-belief theory of enquiry 3609, 3610
Dougherty, K. J. 622
Douglas, C. M. W. 4100–4
Douglas, J. 1520–1
Douglas, M. 333, 683, 721, 741, 743, 923, 1940,
 3632, 3933, 3937, 3974, 4857–8, 4907,
 5044, 5219
Douglas, S. J. 939, 940
Douglass, F. 15
Dowd, T. 2557
Downes, D. 1135–40
Downey, D. 2117

Downs, H. 1197–9
downshifting 729
downsizing 2715, 3398
dowries 1315, 3534
Dowty, R. 854–7
Doyle, R. 3396–9
drag queens and drag kings 1223–6, 2160,
    2611, 5040, 5042
    and female masculinity 1658
Dragnet 1109
Drake, E. 2833
dramaturgy 1226–9
    dramaturgical self 1228, 4158
    Goffman and 1519, 1997, 2362, 2670
    and helping behaviors 3680
    and management consultancy 2721
    and place 3410
    and social interaction 2362
Dreaming 3633
dreams 3629
    and animism 141
Dreeben, R. 3273
Dreiser, T. 743
Drentea, P. 401–2
dress reform activists 1673
Drew, P. 2363
Dreyer, C. 1753
Dreyfus affair 2531
drive reduction theory 257
Driver, T. 754
dromocratic revolution 2692
Dronkers, Jaap 1362–4, 4052–5
dropping out of school 1229–32
    childhood predictors 1232
    and extracurricular activities 1230–1
    and family demography 1326
    and gender 1230–1
    high school dropouts 1230–2
    and literacy differentials 2655
    private school dropouts 1232
    and race/ethnicity 1344
    and randomized trials 2404
    religious schools 1326–7
    and school transitions 4028
    sport, and dropout rate reduction 2121
    stepchildren 1623
    tracking students 1230
drug advertising 1233
drug dealing 820, 834
    black/white dealers 3738
    as career 1143
    and deviance 1093, 1102, 1129, 1224

in public housing neighborhoods 3708
    and subculture 1129
drug use 1232–6
    addiction and dependency 1235
    and casual leisure 2599
    and counterculture 809
    criminal justice approach 1237
    culturally endorsed use 1234
    definitions of "drug" 1236
    and deviance 1093, 1107
    and deviant friendships 1799–800
    and disease prevalence 1184
    drug use continuum 1233–4
    drug–crime relationship 1234–5
    and epidemiological method 1434
    experimental use 1233–4
    and gender 1235, 2819
    and health lifestyles 2061
    and HIV infection 1660
    and homelessness 2149
    medical uses 1238
    opiate addiction 134–5
    parents in cohabiting unions 1624
    performance-enhancing drugs 1241
    and popular music 2826
    predictors for 1232
    prescription drugs 1233, 1234, 1235
    public health approach 1237
    recreational use 1234
    sociological analysis of 26
    see also smoking
drugs
    clinical trials 1865
    sexually enhancing pharameutics 2541
drugs, drug abuse, and drug policy 1236–7
    addiction and dependency 26, 1235
    and child abuse 449
    deviant labeling 26
    discriminatory legislation and policies 3736,
        3738, 3739, 3766
    and divorce 1207, 1208
    female users 1858
    and HIV infection 4217
    and homicide 2152
    and incarceration 804
    intervention and treatment 1144
    media portrayal 1109
    medicalization of drug abuse 1112
    rehabilitation 1144
    and socially disorganized communities 1102
    societal reaction 26
    and sport 1132–3

substance abuse programs 997
see also alcholism and alcohol abuse
drugs and the law 1238–9
asset forfeiture 1238
misuse laws 1239
paraphernalia laws 1239
possession laws 1238
trafficking laws 1238
use laws 1238–9
drugs moral panic 3088, 3090, 3091
drugs research, ethics of 1449
drugs/substance use in sport 1132–3, 1135,
    1239–42
additive drugs 1135
performance enhancing drugs 1134
steroids 1132, 1134
druidism 3875
drunk driving 63
underage 114–15
Drysdale, J. 5226–35
Du Bois: "Talented Tenth" 1242–4
and affirmative action policies 46
Du Bois, W. E. B. 1244–7, 2407, 3266,
    3739, 3740
and the ASA 131
and the color line 604–5, 3746, 4149
and double consiousness 274–5, 1149,
    1220–3, 3368–9
and eugenics 1489
materialist analysis 2838
and Park 131
and racial integration 129
and residential segregation 3888
and Washington 9
dual-earner couples 1247–9
and absenteeism 6
and child outcomes 1625
and childcare 1692
and division of household labor 1844, 1881
and earner–carer model 1272
and family conflict 1582
and fatherhood 1648
LAT relationships 811
and marriage 675
non-standard work schedules 1882
and working hours 1032
dual labor markets 1249–50
dualism
art/science dichotomy 2981
Cartesian 335, 1684, 4094
Durkheim and 1253
ecofeminist critique 1275, 1276

and heterosexism 1275
mind–body dualism 327, 335, 337, 1749,
    1846, 2081, 2431, 2918, 3699, 4094
reason/emotion duality 1391
western 1274
Duany, A. 504
Dubai, fantasy cities 1641
Dubin, C. 1239
Duby, G. 143
dueling 1819
Duesenberry, J. 399, 683
Duff, A. 2328
Duhem, P. 1571
Duhem–Qine underdetermination thesis
    4087, 4098
Duleep, H. O. 3025–31, 3026
Dumais, D. 3–4
Dummer, E. S. 131
dummy coding 1898
Dunayevskaya, R. 1149
Duncan, B. 2419, 2960
Duncan, G. 1613
Duncan, H. D. 1227
Duncan, O. D. 313, 1334, 1336, 2419, 2629,
    2960, 3062, 3063, 3249, 3251
Duncombe, J. 2325
Duncombe, S. 911–13
Duncicr, M. 2362
Dunlap, R. 1417–22, 1419, 3164
Dunlop, J. 2290, 2509
Dunn, J. 2669–71
Dunning, E. 1749–52, 1751, 1877
duration analysis 1017
Durham coal-mining studies 429
During, S. 2982
Durkheim, A. 1252–3
Durkheim, Émile 1250–61
and animism 141, 142
and anomie 144, 145, 516, 593, 595, 1102,
    1199, 1200, 1261, 3124, 3230
and anthropology 149
and *'asabiyya* 180–1
biography 1250–1, 1252–3
and bonding 1253, 1254
and capitalism 390, 516
and the church 485
and the city 500
and civil religion 506, 2276
and civil society 512
and collective consciousness 581–2, 591, 923,
    1966, 2474
and Comte 654

Durkheim, Émile (*cont'd*)
   and crime 249, 819, 1809, 4586
   and cults 884, 3872
   and cultural anthropology 1251, 1259
   and cultural reproduction 910, 911
   and deviance 1114, 1136
   and discourse 1251
   and division of labor 1261, 1319, 2298, 2561,
      2969, 3229, 4484
   and dualism 1253
   economic sociology 932, 2780, 2781, 2784,
      2786–7
   and education 1262, 1323, 1327, 2116
   and egalitarianism 1252, 1255
   and emotions 1376, 1384, 1385
   and empiricism 1397, 2836
   and food 721, 1808
   and individualism 1251, 1256, 1259, 1260,
      1262, 2285, 3230, 3689
   and industrial capitalism 3550
   and law–economy relationship 2557
   and magic as social phenomenon 2699, 2700
   mana 433
   medical sociology 2932
   and the modern state 2356
   and modernity 1253, 1258
   and myth 3137
   and nationalism 3146
   and penal institutions 1262
   and positivism 2186, 2836
   and postmodernism 1251
   and poststructuralism 1251
   and pragmatism 1258
   and private property 3678
   and the professions 2075, 3663
   and public/private spheres 736
   and punishment of criminals 2506
   and racial and gender inequality 1257
   and reason 1254, 1257, 1259
   and religion 259, 1256–7, 1576, 1810, 1996,
      1997, 2081, 3630–1, 3856, 3857, 3867,
      3937, 3972–3, 4484
   and ritual 1254, 1257, 1376, 1385, 1389,
      2032, 2366, 2474, 3146, 3936–7
   and sacredness 742, 1257, 1263, 2081, 3973–5
   and school discipline 4019
   and scientific knowledge 1256
   and social change 1261–3
   and social class 548
   and social cohesion 2143
   and social control theory 844
   and social economics 1318, 1319
   and social evolution 1261–3, 1506, 4361–2
   and social facts 1256, 1417, 2964, 3164,
      4155–6, 4414
   and social institutions 2344
   and social integration 3007–8, 3904, 4429–30
   and social justice 1258–9, 1260
   and social morphology 2047
   and social order 1199
   and social realism 1261
   and social structure and task differentiation
      3229
   social theories 3229, 3230
   and socialism 1258
   and socialism–communism distinction 614
   sociological methodology 1251, 1254, 1255,
      1281, 1397, 2353, 4603
   and sociologism 1520
   and solidarity 181, 1199, 1200, 1253, 1256,
      1258, 1262, 1965, 2003, 2560, 3074, 3464,
      3621, 3670, 3918, 4399, 4615, 4616–17,
      5102, 5104
   and statistics 1255–6
   and strain theory 4779–80
   and structural functionalism 1251, 1254–5,
      1810, 3581, 3582, 4852, 4861
   and suicide 144, 845, 1252, 1254, 1255, 1256,
      2047, 2799, 3008, 3230, 3689, 4414, 4484,
      4527, 4881
   and symbolic classicication 4906
   and totemism 1254, 5020–1
   and traditional/modern societies, contrast
      in 598
Durkheim, Émile, and social change 1261–4
Dworkin, A. 905, 1679, 2605, 3541, 3775, 5271
Dwyer, R. 3825–8
dyad/triad 1264–7
   dyadic friendships 1789, 1791, 1795,
      1797, 1802
   dyadic power-dependence theory 1512
   and elder care 1350, 1351
   and exchange theory 1368–9, 1512
   and interpersonal relationships 2392
   and nation-state interaction 1968
   and networks 3184
   power relations 3599
   pure dyads 1264
   and relational cohesion theory 3845
   representative dyads 1264
   Simmel and 4326
   supra-individual dyads 1264
   see also groups; patient–physician
      relationship

Dyadic Adjustment Scale (DAS) 2773
Dyer, R. 416
Dykstra, P. 88–93
Dylan, Bob 3503–4
dynamism, and *'asabiyya* 182
Dynes, R. 1175
dystopia 3495–6
Dziegel, L. 1520

e-business 3269, 3270
e-commerce 732, 733, 1161–2, 1895, 2330, 2750
e-health 2389
e-management 2750, 2751
e-money 3079, 3080
Earl, J. 4475–9
early childhood 1269–71
   kindergarten 2462–5
   preschool programs 4050–1
   see also childhood
earmarking (money) 3080
earner–carer model 1271–3
   breadwinner/homemaker model 1272, 1883,
     1884, 2309, 2416
   caregiver parity model 1272
earnings gap *see* wages gap
Earth Action International 1432
Earth First! 1431
East Timor 1487, 3382, 4167, 4376
   separatism 4188
Easterlin, R. 626, 1042, 4124
Eastern Europe
   abortion politics 3
   life expectancies 3097
   medical sociology 2935
   migration from 3031
   new religious movements in 3204
   popular religiosity 3524
   regional language minorities 280
   Soviet influence 1295
   transition economies 5050–3
   transition from communism 506–8
   see also individual countries
Eastern Orthodox Church 3345–9
Eastman, G. 3407
Easton, M. 1502–3
Easton Town Center, Columbus, Ohio 735
eating disorders 326, 334, 336–7, 722, 1111, 1850
   child abuse and 449
   and deviance in sport 1134
   and family theory 1632
   and gender 2819
   and hyperconsumption 611

Eaves, L. 131
Eberhard, W. 549
ecclesiology *see* church
Echavarría, J. M. 2948
Echols, A. 2601, 3776
Eck, J. E. 1427
eclecticism 4086
Eco, Umberto 2195, 2236, 4330–1, 4332
eco-efficiency 1422
ecofeminism 947, 1273–7
École Pratique des Hautes Études 242, 361,
   362, 406
École Pratique des Hautes Études en Sciences
   Sociales 362
ecological activism 1166
   and the Internet 2387
ecological anthropology 2250
ecological crisis, and consumer culture 727
ecological economics 728
ecological epistemology 249
ecological feminism 1274
ecological footprint 967, 1420, 1422, 1425
ecological models of urban form:
   concentric zone model, the sector
   model, and the multiple nuclei model
   1277–81
   and the central business district 422–3
   concentric zone model 176–7, 1277, 1277–9,
     1918, 2991, 3113, 3944
   and ethnic enclaves 1454
   and gentrification 1918
   and megalopolises 2943
   and urban ecology 1289–90
ecological modernization 728, 1420, 1421,
   1422, 1425
ecological problems 1281–6, 1417–22
   constructivist approach 1418–19
   deconstruction 1419
   definition as 1418
   emergence theories 1281–3
   and life environmentalism 2640–1
   realist approach 1418, 1419
   social dimensions 1418
   solutions 1421–2
   and urbanizaton 1423
ecological push incentives 1284
ecological state 4728
ecological view of history 1286–9
   and collective trauma 595
   and ecological anthropology 2250
ecologism 1430
ecology 1289–91, 3944

ecology (*cont'd*)
  animal ecology 2418
  behavioral ecology 291, 292
  of crime 828
  evolutionary ecology 4087
  family ecology 1633
  green citizenship 499
  organizational ecology 2353, 3301
  plant ecology 2418
  population ecology 2586
  regional ecologies 3123
  and ritual 3935
  sociocultural ecology 2392
  strategy ecology 293
ecology and economy 1291–3
ecomuseums 921
econometrics 1500
economic anthropology 932, 1306
economic bureaucracy 1074
economic capital 383–4, 742, 2628
  and cultural capital 887, 889
  and lifestyle 2647
  and status 685
economic class 533
economic cycles 1263, 2489–90
  Juglar cycle 2489
  Kitchin cycle 2489
  Kondratieff cycles 1263, 2489–92
  Kuznets cycle 2489
economic democracy 3195
economic dependency theory 1205
economic determinism 896, 897, 1293,
  1293–4, 1955
economic development 1294–7, 1413
  and democracy 1001
  and ecology 1291–2
  and education 1331–3
  and environmental deterioration 1297
  Latin America 1561
  population and development 3525–7
  sustainable development 1563
economic and financial forecasting 1387
economic generations 1903–4
economic geography 1297–300
  fragmentation 1299
economic globalization 1061, 1455, 1956
  and development 1852
  and global justice movements 1977
  and spatial contexts of urban regimes 2035
  and trafficking in persons 1717
economic imperialism 2755, 3802
economic individualism 679

economic inequality and crime 840, 841
economic innovation 1455
economic interventionism 2625
economic justice, and environmental
  movements 1431
economic liberalism 2285
economic migration 1600, 1716
economic nationalism 1074
economic power 548, 550, 602
economic reductionism 1293, 1955
economic regionalization 3436
economic resources, and conflict theory 662
economic sociology 1299, 1304, 1410,
  1760, 2781
  Bottomore and 344
  Durkheim and 932, 2780, 2781, 2784, 2786–7
  Jevons and 2442, 2443
  of the market 2775
  new economic sociology 2782–3, 2784, 2785
  and rational choice theory 3802–5
  Weber and 1318, 2781–2, 2783, 2785, 2786,
    3803, 5228–31
  see also financial sociology
**economic sociology: classical political
  economic perspectives 1300–3**
  law–economy relationship 2557–9
**economic sociology: neoclassical
  economic perspective 1303–6**
economic subordination 1395
economies of scale 2295, 2828, 2940, 3436
economy, culture and 1306–11
economy, networks and 1311–14
  and industrial communities 2743
  and profit expectations 3183
economy, religion 1315–18
economy (sociological approach) 1318–23
  culture and economy 932–6
  financial sociology 1759–62
  and ideology 2232–5
  and institutionalism 2355–6
  money in the domestic economy 3079
  and rational choice theory 3802–5
  and regulation theory 3840–1
  and science 4069
  and trust 5082–3
ecospirituality 752
ecosystems 4544–5
ecowomanism 1274
Ecstasy 1233, 1234, 1236
Ecuador
  capitalist growth 390
  indigenous movements 2279

ecumenopolis 2992
Ed Sullivan Show 3131–2
Edelman, L. B. 2559
edge cities 1550–1, 2992, 3113
Edgeworth, F. 1304, 2442, 2443, 2776, 2777
Edict of Nantes 2529, 5011–12
Edin, K. 1737
Edison, Thomas 2478, 3130
Edison Corporation 1752
education 1323–8
  access to, and class differentials 2628
  African American 605
  Birmingham School and 297
  capitalist definitions 866
  chastity prerequisite in Islamic culture 2429
  children of divorced parents 470
  and class system maintenance 2117
  coeducation 4055–6
  compulsory 464, 773, 1035, 2630
  conflict paradigm 1323
  costs, direct and indirect 384
  and cultural trauma, sensitivity to 596
  decentralization 1972
  and democratic beliefs 1001–2
  detraditionalization 3579
  early childhood 2462–5
  equality of opportunity 1323, 1326
  evolution of, Durkheim and 1262
  expansionary trends 1339, 1971–2
  and fertility rates, impact of 1859
  flow of education 1334
  functionalist perspective 1323
  gender differentials 1339–40, 1345, 1844,
    1859, 1859–61, 1974, 2319
  and gender mainstreaming 1870
  goals 1323
  human capital perspective 1323
  and human rights 2184
  immigrant access to 3033
  industrialization, effects of 2295
  institutionalization 2631
  interventions 2404
  and learned helplessness 2569
  learning opportunities 3271–5
  marketization 1972
  and marriage and childbearing 1727
  mass education 1361
  and maternal and child health outcomes 1727
  media literacy education 2892–4
  and meritocracy 2955–7
  and nationalism 1839
  and nonmarital childbearing 1735

  overeducation 4031
  and physical health 50
  in post-industrial society 3551
  predictor for social mobility 1229
  primary education 1971, 1973, 1974
  privatization 1972
  and psychological well-being 50
  qualifications 1399
  racial disparities 3733
  religious education 3689
  secondary education 1698, 1973
  and social capital 4354–8
  and social inequalities 2116, 2117
  standardized educational tests 4721–5
  street education 456
  and subjective age identity 50
  tertiary education *see* colleges and
    universities
  urban education 512–13
  and voting behavior 552
  see also kindergarten; sex education
education, adult 1328–31, 4564–5
  andragogy 4565
  geragogy 4565
  graduate study 209–12
  professional schools 4045–8
education and economy 1331–3
  coeducation 4056
  schooling and economic success 4029–31
Education For All (EFA) 1974, 1975
educational attainment 347, 1333–6, 1334,
    1342–4
  and anti-Semitic views 153
  and career choice 2852
  charter schools 4036
  child abuse, effects on 449
  children in single-parent families 1623
  class differentials 1861, 2628
  cohabitation and 566, 567
  Coleman on 570
  colleges and universities 601
  and community colleges 622
  and conservatism 1868
  cross-national comparisons 1343
  and cultural capital 1337
  desegregation effects 4025
  determinants 1336–7
  and divisions of household labor 1204, 1205
  and divorce, effects of 1616
  and ethnicity 1344, 1861
  and extracurricular activities 1547
  family factors 1337–8

educational attainment (*cont'd*)
  and fathering attitudes 1603
  and friendships 796
  and gender 1335, 1343–4, 2308–9, 3272, 3378–9
  and health 1327, 1335
  home schooled children 4033
  and income 70
  intelligence test score relation 2360
  and intergenerational mobility 2373
  and marriage 676, 2415
  math, science, and technology education 2851
  measurement 1333–4
  and merit 2954
  and migrants 2259
  and morbidity and mortality variations 2087
  and parental involvement in schooling 1604, 3358, 3359
  and patriarchy 3378–9
  poor levels of, and family conflict 1581
  and post-retirement age income 3256
  professional schools 4047
  racial gap 1335, 1344
  and rates of marital dissolution 2415
  and religious activity 1315
  religious schools 4054
  salutary benefits 1335–6
  and school choice 4015
  and school climate 4015, 4017
  and school dropout 1230
  and school transitions 4028
  and self-fulfilling prophecy 4176
  single-sex schools 4056
  and sport, value of 2121
  and stratification 1326
  systemic factors 1338–40
  urban schools 5113
  women 736
educational homogamy 676, 2416, 4810
educational inequality 1336–40, 1974
  and charter schools 4037
  Coleman on 569–70, 571, 3272
  and cultural capital 891
  and curricular hierarchies 1339
  and the hidden curriculum 2116–18
  intelligence test score relation 2360
  and kindergarten 2462, 2463
  and learning opportunities 3272
  and literacy differentials 2654–5
  and marriage 676

  and parental involvement in schooling 3357
  race/ethnic differences 571
  see also school segregation, desegregation
educational and occupational attainment 1340–5
  and class 1345
  and cultural capital 891
  and cultural reproduction 911
  economic, cultural, and social resources and 383
  and expectations/aspirations 1529, 1530
  family factors 1337–8
  and gender 1345
  and intergenerational mobility 2373, 3243
  intergenerational transmission of educational opportunities 383, 384
  and literacy levels 2654
  and the *nenko* wage system 3171
  and race/ethnicity 1345
  schooling and economic success 4029–31
  single-sex schools 4057
  and stratification 1334–5
  systemic factors 1338–40
educational praxis 3613
educational segregation *see* school segregation, desegregation
educative assumption 1445
educative authenticity 214–15
edutainment 1642
Edwards, Jennifer 4374–80
Edwards, John 3267–71, 3893–8
Edwards, R. 2410, 4353–4, 4768–70
Edwards, T. 4243
Eeden-Moorfield, B. van 1589–94
EEOC *see* Equal Employment Opportunity Commission
effect coding 1898
effect sizes 1345–7
  correlation and 807
  and replicability analyses 3878
effectiveness trials 2404
effects research 2877
effeminacy, and homosexual equation 2161
efficacy trials 2404
efficiency
  allocative efficiency 4134
  bureaucracy 2689, 3313, 3807
  division of labor 2712
  dynamic efficiency 4134
  effectiveness-efficiency dilemma 2745
  knowledge management 2716
  McDonaldization 2689

organizational 2746
outsourcing arrangements 3353
see also scientific management
efficiency movements 2720
see also Taylorism
Efron, N. 4955–60
egalitarianism 3929
and *'asabiyya* 183
and class 533
and communism 614
counterculture and 810
democratic 1007
Durkheim and 1252, 1255
and household division of labor 1203,
1205, 1881
in marriage 2769
networks and 673
peer marriages 2303
Egan, G. 3497
Eggebeen, D. J. 1628
Eggertsson, T. 3313
ego identity 2221
egoism 840
and individualism 2285
and suicidal inclinations 3008
threat to social harmony 651
Egypt
female genital mutilation 1654, 1656
heritage tourism 920
honor killings 2303
protoscience 2140
public housing 3710
revolution 3907
Ehrenberg, R. 1315
Ehrenreich, B. 736, 1721
Ehrhardt-Martinez, K. 1425
Ehrlich, A. H. 1283
Ehrlich, P. 1041, 1281, 1283, 1420, 3526
Eibl-Eibesfeldt, I. 2362
Eichmann, Adolf 3034
eidetic reduction 3402
1848 revolutions 2810
Eikeland, O. 1445
Eisenberg, A. F. 2045–6, 4484–6, 4508–17
Eisenhardt, K. M. 2733
Eisenhower, Dwight D. 3051, 3052, 3179, 3438
Eisenstadt, S. N. 184, 519–29, 1815, 2133,
2135, 3070, 3670
and social change 4370–3
Eisenstein, Z. 2841
Eisinger, P. 3448
Eisner, E. 2972, 2973

Eitzen, D. S. 1132, 4665–8
Ekelund, R. 1316
Ekins, R. 5037–43
Ekman, P. 2362
El Saadawi, N. 1655
El Salvador
capitalist growth 390
feminist activism 1685, 1686
peace processes 3381, 3383
protest waves 781
revolution 3907
Truth Commissions 5085
El Shaddai 441–2
El-Ojeili, C. 136–7, 5018–19
Elazar, D. 1652
Elchardus, M. 1651
elder abuse 403, **1347–9**
active neglect 1348
financial abuse 1348
passive neglect 1348
perpetrators 1348
physical abuse 1347
psychological abuse 1348
verbal abuse 1348
elder care 1349–51, 1591, 1730
and absenteeism 6
agency–client relationship 1349–50
carework 402, 403, 2071
and family migration 1607
gendered patterns of 2301
grandparents 2019
and intergenerational support 2633
kinship obligations 2470
and kinship ties 1350
oldest old 2668
public policy 1884
Elder, G. 74, 76, 2631, 2632, 2634–9
elderly
agism 56–9
and the dependency ratio 2367
family life 2633
generational equity debate 2367
income and wealth patterns 3255–6
intergenerational conflict 234–6, 1902
late-life sexuality 2539–42
later-life marriage 2546–8
and leisure 2592–4, 2595
and non-family living 2572
oldest old 2668–9
post-parental life 2633
and poverty 3900
and sibling relationships 4314–15

elderly (*cont'd*)
   see also aging, demography of; aging and
     health policy; aging and the life course,
     theories of; aging, longitudinal studies;
     aging, mental health, and well-being;
     aging and social policy; aging, sociology
     of; aging and technology; aging and work
     performance; older adults, economic well-
     being of
elective affinity 1352, 3075
electoral mobilization 3065
   see also voting behavior
electric chair, execution by 386
electroconvulsive therapy 2694
electrodynamics 1757
electronic gaming *see* computer games
electronic media 1107
   and diaspora 1152–3
   and pre-literate sociality 2691
   and visual saturation 756
electronic monitoring 803, 854, 855
elementary theory 1352–7
   coercive structures 1356
   and exchange network theory 1512
   modeling procedure 1353
   principles and laws 1353–4
   structural conditions 1354–5
Elger, T. 1249–50
Eliade, M. 2698
Elias, Norbert 325, 344, **1357–60**, 2627
   biography 1357–8
   and the civilizing process 530, 531, 532,
     721–2, 1749–50, 1962, 2629
   and distanciation 1188, 1189
   and emotions 1376
   figurational sociology 1358, 1749–51,
     1767, 1962
   and interdependency chains 1359
   and social constraints 1359
   and the sociogenesis of civilization 1358
   and sport sociology 1750–1, 1877
Eliasoph, N. 2238
Eliot, George 218, 655
Eliot, T. S. 2822, 2877, 3136
elite bilingualism 282
elite culture 518, **1360–2**, 2821
   and censorship 421
   and cultural capital 889–90, 1190
   high modernism 2822
   highbrow/lowbrow 2123–5
elite disability sport 1172
elite schools 1325

elite selection 2759
elite sport 1135
elites 1362–4
   aristocratic 701
   Bottomore and 344
   and CAM 631
   circulating elites 547, 1362, 3597
   and civilizations 520
   and collective memory 593
   competitive elitism 3452
   and consumption 741, 1308
   corporate elites 1004, 1008, 1010, 3714
   and distinction 1190
   and enterprise unions 1416
   and fashion 719
   food and cultural consumption 722
   fragmented 3443
   idleness 682, 701
   indigenous elites 1392
   individualistic/structural approach 1363
   and meritocracy 2954
   and moral panics 3090
   Mosca and 1361, 1362, 3102–3, 3361, 3442
   nationalist elites 3155, 3157
   Pareto and 1361, 1362, 3102, 3361, 3442
   pension elites 3900
   pluralism 3443
   political 1002
   and political parties 3452
   and political sociology 3459
   and power 3597
   and public opinion 3713
   radical elite theory 3459
   reproduction of 1362
   scientific 3222–3
   social class and 536
   "Talented Tenth" 1242–4
Elizabeth, V. 3081–4
Eller, Andrea 1650–1
Eller, J. 1382–4, 1650–1
Ellingsaeter, A. L. 1272
Elliott, D. L. 3609–12, 3620–2
Elliott, J. R. 2304–7
Ellis, Havelock 1364–6, 2132, 4285, 5269
   and female sexuality 5269
   and fetishism 608
   and homosexuality 302, 331
Ellis, L. 822–5
Ellison, C. 2081
Ellison, Ralph 129, 1222
Ellul, J. 2333, 3673, 3674
Ellwood, C. 318, 3229

Elo, I. T. 3096–102
Elton, C. 2250
emancipatory historiography 306
emancipatory theory 874
Emanuelson, P. 1352–7
embarrassment 1378, 1379
  threshold of 1358–9
embeddedness
  biological embeddedness of social interaction
    3186
  cultural embeddedness of organizational
    practices 3332
  and spatial relationships 4633–4
  of work careers 3288, 3289
  see also distanciation and disembedding;
    social embeddedness of economic action
embezzlement 3305, 3675, 4192
embodiment 336, 337
Embong, A. R. 3198–201
embourgeoisement 2628, 2646
embryo research 557, 1907, 2172, 3207, 4067
emergence 634
emergence strategy perspective 2749
emergent market economies 1567
emergent norm theory 1366–8
  and crowd behavior 882
emergent systems 633
  see also complexity and emergence
Emerson, Richard M. 1368–71
  exchange theory 314, 1368–9, 1512,
    3599, 3600
  power-dependence theory 2146, 3598–9,
    3600, 3604, 3848
  relational cohesion theory 3848
emic ethnography 1372
emic/etic 1371–4, 2539
  and ethnic groups 1457
Eminem 2826, 3487
Emirbayer, M. 3609
Emmanuel, A. 1395, 1545
emotion: cultural aspects 1374–7
  and affective roles 1378
  constructionist paradigm 1378, 1380
  determinist perspective 1378
  and emotion work 1383
  fear 1650–1
  macrostructural theory of 1650
  and popular religiosity 3523
  positivist perspective 1378, 1380
  and ritual 3934
**emotion: social psychological aspects 1378,
  1378–82**

and attraction 202
  collective effervescence 3937
  and medical sociology 2935
emotion culture 1389
emotion equations 38
emotion intelligence 1383
emotion management 1375, 1382, 1383,
  2684, 3007
  culture of instrumental control 1390
  gender strategy 1379, 1383
  see also emotion work
emotion work 1382, **1382–4**, 3950
  and carework 402
  gendered expectations 1382
  use value 1382
emotional climates 1376, 1385
emotional culture 1521
emotional dialectics 4749
emotional dynamics 1390
emotional intelligence 3444
emotional interaction 1379
emotional labor 365, 1187, 3565
  exchange value 1382
  gendered expectations 1382
  use value 1382
  see also emotion work
emotional solidarity 1389
emotions
  affect control theory 38
  biological arousal 1378
  circumplex model 3847
  deviant emotions 1383
  emotion categories 1384
  and existential sociology 1521
  hormonal activity and 292
  and identity politics 2215, 2219
  institutionalization 1387
  and irrationality 1384
  premodern emotions 1385
  reason/emotion duality 1391
  reflexive process 1378
  signal function 1382
  social construction 1389, 1390, 1650
  and social movements 4446
  symbolic expression 1389
  universality 1378
  variability 1378
emotions and economy 1384–9
  and the Great Depression 2021–2
**emotions and social movements
  1389–92**
  emotion management 1383

empathic understanding 2108
empathy–altruism hypothesis 3681
emperor system 2803
empire 1392–7
  in antiquity 1392–3
  and capitalism 1394
  and civilization 1392
  maritime empires 1393
  modern European empires 1393–4
  and nationalism 1393–4
  non-national vision 1396
  premodern empire 1392–3
  territorial dimension 1392
  see also colonialism (neocolonialism);
    imperialism; Orientalism
Empirical Program of Relativism (EPOR)
  4097
empiricism 1397–8
  abstracted empiricism 2960
  contextual empiricism 1682
  and criminology 857
  feminist empiricism 1682, 1683
  and humanism 2186
  hyperempiricism 2042
  logical empiricism 3577
  materialist empiricism 871, 2836
  and objectivity 1682
  and positivism 1079
  totality empiricism 28
empiricist epistemology 1434–5
employability 105
employment
  and absenteeism 5
  alienation 119
  and compositional theory of urbanism 637
  and consumption 1032
  and disengagement theory 1928
  employment protection 1400
  employment status classifications 3241
  employment-to-residence (ER) ratio 3116
  gender bias 1844
  industrial classifications 3241
  occupational classifications 3241
  public employment 4734–6
  self-employment 1461–2
  shushin koyo 4311–14
  social organization of 429
  and spatial mismatch hypothesis 4629–32
  status classifications 3241
  and stress 4840–2
  teenagers 774
  time allocation by gender 1881

transition from school to work 1231, 1399,
    4031, 5054–7
  unpaid work 2666
  see also child labor; job satisfaction; labor
    markets
employment law 4737–8
employment status changes 1398–400
empowerment
  black economic 2467
  black feminist 305
  children 696
  and disabled athletes 1172
  and ethics 1439
  female 5273–5
  and feminist pedagogy 1707
  and Gender and Development
    (GAD) 1854
  and gender mainstreaming 1878
  and the Internet 2385, 2387
  women in sport 1879
"empty locker" of distributional equity 1562
en **1400–2**
Enan, M. A. 2461
enclave economy 1452–6, 1460, 3026–7
encoding/decoding 1403–4, 3817
encouragement mechanisms 1389
Encuentros 1687, 1949
endocrine disruption hypothesis 4083
endocrinology 291
endogamy 1404–6, 1615
  ethnic endogamy 1457
  racial endogamy 1405
endogenous development 1406–7,
    1561, 1562
energy consumption 1421, 1424
energy efficiency 1421
energy shortages 1420
energy technology assessment 691
engaged pedagogy 1708–9
Engels, Friedrich 1408–10
  and the 1848 revolutions 2810
  biography 1408–9
  and the city 500
  and colonialism 603
  Communist Manifesto 614, 955, 989, 1148,
    1242, 1318, 1394, 2808–9, 3613
  dialectical conception of nature 1150
  and employment, nature of 2289
  English working class, study of 2808
  evolutionary theory 1596
  and false consciousness 1568
  and gender role relationships 1596, 2308

and Hegelian dialectic 1148, 1408, 2837
historical materialism 350, 2840
and the Industrial Revolution 2298
and Marx, collaboration with 1408, 1409–10
and modernity 3068
and modes of production 515
and nationalism 3146
and patriarchal relations 3378
scientific socialism 245, 4550
and social evolution 1506
and socialism 1596
and working-class diets 721
engineers as bricoleurs 365, 366
England, P. 1737, 1882
Englehardt, T. 695
English Civil War 407, 3468, 3469, 3908
English disease *see* football hooliganism
English language 277, 2534
"English Only" language movement 278,
     1454, 2280
Engwall, L. 2721
Enlightenment 259, 515, 1147
anthropological thinking 148
and anti-Semitism 155
anticlerical dimension 2530
and authorship/originality 730
evolutionism 651
and human rights, emergence of 2183
and humanism 2186
individualism 2285, 2706
and magic 2697
materialism 2837
and modernization theory 3071
and nationalism 3144, 3155
progressivism 3669, 3670
rationality 897, 909, 2294, 2907, 3213, 3635
and religion 3865
and religious skepticism 2297
science–culture distinction 4070
Enloe, C. 1887
Ennis, P. 2340
Enron 1217, 1441, 3339, 3340, 3566, 3664, 3665
enterprise 1410–13
enterprise bargaining 1417
Enterprise Resource Planning (ERP) 2715,
     2729, 5005
enterprise unions 1413–17
entertainment industry 419, 609, 765
Entralgo, P. L. 3375
entrepreneurial professions 3664
entrepreneurship 1410–13, 1461, 2811
civic entrepreneurship 2189

ethnic 1455, 1460, 1462, 1464
hybridity 2189
institutional context 1412
and management education 2728
and masculinity 1891
and organizational learning 3307
political entrepreneurship 3443
in teamworking 3327
women micro-entrepreneurs 1854
see also moral entrepreneur
environment of evolutionary adaptedness
     (EEA) 293, 294, 1509
environment, sociology of the 1417–22
and cultural formations of nature 946–8
rationalized environments 2690
and semi-domestication 4179
and social accountability 4352
sport and the environment 4680–1
and technological assessment 687
environment and urbanization 1423–6
built environment 374–6
civil minimum 505–6
daily life pollution 967–8
and regional ecologies 3123
technological advances, impact of 102
and urban–rural population movements 3018
environmental concern 1283
environmental criminology 828, 1426–7,
     3958
environmental degradation 727, 1417–18,
     1431, 3342
causes 1419–20
and development projects 1948
and economic development 1297
and environmental sociology 1418
and global communication systems 2388
and global justice movements 1976
impacts 1420–1
and McDonaldization 2690
and overpopulation 1041
rural 1423
social structure of victims 4526
and tourism 762
and urbanization 1423–4, 1425
environmental feminism 1274
environmental justice ecofeminism 1274
environmental justice movement (EJM) 1273,
     1275, 1285, 1419, 1421, 1428, 1429, 1781
environmental Kuznets curve 1425
environmental movements 1428–33
animal rights movement 138–9
and consumer movements 699

environmental movements (*cont'd*)
  and development debates 1297, 1949
  and documentaries 1211
  ecofeminism 947, 1273–7
  elitism, alleged 1432
  environmental movement organizations
    (EMOs) 1428, 1432
  and environmental sociology 1422
  formation 1428–9
  and gender 1874
  grassroots movements 1429
  institutionalization 1430–1
  local residents' movements 2657–9
  maternal politics 2847
  radical groupings 1431
  transnational movements 1432
Environmental Protection Agency (EPA) 3304
environmental racism 968, 1275, 1421, 2078,
  2280, 3533
environmental refugees 3533
environmental science 728
environmental sociology 265, 1281, 4179
environmental stressors, and aggressive
  behavior 66
environmentalism 1430
  criticalism 2969
  life environmentalism 2640–1
  nature environmentalism 2640
environments, themed 704, 713
enviropreneurs 729
ephebophilia 3386
Epictetus 197
Epicurus 197, 2836
epidemics 3535
  see also HIV/AIDS
epidemiology 1433–4
  and biodemography 283, 284, 286–7
  and bisexuality 304
  clinical epidemiology 1434
  of crime 1094
  of death 973
  epidemiologic paradox 3757
  epidemiologic transition, and health care
    delivery systems 2054
  epidemiological forecasting 284
  and intervention studies 2403
  and log-linear models 2660
  and population management 338
  social epidemiology 1434, 4403–6
epidemography *see* biomedical demography
epilepsy 2246
episcopal collegiality 410

Episcopalian Church 440, 1053, 1054
episteme 1775
epistemological nihilism 1436
epistemological relativism 908
  and environmental issues 1419
epistemology 1434–6
  and bisexuality 304
  and controversy studies 785
  ecological epistemology 249
  feminist epistemology 904, 1668, 1681–4,
    3561
  foundationalist epistemology 3235
  and language usage 2536
  and naturalistic enquiry 3161, 3162
  and organizational culture 949
  postmodern epistemology 2534, 2969
  poststructural epistemology 2534
  quantitative research paradigm 2978
  representationalist epistemology 3235
  and scientific knowledge 785, 787
  social epistemology 2475, 4406–8
epistephelia 1210
Epstein, D. 4193–6
Epstein, S. 778
Equal Employment Opportunity Commission
  (EEOC) 40–1, 1674–5, 4737
equal pay 1669
  see also wages gap
Equal Rights Amendment (ERA) 250,
  1676, 3378
equality *see* equity
equality of opportunity 46, 1440
equality of outcomes 46
equality-promoting legislation 2558
equilibrium theory 1823, 3361
equity
  equity ideology 2585
  equity issues 1561, 1671
  equity theory, and helping behaviors 3680
  generational equity 1903–4
  and health care implications 2056
  see also distributive justice
equivalence theorem 2777
Erasmus, Desiderius 2186
ERASMUS exchange program 279
erectile dysfunction 4274
Eribon, D. 1778
Ericksen, E. P. 4287–90
Ericksen, J. A. 4287–90
Erickson, F. 1445
Erickson, M. L. 1066
Erie, S. P. 3446

Erikson, E. 1071–2, 2760
Erikson, K. 947, 1114, 1125, 1137, 1175, 2207, 2209
Erikson, R. 2369, 2370, 2371, 2372, 2373, 3060, 3062, 3251
Eriksson, L. 4093–100, 4846–8
Eritrea 3020, 4167
    female genital mutilation 1654
    separatism 4188
eros love 2671
erotica *see* pornography and erotica
error effects 1534
error in the social sciences 426
Esalen Institute 3189
"escalator" regions 1608
escorts 1660, 1661
Esperanto 2535
Esping-Andersen, G. 2664, 3121, 4365–6
Essenes 3048
essentialism and constructionism 1436–8
    Deleuze and 999
    and ecofeminism 1275
    and feminist epistemology 1684
    and fetishism 1746
    gender essentialism 1438, 1682, 2396
    and homosexuality 2610
    hybridity as critique of 2190
    and lesbianism 2610
    and positivism 1079
    and standpoint theory 1712, 1714
    strategic essentialism 4789–91
Esser, H. 795
Essletzbichler, J. 1297–300
establishment criminology 3197
Esterchild, E. 5259–62
Estes, C. 1929
Estonia 1451, 1487, 4168
    race and ethnic conflict 1469
    and secession 1487
ETA 3470
ethanol 116
ethic of care 1438–9
ethic of justice 1438–9
ethical glocalization 1993
ethical guidelines 1449
ethical, legal, and social impacts (ELSI) 1907
ethical relativism 3814
ethical universalism 2140, 2141
ethics
    communal ethics 1441
    covenantal ethics 1444

defining 1442
genetics 1490, 1908
and genomics 2174
and human resource management 2182
and interviewing 2410–11
legal profession 2562
management 2751
Milgram experiments 3036–7
observational research 3240
rational ethical theory 2140
reality TV 3491
sexual ethics 2160
sexuality research 4280–3
societal frames 1447
ethics, business 1439–42
    applied ethics 1440
    individualization 1441
    normative ethics 1439–40
ethics, fieldwork 1442–7
    anonymity 1443
    deception 1444
    informed consent 1443
    "insider" studies 1443
    "outsider" studies 1444
ethics, research 1447–50
    and institutional review boards 2346, 2347–9
    and rapport 3790
Ethiopia 3020
    Coptic Church 3346
    and federalism 1652
    female genital mutilation 1654
    pastoral theism 3870
Ethiopian Jews 1655
ethnic cleansing 1450–2, 1466, 3108
    Burundi and Rwanda 380–2, 661, 1183, 1451, 1909, 1910, 1912, 3673, 3749
    class enemies 1451–2
    ethnic groups 1451
    expulsion of ethnic groups 1458
    former Yugoslavia 660, 3108
    and genocide 1910
    homogenization impulse 3143
    through women's reproductive capabilities 1887
    see also Holocaust
ethnic consciousness 433
ethnic consumption 768
ethnic enclaves 1452–6, 1464
    economic enclaves 196
    and models of urban form 1280
    xenophobic reaction to 1454

ethnic groups 1457–9
  altruism 294
  and assimilation 1457, 1458
  boundary maintenance 346
  collective identity 294, 3013
  communities of attachment 1578
  and consumption 715
  cross-movement coalitions 124
  and diaspora 1151–3
  and discrimination 1183
  and education, privileging of 2117–18
  enclosure tactics 1457
  environmental activism 729
  expulsion 1458
  and higher education 621
  indigenous cultural tourism 921
  and integration 1458
  and kinship 2470
  and kinship groups, distinguished 1457
  and marginalization 2766
  middleman minorities 3008–10
  objectivist perspective 1457
  occupational stereotyping 3249
  and remittances 3081
  and research ethics 1447
  and school dropout 1230
  subjectivist perspective 1457
ethnic homogamy 675
ethnic identity 294, 745, 926, 1152, 1405,
    1458, 1459, 1469, 1471, 1476, 1477,
    2222, 3013, 3480
  pan-ethnic identity 1458
  sport, reinforcement by 2122
ethnic/informal economy 1459–63
ethnic movements 1465, 1466, 1467, 1473–4
  activation 1471
  and authority 1471
  diffusion properties 1472
  free-rider problem 1469
  and game-theory models 1470
  prisoner's dilemma model 1469–70
  violence 1468, 1469, 1470
ethnic nationalism *see* ethnonationalism;
    nationalism
ethnic pluralism 1458, 1459
ethnic and racial division of labor 1463–5
  ecological approaches 1463
  and the ethnic economy 1460
**ethnic, racial, and nationalist movements
    1465–75**
  boundary perspectives 1465
  competition theories 1469

emergence and persistence 1467, 1468
  indigenous movements 2278–80
  rational choice perspective 1469
  social construction theories 1468
  violence 1466
  see also racist movements
ethnic resettlement programs 1470
ethnic separatism 1470
ethnic wars *see* conflict (racial/ethnic)
ethnicity 661–2, 1475–8
  and assimilation 194–5
  biological thesis 3479
  and community 637
  and the criminal justice system 2207
  cultural characteristics 2058, 2701
  definitions 1475, 2701
  and discrimination 1182
  and diversity 1197, 1198
  and domestic violence 1219
  and educational attainment 1344
  and elder care 2381
  and ethnic enclaves 1455
  and ethnic relations 1476
  and feminist standpoint theory 1711
  and friendships 795
  and human resource management 2180
  and hypersegregation 2196–9
  and illness and health-related behavior
    2058–9, 2080
  and interests 1477–8
  and interpersonal relationships 2392
  and intimate union formation and dissolution
    2415
  and kindergarten 2462, 2463
  and literacy differentials 2654, 2656
  and lone parenthood 2666
  and *minzoku* 3057–8
  and nationalism 1466, 1839, 2755,
    3151, 3155
  and nest-leaving 2572
  and occupational prestige 1342
  and partner choice 674, 675
  pluralist conceptions 1458
  polyethnicity 3479–80
  and poverty 1719
  and privilege 3649, 3650
  social construction 3479
  and sport 4681–4
  status exchange hypothesis 2394
  and stratification 4815–19
ethnie 2000, 3058, 3059
ethnoburbs 1454

ethnocentrism 260, 1251, **1478–9**, 2798, 3749, 3750, 3751
  and alliances 122
  and beliefs 260
  bias 2271
  and cultural diversity 900
  and ecofeminism 1273
  and Eurocentrism 1491–4
  and feminist anthropology 1690
  interactionist perspectivism 1478–9
  and lesbian and gay studies 1985
  and majorities 2702
  and nationalism 3144
  and racial/ethnic conflict 661
ethnocide 341
ethnocracy 1487
ethnogenesis 661, 2281
ethnographic documentaries 1210–11
ethnography 1479–83
  anthropological ethnography 1482
  arts-based methods 2971
  audience ethnography 210–11
  autoethnography 231, 1480, 2178, 3141
  and biography 288, 290
  Boas and 321
  case study methods 1129–32, 2976
  and childhood 460
  and criminology 861, 863
  and cultural criminology 894, 895
  and cultural reproduction 911
  cultural research 298
  and deviance 1129–30
  emic ethnography 1372
  ethnographic methods 1479
  ethographies of science 4074–5
  and evaluation 1500
  and facework 1554
  and fan communities 1640
  features 1480
  feminist 1702, 1703
  field research 1129
  Goffman and 1999
  and human–animal interaction 2178
  hypermedia ethnography 3725
  indigenous ethnography 1482
  institutional ethnography 274, 1503
  and institutional review boards 2349
  and investigative poetics 2422
  key informants 2457–8
  laboratory ethnography 2526
  Liebow and 2625–6
  and the life course 2631

  longitudinal ethnographies 1481
  Marxist 1482, 2816
  and mental illness 1998
  and microsociology 3005
  and network research 2742
  and "othering" 1482
  participant observation 3238, 4513–14
  performance ethnography 3391–6
  phenomenological perspective 3404
  photography, use of 2866
  postcolonial ethnography 2983
  and rapport 3790
  reflexive ethnography 3833
  research ethics 1449–50
  and symbolic interaction 2362
  and total institutions 1482, 3334
  and unstructured interviewing 2408
  urban ethnography 3943, 5106
  video ethnography 1523
  visual ethnography 1483, 2986, 2987
ethnolinguistics 2535, 2536
ethnology 1479, 1940
  and gift giving 1940
ethnomethodological indifference 1485
ethnomethodology 1483–6, 4982
  and agency 61
  and comparative sociology 2135
  and controversy studies 785
  and conversation 790
  and conversation analysis 791, 2032–3
  and criminology 861
  and cultural reproduction 911
  and deviance 1077, 1137
  and discourse analysis 1214
  and doing gender 1218
  and dramaturgy 1228
  and existential sociology 1519
  and facework 1553
  and gender inequality 1216
  and interaction 2363
  and intersubjectivity 2401
  and the lifeworld 2652, 2653
  and linguistics 2535
  phenomenological perspective 3403
  and the social definition paradigm 2964
  and social psychology 4510
  and sociology of science 785
  and structuration theory 4860
  and telephone talk 4961–2
ethnomusicology 3129
ethnonationalism 1486–8, 3108, 3157
ethnoscapes 1990

ethnosymbolism, and nationalism 3149, 3151, 3157
ethology 291, 2362
etiquette 530, 1997
  race and ethnic etiquette 3743–5
Etzioni, A. 624–6, 3065, 3310, 3311, 3335
eugenics 1488–91, 2015, 4115
  class issues 1489, 1490
  cloning and 557, 558
  and disability 1169
  Ellis and 1365, 1366
  eugenic management of the body 325
  and euthanasia 1490
  and genomics 2173
  liberal eugenics 1490
  and millenarianism 3047
  new eugenics 1490, 11491
  positive eugenics 1489
  and "racial hygiene" 1908
  racist/ethnic bias 1490
  reform eugenics 1489
  and selective reproduction 2938
  voluntary eugenics 1490
euro 3080
Eurocentrism 399, **1491–4**, 3215, 3670
  and capitalism 1491
  and cultural tourism 920
  and Orientalism 3343
  and religion 1982
  subject–object dichotomy 1492
European Convention on Human Rights 2184
European Court of Human Rights 2184
European Family and Fertility Survey 810
European Fertility Project 1035, 1041, 1046
European Media Technology and Everyday Life Network (EMTEL) 2903
European monetary system 1473
European public sphere 3722
European Scientific Revolution 4073
European Union
  acculturation 16
  bilingual education promotion 279
  and capitalism 393
  cities 496
  economic growth 390
  and gender mainstreaming 1869
  human rights protocols 499
  information society policies 2330
  integration 1473
  migration management 3020
  and the nation-state 1472
  public sphere concept 2909

regulatory commissions 393
regulatory measures 2915
suprastate political functions 1951
euthanasia 974, 1178, **1495–8**
  active euthanasia 1495, 1497
  and agism 57
  altruistic euthanasia 1496
  decision-making variations 1495
  decriminalization 1497
  Ellis and 1365
  and eugenics 1490
  infants 1490, 1495
  informal euthanasia 1495
  involuntary euthanasia 1495
  negative euthanasia 1495
  passive euthanasia 1495, 1497
  positive euthanasia 1495
  quality-of-life view 1497
  religious condemnation of 1497
  sanctity-of-life view 1497
  voluntary euthanasia 1495, 1496
evaluation 1498–502
  evaluation design 1500
  formative evaluation 1499
  key informants 2458
  metaevaluation 1501
  methodology 1499
  models for evaluation 1499–500
  summative evaluation 1499
  techniques and procedures 1500–1
Evangelicalism 2302, 3409, 3518, 3693
  and patriarchal authority 2302
Evans, D. T. 3385–7, 4205–9
Evans, G. 551–4
Evans, M. D. R. 1194
Evans-Pritchard, E. E. 3519, 3629, 3633, 3634, 3772, 3974, 3983
event history analysis 1017–21, 3062
event history calendars 1018
everyday life 1502–3
  aestheticization of 756
  commodification of 610, 703–6, 2646, 4685
  and existential sociology 1519
  intersubjectivity in 2401
  and macro/microsocial porcesses 2579
  and modernity 703, 2581
  and networks 2904–5
  politicization of 3209
  and postmodernism 3554
  presentation of self 1228
  seikatsu/seikatsusha 4150–3
everyday world sociology 1711

evidence-base medicine (EBM) 2931
evolution 1503–12
  agriculture 2141
  anthropological evolutionism 2697
  Darwinian theory 292, 1504, 1507, 1510,
    1595, 1896
  decline of evolutionary theory 1597
  ethnocentric/racist theories 1596, 1597, 3751
  and helping theories 3680
  matriarchal stage 1596, 2858
  mental evolution 2140, 2141
  morality evolution 2140
  natural selection theory 2249–50, 3680, 3751
  neo-Darwinian evolutionary theory 292
  organic evolutionary theory 293
  and organization theory 3284, 3329
  pastoralism 2141
  patriarchal evolutionary theory 1596
  progressive evolution 1506
  sexual selection 4248–9, 4284
  sociocultural evolution 293
  stage theories of evolution 293
  unilinear evolution 1595, 1596
  see also social change; social Darwinism
evolutionary biology 291, 292, 1487, 1757, 2174
  and the animal rights movement 140
  and attraction 204
  and bisexuality 302
  and sexual selection 294
  and Social Darwinism 1488
evolutionary ecology 4087
evolutionary economics 292, 1299
evolutionary game theory 293
evolutionary neuroandrogenic (ENA) theory 824
evolutionary psychology 292, 635, 1508–9
  and fathering 1603
evolutionary sociology 291, 292
evolutionary theory
  and helping theories 3680
  and organization theory 3284, 3329
  and racism 3751
evolutionary view of religious innovation and
  denomination 1051
evolutionism
  academic discrediting of 1068
  and Freudian psychoanalytic theory 2698
Ewen, E. 2615, 2826
Ewen, S. 2826
Ewick, P. 2562
ex post facto laws 2556
excellence, culture of 2750, 2954
exceptionalism 2755

genetic exceptionalism 2940
exchange network theory 640, 641, **1512–15**,
  3183, 4485, 4980
  capitalist exchange 757, 2810
  and dyadic exchange formulation 1368–9
  and elementary theory 1357
  Emerson and 314, 1368–9, 1512,
    3599, 3600
  equal power networks 3605
  and experimantal methods 1539
  gift exchange 1938–41
  Homans and 314, 1368, 1512, 2032, 2361
  and identity 3183
  and interaction 2361
  and markets 2783, 2785, 2786
  multilevel theory 3003, 3004
  and outsourcing arrangements 3352, 3354
  and power-dependence theory 3599–600
  and rational choice sociology 3798
  and the social behavior paradigm 2964
  symbolic exchanges 1940
  weak power networks 3605
  and weak tie networks 2743, 3605, 3754
exchange relationships 640, 641
  capitalist exchange 757, 2810
  and elementary theory 1357
  gift exchange 1938–41
  and markets 2783, 2785, 2786
  and outsourcing arrangements 3352, 3354
  symbolic exchanges 1940
Exchange Theory of Marital Quality 2773
exchange transactions 396
exchange-value 1515–16, 2691
  emotional labor 1382
  land exchange value 2034
  sex 3684
exclusion
  and affirmative action 39
  and class 533
  and cultural critique 897
  and deviance 2208
  and heterosexuality 2112
  and human rights 2182
  and the information society 2330, 2334
  and poverty 3590
  and urban crime 5108
  see also marginality; marginalization,
    outsiders
exclusivity, ethnic 1475
excremental sex 3569
excuses 10, 11, 13
exeptionalism 1570

exercise and fitness 1516–18
  body governmentality 325
  and disease prevalence 1184
  exercise-related injuries 2093
  and health behavior 2051, 2061
  and health lifestyles 2061
  older people 104
exhibitionism 1518–19
  by women 1518
  Internet exhibitionism 1519
existential sociology 1519–24, 3819
  emotions and
  and Fromm 1805
  postmodernism and
existential strategies 1523
existentialism 1434
  and agency 61
  and atheism 197
  Barthes and 242
  de Beauvoir and 252, 253
  existential self 1512–22
  Fromm and 1805
  Lukács and 2680
exogamy 1404, 1615, 3228
  racial exogamy 1405
  and totemism 5020
exopoles 3113
expectation states theory 1524–8
  and identity 2219
  and impression formation 2270, 2271–2
  mathematical models 2856
  and social influence theory 4428
  status characteristics theory 1525
  see also self-fulfilling expectations
expectations and aspirations 1528–31
  extracurricular activities and
  professional school students 4047
  separatist 4188
  see also self-fulfilling prophecy
expected value model 1512, 1514
experience economy 353, 355
experiential consumption 716–18
experiential learning strategies 1707
experiential sampling method 1033
  time use 1033
experiential systems 1005
experiment 1531–3, 1537
  control conditions 1538
  experimental data 1538
  exploratory experiments 1538
  field experiments 1539–40
  and group processs 2028

independent variables 1533
  initial conditions 1538
  laboratory experiments 1540–1
  natural experiments 1539
  objectives 1538
  quasi-experiments 1534, 4514
  survey experiments 1540
  theory-driven experiments 1538
  underuse 1537
experimental design 1533–7, 1538
  analytical induction 134–5
  classical experimental design (CED) 2967
experimental methods 1537–41, 4514
  experimental situations 1539–41
  Milgram experiments 3034–6
  random sample 3782–3
  randomized controlled trials 2403, 2404, 2405
  units of analysis 1539
expert knowledge 1542
expert patient concept 2246
expert systems 2922
expertise
  crisis of 3930, 3931
  democratization 3931
  institutionalization of 2583
expertise, "scientification," and the
  authority of science 1541–3, 3930–1
exploitation 677, 1543–6
exploratory factor analysis 643, 1558
explusion from school 4021
export processing zones (EPZs) 1854,
  2382, 5067
exposure learning 257
expressive group dimension 1581
expulsion from school 4021
extended families, and family sociology
  1617, 1619
extended households 1597, 1617, 1619
externalization 1088
extra-marital and premarital sex
  associated guilt 2487
  and family sociology 1616
  high school sports 2120–3
  in Islamic culture 2429
  Kinsey Institute research 2468
  tolerance of 1735, 2414, 2792, 2794
  see also nonmarital fertility
extracurricular activities 1546–9
  and friendships 1801
  and the hidden curriculum 2118
extranets 2387
extrasensory perception 1140

extraversion 838
extreme sports 4652, 4701
exurbia 1549–51
Eyerman, R. 1430, 3134–6
Eysenck, H. 8387

F Scale 1806
Fabianism 1542
  and laborism 2526
facework 1553–4
  expert systems, and facework commitments
    2922
  and identity politics 2214
  and impression formation 2269
fact, theory, and hypothesis: including the
  history of the scientific fact 1554–7
  and falsification 1570–2
fact/value distinction 344
factor analysis 1557–9
  analysis of variance and covariance 1534, 1535
  and multivariate analysis 3121
factor rotation method 1558
  oblique rotation 1558–9
  orthogonal rotation 1558, 1559
factor scores 1557
factory system 363, 2294
  child labor 455
  and family roles 1594
  new factory regimes 428–9
facts 1554
  conceptual character 1555
  see also fact, theory, and hypothesis:
    including the history of the scientific fact
Faderman, L. 2602, 2604
failure-time analysis 1017
Fairchild, G. 2730
Fairchild, Henry P. 131
Fairness and Accuracy in Reporting (FAIR)
  3674
Fairtlough, G. 2717
faith
  faith/belief dichotomy 258
  religious faith 641
  value-rational 229
  see also belief
faith healers 2079, 2080
Fajnzylber, Fernando 1559–64
Faletto, Enzo 1564–8, 3538
Falk, P. 716–18
Falk, W. W. 3963–7
Falklands War 2878
fallibilism 3609

Fallows, J. 3471
false consciousness 1568–70, 2231, 2629,
  2758
  and class consciousness 540
  and ideology 1568
  Marx and 1221, 1568
  and nationalism 3156
  psychological dimension 1569
falsification 1570–2
  and demarcation 1571
  naïve falsification 1571
  Popperian 1570–1, 2286, 2968, 3577, 3814,
    4079, 4084
Falun Gong 672, 886, 3203
Falwell, J. 4279
familialism 2849
familiarity
  and attraction 202
  and proximity 203
families, consumer roles 725
families and childhood disabilities 1572–4
  advocacy work 1572, 1573
  carework 1572, 1573
familism 1576, 3751
The Family (new religious movement) 3202,
  4144, 4277
family
  biblical family form 1595
  breakdown 1617
  companionate family 1598
  definitions 1574–5, 1584–5, 1589, 1590–1
  demise of "traditional" family 1577, 1735
  desired family size 1740
  drag community 1224–5
  and dyads/tryads 1264
  elder support 84, 86
  emotional bond 845
  and entrepreneurship 1462
  extended-family system 1598
  family groups 1585
  family size 1609, 1732, 1738, 2633
  gay and lesbian families 1618
  gender bias within 1844
  as ghetto 1582
  horizontal families 2254
  and household, distinguished 1618–19
  institutional family 1598
  and kin relationships 1575
  multiple transitions 1622
  network characteristics 3182
  power and authority distribution 1618
  pre-industrial family 1594

family (*cont'd*)
  reduced size of 1586
  same-sex families 2161
  and social capital 1326, 1338
  social support provision 90, 91, 92
  and socialization 4566–7, 4570
  subfamilies 1584–5
  transitions 1624
  see also divorce; households; immigrant
    families; kinship; life course and family;
    marriage; parenting
family and community 1574–80
  Confucianism and 671
  industrialization, threat of 1577–9
  and kinship relations 1576, 1579
  and spatial location 1575–6
family conflict 1580–3
  conflict management 1583
  and elder abuse 1349
  and family structure 1593
  gay and lesbian couples 1593
  impact on children 1623
  models of 1581–2
family demography 1583–9
  beanpole structure 1588
  child custody and child support 451–4
  composition 1584, 1586
  decomposition 1584
  demographic transition theory 1035
  differential treatment of children by sex
    1155–9
  and divorce 1206–9
  and early childhood 1270
  family generations 1904–5
  family reconstitution 1045–6
  family size 1042
  intergenerational family 1588
  and modernization 1042
  older adults, support for 70
  pyramid structure 1588
  and role discrimination 1183
  social demography of the family 1587
  see also infant, child, and maternal health and
    mortality
family diversity 1589–94
  cohabitation and 565–9
  family process 1592–3
  and family structure 1592
  and gender 1198, 1591–2
  lesbian and gay families 2606–9
  lesbian partners 1590
  and race/ethnicity 1591

  and sexual orientation 1592
  and socioeconomic status 1591
  see also lesbian and gay families
family ecology 1633
family economy 1411
family firms 1880
family generations 1904–5
family, history of 1594–601
  and the Industrial Revolution 2296
family leave 1883–4
  paternity leave 1649
  women's use of 1884
family limitation 1035
Family and Medical Leave Act (FMLA)
family, men's involvement in 1601–5
  household labor 1882
  see also divisions of household labor;
    fatherhood
family migration 1605–8
  family reunification migrants 3021
  gendered dimensions 1607
  immigrant families 2252–4
  noneconomic outcomes 1606
  socioeconomic effects 1606, 1607
family planning 971–2, 1158
  and child sex preferences 1158
  Davis and 971–2
  and eugenics 1490
  and family sociology 1617
  government coercion 1738
  government programs 3526
  information and edcuation 1609
  men and 1610
  voluntary programs 1738
  see also contraception
**family planning, abortion, and
    reproductive health 4, 1609–12**
  and stratified reproduction 4828
  see also abortion; infant, child, and maternal
    health and mortality
family poverty 1612–14
  lone-parent families 2664, 2665–6
  and money management 3081
  see also public housing
family processes 1592–3, 1632
family, sociology of 1597, 1614–18
  alcoholic members 117–18
  Bernard and 271
  biblical family form 1595
  breakdown 1617
  companionate family 1598
  consumer roles 725

definitions 1574–5, 1584–5, 1589, 1590–1
demise of "traditional" family 1577, 1735
drag community 1224–5
and dyads/tryads 1264
elder support 84, 86
elder support for 70, 84, 86
emotional bond 845
and entrepreneurship 1462
evolutionary perspective 1615
extended-family system 1598, 1617, 1619
family groups 1585
family size 1609, 1732, 1738, 1740, 2633
gender bias within 1844
as ghetto 1582
horizontal families 2254
and household, distinguished 1618–19
institutional family 1598
intergenerational relationships and exchanges
    2380–1
and kin relationships 1575
multiple transitions 1622, 1624
network characteristics 3182
power and authority distribution 1618
pre-industrial family 1594
reduced size of 1586
and social capital 1326, 1338, 4354
social support provision 90, 91, 92
subfamilies 1584–5
Taylorization of family life 458
work–family strategies 458
see also divorce; households; immigrant
    families; kinship; lesbian and gay families;
    life course and family; marriage; parenting
family structure 1592, **1618–21**, 1626, 3223
alcoholic members 117–18
child custody and child support 451–4
and child well-being 1621
and childcare 1619
children, priority given to 1619
conjugal family 1620
decomposition of traditional structure 499
egalitarian structure 2818
ethnic variation 1620
extended families 1597, 1617, 1619
and gender 1620
and generational change 1900–5
grandparenthood 2017–20
headship patterns 1626
and individualization 1620
and industrialization 1922
inter vivos family transfers 1905
and kin relationships 1619

marital histories 1626
patriarchal structure 2818, 3378
post-divorce 467, 468
see also couples living apart together;
    households; lesbian and gay families
family structure and child outcomes
    1621–6
and child well-being 1621
cohabitation and 567, 568
and differential treatment of children by sex
    1155–9
and family diversity 1592
immigrant children 1270–1
and lone-parent families 2667
and monetary support 2571
and paternal involvement 1603
and poverty 1591
and residential support 2571
family structure and poverty 1591, **1626–9**
child poverty 450, 1591, 1614, 1622,
    1624, 3587
lone-parent families 1591, 1612, 1613, 1626,
    1627, 1719, 1721, 1736, 2254, 2664, 2665
family systems models of therapy 1635
family theory 1630–4
deinstitutionalization of family life 1633
exchange theory 1630–1
and family ecology 1633
feminist theory 1632–3
Freudian 1786
and individualization theory 1633–4
and life course development 1631
and symbolic interactionism 1631
and systems theory 1632
family therapy 248, **1634–6**
boundaries and organization 1635
communication patterns 1635
function/purpose of symptoms 1635
multidirectional/circular causation 1635
postmodernist models 1636
family violence *see* domestic violence
family wage model 1271, 1272, 1721
famine 3533
Fan, Xitao 1897–9, 2974–6, 4848–51
fandom 1637–40
fanfic 1638
Fanning, S. 3133
Fanon, Frantz 1636–7
and colonialism and resistance 275, 603,
    1149, 1396, 2838, 2984, 3370
materialist analysis 2838
and paternalism 3370

fans and fan culture 1637–41, 4674
  authenticity issues 760
  and celebrity culture 416, 420
  and censorship 421
  and consumption 760
  Deadhead community 3504, 3505, 3506
  fan social capital 1639
  fan/spectator dichotomy 760
  and nationalism 3159
  sports fandom 1639, 4674–5
  Star Trek 3517
  "traditional"/"new" fans 760
  transnational fan cultures 1640
  and violence 1132, 5202–5
Fantasia, R. 2518–21
fantasy city 1641–4
fanzines 1638, 3920
Faraday, A. 2611
Fararo, T. J. 314, 315, 1318–23, 2144–6,
    2853–7, 3577–8, 3802–5
Faris, E. 271, 443
Farkas, G. 2653–6
Farley, J. E. 2993–6
Farnsworth, J. 2902–6
Farrakhan, Louis 1665
Farrar, M. 267–70, 1774–8
Farrell, M. P. 2238
fascism 660, 897, 959, **1644–7**, 2298, 3147
  and Cesarism 413
  class perspective 1646
  F Scale 220–1
  Frankfurt School and 865, 875
  from below/from above 2804
  historical fascism 1644–5
  and homophobia 2156
  and ideology 2231
  Italian 325, 1644, 1753
  Italian fascism 325, 1644, 1646, 2014, 2015,
    2102, 2747, 2804, 3361, 3453, 3462
  Japanese fascism 2803, 2805
  of the mind 999
  Nazi fascism 152, 1489, 1569
  neo-fascism 3780
  and peronism 1925
  propaganda 875, 1753
  propagandistic cinema 1753
  protofascism 3217
  and racial/ethnic conflict 660
  rise of 874
fashion
  dynamism 774
  ephemerality 774

gendering 719
  leisure class fashion 2595
  and lesbian feminism 2603
  masculine renunciation of 718
  mass-produced clothing 726
  rapid innovation 740
  sport/leisure-wear industry 1986
  teenagers and 774, 775
  trickle down theory 4932
  see also management fashion
fashion and consumption 741
  commodity depreciation 702
  dynamism 774
  ephemerality 774, 1959
  gendering 719
  identification and differentiation 718, 720
  leisure class fashion 2595
  and lesbian feminism 2603
  masculine renunciation of 718
  and masculinity/femininity 736
  mass-produced clothing 726
  rapid innovation 740
  Simmel and 683
  sport/leisure-wear industry 1986, 3441
  teenagers 774, 775
  see also clothing styles
fashion–beauty complex 1850
  see also beauty industries
fashionability 683
fast food 704, 723, 752
  see also McDonaldization
fatalism 2016, 3929
fatalist culture 3929
fatherhood 1647–50
  better-educated fathers 1603
  biological 1649
  and child custody 452
  childcare 457, 1602, 1649, 1881, 2301, 2667
  cultural variation 1603
  deadbeat dads/feckless fathers 1649, 3224
  and divorce 2381
  father absence 1601, 1623, 1649, 3223, 3224
  father–child relationship 1603, 1648, 1883,
    2381, 2487
  low-income fathers 1604
  male role models 1649
  and masculinities 1665
  "new" fatherhood 1648–9
  non-custodial fathers 1620
  non-residential fathers 1602, 1604, 1624
  qualitative approaches 1648
  stepfathering 4768–70

time engaged with children 1602, 1881
unmarried fathers 1601, 1736–7
verification 1605, 1649
and wages increase 1882
fathering 1648
fatherless families 1649
fatness
  as disability 1699
  fat bias 1679
  and stigma 1699
  see also obesity
Faunce, W. 974
Fausto-Sterling, A. 1681, 1846
faux queens 1223
Fayol, H. 428, 2746
Fazio, E. 3954–6
FBI Crime Index 820, 821, 1093, 1128, 2277–8
fear 1650–1
  concrete fear 2342
  of crime 2339–43, 3716
  formless fear 2342
  and homophobia 2152
  of litigation 2929
  of rape 211, 2113, 2341
Fearfull, A. 2514–18
Fearon, J. 1468, 1469
feast days, religious 3522, 3523
Featherman, D. L. 2369
Featherstone, M. 709, 710, 1930, 2650, 3552
Feaver, P. 3043
Febvre, Lucien 362
  and Annales School 142, 143, 144, 2047
  and civilization 529
federal court system 812–15
federalism 1651–3
  ancient Greece 3885
  esential institutions 1653
  essential institutions 1653
  Nigerian experiments 240
Federation of Cuban Women 1687
Fedigan, L. 3627
feedback 1380, 2616–17
  from teachers 2655
  morphostatic processes 4916–17
Feenberg, A. 876
Feeney, G. 1731
Fei Xiaotong 671
Feifel, H. 974
Fein, C. 2714
Fein, H. 2143
Feld, S. L. 796
Feldman, S. P. 3335–40

fellatio *see* oral sex
Fellman, G. 5291–5
felonies 2554, 2555, 2556
felony 813, 814, 819
Felson, M. 684, 1427, 3958–9, 3960
female body
  hysterization of 332
  "inferiority" 331
  male gaze 334
  medicalization 331
  naturalistic conceptions 332
  patriarchal regulation 336, 905
  site of abjection 333
female bonding 903
female circumcision *see* female genital
  mutilation
female criminality 1695
female genital mutilation 1083, 1609,
  1653–7, 2302–3, 2309, 2399, 2429
  health consequences 1655
  medicalization 1656
  and national laws 1099
  non-Muslim practice of 1655
female masculinity 1657–8, 1664
female sex work as deviance 1659–62
female sexuality 254, 333, 904, 1678,
  2611, 2613
  medicalization 5271–2
  patriarchal control of 1656, 2613
female subordination 251, 252, 331, 2302, 2841
  see also patriarchy
feminine identity 1850
femininities/masculinities 1662–6
  social construction 1665
  and subordination of racial/ethnic minorities
    1663
  see also femininity; gender; masculinity
femininity
  and advertising 1849
  Beauvoir and 254
  changing understandings of 2793
  and classroom dynamcis 1860
  deconstruction 1223
  default position 1681
  denigration of 735
  and the domestic sphere 1871
  emphasized femininity 1668
  fetishization 4258
  hegemonic femininity 1663, 1665, 1755, 1851
  idealized femininity 1850, 1851, 1877
  normative 1665
  and the Olympics 3264

femininity (*cont'd*)
 performing 1223
 postmodernist/poststructuralist perspective
  1891
 psychoanalytic feminist perspective 3697,
  3698
 qualities 1871, 1876
 reclaiming and redefining 1677
 social construction 254, 905, 1591, 1663
feminism 1666–71, 4982
 and advertising 1849
 alternative discourses 1666
 and bisexuality 304
 black feminism 305–10
 black–white alliances 308
 and childcare 457
 and constructionism 1087
 and consumption and the body 711
 and content analysis 778
 cultural feminism 902–6
 and cultural studies 301, 736
 difference feminism 251, 1155
 and discrimination 1183
 and division of household labor 1202–3
 and documentaries 1211
 and earner–carer model 1272
 ecofeminism 947, 1273–7
 environmental feminism 1274
 and ethnography 1482
 and family theory 1632–3
 feminist epistemology 1668
 feminist sociology 1667, 1668, 1670–1
 feminist spirituality 752
 and film 1755
 and food and cultural consumption 722
 and gender inequalities 2308, 2310
 and girls' consumption 724
 goals 1686
 grassroots feminism 1688
 hegemonic feminism 1679
 history of 1685–6
 and homophobia 2602
 individualism 726, 1207
 and individualism 1207
 international and transnational 678
 and the Internet 2387
 and Islamic sexual culture 2429
 liberal feminism 1666
 Marxist feminism 1711, 2621
 materialist feminism 1666
 and maternalism 2847, 2848
 methodology 1669

 middle-class 308
 and motherhood 939
 multiracial feminism 1679
 national feminisms 4996
 naturalist feminists 332
 and organizational communication 3295
 and peacemaking 3385
 as political movement 1669
 and polyamory 3477
 and postcolonialism 2982, 4996–8
 postmodern feminism 937, 1666, 3558–62
 and poststructuralism 937
 psychoanalytic feminism 1666
 radical feminism 1666
 and reception theory 210
 revolutionary feminism 1685
 self-identification with 1868
 sex work feminists 3683
 and sexual politics 4245
 and sexuality research 2468
 and the sexualization of organizations 3319
 socialist feminism 1711
 and sport 4659
 standpoint feminism 274, 1669, 4067–8
 and the tourist gaze 763
 and welfare reform 4538–9
 womanist feminism 1666
 see also black feminist thought; liberal
  feminism; radical feminism; transnational
  and global feminisms
feminism, first, second, and third waves
  332, 1666, **1672–81**
 backlash against 937, 940
 black feminism 309
 bra burning myth 3774
 and cultural feminism 902
 ecofeminism 1273–6
 and fashion 719, 720
 first wave 1666, 1669, 1672–4, 2308, 2618,
  3117, 5281
 and gendered social arrangements 937
 generational discord 1678
 and Latin America 1685
 post-feminist era 1676
 racial-ethnic inclusion issue 1678
 second wave 1666, 1667, 1673, 1674–6, 1693,
  1694, 1695, 1845, 1847, 2112, 2308, 2793,
  2818, 3117, 3118, 3319, 3378, 3653, 3921,
  5281–2
 submerged networks 1679
 third wave 1666, 1667, 1676–8, 3117,
  3920, 5282

women's liberation branch 1675
women's rights branch 1675
see also black feminist thought
**feminism and science, feminist
epistemology 1681–5,** 4067
  and ecofeminism 1274
  operationalization of feminist epistemology
    1682, 1683
feminist activism in Latin America 1685–9
feminist anthropology 1689–93
  and Engels 1410
  ethnocentric bias 1690
  neo-Marxist perspective 1690
feminist case studies 2977
feminist click 678
feminist criminology 841, 858, **1693–6**
  and female gangs 1826–7
  female offending 1694, 2818–19, 4191–3
  and patriarchy 1106, 1121
  and peacemaking 3385
feminist disability studies 1696–701
  and disability sport 1173
  and gendered bodies 1847
feminist environmentalism 1274
feminist epistemology 1435
  and feminist criminology 1695
  and science 4072
feminist evolutionary theory 1504
feminist gerontology 1929
feminist media studies 3817
feminist methodology 1701–6
  and everyday life 1502, 1503
  and feminist criminology 1695
  reflexivity 1702–3
feminist pedagogy 1706–10
  basic principles 1707
  engaged pedagogy 1708–9
  liberatory pedagogy 1707–8, 1709
  multicultural pedagogy 1707
  positional pedagogy 1709, 1798
  psychologically oriented pedagogy 1707
feminist pragmatism 24
feminist sociobiology 1511
feminist standpoint theory 274, 1669, **1710–15**
  black feminist 306, 1683, 2859
  black feminist theory 306, 1683, 1712, 2859
  Chicana theory 1712
  and cultural feminism 904
  and ethics in fieldwork 1444
  feminist 1683
  and feminist pedagogy 1708
  postmodern feminist 3561

relational perspective 1712–13
  and science 4067–8
  as site of inquiry 1713
feminization of labor migration 1715–17,
  2252, 2254, 2383, 3027
feminization of poverty 1613, **1718–25,** 2308
  cross-national picture 1722–5
  and culture of poverty 952, 1613
  and social construction of femininities 1663
feminization of society 1877
feminization of welfare 4539
femme queens 1224
Fenstermake, S. 1216–19
Ferber, A. 2398
Ferguson, A. A. 1861
Ferguson, Adam 244, 512
  and civil society 512, 4600–1
Ferguson, C. 282
Ferguson, K. 1892
Ferguson, R. B. 2282
Fermin, B. J. 2011–14
Ferrari, Lolo 326
Ferraro, K. F. 2341
Ferrell, J. 892–6
Ferri, E. 2663
fertility
  age-specific fertility rates 1026
  average fertility in developed world 1739
  baby boom 74
  and biodemography 284
  and birth rates 1014
  cohort fertility measure 1729
  cost-benefit framework of fertility decisions
    1042
  data collection 1013, 1014
  decline 1611
  developing countries 1043
  fertility-related medical decisions 3535
  General Fertility Rate (GFR) 1015–16
  intrinsic rate of growth 1745
  male 1604
  maximal fertility 1729
  and physical attractiveness 204
  replacement-level fertility 1729, 1730, 1744,
    2314, 4123
  teenage mothers 1019, 1020
  time-series analysis 1026
  total fertility rate (TFR) 1039, 1729–30,
    1731, 1732
  World Fertility Survey (WFS) 1013
  see also nonmarital fertility
fertility: adolescent 1725–9

fertility control 1035, 1609, 2308, 2793
fertility: low 1729–33
 and aging, demography of 68
 causes 1732–3
 decomposition approaches 1730–1
 demographic transition theory 1035
 and economic growth 1042, 3525, 3526, 3527
 and family demography 1587
 global spread of 1730
 and grandparenthood 2018, 2020
 immigrant families 2254
 in industrialized economies 1588
 and infertility 2322
 and mortality levels 1041
 proximate determinants 1730, 1731–2
fertility: nonmarital 1734–7
 see also nonmarital childbearing
fertility and public policy 971, **1737–41**
 fertility reduction policies 1738–9
 one-child policy 1159
 pronatalism 1740
 state family planning programs 3526
fertility tempo 1741
fertility: transitions and measures 1033,
  1034–5, 1036, 1038, 1039, 1729, 1730,
  1733, 1739, **1741–5**
 age-based methods and models 1742–3
 age-specific fertility rates (ASFR) 1026,
  1039, 1587, 1742
 AIDS, impact of 2137–8
 average fertility in developed world 1739
 baby boom 74
 biodemographical models 284, 1743
 birth interval analysis 1744
 and birth rates 1014
 cohort fertility measure 1729, 1741
 cost-benefit framework of fertility decisions
  1042
 crude birth rate (CBR) 1742
 data collection 1013, 1014
 decomposition and standardization analysis
  1014–17
 demographic quantum 1741
 demographic transition theory 93–4, 1037
 developing countries 1043
 direct measures of fertility 1741–2
 dispersion 1741
 event history analysis 1017–21
 fertility decline 1026, 1042, 1043, 1044, 1611
 fertility tempo 1741
 fertility-related medical decisions 3535
 first demographic transition 4125

general fertility rate (GFR) 1015–16, 1742
 high, and child mortality 2314
 high, and child sex preferences 1156
 high fertility 1729, 1738
 and historical demography 1046–7
 HIV effects 2138
 intermediate fertility variables 1743
 intrinsic rate of growth 1745
 life table analysis 1039
 male fertility 1604
 maximal fertility 1729
 mean age of childbearing 1742
 and mortality decline 1035
 and mortality levels 1041
 non-biodemographical mdoels 1743
 parity-based measures 1743–4
 period fertility rates 1741
 proximant determinants of fertility 1743
 replacement-level fertility 1729, 1730, 1744,
  2314, 4123
 reproductivity 1744–5
 second demographic transition 4125–6
 teenage mothers 1019, 1020
 time-series analysis 1026
 total fertility rate (TFR) 1039, 1729–30,
  1731, 1732, 1742
 World Fertility Survey (WFS) 1013
 see also nonmarital fertility
Festinger, L. 561
festival marketplaces 767, 768, 1643
fetal loss, HIV effects 2138
fetishism 1745–7, 2158, 2493
 and animism 141
 the body and 711
 commodity fetishism 608–9, 611
 Comte and 651–2
 dependency fetishism 5236
 and religion 3629, 3631
 and totemism 5020
 see also commodities, commodity fetishism,
  and commodification
feudalism 493, 514, 530, 537, 550, 613, 2311,
  2812–13, 3468
Feuer, L. 577
Feuerbach, Ludwig 1199, **1747–9**, 2837
 and alienation 1748
 Christian dogma critique 1747–8
 Hegelian critique 1408, 1747
 and Marx 1747, 1748
 materialism 1408, 1748, 2837
 and reification 1748
 transformative method 1748

Few, A. L. 305–10, 3764–5, 5257–9
Feyerabend, P. 4086
Fichte, J. G. 2533, 2924
Ficino, Marsilio 2697
fiduciary system 1320
field experiments 1539–40
Field, H. 2407
Field, Mark G. 4555–8
Field, Marshall 1057
field theory *see* habitus/field
Fielding, A. J. 1608
fieldwork
    African religions 3869–70
    anthropology 2539, 2704
    ethics 1442–6, 2349
    ethnography 1483
    experiments 1539–40
    and the Internet 1445
    and key informants 2457, 2458
    and reflexivity 3832
    self-representation 1444
    and unstructured interviewing 2408
Fifth Monarchy Men 3048
Fifty Years is Enough 1949, 1978
50 Cent 2826
Figgis, J. N. 3423
figurational sociology 1358, 1749–51,
    1767, 1962
**figurational sociology and the sociology of
    sport** 531, **1749–52**, 1767
Fiji
    affirmative action 42, 44
    affirmative action for majority groups 42, 44
    folk religious practices 1764
file-sharing networks 1162, 2358, 2904, 3489
filial piety 2380
filking 1638
film 1752–7
    African American 708
    alleged anti-social messages 2826
    art film tradition 1753
    author/auteur theory 218
    Benjamin and 268
    blockbuster movies 2889
    and bodily display 709–10
    and censorship 421
    and cultural production 953
    denigration of 2124
    and documentary 1210–12
    filmmakers and occupational devotion 2599
    and genre 1914, 1915
    and hegemonic codes 2103

and marketing communication 770
and mass culture concept 2823
mass medium 2873–4
motherhood, representation of 940
and multimedia 3111
pop-cultural analysis 3881
pornographic 3541
and portrayal of deviance 1109
postmodern 3556–7
product placement 3672–3
Production Code 2874
and propaganda 1753
ratings 3792–3
regulation 2913–14
science fiction 3497
science, influence of 4958
silent films 1752
and visual consumption 755, 771
see also cinema
film studies
    and genre 1916
    and masculinity 736
finalization in science 1757–9
finance, unpredictability of 1387
finance capital 1395
financescapes 1990
financial investment, and ethics 1439
financial markets 934, 3324
financial scandals 1320, 3324, 3339, 3340,
    3664, 5074
financial shocks 3176
financial sociology 1759–62
    corporate finance 1759
    personal finance 1759
    public finance 1759
    see also economic sociology
financialization, trend towards 3324, 3325
Finch, E. 4719–20
Finch, J. 2470
Fincham, R. 2719–22, 2721
Fincher, W. 2651–3, 2660–2
Findhorn community 3189
Fine, B. 749
Fine, G. A. 320, 2237, 2366, 2962, 3886–8
Fine, M. A. 467–71
Finger, A. 1697
fingerprints 2870
Finke, R. 751, 1315–16, 1317
Finkelhor, D. 1348
Finkelstein, J. 723
Finland
    bilingual education 279

Finland (*cont'd*)
    bilingualism 281
    cohabitation 566
    demographic data collection 1012
    family leave 1883
    health care system 2055
    life expectancy 2087
    medical sociology 2935
    technology assessment 689
    teenage motherhood 1728
Finlay, W. M. L. 2214
Fiol, C. M. 3309
Fiore, Q. 2692
FIRE (finance, insurance, and real estate) 1918
fire guard, as coercive institution 3315, 3316,
    3317, 3318
Firebaugh, G. 2274–5
Firestone, J. M. 241–2, 1340–5, 4189–91,
    5225–6
Firestone, S. 677, 677, 3400, 3773, 3775
firing squad, execution by 385, 386
First Amendment 2357, 2358, 2912, 3490
first demographic transition 4123, 4124–5, 4126
First Great Migration 316
First International 2809
first-past-the-post voting system 553
firstfruit offer 3981
Fischer, C. 637, 1796, 3719–20
Fishbein, M. 2105
Fisher, I. 1304, 2776
Fisher, R. A. 1533–4, 2974
Fishman, J. 282
Fiske, D. W. 2978
Fiske, J. 611, 707, 912, 1639, 3499
Fiske, S. T. 639
Fisse, B. 827
fitness, commodification of 482
Fitzpatrick, K. 2073
fixed-term contracts 1400
FJH hypothesis 2369–70, 2371
Flacks, R. 3192–6
Flaming Faggots 1225
Flanders, A. 2290
flânerie 1762–3
    Benjamin and 268–9, 757
    and experiential consumption 717
Flannery, D. J. 842–4
"flashers" *see* exhibitionism
flattened organizational hierarchy 2512
Flaubert, Gustave 1492
Flax, J. 3696
Fletcher, J. 1490

flexible capitalism 3181
flexible firm model 2514
flexible labor 2383
flexible manufacturing 1769
flexible specialization 1411
flextime 1248, 1272
Fligstein, N. 1309, 2356, 2558
Flint, J. 1643
Floden, R. E. 3274
flogging 2556
Flood, R. L. 16–20
Flores, D. 4383–6
Florida, R. 3077, 3466
flow networks 1356
Flowers, A. 1661
Floyd, S. W. 5016–18
fluid mechanics 1757
Flynn, N. 992–4
Fo Guang Shan 1982
focus groups 2564
    interviewing 2407, 2408
focus theory, and friendships 795
Foley, D. 2122, 2550
folk bilingualism 282
folk crafts 2762
folk culture 2821
folk devils 3089, 3090, 3091, 3387, 4199
    see also moral panics
folk festivals 2762
folk Hinduism 1764–7
folk medical systems 629, 631, 2079, 2080, 2694
folk theorem 4393
folk wisdom 24
folkloristics, Japanese 5302–4
folkways 3231–2, 4885
Follett, M. P. 2712, 2713, 2715, 2746–7, 2750
Foner, A. 1934–5
Foner, N. 1175
Fonow, M. M. 1702
Fontana, A. 1521, 1523, 2407–11
food and cultural consumption 721–3
    ambivalent relationships 723
    and asceticism 188
    comfort eating 722
    consumption rituals 753
    culinary tourism 764
    cultural variations 4568
    culturally sacred position 753
    differential feeding of children 1156
    and experiential consumption 716
    family food, and decision-making 2771
    food and drink preferences 347

gastronomic tourism 921
haute cuisine 722
provisioning and consumption 749, 2706
school franchises 775
shopping mall food 764
see also fatness
food and drink preferences 347
food manufacturing industry 1890
food production 1040–1
food riots, eighteenth-century 3084
food safety 697
food security 1041
food stamps 1720
football *see* soccer
football hooliganism 1133, 1751, 1767,
   1767–9, 4348, 5202–5
footbinding 4213
Foote, N. 2217
footing concept 1998
foraging 293
Foran, J. 3906–15
Forbes-Edelen, D. 3707–11
force-field analysis 430
Forché, C. 2420, 2421
Ford, Henry 363, 702–3, 765, 1769, 2510, 2828
Ford, John 218, 219, 1916
Ford Motor Company 2740, 2887
Fordham, S. 1327
Fordism/post-Fordism 1769–71, 2710–11
   and consumption 702, 706, 762, 763
   economies of scale 2940
   and enterprise 1411
   Marxist perspective 2816–17
   mass production 701, 702, 1410, 2828, 3565
   pharmaceutical companies 2940
   and political economy 3435
   post-Fordist economy 764
   and regulation theory 3841–2
   unintended consequences 2746
   and urban development 1917
foreign direct investment (FDI) 5067
formal apriorism 2757
formal democracies, democracy 1000, 1001
forms, sociology of 2692
   Simmel and 2692, 2998, 4325–6
Formula One motor racing 2739, 2741
Forrester, J. 4088–91
Forsyth, A. 1803
Fortress Europe 3838
fossil fuel combustion 1424
Foster, Janet 618
Foster, John Bellamy 1420, 1424

fostering, gay and lesbian parents 2608
Foucauldian archeological analyses
   1771–4, 3575
   and genealogy 1897
Foucault, Michel 125, 126, 242, 869, 999,
   1774–8
   auteur theory 216–17, 219
   biography 1774–5
   and biopower 2711, 3884
   and capital punishment 976
   and the civilizing process 530
   and crime and punishment 1776, 1777,
     3582–3, 5044
   and cultures of nature 947
   and the disciplinary society 1176, 1177–8,
     2523, 3335, 4020
   and discursive formations 1214
   and economic geography 1299
   and genealogy/discourse analysis 1896, 3583
   and government of the body 324, 337, 338
   and governmentality 378, 1122, 2008, 2010,
     2077, 2744, 3566, 4389–90
   and homosexuality 3883–4
   and linguistic categroies 2533
   and medicine 335
   and mental illness 1775, 3575
   and panoptics 1122
   political sociology 3462
   postmodernism 3570, 3573, 3574–5, 3582
   poststructuralism 244, 3573
   and power/knowledge 786, 787, 915, 958,
     1170, 1775–6, 1777, 2008, 3472, 3575,
     3583–4, 3597, 3598, 3937
   and the professions 3662
   and queer theory 1777, 2114, 3728
   reason, problematization of 1773, 1774
   repressive hypothesis 3883
   and sexuality 332, 335, 1436, 1776, 2114,
     2157, 2158, 2160, 2493, 2609, 3540, 3583,
     3882–4, 4248, 4264, 4290
   social constructionism 2935
   subject, problematiation of 1774
   and surveillance 1122, 3314, 4896
   and technologies of the self 1215
foundationalist epistemology 1435, 2969, 3235
four noble truths 372
4I organizational learning model 3309
Fourcade-Gourinchas, M. 932–6, 1306–11
Fourier, C. 3046, 4549
Fowler, B. 590–3
Fox 2898
Fox, A. 2290

Fox, E. 2550
Fox, J. 1317
Fox, R. 2934
Fox, Terry 4712
Fox Keller, E. 1683, 4094
Fox News 877, 3674
Fox Talbot, W. H. 3405
frame 1778–80
    articulation mechanisms 1779
    attention focus 1779
    ba 238
    Bateson and 248
    and biography 290
    core framing tasks 1781
    diagnostic framing 1781
    and gay and lesbian movement 1836
    Goffman and 248
    and innovation 3687
    master frame 1781
    prognostic framing 1781
    sampling frame 3782–3
    and social movements 1874
    and Thomas theorem 992
    transformative function 1779
frame alignment processes 1781–2
frame amplificiation 1782
frame analysis 776, 777
frame articulation 1779, 1782, 1783
frame bridging 1782
frame elaboration 1782, 1783
frame extension 1782
frame resonance 1782
frame transformation 1782
framing and social movements 954–5,
    1780–4, 1999, 4468
    collective action frames 3067, 3687
    collective identity and 587, 954
    and consensus mobilization 3067
    gay and lesbian movement 1836–7
    and political process theory 3455, 3456, 3457
    and social problems 4505
framing theory
    Bateson and 248
    Goffman and 248
Framingham Heart Study 1866
France
    acculturation 16
    aging and social policy 86
    anarchism 136
    anti-trust institutions 2356
    Bonapartism 411, 412, 413, 414
    Brumaire 2809–10

    business schools 2726
    capitalism 396
    charismatic movement 440
    cities 494
    civil religion 4142
    cohabitation 566
    colonialism 603, 985
    complementary and alternative medicine
      2068
    crime 821
    cultural studies 914
    cultural tourism 920, 921
    culture industries 943–4
    democracy 1001
    diffusion of protest 3686
    empire 1393
    family leave 1883
    film industry 1753
    film theory 218, 1755
    French Marxism 755
    gender poverty ratios 1723
    global justice groups 1978–9
    governing elites 1363
    graduate education 2013
    health technology assessment 692
    immigrant identity politics 3748
    immigration 2257–8, 2261, 3024
    immigration policies 3020
    industrial relations 2289
    industrialization 494
    Jewish population 2453
    kindergarten programs 2462
    laicism 2529–30, 2531, 4145
    LAT relationships 811
    lone parenthood 2665
    May riots (1968) 2580, 3460
    nationalism 1473
    new religious movements 3205
    nonmarital fertility 1587, 1734
    nuclear technology 3038
    oldest old 2669
    parliamentary bureaucracy 2809
    political project 297–8
    prostitution 1659
    Protestantism 3692
    public school system 4049, 4051
    racism 3762
    religious belief 198
    religious discrimination 2440
    religious schools 4053
    revolution 170
    school system 1324

social fluidity 2370
social security system 2055
socialism 614
socioeconomic policies 393
Taylorism 2746
technology assessment 689
teenage motherhood 1728
unions 2289, 2511
veiling controversy 1992
wealth inequalities 2312
welfare strategies 4538
Franceschet, S. 1688
franchise 1784–5
business-format franchising 1784
McDonald's 2739
product franchising 1784
sport/leisure-wear industry 1986
trade name franchising 1784
franchise (voting) *see* suffrage; voting behavior
Francis, R. 1440
Francke, A. H. 3408
Frank, A. G. 603, 1060, 1295, 1566, 2247, 3179
development theory 1395, 1853, 1944
Frank, Arthur 481
Frank, D. J. 1291–3
Frank, G. 287–91, 1698
Frank, K. A. 622
Frank, R. 685
Frank, T. 518
Frankel, B. 4725–30
Frankenberg, R. 1575
Frankfurt School *see* critical theory/Frankfurt School
Franklin, A. 150–2, 910–1, 1360–2, 3163–6, 3484–6, 3488–9, 3498–503, 3548–50, 4583–5
Franklin, B. 3470
Franklin, R. 2171
Franklin, S. 2172
Franks, D. D. 3055–7, 3185–9, 3945–8
Franquism 411
Franz Ferdinand of Austria, Archduke 239
Franz, F. 2440
Fraser, N. 876, 1177, 2653, 3560, 3610, 3821
fraternity gang rape 2153
fraud 1440
welfare fraud 5238–40
Frazer, Sir James 3630, 3981–2, 5020
Frazier, D. 307
Frazier, E. Franklin 131, 443, 1597, **1785–6**, 2444, 2838

Fredrickson, G. 3740
free market
and cultural imperialism 907
and health care delivery systems 2054
and industrialization 2299
and liberalism 2624
and neoliberal globalization 1947
and neoliberalism 3177
free-market capitalism 2296
free-market conservatism 681
free-rider problem 577, 587, 1282, 1315
and collective action 1823
and ethnic mobilization 1469
and religious movements 2441
and social movements 1781
free school movement 866, 4111
free school system *see* schools, public
free speech 2556, 3490
and censorship 421
in cyberspace 966
and media regulation 2916
Free Speech Movement 1674
free trade 393, 1303, 2299
and decolonization 985
global free trade regime 2890
and poverty 3595–6
free will
Beccaria and 256, 3800
free-will–determinism issue 257
and humanism 2186
James and 2434
Kant and 2187
Lombroso and 2662
free will hedonism 1118
Freedman, C. 3496
Freedman, D. A. 788, 789
Freedman, J. 625–6
freedom
and agency 2041
arbitrary liberty 2041
creative liberty 2041
decisive liberty 2041
and determinism 2041
epistemological justification 2187, 2188
freedom/determination dilemma 347
Gurvitch and 2041
Gurvitch on 2041
and human rights 2183
innovative freedom 2041
intellectual freedom 3468
and liberalism 2623
negative/positive liberty 2624

freedom (*cont'd*)
　press freedom 2912, 3490
　and wealth 2311
freedom of information laws 5072
Freedom Rides 1165, 1166, 3193, 4472
Freedom Singers 3135
Freedom Summer campaign 3067
Freeman, H. 2934
Freeman, J. 677, 1674, 3776
Freeman, L. 3183
Freese, J. 1868
Freidan, B. 2485
Freidson, E. 2076, 2246, 2930, 3657,
　3661, 3662
Freidson, M. 2105
Freire, P. 865–6, 3613
Fremont, A. 2934
French Regulation School 3179, 3434
French Revolution 407, 614, 660, 665, 1067,
　1147, 3909, 3915
　and collective trauma 595
　and conservatism 678
　individualism 2285, 2706
　and intellectual freedom 3468
　and liberalism 2622–3
　and nationalism 3145, 3155
Freston, P. 439–42
Freud, Sigmund 1261, 1366, **1786–7,**
　4248
　and Althusser 126
　and civilization 530
　and cultural critique 896
　and the death instinct 65
　depth psychology 875
　dream analysis 3881
　and fetishism 608
　and happiness 33
　and hermeneutics 2109
　and hypnosis 3695
　identification theory 4571
　and Lacan 2527
　and masturbation 2834
　misogyny 2528
　and Nietzsche 3215
　object relation theory 3697
　and personality development 837, 1070–1
　and play 3414
　and psychiatry 2694
　psychoanalytic method 865, 1070–1, 1897,
　　2695, 2698, 2760, 3694, 3696, 4264
　psychodynamic psychology 837
　psychosexual theory 462, 4264

　and sexual desire 3698
　and sublimation 2708
　and the super-ego 530, 837, 2434, 4156
　totems and taboos 3344, 3972, 5045
Freudenberg, W. 1175
Frick, H. C. 2005
Friedan, B. 677, 1666, 1674, 2602, 2619,
　2621, 2866
Friedman, J. J. 4878–81
Friedman, M. 2777, 3176, 3177
Friedman, T. 1994
Friedrichs, D. O. 3303–6
Friedson, E. 2934, 2935, 3374
Friends of the Earth (FoE) 1428, 1429, 1430,
　1432, 3212, 3259
friendship during the later years 1787–8,
　1796
　cross-sex friendship 878
　and gender 1788, 1791, 1795
　and network density 1796
　retirement communities 3905
friendship: interpersonal aspects 1788–91,
　2390
　adolescent friendships 1799
　affective nature 1789
　cross-cultural and ethnic variations 1790,
　　1796, 1798, 3754–6
　cross-sex friendship 795, 877–9, 1791
　cross-species companionship 947, 2175
　delinquent friends 845
　and equality 1789
　and gender 1790–1, 1862–3
　homophily 203
　and mutuality 1789
　personal nature 1789
　and polyamory 3477–8
　and proximity 203
　social support provision 90
　voluntary nature 1789
friendship, social inequality, and social
　change 1792–5
　child friendships 1802
　and gender 1792
　and race/ethnicity 3754–6
friendship: structure and context 1795–9
　and balance theory 795
　choice-constraint approach 795
　convivium 795–6
　demand-side perspectives 795
　during later years 1787–8
　focus theory and 795
　and gender 1795, 1797

and geographical proximity 795
and race/ethnicity 3754–6
social capital and 795
supply-side perspectives 795
friendship-based love 2671
friendships of adolescence 1799–801
cross-sex friendship 878
friendships of children 1801–3
bridging relationships 1802
cliques 1802
cross-sex friendships 878, 879, 1802
friendship choice 1802
interracial friendships 1801–2
and school climate 4016
friendships of gay, lesbian, and bisexual
people 877, 1794, **1803–4**
and polyamory 3477, 3478
and sexual activity 1804
Frieze, I. H. 1803, 2671–4, 5047–50
Frisbie, P. 3756–60
Frisby, D. 344
Frisco, M. L. 4028–9
Frith, S. 1915
Frito Bandito cartoon character 2549
Froebel, F. 2462
frog/pond theory 2119
Fromm, Erich 875, **1804–8**
and authoritarianism 1805–6
and education 1807
and false consciousness 1569
and the Frankfurt School 865, 874, 875, 1569
Freudian critique 1806
Fromm–Marcuse debate 1806
Fromm–Riesman collaboration 1807
and Horkheimer 2164
and the new left 3193
and public sociology 1807
sociological imagination 1807–8
Frontier Myth 3511–13
Frostbelt 993, 1454
frustration–aggression hypothesis 66, 4013
frustration–reaction theory of racist movements
3768–9
Fuchs, S. 60–2
fudo 1287
Fuentes, C. 2550
Fujimura-Fanselwo, K. 1692
Fukata, A. 2445, 2446
Fukuyama, F. 337, 3174, 3497
full information maximum likelihood (FIML)
2544
Fuller, Samuel 218

Fuller, Steve 21–3, 1896–7, 2474–6, 3222–3,
3544–7, 4406–8
Fulton, J. 3047–50
Fulton, R. 974
Funabashi, H. 265–7
function 1808–10
functional differentiation 2231
and secularization 4141, 4142–3
and social change 1812, 4362
functional rationalization 378, 4143
functionalism/neofunctionalism 1808,
1809, **1810–13**, 4980–1, 4982
autopoietic systems 233
and Christianity 478
and conflict theory 662
critics of 1812
Durkheim and 1251, 1254–5, 1810
and ecological problems 1282
and economic sociology 1319–20
and education 1323, 1332
Eisenstadt and 2135
and ethnography 1481
functionalist lawmaking 667
and gerontology 1928, 1929
and the hidden curriculum 2116, 2117
and labeling 2501
Luhmann and 2675–6
macro-functionalism 1811
and magic 2698–9
Malinowski and 2705
organic analogy 1810
and professions 2075
psychological funtionalism 2431
and racial conflict 659
and social anthropology 3772
and stratification 4797–8
fundamental attribution error 206
fundamental Marxian theorem (FMT) 1544–5,
1546
fundamental nationalism 1474
fundamentalism 1813–16
and conservatism 1868
and creationism 1510
and globalization 1957
and homophobia 1984
and modernity 1815
and secularization 1815
see also Islamic fundamentalism; religious
fundamentalism
funeral gatherings 881
fur seals 1291
Furies 2602, 2603–4

Furnivall, J. S. 603, 661, 3420
Furstenberg, F. F. 2342
Fusco, C. 4290–3
Fussell, P. 1190
fuzzy logic 3725

G7 summits 1977
G8 summits 1977, 1978
Gaard, G. 1275
Gabriel, K. 4974–6
Gadamer, H.-G. 2108, 2109, 3820
Gadsden, G. 1856–8
Gaelic games 3160
Gafford, F. 5104–7
Gagnon, J. 2112, 2159, 2468, 4122, 4248
Gaines, Larry 1232–6
Gaines, Lloyd 368
Gaither, B. J. 1829
Gaitskell, Hugh 2141
Galanter, M. 2562
Galarza, E. 2549
Galbraith, J. K. 684, 702, 741, 748, 2021, 2192,
    3288, 3438
Galen 5268–9
Galileo Galilei 1352, 2896, 3572–3, 3999,
    4091, 4116
Galison, P. 1532
Gallagher, E. 2056, 3374–7
Gallagher, S. K. 5265–7
Galle, O. R. 2341
Galligan, B. 1651–3
Galliher, J. F. 3088
Gallini, C. 2700
Gallup, George 2407
Gallup Polls 1013, 1317, 2407
Galor, O. 1332
Galton, Sir Francis 1488, 1506, 3044
Gambia, female genital mutilation 1654
Gamble, A. 678–81, 2622–5, 3172–8
Gamblers Anonymous 1817
gambling as a social problem 1111, **1817–18**
    disease concept 1817
    pathological gambling 1817, 1818, 2599
gambling and sport 1818–21
    and deviance 1132, 1133
game stage 1821, **1821–2**, 1899, 3415, 3418,
    3617, 3949, 3952
    and the generalized other 1899, 3417, 3617,
        3949, 3952
    see also play stage
game theory 1822–5, 3434, 4134
    analytical game theory 1824

    Bernard on 272
    and ethnic movements 1470
    evolutionary game theory 293, 1824
    and exchange network theory 1514
    Goffman and 1997
    and network structures 1512
    and norms 3232
    and rational choice theory 1557
    and social dilemmas 4393
    and social interaction 1997
gameshows 3491
Gaming Act 1667
Gamio, Manuel 339
Gamoran, A. 1335, 3271–6, 3274
Gamson, J. 1166
Gamson, W. 781, 3067
Gance, A. 1753
Gandhi, Indira 1814
Gandhi, Mahatma 165, 912, 2130, 3147, 3854
    assassination 2132
    and direct action 1165
    and frame articulation 1782
    non-violence 4458–9
    pluralism 2131
    positive deviance 3543
Gandhianism 2969
Gangl, M. 5242–6
gangs, delinquent 833, **1825–8**, 2826
    cultural transmission 585
    definitional issues 1825–6
    female gang members 1826–7, 1857, 1858,
        2820
    formation 1825
    hate groups 2049
    and juvenile delinquency 2454
    and mass media influences 2826
    membership 1767–8
    motorcycle gangs 1129
    narcotics trafficking 834
    and organized crime 834
    participant observation methods 2031
    and rape culture 3783
    schools and 842
    and strain theory 4780–1
    structures and typologies 1826
    subcultural deviance 4875–6
    tattoing 329
Ganong, L. H. 4765–8, 4770–2
Gans, H. 637, 777, 1455, 2124, 2615, 5105
ganymedes 2160
garbage collection 1421
Garber, E. 3496

garden cities 502, 967
Garey, A. I. 3104
Garfield, E. 4120
Garfinkel, Harold 1130, 1257, 2652
    breaching experiments 1484, 4387
    and documentary analysis 1214–15
    ethnomethodology 791, 1087, 1449, 1483,
        1484–6, 2032–3, 2363, 3403, 4065, 4487
    and gender 1484
    and intersubjectivity 2401
    and phenomenology 1484, 3403
Garland, R. 1697
garment manufacture 1453, 1454, 1461, 3184
Garner, L. 514–19
Garner, R. 138–41, 514–19
Garnham, N. 942–5, 2327
Garofalo, R. 857, 1136, 2663
Garrick, J. 2717
Garrison, E. 1680
Garth, B. G. 1310, 2558
Gartner, R. 5206–8
Garvey, A. J. 306
Garvey, Marcus 4188
Gasset, Ortega y 1229
gastronomic tourism 921
gated communities 619, 1643
gatekeepers
    art worlds 179
    law enforcement officers 853
    media 2877
    observational research 3238–9
Gates, Bill 2876
Gates, Henry Louis 309
gateway pleasures 2833
Gavron, S. J. 1171
Gay Activists Alliance 1834
gay bashing 1828–30
    and the heterosexual imaginary 2110
gay culture 2162
Gay Games 1134, 1879, 1985, 4293, 4701
gay gene 331, **1830–3**
gay ghetto 2159
gay and lesbian movement 1833–8, 2157
    and the AIDS epidemic 1834–5, 2606,
        2607, 2608
    and civil and family rights 1592
    and collective identity 588, 589
    countermovement 1834
    and drag subculture 1225
    and framing 1836
    goals 956, 1836
    and the Internet 2387

liberationist approach 1834
    research issues 1836
    rights–based approach 1834, 1835
    rsearch issues 1836
    and sexual citizenship 4205, 4206–7
    see also coming out/closets
Gay Liberation Front 1834
gay pride movements 3106
Gazzaniga, M. 3187
GDP, and economic development 1296,
    1332, 1852
Geddes, P. 3123
Geertz, Clifford 2973, 3141, 3292, 3950
    and cultural sociology 823, 2971
    and ethnicity 1475, 2642
    and magic 2698
    and religion 3524, 3860–1
    and social change in Southeast Asia 4377–8
    and structuralism 2427
    and the western self 238
    on the western self 238
Gehlen, A. 2344
Geis, G. 826–8, 850–1, 4900–3
Gell, A. 288
Gellner, Ernst 344, 1466, **1838–40**
    anthopological studies 1838–9
    biography 1838
    linguistic philosophy critique 1838
    and nationalism 1466, 1839, 2900, 2901,
        3147, 3148, 3150, 3156
Gemeinschaft/Gesellschaft 183, 500, 594, 598,
    620, 661, 1401, 1458, 1576, 2003, 2031,
    3621, 3964, 4130, 5015, 5104
gender 677
    and affirmative action 4204
    and age identity 50
    and alcoholism 117
    and anatomy 335
    and anti-Semitic views 153
    behavioral differences 292
    biological ideology 1846
    Birmingham School and 297
    and consumption 735, 1848–51
    and cultural feminism 904
    and cultural sociology 926
    and cyberculture 963
    De Beauvoir and 326
    and depression 82
    development 1681
    and disability 1172, 1864, 2097
    and discrimination 1182
    and diversity 1197

gender (*cont'd*)
  and division of labor 1273, 1716, 1848, 1893, 2307, 2486, 2516, 2619
  and divisions of household labor 673, 1202–6, 1580–1, 1582, 1591, 1620, 1633, 1669, 1840, 1859, 1881, 2112, 2301, 2310, 2547–8, 2790–1, 3081
  and domestic violence 1219
  and dropping out of school 1230–1
  and drug use 1235
  and educational attainment 1335, 1343–4
  essentialist notions of 2396
  and fashion 719
  and feminist anthropology 1690
  and feminist standpoint theory 1711
  gender identity 1662–3, 1664, 2114, 2215
  historical use 1667
  and human resource management 2180
  and inclusion 901
  inequalities 336
  and intersectionality 2395, 2396
  intersectionist approach 2852
  Luxemburg and 2687
  and mate selection 204
  and migration 1715–17
  modern understandings 1667
  and patriarchy 3379
  performance 333, 1998
  population and 3533–6
  and postmodern feminism 3559–60
  postmodern perspective 3699
  psychoanalytic critique 3696
  racialized 3764–5
  radical feminist critique 3773
  sex–gender conflation 1895
  sex–gender distinction 1847
  and sexuality 4265–6
  social construction 326, 332, 336, 1843, 1845, 1846, 1847, 1864, 1875, 1998, 2110, 2307, 2396, 3104, 3696, 4197
  and sport 1875–9, 4666–7, 4672–3, 4700
  and stratification 4799–801
  and suicide 4883
  "third gender" 4214–15
  and victimization 66
  see also doing gender; inequality/ stratification, gender
gender, aging and 69, **1840–3**
  and caregiving 403, 2546
  and friendship 1931
  and marital satisfaction 2546–7
  and retirement 3900

gender bias 1843–5
  differential treatment of children by sex 1155–9
  in the economy 1844
  in education 1844
  in health 1844–5
  within the household 1844
  see also inequality/stratification, gender; sexism
gender, the body and 326, 332, 333, **1845–8**
  gender verification 1847–8
gender consciousness 1873–4
gender, consumption and 1848–52
  and the department store 1057–8
  girls 724–7
  and shopping 1057–8
gender, development and 1274, **1852–6**
  and female poverty 1724–5
  and gender mainstreaming 1870
Gender and Development (GAD) initiatives 1854, 1855, 4996
gender, deviance and 1856–8
  female criminality 2663, 3676, 4191–3
  and female gangs 1826–7
gender dysphoria 111, 4246
gender, education and 1859–61
  and the hidden curriculum 2117, 2118
  and school dropout 1230
  single-sex schools 4055–8
gender equality 1156
  and gender mainstreaming 1869
  and nonmarital fertility and cohabitation 1735
gender equity 1677
gender essentialism 1438, 1682
gender, friendship and 1862–4
  child friendships 1802
  older people 1931
gender, health, and mortality 1864–7, 3535
  fertility-related medical decisions 3535
  HIV/AIDS 333, 2309, 2319, 2398, 3535
  see also infant, child, and maternal health and mortality; maternal morbidity and mortality; women's health
gender identity 1662–3, 1664, 2114, 2215
gender identity disorder 1112
gender ideology and gender role ideology 1867–9
  Bernard and 270, 272
  children and gender formation 3697
  and divisions of household labor 1205, 1591
  doing gender 1216–18
  dominant ideologies 1846, 1877
  and earner–carer model 1271–2

and family diversity 1591–2
gender role egalitarianism 1596
and helping behaviors 3681
and Islamic culture 2428
and liberalism 1868
and patriarchy 3377–8
scales 1868
see also femininity; masculinity
gender inequality/stratification
and family theory 1633
and gender mainstreaming 1869–70
and occupational sex segregation 1892
gender mainstreaming 1855, **1869–70**
gender oppression 1871–2
in household labor 2841
Playboy and 3419
and purdah 3723
in sport 1875–9
in war 1885–7
see also inequality/stratification, gender;
patriarchy; rape culture
gender panic theory 2155, 2156
gender performativity 1664, 1667
gender policing 2100
gender role egalitarianism 1596
gender, social movements and 1872–5
ecofeminism 1273–6
and feminist collective activism 2768
see also feminism, first, second, and third
waves; feminist activism in Latin
America; women's movements
gender socialization 1591–2, 1667–8, 1792,
1846, 1851, 3698, 4198, 4571–4
gender, sport and 1875–80
and disability sport 1172
female athletes 1172
female sports writers 2920
liberal feminist perspective 2918
media representation of sportswomen 2918
gender studies 1777
gender subordination 1663
gender substructure 1894
gender, work, and family 1880–5
caregiving 403
and earner–carer model 1271–2
working hours 1032–3
see also divisions of household labor; family,
men's involvement in; fatherhood;
motherhood
**gendered aspects of war and international
violence 1885–8**
rape culture 1885–7

gendered enterprise 1888–91
gendered interviewing 2409–10
**gendered organizations/institutions
1892–5**
gender bias 1844–5
occupations 2100
and office ladies (Japan) 3251–4
sexualization 3319–21
and social movements 1874
gene–culture coevolution 294
gene sequencing 2172
gene therapy 1907–8, 2940
genealogy 1896–7
and Nietzsche 896
General Educational Development (GED)
examination 1329
General Electric 2898
General Fertility Rate (GFR) 1015–16, 1742
General Household Survey (UK) 2590
general linear model 1897–9
ANOVA (analysis of variance) technique
146–7
correlation and 807
General Motors 697
General Social Survey (GSS) 1868
generalizability theory 3849, 3850
generalized other 1899–900, 3946, 4170
and facework 1554
and the play stage/game stage 189,
3417, 3617
generation gap 1902
generational accounting 1904, 2367
generational change 1900–6
economic generations 1903–4
family generations 1904–5
political generations 1902–3
social and intellectual context 1900–1
generational conflict 1902, 2367
see also intergenerational relationships and
exchanges
generational equity 1903–4
and intergenerational conflict 2367
generational justice 2367–8
generative grammar 2535
genericide 731
genetic determinism 2174
**genetic engineering as a social problem
1906–9**
cloning 556–9
and eugenics 1490
and genomics 2172
germ line engineering 1490

genetic engineering as a social problem
   (*cont'd*)
   and human dignity 1491
   legal regulation 1908
   reprogenetics 1490
   and risk 2840
   social regulation 1908
genetic exceptionalism 1907, 2940
genetically modified organisms (GMOs) 1273,
   4103
geneticization 2173, 2940
genetics 1757, 3376
   APOE gene alleles 284
   behavioral genetics 635
   body mapping 328
   communication issues 2938–9
   corporate ownership of genetic materials
      1274
   divorce and 470
   and environment 1508
   ethics 1490
   and ethnicity 661, 2080
   and eugenics 1489
   forensic genetics 337
   genetic drift 293
   genetic surveillance 337
   homosexual gene 331, 1830–3
   Human Genome Project 337, 1490, 1684,
      1830, 1906, 2937
   and hybridity 2189–90
   and medical sociology 2937–40
   and medicalization 1113
   Mendelian genetics 292
   modification 328, 558
   mutations 286, 293
   population genetics 291
   and racial difference 3731–2
   recombination 293
   screening 337, 2173
   sexual orientation and
   and social behavior 1907
   social consequences 337
   and surveillance issues 2172
Genette, G. 1916
Geneva Refugee Convention 2256
Genghis Khan 522
genital piercing 324, 330
genital surgery 1656
   see also female genital mutilation
Gennep, A. van 3932–3, 3937
genocide 531, 1466, **1909–13**
   bystanders 1910

and the civilizing process 531
and critical theory 876
cultural genocide 2755
elements 1910
and ethnic cleansing 1451
and failed democracy 1911, 1912
and ghetto 1937
indigenous peoples 2281
modernity and 525
perpetrators 1910
prevention and intervention 1912
types and periods 1910
see also Burundi and Rwanda (Hutu, Tutsi);
   Holocaust
genomics 1215, 2171–5
Genosko, G. 2037–8, 2690–3
genotype 1508, 1897
genre 1913–17
   communicative genres 1916
   documentaries 1210–12
   sub-genres 1913–14
   television and 219
genre theory 1756
Gentile, E. 1646
gentrification 501, 502, 767–8, **1917–20**,
   5147–8
   agents of 1918
   and community 618
   and cultural studies 916
   demand-side analysis 1919
   and growth machine thesis 2035
   and invasion-succession 2419
   supply-side analysis 1919
Geoffrey, W. 1445
geography
   and colonialism 1297, 1295, 1297
   cultural geography of the nation-state 2901
   economic geography 1297–300
   gay geography 2159
   idiographic approach 1298
   Marxist 2816
   quantitative economic geographers 1298
   queer geography 2162
geometry 4116
geopolitics 1295, 4731
George, L. K. 79–84, 93–101
George, N. 798
Georgia
   ethnic mobilization 1470
   Orthodox Church 3345
   and secession 1487
geragogy 4565

Gerami, S. 1885–8
Gerbner, G. 2826
Gergen, K. 1087
Gerhardt, U. 2059
germ line engineering 1490, 1908
German Expressionism 1753
German National Socialism 1644, 1903,
    2142, 2804
German Social Democratic Party 1409,
    2996, 3258
Germani, Gino 1920–6
Germany
    acculturation 16
    aging and social policy 86, 1028
    bilingual education 279, 280
    Bismarckism 411, 413
    bureaucratic model 2747
    citizenship 497
    cohabitation 566
    communism 2685
    complementary and alternative medicine 631
    cultural imperialism 907
    cultural studies 914
    democracy 1001
    diaspora 1152
    diffusion of protest 3687
    drag queens and kings 1224
    economic geography 1298
    economic growth 2726
    educational system 1363
    elites 1363
    environmental movements 1430–1
    ethnic violence 1470
    eugenic management of the body 325
    family leave 1883
    and federalism 1652, 1653
    film industry 1753, 1754
    gambling 1817
    gender poverty ratios 1723
    global justice groups 1978, 1979
    graduate education 2013
    guest workers 1153
    health care system 3657–8
    health care-seeking behavior 2069
    home schooling 4033
    immigration 1459, 2259, 2262, 2263
    immigration policies 3020
    industrial democracy 2750, 2753
    industrial relations 2289, 2753
    industrialization 494, 3072, 3076
    inter vivos family transfers 1905
    Jehovah's Witnesses 2439
    Jewish population 2453
    job history analysis 3062
    kindergarten programs 2462
    labor skill levels 364
    LAT relationships 811
    liberalism 2624
    lone parenthood 2665
    medical sociology 2935
    metropolises 495, 2992
    migration 2264
    nationalism 1473, 3142, 3145, 3215
    neoliberalism 3175, 3176
    nonmarital fertility 1734
    prewar German sexology 2158
    prostitution 1659
    public broadcasting 3703
    public school system 4049
    religious schools 4053
    retirement policies 3902
    Romantic movement 2758
    school system 1324
    social fluidity 2372
    social movements 3260
    social science 2186–7
    social security systems 2053, 2055
    socialism 614
    socioeconomic policies 393
    sterilization policies 1169
    Taylorism 2746
    technology assessment 689
    unions 2289
    universities 621
    vocational training systems 1399
    war crimes 226
    war reparations 3876
    wealth inequalities 2312
    weapons R&D 3039
    women's movements 2768–9
Gernsback, H. 3494
Geronimus, A. T. 1629, 1727
gerontology 337, **1926–30**
    biological 284–5
    biological gerontology 284–5
    biomedical gerontology 1927
    and caregiving 402
    and death and dying 974
    and early life patterns 76
    and elder care 1349–51
    feminist gerontology 1929
    Foucauldian gerontology 1930
    functionalist perspective 1928, 1929, 1930
    male and female chronology 1929

gerontology (*cont'd*)
  Marxist gerontology 1929
  political economy of old age 1929, 1930
  postmodern gerontology 1930
  social gerontology 1927–8, 1930
gerontology: key thinkers 1931–6
Gershuny, J. 2516
Gerson, K. 1721
Gerstel, N. 811
Gerstle, G. 3422
Gerteis, J. 3421–3
Gerth, H. H. 3050, 3949, 3950
gestalt 2616, 2692
Ghana
  capitalist growth 390
  charismatic movement 441
  educational opportunities 1157
  public housing 3710
Ghelke, E. 1258
ghetto 1936–8, 3743
  cross-border networks 1050
  family as ghetto 1582
  gay ghetto 2159
  and genocide 1937
  and models of urban form 1280
  and public housing 3711
  and segregation 2197
ghetto mentality 1937
ghetto walls 1890
ghettoization 1938
  of children 696
Ghezzi, S. 4906–8
Ghiaroni, S. 3980–5
Ghosh, A. 2130
Ghost Dance movement 3048–9
ghost-writing 1085
ghosts 1140, 3629, 3631
Giard, L. 424
Gibbs, J. P. 1065, 1066
Gibbs, R. 3426
Gibson, D. 1840
Gibson, W. 961, 3497
Giddens, Anthony 1199, 1607, 1633,
    1794, 2761
  and agency–structure problem 438, 871, 872
  and disembedding of social interactions
    1188, 1189, 1575
  and family relationships 1634
  and globalization 1956, 1958, 1961, 1994
  and hermeneutics 2109
  and identity formation 3141
  and improvisation 2734

  and "life politics" 2910
  and lifestyle selection 2062
  and marital and partner commitment
    2323–4
  materialist analysis 2838
  and mediation 2926
  and money 3079
  and plastic sexuality 3411, 3412, 3568
  and reflexive modernity 2650, 3070,
    3830, 4238
  and reflexive self-fashioning 711, 1577–8
  and the risk society 2084
  and scientific disciplines in modernity 2389
  and self-disclosing intimacy 2412, 2413
  and sequestration 2926
  and sexuality 334
  and spatial relationships 4633
  structuration theory 1087, 1640, 2400, 2515,
    2962, 2998, 3295, 4859–61, 4863
  and time/space distanciation 1958, 2889,
    2922, 3070, 5003
Giddens, F. 603
Giddings, F. 130, 3227
Giddings, P. 308, 309
Gieryn, T. 2960
gift 600, 745, 754, 946, **1938–40**, 4908
  competitive gift giving 1940
  reciprocity 1839, 3227, 4908
  redistribution 1939
  self-interested gift 3981
  transactional sex 4211
  see also symbolic exchange
gift relations 1940–1
  Bataille and 1940
  Christmas 753
  gift/counter-gift cycle 1940, 3228
  and justice analysis 1194
  and networks 1252
  and paternalism 3370
  and ritual 3937
  social nature 1940
gift-sacrifice 3981
Gilbert, E. 694
Gilded Age 685
Giles, D. 418
Gill, E. 2653
Gillespie, M. 2886
Gillespie, W. 3384–5, 4746–9
Gilligan, C. 904, 1072, 1438, 1682, 1707,
    3699, 3776
Gilman, Charlotte Perkins 1941–2, 2767
  and cultural feminism 902

feminist sociology 2769
and food production 1668
and gender 1667
Gilroy, P. 300, 3135
Giménez, H. 440
Gimenez, M. 2838
Gimlin, D. 323–4
Gin, C. 2499
Giner, S. 2822
Gini, C. 1942
Gini index 1942
Gini mean difference 1743
Gini coefficient 1942–3
and inequality 1196, 1942–3, 2275–6
Ginn, J. 1929
Ginsberg, M. 2141
Gintis, H. 1323, 2116
Giordan, Giuseppe 185–9, 3871–6, 5168–72
Giovanni, N. 308
Girard, R. 3984
girl power 726
Girling, E. 976–8
girls' consumption 724–7
Giroux, H. 866, 890, 1155, 2101, 2826
Girschick, L. 1856
Gitlin, T. 2229
Giuliani, Rudy 825
Giulianotti, R. 760, 1751, 4345–50
Gladstone, William 2895
Glaeser, E. 1315, 1333
Glaser, B. 233, 973, 2023, 2024, 2025, 2026, 2631, 2934
Glasgow Trades Hall 590
Glasius, M. 1959
glass ceiling 937, 1669, 1889, 2310
and gender 3649
and patriarchy 3378
racial/ethnic exclusion 3371–2
glass escalator 1894
Glass, R. 1917
Glassner, B. 2827
Glazer, N. 2945, 3106–7, 3445, 3917
Glendenning, F. 1348
Glenn, N. D. 52–6
Glick, P. 2572
Glissant, E. 818
Global Campaign for Education 1974, 1975
global capitalism 1991, 2842, 3114
global civil society 1959–60
global consciousness 1957, 1960
global culture 1962, 1988, 1991
global economy 1943–6, 1961, 1988

and gender and development 1852–5
and global justice movement 1947
and international division of labor 2382
and neoliberalism 1948, 3176
restructuring 2382–3
and world-system theory 1061
global exchange structures 1295
ideological dimension 1987
media dimension 1987
global factory 2382
global flows
cultural flows 1990
economic dimension 1987
ethnoscapes 1990
financescapes 1990
flow determinism 2329
ideoscapes 1990
international movement of people 1986–7
mediascapes 1990
migratory flows 2252, 2255, 2257, 3012
network of flows 2329
and sports development 1989
technology dimension 1987
technoscapes 1990
global futures trend 1969
global justice as a social movement 1947–50, 1976–9, 3913
collective identity 1949
different ideological currents 1978
and direct action 1166
environmental justice movement (EJM) 1273, 1275, 1285, 1428, 1429
global cultural values and infrastructures 1979
participatory democratic character 1949
pro-global elements 1977
global modernity 3070
global politics 1950–3
periodization 1951
global village 1958, 2330, 2692
global warming 33, 728, 968, 3342
global/world cities 1953–6, 1957
and the central business district 423
command and control functions 2304, 2305
ethnic enclaves 1454
and homelessness 2148
hybridity 2190
and inequalities 2304–5
and metropolises 2992
and network analysis 3182
power theory 3182
primate cities 3622–5

globalization 1956–60
and alienation 120
and authority and conformity 228
and biracialism 296
capitalist globalization 1062
and celebrity culture 417
and consumer culture 740, 745
and criminal law 1099
and critical theory 876
and cultural imperialism 907
and cultural studies 916
of culture 518, 953
definitions 1990
and deindustrialization 994
and denationalization 1048–51
and diaspora 2885
and economic determinism 1293
economic globalization 1061, 1293
and economy–sociology relation?
and education 1334
and elder poverty 1930
and entrepreneurship 1412
and family and community 1577
and family sociology 1600
from below 1969
and global/world cities?
and immigration
and imperialism 1960
and inequality 390–1
and information technology 2334, 2335
and job losses 120
and laicism 2532
and management theory 2749
Marxist analysis 2816
materialist analysis 2838
media 418–19
and metropolises 2990
and migration 3011, 3012
myth of 349
neoliberal globalization?
and occupational communities 1579–80
and organizational communication 3297
and political economy 3435–6
and racial/ethnic conflict 661
reflexivity 1990
religious 488
of social and cultural relations 611
sport 4651
and wealth inequalities 2313
and world-systems theory?
globalization, consumption and 1960–4
and children's consumer culture 696

food and cultural consumption 723
and the global economy 1946
globalization, culture and 518, 953, **1964–70**
and diaspora 1153
and the information society 2329
globalization, education and 1971–6
conflict theories 1971, 1972
expansionary trends 1971–2
institutional theories 1971–2
internationalization 1974–5
nationalization 1972–3
standardization 1973–4
globalization and global justice 1976–80
globalization, religion and 1980–3, 3867
and denominationalism 1055
Islam 3867
Jehovah's Witnesses 2439–40
Pentecostalism 3867
globalization, sexuality and 1983–6
and AIDS pandemic 106
see also sex tourism
globalization, sport and 1986–90
figurational sociology and?
see also Olympics
globalization, values and 1990–3
glocalization 1992, **1994–5**
and distanciation 1189
ethical glocalization 1993
and global consumption 1963
and global culture 1965, 1968–9
healthy glocalization 1994
and heterogeneity 2022
glossolalia 439
Gluck, E. 838, 1143, 1144
Gluck, S. 838, 1143, 1144
Glymour, C. 426
GNP
income/GMP-environmental concern
correlation 1283–4
as predictor of democracy 1001
Go, J. 602–4, 984–6
goal attainment 1809, 3367
goal displacement 3397
goal-oriented rationality 3313, 3338, 4644
Godbey, G. 1032
Goddard, H. H. 837
Godwin, William 524–5, 2706
Goebbels, Josef 2879
Goetz, E. T. 1220, 2868–9, 5180–6
Goffman, Erving 1257, **1995–9**
and the asylum 1122, 2934
biography 1995

and the body 325, 736, 2363
and the body, and interaction 2363
and the Chicago School 1227
and consumption 736
and discourse 2537
dramaturgical sociology 1997, 2211, 2670,
    3410, 3950, 4158
and emotions 1379
and facework 1553–4, 3937
and the felicity condition 1227
and framing 248, 1778–9, 1780, 1998
and game theory 1997
and games 4648
and the health professions 2076
and identity management 2218, 4325
and identity politics 1143, 2214
and impression management 2215, 2221,
    2433, 3007
influences on 1996
and interaction 1997, 2211, 2214, 3415
and interaction order 1995, 1997, 2032,
    2365, 2366
and interaction rituals 990
medical sociology 2934
and mental illness 1998, 2695, 3332–3, 3334
and photography 770
and presentation of the self 1228, 1996–7, 2362
and self-management 965, 4325
social interaction analysis 990, 1995, 1997,
    2032, 2211, 2214, 2365, 2366, 3331, 3415
stigma theory 323, 479, 583, 584, 1087, 1094,
    1125, 1169, 1572, 1998, 2214, 2502,
    2832, 3505
symbolic interactionism and 325, 1812
and total institutions 3331–2, 3891–2
and visual sociology 2986
Gökalp, Ziya 1999–2004
Gold, S. 1247–9, 1459
Gold, S. J. 3740–3
Goldberg, G. S. 1723
Golden Age of Capitalism 1398–9
Golden Temple in Amritsar 1814
Goldhagen, D. J. 1646
Goldman, Emma 2004–7, 2618, 2841
    and anarchism 136
Goldscheider, F. 2570–5
Goldschmidt, R. 1830
Goldson, A. 1210–13
Goldstein, J. S. 2491
Goldthorpe class schema 2373, 2374, 3060, 3251
Goldthorpe, J. H. 2369, 2370, 2371, 2372,
    2373, 2376, 2628, 3060, 3061, 3062, 3251

Goldwater, Barry 2233
Goleman, D. 3444
Gomart, E. 746
Gomes, R. 2836–9
Gómez-Morales, Y. J. 489–93
Gomez-Smith, Z. 830–3
Gong Lum v. *Rice* 368
GONGOs (government-organized NGOs) 3212
good death 975
Goode, E. 583–4, 978–80, 979, 1075–82, 1087,
    1090, 1092–5, 1100–17, 1124, 1140, 1233,
    2411, 3088, 3089, 3090
Goode, L. 1159–64
Goode, W. J. 1599, 2469–70, 2789
Goodman, L. 2378, 2659
Goodman, P. 3193
Goodman–Hauser model 2378
Goodwin, J. 3449, 3457, 3909
Goody, J. 1213, 2840
Google 2880
Gordon, K. 4940–1
Gordon, M. 192, 1458, 2394, 2944–5
Gordon, R. 437–8
Gordon, S. L. 1379
Gore, J. 1708
Goring, C. 837
Gorman, L. 2873–80
Gorski, P. S. 3461
Gotham, K. F. 2942–4, 5132–4
Gottdiener, M. 704, 2194, 2884, 3114
Gottfredson, M. 819, 838, 847, 851, 1104,
    1120, 4163–6
Gottlieb, R. 1275
Gottmann, J. 2942–3
Gough, B. 1518–19
Gould, Steven Jay 1508
Gouldner, A. 1138, 1807, 2202, 2960, 2968,
    2969, 3227, 3232, 3466, 3546, 3679
Gouthro, P. 1708
Gove, W. 2695
governmentality and control 2008–11
    body and 338
    and conservatism 680
    conservatism and 680
    and the disciplinary society 1176–8
    and football 4346
    Foucault and 378, 1122, 2008, 2010, 2077,
        2744, 3566
    and information technology 2332
    new genetics and 338
    technologies of government 2009, 2010
    see also social control

governmentality studies 2008, 2010, 2011
Gowaty, P. 1511
Graaf, P. M. de 383–4, 4797–9, 4810–12
Grace, A. 1708
grade inflation 1085
graduate study 2011–14
   doctoral studies 2012
   master's programs 2012
   women students 2013–14
Grady, J. 2986–9
Graefe, D. R. 1727
graffiti 893–4, 3486
Gramsci, Antonio 2014–16, 2648, 2711,
      4260, 4261
   Althusser on 125
   and Cesarism 412–13
   and civil society 513
   common sense theory 2016
   and cultural resistance 912
   and false consciousness 1569
   and hegemony 2101, 2103
   and ideological hegemony 299, 914, 1569,
      2101, 2103, 2227, 2228, 2838, 3264
   and the intelligentsia 2758
   Marxism 299, 914, 2102
   and mass production 2828–9
   and popular culture 3481–2
   sociological theory 2015–16
   and the subaltern 4998
grand narratives
   collapse of 312, 3557, 3570, 3671
   resistance to 306
grandparenthood 2017–20
   and childcare 1622, 1626, 1841, 2017, 2019,
      2020, 2632–3
   and cultural transmission 2017, 2020
   custodial 95
   demographics 2017–18
   and dependence 2019
   in family systems 2017, 2018–19
   and family transfers 1905
   grandparent role 2019–20
   grandparent–grandchild relationships
      2018, 2019
   individual level 2107
   intergeneration relationships and exchanges
      2380, 2381
   racial/ethic differences 1842, 2018
   socialization agents 2020
   societal level 2017–18
Granovetter, M. 1299, 3332
   and economic sociology 1321, 1760

and embeddedness 1311
and network sociology 2744, 3184
weak-ties principle 315, 2743, 2903, 4485,
   5222–5
Grant, G. 2333
Grant, L. 4941–5
graph-theoretic power index (GPI) 1514
graphical user interfaces (GUIs) 3110
Grasmick, H. G. 1825, 1826
Grateful Dead and Deadheads 3493,
   3504–7
Graunt, J. 1021, 1184, 2087, 4746
gravity theory 4116
Gray, B. H. 2167
Gray, C. 3497
Gray, G. 2830
Gray Plan 2830
Great Awakening 3202
Great Confinement 2694
Great Depression 85, 158, 702, **2020–2**, 2298
   and divorce rates 1207
   and homelessness 2148
   and the life course, effects on 2636, 2638–9
   and nationalistic tendencies 3147
   unemployment 2021, 5090
   and unionism 2519
   and viability of capitalism, doubts about 3647
Great Migration 3747, 3898, 5126
Great Society programs 3173
Greco-Roman classical culture 475
Greece
   axial civilization 520, 521
   births outside marriage 2663
   cultural tourism 920, 921
   diaspora 1151, 3345
   divorce rates 2664
   ethnic cleanisn
   health care system 2055
   immigration 3031, 3032
   lone parenthood 2663, 2664
   nationalism 3145, 3347
   Orthodox Church 3345, 3346, 3347
   polis 497
   population exchange 1451
   religiosity 1056
   slavery in ancient Greece 1463
   teenage motherhood 1728
Greece, ancient
   and ethical universalism 2140
   and federalism 3885
   and magic 2696
   Olympics 3262–3, 4690

polis 2990, 3717
  and public life 3645
greedy institutions 3334
Green Belt movement 1274
green citizenship 499
Green, D. A. 3026
Green, E. 2589
Green, K. 1751
Green, N. 3609, 4960–3
Green, N. S. J. 3609
Green, Nicola 4960–3
Green parties 550, 954, 1417, 1428, 1430, 1431
green politics 3821
Green Revolution 3439
green state 4728
Greenberg, C. 2124
Greenfeld L. 3144, 3155
greenhouse gases 266, 728, 1281, 1423,
  1424, 1425
Greenpeace 1284, 1428, 1429, 1430, 1441, 3212
  organizational form 3259, 3260
  resource mobilization 3067
Greenspan, Alan 2021
Greenwood, R. 3281–5
Greer, Germaine 336
greetings and farewells 1553
Greg, W. R. 3044
Gregson, N. 5217–21
Greil, A. L. 2320–3, 2321
Greimas, A. J. 242
Grenada
  revolution 3907
  US invasion of 2878
Greyser, S. 698
Grierson, J. 1210
Griffin, R. 1644
Griffin, S. 833–4, 1274, 3774
Griffin v. *County School Board of New Kent
  County* 369
Griffith, D. W. 1752
Grills, S. 1126, 1126–31, 1127, 1130
Grimes, M. 3119
Grimke, Angelina 2618, 2838
Grimke, Sarah 2618, 2838
Grimm's law 2539
Grint, K. 2846
grobalization 1963, 1994, **2022–3**
Groenemeyer, A. 1142–5, 2471–4, 4495–507
Groff, R. 873
Gronow, J. 4930–5
Grosby, S. 3156
Gross, E. 1379

Gross, H. 811
Gross, P. 1088, 1509
gross reproduction rate (GRR) 1744
Grossberg, L. 301, 2101
Grossman, H. 245, 865
Grosz, E. 1846, 2612, 3497
Grosz, G. 874
grounded theory 644, **2023–7**, 2968
  and awareness contexts 234
  and case study methods 2977
  constructivist theory 2025–6
  objectivist theory 2026
  and research ethics 1449
grounding 2962
group cohesion 1576–7
  industrialization as threat to 1577
group dynamics 636, 2747, 2748, 2855, 3701
  field theory 2616
  process model 2855
  and reference group theory 3828
group identity *see* collective identity
group interaction *see* collective action; social
  network theory
group organization, *ba* 237, 238
group processes 2027–9
  dyads and triads 1264–7
group randomized trials 2404
group religious practices 1576
group sex 2599
groups 2029–33
  and accommodation 8
  aggregates 2029
  collectivities 2029
  completeness theorem 561
  and deference 990
  democratic group structues 2617
  fight-flight groups 3443
  group formation and maintenance 2031, 2616
  identity politics 2214, 2224
  idioculture 2238
  and impersonal duties 2030
  in-groups and out-groups 315, 2338–9
  pairing groups 3443
  and personal relationships 2030
  primary group functions 2030–1
  secondary group functions 2030–1
  and social distance 4398
  solidarity 2799
  status within 4751
  structure theorem 561
  task interdependence 2616
  see also collective action; intergroup relations

groupthink 2271
Grove, W. R. 1128
Groves, B. 2455
growth coalitions 3115
growth machine 2033–7
growth networks 3115
Gruenbaum, E. 1655
Grünberg, C. 964
Grunstein, A. 1920–6
Grusky, D. 3246–7, 4801–90
Grzywacz, J. G. 1516–18
Guantanamo Bay 1404
Guare, J. 1312
Guatemala
    capitalist growth 390
    charismatic movement 441
    peace processes 3381
    revolution 3907
Guattari, Félix 999, **2037–8**
    and capitalism 3566
    and desire 3574
    and schizoanalysis 2037
    and subjectivity 2038
    and the unconscious 2038
Guba, E. G. 2980, 3355–6
Gubrium, J. 2410, 3137
Gudergan, S. P. 121–3
guerilla activism 340
    anti-branding movement 359
    and anti-imperialism 616
    and nationalist movements 1465
Guerry, A.-M. 828
guestworkers 280, 1342, 1461
Guevara, Ernesto "Che" 36, 394, 616
guided missile technology 3040
guilds 1200
Guillaumin, C. 2113
Guillén, M. F. 1296
Guinea, female genital mutilation 1654
guitar music 3493, 3507
    see also rock 'n' roll
Guldner, G. 811
Gulf Wars 876, 2801
    media management 2879
Gumplowicz, Ludwig 2038–40, 3102
    conquest hypothesis 2039
    and differential power relations 2040
    and Ibn Khaldun 1493
    and individualism 2040
    and intragroup solidarity 2039
    and positivism 2039
    social Darwinism 2039

guns
    gun availability, and the homicide rate 2151–2
    gun control issues 2234, 3087
    pro- and anti-gun movements 1115
Gupta, P. D. 1014–17
Gurock, J. 1937
Gurr, T. R. 954, 1470
Gurvitch, Georges: social change 362, **2040–3**
    dialectics 2042, 2043
    and freedom 2041
    hyperempiricism 2042
    and microsociology 2042
    and the total social phenomenon 2041–2
    and Weber 2040–1
Gurwitsch, A. 1484
Gusdorf, G. 3983
Gusfield, J. 954, 959, 1097, 1227, 1228
Gutenberg, Johannes 2691, 2896, 3635
Gutting, G. 1772
Guttman, A. 1132
Guttman scales 1868
Guyana 8
Guzman, G. 1685
gynecocentric social theory 1941
gypsies *see* Roma people

Haan, J. I. de 2158
Haber, A. 3194
Habermas, Jürgen 406, 1177, 1491, 1758,
        2761, 4187
    and civilization 518
    and communicative action 876, 1146, 1813,
        2030, 2907
    and critical theory 875–6, 2651, 2652
    defense of modernity 3069
    and democracy 2807, 2907
    and ethnic divisions 1458–9
    and Foucault 1777
    and Frankfurt School 865, 875–6
    and hermeneutics 2109
    and ideal speech situation 945, 2653
    and ideological hegemony 2228–9
    and the information society 2327
    and legitimacy 229
    Marxism 3195
    and money 3079
    and neofunctionalism 1812, 1813
    and new social movement theory 3209
    and postmodernism 3570
    public sphere concept 628, 915, 944, 2906–7,
        2908, 3467, 3468, 3470, 3718, 3719,
        3721, 3778

structure and agency 4864
validity claims 3824
habit 260, 1146
habitus/field 327, 336, 346, 1513, **2045–6**, 2616
  Bourdieu and 327, 336, 346, 347–8, 710, 742,
    934, 1309, 2045, 2062, 2534, 2536, 2648,
    2962, 3452, 3582, 3583
  and the civilizing process 530
  and lifestyle reserach 2062
  and management innovators 2731
Habsburg empire 239, 1393, 3145, 3147
hacker and crackers 835, 960, 1162
Hacking, I. 4093–4
Hackworth, J. 1918
Hadfield, L. 4768–70
Hadjicostandi, J. 3031–4, 5146–51
Haeckel, E. 302, 1896
Hafferty, F 2930–2
Hagan, J. 820, 2818
Hagedorn, J. M. 1825, 3967–9
Haggett, C. 4076–9
Hagin, K. 440
hagiography 589
Haignere, L. 1705
Haiti 985
  revolution 3907, 3911, 3915
Hajnal, J. 1047
Hakim, C. 4799–801
Halberstam, J. 1658, 1664
Halbwachs, Maurice 654, **2047–8**
  and collective memory 589, 591–3, 2047–8
Haldane, J. B. S. 1489, 1507
Haley, J. 248
Halfacree, K. H. 1607
Halfon, S. 4082–3
Halfpenny, P. 2968
Hall, D. T. 3286
Hall, E. 239, 1372, 2363, 4626
Hall, Jeffrey E. 4829–33
Hall, John R. 142–4, 4061–4
Hall, L. A. 4283–7
Hall, M. 3014–19
Hall, P. M. 2961, 2962, 4909–14
Hall, Radclyffe 1657–8
Hall, Stuart 344, 611, 1850
  and articulations 2926
  and Birmingham School 297, 298, 299, 301,
    912, 914
  encoding/decoding model 300, 1403–4,
    2882, 2918
  and media ideology effect 2104
  and the new left 3192

and Oriental discourse 3344
and racism 3013
reception theory 210
and youth subcultures 2102, 2649, 3937
Hall, T. D. 2280–5
Halle, D. 2123–6
Haller, A. 1530, 3250
Hallett, T. 2237–8
Halley, Edmund 1021
Hallinan, Maureen T. 131, 1801–3
hallucinogens 1234
Halnon, K. B. 2268–9, 3485–8
halo effect 2270
Halton, E. 3609
Hamaguchi, E. 3218, 4154
Hamas 1315, 2801
Hamelink, C. 966
Hamer, D. 1830, 1831, 1832
Hamilton, L. 2116–18
Hamilton, W. D. 292
Hamish, C. 3400
Hamm, M. 2892
Hammersley, M. 1479–83, 3236–40
Hamoudi, A. 2427
Hanafite School 2426
Hanbalite School 2426
Handelman, J. M. 945–6
handicraft production 2829
Handler, J. 698
Hanegraaff, W. 3192
Haney, L. 2849
Haney, T. J. 2304–7
hanging, execution by 385–6
Hankins, F. H. 131
Hanlon, G. 3664
Hannerz, U. 818
Hannigan, J. 767, 1641–4
Hanukkah 2452
happiness
  age patterns 55–6
  Arendt on 171
  Aristotle on 33
  divorce, effects of 1208
  Freud on 33
  and justice analysis 1196
  public happiness 171
  pursuit of 1207
  and socioeconomic status 625–6
Harary, F. 2854
Haraway, D. 274, 333, 947, 1275, 1668, 1682,
    1711, 2834, 3165, 3496, 3548, 3552, 3561,
    3625–8, 4095

Harcourt, B. 826
Hardey, M. 2388–90
Hardin, G. 1281, 3532
Harding, D. J. 5125–8
Harding, E. 2672
Harding, S. 274, 904, 1154, 1682, 1683, 1701,
    1703, 1711, 1712, 1893, 2396, 3560,
    3561, 4094
Hardt, M. 1396, 2268, 3563, 3564, 3565,
    3567, 4334
Hardy, D. E. 329
Hardy, M. 103–6
Hardy, Simon 3540–2
Hare, R. 838
Hareven, T. K. 2633
Hargreaves, J. 1847, 1879
Harlan, J. 3752
Harlem Renaissance 2444, 3610
Harmonized European Time Use Study 1031
Harney, N. D. 5294–5
Harré, R. 873, 1087
Harreau, J. 1551
Harriet Martineau Sociological Society 133
Harrington, A. 2107–9
Harrington, M. 1613
Harris, B. D. 71–3
Harris, C. 1280
Harris, D. 2101–4
Harris, J. 2174
Harris, M. 1372, 3984
Harris, R. J. 1340–5
Harris, Z. 1179
Harrison, B. 994
Harrison, K. 2323–5
Harrod, M. M. 2206
Harry, J. 2159
Harry, Prince 415
Hart, B. 2655
Hart, C. W. M. 1995
Hart-Cellar Immigration Act 1967 2263
Harter, S. 1797
Hartmann, H. 1705, 1892, 2840, 2842
Hartmann, N. 1363
Hartnett, S. 2420–4
Hartog, J. 3028
Hartsock, N. 1682, 1710, 1712, 1713, 1714
Hartwell, M. 3176
Harvard Business School 2732
Harvey, David 759, 3558, 3589–94
    and American imperialism 2268
    and cultural change 2649
    and globalization 1958–9, 1961

and primitive accumulation 2817
    urban sociology 389, 501
Harvey, J. 2092, 4693–5
Hasegawa, K. 967–9, 2126–7, 2325–6, 2656–9,
    3476–7, 4526–7, 4855–6
hashish 2800
Hasidism 2302, 2764
Hassan, I. 3496
Hassan, N. 2801
Hassan, R. 2801
Hassrick, E. M. 4045–8
Hatch, J. A. 5083–5
Hatch, M. J. 2733
Hatcher, R. 310
hate crime laws 1099
hate crimes 1218, **2048–50**
    against immigramts 3012
    anti-Semitism 153
    defensive hate crimes 2049
    gay bashing 1829–30
    and homophobic violence 2156
    mission offenses 2049
    retaliatory hate crimes 2049
    thrill hate crimes 2049
hate groups 1825
    maternal rhetoric 2848
    see also white supremacists
Haug, M. 2076, 3658
Hauriou, M. 2344
Hauser, P. 132
Hauser, R. M. 2369, 2378
Haussmann, Baron 1763
Hawai'i 2280
Hawkes, G. 3411–13
Hawkins, N. 2934
Hawks, Howard 218
Hawthorne Effect 429, **2050**–1, 2712,
    2716, 2747
Hay, D. F. 830
Hayami, A. 1046
Hayashi, A. M. 982
Hayden, C. 1674
Hayden, D. 1551
hayden, T. 3194
Hayek, F. 5–17, 808, 1188, 2622, 2777, 2779
Hayes, J. H. 3153, 3155, 3176
Hayles, K. 3497
Haymarket Square Riot (1886) 2004, 2007
Hays, S. 939, 940, 3104
Hayward, K. 165–6
Hayward, M. 2097
Hayward, M. D. 2095–8

Haywoode, T. 1705
Hazama, H. 2436, 3170
hazing rituals 2122, 4226
Head Start 1604, 1613, 1884, 2463, 4050–1
headscarf controversy 2532, 3108
Healey, D. 4223–7
health
    and age identity 50
    aging and health policy 71–3, 899, 900–1
    cultural definitions 2070
    definitions 1864, 2070, 2078
    divorce, effects of 1208
    and educational attainment 1327
    and gender 1864–5
    and human rights 2184
    and interpersonal relationships 2391
    intervention studies 2403
    medicalization 1699
    and poverty, impact of 2315
    racial/ethnic disparities 1842, 3733
    and racism 2078–9
    self-reported health (SRH) 2085
    sex-based differences 1864–5, 1865
    and social capital 4359
    and socioeconomic status 99–100, 4590–3
    symbolic definitions 2070
    WHO definition 2313
    wired self-help 2389
    see also medical sociology; mental disorders;
        women's health
health behavior 2051–2
    cultural determinants 2060
    ethnic differences 2058, 2060
    exercise and fitness 1516–17
    and health inequalities 2089
    and health locus of control 2063–4
    and help-seeking 2104–7
    and religious involvement 2081
    see also illness behavior
Health Belief Model (HBM) 2058, 2083
health care
    access to 2074, 2079
    acute care service 72, 73
    bureaucratic control systems 2709
    buyer-based system 2709
    chronic care service 72, 73
    and cultural feminism 904
    cultural means of health promotion 2080
    and decision-making 984
    and demography of aging 69
    ethical dilemmas 2710
    and gender mainstreaming 1855, **1869–70**

government sponsored 840
    and health inequalities 2089
    health-care seeking patterns 2067–8
    immigrant access to 3033
    interventions 2404
    lay-referral network 2080
    and marital status 2110
    older people 102
    provider-driven 2709
    public system 2080
    rationing 1903
    and religiosity 901
    service utilization 2104
    utilization, class differentials 2628
    utilization, determinants of 2068, 2315
health care delivery systems 2052–8
    aging and health policy 72
    boundary maintaining autonomy 2052
    and complementary and alternative
        medicine 632
    consensus conferences 691
    coordination 2052
    decentralization 2056
    and deinstitutionalization 993–8
    free market model 2054
    functional specificity 2052
    gender bias 1844–5
    and gender mainstreaming 1870
    goal-setting 2052
    health maintenance organizations 2065–6
    home health care services 2070
    hospitals 2165–8
    and illness behavior 2242–3
    and impact of litigation 2928
    and infant, child, and maternal health and
        mortality 2320
    managed care 1111, 2709–10
    and medical sociology 2932, 2933, 2935
    NHS model 2055, 2056
    and professional dominance in medicine
        3657
    social insurance system 2054–6
    socialist medicine 4555–7
    socialized medicine 4580–1
    Soviet model 2055, 2056
    state funding 2054
    structural differentiation 2052
    see also community-based care
health and culture 2058–61
    health care delivery systems 2056
    and illness behavior 2243
    see also smoking

health expectancy research 2098
health inequalities
  and adult living conditions 2089
  Black Report on Inequalities in Health 2086
  causes 2088–9
  changes over time 2089–90
  and class 2935
  and early life conditions 2089
  gendered 2089
  and health behaviors 2089
  and health care impacts 2089
  and life stage 2089
  and medical sociology 2935
  and social class 2086–91
  social selection explanation 2088
health insurance 86, 550, 1111, 1904, 2054,
  2068–9
  uninsured patients 2069, 2070, 2244
health lifestyles 2061–3
  and class 2062
  and gender 2062
  and health behavior patterns 2052
  and illness behavior 2242
  and religious behavior 2081
health locus of control 2063–4
  and class 2063
  scales 2063
Health Locus of Control scale 2063
health maintenance organization 998, **2065–6**
  group HMOs 2065
  independent pratice associations (IPAs) 2065
  and managed care 2709
  mixed HMOs 2065
  network HMOs 2065
  preferred provider organizations (PPOs) 2065
  prepaid group, practices (PGPs) 2065
health and medicine 2067–72
  health care utilization 2067–9
health, neighborhood disadvantage 2072–5
health problems
  school drop-out as predictor for 1229
  social role 2076
  unemployment and 1591
  see also chronic illness and disability;
    disability; disease; mental disorder
health professions and occupations 2075–8
  medical school socialization 2930–1
health and race 2078–81, 3756–60
  and help-seeking patterns 2069
  personally medicated racism 2080
health and religion 2081–3
health risk behavior 2083–5

  and neighborhood influence 2073
  see also alcoholism and alcohol abuse; drug
    use; smoking
health and social class 2086–91
  and health lifestyles 2062
  and health locus of control 2063–4
health sociology *see* medical sociology
health and sport 2091–5
  sports injuries 2093–4
health technology assessment (HTA) 691–2
health and wealth gospel 439
healthy life expectancy 394, **2095–8**, 2668,
  3098, 3901
  active life expectancy 94
  capitalist growth and 390
  and death 973
  delining 1026
  demographic transition theory 1036
  and demography of aging 68, 70
  disability-free expectancy 2096
  disease-free expectancy 2096
  and family demography 1585–6
  and family diversity 1589
  and gender 1156, 1586, 1864, 2097, 2668,
    3902, 5276
  health-adjusted expectancy 2096
  and industrialization 2298
  life-table analysis 1023, 1024–5
  measures 2095–7, 3096–7
  and Physical Quality of Life Index 1001
  prevalence rates 2096, 2097
  social indicators 4420
  Sullivan method 2096–7
  technological developments, benefits of 101
  UN estimates 3097
  variation across countries 1044
  see also mortality; specific countries
Heaphy, B. 2606–9, 3995–8
Hearn, J. 1891, 1895, 3319–21
Hearst, William Randolph 2873, 2897
Heath, S. 2655, 5305–8
Heaven's Gate 886
Hebdige, D. 298, 301, 742, 912, 914, 1915,
  2649, 3135
Hebert, R. 1316
hebophilia 3386
Hecataeus of Miletus 147, 909
Hechter, M. 1464, 1466, 1468, 3149, 3232
Heckert, D. A. 3542–4
Heckert, D. M. 3542–4, 3543
Hediger, H. 2362
hedonical relevance 205

hedonism 325, 751, 2826
Heelas, P. 3190
Heeren, J. W. 1084–6
Heffetz, O. 683
Hefner, C. 3418
Hefner, H. 3418
Hegel, G. W. F. 874, 1287, **2098–9**, 2806
   and Absolute Spirit 2807, 2808, 2925,
     3819, 4637
   Althusser and 125
   and civil society 513, 2099
   and consciousness 1147, 1148, 2097, 2807
   and contradiction 1147
   and determinate negation 2808
   and difference 1147
   and Engels 1408
   Hegelian dialectic 999, 1146, 1147, 1149,
     1408, 2098, 2099, 2760, 2837, 3820
   Hegelian philosophy 2760
   historicism 2808
   historicizing phenomenology 2760
   and identity 1147
   and knowledge 1147
   master–slave dialectic 2808
   and mediation 2924–5
   moral system 1083
   philosophical idealism 2837
   and positivism 2187
   radical conflict perspectives 666
   and the state 2806, 2807, 2925
hegemonic complicity 2100
hegemonic masculinity 735, 1663, 1664,
   1665, 1668, 1755, 1878, **2099–101**, 2222,
   4265, 4673
hegemony 677
   Birmingham School and 297, 299
   cultural hegemony 297, 3597
   and cultural resistance 912
   ethnic 660
   resistance to 299
   see also ideological hegemony
hegemony and the media 2101–4
   and encoding/decoding 1404
   and music 3129–30
Hegtvedt, K. A. 4432–6
Heidegger, Martin 874, 2680
   and Adorno 28
   and deconstruction 986
   existentialism 2760, 3402
   and hermeneutics 2108
   ontological concerns 2108
   and technology 2333

Heider, F. 205, 559–62, 3701
   balance theory 559–62
Heilbroner, R. 1384, 1386
Heilbrun, B. 3555
Heinemann, G. D. 1935
heirlooms 745
Heise, D. R. 35, 1380, 1383
Hekma, G. 1745–7, 2157–63, 3985–7
Held, D. 1961
heliotropism 3484
Heller, A. 1375–6, 3068, 3069, 3466
Hell's Angels 1078
help-seeking 2104–7
   health care 2070, 5277
helping behaviors 3678–9
   evolutionary theory 3680
   and symbolic interactionism 3680
   see also altruism
Hemlock Society 1497
Hendershott, A. 978–9
Henderson, C. R. 24, 442, 443, 446
Henderson, L. 1555, 2932, 3375
Hendricks, J. 1932–4, 2592–4
Hendrix, Jimi 3503, **3507**
Hennessy, R. 1714
Henning, C. 1188–9, 2230–2, 2344–5, 3595–6
Hennion, A. 20, 746, 2905
Henricks, T. 3413–17
Henry, L. 1045
Henry, S. 1086–92
Henry, W. 1928
Henschel, M. 2440
Henson, R. K. 805–7, 3848–51
Hepatitis B 2078
Hepworth, W. 1930
Heraclitus 197
herbalism 631, 632, 2079
Herberg, W. 1052
Hercowitz, Z. 3028
herd mentality 896
Herder, J. G. 148, 3153, 3154
Hering, S. 4537–41
heritability
   intelligence 263–4, 2360
   sexual orientation 1830–1, 1832
Heritage, J. 2363
heritage sites 763
heritage tourism 919, 920
Hermalin, B. 950
Herman, D. 1984
Herman, E. 2887, 3674
Hermanowicz, J. C. 3665–9

hermaphroditism 301, 302
  stigma 323
hermeneutic circle 2108, 3695, 3823, 4107
hermeneutics 1434, 2107–9
  and biography 287
  and ethnography 1480
  Gellner and 1838
  hermeneutic approach to sociology 1397
  metatheory 2964
  and organizational culture 951
  philosophical hermeneutics 1435
  of suspicion 1481, 2231
Hermet, G. 3539
Hernandez, D. J. 970–2
Herndon, A. 1699
Hero, R. 2550
Herodotus of Halicarnassus 147, 186, 909
heroin 797–8, 1233, 1234, 1236, 1238
Herrnstein, R. J. 263–5, 837
Herskovits, M. 1083
Herskovits, N. 909
Herzlich, C. 2051
Herzog, H. 3779, 3780
Hess, Beth 1931–2
Hess, Martin 4633–5
Hess, Moses 1408, 2808
hetaerism 2858
heterarchy 5069
heterogeneity
  and global culture 1965
  and glocalization 2022
  heterogeneity principle 74
heteronomy 407
heteronormativity 2111, 2114, 2154–5, 2613, 4266
heterosexism 639, 2154
heterosexual feminism 2113
heterosexual identity 2115
heterosexual imaginary 2109–11
heterosexuality 334, 2111–16
  compulsory heterosexuality 638–9, 2113,
    2155, 2253, 2602
  construction of 332
  and cultural feminism 904
  dominant discourse 332
  dualist structures of 1275
  economy of 302
  and eroticism 2111
  feminist critique 2113–14, 4266
  framing 1836
  and gender 2111–12, 2114
  hegemonic understandings of 638, 1679
  heterosexual identity 2115, 2153, 3651

heterosexual–homosexual continuum 2468
heterosexual/homosexual distinction 2112,
    2113, 2114
  institutionalization 606, 638–9, 2110,
    2111, 4266
  and legal studies 4268–9, 4270
  naturalization of 638
  and non-human animals 639
  and patriarchy 2601, 2602
  and plastic sexuality 3412
  postmodern feminist critique 3559–60
  and privilege, reproduction of 3651
  privileging 1681, 2113, 2115
  ritual 3729
  and same-sex activity 2610
  social construction 3728
  social practices 2110
  state recognition 2111
Hetherington, E. M. 1208
Heugens, P.M.A.R. 395, 3326–31
heuristic, positive/negative 4085
Heusch, L. de 3983–4
hexis 327, 336
Hicks, M. 2774
Hidalgo, M. 414
hidden curriculum 2116–18
  conflict perspective 2116–17
  and educational segregation 1860
  functionalist perspective 2116, 2117
  and gender bias 1844
  and learning opportunities 3271
  and school sport 2121–2
  and stratification 2117
  symbolic interactionist perspective 2116, 2117
hidden economy 1411
hierarchical culture 3929
hierarchical linear models 2118–20
hierarchy
  academic 600–1
  authority of 3463–4
  and biomedicine 631
  bourgeois status hierarchies and commodity
    relations 609
  church 483
  and conservatism 679
  and consumption 934
  and cultural feminism 903
  curricular hierarchies 1339
  and democracy 1004
  flattened hierarchies 1895
  and the hidden curriculum 2118
  hierarchical self-ranking 2100

managerial 3328
and medical pluralism 630
organizational hierarchy 1892, 3464
post-hierarchical society 3464, 3465
and power networks 1355
racial and ethnic hierarchies 3760–3
see also status
hierophany 3520
Higgins, M. 353–7
Higgs, D. 2159
high modernism 2822, 2823
high school proms 725–6
high school sports 2120–3
and ethnic identity 2122
gendered nature 2122
prioritizing of male sports 2118
highbrow/lowbrow 2123–6, 4934
and high art 1753, 1754
high-speed transportation pollution 2126–7, 4855
linear and planar zones 3476
and local residents' movements 3477
structural strains 4855–6
higher education
affirmative action 39–40
graduate and professional 601
mass higher education 602
roots of 599
utilitarian approach to 600
see also colleges and universities
highly active antiretroviral therapy (HAART) 2542
hihra 4214–15
Hilferding, R. 344, 2267
Hilfiger, Tommy 704
Hill, Anita 309
Hill, Annette 3490–2
Hill, M. R. 130–4, 1941–2, 2170–1, 3585–7, 5216
Hillary, Edmund 4712
Hilliard, B. 1574–80
Hills, M. 421–2, 1637–41, 1639, 2402–3
Hillsman, S. T. 132
Hillyard, D. 1095–100
Hilton-Morrow, W. 2107–9
hinayana Buddhist tradition 371
Hindeland, M. 837
Hindess, B. 807–9
Hindin, M. J. 2313–20, 3951–4
Hindu-Bali 671
Hinduism 520, 523, 1980, **2128–32**, 4374
al-Biruni and 112

and asceticism 188
caste system 404–5
Christian synthesis 2131
folk Hinduism 1764–6
fundamentalism 1813
global activities 1982
global Hinduism 2131
and Indology 1492
millenarianism 3047
nationalism 1982
and political mobilization 2132
roots of 2128–9
and the sacred 3972
social framework 2129–30
theistic devotionalism 2131
theocracy 3094
Vedantic Hinduism 2131, 3854
Hinote, B. P. 2063–4
Hinton, J. 1364
Hinze, S. W. 1718–25
hip-hop 309, 327, 704, 3128, **3486–8**
and consumption 708
and cultural studies 916
digital aesthetics 1163
graffiti 893–4
and nationalist consciousness 3135
and women 3487
hippies 809, 2832
Hippocrates 2694
Hirsch, F. 2192
Hirsch, P. 1760
Hirschfeld, Magnus 2132–3
and sexual reform 331
sexuality research 2132–3, 2158
Hirschi, T. 819, 837, 838, 845, 847, 851, 1104, 1120, 3959
Hirschman, A. 618, 1760
Hirschman, C. 4374–80
Hirst, P. 1961, 3424
Hispanics
adolescent fertility 1728
and division of household labor 1204
education 370, 1330
educational attainment 1335, 1343–4
exogamy 1405
families 1591
fatherhood 1603, 1626
and fertility 2018
grandparenting 1842, 2020
health problems 2078
and helping behaviors 3681
hypersegregation 2196, 2198

Hispanics (*cont'd*)
  identity 3757
  and kindergarten 2463
  marriage 566
  morbidity and mortality 3757
  and nest-leaving 2572
  nonmarital births 1721, 1735
  and occupational prestige 1342
  and parental involvement in education 3358
  and poverty 1591
  residential segregation 3888, 3889
  and school dropout 1230
  unemployment 4030
historical and comparative methods
  2133–6
  Hegelian notion of history 2804
historical demography 1045–6
historical institutionalism 3461
historical linguistics 2535
historical materialism 350–1, 2837–8
  capitalist critique 2836
  and dialectical materialism 2837
  Engels and Marx and 350, 865
  feminist 1710–11, 1713
  Gramsci and 2015
  Lukács and 2679
  Marxist 350, 865, 896, 1067, 1150, 1293,
    1711, 2298, 2806, 2808, 2812, 2813–14,
    3437, 3670
  revisionism 350–1
  Simmel and 2679
historical particularism 149
historical sociology 176
  event history analysis 1017–21, 3062
  life histories 2641–4
  Marxist 2816
historical time 73
historicism 2757
historiography, Annales School 517, 1395
history
  Certeau's project 424
  and collective memory 588–9
  cyclical processes 361
  historiographic operation 424
  mythologization of 3139
  path dependent 642
  positivism 592
  total history 360
Hitchcock, Alfred 218, 1916
Hitler, Adolf 240, 616, 865, 876, 1805, 2031,
  2142, 2875, 3143, 3657, 3876
  authoritarian personality 220

charismatic leadership 2566, 3597
  and Nietzsche 3214
  and racial myths 3673
HIV/AIDS
  in Africa 106, 4210–11
  in Asia 4217
  caregiving 401
  children 2137, 2139, 2319, 3099
  community responses 2606, 2608, 3995–6
  and condom use 1610
  demographic effects 10444
  and disease burden 1864
  and ethnicity 2080
  and identity reconstruction 2248
  and illness behavior 2241
  and the illness experience 2248
  impact on gay and lesbian movement 1834–5
  and moral entrepreneurship 3087
  mortality impacts 3099
  and older people 2542
  pandemic 1984–5, 2137, 4093
  and pornography performers 3542
  prevention/response 2060
  and public health authorities 2105
  research 2347
  and risky sexual behavior 1609
  and safer sex 3278, 3987–9
  and sex education 4195–6
  sex panic 4199
  and sex tourism 4202
  and sex work 1660
  sex-specific susceptibility 3535
  and sexual health agendas 4236–7
  and sexual politics 4247
  spread of 1610, 1611, 2059
  transmission 1237
  women's vulnerability to 333, 2309, 2319,
    2398, 3535–6
  see also AIDS, sociology of
HIV/AIDS and population 106–10, **2136–40**
  demographic dimensions 2137–9
  demographic transition paradigm 2136
  epidemiological transition paradigm 2136
  modeling HIV impacts 2137
  spread of 2136
Ho Chi Minh 2838, 3147
Hobbes, Thomas 512, 3463, 3466, 3597,
  4133, 4601
Hobbs, S. 3032
hobby farming 1550
hobbyists 2597
Hoberman, J. 1241

Hobhouse, L. T. **2140–2**, 2622
hobohemias 2147
Hobsbawm, E. 414, 2267, 2648, 2901, 3156
Hobson, D. 914, 2922
Hobson, J. 603, 1394, 2267, 2686
Hoch, P. 3473
Hochschild, A. 365, 1032, 1379, 4565
   and dual-earner households 1881
   and emotions 1382, 1390, 3950
   and intimacy 2413
Hodson, R. 119–21
Hoess, R. 2143
Hofferth, S. L. 1601–5
Hofstadter, R. 4391
Hogan, J. 2178–82, 2287–93
Hogan, T. 3423–4
Hoggart, R. 297, 298, 897, 913, 914, 2649, 2691
holidays
   beach holidays 3484–5
   consumption and 740
   and consumption rituals 753
   Jewish 2452
   religious holidays 752
holism 1436
holistic health movement 630, 631–2, 752
Holland, D. 2642
Hollands, R. 1643
Hollingshead, A. 773, 2933
Hollis, F. 4542
Hollywood film industry 1753, 1754–5, 2124,
   2873–4, 3483
Hollywood star system 419
Holmes, M. 810–2
Holmes, O. W. 3609
Holocaust 1451, 1458, **2142–3**
   and authoritarian cultural traits 3034
   bureaucratic organization 3304
   and collective memory 589
   and collective trauma 595
   German civilian involvement 1646
   and Jehovah's Witnesses 2439
   and postmodern social theory 3571
   and race hygiene 4115
   and reparations 3876
   role and scope of anti-Semitism 152, 159
   and secrecy 4134
Holstein, J. 2410, 3137
Holt, D. B. 685, 742, 1189–91
Holt, J. 4032
Holton, R. J. 1969
Holy Land 591
Holy See 408, 409–10

Holzner, B. 3647–9, 5071–5
Homans, George 640, **2144–6**
   and behaviorism 1812
   exchange theory 314, 1368, 1512, 2032, 2361
   and group dynamics 2032, 2355, 2855
   and relational cohesion theory 3848
   and social process 642
   and social reality 2144, 2998–9
   social system theory 2144
   and theory 2144
home economics movement 1202, 1205
home ownership, and wealth 2313
Home Shopping Network 759
homelessness 998, **2146–51**
   causes 2149
   characteristics 2148–9
   criminalization 1097
   and domestic violence 1220
   estimates of 2148
   pre-industrial 2147
   responses to 2149
   survival strategies 2149–50
   and transcarceration 5035
homeopathy 630, 631, 632, 4092
Homer 186
homicide 820, 974, **2151–2**, 2555, 5194
   biosocial theory 293
   black males 544, 3734
   and the death penalty 977
   and domestic violence 1219
   and epidemiological method 1434
   female offenders 4192
   female victims 1219
   and gun availability 2151–2
   and hate crime 2048
   homicide rates and rape rates 3783, 3786
   honor killings 2303
   index crime 2277, 2278
   inductive approach 1398
   and infidelity 2324
   interracial and intraracial 544, 3735
   and mental illness 998
   and mercy killing 1497
   racial patterns 3735
   school-aged youth 842
   spousal homicide 1857, 2324
   UCR definition 2278
   US 821
homo economicus 936
homoeroticism 2155
   and sport 4293
homogamy 203, 674–6

homogeneity
  cultural 345, 1991
  linguistic homogeneity 3156
  and nationalism 3150, 3158
homogenization 818
  and assimilation 3143
  of body cultures 1989
  cultural 1963
  and ethnic cleansing 3143
  and global consumption 1963
  and global culture 1965, 1970
  and globalization of sport 1989
  and indigenous peoples, integration of 2948–9
  political 3153–4
homomorphism 2856
homophily 203, 795, 1793, 1931, 3529
homophobia 2152–4, 4273
  assessing levels of 2152–3
  and compulsory heterosexuality 639
  and deviance in sport 1134
  and feminism 1677, 1679, 2602, 3775
  and fundamentalism 1984
  and gay bashing 1828–9
  and masculine sexuality 4273
  and patriarchy 3651
  in political life 2611
  and privilege, reproduction of 3651
  and sport 1877, 1878, 2122
  in women's liberation groups 1834
homophobia and heterosexism 2154–7
  gay and lesbian movement and 606
homosexuality 2157–63
  and aging 901
  Asian 4214–5
  biological theory 2132
  biomedical claims 2613
  changes in sexual identity 2162
  Christian alliances against 1984
  coming-out narratives 303, 606
  conservatism and 680
  and consumption 4257
  convenience sample studies 789
  conversion therapy 1112
  criminalization 2156
  deconstructive perspectives 2159
  decriminalization 2610
  degeneracy thesis 2493
  demedicalization 1112
  denigration of in sport 1878, 1879
  and deviance 1082, 1096, 1112, 1835,
    2599, 4264
  disease metaphor 1833

  and drag queens 121–4
  early medical research 2158
  Ellis and 1365
  and fashion 719
  and friendship 1804
  gay bashing 1828–9
  and the gay gene 331, 1830–3
  genetic component 111
  and gentrification 1919
  global gays 2161
  and heterosex 2610
  historical-sociological perspectives 2159–60
  and the Holocaust 1489, 1496, 2156
  homo–heterosexual scale 2161
  homosexual gene 331
  homosexual identity 1835, 1878, 3730, 4239–40
  identity 4239–40
  illegality 331–2
  and Islamic culture 2429
  Kinsey Institute research 2468
  Krafft-Ebing and 2493
  Latin American culture 4219
  and male rape 2703
  marginality 2763
  medicalization 3651
  minority group perspective 1835
  othering 331
  pathologizing 606, 639
  politicization of 4246
  premodern societies 4247
  psychological perspective 2158, 2159
  religious responses to 4277
  ritual context 1078
  self-identification 2161
  self-reporting 1129
  sexual citizenship 4206
  sexual migration 4220–1
  sexuality research 302, 331, 4289
  social construction 1437, 3728
  social context 2157
  sociological perspective 2158
  sociology of 2158, 4264, 4265
  and sport 2222
  stigma 324, 583, 639, 1833, 2009, 2159
  sublimated homosexuality 2153
  and subordinated masculinity 2100
  symbolic interactionist perspective 2159
  urban living and consumption 766, 768
  violence against 1098
  young gay men 466
  see also friendships of gay, lesbian, and
    bisexual people; lesbianism

homosociality 4214
Honea, Joy Crissey 4653–6
Hong Kong 765, 4376
  colonial language 2260
  Confucianism 670
  economic success 2299
  migrant domestic workers 1716
  public school system 4049
  Taoism 4929–30
Honneth, A. 876, 1177
honor killings 2303
hooks, bell 306, 308, 866, 1708, 3119
  and cultural critique 897
  and educational praxis 3613
  and engaged pedagogy 1708–9
  and multiracial feminism 3119
Hopkins, T. K. 2838
Horkheimer, Max 2163–5
  and Adorno 27, 2163, 2164, 2165
  biography 2163–5
  and Brecht 268
  and consumption 741
  cultural critique 610, 1754, 2881, 3482
  culture industry thesis 416, 942, 2824
  and the Frankfurt School 865, 874, 875, 897,
    1569, 2163, 2165, 2881
  neo-Marxism 869
  and sport 2235
hormonal activity patterns
  sex hormones 331
  and social behavior 292–3
hormone replacement therapy (HRT)
    2541, 2542
Horney, K. 2760
Hornsby, A. M. 4615–17
Horowitz, D. 1826, 3922–3
Horrocks, R. 1913–17
horror movies 1639, 1915
horse racing 1820, 1821, 4671, 4696
Horsman, R. 2755
horticultural societies 293, 4821–2, 5259–60
horticulture, and hybridity 2189
Horton, D. 2921
Horton, R. 2698
Hoskins, J. 287–91
hospice movement 973
  lifeworld and system perspectives 2653
hospitals 2165–8
  "community benefit" requirement 2166
  deinstitutionalization 993–8, 2695
  for-profit hospitals 2167
  and health care delivery systems 2054

not-for-profit hospitals 2166
  program and performance auditing 213
  public hospitals 2167
  rationalization process 2883
  "relief of poverty" requirement 2166
  see also mental hospitals
host hostility 3008
hot spots of crime 828–9
hot towns 1551
Hotz, V. J. 1727
Houellebecq, M. 3497
Houlihan, B. 3472–6
Houlihan, Barrie 3472–6
Hoult, T. F. 534
house arrest 803
House, D. 2214
House, J. 4403–6
House, James 4403–6
House Un-American Activities Committee
    2874
household appliances 1202
household consumption
  children and 695
  women and 1202
household division of labor
  biosociological theory 293
  food preparation 722
  ritual performance roles 753
household economies 1299
household formation 1046, 1047
household labor, and bifurcated consciousness
    274
households 2168–70, 3720
  adult children in the parental home 2169,
    2438, 2570–2, 2573–4
  chonaikai 472
  commercialization of household life 1849
  composition 1584, 2169–70
  conspicuous consumption and 683
  consumption, children and 695
  consumption, women and 1202
  definitions 1584, 1619, 2168–9
  economies 1386
  and *en* 1401
  and family demography 1584
  and family, distinguished 1618–19
  family household 1584
  and framing theory 238
  gay and lesbian-headed households 1592
  gender bias 1844
  and *ie* 2238–41
  lesbian partners 1590

households (*cont'd*)
  money economy 1385
  non-familial shared households 1584,
    1585, 2169
  oikonomia 1385
  one-person non-family households 1586
  patriarchal households 1844
  pre-industrial 1202
  and the private sphere 3717
  reduced size of 1586
  self-provisioning 748
  size 1586
  see also family structure
housekeeping system 3081, 3082
Houser, Jeffrey 4484–6
housework, Marianne Weber on 2768
  see also divisions of household labor
housing
  affordable 503
  community housing 997
  and the concentric zone model 1278
  and consumption 748
  houshold patterns, impact on 2170
  and human rights 2184
  and invasion-succession 2419
  multifamily housing 1424
  public housing assistance 1720
  and redlining 3825–7
  residential segregation 316–18
  retirement communities 3903–6
  see also gentrification; public housing;
    residential segregation
housing inequality 503
Houston, ethnic enclaves 1452, 1454
Houston, C. H. 369
Houston, Charles Hamilton 369
Hout, M. 2369, 2379
Hovland, C. 3672
Howard, Ebenezer 502
Howard, George Elliott 130, **2170–1**
  ASA president 130
Howard, K. 2214
Howson, C. 2287
Hoyt, H. 3, 1279
Hoyt, Homer 3, 1279
Hrdy, S. 1511, 3104–5
Hsiao, M. 3199
Hsu, F. 1402
Hsu, Francis 1402
Hubbard, L. R. 3202, 4117, 4118
Hubbard, P. 1643
Hudis, Peter 1146–50

Huffer, David 3715–7
Hughes, E. C. 320, 1996, 2075–6, 2362, 2472,
    2961, 3286, 3331, 3661
Hughes, G. 2208
Hughes, Helen McGill 1670
Hughes, J. 4343–5
Hughes, Langston 2444
Hughes, Robert 1241
Huizinga, J. 3413, 3415, 3416, 4647
Hull, C. 257
Hull, Gloria 308
Hull-House 23, 444, 446, 3512, 3611
  see also Addams, Jane
human capital 1321
  and economic development 2653–4
  and education 1323, 1331, 1332, 1333
  and homelessness 2149
  and status attainment 4754
Human Development Index (World Bank), as
    predictor of democracy 1001
human dignity 1447
  and genetic engineering 1491
Human Genome Project 337, 1490, 1684, 1830,
    1906, 2937
human genome and the science of life
    2171–5
Human Growth Foundation (HGF) 1111
human needs, hierarchy of 2629, 4124
Human Relations School 2713
human reproduction, selective reproduction
    2937–8
human–non-human interaction 2175–8,
    3627
  animal rights movement 138–9
  anthrozoology 150–1
  companion species 150
  zoos 3500–3
human resource management 355,
    2178–82, 2289
  and diversity issues 2180
  ethical dimension 2182
  and the Hawthorne experiments 2747
  and knowledge management 2479
  and labor–management relations 2509,
    2510
  and occupational mobility 3288
  in voluntary organizations 3341
  within transnational corporations 5070
  workers' participation in management
    (WPM) 2752–4
human rights 2182–5
  AIDS and human rights violations 108–9

children 455
civil minimum 505–6
and community media 628
conservatism and 680
crime and 819, 835
and cultural relativism 909, 2183
and the death penalty 976
definitions 2182
and discrimination 1183
early declarations 2183
female migrant workers 1717
and gay and lesbian movement 2610
and global justice movements 1976
human rights INGOs 3212
and infant, child, and maternal health and
    mortality 2317
internationalization 2182–3
legal discourse 2156, 2182, 2183–4
and the market 1310
and media regulation 2913
moral discourse 2182
normative approach 4587
and sovereign rights 1952
and sport 4348–9
universal rights 1952, 2183
violations 835
see also Civil Right Movement
human rights movements 1472
Human Rights Watch 2156
Humanae Vitae 4141
humanism 1436, **2186–8**
and agency 60
humanist atheism 197
humanist sociology 2187–8
Marxist humanism 324
materialist humanism 1748
and modernization theory 3071
and natural magic 2697
see also posthumanism
humanitarian intervention 2184
Hume, David 2706
and causality 653
and empiricism 1397, 1434
and inductive inference 2286
philosophical idealism 2837
and prosocial behavior 3679
and religion 3629
Hummer, R. A. 3756–60
Hummon, Norman 314
Humphery, K. 4888–90
Humphreys, L. 2159, 2610
Humphries, D. 1856

Huneker, J. G. 2958
Hunert, H. 3982
Hungary
    anti-Jewish violence 3428
    and cultural reproduction 911
    Jewish population 2453
    religious schools 4053
    social fluidity 2372
    social security system 2055
    stratification system 889
hunger and malnutrition 1852
Hunt, M. 2958
Hunt, S. 433–7, 537–9, 2832, 3233, 3310–15,
    3972–6, 4524–6, 4532–3
Hunter, A. 3719, 3720
hunter-gathering societies 4821
Huntington, S. 1970, 1991, 3042, 3174
Huntington's disease 2173, 2938
Hurd, R. 1279
Hurst, Damian 1361
Hurston, Zora Neale 2444
Hurtado, A. 3118
Hussayn, T. 181
Husserl, Edmund 2680, 2756
    eidetic reduction 3402, 3403
    and intentionality 3402
    and the lifeworld 2651
    phenomenology 326, 2108, 2651, 2760,
        3401–2, 3403, 4062
Hussites 3409
Hutchinson, A. 1114
Hutchinson, J. 3154, 3157
Hutchison, Ray 388–9, 442–5
Hutter, Jakob 3048
Hutter, Mark 1594–601
Huxley, Aldous 1489, 3495
hybrid consumption 1187
hybridity 288, 1477, **2188–91**
    cultural hybrids 1152
    hybrid consumption 1187
    and management innovation 2737,
        2741–2
hybridization 1992, 1994, 2188, 2189
    and postcolonialism 2983, 2984
Hydén, Lars-Christer 2246–8
hydrodynamics 1757, 1758
hygiene movement 631
hygiene and sociology 2932
Hymes, D. 1181
hyperactivity disorder 1111
    and children and divorce 1623
hypercommodification 760

hyperconsumption/overconsumption 727,
   2191–4
   and advertising 33
   and commodity relations 611
hyperempiricism 2042
hypermedia 3110
hypermedia ethnography 3725
hypermodernity 3566, 3575
hyperrationality 3803
hyperreality 1163, **2194–6**, 2590, 2922
   Baudrillard and 2194, 2195–6, 2925–6
   Eco and 4330
hypersegregation 2196–9
   criteria 2197–8
hypertexts 1164, 3817
   see also text/hypertext
hyperurbanization 3624
hypnosis 3695
hypoactive sexual desire disorder 2541
hypotheses 1554, **2199–200**
   analytic induction 134–5
   endorsement 3167
   hypothesis testing 263, 2199, 4741–3
   hypothesis–evidence relation 1571
   invention stage 3167
   and negative case analysis 3166, 3167
   null-hypothesis significance testing 1346
   refutation stage 3167
   statistical hypotheses 1533
   statistical significance testing and
   see also fact, theory and hypothesis: including
      the history of the scientific fact
hypothetic-deductive method 2968
hypothetic-deductivism 1555, 1556
hypothetico–deductive model of scientific
      enquiry 2286

Iatmul culture, New Guinea 247
Iawo, S. 1692
Ibarra, P. I. 1089, 1091
Ibn Arabi 2003
Ibn Batuta 147
Ibn Khaldun 1493
Ibsen, Henrik 1896–7, 2006
ice hockey 2222
Iceland, health care system 2055
Iceland, J. 2198, 3587–9, 3888–91
Ichthus 440
iconoclasm 408
icons
   high culture icons 3543
   religious 3346

Idahosa, B. 440
ideal speech community 2653
ideal type 2134, **2201–2**
   Lukács and 2678
   Weber and 2201–2, 2678, 5228
identity
   adolescent 773, 1547
   ambiguity 720
   ambivalence 720
   athletic identity 2221–3, 4709
   and behavior 2225
   biracial identity 296
   bisexual identity 303, 304
   border identity 296
   class identity 533, 541
   and community 618, 1476
   and community media 628
   consolidation 1793
   and consumption 745
   corporate identity 353, 354, 355, 730
   corporeal identity 709
   and cultural sociology 926
   definitions 2210–11
   deviant identity 1124, 2207–10, 3505
   dialectic perspective 2211
   diasporic identity 288
   and emotion work 1383
   essentialist perspective 2211, 2215
   ethnic identity 294, 745, 926, 1152, 1405,
      1458, 1459, 1469, 1471, 1476, 1477, 2222,
      3013, 3480
   and exchange network theory 3183
   and false consciousness 1569
   fan identity 1638, 1639
   feminine identity 1850
   food and 721
   and friendships 1793
   gay and lesbian 606, 1834, 1984, 1985, 3729
   gender identity 1662–3, 1664, 2114, 2215
   group identity 298, 1466, 1471
   heterosexual identity 2115, 2153, 3651
   higher-/lower-level identities 2205
   homosexual identity 1835, 3730, 4239–40
   identity change 2208
   identity transformations 2218
   indigenous peoples 2281
   interpretive approaches 2213
   lesbian identity 2604, 2611, 4239–40
   local identity 1476
   marginalized identity 2766
   masculine identity 1862, 1891, 2153, 2222
   micro-politics of 337–8

mixed race identity 295
multiple identities 308
multiracial identity 2219
national identity 745, 926, 957, 1458, 1468,
    1476, 1839, 2248, 2249, 3149, 3156, 3159
online identity 962
organizational identity 353, 354, 355, 356, 2477
performance 1678
and photography 770–1
poststructuralist perspective 2212
product identity 771
protean identity 296
racial 295, 296, 661, 2222, 3761
regional identity 1476
religious identity 198, 2225
rhetoric of identification 354
scripting theories 4122–3
self-definition 1476
self-identification 296, 303, 1457, 2219
self-identity 962, 963
self-reported 1547
self-verification 2219
sexual identity 303, 336, 926, 1437, 2114,
    2793, 3568
sibling identity 558
signifying functions 759
singular identity 296
social constructionist models 2215, 2216
social relationship perspective 2211
spoiled identities 2207, 2208
and stigma 2218
techno-identities 965
transcendent identity 296
verification processes 2206
virtualization 1897
and visual culture 755
worker identity 2724
see also collective identity
Identity Church 2049
identity claims 2221–2
identity construction 2212, 2221, 2222
    biracial 295
    bisexual 303
    consumer 352
    and consumption 710
    and cultural studies 916
    and documentary analysis 1215
    gender identity 1662–3, 1664, 2114, 2215
    girls 726
    identity change 303
    and the lifeworld 2652
    and music 746, 3128

and narrative 3141
and pop culture 730
psychoanalytic perspectives 295
sexual identity 303, 326, 336, 926, 1437,
    2114, 2793, 3568
through cultural oppositions 2153
and values 5170
identity control theory 2202–7, 2226
    resources 2204–5
    symbolic interaction perspective 2203
identity, deviant 1124, **2207–10**, 3505
identity maintenance 2221, 2222
identity: the management of meaning 32,
    2210–14, 2218, 3410
identity performance 2211
identity politics/relational politics 1477,
    1998, 2209, **2214–15**, 2551, 3400
    and assimilation 2945
    civil/territorial perspective 2214
    cultural perspective 2214
    and emotions 2215, 2219
    ethnic perspective 2214
    gay and lesbian identity 4240
    and intersexuality 2399
    and multiculturalism 3106
    Native American 2284
    politics of recognition 4271
    and race/ethnicity 3748
    and the split of the subject 2528
    and tradition 5027
identity reconstruction 2248
identity salience 2224, 2225, 2226
**identity: social psychological aspects
    2216–20**
    age identity 49–51
    autoethnography and 231
    Deadhead community 3505
    and identity control theory 2206
    interactionist perspective 2217
    looking-glass self 2669–71
    personal identities 2217
    and self-narratives 2217–18
    situational perspective 2216–17, 2219
    social construction 2216
    social identities 2216
identity, sport and 2220–3
    national identities 3158–60, 3264
identity standards 2203, 2205, 2206
identity theft 960, 1107
identity theory 2223–6
    and accounts 11
    and the concept of self 4159, 4161–2

identity theory (*cont'd*)
  identity control theory 2202–6
  and justice analysis 1195
  and narrative 3141
  and personal identities 2224
  role identity theory 2211, 2224
  and social categories 2223
  and social identities 2224
  symbolic interactionist perspective 2223, 2224
  see also role theory; self-concept; social
    identity theory
identity-vignettes 1868
ideo–motivation 2432
ideological criticism 2230
ideological hegemony 1964, **2227–30**
  and print media 3639
  reproduction through interpersonal
    interaction 2229
ideological state apparatuses (ISAs) 245–6
ideologues 2230
ideology 2230–2, 2925
  Althusserian theory of 126
  anarchism 136
  apartheid ideology 162
  Aron on 176, 177
  and Birmingham School 297, 299
  collectivist ideologies 2624
  and consciousness 877
  and consumer movements 699
  and critical theory 874
  and direct action 1167
  dominant ideology thesis 931, 1568, 1570,
    1867, 1964
  "end of ideology" thesis 2231
  equity ideology 2585
  expansionist ideology 2267
  and fascism 1655
  and framing 1779
  gender ideology 1668, 1846, 1867–9
  global ideology 1991
  hegemonic masculinity 735, 1663, 1664,
    1665, 1668, 1755, 1878, 2099–101, 2222,
    4265
  ideological belief systems 2756
  and the Industrial Revolution 2296
  lesbian feminism 2602
  magical ideology 2700
  Mannheim and 2483
  Marxist theory 2111
  and myth 3139
  nonevaluative treatment of 2483
  political ideology 925

  poststructuralist critique 913
  Protestant 3690
  public opinion, impact on 3714
  racial ideology 3731
  secular ideologies 2296
  social movement organizations 955
  structuralist critique 913
ideology, economy and 2232–5
  and commodification 610
ideology, sport and 2235–7
ideoscapes 1990
idiocentrism 598
idioculture 2237–8
  and interaction order 2366
idiographic studies 2134
ie 238, **2238–41**
Iijima, N. 4526
Iizuka, K. 3218
illegal immigration 3031–3
  and stress 4833–4
illegitimate births *see* nonmarital fertility
Illich, I. 866, 3657
illiteracy *see* literacy/illiteracy
illness
  biologization of 2172
  recognition and response to 2242
  self-reported symptoms 2243
  somatization 2242
illness behavior 2241–5
  ethnic differences 2058
  gendered 5277
  and health locus of control 2063–4
  and help-seeking 2104–7
  immigrants 2243
  see also sick role
illness or disability career 2106
illness experience 2245–6
  body and 335
  and disease, social causation of 1184–6
  and HIV/AIDS 2248
  and Internet medicine 2389–90
  and marginality 2763
  and medical sociology 2935
  response to 2105
illness narrative 2246–8
  and illness experience 2246
illness/disease dichotomy 2245
image economy 353, 770
image management 2878
images
  cultural and historical framework 771
  image archiving and analysis 2988

image-making 770, 2987
interpretation 770, 772
polysemy 772
in popular culture 2989
representational and rhetorical power 772
and visual sociology 2986–7
see also signs
images, culture of 1969
images of the world 1969
the imaginary 2528
imagination, and action 199
imaginative reconstruction 801
imagined communities 618, 628, **2248–9**
nations as 1468, 2900–1
Imanishi, Kinji 1287–8, **2249–52**
imitation theory 799
and social learning theory 848
immanent difference 999
immanentism, and atheism 197
immaterial labor 3565
immigrant children 2254
adaptation 1270–1
language difficulties 2259
second-generation immigrants 2254
immigrant families 2252–5
demography of 2254
and family migration 1605–8
family reunification migration 3021, 3022
fertility rates 2254
health and survivorship 3758
and illness behavior 2243
lone-parent families 2254
multilocal and multinational 2252
residential segregation 3888
work–family balance 2254
immigrant human capital investment
(ICHI) 3026
immigrant underclass 2306
immigration 2255–8, 3019, 3031, 3032
anti-immigrant sentiment 3748, 4835–6
and assimilation 191–6
and collective trauma 595
and community 618
ethnic enclaves 1452–6
feminization of labor migration 1615–17
and human rights 2256
internal colonialism 603
and the melting pot concept 2944
and occupational segregation 1342
and offset of low fertility levels 1730
settlement patterns 2419
and urban concentration 2306

immigration competition hypothesis 2306
immigration and language 2258–62
immigration policy 2262–6, 3022, 3747
control mechanisms 2256
family reunification criterion 2263, 2264
and the Geneva Convention 2256
and human rights 2256
and language skills 2260–1
and non-immigrants 2262
open-ended regulation 2256
quotas 1453, 2263, 3747
welfare states 2256
Immigration Reform and Control Act (IRCA)
2263, 2265
immitative magic 32
impaired fecundity *see* infertility
imperialism 2266–8
academic imperialism 398, 399
and anthropological ethnography 1482
and assimilation 1393
and capitalism 1394–5
capitalist imperialism 1394–5, 2268
civilizing mission 1505
and colonialism 602–3
"communist imperialism" 2267
cultural imperialism 739, 906–7, 1993
and cultural tourism 920
and the developmental state 1074
and diaspora 1152
and documentaries 1211
economic imperialism 2755
and empire 1393
expansionist ideology 2267
and family systems 1595
and globalization 1950, 1960
imperialist convergence 2267
and industrialization 2297
inter-imperialist rivalries 1394
and the international economy 1944
Islamic 1981
liberal opposition 2267
Luxemburg and 2686
manifest destiny doctrine 2754
medical imperialism 1111
"new" imperialism 2268
and Orientalism 3990
over-stretch 1396
political critique 2267
postcolonial studies of 2982
and separatism 4187–8
and social anthropology 340
and social evolution 1505

imperialism (*cont'd*)
and tourism 1994
and traumatogenic change 595
see also colonialism (neocolonialism); cultural
imperialism
implosion 2268–9, 2692
impression-change equations 37
impression formation 2269–74
and affect control theory 37
balance effect 2273
central organizing traits 2271
confirmation bias 2270
congruency effects 2273
consistency principle 2273
halo effect 2270
and identity 2221
implicit personality theories 2271
morality effect 2272
object salience 2270
primacy effect 2270
recency effect 2270–1
stability principle 2272
trait schemas 2271
transient impressions 37
impression management 1999, 2215, 2221, 2433
devious accounts 13
Impressionism 952, 2238
Imus, D. 2337
in vitro fertilization (IVF) 558, 1907, 2322,
2323, 3206, 4067
incarceration
intelligence test score relation 2360
parents in cohabiting unions 1624
racial variations 3733, 3736, 3738, 3739, 3766
women 1858
see also prisons
incest 309, 1078, 2682, 3228, 5045
inclusion
and collective memory 590
community and 618
and cultural diversity 900–1
and deviance 2208
and disability 1169
and disabled athletes 1172
and gender 901
and poverty 901
inclusive fitness 293
inclusivity, ethnic 1475
income inequality, global 351, **2274–5**
between-nation income inequality 2274, 2276
and ethnicity 1943
and gender 1724

Gini coefficient 1942, 1943
and industrialization 2297
and social class 536
**income inequality and income mobility
2275–7**
and age 58–9
and the elderly 3254–6
and gender 1204
and justice analysis 1196
and literacy differentials 2656
longitudinal studies 3256
methods of analysis 2373–9
and the *nenko* wage system 3171
and race 993
Robin Hood hypothesis 2276
stratification theories 98, 4803–4
and wealth inequality 2310
see also comparable worth; poverty; wages gap
income poverty 3587, 3588
income redistribution 392
incompatibility thesis 5078
indemnity health insurance 2065, 2066
Independent Living Movement 480
independent pratice associations (IPAs) 2065
independent variables 1897, 1898
Indergaard, M. 422–3, 2297–300
index crime 2277–8
and juvenile delinquency 2454
property crime 3675
Index of Dissimilarity 2197
Index of Incapacity 1935
Index Librorum Prohibitorum 490
Index of Power Resources 1002
indexes, citation indexing 489–90
India 344
affirmative action policies 45
AIDS 106, 109
capitalist growth 390
caste system 45, 404–5
censuses 1011
child health disparities 1157
Chipko movement 1274
colonialism 947–8
community media 627
consumer culture 744, 745
consumer movements 697, 698
diaspora 1151
ethnic conflict 1470, 1471
family planning programs 1738–9
and federalism 1652
film industry 1753
food and cultural consumption 722

fundamentalism 1813–14
heritage tourism 920
Hinduism 1766, 2128–32
Indian medicine 631
industrialization 704, 2299
and information technology 2335
Islam 2130–1
kindergarten programs 2462
life expectancies 3097
marriage 2303
medical sociology 2935
mortality 3097, 3535
mortality decline 3100
and multiculturalism 3108
Muslims 2128
"new woman" stereotype 1692
Non-Resident Indians (NRIs) 2885
nuclear technology 3038
Orissa famine 2686
out-migration 1344
partition 1451, 3020
population 1044
religions, al-Biruni's study of 111, 112–13
sex ratios 1029
television corporations 2890
underdevelopment theory 4008
world holidays 740
indigenismo 339, 340, 341, 342
indigenization 818
indigenous elites 1392
indigenous ethnography 1482
indigenous feminism, and intersectionality 2395
indigenous movements 2278–80, 2280
feminist movements 1992
and global cultural values 1993
see also self-determination
indigenous peoples 2280–5
and anthropology 147–9
assimilation 2281
autonomy 341, 342, 343
and bioprospecting 2172
control of resources 2280
cultural renewal 2280
demography 2282–3
first-contact accounts 2282
genocide 2281
and governing 2279–80
identity 2281
indigenous consciousness 2280
integration 339–40
land claims 2280
languages and cultures 2280

modernist perspective 2948–9
naming 2281
sacred sites 2280
social change and evolution 2282
see also tribalism; individual peoples
Indigo Girls 1677
individualism 2285–6
and altruism 1940
American individualism 3718
and atheism 197–8
and attribution biases 207
and business ethics 1441
and business organizations 2292
and civil society 512
and collectivism 598
and communism 617
conservative critique 678, 679
and demographic transition 1043
and divorce rates 1207, 1615
Durkheim and 1251, 1256, 1259, 1260, 1262,
     2285, 3230, 3689
and economic development 1295
economic individualism 679
and egotism 2285
and family and community 1577–8
and family conflict 1582
and family size restriction 1732–3
and family theory 1620, 1633–4
feminist 726
and home schooling 4033–4
and identity 2211
and jazz 3489
laissez faire individualism 679
liberal 807
and liberal feminism 2619
and the life course 2631
market individualism 3196
and marriage, effects on 2790
methodological individualism 635, 1298
and nonmarital fertility and cohabitation 1735
and plastic sexuality 3412
possessive individualism 2712
and postsocial theory 3579
and the public sphere 1862
and reflexive modernization 3830
religious individualism 3689
and second demographic transition 1733
and separate spheres ideology 1880
and socialism 614
individualistic market culture 3929
Individuals with Disabilities Education Act
     (IDEA) 1573

Indology 1492
Indonesia 4377
    Confucianism 670–1
    cultural tourism 921
    decolonization 985
    female genital mutilation 1654
    female migration 1716
    genocode 2420, 2421
    and multiculturalism 3108
    religions 671
induction and observation in science 2286–7
inductive approach to crime 1397, 1398
inductive conceptualization 234
inductive inference 2286, 2287
inductive theory 643–4
inductivism 1555, 1556
industrial architecture 1308
industrial betterment 2723–4
industrial bureaucracy 3287
industrial capital 1395, 2627
industrial capitalism 534, 535, 3550
    and family structure 1619, 1836
    and leisure class values 2595
industrial centralization 1314
industrial cities 765–7
industrial communication 3291
industrial democracy 2510, 2750
industrial democracy movement 19
industrial districts 1411
industrial psychology 2748
    see also management theory
industrial reengineering 2513
industrial relations 2287–93
    and alienation 119
    and human resource management 2178–82
    and Japanese-style management 2436
    and management 2712–13
    systems model 2288
    and workers' participation in management
        (WPM) 2752–4
    see also unions
industrial relocation 2382
Industrial Revolution 2293–7, 3915
    and capitalism 390
    causes 2294
    child labor 455
    and consumerism 751
    and decivilization 2747
    demographic consequences 2295–6
    and empiricism 1397
    European cities and 494
    and gender stratification 2308

    historical episode 2293, 2294
    and household organization 1202
    long-term developments 2294–7
    phase of sociocultural evolution 2293–4
    short-term consequences 2294
    work/leisure demarcation 761
    and working-class exploitation 840
industrial society 293, 4823
    Aron on 176
    classes 534, 535
    and division of labor 1922
    and families 1594
    instability 1199
    and kinship solidarity 2469
    life expectancies 3097
    Marx on 534, 535
    and secularization of knowledge 1922
    social mobility 3287
    social order 1199
    and transformation of the family 1922
industrial sociology 1287, 2298
industrialization 701, 2297–300
    and alienation 1839
    Blumer on 320
    capitalist industrialism 1428
    and the city 500, 501
    and collective trauma 595
    and communism 616
    and community–economy relation 624
    and consumption 740
    convergence thesis 2299
    and cultural sociology 923
    decline 1917
    and democracy 1002, 1003, 3076
    and demographic transition 1034
    and development 1852, 1853
    and eco-efficiency 1422
    and ecological exploitation 1281, 1291
    and ecological problems 1281
    and education 1332
    European cities and 494
    export-oriented industrialization 3441, 3536
    and family and community 1041, 1577–9,
        1597, 1598, 1619
    and family demography 1041
    and family structure 1619
    and financial sociology 1761
    free-market accounts 2298
    and friendships 1798
    and functional specialization 1619
    of the home 1202
    and homelessness 2147

homgenizing logic 2581
ideologies of industrialization 1925
indigenous peoples, impact on 2280
and institution of marriage 675
late industrializers 2299
and low fertility rates 1588
and modernization 3076
multiple-path thesis 2298, 2299
and nationalism 3150
one-path thesis 2298
and organic society 581
and the public school system 4048–9
role in shaping human behavior 320
and separation of spheres 1849
and social mobility 1967
and the working-class movement 498
industry networks 1313
Indymedia 1979
inequalities in marriage 2301–4, 2790
and family conflict 1581, 1582
gender-based 2301
and money management 3081, 3083
inequality and the city 2304–7
black urban regime 310–12
and homelessness 2146–50
inequalities among cities 2304–5
inequality within cities 2305–6
and megalopolis growth 2943
observation studies 2625–6
redlining 3825–7
see also residential segregation
inequality/stratification, gender 336, 1663,
2307–10
biosociological theory 293
and carework 403
conflict theory perspective 2309–10
and differential treatment of children by sex
1155–9
and doing gender 1218
and earner–carer model 1272
economic perspective 2307–8
and family theory 1633
feminist critique 2310
and gender mainstreaming 1869–70
and gender oppression 1871
and intersectionality 2859
and occupational segregation 1892, 3234–5,
3246, 3247
and occupational sex segregation 1892
organization settings 2750
political perspectives 2308
structural functional perspective 2309

inequality, wealth 2310–13
and Gini coefficient 1942
historic 2311
short-term changes 2313
infant attachment theory 2674
infant betrothal 1158
**infant, child, and maternal health and
mortality** 1035, **2313–20**
causes 2314–16
differential treatment by sex 1155–9
education, effects of 1727
health promotion interventions 2315,
2316–17
and human rights 2317
inequalities 2314
intermediate and proximate causes 2315–16
and maternal education 1156
measuring 2317–19
socioeconomic and sociocultural factors
2315, 2316
teenage mothers 1726
infant mortality
calculating 2318
causes 2314, 3758
class differentials 2628
definition 2313
and family demography 1041
infant mortality rate (IMR) 1039, 2313
intervention programs 2316–17
and maternal age 3535
Physical Quality of Life Index 1001
and poverty 1613
racial variations 3758
sex ratio 1157
and sex-selective abortion 3535
and teenage mothers 1726
see also child mortality
infanticide 1156, 1157
and euthanasia 1490
female 2302
and female deviance 1856
and fertility control 2707
inferences, dispositional 206
infertility 1609, 1626, **2320–3**
incidence of 2321
and men 2320
primary 2320, 2322
secondary 2320, 2321, 2322
social and cultural context 2321–2
infertility distress 2321–2
infertility treatment 1907, 2322–3
infibulation 329, 1654, 1655, 1656

infidelity and marital affairs 2323–5
and divorce 1207
and Islamic culture 2429
social attitudes toward 2324, 2325, 2793
inflation 3079, 3176
informal economy 1411
informalism, and masculinity 1891
informalization of work 2383
informated labor 3565
Information Age 3180
information associations 1402
information flow
cross-border flows 1396
and interform networks 1313
information integration 643
**information and resource processing
paradigm 2325–6**
information society 353, 2326–31
economic perspective 2328
information society debates 2329–30
informational privacy 3644
information technology 2331–6
and audience research 211
cultural perspective 2333
cyberculture 961–4
diffusion of 2749–50
ethical perspective 2333
female use of 5263–4
image archiving and analysis 2988
industrial relations, impact on 2292–3
industrialization of information 2300
and innovation 2740–1
and management consultancy 2720
and medicine 2388, 2390
and the network society 3180
networks 2742
and older people 102
photography and 771
political economy perspective 2333, 2335
and social life organization 2927
sociological analysis 2335
and technological innovation in warfare 3040
and technology assessment 691
virtual-*en* 1402
and visual consumption 771, 772
see also multimedia
Information Technology Revolution 2300
informational capitalism 3180
informational economy 3181
informationalism 518
informed consent 1443, 1444, 2174
sociological research 2347, 2348

informetrics 4120
infotainment 2336–7, 2908, 3491
infractions, legal 2554–5
Ingham, B. 3471
Ingham, G. 3079
Inglehart, R. 1317, 1902, 2234, 3071–8, 4124
Ingold, T. 3165
Ingraham, C. 2109–11, 2114–15
Ingram, J. K. 3045
Ingram, P. 2353–7
in-group marriage *see* endogamy
in-groups and out-groups 315, 2338–9
and collectivism 598
in-group association 795, 796
and prejudice 3615
Ingush 1451
inheritance
discriminatory practices 1724
and *ie* 2239
and marriage 2414
Mendelian principles 1505, 1897
inheritance taxes 2628
Inhorn, M. 2322
initiation studies 563
Innacone, L. 1315, 2438, 2441
inner-city decay 501
inner-directed personality 3918
Innis, H. 1108, 2333, 2691, 3635, 3778
innovation, innovators 293
and anomie 597
and deviance 1102
discontinuous innovation 2730
early adopters 3685
economic innovation 1455
fashion and 740
and hate crime laws 1099
later adopters 3686
and management education 2728
non-adopters 3685, 3687
organizational innovation 1309
police 3431
and the population–environment relationship
3532
positive deviance 3543
social innovation 1901
and sport 1134
strategic framing 3687
and technological spillovers 1313
innovative freedom 2041
Inoue, K. 1971–6
Inoue, T. 1402
Inquisition 1140, 2453, 2896

insanity 2694
see also mental disorder
insecurity and fear of crime 1650, 1651, **2339–44**, 3941
insecurity in the work context 379
insider trading 850
instinct psychology 799
institution 2344–5
gendered organizations/institutions 1893–5
and law–economy relation 2558
and market-economic behavior 2443
new institutional theory 2351–2
total institutions 2934
institutional change 2356
institutional determinism 3283
institutional economics 1299
and development studies 1296
institutional ethnography 274, 1503
institutional inertia 5025
institutional isomorphism 2351
institutional migrants 3021–2
institutional review boards and sociological research 2345–51
and fieldwork ethics 1442–6
and research ethics 1442–6, 1448
institutional theory, and organizational action 2476, 2478
institutional theory, new 2351–2, 2354, 2355, 2714, 3283, 3301, 3461
amd social movements 4442
commitment to macro structures 3337
field-level processes 3283
and management fashion 2729
and management theory 2714
and organizational action 2478
and study of tradition 3337
institutionalism 2353–7
and charisma 438
gendered character 1217
historical institutionalism 3461
interdependencies 2356
new institutional theory 2351, 2714, 3461
organizational institutionalism 3461
rational-choice institutionalism 3461
and risk 1387
institutionalization
and asylums 1169
and crime 839
and cultural capital 888
of emotions 1387
environmental movements 1430–1
hospitals 2695

masculinity 2820
mathematical sociology 2856–7
institutionalized logics 2586
institutionalized norms 2585, 2586
instrumental activities of daily living (IADLs) 2546
instrumental aggression 64
instrumental group dimension 1581
instrumental rationality 518, 876, 2235, 3233, 3312, 3314
instrumental reason 518, 2235, 3312
instrumentalism 1145
and the state 3458
insulin treatment 2694
insurance
and disasters 1175
life insurance 1386
insurance industry 1890
Integrated Management of Childhood Illness (IMCI) 2317
integration
and accommodation 7–9
and assimilation 191–6
attunement 3007
and bilingual education 278
Catholic Church and 409
Comte and 654, 655
and disability 1169
and disabled athletes 1171
and ethnic groups 1458, 1461
and homogenization 2949
horizontal/vertical 1363
indigenous peoples 339–40, 341
and life chances and resources 2628
and massive resistance 2830
migrants 1981, 2257
and mobilization 1922
natural and social sciences 687
and organizational culture 950
and organizational environment 950, 3300
and participation 1922–3
perfect occupational integration 3244
pride/shame component 3007
religious institutions, role of 1981
reverse integration 1173
social disintegration 1922
and social systems theory 3366, 3367
state policies 3761
and state-controlled education 1972
and systemic needs 1809
integrative medicine *see* complementary and alternative medicine

intellectual capital 2477
intellectual freedom 3468
intellectual functions, decrements in 104
intellectual property 2357–8
copyright issues 3489–90
and digital media 1159, 1162
and the Matthew effect 2860
intellectual property laws, consumption and
729–32
intellectuals, sociology of 2758
organic intellectuals 3481–2
revolutionary role of intellectuals 4295
intelligence
Bell Curve, The and 263–4
and child abuse 449
and crime 837
defining 2358
and effort, sum of 2954, 2956
emotional intelligence 3444
environmental determination 264
heritability 263–4, 2360
low intelligence and social pathologies 264
and merit 2954, 2956
intelligence services 2334, 2335
intelligence tests 2358–61, 3731
black–white test score differences 2359, 2360
cultural bias 264
heritability estimates 2359, 2360
Pygmalion effect 4176
racial and ethnic differences 264, 265
standardized educational tests 4722–3
WAIS III intelligence test 2359
intensive supervision probation (ISP) 803
intentional fallacy 216
intentionality
and agency 60–2
and attitudes 200
attribution theory 205
and phenomenology 3402
inter vivos family transfers 1905
INTERACT computer program 2272
interaction 2361–5
affect control theory 35–8
communicative interaction 2033
and conversation analysis 791, 792
conversation analysis and 790–1
and deference behaviors 990
and deviance 2506, 3087
deviant labeling, effects of 2502
dyads and triads 1264–7
and ecological problems 1283
and economic geography 1298

and elementary theory 1352–3
emotional interaction 1379
euphoric interaction 4648
face-to-face interaction 1997, 2218, 2269,
2906, 2921, 2922, 2961, 3937
focused/unfocused 1997
friendships 795, 1788–91, 1863
functionalist approach 2361
gender, work and family 1880
Goffman and 1995
grammar and 794
and group processes 2032
human–non-human interaction 2175–8
and identity politics 2214, 2215
and identity processes 2218, 2224
and institutions 2345
interactional frameworks 1863
and interpersonal relationships 2392
interpretive interactionism 2448
and leisure 2589
and management discourse 2723
mediated interaction 2921
and moral entrepreneurship 3088
nation-states 1968
and the public realm 3720
and the public sphere 2908, 3720
and reproduction of hegemony 2229
role-taking 3948
as self-referential circle 2677
and sexual practices 4249
spatial and bodily conduct 2363
video-based studies 2363–4
see also social comparison theory; symbolic
interaction
interaction order 2365–6
and idiocultures 2366
Interaction Process Analysis (IPA) 2027,
2031–2
and group processes 2031–2, 2362
interaction ritual chains 1999
interaction rituals 3937
interaction theory *see* coalitions; collective
action; conversation analysis; exchange
relations; game theory; symbolic
interaction
interactional psychology 122
interactivity, digital 1159, 1160, 2923
interconnectedness, and globalization 2889
interdenominationalism 1052
interdependence of generations perspective
2368
interdependency chains 1750

interdependent lives hypothesis 76
interdisciplinarity in science 2190
interest 1385
interest group pluralism 3451, 3452
interface 1163
 human–computer interface (HCI) 4972
intergenerational conflict 1902, **2366–8**, 2691
**intergenerational mobility: core model of
 social fluidity 2368–73**, 2377
**intergenerational mobility: methods of
 analysis 2373–80**
 dissimilarity index 2376
 FJH hypothesis 2369–70, 2371
 and partner choice 675
 scaled association models 2377–8
 social fluidity model 2368–72, 2377
**intergenerational relationships and
 exchanges 2380–2**, 4810
 and elder care 1349–51, 2381, 2633
 inter vivos family transfers 1905, 4810
 life course perspective 2381, 2633–4
 monetary support 2571
 and parenting roles 2633
 residential support 2169, 2438, 2570–2,
  2573–4
 social contexts 2381
 see also grandparenthood; parenting
intergenerational transmission 2380
intergovernmental organizations (IGOs) 1951
intergroup relations
 applied social psychology 4519
 attribution theory and 207
 macrostructural theory 315
 and social psychology 4515–16
 see also organizational structure; social
  network theory
intermarriage 315
 Jews 2452, 2453
internal consistency reliability 3850
internal labor markets 1249, 1416, 3287
internalization 1088
internally displaced persons (IDPs) 3835
International Association of Economic
 History 362
International Bill of Rights 2183–4
International Committee for Assigned Names
 and Numbers (ICANN) 2914
International Council of Social Welfare (ICSW)
 4537–8, 4539–41
International Court System 1224
International Covenant on Civil and Political
 Rights (ICCPR) 2184

International Covenant on Economic, Social,
 and Cultural Rights (ICESCR) 2184
International Feminist Congresses 1685
International Fur Seal Convention 1291
**international gender division of labor
 2382–4**, 3245
 and earner–carer model 1272
 new international division of labor (NIDL)
  1715
International Labor Organization 1716, 2319,
 2509, 4456, 4539
International Lesbian and Gay Association
 1984, 1985, 2156
International Lesbian and Gay Human Rights
 Commission 2156
International Monetary Fund 349, 745, 1294,
 1945, 1956
 and AIDS pandemic 107
 anti-IMF riots 1062
 and decolonization 986
 and democratic accountability 1947, 1960
 economic globalization strategies 1852
 and global South economies 2382
 neoclassical economic precepts 1295
 and neoliberalism 1948
 organizational deviance 3304
 protests against 981, 1062, 1977, 1978
 structural adjustment programs (SAPs) 1724
international non-governmental organizations
 (INGOs) 1951
International Olympic Committee (IOC)
 1171–2, 1239–40, 1988, 3474, 3476
international relations (IR) 1950, 1951
International Society for Krishna
 Consciousness (ISKCON) 885, 2131
International Sociological Association 366
International Standard Classification of
 Occupations (ISCO) 3250
International Union of Penal Law 969
international violence 1885–8
 see also war
internationalization of business 355
Internet 2384–8
 activism 780
 banditry 3490
 and brand communities 359
 and censorship 421–2
 and children's consumer culture 696
 communication networks 2387
 communities 5150
 and computational sociology 643–4
 conservatism and 680

Internet (*cont'd*)
consumption and 732–4
conversations 791
culture 2386
cybercrime 960–1
cyberculture 961–4
cyberfeminism 1678
cybersexualities 965–6
and diaspora 1153, 2885, 2886
and digital media 1160, 1161
e-commerce 732, 733, 1851
e-money 3079
electronic interviewing 2410
entertainment environment 1756
environmental impact 2388
and ethnography 1483
exhibitionism 1519
fieldwork ethics 1445
file-exchange networks 1162, 2358, 2904,
   3489–90
fraud 1107
and gambling 1133, 1820
and genres 1914
and global justice movement 1949
global take-up 2876
industrial relations, impact on 2292
and the information society 2329, 2330
and information technology 2334
intellectual property issues 741, 2358
and intellectual property laws 731
interactivity 2886
interfaces 2909
Internet communities 620, 1578
marketing 774
mediated interaction 2923
multimedia 3110, 3111
music file sharing 3133
networks 2902
and new religious movement information
   exchange 3205
political party activism 3454
and the polyamory community 3477
and propaganda diffusion 3674–5
and the public sphere 2910
and racism 966, 3768
ratings 3793
regulation 2911, 2914–15
research 2387
s/m sites 3986
and secondary data analysis 4127
sex work online 1661–2
and sexual identities, shaping 1985

sexual interaction 2541
and sexuality research 4282
social support networks 101–3
social use 2905
sociological account 2384–8
and transnational activism 1985
virtual communities 628
and visual consumption 771
visual data integration 2988–9
and youth culture 774
Internet medicine 2388–90
quality debate 2389
Internet studies 733
interpersonal politics *see* identity politics/
   relational politics
interpersonal relationships 2390–3
and collective consciousness 2474
and ethics 1439
religious 3863
and significant others 4320–1
and social influence 4426–9
social support 4527–30
see also dyad/triad; friendship: interpersonal
   aspects; interaction; marriage
interpersonal scripting 4122
interpersonal trust 1634
interpretive interactionism 2448
interpretive sociology 2968
interpretive theories 1557
interpretive turn in the social sciences 1435
interpretivism 1436, 2968, 3293
interracial unions 2393–5, 3732
and biracialism 295
and diversity 1198
and endogamy 1405
and the melting pot theory 2944
and one drop rule 3266
and polyethnicity 3479
interrogation 791
interscience 360, 361
intersectional analysis 1701, 2838
intersectionality 1701, **2395–8**, 2838
and collective identity 587, 2901
and disability 1700
and feminism 1668, 2395, 2397, 2842, 2859,
   3117, 3119–20, 3776
identity politics 3400
leisure 2592
and lifestyle consumption 2646
and lived experience 1668
power relationships 1707
of social life 1217

and social mobility 3064
of women's lives 1695
Intersex Society of North America (ISNA)
2397
intersexuality 1846–7, **2399–400**
medical management 1846–7, 2399
sexuality research 2132
intersubjectivity 2108, **2400–2**
knowledge sharing 2651
and phenomenology 3402
postsocial theory 3580
intersystemic relations 2677
intertextuality 216, 918, **2402–3**, 3581
and celebrity 416
Kristeva and 216
intervention studies 2403–6
interventionist policies 2625
humanitarian intervention 2184
and manifest destiny doctrine 2755, 2756
neo-Keynesian 3592, 3593
interventionist state 2623, 2624
**interviewing, structured, unstructured,
and postmodern 2407–11**, 4514
active interviewing 2410
creative interviewing 2407, 2409
electronic interviewing 2410
ethical issues 2410–11
focus group interviewing 2407, 2408
gendered interviewing 2409–10
key informants 2458
life history interview 2641, 2642
and network research 2742
open-ended interviews 1868
oral history 2407, 2409
and peer debriefing 3387–8
postmodern interviewing 2407, 2409, 2410
power relations 2401
and sexuality research 4288
and transcription 5036–7
unstructured 2407, 2408–9
intimacy 2411–14
and attraction 204
broadcasting, relationships with 2922
and chaos and complexity theories 432
and dyads and triads 1264
and fandom 1638
and female sexuality 904, 2612
and gender difference 1862–3
and interpersonal relationships 2390
and LAT relationships 811
and lust balance 2681
and marriage 2791

mutuality of revelation 3644
and polyamory 3477, 3478
postmodern 3412
rapport 3789–90
self-disclosing intimacy 2411–13
and stranger typology 4783–4
within cohabitation 1634
within marriage 1634
**intimate union formation and dissolution
2414–18**
and class 2415
co-residence 2417
cohabitation 565–7, 1587–8
economic and cultural explanations 2415–16
and race/ethnicity 2415
see also divorce; intimacy; marriage
intolerance 2826
intra-cytoplasmic sperm injection (ICSI) 2322
intraclass correlation (ICC) 3850
intranets 2387, 2479
intrapsychic scripting 4122
Introvigne, M. 2438–41, 3189–92, 4010–11
Inuit 321, 1263
and cultural tourism 921
invasion-succession 2418–20
reverse succession 2419
and urban ecology 1289–90
invention 293
inversion 2493
investigative poetics 2420–4
and arts-based research 2971–2
Investigative Review Boards (IRBs)
investigator triangulation 5076, 5077
investment, freedom of 393
invisible colleges 2948, 4107–8
and scientometrics 4120
"invisible continent" 1958
Iowa School 2220, 2362, 4912
Ipat formula 1283
iPod 3133
Iran 704
axial civilization 520
death penalty 977
diaspora 2885–6
Gulf Wars 2801
Islam 1814
Jewish population 2453
Iranian Revolution (1979) 665, 1813, 1982,
3867, 3907, 3910
Iraq
civil wars 1473
Gulf Wars 2801

Iraq (*cont'd*)
  Jewish population 2453
  male/female median earnings ratios 1724
Iraq, invasion and occupation of 876, 1396,
    1679, 2268, 3175
  media role 2879
Ireland
  Catholicism 2531
  cohabitation 567
  collective bargaining 2512
  colonialism 947, 1394, 3731
  cultural tourism 921
  diaspora 1151
  divorce rates 2664
  education system 1399
  family and community 1576
  famine 3525
  identity construction 2214
  Irish land question 3044–5
  lone parenthood 2663, 2665
  migration 1044, 2264
  nationalism 3146, 3159
  and slavery 4338
  social class inequalities in mortality 2090
  sport and nationalism 3159, 3160
Irigaray, L. 869, 3698
Irish Republican Army (IRA) 3470
Irnerius 599
irrationality, emotional 1384
Irvine, L. 2177
Isherwood, B. 683, 741, 743
Islam 520, 521, 524, 671, 672, 1980, 2003,
    2424–8, 3855
  activism 781
  al-Biruni and 113, 114
  and American voluntarism 1055
  anti-Semitism 160
  'asabiyya 180–5
  and capital punishment 976
  conservatism 680
  and economics of religion 1316
  and empire 1392–3, 1981
  etymology 2424
  and female genital mutilation 1654,
    1655, 1656
  global activities 1982
  and homosexuality 1828
  Islamic identity 2425, 3108
  Islamic law 2552
  juridical interpretation 2426
  legal systems 1981
  liberation theology 1814
  and marital infidelity 2324
  and martyrdom 2800
  millenarianism 3047, 3048
  nationalism 1465, 1467, 2427, 2453
  and Orientalist discourse 3344
  origins 2424
  and political authority 229
  and popular religiosity 3518
  and purdah 3723
  Qur'an 1655, 2003, 2424–5, 2428, 2552, 3723
  radical Islamism 2426
  re-Islamization of society 2427
  revolutionary role 4295, 4296
  scholarship 4073
  and sexuality 1828, 4279
  Shiite Islamism 1814, 2425–6, 2800, 3048
  social cohesion 2460
  Sunni Islamism 2425–6, 3048
  theocracy 3094
  theology 2424
Islamic fundamentalism 256, 876, 1645,
    1813, 2324
  suicide attacks 2800–1
Islamic mysticism 2000
Islamic sexual culture 2428–30
Islamism 2000
isomorphism 2351
  mimetic isomorphism 2714
Israel
  and American neoconservatism 3173
  axial civilization 520
  civil religion 507
  creation of 1451
  ethnic violence 1470
  fundamentalism 1813
  immigration 2259
  Israeli–Palestinian dispute 159, 160
  kibbutzim 2753
  maternal politics 2848
  medical sociology 2935
  nuclear technology 3038–9
  secularization 2532
  see also Judaism
Isvan, N. 2839–44
Italian Americans
  clothing styles 715
  ethnic enclaves 1452, 1454
Italian barbershops 715
Italian Elitist School 3361
Italy
  anarchism 136
  Catholicism 2530

centralized control 1488
civil religion 507
cohabitation 567
communism 2014
cultural tourism 920
democracy 1001
demographic data 1033–4
diaspora 1151
divorce rates 2664
economic geography 1298
environmental movements 1430
extramarital births 2663
fascism 325, 1644, 1646, 2014, 2015, 2102,
    2747, 2804, 3361, 3453, 3462
film industry 1753
ghettos 1937
global justice groups 1978
health care system 2055
immigration 3031, 3032
industrial relations 2289
industrialization 494
Jehovah's Witnesses 2439
laicism 2532
liberalism 2624
lone parenthood 2663, 2665
medical sociology 2935
migration 2264
nationalism 3145
nonmarital fertility 1734
religious schools 4053
republicanism 3885
secret societies 4132
teenage motherhood 1728
unions 2511
weapons R&D 3039
Itani, J. 2250
item response theory 3849, 3850
IUD 1738
'Izzat, 'Abd al-'Aziz 2461

jack-off (JO) clubs 2834, 3989
jackknife replicability analysis 3878
Jackman, R. W. 1001
Jackson, B. 2730
Jackson, D. 248
Jackson, J. 901
Jackson, Mahalia 3135
Jackson, Maynard 311
Jackson, Michael 3507–10
Jackson, P. 2116
Jackson, R. M. 796
Jackson, S. 2111–16, 4711–13

Jackson, S. A. 2701–2
Jacob, L. 1755
Jacobin movement 524, 4168
Jacobs, A. J. 5096–9
Jacobs, H. 306
Jacobs, J. 501, 1330, 1331, 1427, 1721, 3125
Jacobs, M. D. 1145–6, 2365–6
Jacobsen, M. M. 1179–82, 3278–81, 3971
Jaggar, A. 1712
jai alai 1821
jails 803
Jainism 2130
Jakarta 2991
Jakobson, R. 2534
Jalali, R. 404–6
jam bands 3506
Jamaica 1855
    male prostitution 1661
James, A. 460
James Bond movies 2103
James, C. L. R. 1149, 1637, 3473
James, Henry 2431
James, J. 309
James, S. 309
James, William 799, 1145, 1258, 1483, 2203,
    2431–5, 3363
    and consciousness 2431–2, 2434
    figured reality principle 2432
    and free will 2434
    functionalism 2431, 2434
    parallelism 2431, 2434
    and positive psychology 2566
    pragmatism 2431, 2432, 3051, 3609–10
    and religious experience 3857
    and the self 2217, 2432–3, 2434, 2670, 4157
    and self-esteem 2433–4, 4170
    social psychology 2431
Jameson, F. 518, 759, 916, 3496, 3557–8, 3570,
    3573, 3575, 3879–80
Jamieson, L. 2402, 2411–14, 3412
Jamison, A. 1430
Jancovich, M. 1639
Janesick, V. J. 2447–8, 3387–8
Janis, I. L. 3444
Janowitz, M. 445, 714, 1146, 3041, 3042
Japan
    adolescent fertility 1725
    aging population 1028
    axial civilization 523, 526
    ba 237–9
    Buddhism 371, 750, 1982
    caste system 404

Japan (*cont'd*)
citizenship 497
civil minimum 505–6
civil religion 507
Confucianism 672
consumer culture 744
consumer movement 698
consumption 702
democracy 1001
demographic data collection 1012, 1046, 1047
and the developmental state 1075
ecological view of history 1286–8
economy 393, 1073–4, 1296, 2299, 2726, 2750
emperor system 2803
empire 1395
en 1400–42
enterprise unions 1413–17
environmental burden 266
environmental sociology 265, 4179
ethnic groups 3059
and extracurricular activities 1549
and "face" 2215
fascism 2803, 2805
female labor force participation 1204
feminism 1690, 1692
fertility levels 1738, 3527
feudalism 514
filial piety 2380
folkloristics 2445–7, 5302–4
and the ghetto 1936
and ghetto 1936
graduate education 2013
high-speed transportation pollution 2126–7
home schooling 4033
human resource management 2180
ie 2238–41
immigration 2263, 3058–9
indigenous movements 1992
industry 429–30, 2299, 3072
internal migration 3017
Japan–US relationship 1968
jōmin 2445–7
laboratory practice 2525
life expectancy 1023–4, 1864, 3096–7
local residents' movements 2656–9
lone parenthood 2663, 2664, 2665
low fertility levels 1588
machine politics 3445
management innovations 2741
marginal art 2761–3
medical sociology 2935

megalopolises 2943
metropolises 495, 2992
middle class 3200
migration 2472
militarism 3147, 3218
minzoku 3057–9
mortality 1023
nationalism 2802, 2803, 3057, 3058, 3142–3, 3145, 3147, 3218, 3220
neighborhood associations 471–4
new religious movements 3202
nihonjinron 1494, 3058, 3217–21
occupational segregation 3245
office ladies 3251–4
operations mangement in 3268
organizational culture 949
pollution 967–8, 3476, 3477
production per worker 1959
public broadcasting 3703
public school system 4049
quality management movement 19
recession 2022
reintegrative shaming 2506–7
retirement policies 3902
revolution 3907
rural sociology 4903–4
school system 1324
secularization 4300
seikatsu/seikatsusha 4150–3
seken 4154–6
sex workers 1717
Shintoism 1980, 2499, 3855, 4297–303
single motherhood 1723
social change 4370–1
social security system 2055
socioeconomic policies 392
statist model 4733
tatemae/honne 4155, 4935–8
teenage motherhood 1728
transnational corporations 1944
unions 2512, 3170–1
urban sociology 4904–5
weapons R&D 3039
world holidays 740
Japanese Americans 1114, 1460
middleman minorities 3009
and reparations 3876
upward mobility 1460
Japanese-style management 1287, 1413–17, **2435–8**
corporate familism 2240
labor–management relations 2512–13

nenko chingin 3170–2
and office-ladies 3251–4
operations mangement 3268
salary men 3992–4
shushin koyo 4311–13
Jaques, E. 948
Jardine, L. 1966
Jarmon, Charles 3370–3, 3743–5
Jarvie, Grant 1751
Jarvie, Ian 1755
Jasper, J. M. 3457, 4443–51
Jaspers, K. 520, 3673
Jasso, G. 1191–7
Jaurès, J. 2531
Java 3420
jazz 913, 2124, 2734, 2826, 3128, **3488–9,**
3492
jealousy 1377
Jefferson, G. 791, 793, 2363
Jefferson, M. 3622
Jefferson, Thomas 2618, 2954, 4088
Jefferys, M. 2669
Jeffrey, C. R. 848
Jehle, A. 562–5
Jehovah's Witnesses 886, 1056, **2438–41,**
3202, 3203
millenarianism 3048
Jekielek, S. M. 1621 6
Jenkins, H. 366, 1637, 1638, 3497
Jenkins, P. 3087–8, 3090
Jenkins, R. 1475–8, 2517
Jenks, C. 460, 910, 911, 928–32
Jenness, V. 1096, 1098, 1099, 1828–30
Jennings, L. 3613–17
Jensen, L. 1461
Jensen, M. C. 3327
Jerusalem 2449, 2450
Jessop, B. 3179, 3840–3
Jesuits 1262
Jesus Movement 885
Jesus of Nazareth 230, 335, 474, 911, 2450
charisma 3597
and Confucianism 670
and cultural resistance 911
and martyrdom 2800
see also Christianity
Jette, A. 2095
Jetter, A. 2848
Jevons, William 2441–3, 3046
and marginalism 1304
and neoclassical economics 1304, 1305
Jewish Americans 1452, 1454

Jews
alcoholic abstinence 117
American Jews 154
Ashkenazic Jews 2450
assimilation 2452
biculturality 270
blood libel 155, 260
businesses 1457
and collective memory 590
Conservative Judaism 2452
cross-movement coalitions 124
and cultural resistance 911
and the Deadhead community 3506
defining 2449
diaspora 1151, 2885
emancipation 2296
Ethiopian Jews 1655, 2453
and the ghetto 1936, 1937
Hasidic Jews 2302, 2764
identity 911, 3741
ingroup association 795
intermarriage 2452
IQ scores 264
Jewishness 1475
Judeo–Bolshevism 158–60
middleman minorities 3009
Orthodoxy 2452, 2532
and patriarchal authority 2302
pogroms 2006, 2142, 3426–8
population estimates 2453
premodern nation 3151
Reconstructionism 2452
Reform Jews 1053, 2452
scapegoating 875, 4013
Sephardic Jews 2450–1, 2453
Soviet Jews 1152
and stigma 584
Ultra-Orthodox Jews 1315
whiteness literature 195
world conspiracy myth 158, 159
see also anti-Semitism (religion); anti-
Semitism (social change); Holocaust
Jhally, S. 611, 2101, 2826
Jihad 1994
Jim Crow regime 15, 368, 507–8, 509, 510, 708,
1463, 3369, 3616, 3746
Joas, H. 3609
job creation and training programs 840
job satisfaction 2077
and absenteeism 5
determinants 120
jock identity 2122

Joffe, C. 3651–6
Jogiches, L. 2685
John Paul II, Pope 159, 441, 3541
John of Poinsot 4180
Johns, G. 4–7
johns (sex customers) 1660–1
Johnson, B. 1239
Johnson, C. 1073, 1074
Johnson, Charles Spurgeon 1785, **2444**
Johnson, D. 4886–8
Johnson, H. 1689–93, 5262–5
Johnson, J. 1520–1, 1523
Johnson, Jack 4687–8
Johnson, L. 510, 2233, 3173
Johnson, N. R. 1367
Johnson, P. 5016–18
Johnson, R. B. 2978
Johnson, T. 3663
Johnson, V. 4286
Johnston, B. V. 2958–61
Johnston, H. 3065–8
Johnston, J. 2602
jōmin **2445–7**
Jonas, A. E.G. 2033–7
Jones, F. L. 2369
Jones, P. R. 2248–9, 5299–300
Jones, S. H. 230–2
Jonestown, Guyana 886, 3047
Jordan, D. S. 2170
Jordan, Michael 4716
Jöreskog, K. G. 1559
journaling, reflexive 2447–8, 5084
journalism 48, 2907, 3470
    adversarialism 3471
    arts-based methods 2971
    Fourth Estate 3468
    objective reporting 3638
    pauper press 3469
    penny press 3469
    photojournalism 3406–7
    sports writers 2920, 4709
    and surveillance 3467–8
    tabloid journalism 3491
Jowett, G. 1755
Joyce, James 2580
Joyce, P. 947, 2904
Jubilee 2002 1949
Judaism 520, 1980, **2448–54**, 3854
    and capital punishment 976
    defining 2449
    fundamentalism 1813
    holidays 2452

international organizations and
    movements 1982
life-cycle events 2452
millenarianism 3047, 3048
and purdah 3723
Reconstruction Judaism 2449
Reform Judaism 2449
and religious anti-Semitism 152
Second Temple Judaism 524
synagogue tradition 1054
Judson, R. 1332
Juglar cycle 2489, 2490
Jung, Karl 2672, 3213
Junisbai, Azamat 1568–70
junkie subculture 797
Jürgensmeyer, M. 2801
jury deliberations 1383, 1484
jury nullification 1497
jury trial 814
just reward 1192
    disclosed just reward 1194
    non-reflexive 1194
just society 2955
Just-In-Time (JIT) management 430, 1411,
    1959, 2437, 2817, 3269, 4893
justice
    distributive justice 6, 1191–6, 2145
    ethic of justice 1438–9
    justice analysis 1191–6
    microjustice/macrojustice 1192
    participatory model 2
    restorative justice 2
justice analysis 1191–6
    empirical 1194–5
    framework 1191–2
    theoretical 1193–4
justifications 10–11, 13
Justinian Code 2552, 2696
juvenile courts 814–15, 855
juvenile delinquency 543, **2454–5**
    age–crime curve 830–1
    child abuse and 449
    criminology and 861
    deviant accounts 13, 1123
    and deviant friendships 1799–800
    and gangs 1825, 1827
    girls 1858, 4192–3
    and imprisonment 804
    measuring 2455
    and musical influences 3128–9
    predictors for 1232
    self-control theory 4164–5

social control theory 845, 846
and social support 4531
and socially disorganized communities 1102
underage drinking 114
juvenile justice system 855–6
community-based corrections 856
diversion programs 855–6

K-12 schooling 1329, 2893, 3666, 4035
Kabbadi 1989
Kabbalah 4275
Kabir Panth 2131
Kada, Y. 2640–1, 4178–9
Kafka, Franz 874, 3809
Kahl, J. A. 1529
Kahn, J. P. 2350
Kahn, J. R. 1028–30
Kain, J. 2305
Kaiser, S. B. 718–21
Kalaitzidakis, P. 1332
Kaldor, P. 3039, 3040
Kallen, H. 3421
Kalmyks 1451
Kameda, A. 1692
Kamenev 159
kamikaze 2800, 3143
Kamoche, K. 2734
Kampwirth, K. 1686
Kane, J. 3444
Kane, N. 4820–4
Kaneko, Y. 3170
Kang Youwei 670
Kangas, O. E. 5247–9
Kannarese language 1371
Kansas Marital Satisfaction Scale (KMSS) 2773
Kant, Immanuel 3949
and aesthetic taste 1361, 4931
and autonomy and free will 2187
and causality 653
and the church 483
and constructionism 1087
critique of reason 874, 896, 897
and cultural critique 896
and direct knowledge, possibility of 2924
and Durkheim 1258
Kantian ethics 2679
moral philosophy 2187
and *moralpolitik* 3094
Kanter, Rosabeth Moss 1880, 1881, 1889, 1892
Kantzara, Vasiliki 4749–53
Kaplan, E. A. 940
Kaplan, M. 2596

Karabel, J. 622
Kardash, T. 1483–6
Karim, K. 2886
Karim, W. J. 1690, 1691, 1692
karma 371, 2130
Karstedt, S. 1909–13, 2182–5, 5011–14
Kasel, S. 2051
Kashmir 2801, 4188
Katona, G. 741
Katz, E. 1437, 3621
Katz, F. E. 2142–3
Katz, J. 1398, 1828, 3801
Katz, S. 1930
Katz-Fishman, W. 2836–9
Katz-Gerro, T. 2644–6
Katzenstein, M. 1679
Kaufman, A. 3194
Kaufman, B. E. 2513
Kaufman, E. 39–42, 367–70
Kaufman, F.-X. 485, 3618–20, 4490–5
Kawanishi, H. 2437, 3172
Kawashima, T. 3218
Kazakhstan 1451, 3039
kazoku 2239
Keating, N. 1349–51
Keaton, Buster 1752
Kedourie, E. 3153
Keeney, R. 984
Kehily, M. 2153
Keller, E. F. 4072
Keller, S. 637, 3905
Kellerhals, J. 1580–3
Kelley, H. H. 1512, 2390
Kelling, G. 1397–8
Kellner, Douglas 1752–7, 2195, 2838, 2881–5,
4896–8, 4969–71
and critical theory 876
and implosion theory 2269
Kelly, E. L. 1718, 1720, 1721
Kelly, G. 1087
Kelly, L. 4249–54
Kelly, R. 4323–8
Kelly, W. W. 1638
Kemal, A. 2001
Kemmelmeier, M. 3034–7, 5313–16
Kemp, J. 3709
Kempadoo, K. 1984
Kemper, T. D. 990, 1380, 1383, 1384, 1390, 1650
Kendon, A. 2362, 2363
Kennedy, F. 307
Kennedy, John F. 995, 1370, 1666, 2878, 3052,
3516, 3517

Kennedy, R. J. R. 2944
Kennedy, Rose 2857
Kent, Donald P. 1932–4
Kenya
    capitalist growth 390
    failed revolution 3910
    female genital mutilation 1656
    Green Belt movement 1274
    pastoral theism 3870
    sex tourism 4201
Keohane, R. O. 1951
Kepel, G. 2427
Kern, R. 2935
Kern, R. M. 1361
Kerouac, Jack 798, 3844
Kerr, A. 1681–5, 2171–5, 2173, 5267–8
Kerr, C. 1410, 2290
Kertbeny, K. M. 2157
Kessler, S. 1846–7, 2399
Kett, J. F. 1328
Key, E. 2767
key informant 2457–8
    and unstructured interviewing 2408
Keyes v. *School District No. 1, Denver,*
    Colorado 369
Keynes, J. M. 1387, 2021, 2817, 3079, 3178
Keynesianism
    economics 1061, 2625
    and expectations 1384
    and ideology 2231
    liberalism 3176
    welfare state 1298
Khaldun, Ibn 147, **2458–62**
    and *'asabiyya* 181, 182, 184
    civilization theory 180
    Muqaddima 180, 181
    and political sociology 3458
Khmer Rouge 1452, 1910
Khomeini, Ayatollah 1378, 1814
Khong Kauw Hwee 670–1
Khosrokhavar, F. 2801
kibbutzim 2753
Kibria, N. 1404–6
Kidd, B. 4656–8
Kiely, R. 2214
Kigler, A. 3028
kigyobetsu kumiai 1413–17
Kilbourne, J. 1850
Kilday, K. 1654
Kilker, E. 3660
Killian, L. M. 1367, 3065
Kilmann, R. 1583

Kilpatrick, J. 2851–2
Kim, A. H. 5109–12
Kim, C. 3112–17, 3763
Kim, S. 3093–6
Kimball, S. 1575, 1576, 1577, 1579
Kimmel, M. S. 736, 1664, 4272–5
Kinberg, O. 970
Kincheloe, J. 867
kindergarten 2462–5
kinesics 1995
Kinfdleberger, C. 2021
King, C. R. 3547–8, 3789–92, 4681–4
King, Dave 5037–43
King, Deborah 308
King, Martin Luther 508, 509, **2465–7**, 3680
    and direct action 1165
    and frame articulation 1782
    non-violent resistance 4459
    and social justice 2465
King, Mary 1674
King, S. 2058
king-gods 521
kinging 1224
Kingsbury, S. M. 131
kingship 1359
    divine right of kings 2529
    "two bodies" theory 229
Kingston, P. 891
kinky sex *see* sadomasochism
Kinney, W. J. 64–7, 189–91
Kinsey, Alfred 2158, 2161, **2467–9**, 3418,
    4264, 4286, 4287, 4288, 4289
    and bisexuality 302–3
    and female sexuality 5269
    and homosexuality 4289
    and masturbation 2833–4
    and oral sex 3277
Kinsey Institute 2159, 2468
Kinsey Report 331
Kinsey scale 303
kinship 2469–71
    and altruism 3680
    and *'asabiyya* 181, 182
    and capitalism 397
    and caste 404
    collective networks 2471
    and community 636
    and conjugal roles 672
    and culture of poverty 1612, 1614
    demographic data 287
    and elder care 1350
    and *en* 1401

and ethnic groups, distinguished 1457
and ethnicity 1476
and family and community 1576
and family sociology 1575
and family structure 1619
and framing theory 238
and gender stratification 2308
and gift exchange 1938
grandparenthood 2017–20
and homicide 293
impact of new reproductive technologies 3207
Japanese 2239
kin recognition 294
kin selection 292, 294
matrilineal 2469, 2858
and *minzoku* 3058
and nationalism 3156
networks 2471
and patriarchy 2302
patrilineal 2469
and reciprocity 3227
social support provision 90
and structural balance 2144–5
and traffic in women 2155, 3775
see also family structure; households
kinship-based economies 514
Kippax, S. 106–11
Kipping, M. 2720
Kirk, R. E. 1533–7, 3349–50, 3782–3
Kirkey, K. 1803
Kirmeyer, S. 1741–5
Kirton, G. 1888–91
Kishor, S. 3533–7
Kissinger, Henry 3380
Kitano, S. 2239
Kitchin cycle 2489, 2490
Kitsuse, John I. 1089, 1091, 1123, 1137, 2207, 2209, **2471–4**
    constructivist perspective 2472, 2473
    and deviance 2472
    labeling theory 2472–3
Kitzinger, C. 2611
Kivisto, P. 128–30, 3362–5
Kiznets, S. 1425
Klandermans, B. 3067
Klein, D. 1630
Klein, L. 815–17
Klein, M. W. 1825, 1826
Klein, N. 356, 359, 4333
Klein Sexual Orientation Grid (KSOG) 303
Kleinman, A. 2245
Kleinman, D. L. 2524–6, 4068–9

Kleinman, S. 1379
Klenow, P. J. 1332
Klesse, C. 301–5, 3477–9, 3882–5
Kliman, A. 1543–6
Kline, F. 797
Kline, N. 3626
Klinenberg, E. 1174
Klute, M. M. 1868
Knight, F. 1387, 2777
Knight, J. Z. 3191
Knights of Labor 2518, 2519
Knöbl, W. 5213–16
Knorr, N. H. 2439
Knorr-Cetina, K. 2525, 4957
knowledge 2474–6
    androcentric 1701, 1706, 1712
    authority structure of 601
    black-boxed knowledge 2730, 4065
    causal knowledge 426
    codified knowledge 2328
    commodification of 2726
    connaissance 1772, 1773
    construction 2525
    defining 2480
    differentiated knowledge 377
    diffusion 2478
    epistemology 1434–6
    genetic knowledge 2939
    and hierachies, maintenance of 2484
    innovative 2844
    instrumental knowledge 2432
    knowledge chains 2738
    knowledge sector, growth of 601
    and management innovation 2737, 2738
    management knowledge 2727
    mediated knowledge 2924
    metaphysical 651
    patriarchal control of 1708
    positive 651
    practical knowledge 3606–7
    professional 3619, 3661
    redundancy 2717
    savoir 1772, 1773, 1774
    scientific 2624, 2844, 3222
    secularization of 1922
    sharing 2479, 2480
    situated knowledges 1711
    tacit knowledge 2478
    theological 651
    transient knowledge 2721
knowledge associations 1402
knowledge economy 944, 1009, 2728

knowledge-intensive firms 2524
knowledge management 2476–80,
  2716–17, 2729
  commodification of knowledge 2716
  efficiency 2716
  and human resource management 2479
  and ICT 2479
  knowledge workers, domination of 2716
  and organizational learning 3308
knowledge production 944, 2844, 3181
  feminist reconceptualizations 1705
  and feminst pedagogy 1708
  and the outsider-within concept 3351
  politics of 963–4
knowledge representation 3725
knowledge societies 1758, **2480–2**
  see also information society
knowledge, sociology of 2482–5
  and biography 289
  and classification 554–6
  and controversy studies 784
  and Durkheim 1259
  and the ecological view of history 1287
  formal apriorism 2757
  French tradition 2474, 2475
  German tradition 2474, 2475
  historicism 2757
  and identity 2220
  and ideology 2483, 2484
  Mannheim and 589, 2757–8
  material apriorism 2757
  and phenomenology 3403
  positivist perspective 2757
  Strong Program 4846–7
knowledge workers 1009, 2477, 2716
Knowles, H. 1639
Knowles, J. G. 2641, 2642–3
Known, Useable, Functional, Appropriate, and
  Triggered (KUFAT) process 2237, 2238
Kobayashi, M. 2803
Koedt, A. 2112, 3400
Koehler, W. 1749
Kofman, E. 1606
Kofta, M. 2569
Kohlberg, L. 837, 876, 1072, 3679, 3680, 3699
Kohli, M. 1900–6
Kohn, H. 3153, 3155
Kohn, R. 3043
Koike, K. 3171
Kokosalakis, N. 3345–9
Kolakowski, L. 3069
Kolar-Panov, D. 2886

Kollontai, A. 2838, 2841
Kolodny, A. 1274
Komarovsky, Mirra 131, **2485–9**
Kondo, D. 1692
Kondratieff cycles 1263, **2489–92**, 3437
  and economic change 3437
  Kondrative B-phase 362
Kondratieff, Nikolai 1263, 2489
Kong, T. S. K. 4213–18
Konty, M. 225–9, 2501–54
Kool Herc 3486
Kopytoff, I. 742
Koran *see* Qur'an
Korea
  adolescent fertility 1725
  boy:girl ratio 1158
  Buddhism 371
  Confucianism 672
  higher education 602
Korean Americans 1454
  middleman minorities 3009, 3010
Korean War 3041
Korenman, S. 1629, 1727
Koresh, David 3047
Kornberger, M. 1439–42
Kornhauser, R. R. 847
Kornhauser, W. 2822, 3065
Korsch, K. 1151
Kosaka, K. 2497–500
Koselleck, R. 3069
Kosovo 1451, 4188
  civil wars 1470
  marginalized groups 2764
Kotarba, J. A. 1519–24, 4563–6
Kovalevsky, A. 302
Kowinski, W. S. 713
Kozinets, R. V. 945–6, 3554
Kracauer, S. 1754
Krafft-Ebing, Richard von 2132, **2492–3,**
  4284, 5269
  and homosexuality 302, 331
  and pedophilia 3386
  and sadomasochism 3985–6, 4285
Krase, J. 3898–9
Krasmann, S. 1176–9, 2008–11
Krasner, S. D. 4623–6
Krause, E. 3659
Krause, N. 2074
Kremen, E. 1723
Kress, G. 3112
Krieken, R. van 529–33
Krishna Consciousness 3202, 3506

Kristallnacht 2142
Kristeva, Julia 869, 3552, 3581
  and genre 1916
  intertextuality 216, 2402, 4974
  poststructuralism 244
  and pregnancy 333
Kristol, I. 3172
Kritz, M. M. 3019–25
Kroc, Ray 2689, 3705
Kroeber, A. L. 909
Krohn, W. 1757–9
Kroker, A. 3569
Kroker, M. 3569
Kropotkin, P. 136, 1165
Kroska, A. 1867–9
Krueger, D. 1332
Krueger, M. 1751
Krupskaya, N. 2841
Ku Klux Klan 508, 833, 2049, 3733, 3746, 3769
Kubler-Ross, Elizabeth 234, 973
Kubrick, S. 3880
Kucretius 3669
Kuehlewein, K. 1087
Kuhn, M. H. 2218
Kuhn, Thomas 1509, 1531, 3222, 3293, 3546
  and finalization theory 1757
  and knowledge, sociology of 784, 2844
Kuhn, Thomas and scientific paradigms
  2493–7, 2964, 3355, 3547, 3577, 3814–15,
  3831, 4065, 4070, 4086, 4116, 4598
Kuhse, H. 1490
Kulik, L. 2546–8
Kumar, K. B. 1332
Kumazawa, M. 2437
Kunda, G. 2723
Kundera, M. 3005, 3006
Kunkel, S. 1927
Kunz, E. 3835
Kuper, L. 3420
Kuran, T. 1316–17
Kurasawa, S. 5143–4
Kurauchi, Kazuta 2497–500
Kurdish nation 1152, 1466, 1469, 1470, 1486,
  2003, 4188
Kurihara, T. 3251–4, 3992–4, 4154–7
Kurita, Y. 1402
Kusow, A. M. 4778–9
Kuwayama, T. 237–9, 2238–41, 2445–7, 5301–5
Kuznets, S. 1566, 3526
Kuznets cycle 2489
Kymlicka, W. 1459, 1938
Kyoto School 1286

labeling 2501–4
  and affect control theory 2272
  apartheid and 162
  destigmatizing labels 2209
  and deviance 1078, 1086, 1105–6, 1124,
    1125, 1143, 2207–8, 2472, 2501–3, 2505,
    2766, 2832, 2951, 2952, 3543
  and drug use 26
  and gangs 1827
  and the hidden curriculum 2117
  internalizing 2504
  Kitsuse and 2472–3
  positive functions 2506
  and self-fulfilling prophecy 2117
  and social control 2952, 4388–9
  see also stigma
labeling theory 2504–7
  and conflict theory 667
  and criminology 858
  and deviance 1102, 1120, 1123, 1124, 1136,
    1137, 1138
  and disability 1170
  and juvenile delinquency 2454
  and mental disorder 2695
  and moral entrepreneurship 3088
  and sexuality 4264–5
labor/labor power 2507–9, 2522
  alienation of 119, 874, 929, 1200, 1201, 1502,
    2580, 2750, 2752, 2807, 2816
  automation of 1200
  class exploitation of 1201
  commodification 1201
  emotional labor 1187
  exchange value 1201
  exchange-value 1515
  flexible labor 1959
  hierarchical division 275
  and the Industrial Revolution 2295
  mental and manual 1200, 1201
  ontological nature 2507–8
  performative labor 1187
  social disrepute 682
  social relations of 611
  underpaid labor 1852
  unpaid labor 939, 1841, 1852, 1881
  use-value 1201
  see also division of labor; labor markets;
    occupations
labor contract 552
labor law 4737, 4738–40
labor–management relations 2509–14
  and absenteeism 4

labor–management relations (*cont'd*)
  Anglo-American model 2510, 2512
  core labor standards 2509, 2510–11
  European model 2510
  evolution of 2510
  and human resource management 2509, 2510
  industrial relations perspective 2509, 2512
  institutions 2510–11
  neoliberal perspective 2512
  social pacts 2511
  under capitalism 396
  workers' participation in management
    (WPM) 2753
  see also collective bargaining; Japanese-style
    management
labor markets 2514–18
  casualization of work 350
  child labor 455–6
  and class consciousness 2515
  comparable worth issue 1669
  competition theory 1469
  diversification 3289
  domestic service 3031
  effects of immigration labor on natives
    3028–9
  and employment status changes 1399–400
  ethnicity, inequalities and 2517
  family positions and labor market outcomes
    1882, 1883
  feminization of 1399, 1663, 2750, 3245
  immigrant labor 2305, 2306, 2307, 2383,
    2519, 3012, 3027, 3031, 3445, 3745–6
  inequalities 1844, 2397, 2516–17, 3245
  informal labor market 3031
  internal labor markets 1249, 1416, 3287
  internal markets 1769, 2290
  Japanese 2438
  labor market dualism 1249–50
  labor market segmentation 1463
  and lone parents 2665–6
  metropolitan labor markets 1463
  older workers 103–5
  out-migration, and labor shortages 1039
  primary markets 1892, 2514
  and public/private spheres intersection 1889
  regulation 1399–400
  secondary markets 1892, 2514
  segmentation 1250
  sexual domination 3320
  shortages 3527
  skilled labor 3286, 3289
  and spatial mismatch hypothesis 4629–32

  split labor market theory 664, 1463,
    1469, 3012
  unskilled labor 3286
  see also division of labor; occupations; women
    in the labor market
labor migrants 3021, 3022
labor movement 2518–21
  American 702, 1570, 2289
  and Fordism 702
  and injustice accounts 11
  laborism 2526–7
  organizational forms 3259
  and women 609
labor process 2521–4
  alienation of labor 119, 874, 929, 1200, 1201,
    1502, 2580, 2750, 2752, 2807, 2816
  deskilling thesis 364–5, 366
  Marxist theory 363, 364, 538, 2507–8
  see also scientific management
labor socialism *see* laborism
labor turnover 1769
labor unions *see* unions
laboratory ethnography 2526
laboratory experiments 1540–1
**laboratory studies and the world of the
    scientific lab 2524–6**, 4098
  ethnographic studies 4074–5
  and methodology 2968
  and scientific practice 2844
  sociology of scientific knowledge (SSK)
    studies 4098
laborism 2526–7
  Anglo phenomenon 2526
  and managerialism 2526–7
Labour Party 2628
Labov, W. 1181, 1373
Lacan, Jacques 125, 242, **2527–9**
  and Guattari 2037
  and the imaginary 2110
  postmodernism 3570
  and queer theory 2114
  and sexual desire 3698
Lacey, H. 1449
Lackey, G. F. 4837–40
Laclau, E. 2815, 3538
Lactantius 3854
Ladson-Billings, G. 1446
Ladurie, L. R. 144
LaGory, M. 2073
Lagos, R. 1564, 1565
Lahelma, E. 2086–91
Lahm, K. 1064–5, 5165–7

laicism **2529–33**, 4145
  characteristics 2531
  political process 2529
Laing, R. D. 248, 3333
Lair, C. D. 1940–1, 3917–20
laissez faire leadership 2617
laissez-faire capitalism 515, 1296, 1506, 2232
laissez-faire economics 1306, 2233, 2298,
  2779, 3361
laissez-faire liberalism 2624, 3176
laissez-faire philosophies 624
laissez-faire racism 3616
Laitin, D. D. 1468, 1469, 1470
Lakatos, I. 1571–2, 1757, 4079, 4080,
  4084, 4085
Lal, B. B. 3943–5
Lalitha, K. 1692
Lamarck, chevalier de 1505
Lamb, J. 3726–8
Lamnek, S. 3120–3, 5238–41
Lamont, M. 890, 891, 958
land claims
  indigenous 2280
  Native American 2283
land development interests 2035, 3115
Land, K. C. 4420–6
land ownership, indigenous 2279
land use and land cover change 3532, 3533
landfills 1425
landlord class 1002
landmines 1978, 1979
Landow, G. 3111
Lane, P. 2282
Lang, A. 3631
Láng, J. 2756
Lang, R. 5050–4
Langenkamp, A. G. 4042–5
Langer, B. 1960–4
Langman, L. 30–4, 873–7, 876, 2336–7,
  4308–11, 4328–31, 5043–7
language **2533–8**
  abusive 1183
  and acculturation 817
  ancient languages 2534
  artifical languages 2535, 2536
  child language acquisition and development
    1269, 1270, 2654
  colonial languages 2260–1
  and cultural imperialism 907
  and deconstruction 986–7, 988
  definition 2534

  and discrimination 1182
  diversity 1197
  and ethnicity 1476
  feminist alternative language 2603
  geolinguistic regions 2889–90
  hybrid languages 1152
  immigrant language maintenance
    programs 2261
  immigration and language 2258–61
  indigenous languages 278, 2280
  intergenerational language shift 2259–60
  linguistic segregation 370
  and media globalization 2889–90
  pidgin language 1179, 3280
  and power 786
  regional minority languages 279–80
  and resistance 2984
  and self-definition 306, 3186, 3187, 4158
  and social interaction 2362
  of sport 4673
  vernacular languages 2534
  see also converation analysis; conversation;
    linguistics; sociolinguistics
language acquisition
  "English-only" movement 2280
  immersion programs 277, 279, 2260, 2261
  Lacan and 2528
  second-language acquisition 281–2
  Skinner and 258
  submersion programs 277
language shift 634
  emergent phenomenon 634
  and identity politics 2214
language standardization movements 282
langue **and** *parole* 2537, **2538–9**, 4181
  structuralist approach 2539, 4181
Lao Siguang 670
Lapouge, V. de 2002
Laqueur, T. 335, 1437, 5269
larceny-theft 2278, 2555
Lareau, A. 887–92, 1326, 2655
Laroui, A. 2427
Larsen, U. 1864–7
Larson, M. 3657, 3661, 3663
Las Vegas
  architecture 2124
  casinos 2194
  fantasy city 1641
  gambling 1821
  simulacra 3567, 4330
  strip 734–5, 759
Lasch, C. 312, 2650, 3193

Lash, S. 2402, 2649, 3567, 3830
Lask, E. 2040, 2041, 2756
Laski, H. 2141, 3423, 3424
Lasn, K. 359
Lasswell, H. 3443, 3472, 3474, 3672
Latané, B. 3679, 3680
late-life sexuality 2539–42
latent content 777
latent growth curve models 98–9, 2542–6
latent learning 257
latent semantic analysis 639, 643
latent structure analysis 2565
later-life marriage 2546–8
Lather, P. 5161–5
Lathrop, J. 131
Latin America
    adolescent fertility 1725
    anti-globalization movements 1948
    authoritarian states 2576
    bankruptcy law 241
    bourgeoisie 1923
    caudillismo 411–15, 1923
    civil wars 1923
    colonialism 602, 603, 985
    community media 627
    democracy, transition to 1688, 2576,
        2577, 2578
    dependency theory 1060, 1068
    dictatorships 1852, 1923
    economic development 1565, 1566, 2577
    and federalism 1652
    feminist activism 1685–9, 1873
    fertility levels 1738, 1739
    film industry 1753
    hybridity 2190
    ideologies of industrialization 1925
    indigenous movements 2278–80
    industrialization 1566
    life expectancies 3097
    medical sociology 2935
    modernization 1922–6
    mortality 3099
    popular religiosity 3519, 3520, 3522, 3523
    populism 413, 3528, 3537
    Protestantism 441
    sex tourism 4220
    sexual cultures 4218–21
    social urban movements 415, 1948
    and state theory 2575
    teenage fertility 1726
    transition model 1923–4
    truth commissions 3382

    see also individual countries
Latin language 2896
Latinidad and consumer culture 2548–52
Latino/as and Chicano/as 661, 1459, 3118
    Chicano theory 1712, 2984–5
    cultural heterogeneity 901
    and drag subculture 1224, 1225
    education 370
    educational attainment 1335, 4150
    educational segregation 3752–3
    and elder care 2381
    ethnic enclaves 1453, 1454
    feminism 3118, 3776
    folk medicine 2079
    interracial marriage 2394
    patriarchal authority 2302
    and poverty 1719
    rates of pay 1844
    and social movements 1873
    and sport 2222
    see also Hispanic Americans; specific groups
        e.g. Mexican Americans
Latour, B. 20, 21, 22, 23, 786, 2525, 2844–5,
    3165, 3549, 4096
    actor-network theory 219, 2364, 2904, 3548
Latvia 1451, 4168
    race and ethnic conflict 1469
Lau Remedies 278
Laub, J. H. 830, 831
Laudan, L. 4085
Lauderdale, P. 1114–16
Laughlin, H. 4115
Laumann, E. O. 1796
Lavender, A. D. 2448–54
Lavender Menace 2602
LaVey, A. S. 4010, 4011
Law, I. 22, 1182–4
Law, J. 20, 2364, 3165, 3548, 3549
law
    canon law 3348
    common law of England 1092, 2183, 2454,
        2552, 2554, 2555
    and cultural norms 1207
    and decision-making 983
    definitions of 1238, 2583
    employment law 4737–8
    functionalist lawmaking 667
    institutional embeddedness 2561
    labor law 4737, 4738–40
    legal consciousness 2561
    sexuality and the law 4268–71
    sociological jurisprudence 3585–6

law, civil 2552–3
law, criminal 2553–7, 3586
law, economy and 2557–60
   and institutionalism 2353, 2355–6
law enforcement 852–3, 1108–9
   discretion 852, 853
   specialized agencies 852
   see also courts; criminal justice system; police
law schools 4047
law, sociology of 2560–4
Lawler, E. 1369, 1380, 3601, 3604
Lawrence, B. 1815
Lawson, J. H. 1755
lawyers and paralegals 1894, 3649, 4047
Layte, R. 1398–400
Lazaridis, G. 3031
Lazarsfeld, Paul 2486, **2564–5**, 3779
   and Adorno 27
   and Blau 313
   communciation research 208
   empirical method 2960
   and friendship 795
   and Fromm 1806
   and mass culture 2821
   and mass media 2825, 2882, 3635
   and Merton 2959, 2960
   and Mills 3053
   and quantitative methods 2023–4, 2407
Lazarus, C. 1059
Le Bon, G. 1767
Le Cour, P. 3190
Le Galès, P. 493–7
Le Guin, U. K. 3495, 3496
Le Play, F. 1574, 1576, 3123
Leach, E. 1751
Leach, W. 743, 1057
leadership 2565–7
   authoritarian 220–1, 2031, 3701
   autocratic 2617
   black leadership 2466
   caudillismo 411–15
   charismatic 259, 412, 413–15, 433–7, 508, 886, 2565, 2566, 3203, 3510
   communicative phenomenon 3293
   communist 616
   and consumer movements 699
   democratic 2031, 2617
   dispersed leadership 2566
   and dyads/triads 1267
   and ethics 1439
   and gender 1874
   heroic 3564

   and human resource management 2179
   and improvisation 2736
   insecurity of leadership status 1008
   laissez faire 2617
   leadership vacuum 418–19
   legal leadership 2565
   and management education 2728
   myth and 415
   neoconservative 3174
   organizational 3300–1
   philosophical analysis 3444
   political 412–13, 3441–4
   political professionalization 1008
   positive deviance 3543
   positive psychology of 2566
   postmodern leaders 2566–7
   professionalization 1008
   relationship-oriented 3301
   situational leadership theory 2565–6
   in social movements 4453–4
   task-oriented 3300–1
   traditional leaders 2565
   trait-based approaches 2565
   transactional 438, 2566
   transformational leadership 2566
League of the Just 1409
league tables 213
Lealand, G. 3792–3
lean manufacturing 3269
learned helplessness 67, **2567–70**
learning
   exposure learning 257
   latent learning 257
   learning opportunities 3270–6
   organizational learning 3307–10
   prepared (biased, directed) learning 294
   see also education; social learning theory
learning models 3795
Learning Organization 2729
Learning Society 1329, 1330
Lears, Jackson 743
leaving home in the transition to adulthood 2570–5
Leavis, F. R. 2877
Lebanon 2801
Lechner, F. J. 1967, 1968, 1990, 1992
Lechner, Norbert 2575–80
Leclerc-Madlala, S. 4209–13
Lederberg, J. 1489
Lee, A. M. 132
Lee, B. A. 2418–20
Lee, C.-Y. 4924–30

Lee, J. 2671, 2672, 3480
Lee, R. 1297
Lee, S. 1445
Lee, Sooho 4112–13
Lee, Spike 708
Lee, Susan Hagood 1653–7, 5031–4
Lee, V. 622, 2462–5
Lees, L. 1919
Lefanu, S. 3496
Lefebvre, Henri 2195, **2580–2**
  and circulation of capital 389
  and commodity fetishization 757
  and consumption 703, 704, 2195, 3554
  and Debord 980
  and everyday life 1502
  and modernity 702
  situationism 4335
  and social space of the city 501
  urban sociology 389
Lefort, C. 2815
left-handedness 326
legal personhood concept 2557
legal profession 2562, **2583–4**
  capital accumulation strategies 3664
  ethics 2562
  and management consultancy 2720
Legion of Decency 1753
legitimacy 1356–7, 1527, **2584–7**
  Arendt and 229
  bases of 229–30
  crisis of legitimation 231
  democratic 230
  and feminist epistemology 1683
  and institutionalism 2353, 2354
  legitimate power 229
  market legitimization 2550
  mixed methods research 2980
  and resource mobilization theory 3895
  and social movements 4472
  sociological approaches 229
  sport legitimization 4650
  state legitimacy 3233
  Weber on 229–30
Legitimation League 1365
Legrain, P. 1959
Lehmann, J. 582
Lehn, D. vom 2361–5
Lehnerer, M. 1885–8
Lehrer, E. 1315
Leicester School 1768
leisure 2588–92
  age-related differences 2592–4, 2595

androcentric theories 2589, 2592
casual leisure 2598–9
class differentials 2628
commercialized leisure 766, 767, 2125, 2594
as compensation 2588
cultural tourism 919–21
definition 2588
as deviance 2593, 2596, 2598–9
feminist perspective 2589
gendered experience 2589, 2592, 2593
intersectionality 2592
involuntary and problematic leisure 2595
leisure careers 2597
Marxist theory 2589
and masculine sexuality 736
materialist perspective 2589
phenomenology of leisure 2590
and play 3414
pluralist model 2588–9
post-industrial 768
postmodern perspective 2590
range of activities 2596–7
as residual time 2588
social interactionist perspective 2589
structuralist perspective 2589
surveys 2590–1
uncoerced activity 2596
work–leisure relationship 2588, 2591
work–leisure–family balance 2591
see also holidays; sport
leisure, aging and 2592–4
  and friendship 1787–8
  the oldest old 2669
leisure class 2594–6, 2645
leisure industries 325
leisure, popular culture and 2596–600
  cultural tourism 919–21
  and *flânerie* 1762–3
leisure society 2595
Leiter, V. 1572–4
Leites, N. 1754
Lemarchand, R. 380–2
Lemelle, A. 3265–7
Lemert, C. 1087, 1124
Lemert, Edwin M. 1123, 1136, 1137, 1138, 2208, 2209, 2472, **2600–1**
  labeling theory 2472, 2501, 3005
  and primary/secondary deviance 2501, 2505
  and social control 4388
Lemkin, R. 1909
LeMoyne, T. 4782–4
Lengermann, P. 1666–71, 2766–70

Lenin, V. I. 2685, 4224
and cinema 1753
and colonialism 603
and communism 615
and Hegelian conssness 1148
and historical materialism 2837
and imperialism 1068, 1394–5, 2267, 2686, 3179
and self-determination 4167
and Taylorism 2746, 2828
Leninism 3585
Lenski, G. 2297, 2626–7, 2795, 3073, 4820
Lenskyj, H. 1134–5
Leopold, E. 749
Leoussi, A. S. 3152–8
Lerner, D. 2899
Leroux, P. 614
Lesbian Avengers 1677, 1835
lesbian feminism 1675, **2601–6**, 2610, 3775
central tenets 2601
critiques of 2605
and cultural feminism 902, 2603
heterosexual critique 2115
ideology 2602, 2603, 2604, 2605
lesbian separatism 2603–4, 2605
origins 2601–2
political statements 2602, 2604
radical feminist ideology 3775
research 2604–5
women-identified women 2602, 2603
lesbian, gay, bisexual, and transgender (LGBT)
equality rights 2156
LGBT studies 1663, 1664, 2157
violence against 2162
lesbian and gay families 2161, **2606–9**
and carework 2608
and children 1624, 2607
and domestic duties 2608
and family terminology 2607
friendship model 2607
lesbian lone mothers 2666
self-disclosing intimacy 2412–13
see also same-sex marriage/civil unions
lesbian separatism 2603–4, 2605
lesbian sex 2613
lesbian sex wars 2603
lesbianism 2609–14
and aging 901
biomedical research 2612
black lesbian separatism 307
butch lesbians 1224
coming-out narratives 303

consciousness-raising 677
and consumption 4257
criminalization 2612
definition issues 2609
denigration of in sport 1878
desexualization 2610
essentialist/constructivist debate 2610, 2612
etymology 2609
and family membership 1590
female masculinity 331, 1657–8
and friendship 1804
and gentrification 1919
and the homosexual contract 2113
and household membership 1590
and Islamic culture 2429
lesbian continuum 2113, 4265
lesbian identity 1878, 2611, 4239–40
political lesbianism 5270
radical lesbianism 2113, 4265
and resistance to patriarchy 2113
and self-determination 2155
self-reporting 1129
sexual citizenship 4206
sexual health agenda 4236–7
sexual migration 4220–1
and sport, denigration in 1878, 4291
and stigma 2609, 2613
urban living and consumption 768
violence against 1098
young lesbians 466
see also friendships of gay, lesbian, and bisexual people
Leslie, L. A. 1634–6
Leslie, T. E. C. 3045
less developed countries (LDCs)
product manufacture 3441
unequal exchange theory 1545
see also developing countries
Lessenich, S. 5241–2
Lesthaeghe, R. J. 1733, 4123–7
Lesvos/Lesbos 2609
lethal injection, execution by 386
Leufgen, J. 2146–51
Leur, J. C. van 1492
Levelers 3048
Levene, R. 2948
Leventhal, H. 2242
Lever, J. 1661
Lévi-Strauss, Claude 219, 242, 252
and bricolage 365
and food 721
and law of reciprocity 3228

Lévi-Strauss, Claude (*cont'd*)
  and mythical thinking 556, 1916, 2700, 3136
  and patriarchal relations 3378
  structuralism 4182, 4856–7
  and symbolic anthropology 1257
  and symbolic classification 4907
  and symbolic systems 1251
  and totemism 5021
  and twins, cultural significance of 556
Levin, J. 2048–50
Levinas, E. 3673
Levine, I. 810, 811
Levine, M. 2159
Levine, S. 2934, 3658
Levinthal, D. 3308
Levi's 739
Levitt, N. 1088–9, 1509
Levittown 2614–15
  and popular culture 2124
Levy, D. 2099–101, 3377–80
Levy, J. A. 2539–42
Levy, M. 1406, 1811
Lévy-Bruhl, L. 259, 262, 1251, 1257, 2474,
    2698, 3630, 3632, 3633
Lewin, Kurt 1749, **2615–18**
  and action research 19
  applied social psychology 4517, 4518
  and change management 430
  field theory 2616, 3701
  and group dynamics 3701
  social psychology 2616, 3679
Lewinsky, Monica 417
Lewis, J. E. 2516
Lewis, Meriwether 2282
Lewis, O. 288, 951, 1612
Lewis, R. 2773, 3344
Lewis, T. E. 896–8
Lewontin, R. 1507, 1508
Ley, D. 1919
Lezaun, J. 1531–3, 4635–7
Leznoff, M. 2159
Lhotshampas ethnic groups 1458
Liang Shumin 670
liberal capitalism 3124
liberal conservatism 681
liberal democracy 1004, 2623, 2624, 2757, 3076
  and totalitarianism 5019
liberal democratic citizenship 4206
liberal feminism 1666, 1675, **2618–22**
  elitism 2621
  and female criminality 1694
  Marxist critiques 2841

  and sport 1876, 4291
  theoretical foundation 2618
  and women's inequality 1888–9
liberalism 2622–5
  classical liberalism 2624, 2625, 3451
  conservative opposition to 678, 680
  core beliefs 2622
  counter-movements 2624
  cultural doctrine 2623
  and cultural issues 2234
  and democracy 2623, 2624
  economic liberalism 2285
  and governmentality 2008–9
  ideological disagreement 2624
  and imperialism 2267
  individualism 678, 807, 2622
  laissez-faire liberalism 2624, 2625
  left-liberal agenda 2625
  liberal–conservative continuum 2232
  and marital quality 1868
  national traditions of 2624
  new liberalism 2624
  political doctrine 2623
  political economy 2623
  and private property 3677, 3678
  progressive liberalism 4367
  "rational" liberalism 2624
  religious liberalism 4278
  revival 2624
  and sadomasochism 3986
  universalism 678
  and utilitarianism 2624
  see also neoliberalism
liberation hypothesis, and deviance and crime
    1857
liberation movements 1885
liberation theology 441
  Islamic 1814
liberatory feminist pedagogy 1707–8
Liberia 1725
libertarianism 1162, 3177
liberty choice 2041
liberty principle 3812
libido 2541
libraries, and multimedia 3109
library classification 1914
Libya 1724
licensing 2912, 2915
Lichter, D. T. 1626–9, 1628, 1727
Lichter, M. 1463–5
Lichterman, P. 2238
Lidz, V. 3365–8

Lie, J. 1494, 3458–63, 3915–17
Lieberson, S. 1463, 1464, 2257
Liebig, J. von 599
Liebknecht, K. 2685
Liebow, Elliot 2457, **2625–6**, 2976, 2977
life chances and resources 2626–30
  and health lifestyles 2062
  ideology hypothesis 2626, 2627
  schooling and economic success 4029–31
  social class and 535, 541, 547, 550
  technology hypothesis 2626–7
life course 2630–2
  biographical approach 2632
  and embodiment 327
  and marriage 2789, 2791, 2792
  in primitive societies 2631
  sociostructural approach 2632
  status passages 2631
  stressful life events 4843–4
  time concept 2633
  transitions 2631
  see also gerontology
life course and family 2632–4
  developmental stages 1072–3
  and family demography 1584
  and family structure 1620
  and family theory 1631
  family time 2633
  and generational change 1901
  and grandparenthood 215–18
  historical time 2633
  individual time 2633
  post-parental life 2633, 2774
  transition to adulthood, and leaving home
    2570–4
life course perspective 2632, 2634–9
  age identity 49–51
  age, period, and cohort effects 52–6
  and aging 73–6, 98–100, 1930, 1934
  career pattern 1142
  and employment status changes 1399
  and friendships 878, 1796, 1802
  and gender relations 1841
  health and illness differentials 1186
  and health inequalities 2089–90
  human agency principle 2636
  intergenerational relationships and exchanges
    2381
  leisure and aging 2593
  life course theory of crime 830–2
  linked lives principle 2636, 2637
  trajectories and transitions 2632, 2634–5

life cycle 2635, 2637, 2638
life environmentalism 2640–1
  daily life pollution 967–8
  and semi-domestication 4179
life events, transformative 241, 1185
life expectancy *see* healthy life expectancy
life history 2641–4
  and biography 289, 290
  and journal writing 2448
  and migrant research 1716
  and social movements 449–51
  see also event history analysis
life insurance 1386
"life politics" 2910
life satisfaction 50, 80, 1548
  later life 80–1, 82, 97, 98
  predictors of 82
  quality of life measures 1296–7
  scales 80
  school students 1548
  social indicators 4420
life span 2635, 2637
  see also healthy life expectancy
life stage hypothesis 76, 2631
life-support systems 973
life-table analysis
  fertility 1039
  and healthy life expectancy 2095–7
  mortality 1021–5, 1026
Lifelong Learning 1329–30, 1974
lifestyle 2644–6
  and community 636
  digital lifestyles 2880
  and disease onset 1866
  and health and illness 2059
  health lifestyles 2061–2
  and hyperconsumption/overconsumption
    2192
  in old age 2669
  risky lifestyle 2073
  as status emulation 2647
  transnational lifestyle 5065
  urban–rural differences 637
lifestyle consumption 715, 2646–51
  and environmental sustainability 728
  and health lifestyles 2061–2
  and leisure 2599
lifestyle magazines 1850
lifestyle migrants 3021, 3022
lifeworld 876, 2108, 2534, 2651–3
  characteristics 2651–2
  "colonization" of 2652

Light, D. 2709, 2935, 3656–60, 3657, 3658
Light, I. 1459
Likert, R. 2407
Limbaugh, R. 2337
limerance 2672
liminality 3933
limited liability principle 2295
Limón, J. 2550
Lin, J. 1452–6
Lincoln, Abbey 308
Lincoln, Abraham 592
Lincoln, K. D. 4527–31
Lincoln, Y. S. 213–16, 1448, 2349, 2980, 2981, 3161–3, 3355–6
Lind, A. 1662–6, 4203–5
Lind, B. 4453–5
Lindenberg, S. 3804
Lindert, P. H. 2311
Lindesmith, A. 134–5
linear thinking 249
linearity 426
LINGUA exchange program 279
linguistic determinism 3280
linguistic minorities 283
linguistic philosophy critique 1838
linguistic poststructuralism 3580–1
linguistic relativity 3280
linguistic turn 2539
linguistics 2534
    anthropological linguistics 2535, 2536
    apparent-time hypothesis 4595–6
    and discourse 1180
    ethnolinguistics 2535, 2536
    historical linguistics 2535
    life stories 288
    multimodality 3112
    philosophical problems 2534
    phonetics 1371
    psychological linguistics 2535
    Saussurean 1154
    social science questions 2534
    sociolinguistics 4593–6
    structural linguistics 1154
    taxonomic linguistics 2535
    see also language
Linnaeus, C. 2857, 4114
Lins, M. 2948
Linstead, S. 3563–8
Linton, R. 3945, 3952, 4750
Lipovetsky, G. 3575
Lippitt, R. 2617
Lippman, A. 2173

Lippman, W. 2906, 3193, 3442, 3467, 3469, 3672, 4775, 4776
Lipscomb, M. 1062–4
Lipset, S. M. 547, 549, 570, 1001, 1007, 1008, 1921, 2795, 2796, 2960, 3061, 3172, 3259, 3460
liquor industry 766
Lisbon 765
Lister, M. 3404–8
Lister, R. 1438
Liston, K. 1751
Liston-Heyes, C. 3268
literacy/illiteracy 2653–6, 4382
    adult literacy programs 1329
    biliteracy 277
    critical pedagogy and 865
    definitions 866, 2653, 2892
    democracy, literacy as predictor of 1002, 1003
    and early childhood 1270
    and educational attainment 1334
    and industrialization 2298
    mass literacy 3469, 3635–6
    measuring 2653, 2654
    media literacy 2891–4, 3635–6
    Mexico 340
    migrants 2259
    multiple literacies 2892
    and nationalism 2249, 3154
    and orality 3279–80
    and Physical Quality of Life Index 1001
    and print capitalism 628
    and second language learning 2259
    secondary literacy 3279
    see also media literacy
literary poststructuralism 3581, 3583
literature
    adolescent 726
    and arts-based research 2972
    black feminist 308–9
    book, origin of the 2896
    and cultural capital 891
    and cultural studies 913
    and cyberculture 962
    and genre 1915
    and intertextuality 2402
    Latino/a 2550
    literary value criteria 916
    and mass media 3638
    organizational literature 949
    postmodern 3556, 3557, 3570
    religious fiction 752
    romance novels 1915

science fiction 3495, 3497
slash fiction 3497–8
sociology of 2678–9
Lithuania 1451, 4168
    anti-Jewish violence 3428
    race and ethnic conflict 1469
    and secession 1487
litigation
    medical-related 2928
    see also law
Litt, T. 2498
Little, C. B. 1082–4, 4359–60
Little, R. 3041
Little Science 275, 276
Littler, C. R. 2515, 2516
Litwak, E. 1798, 3621–2
Liu, T. J. 562–3
Liveley, K. J. 1383
living apart together (LAT) relationships
    810–12
living wills 1497
Livingstone, S. 732–4, 3816–18
Lizardo, O. 313–16, 3845–8
Lloyd, J. 3471
Lloyd, R. 5141–3
lobbying 779, 780
lobotomy 2694
Local Exchange Trading Scheme (LETS) 3079
local residents' movements 2656–9
    characteristics 2657
    chonaikai 471–4
    civil minimum 505
    high-speed transportation pollution 2127,
        3477
    participants 2657
    proactive strategies 2658
location, politics of 306
Locke, A. 1243, 3610–11
Locke, John 148, 2618
    and civil society 513
    and empiricism 1397, 1434
    and language 4593–6
    on property 613
    and self 2032
    and semiotics 4180
    and social science 2186
Locke, R. 2726
Locke-Wallace Short Marital Adjustment Test
    (LWMAT) 2773
Locker , D. 481
Lodziak, C. 744
Loe, M. 5188–9

Loeber, R. 830, 831
Loewen, J. 3010
Loewenthal, L. 2164
Lofland, J. 320, 1995, 3718–21
Lofland, L. 320, 3719, 4130
Löfström, J. 4227–30
log-linear models 2565, 2659–60
    capture-recapture models 2660
    and demographic data 1016
    latent class models 2660
    logit models 2659
    and segregation analysis 3247
    and social mobility analysis 2368, 2369, 2377,
        2378–9
    symmetric models 2659, 2660
Logan, J. 1453, 2034
logic and myth 262
Logic Theorist computer program 640
logical empiricism 3577
logical positivism 1434, 3545
logocentrism 986, 2660–2
    multimedia 3111
logos 730
Lohmann, S. 580
Lois, J. 1380
Loisy, A. 3983
Lombroso, Cesare 857, 2662–3
    and positivism 1101, 1118, 2662
    social Darwinism 2015, 2662
London 765, 3623
    biosocial theories of crime 822
    global city 1954
    Victorian London 2991
London, Jack 3495, 3589
London School of Economics 367
London Zoo 3501–2
lone-parent families 2663–7
    child custody and child support 453
    and child outcomes 1621, 1623, 1625, 1736
    and early childhood 1269
    and educational attainment 1338
    employment patterns 2665–6
    and family sociology 1617
    and family structure 1620
    female-headed families 1586, 1613, 1626,
        1719, 1721, 1844–5
    and health care 1844–5
    and high school dropout 1326
    homogeneity/heterogeneity 2667
    households 2169
    immigrant families 2254
    and low social outcomes 265

lone-parent families (*cont'd*)
  negative outcomes 1736
  and poverty 1591, 1612, 1613, 1626, 1627,
    1719, 1721, 1736, 2254
  single-father families 1586, 1591, 1719
  social acceptance of 1622, 1735
  and social security policies 2664–5
  welfare support 2664
  and working hours 1032
  see also non-resident parents
"Lonely crowd" 2822
Long, E. 913–18
Long, J. F. 1025–8
long-distance truckers 2138
**longevity, social aspects (the oldest old)
  2668–9**
  and biodemography 284, 286
  elder care 1349–51
  and grandparenthood 2018
  longevity definition 2668
Longhurst, B. 1638
Longino, H. 1682
Longino, Jr., C. F. 67–71
longitudinal study design 78–9, 97, 98
longue durée 360, 361, 363
Lonsdale, C. 4890–5
looking-glass self 799, 1380, **2669–71**, 3952
  Cooley and 2208, 2669–70, 3007, 4157
  and deviant identity 2208
looting 779
Lopez, Jennifer 416
López, N. R. 1559–64
Lorber, J. 1867
The Lord of the Rings film trilogy 1640
Lorde, Audre 308
Lorenz curve 1942
Loria, A. 2015
Lortab 1233
Los Angeles 494, 495
  ethnic enclaves 1454
  fantasy city development 1642
  homicide rates 2151
  prostitution 1661
  riots (1992) 707, 881, 1454
  urban redevelopment 1455
Los Angeles Police Department 1109
Los Angeles School 445, 503
Lost Tribes 2449, 2453
lotteries 1820
Lovaglia, M. J. 4408–10
love and commitment 2671–4
  and attraction 204

cohabitation 565–9
confluent love 2323–4
Confucian love 669
desexualized love 2682
and family structure 1620
and LAT relationships 811
and marriage 2790
and polyamory 3478
romanticization and idealization of love
  2681
types of love 2671–2
see also intimacy
Lovell, D. W. 612–17, 5155–9
Loveridge, R. 5066–71
Lowenthal, L. 2881
Lowie, R. H. 909
Löwith, K. 344, 3214
Lowney, K. S. 1100
Loy, J. W. 4643–53
Loyal, S. 3837–8
loyalty 3008, 3621
  civic loyalty 3142
  to nation 3142
  to state 3142
  see also nationalism; patriotism
LSD 1233
Lu, C.-C. 1206–10
Lü, D. 3861
Lubavitch, C. 3048
Lucas, J. W. 2027–9, 4852–5
Luccarelli, M. 3123–5
Lucio, M. M. 2178–82
Lucke, G. 4260–3
Luckmann, T. 484, 886, 1087–8, 1436, 1520,
  1812, 1916, 2345, 2584, 3403, 3856, 3874,
  4094, 4144
lucky numbers 1140
Lucrecian 197
Luddite riots 3065
ludenic reading 3637
ludic activity 464–6, 4649
  see also sport
ludus love 2672
Luhmann, Niklas 1812, **2675–8**
  and autopoiesis 233
  and Christianity 478
  and the church 486, 487–8
  and emotions 1384, 1385
  and money 3079
  and neofunctionalism 1812–13, 2361
  sociology of religion 486, 487–8, 3874
  systems theory 1813, 3076

Luijkx, R. 2373–80
Lukács, Georg 874, **2678–81**, 2756
  and atheism 197
  and bourgeois hegemony 2227
  and class consiousness 2227, 2838
  and commodity fetishism 1148
  and commodity relations 610, 757
  and consciousness 874
  and dialectics 1148, 1151
  and false consciousness 1569
  historical materialism 2679
  and Luxemburg 2685
  and reification 757, 3845
Luke, C. 1708
Luke, T. 876
"Luke theorem" 1243
Luker, K. 3093, 3655
Lukes, S. 1261, 2771, 3472
Lumière brothers 1210, 1752
lumpenproletariat 534, 3589
lunch counter protests 706
Lundgren, D. C. 1380
Lunnenborg, C. E. 788–90, 2975
Lupton, D. 334, 2083–5
lust balance 2681–5
Luther, Martin 258, 2147, 3636, 4975
  and individualism 2285
Lutheranism 188, 407–8, 3408, 3689, 3690
Lutz, A. 277–81
Luxembourg
  bilingual education 279
  immigration 2263, 3020
  immigration policies 3020
  social security system 2055
  teenage motherhood 1728
Luxemburg, Rosa 245, **2685–8**, 2817
  and colonialism 351
  and imperialism 2267
  and militarism 2267
  and participatory democracy 3259
luxury 4619
Lyles, M. 3309
Lyman, S. M. 320, 1523, 2978
Lynch, M. 2525
lynching 307, 3448, 3456, 3512, 4013
Lynd, H. 619, 684, 2407, 2647
Lynd, R. 619, 684, 2407, 2647, 3051
Lynn, R. 2959
Lyon, D. 2331–6, 4895–8
Lyon, S. 1639
Lyotard, J. 916, 2333, 3552, 3553, 3556, 3567, 3570, 3573, 3575

Lysenko, T. 1505, 1507
Lyson, T. A. 3963–7

Maastricht Treaty 3157
Maathai, W. 1274
Mac Innis, K. 3418–9
McAdam, D. 574–81, 1166, 3066, 3067, 3448, 3449, 3455–6, 3457, 3909
Macao
  Confucianism 670
  fertility levels 1737
Maccabees 2450
McCall, G. J. 2218, 2225
McCallion, M. J. 2338–9, 4759–62
McCallum, E. L. 1747
McCammon, H. J. 4737–41
MacCannell, D. 763
McCarthy, E. D. 2482–5
McCarthy, John D. 697
McCarthy, Joseph 1115
McCarthyism 533, 2156, 2520, 2760, 2803, 2838
McChesney, R. 2887, 3674
McCleary, R. M. 1315–18
McClintock, A. 2985
McClintock, M. A. 2618
McCloud, S. 1640
McCormick, C. 1397–8, 3580–4
McCracken, G. 743, 744
McCreadie, C. 1348
McCulloch, B. J. 3961–3
McDevitt, J. 2049
McDisneyization 763
MacDonald, K. 3660–2, 3663
McDonald, P. 3525–8
McDonaldization 2189, 2193, **2689–90**, 3807
  and alienation 2690
  automation 2689
  bureaucracy 3567
  calculability 2689
  and commodification 1991
  and conformity 228
  control 2689
  and the department store 1058
  and Disneyization 1187
  economic rationalization 2300
  efficiency 2689
  and environmental degradation 2690
  and global consumption 1962, 1963
  and global cultural values 518
  and grobalization 2023
  immateriality 3567
  irrationality of rationality 2690

McDonaldization (*cont'd*)
and litigation, increased 2927
and mass production 2829
of non-commercial institutions 2690
organizational innovations 1309
predictability 2689
rationalization 723, 2300, 2689, 2690, 2883, 2965, 3312, 3567
Ritzer and 704, 738, 759, 763, 1187, 2689, 2690, 2883, 2928, 3312, 3567, 3810
Taylorism 704, 2746
and Weberian bureaucracy 704, 3567
McDonald's 352, 739, 934, 2883
and corporate logics 935
cultural imperialism 907
franchisees 2739
McDougall, W. 3700
Macedonia 4188
McGann, P. J. 1110–14
McGannon, K. 1517
McGinty, P. H. W. 4129–31
McGuire, M. 1643
Mach, E. 3545, 3546
Machalek, R. 291–5
Machiavelli, Niccol 547, 1242, 3444
and conflict theory 662
language of nation 3145
The Prince 1362
machine learning 639
machine politics 3445–6
Machlup, F. 2327–8
McIntire, C. 2932
McIntosh, M. 2157, 2159–60, 2610, 3682
McIver, R. 2959
McKay, Henry 828
Mackay, Hugh 2326–31
McKay, J. 4684–6
McKay, N. 309
MacKenzie, D. 1532, 3039
McKenzie, R. 443, 1289, 1290, 3112–13
McKeown, T. 3099
McKercher, B. 920
McKinlay, A. 2521–4
McKinlay, J. 2076
McKinley, W. 2006
MacKinnon, C. 1892, 2114, 2605, 3419, 3541, 3775, 5271
McLanahan, S. 1718, 1720, 1721
McLaren, P. 867
McLaughlin, N. 1804–8
McLaurin v. *Oklahoma State Regents* 368
Maclean, C. 1578

Maclean, M. 1444
MacLean, V. M. 251–5, 270–3, 1706–10, 2485–9
McLennan, J. 608
Macleod, K. 729–32, 3497
McLuhan, Marshall 1108, 2195, **2690–3**
and the global village 2330, 2882, 3778
and information technology 2333
and media communication 3111, 3636
and media culture 2882, 3635
"medium is the message" 3636
McMahon, M. 3104
McMichael, P. 1061
Macnaghten, P. 3164, 3165
McNair, B. 3467–72
McNamee, S. 459–62
McNeal, Jr., R. B. 1229–32
McNeill, W. 3038
McPhail, C. 577, 880–4, 881
McPherson, M. 796
McQuail, D. 2911–16
McQuillan, J. 2321
macro-functionalism 1811
McRobbie, A. 301, 914, 3091
macrosociology 2997
McShane, M. D. 255–6, 2662–3
Macy, M. W. 641, 1822–5
Madagascar 1727
Madan, T. N. 2128–32
MADD (Mothers Against Drunk Driving) 1115
madness 2693–6
see also mental disorder
Madonna 326, 419–20
Madres Demandantes 1686
Madrid bombings (2004) 3469
Maffesoli, M. 2157, 3569
Mafia 3515, 3516
magazines
lifestyle magazines 1850
teen magazines 1850, 1851
women's magazines 2897, 3638–9, 4259
Magdalinski, T. 4690–3
magic 2696–701
and animism 141
and charisma 433
contagious magic 2697
evolutionistic approach 2698
functionalist approach 2698–9
magic alterity 2700
magico-religious symbolism 2700
natural magic 2697
and popular religiosity 3524

professional magicians 4135
and religion 433, 2696, 2697, 2698, 2699,
3630, 3631
and the sacred 3976
and secrecy 4135
as social phenomenon 2699
magical thinking 2631, 2698, 2700
magistrate judges 813
magnet schools 4042–5
Maguire, Joseph 1751, 1986–90, 4710–11
Mahathir Mohamad 43, 44
mahayana Buddhist tradition 371, 373
Mahdi Caliphate 3048
Maher, F. 1708
Mahutga, M. C. 2227–30
mail order selling 740
mail-order brides 1717, 1984, 1985
Mailer, Norman 798
Main, Regan 3025–31
Maine, Henry Sumner 1595
Maine, Sir Henry 2560
Maines, D. 320, 1130, 2961, 2962, 3609
mainstreaming 2505
Mairs, N. 1697
Maison des Sciences de l'Homme (MSH) 361,
362
Maisonneuve, S. 746–7
Maistre, J. de 651, 652, 653, 679, 2837
Maitland, F. W. 3423
majorities 2701–72
conflict perspective 2702
functionalist perspective 2702
malaria 3099
Malaw, discriminatory inheritance practices
1724
Malaysia 4376, 4377
and accommodation 8
affirmative action policies 42, 43, 44, 45, 47
Ali-Baba corporations 47
communal democracy 3423
Confucianism 670
consumer movements 697, 698
ethnic divide 42
fantasy cities 1641
and federalism 1652
female genital mutilation 1654
and feminist anthropolgy 1691
folk religious pracctices 1764–5
Hinduism 1765
Islam, revitalization of 1692
migrant domestic workers 1716
and multiculturalism 3108

nation-building 1692
New Economic Policy (NEP) 42
public school system 4049
working class 1410
Malcolm, D. 1751, 4345–50, 4713–17
male gaze 334
male rape 2278, **2702–4**
male role models 1649
Mali
capitalist growth 390
consumer movements 697, 698
female genital mutilation 1654
infant mortality 1726
teenage marriage 1727
Malikite School 2426
Malinick, T. E. 5222–5
Malinowski, Bronislaw K. 2704–5, 3843
functionalism 1809, 1810, 2698, 2705
and magic and religion 2698, 2699
and myth 2705
social anthropology 149, 2698, 2699,
2704–5, 3228, 3771, 3772
and social institutions 2344
Mallarmé, S. 216
Mallon, T. 2448
malnutrition 1157, 1158
Malthus, Thomas Robert 2705–8
and ecology 1289
exclusionist ideology 3590
and markets 2776, 2778
and political economy 1300, 2797
and population growth and poverty 1040,
1506, 2706–7, 3071, 3590–1
Mamo, L. 234
Man, H. de 2015, 2016
mana 433, 608, 610, 3630, 3631
managed care 2709–10, 3658
capitation 2709
ethical dilemmas 2710
and health maintenance organization
2065–6
and medical sociology 2935
pre-certification 2709
purchaser contracts 2709
utilization review 2709
managed professional businesses 3664
management 2710–19, 4791–2
and academics 2745
and consultants 2745
and ethics 1439
and human resource management 2178–82
long-term cycles 2740

management (*cont'd*)
 new institutional theory (NIT) 2351–2
 paternalistic 3170
 and practitioners 2745
 professionalization of 2727
 radical maangerialism 2523
 results-orientated management 213
 as social process 2745
 women in 1889
 see also Japanese-style management; strategic
  management (organizations)
management consultants 2520, **2719–22**,
 2750
 and innovation 2738–9
 interactive relations 2721
 and management fashion 2721
 rhetorical discourse 2721
management discourse 2722–5
management education 2725–8, 2745
management fashion 2715–16, **2729–31**
 and management consultants 2721
 and new institutional theory (NIT) 2352
management history 2731–3, 2744–5
management improvisation 2733–6, 2737
management innovation 2736–42
 core research programs 2737–8
 early and late adopters 2739
 and hybridity 2741–2
 local domestication 2741
 long-wave theory 2740
 national systems 2741
 non-human elements 2740
 pro-innovation bias 2737
management networks 2742–4
 alliances 122
 see also supply chains
management science 1287
management sociology, and cultural geography
 1299
management theory 949, 1387, 2714–15,
 2744–52
 American 2748–9
 and business ethics 1441
 and the Hawthorne studies 2050–1
 key issues 2745
 knowledge management 2476–80
 and management innovation 2738
 modern theories 2714
 and network sociology 2744
 and organization theory 3281
 and organizational structure 3301
 and performance measurement 3396

management, workers' participation in
 2511, **2752–4**
 and human resource management 2179, 2180
managerialism 3324, 3664
 and laborism 2526–7
Managua Declaration of the Organization of
 American States 2184
Manchester 1954
mandated science 4636
Mandel, E. 2267
Mandela, Nelson 163, 164–5, 3381
Mandes, E. 256–8, 4012–14
Manhattan Project 275, 3038, 3039
mania love 2671
manifest content 777
manifest destiny 1455, **2754–6**
Mann, C. 1445
Mann, H. 4041
Mann, M. 1451, 1452, 1646, 1647, 2133,
 3150, 3461
Mann, S. 3119
Mann, Thomas 874, 3213, 3216
Mannheim, Karl 1902, **2756–9**
 biography 2756–7
 and democratization 2758–9
 and Elias 1358, 1749
 functional rationalization 378
 and ideology 2231, 2483
 rationalization theory 3809
 relationism 2231
 sociology of knowledge 589, 931, 2474,
  2482, 2483
Manning, Peter Kirby 1226–9
Manning, Philip 1229, 3334
Manning, R. 1761
MANOVA 1557, 1559
Mansfield, L. 1751, 1875–80
Manson, Marilyn 2826
manufacturing industries 2295, 2300, 2478
 decline of 2329–30
 global networking 3565–6
 see also industrialization
Mao Zedong 616, 677, 2837
Maori identity 2222
marathon running 2599
Marber, P. 1761
Marcel, G. 3673
March, J. 3282, 3307, 3308, 3323, 3333
March for Women's Lives 3654
Marchand, R. 743
marches 779, 780, 1166
Marches for Jesus 440

Marconi, Guglielmo 2874
Marcuse, Herbert 943, 1806, **2759–61**, 3217
and advertising 33
and civilization 518
and class consciousness 2228
and commodity fetishization 757
and consumer society 702, 2228
and dialectics 1149, 2759
and the Frankfurt School 865, 874, 875, 897, 1569, 2881
Fromm–Marcuse debate 1806
and Horkheimer 2164
and marketing 684
neo-Marxism 869
one-dimensional society theory 416, 875, 929
revolutionary praxis 2759, 2760
and sexual liberation 2160
and technology–rationalization relation 3810
Mardin, S. 1999–2004
Marduk, myth of 261
Mare, R. 1339
Marett, R. 3629–30
Marger, M. N. 1183
marginal art 2761–3
marginal-utility value theory 1304, 2441
marginalism 2441, 2777, 2780, 3360
and neoclassical economics 1303–4, 1305
marginality 2763–5
and disability sport 1172
dual marginality 2764–5
and entrepreneurship 1412
imposed marginality 2764
marginality by choice 2764
Park–Stonequist model 2763, 2764
personality features 2763
marginalization, outsiders 2765–6
bisexuals 303
and critical pedagogy 864
and cultural critique 897
and gentrification 1919
and martyrdom 2801
poverty and 699, 700
and school curricula 1708
and subordinated masculinity 2100
and women of color 1701
of women in sport 1877
see also exclusion
Margolis, E. 4009–10
Margolis, M. 2910
Marian devotion 442
Marianne Weber on social change 1234, **2766–70**

marijuana 1078, 1107, 1143, 1233, 1235, 2832, 3086, 3088
medical marijuana 1109
Marini, R. M. 1567
marital conflict 2773
marital power/resource theory 2770–2
and divisions of household labor 1205
and dual-earner couples 1247
inequalities 2301–2, 2790
later-life marriage 2547
and money management 3083
marital quality 1631, **2772–5**
and child well-being 1623
children, effect of 2774
and liberalism 1868
multidimensional measures 2772–3
and poverty 1614
sociocultural contexts 2774–5
two-dimensional structure of affcet perspective 2774
unidimensional measures 2773
marital satisfaction 2772, 2773
attribution theory 207
diminution 2325
and family sociology 1617
and later-life marriage 2546–7
low marital quality and effects on children 469
unemployment, impact of 2486
Victorian ideal 2682
working class marriage 2487
Marital Satisfaction Inventory (MSI) 2773
Marital Satisfaction Scale (MSS) 2773
maritime empires 1393
Mark, N. 641
marker goods 741
market capitalism 3429
market collapse 594
market economics 2775
market fundamentalism 2775, 3178, 3592, 3593
market incentive thesis 4824
market individualism 3196
market integration 935, 1310
market interventions 624
market opportunity thesis 4824
market research, and decision-making 983
market segmentation 744
market societies 514, 515, 517
market transition theory (MTT) 4824–5
marketing
and digital capitalism 1162

marketing (*cont'd*)
  of ethnicity 1456
  niche marketing 1851
marketing communication 770, 771
  as face of capitalism 771
marketization 553, 2749
  and monetization of life 517
  of peasant societies 3084–5
markets 2775–88
  child- and adolescent-centered markets 1619
  cities as marketplaces 765
  commodity chains 749
  cultural orders 2786–7
  and cultural production 953
  deregulation 2513, 2887
  disembedding 1188
  economic dimensions: mechanisms
    2776–80
  equilibrium 2777, 2778
  free competition 2777, 2778, 2779
  human rights and the market 1310
  institutional conceptions 2781–2
  interdependencies 2356
  invisible hand principle 2779, 3840
  juvenile 724–7, 774
  liberal market model 2512
  and neoliberalism 3175–6, 3177
  networks and relations 2783–4, 2785
  optimal market adaptation 2776
  power configurations 2785–6
  and price determination 2780
  regulation 1947
  religion as a marketplace 751
  and resource allocation 2779–80
  Say's law of regulating markets 2776
  schools as 775
  self-regulating mechanisms 2777, 4402
  and social institutions 2345
  social relations and networks 2783–4
  as social systems 2784–5
  as societal phenomena 2780
  sociological dimensions: social constructions
    2780–7
  sociology of the market 2443
  spontaneous coordination 2779, 2782
  supply and demand 2776, 2777
Markovsky, B. 641, 1369, 2997–3005, 4979–95
Markowitz, H. 3323
Markson, E. W. 1931–2
Markula, P. 4658–60
Marley, Bob 3510
Marlin, R. 3671–5

marriage 334, 2789–91
  age at first marriage 1587, 4124
  and appropriation of women's labor 2113
  arranged marriages 2671, 2789
  biosociological theory 293
  caregiving 2546
  child marriage 4003, 4004
  commuter marriages 810, 811
  companionate marriage 2487, 2620,
    2769, 2770
  comparative research 2789
  conjugal roles and social networks 672–4
  connubium 674–6
  cost-benefit calculations 2415
  and cross-sex friendhsip 878, 879
  declining marriage rates 1587, 1734, 2790, 2792
  definitions 2789
  deinstitutionalization of 2772
  delayed marriage 736, 1586
  and demographic transitions 4124–5
  disincentives 1734, 1735
  dissolution *see* divorce
  and dyads/triads 1267
  and economic well-being 1628
  effect on engaging in crime 637
  en 1401
  endogamy 1404–5, 1457
  exogamy 1404
  and female genital mutilation 1655–6
  and friendships 796, 1798
  functionalist theories 2145
  Goldman and 2005
  and happiness 1207
  heterosexual character 639, 2113, 2791
  and homogamy 203
  Howard and 2171
  indigenous intermarriage 2283
  inequalities in marriage 2301–3
  and infidelity 2323–5
  and interpersonal relationships 2390
  interracial 1198, 2393, 2394
  interreligious 1198
  Islamic 2428–9
  later-life marriage 2546–8
  "legalised prostitution" 2005
  life course perspective 2636
  male economic prospects as predictor of 1734
  marital power/resource theory 2770–2
  median age at marriage 2414
  partner effects 4810–12
  patriarchal marriage 2302, 2303, 2769, 2789
  peer marriages 2303

postponement 675, 1037, 1585, 1589, 1728,
    2415–16, 2429
predictors 1734, 2415
and prior cohabitation 566
racial intermarriage 2416
records 565
and regulation of sexuality 2110
religious intermarriage 2416
and religious preferences 1315
spousal similarities 2394, 2426
spouse selection 1631, 2308, 2416–17
status exchange hypothesis 2394
tax and inheritance laws 2414
teenage marriages 1726–7
transnational marriage networks 1665
Western European pattern 1047
working-class 2486–7
see also divorce; family structure; marital
    satisfaction; same-sex marriage/civil unions
marriage counseling 1634
and triadic interaction 1266
marriage market 2394, 2416, 2417
marriage, sex, and childbirth 2789, **2791–4**
    see also motherhood
Marsden, P. V. 569–74
Marsh, P. 1767
Marshall, A. 1304, 1305–6, 2776–7, 2778, 3434
Marshall, B. 736
Marshall, P. 308
Marshall, S. L. A. 3041
Marshall, T. 369, 2444, 4602
Marshall, Thomas Humphrey 2794–6
    and citizenship 498
    and class inequality 2795
    middle distance theory 2795
Marshall, V. 974, 1936
Marshall Aid 2726, 2747, 3179
Marteau, T. 2173
Marti, José 2550
martial arts 325
Martin, David 1051, 4138
Martin, Dominique 3990–2
Martin, J. 949, 950, 1155
Martin, P. Y. 1895
Martin, R. 3321–6
Martin, S. 1017–21
Martindale, D.
Martineau, Harriet 273, 1668, 2618, **2796–9**
    biography 2796–7
    Comtean translations 655
    and feral dogs 2176
    and the social science movement 1670

Martinelli, A. 1410–13
Marty, M. 1052, 1814
martyrdom 2799–882
    active 2799, 2800, 2801
    goals 2801
    passive 2799
    religious doctrines 2799, 2800, 2801
    and sadomasochism 3985
    suicide attacks 2800
    war context 2801
Maruyama, K. 2802
Maruyama, Masao 2802–5
Marvin, C. 2905
Marx, A. 1451
Marx, G. T. 3643–7
Marx, Karl 655, **2805–15**
    and active citizenship 2807
    and alienation 119, 874, 929, 1200, 1502,
        2580, 2807, 2816, 5158
    Althusser and 125
    and base–superstructure theory 539, 839,
        932, 1307, 1318, 2227, 2812
    biography 2806, 2809
    and bureaucracy 2807
    capitalist critique 362, 390–1, 394, 515, 607,
        718, 873, 1394, 1949, 2294, 2518, 2808–9,
        2810–11, 2925
    and causality 2813
    and circulation of capital 388–9
    and the city 500
    and civil society 513, 2925
    class analysis 533, 539, 839, 1966, 2806,
        2810–11, 2811–12, 3466
    class conflict theory 534, 538, 662–3, 1201,
        1961, 2806, 2813
    and class consciousness 2585
    and class polarization 513
    and colonialism 603
    commodity analysis 1515
    and commodity fetishism 741, 756, 758, 864,
        1745, 2679, 2811
    and commodity production 1403
    and commodity relations 607–9, 702–3, 2925
    and communism 703, 2805, 3464, 4550–1
    Communist Manifesto 614, 955, 989, 1148,
        1242, 1318, 1394, 2808–9, 3613
    and conflict theory 666
    and consciousness 932, 1307
    and consumption 701
    and contradiction 1148
    and critical theory tradition 2806, 2808
    and cultural critique 896

Marx, Karl (*cont'd*)
  and Darwin 1506–7
  and dialectics 1146, 1147–8, 2298, 2964
  and dominant ideology 1568
  and economic determinism 1293
  and Engels, collaboration with 2808–9, 2812
  exploitation theory 1543
  and false consciousness 1221, 1568
  and Feuerbach 1748, 1749
  and free speech 2807
  and freedom 2807
  and gender role relationships 1596
  and Hegel 1408, 2806, 2807–8, 2837
  historical materialism 350, 865, 896, 1067,
    1150, 1293, 1711, 2298, 2806, 2808, 2812,
    2813–14, 3437, 3670
  and idealism 2925
  immiseration thesis 1946, 1961
  and industrial capitalism 3550
  and the Industrial Revolution 2298
  and interpersonal relationships 2390
  and labor process 364, 2298, 2507–8, 2811
  and Malthus 2707, 2708
  and marginalization 2766
  and material production 1303
  materialist method 274
  and mediation 2925
  and modernity 3068
  and modernization 3071
  and money 3078, 3079
  and national self-determination 1487
  and nationalism 3146
  political economy critique 245, 702, 1300,
    1302, 1748–9, 5167
  and poverty 2708, 3591
  and power in social relations 3006
  and praxis 3612–13
  and primitive accumulation 2817
  profit theory 1545
  and property relations 244–5
  and relations of correspondence 2812–13
  and religion 33, 3049, 3524, 4145
  revolutionary theory 3908, 3915
  and scientific progress 3437
  and the self 4157
  and self-fulfillment 4162
  and social economics 1318
  and social evolution 1506, 4361
  and social hierarchies 3464
  and social relations of production 244–5, 515
  and socialism 612, 4550, 4551
  sociohistorical analysis 143, 2760
  and Species-Being 4637–8
  and the state 663
  structuralism 4525
  and surplus-labor extraction 1544
  teleology 2969
  theory of ideology 923
  use-value theory 876, 5155
Marxism
  Althusser's structural reinterpretation of 125
  anarchist views of 136
  and atheism 197
  Austro-Marxism 344
  and autoethnography 1480
  base–superstructure model 299, 2648, 2815,
    3880
  Benjamin and 268
  Bottomore and 344
  capitalist critique 874, 2817
  and civil society 513
  class analysis 533, 534, 539, 2086, 2816, 2842
  and class conflict 3550
  and class consciousness 540
  and commodity fetishism 758
  conflict theory 662–4, 2806
  criminology 839–41, 2506
  and critical realism 872
  and critical theory 2816
  cultural critique 736
  and cultural homogenization 2888
  Derridean deconstruction 988–9
  and dialectical materialism 1150
  and dialectics 1149
  and distanciation and disembedding 1188
  and division of labor 1199
  and electoral politics 551
  and ethnography 1482, 2816
  and false consciousness 1568, 2227
  and family history 1595–6
  and family theory 1630
  and fascism 1646
  and Fordism/post-Fordism 2816–17
  French Marxism 755
  and genre analysis 1914
  gerontology 1929
  and globalization 2816
  Hegelian Marxism 2815
  and historical change 785
  historical materialism 1711
  and ideological hegemony 2227
  and ideology 2231
  and imperialism 2267
  instrumental Marxism 3585, 3597

and labeling theory 2506
and leisure 2589
and liberal feminism 2841
Marxist anthropolgy 341, 342
Marxist feminism 1711
and materialist feminisms 2839–40
materialist theory 937, 948, 2838
and nationalism 1838, 3150
neo-Gramscian 299, 301
neo-Kantian 344
non-essentialist Marxism 3430
and the nuclear family 811
organizational sociology 3323–4
political party theory 3451, 3452
political sociology 3458
and popular culture 3481
and populism 3538
poststructural critique of 2103
power, theories of 3597
and private property 3677, 3678
and the professions 3661–2
rational choice Marxism 2816
reductionist tendencies 297
as regional theory 2816
and regulation theory 2816
and reification 3844
religious theory 549
revolutionary theory 575, 3908, 3916
Sartre and 4009
and social control 4389
social theory 344, 660, 667
structural Marxism 298, 3597–8
and systems theories 4916
and utopias 2815
Marxism and sociology 2815–18
Aron and 177
Gellner and 1839
and Latin American states 2575
Lukács and 2678–80
urban sociology 389
Marxism-Leninism 865, 1151
and economic determinism 1293
Marxist feminism 1711, 2621
Marxist humanism 324
Marzal, M. M. 3518–25
masculine identity 1862, 1891, 2153, 2222
masculinities, crime and 2818–21
representation 919
masculinity
and advertising 1849
aggressive masculinity 2093
androgynous masculinity 735

black masculinity 1665
class differences 1891
and coercive institutions 3318
complicit masculinity 2099, 2100
and consumerism 735–7, 1849–50
cultural masculinity, and salary men 3993
deconstruction 1223
and deviance 1134
discourses and practices 1891
female masculinity 1657–8, 1664, 2820
and football hooliganism 1768
gay masculinities 736, 1663–4
hegemonic masculinity 735, 1663, 1664,
    1665, 1668, 1755, 1878, 2099–101, 2222,
    4265, 4673
heterosexual masculinity 2155
and homophobia 2153
and homosexuality 2160
hypermasculinity culture 3785, 3786
ideal–type masculinity 2100
ideology 1877
institutionalization 2820
marginalized masculinity 2099
masculine identity 1862, 1891, 2153, 2222
masculinities and consumption 735–6
"myth" of 3136
normative 1665
and the Olympics 3264
and oral sex 3277
and patriarchy 1663
performing 1223
postmodernist/poststructuralist perspective
    1891, 2816
privileging 1681
psychoanalytic feminist perspective 3697,
    3698
and the public sphere 1862, 1871, 1872
qualities 1871, 1876, 1877, 2122, 2214
reconstruction 720
and risk behavior 1842
and sexual cultures 4211
and sexuality 2115, 4272–5
and sexuality, regulation of 2115
social construction 905, 1591, 3535
and social movements 1872, 1873, 1874
and sport 1876, 1877, 1878, 4292
status insecurity 2155
subordinated masculinity 2099, 2100
masking 1245
Maslow, A. 2566, 2760, 4124
masochism 2157, 2493
Mason, J. 2470

Masorti movement 2452
mass art 1754
mass communication
    and celebrity culture 417
    and consumer culture 744
    and encoding/decoding 1403–4
    mechanistic model 209
    reception theory 210
    sensationalism 2532–3
    transmission model 208
    two-step flow theory 209
    uses and gratifications (U&G) tradition
        209, 2917
    see also audiences
mass communication research (MCR) 208,
    209, 2882
mass consumption 325, 684, 738–9, 740, 762
    and digital capitalism 1162
    Fordist emphasis 2817
    global 1991
    and the working class 2228
    see also consumption, mass consumption, and
        consumer culture
mass culture and mass society 518, 897,
    913, 923, 924, 2123, 2125, **2821–4**
    and experiential consumption 716, 717
    implosion theory 2268–9
    mass culture as high culture's "other" 2822
    see also popular culture
mass customization 739
mass democracy 2296
    anti-democratic outcomes 2759
mass higher education 602
mass killings 1909, 1910, 1911, 1912
    see also genocide
mass marketing 742
mass media 740
    Birmingham School and 297
    and consumption and the body 709
    and culture 1523
    and culture industries 943
    definition 2873
    development 2873–6
    and diffusion of protest 3687
    industrial forms 2923
    and infotainment 2336–7
    and institution of marriage 675
    and mediation 2923
    political impact 2878
    and socialization 2824–7, 4561–2, 4567, 4573
    see also print media
mass media landscape 2901, 2903

mass media and socialization 2824–7
    alleged deleterious influence 2826
    media literacy education 2893–4
    models of media influence 2825–6
    and soap operas 3499
    television 4573
mass merchandising 744
Mass Observation movement 3407
mass production 701, 740, 744, 874, 2299,
    2827–9, 2881
    economies of scale 2828
    optimal organizational structure 3300
    regulation theory 3841
    see also Fordism/post-Fordism; Taylorism
mass society theory 577, 2908, 3065, 3200, 3722
mass traumas 595
massage parlors 1660
Massey, D. 2306
massive resistance 2829–31
Massive Resistance Movement 2830
master narratives 867
master status 2205, **2832**
    and labeling 2832
Masterman, L. 2892
master's programs 2012
Masters, W. 4286
Mastroianni, A. C. 2350
masturbation 2684, **2832–5**
    and cybersex 965
    demedicalization 1112
    infantile 464
    Kinsey Institute research 2467, 2468
    oral sex 3276–8
MATAKIN (Supreme Council for the
    Confucian Religion in Indonesia) 671
mate selection 204, 292, 2391, 2416, 2673
material agency 2846
material apriorism 2757
    see also phenomenology
material culture 2835
    biography and 290
materialism 742, **2836–9**
    and atheism 197
    Benjamin and 268
    and cultural formations of nature 948
    dialectical materialism 268, 1148
    feminist cultural materialism 2843
    heuristic materialism 2813
    historical materialism 268, 2679
    idealism versus materialism debate 2837
    Marxist theory 937
    negative terminal materialism 742

positive instrumental materialism 742
  unhappiness and 745
  see also historical materialism
materialist feminisms 1666, 1710–11, 2838, **2839–44**
  class perspective 2839
  dual systems approach 2841–2
  and global capitalism 2842
  Marxian perspective 2840
  materialist ecofeminism 1274
  postmodern perspective 2842–3
materiality and scientific practice 2844–6
materialization 169
maternal discourse 2847
maternal morbidity and mortality
  calculating 2318–19
  causes 2314
  definition 2313–14
  health intervention programs 2317
  and maternal age 3535
  maternal mortality ratio (MMR) 2314, 2318
  see also infant, child, and maternal health and mortality
maternal thinking 1682, 2848, 3104
maternalism 2846–9
  and childcare 458
  and ethic of care 1438
  and feminism 2848
  maternal thinking 1438
  see also motherhood
maternalist politics 1873, 1874
maternity leave 2319
math, science, and technology education 2849–53
  gender bias 1859, 1860, 1861, 3272
  learning opportunities 3272, 3273–4
mathematical proofs 640
mathematical sociology 2853–7
  Blau and 314
  and chaos and complexity theories 432
  Coleman and 570, 571
  Comte and 653
  discrete-state stochastic process models 571
  institutionalization 2856–7
Mather, Cotton 2833
Mather, M. 1011–14
Matheson, H. 3778
Mathisen, J. 507
Mathy, R. 2159
matriarchy 1596, **2857–9**
  and family structure 1615
matrilineal societies 2858, 5020

matrix of domination 2859
  and intersectionality 2396–7
  and multiracial feminism 3119
  and standpoint theory 1714
Matsueda, R. 2504–7, 2507
Matsushige, H. 3171
Mattachine Society 1834
Matthew effect 2860–1, 3222–3, 4113
Maturana, H. R. 232, 233
Matza, D. 846, 1138, 2472, 3589, 3593
Mau, S. 3084–6
Maudsley, H. 836
Mauritius
  folk religious practices 1764
  mortality decline 3100
Maus, H. 1493
Maushart, S. 3104
Mauss, A. L. 2441
Mauss, Marcel 1252, 1263, 2041, 4415
  and body techniques 327, 336
  and consumption 701, 703
  and gift exchange 1252, 1938–9, 1940, 3228, 3937, 3982
  and individualism 1252
  and magic as social phenomenon 2699, 2700
  and *mana* 608, 610
  and sacrifice 3981, 3982
  and symbolic classification 4906
  and total social phenomenon (TSP) 2041–2
Mauthner, M. 2410, 4315–17
Mauws, M. 1517
Max-Planck Society 1758
maximization principle 292
Maxson, C. L. 1826
Maxwell, C. J. C. 3655
May, J. D. 2996
Mayer, D. P. 3274
Mayer, K. U. 2636, 3062
Mayer, R. N. 697–9
Mayflower Compact 172
Mayhew, B. 314
Maynard, D. W. 1483–6
Mayo, E. 2050, 2512, 2712, 2713, 2847
Mayol, P. 424
Mays, B. E. 2466
Mazarella, W. 744
Mazarin Bible 3635
Mazerolle, L. 828–9
MBA qualification 2351, 2726, 2727, 4046
Mbeki, T. 165
Mead, George Herbert 801, 1145, **2861–4**
  and Addams 24, 25

Mead, George Herbert (*cont'd*)
  and Bernard 271
  biography 2861–2
  and Blumer 318
  and the Chicago School 445, 714, 1227
  and communication 3228
  and constructionism 686
  and the generalized other 1899, 2670,
    3946, 3949
  and institutions 2863–4
  and language 2864
  negative case analysis 3167
  and non-human animals 2176
  and Orientalism 3344
  and the play stage/game stage 3414–15,
    3417, 3948–9, 3951–2
  pragmatism 2187, 2862, 3610
  and punishment of criminals 2506
  and role-taking 2862, 3946, 3948
  and scientific knowledge 3167
  and the self 61, 1821, 1899, 1996, 2217, 2224,
    2433, 2862, 2863, 3187, 3228, 3414–15,
    3417, 3617, 3621, 4157, 4563
  and social behaviorism 3055–6
  and social change 446
  and social groups 2032
  social psychology 274, 1996, 2484
  and sociality 2864
  symbolic interactionism 319, 847, 858, 1087,
    1996, 2030, 2535, 3679, 4186, 4509–10,
    4910
  theory of mind 3055–6, 3057
Mead, Margaret 247, 909, 1083, 2865,
    2865–8, 3387, 4320
  and anthropology 2865–7
  and Boas 322
  ethnography 2976
Meadows, D. 1281
Mealey, L. 823
meaning
  control of 2205
  Cooley and 798
  displaced meaning 743
  and empiricism 1434, 1435
  hermeneutics 2107
  and identity 2217, 2224
  and identity control theory 2203
  idiosyncratic meanings 2224
  indentity-relevant meanings 2203–4
  meaning construction within relationships
    2392
  perceptions of 2203

  and pragmatism 1145
  problem of 2484
  production of 300
  and semiotics 758
  shared meanings 2224
  sign meanings 2204
  signification and practice 919
  site of contest 786
  standard symbols 798
  subjectively intended meanings 2108
  symbolic meanings 2204
meaning-making 785, 922, 923, 924, 925,
    926, 933
  and death and dying 974
  thick description of 925
  through myth 3137
means–end relationships 249
Measor, L. 2642
measures of centrality **2868**–9
  and descriptive statistics 1064–5
  and outliers 1065
measuring crime 820, **2869**–73
  class and crime 542
  computerized criminal history (CCH) files
    2872
  crime reporting systems 1128
  index crime 2277–8
  juvenile delinquency 2455
  National Incident-Based Reporting System
    (NIBRS) 2871–2
  police measures 2869, 2870, 2871
  quantitative methods 862–3
  rape and sexual assault 3788
  recidivism rates 3818
  self-report measures 2869–70, 2871
  victim surveys 2870, 2871
meat production 1424
Mechanic, D. 2105, 2242, 2934
mechanics 1758
Meckling, W. H. 3327
media **2873**–80
  agenda-setting 2877
  and children's consumer culture 694, 695
  and deviance, reporting 1132
  diasporic media 2885–6
  and experiential consumption 716
  gatekeeping 2877
  globalization 418–19
  hegemony and the media 2101–4
  and leisure 2591
  mass society approaches 2877
  media management 2879

moral messages 1107
negative portrayal of women in 1686, 1687
watchdog role 2879
and youth culture 773
youth-oriented media 2826–7
see also mass media; print media; radio;
   television
media conglomerates 1945–6, 2887, 2897–8
media and consumer culture 2881–5
media and diaspora 2885–6
   and the information society 2330
   and satellite technology 2890
media fandom 1638, 1639
media and globalization 2886–91
   and deterritorialization 2889
   and digital technology 1159
   and global justice movements 1979
   and media monopoly 2896–9
media hegemony 2878, 2925
media imperialism 2878, 2880
media influence 2825–6
   agenda-setting model 2825
   cultivation model 2825, 2826
   hypodermic needle model 2825, 2877, 2900
   minimal effects model 2825
media literacy 2891–5
   children 2894
   consumer activist groups 2894
   and mass production technology 3635–6
   national standards 2894
media meta-capital 1639
media monopoly 2895–9, 3639
media and nationalism 2899–902
   atrocity videos 2886
   and cultural imperialism 2888
media, network(s) and 2902–6
   community media 627, 629
media power 2925
media and the public sphere 2906–11
   and agenda setting 63
   audiences 211
   community and media 626–9
   and criminality, reporting of 2340–1
   media regulation 2913
   press freedom 3468
   and public opinion 3637–8
   public relations 3469–71
   and voting behavior 3468
   see also propaganda; public broadcasting;
      public opinion
media, regulation of 2911–16
   broadcasting model 2914, 2915, 3703

and changes in communication technology
   2912
deregulatory trend 2914
external regulation 2915
internal regulation 2911, 2915
self-regulation 2915
media and sport 2879, 2916–21, 4715
   disability sport 1173
   revenue 4667
media-sport production complex 1987
mediascapes 1990
mediated interaction 2921–3
mediation 2923–8
   and triadic interaction 1266
mediatization 2923
Medicaid 86, 995, 1617, 1720, 2167, 2709
   and health care-seeking behavior 2069
medical anthropology 630, 2054
medical deprofessionalization 2928
medical education
   core competencies 2931
   traits perspective 2930
medical imperialism/colonization 1111
medical–industrial complex 3658
medical informatics 2389
medical malpractice 820, 2928–9, 4134
   and compensation 2562, 2928
   and deviance 1085
medical pluralism 630
medical profession 2055, 5277–8
medical school socialization 2930–2, 4047
medical sexology 302
medical sociology 2060, 2932–6
   and documentary analysis 1214–15
   earliest literature 2932
   and ethnicity 2059–60
   Foucault and 335
   and health locus of control 2063–4
   health and medicine 2067–71
   and the illness narrative 2247
   illness-as-deviance perspective 2059
   and infertility 2321–2
   interaction studies 2364
   power-domination perspective 2059
   and socialization 2930
   and sociology of the body 338, 2060
   sociology of medicine 2933
   and sociology of science and technology 2940
   see also physician–patient relationship;
      sociology in medicine
medical sociology and genetics 2937–41
   gay gene 1830–3

medical sociology and genetics (*cont'd*)
  and genetic engineering 1906–9
  and homosexuality 1113
medical technology assessment *see* health
    technology assement (HTA)
medicalization 1111–13, 1542
  and biomedicalization 1113
  of deviance 1110–13
  of female genital mutilation 1656
  female sexuality 5271–2
  of normalcy 1699
  and social control 1112–13
Medicare 72, 73, 86, 995, 1617, 1720, 1904,
    2054, 2065, 2167, 2709
  gender bias 1842, 2367
  Prospective Payment System (PPS) 2166
medicine
  confidence intervals, use of 658
  and decision-making 983
  Internet medicine 2388–90
  medical innovation 570
  private medicine 2055
  professionalization 1846
  social class differences 537
medicine, sociology of 2931–42
  and the illness narrative 2248
  Internet medicine 2388–90
  medical–demographic research 286
  see also medical sociology; sociology in
    medicine
meditation 631, 752
"medium is the message" 2692, 3636
Meeker, B. F. 4611–12
Meeks, C. 605–7, 3728–30
Meese, E. 1109, 3541
mega-event sociology 3263
megacities 3527, 3625
  pollution 1424
  see also global/world cities; megalopolis
megalopolis 2942–4, 2992, 5103
  and the central business district 423
  multinational megalopolises 2943
  network megalopolises 2943
Megan's Law 3385
Meier, R. F. 1116–21, 2277–8
Meiji Restoration 2240, 2803, 3058, 4299, 4370
Meinecke, F. 3144
Meir, Golda 3989
meliorism 3609
Mellors, M. 1275
melting pot 15, 137, 1458, **2944–6**, 3421
  and assimilation 192, 2944–5

  and cultural diversity 899
  and high school sports 2122
  and immigration 2257
  Park and 3364
Melton, J. G. 3190, 3202
Melucci, A. 954, 3209
Melville, Herman 1220
memetics 1509
memory
  alienated memory 592
  collective memory 959, 3911
  counter-memory 592
  cultural memory 591
  and decision-making 983
  dominants' memory 592
  historical memory 290
  and the making of revolutions 3911
  and mythogenesis 3137
  and neurosociology 3185
  see also collective memory
memowriting 2025
Memphis, US 124
men
  infertility 2320
  male prostitution 1661, 2160, 3683, 3684,
    4216–17
  male rape 2703
  and marital infidelity 2324, 2325
  social movements 1873
  see also fatherhood; masculinity; patriarchy
men having sex with men (MSM) 2160
Mencius 669, 670
Mendelian genetics 292, 1897, 4114
Méndez y Berrueta, L. 339–43
Mendieta y Núñez, Lucio 2946–51
Menger, C. 1304, 1305, 2441, 2777, 2779
Menken, J. 1155–9
men's magazines 736
menstruation 333
mental disorder 2951–4
  and aggression 65
  and child abuse 449
  and children of divorced parents 452,
    468, 1623
  combat exposure, effects of 99
  and compositional theory of urbanism 636
  and crime 836–7, 838–9
  and dangerousness 969
  and deviance 2695, 2951
  diagnostic measures 80
  early transitions to adulthood, effects of 2636
  and ethnicity 2080

historic attitudes and treatments 2694–5
and homelessness 2149
and illness behavior 2241
and incarceration 838
involuntary treatment 2105
labeling approach 2695, 2934, 2951,
   2952, 2953
madness 2693–5
and marginality 2763
and marital disruption 452, 468, 1623
organic and non-organic disorders 81
psychiatric medical model 2961
public attitudes towards 996–7
racial/ethnic factors 2953
social causation model 2951
and social class 2933
and social exclusion 2952
and socially disorganized communities 1102
and socioeconomic status 2951, 2952, 2953
Spanish American attitudes toward 239
stigma 583, 2505, 2951, 2952
and stress 2951, 2952
symptoms and diagnoses 2952
and unemployment 1591
mental evolution 2140, 2141
mental health
   age distributions 79–80
   defining and measuring 80
   and interpersonal relationships 2391
   and medical sociology 2935
   and religious involvement, benefits of 2082
   social class variations 2088
mental health system
   and deinstitutionalization 993–8
   organizational processes 997
   political economy perspective 997
   and privatization 2695
mental hospitals 994, 1998, 2694–5
   deinstitutionalization 993–8
   patient–staff interactions 3332–3
   total institutions 3332–3
mental properties 635
mentalities 223
   authoritarian 223
   collective mentality 261
Menzies, Robert 5034–6
mercantilism 1393
merchandising 1187
Merchant, C. 947, 1274, 1275
mercy killing 1497
   see also euthanasia
Meredith, W. 2543

mergers and acquisitions 355, 1058, 3309
merit 418
meritocracy 1200, 1336, 1663, **2954–8**
   and cultural capital 891
   and educational attainment 384
   see also intelligence tests
Merleau-Ponty, Maurice 252, 1774
   and atheism 197
   and cognition 335
   and existential sociology 1522
   and the "lived body" 326–7, 331, 2652
   phenomenology 326
   structuralism 4182
Merriam, C. 443
Merton, Robert K. 1193, 1805, 1921,
   2958–61, 3051
   and ambivalence 127
   and anomie 117, 144–5, 597, 809, 1102,
      1103, 3589
   and anticipatory socialization 4569
   and Blau 313
   and bureaucracy 2355, 3312–13
   and the bureaucratic personality 378, 379
   and Coleman 570
   and consumer culture 420
   cumulative advantage/disadvantage, theory
      of 99, 3222–3
   and deviance 1136, 3589
   empirical method 2959, 2960
   and friendship 795
   and insiderism 909
   and Lazarsfeld 2565, 2959, 2960
   and manifest/latent functions 1809
   and mass media 2825, 3635
   medical sociology 2934
   and medical student socialization 2930, 2934
   middle distance theory 2795
   quantitative methodology 2407
   role-set and role-relations theory 127, 2486
   and science/democracy conflict 1542
   and scientific publication 490–1
   and self-fulfilling expectations/prophecies
      991, 2208, 4172–3, 4175
   sociology of knowledge 2483
   sociology of science 784, 785, 2475, 3667,
      4065, 4067, 4070, 4107, 4109–11, 4121
   status exchange hypothesis 2394
   and strain theory 1134, 4780
   and structural functionalism 127, 1809,
      1810–11
   and Thomas theorem 991
   and urban political machines 3446

Mesopotamia 4180, 5133
mesostructure 2961–3, 2997, 2999, 3003
Messerschmidt, J. W. 2818–21
messianism 2450, 3047
Messinger, S. L. 2472
Messner, M. 1663, 1877, 1878
Messner, S. 821, 841
mestizaje 339, 340, 341, 2190
meta-analysis 2963–4
meta-methods 2965
metabolic rift thesis 1425
metaevaluation 213, 1501
metallurgy 2699
metanarratives of modernism 3553
metaphor 1228
metaphysical beliefs 3355
Metaphysical Club 3609
metaphysical dualisms 1145
metaphysical realism 3235, 3236
metaphysical society 652
metaphysics of science 3355
metapower 2962
metasociology 2964–5
metatheory 2964–7
    paradigmatic 2963
    and postpositivism 3578
metatheory discourse analysis 1179
meterosexual 4259
methadone 1235, 1238
methamphetamine 1233, 1235
methane emissions 1425
methaqualone 1238
Methodism 914, 1053, 1055, 3408,
    3689, 3692
methodological behaviorism 2145
methodological holism 2964, 3794
methodological individualism 635, 1298, 1436,
    2963, 2964, 3794
methodological nationalism 1050
methodological symmetry 785, 786
methodological triangulation 5076, 5077
methodology–method distinction 2967
methods 2967–71
    action research 18
    comparative method 653
    Comtean 653
    deviance research methods 1126–31
    feminist methodology 1701–5
    historical method 653
    methodological questions in research 2135
    and naturalistic enquiry 3161, 3163
    and paradigms 3355–6

quantitative research paradigm 2978
    reflexivity 1145
    triangulation (multiple methods) 778
methods, arts-based 2971–4
methods, bootstrap 2974–6, 3878
methods, case study 2076–8
    and deviance 1129–30
methods, mixed 2978–81
    integration problem 2980
    legitimation problem 2980
    politics, challenge of 2980
    qualitative computing strategies 3726
    representation problem 2979–80
    triangulation 778, 1127, 2969, 2978, 5075–9
methods, postcolonial 2981–6
methods, visual 2986–9
metropolis 2989–93
    in antiquity 2990
    black urban regime 310–12
    and blasé/neurasthenic personalities 312
    and the central business district 423
    and economic growth 2990, 2991
    European cities 494
    and fantasy cities 1643
    and homelessness 2146–50
    and internal migration 3018
    memory sites 591
    new metropolitan regions 2992
    in the third world 2991
metropolitan district 2991
**Metropolitan Statistical Area 2991–2,
    2993–6**, 5103
Metz, C. 1755
Mexican American Women's National
    Association 1676
Mexican Americans 1459
    clothing styles 715
    cohabitation 1208
    folk medicine 631
    health care 2244
    morbidity and mortality 3757
    subtractive bilingualism 283
Mexican Revolution 339, 341
Mexico
    authoritarian regimes 222, 223, 225
    bandits 414
    Cardenism 411
    Catholicism 2530
    civil religion 507
    demographic data collection 1012
    economy 411, 1561
    emigration 3020

and federalism 1652
feminist activism 1685, 1686
film industry 1753
indigenous peoples 2948–9
indigenous struggles 2279
Jewish community 2453
kindergarten programs 2462
labor migration 2263–5
laicism 2532
machine politics 3445
medical sociology 2935
Mexican anthropology 339–43
Mexican Revolution 339, 341, 412, 414,
 2946, 2947
migration 661, 1044, 1459, 3032, 3759
neopopulism 413
peripheral state 1395
social movements 413
sociological tradition 2946–50
television corporations 2890
working class 1410
Mexico City 2991, 3623
Meyer, D. S. 3447–50
Meyer, J. 933, 1307, 1334, 1968, 2351, 2353,
 2585, 2714, 3283, 3333
Meyer, M. 318, 3306
Meyrowitz, J. 2921
Miami 1452–3, 1454, 1461
Michéa, C. F. 2157
Michel, P. 196–9
Michels, Robert 570, 2015, 2039, **2996–7**
 and elite rule 3442
 iron law of oligarchy 1362, 3258, 3312,
  3442, 3459
 political party theory 3452
Michlic, J. 1936–8, 3426–8
Mickelson, R. A. 4023–7
Mickey Mouse 694, 730, 2898
micro and macro in sociological analysis 2961
 see also mesostructure
micro–macro deductive logic in social theory
 2146
micro–macro links 2997–3005
 and agency–structure debate 2999
 bridging 3001, 3002–3, 3004
 and containment 3002
 embeddedness argument 2999, 3000,
  3001, 3004
 multilevel theories 3001–2
 and rational choice sociology 3794, 3796,
  3803–4
 urban ecology 5102

microeconomics 635
microelectronics 689, 2333
Micropolitan Statistical Areas 2994, 2995
microsociology 1812, 2042, **3005–8**
Microsoft 731, 1958, 2876, 2883, 3110
middle class
 activism 781
 ascendancy 3200
 in Asia 3198–201
 black middle class 311, 707, 708, 709,
  2306, 3747
 and consumption 736, 765–6, 2192, 2193
 delinquency 543
 and democracy 1002
 friendships 1792, 1862
 and gentrification 1919
 growth of 535
 habitus 2648
 identification with 546
Middle Way 681
middleman minorities 3008–10, 3836
 economic role 3008
Middletown 2647
midwifery 630, 632
 midwives as witches 1115
Mies, M. 1115, 1275, 2383, 2838
Mies Van der Rohe, Ludwig 3573
Miéville, C. 3495
migration
 and biodemography 284
 brain drain 1040
 chain migration 2253, 3012
 circular migration 3759
 domestic 1027
 economic migration 3011, 3017, 3018
 and environmental degradation 1423
 estimates and projections 1026, 1038,
  1039, 1044
 forced migration 3011, 3838
 gender imbalance 3017, 3536
 host populations, costs and benefits to 3022
 illegal/unauthorize 2263, 2265
 in-migration 3019
 international migration 1027
 joint family migration 2253
 man first migration 2253
 motivations 2253
 net migration rate 1027
 non-economic factors 3017, 3018
 out-migration 1039, 3015, 3019
 positive/negative effects 1039–40
 push-pull model 2253, 3032, 3835

migration (*cont'd*)
 quantitative research methods 1716
 rates of 3017
 regulation 2256, 2262, 3020
 rural–urban migration 1037, 1423, 1715
 and stress 4833–6
 temporary migration 3022
 UN estimates 3021
 undocumented migrants 3011
 unmeasured migration 1027
 urbanization 1423
 see also asylum seekers; immigration;
  immigration policy; refugees
migration, ethnic conflicts, and racism
  3011–14
 and immigrant language issues 2260
migration: internal 2256, **3014–19**
 definitional ambiguity 3015–16
 demographic transition theory 1034
 Great Migration 3747
 and HIV impacts 2138
 international–internal migrant distinction 3020
 measuring 3016
 out-migration 1344
 projections and estimates 1027
 push–pull factors 3017
 rural-to-urban migration 2138
migration: international 1027, 3011–12,
  3019–25
 definition 3019
 demographic effects 1039–40
 economic migration 1600
 European cities and 494
 family migration 1605–8
 flexible labor 1959
 immigrant families 2252–4
 international–internal migrant distinction 3020
 language issues 2258–61
 linguistic adaptation and incorporation 2258–9
 and postnationalism 3576
 process components 3019
 projections and estimates 1027
 and prostitution 3682, 3683
 and race consciousness 3741
 and religious institutions, role of 1981
 sex workers 1984
 statistics 2263
 women 1854
 see also immigration; immigration policy;
  refugee movements
migration and the labor force 3025–31
 labor migrants 3021, 3022

migration transition 1036, 1037
migration: undocumented/illegal 1027,
  2263, 2265, **3031–4**
 people trafficking 3836
Mihlej, S. 2899–902
Milardo, R. M. 672–4
Milgram, Stanley (experiments) 1311,
  1912, **3034–7**, 5315
 and Asch experiments 189–91
 and conformity 226–7, 3034, 3230–1, 3701
Miliband, R. 664, 2838, 3052, 3442, 3597
Milingo, Archbishop 441
militarism 1663
 and capitalism 2686
 and empire 1394
 and gender stratification 2308
 and globalization 1958
 and imperialism 2267
 Luxemburg and 2686
 and manifest destiny doctrine 2755
militarized women 1887
military
 as coercive institution 3315–17, 3318, 3319
 minority group representation 3318
 and the nation-state system 2498
 and patriarchy 3379
military coups 224
military interdependence 1473
military prisons 3640
military research and science and war
  3037–40
 Big Science 275, 276
 decision-making 983
military sociology 3040–3
 coercive institutions 3315–17, 3318, 3319
 and decision-making 983, 3323
 gays in the military 1835, 2100, 2162
 institutional/occupational (I/O) model 3042
 and media management 2879
 post-Cold War period 3042–3
 see also war
military-industrial complex 3051, 3179, 3438
military-industrial-academic complex 3291
military-industrial-government-academic
  complex 275
Mill, Harriet Taylor 2618
Mill, John Stuart 425, 1258, 2108, 2618,
  3044–7, 3469
 bureaucratic-military regimes 224
 and causal relationships 1533
 and Comte 655, 1542, 3044
 economic sociology 1301, 3046

and the Irish land question 3044–5
and the laboring poor 3045, 3046
and liberalism 2622
and markets 2778
method of (indirect) difference 2133
and political economy 1300, 1303, 1304,
  2797, 3044, 3045
positivism 3044
and representative government 4167
and utilitarianism 3046
and wealth distribution 1302
and women's rights 3045
Millar, J. 4601
millenarianism 3047–50
  catastrophic millenarianism 3049, 3190
  Jehovah's Witnesses 2439, 2440
  and the New Age 3190, 3191
  optimistic millenarianism 3190
  pre- and postmillenarianism 3049–50
  progressive millenarianism 3049, 3190, 3191
Millennium Development Goals 1724, 1975
Miller, D. 737, 790–1, 1264–7, 1962,
  3634–40
Miller, F. 1685
Miller, H. 991
Miller, J. 2820, 4102, 4103
Miller, Mark C. 2827
Miller, Michael 743
Miller, Monica K. 562–5, 4383–6
Miller, T. 3480–3, 4965–9
Millet, K. 336, 3682, 4245
Milliken v. *Bradley (Milliken I)* 369
Million Man Marches 1665
Mills, C. Wright 515, 1228, 1807, 1811, 2409,
  3050–5, 3334, 4186
  "cow sociology" 363
  and critical theory 3053
  elite theory 1363, 2838, 3051, 3193, 3442,
    3459, 3597, 3602–3
  and empiricism 2960
  and Lazarsfeld 3053
  Marxism 3053, 3193
  and mass society 2823, 3043
  and the middle class 3052
  and the New Left 3052, 3193
  and Parsons 3053
  and postmodernism 3054–5
  and pragmatism 3051, 3193
  and role-taking 3949, 3950
  and social order theory 4487–8
  and the sociological imagination 1127, 1245,
    2589, 3053, 3400, 4596–7, 4604

Mills, T. 1379
Millward, P. 2235–7
Milner, A. 365–6, 3494–8, 3516–17
Milner, M. 773–6
Milosevic, Slobodan 1814
Milton, John 3468, 3637
mimetic isomorphism 2351
Min, P. G. 3008–10
Minami, H. 3218
mind 3055–7
  philosophy of the mind 799
  and positivistic neuroscience 3187
mind–body dualism 327, 335, 337, 1749, 1846
  Buddhist teaching 373
mind-control 886
mindfulness 3384
mineworkers strike (UK, 1984–5) 2288
Mingione, E. 4399–403
minimum wage 840
Minnelli, Vincent 218
Minobe, R. 505
minority groups *see* ethnic groups; specific
  groups
Mintz, S. 288
Mintzberg, H. 3301
minzoku **3057–60**
miracles 3521, 4092
Mirandé, A. 2550
miscarriage 1629
miscegenation 295, 3479, 3732, 5250
  see also interracial unions
misdemeanours, criminal 2554, 2555
Mises, L. von 2201, 2779, 3176
Mishler, E. G. 2247
misogyny 677, 2155, 2826
  black male 307
  and pornography 905
Misra, J. 402–4, 1271–3, 1438–9
missionary activity 408, 1055, 1982, 2131
  Jehovah's Witnesses 2440
Mississippi Bubble 2022
Mississippi Freedom Summer Project 578
Missouri ex rel. Gaines v. *Canada* 368
Mitchell, I. J. 1444
Mitchell, J. 2841
Mitchell, S. A. 2401
Mitchell, W. J. T. 3141
Mitroff, I. 4111
mixed methods research 2978–80
  and naturalistic enquiry 3161
  and qualitative computing strategies 3726
mixed model designs 2979

mixed race theory 296
"mixed-race" children 1405, 2394
Miyata, N. 2446
Mizruchi, M. S. 2714
mnemonic learning practices 4972
mob rule 2759
   see also crowd behavior
mobility
   absolute 2368
   career mobility 1142
   and globalization 1959
   relative 2368, 2376–7
   see also occupational mobility
mobility, horizontal and vertical 3060–1,
   3064
   caste and 405
   class and 534, 551, 719, 911
   education and 1229, 2654
   and ethnicity 1456, 1460, 1461, 1464
   gender bias 1844
   and industrialization 1967
   log-linear modeling 2660
   and marriage 675, 1664–5
   occupation 1250
   social fluidity model 2368–72
   workers 1769
   see also occupational mobility
mobility, intergenerational and
   intragenerational 2627, 3061–2
   and assimilation 193
   and class 533, 534, 537, 549
   and income inequality 2276–7
   occupational mobility 3240–1, 3242–3
   occupational scaling 3251
   schooling and economic success 4029–31
   and the sick and disabled 337
   social fluidity model 2368–72
   and status attainment 4753, 4754
   women 3956
   see also intergenerational mobility: methods
     of analysis
mobility, measuring the effects of 3063–4
mobility, physical, and the elderly 337
mobilization 3065–8
   collective 594, 3065
   consensus mobilization 3067
   electoral mobilization 3065
   ethnic 1465
   and integration 1922
   Latin America 1923–4, 1926
   moral shock and self-recruitment perspective
     3092–3

political mobilization 223, 3065
   resource mobilization perspective 3065, 3066
   wartime 3041–2
Mochizuki, T 1402
mockumentary 1212
modeling 4437–8
Modell, A. 1132, 1460
Modell, J. 3009
Modelski, G. 1951, 2491
modern technism 2640, 2641
modernity 3068–71
   and actor-network theory 219
   and anomie 3124
   and atheism 197
   and beliefs 260, 261
   and blasé/neurasthenic personalities 312
   and capitalism 2808
   Christianity and 477, 478
   civilization of 526
   and collective memory 590
   Confucianism and 671, 3096
   and cultural dominance of the body 337
   cultural and political program 524–5, 526,
     527, 3069
   and culture and economy 935, 1309–10
   and Eurocentrism 1492
   and everyday life 703
   and fashion 718
   and film 1752–3
   and *flânerie* 1762
   Fordist 2711
   and fundamentalism 1815
   and generational change 1901
   and genocide 1911
   global modernity 3070
   hypermodernity 3575
   and imagined communities 2249
   and information technology 2332
   "iron cage" 3330
   late modernity 3070
   and metropolises 2991
   multiple modernities 527, 3670
   and nationalism 3149–51
   and the Orthodox Church 3348, 3349
   and the public sphere 3722
   and race 3731
   and racial/ethnic conflict 661
   reflexivity 3069, 4248
   and science 136
   and sexuality 334
   tensions within 3070
   and traumatic change 595

modernization 3069, **3071–8**
  asynchronic model 1926
  and community–economy relation 624
  and contentious politics 780
  and decolonization 2267
  and democracy 3076
  and demographic transition 1034
  and dependency theory 1068
  and development 1853
  and development theory 1068, 1853
  ecological modernization 728, 1420,
    1421, 1422
  and ecological problems 1283
  and economic development 1295, 1296
  and elder status 2017
  and endogenous development 1406, 1407
  and exercise/fitness 1517
  and family demography 1042
  and family sociology 1598–9
  and friendships 1798
  and globalization of education 1971
  and industrialization 2298
  and institution of marriage 675
  and laicism 2532
  late modernization 1924, 1925
  Latin America 1920, 1922–6
  liberal theory 3073
  and the life course 2631
  and money exchange 1958
  and new religious movements 3204
  and patriarchy 1600
  and political economy 3435
  and political sociology 3460
  and populism 3537–8
  reflexivity 1174
  and revolutions 3916
  and social capital 3077
  technological modernization 1560
  and urbanization 1423
  see also postmodernism
Modood, T. 3105–8
Mods and Rockers 742, 3089
Moe, A. M. 1693–6
Moerman, M. 2363
Moffit, R. 1735
Moffit, T. E. 830–1
Mohammed 670, 911, 1655, 2424, 2425
Mohanty, C. T. 1692, 1704, 1854, 2396,
  2397, 3344
Mohr, M. 1444
Mokyr, J. 2300
Moland, J. 4339–41

Moldavia 4188
molecular biology 1681
molecular demography 286
molecular medicine 2940
Moll, A. 2132
Moller, S. 3956–7
Molm, L. 1369, 3598–602, 3604
Molotch, H. L. 2034, 2036
Molyneux, M. 1687
Molz, J. G. 761–4
monasticism 612
  asceticism 3689
  hermetic monasticism 3346
  and sexuality 4276
money **3078–81**
  e-money 3079, 3080
  earmarking 3080
  global control of 1388
  money-of-account 3079, 3080
  multiplicity of money 3080
  surrogates 1759
Money, J. 2672
money laundering 834
money management 1759
money management in families 3081–4
  housekeeping system 3081, 3082
  independent system 3083
  marital power theory 2771–2
  pooling 3082–3
  whole wage system 3081–2
Monge, P. R. 3293
Mongolia 371
monkeywrenching 1166
Monnier, C. A. 347–50, 1990–3, 2527–9
monogamy 1615, 2112, 3477
  and AIDS 108
  and commitment 2324
  compulsory 3477
  and same-sex couples 2608
  same-sex unions 2608, 3997
  serial monogamy 3478
monolingualism 277
Monophysites 3346
monopolistic tendencies 362
monopoly 2295, 2776, 2785, 2811
  of media regulation 2914
  monopoly capital 3437
  professionalism as 3657
  state monopolies 2914
monopoly capitalism 1394, 1395, 3179, 3440
monosexism 304
monosexuality 303, 304

monotheism 141, 523, 652, 3629, 3633, 3860
monsoon region 1287
Monsour, M. 877–9
Mont Pelerin society 3176
Montaigne, Michel de 908
Montchrétien, A. de 3440
Montejano, D. 2550
Montesquieu, Charles de 857
   attacks on Judaism 155
   and Durkheim 1251, 1254, 1258
   and pluralism 3459
   and political sociology 1005, 3458, 4599–600
   separation of powers doctrine 2583
Montgomery bus boycott 508–9, 706, 2466
Moodley, K. 162–5
Moonies *see* Unification Church
Moore, B. 1811, 2133, 3460
Moore, C. D. 2269–74
Moore, Joan 1826
Moore, John 2172
Moore, Kelly 1164–7
Moore, Kristin A. 1621–6
Moore, L. J. 2399–400
Moore, M. 1212
Moore, W. 971, 1811, 1950
Moores, S. 2922
Moraga, C. 2398, 2549
moral boundaries 1114, 1115
moral conservatism 3683
moral crusades 2505
moral culture in organizations 3339
moral development 1072
moral economy 900, 1310, **3084–6**, 4378
   and sport 4536–7
moral entrepreneur 1126, **3086–9**
   and mass media 2826
   and moral crusades 2505
   as rule enforcer 3086, 3087, 3088
moral fundamentalism, and neoconservatism
   3174
moral hazard 682
Moral Majority 1813, 3867
moral panics 1089, 1141, 2877, **3089–92**, 4199
   alcoholism 117
   and censorship 421
   and collective mobilization 3065
   and collective trauma 596
   and cybersexualities 966
   and deviant conduct 1136
   and marginalization 2766
   Marxist perspective 3090
   and mass media, impacts of 2877

and moral entrepreneurship 3087, 3088
   mugging 299, 3090
   and new media forms 3779
   and pedophilia 3385, 3386
   Satanism 4011
   and sexuality, globalization of 1984
   social constructionist approach 1089, 1090,
      3090–1
   and youth subcultures 2102, 4871
   see also sex panics
moral reasoning 1072
   development of 3680
moral resources 3895–6
Moral Right 2606
moral shocks and self-recruitment 1389,
   3092–3
   and animal rights movement 139
moral turpitude 2555
moral witnessing 1166
Morales, Y. J. G. 2860–1, 4079–82, 4119–22
morality
   Buddhist 372–3
   religious 2140
   and virtual reality 966
   see also ethics
morality evolution 2140
moralpolitik **(Confucian) 3093–6**
Moran, L. J. 4268–72
Moravian Brethren 3409
Moray, Sir Robert 4107
morbidity
   AIDS-related 2138
   HIV-induced 2138
   life-table model 2095–6
   morbidity rates and economic productivity
      3529
   mortality–morbidity–disability relation 2097
   racial variations 3757
   social class inequalities 2087, 2088, 2089
   see also chronic illness and disability; disease
More, Sir Thomas 612–13, 3495, 5155–6
Morehouse College 2466
Morehouse Family Institute 2466
Morelos y Pavón, J. M. 414
Moreno, J. L. 3182, 4611
mores 3231
Morga, A. de 1492
Morgan, D. H. J. 2789–91
Morgan, J. 870–3
Morgan, L. 1505, 1595, 1927
Morgan, S. L. 1528–31
Morgan, S. P. 1729–33

Morgenstern, O. 1822
Morley, D. 914, 1404
Mormons *see* Church of Jesus Christ of Latter
  Day Saints
morphine 1238
Morrione, T. 318–21, 2962
Morris, A. 507–12, 781, 1166, 3067
Morris, B. 3471
Morris, C. 1227, 4186–7
Morris, William 3495
Morrison, L. 3891–3
Morrissey, M. 4995–5000
Morrow, V. 455–6
Mort, F. 736
mortality
  age-specific 285, 286
  AIDS-related 2138
  and biodemography 284
  causation 1185
  class differentials 2628
  definition 1864
  divorce, impact of 1208
  and gender 1156–7, 1870, 3535
  and industrialization 2295–6
  life-table model 2095
  and morbidity/disability rates 2095
  mortality risk, and health behaviors 1517
  mortality–morbidity–disability relation 2097
  old-age mortality 2095, 2098
  and poverty 1613–14
  racial disparities 3757
  social class variations 2087, 2088, 2089
  and socioeconomic status (SES) 99–100,
    4590–3
  see also death and dying; suicide
mortality: transitions and measures 1033,
    1036, 1037, 1038, 1039, **3096–102**
  and aging, demography of 68
  cause-specific mortality 3101
  and demographic transition theory 93
  and drug therapy 3100
  and fertility decline 1035
  infant mortality rate (IMR) 1039
  life-table analysis 1021–5, 1026, 2095–6
  and medical technologies 3100
  and nutritional status 3099
  Physical Quality of Life Index 1001
  and public health and hygiene 3099–100
  see also child mortality; infant mortality;
    maternal mortality
mortgages 2196, 4762
Mortimer, J. T. 2636

mosaic metaphor 2944
Mosca, Gaetano 2015, 2016, 2039, **3102–3**
  and elites 1361, 1362, 3102–3, 3361, 3442
  political party theory 3452
  and social stratification 547
Moscow–San Francisco Peace March 1165
Moses 2449
Moskos, C. C. 3042, 3043
Moss, L. 4132–5
Most, J. 2005
Mother Teresa 1115
mother-tongue shift 2259–60
motherhood 3103–5
  activist mothering 1679
  Bernard and 272
  and childcare 457
  and cultural feminism 904, 905
  culture of motherhood 940
  and feminism 939
  gender role expectations 3226
  and home schooling 4032
  immigrant women 3033
  intensive mothering 940
  and labor market participation 458, 695, 937,
    1032, 1204, 3033
  maternal thinking 3104
  media representation of 940
  non-resident mothers 3224, 3226
  and patriarchal rule 333
  and school dropout 1230, 1231
  social attitudes to 939–40
  social construction 3103–4
  stepmothering 4770–2
  surrogacy 3104
  teenage mothers 1725–9
  time engaged with children 1602, 1881, 2381
  unpaid labor 939
  voluntary motherhood 1699
Motion Picture Association of America 730, 3792
motivational framing 1781
motor neuron disease 2246
motor vehicle theft 2278
motorcycle gangs 1129, 1825
Mott, L. 1673, 2618
Mouer, R. 1413–17, 2435–8, 2437, 3170–2,
    3172, 3219, 4311–14
Mouffe, C. 1004–5, 1009, 2815
Mouw, T. 4629–33
Movahedi, S. 3694–6
movie theaters, and crowd dispersal 881
Moya, P. M. L. 3562
Moylan, T. 3496

Moynihan, D. P. 1627, 1785, 2945, 3445
Moynihan Report 1627
Mozambique
  infant mortality 1726
  revolution 3907
  teenage marriage 1727
Mozetic, G. 3360–2
MP3 964, 1164, 3133
MTV (Music Television) 739, 774, 914
Mueller, A. S. 1323–8, 1546–9
Mueller, C. 5279–84
mugging 299, 2340
Muggleton, D. 4869–72
Muir, J. 1275
Mukerji, C. 743–4, 784–8, 946–8, 957–9, 2596, 4380–3
mulatto 3265, 3266
Mulkay, M. 4111
Mullany, B. 2313–20
Muller, H. J. 1489
Müller, M. 3629, 3860
multi-agent systems 634, 639
multicultural education 277
multicultural feminism 2395
multicultural pedagogy 1707
multiculturalism 1154, 1468–9, **3105–8**, 3422
  and Anglo-conformity 137
  and assimilation 3364
  and coercive organizations 3318
  and collective memory 589, 590
  and creolization 818
  and cultural diversity 899, 900
  and cultural trauma, coping with 597
  and difference 2945
  and the ghetto 1938
  non-territorial multiculturalism 3108
  state policies 3761
multidimensional scaling (MDS) 3121
multiethnic queer communities 2161
Multilateral Agreement on Investment 1978, 1979
multimedia 3108–12
  CD-ROM interactive media 3109, 3110–11
  computer-based interactive multimenida 3109–12
  definitions 3109
  logocentrism 3111
multimodality 3111–12
Multinational Comparative Time-Budget Research Project 1031
multinational corporations *see* transnational corporations

multinucleated metropolitan region 2992, **3112–17**
  see also megalopolis
multiphasic response theory 3532
multiple correspondence analysis (MCA) 2969
multiple nuclei model 1280
multiple regression 313, 645
multiple sclerosis 2245, 2246
multiple social temporalities 361
multiple triangulation 5077
multiracial feminism 3117–20
  and intersectionality 2395
  issues 3118
  and racialized gender 3764
multiraciality 295, 296
multistage sampling procedure 3782
multisystemic therapy 2406
multivariate analysis 2119, **3120–3**, 4748–9
  path analysis 3373
  structural equation modeling 4848–51
Mumby, D. K. 3290–9
Mumford, Lewis 2992, **3123–5**
  and regionalism 3123
municipal housekeeping 1669
Muñiz, A. M. 357–60
Muñoz, J. 1225
Munroe, P. T. 146–7, 559–62, 990, 2400–42
Münzer, T. 3048
Murchison, C. 837
murder *see* genocide; homicide
Murdoch, Rupert 419, 2873, 2874, 2887, 2897–8
Murphy, Patrick 1751
Murphy, Peter 166–75, 3563–7, 3885–6
Murphy, Raymond 1419
Murphy, Robert 481
Murray, A. 1984, 2862
Murray, C. 263–5, 1735, 3523, 3592
Murray, J. 3110
Murray, P. 306, 307, 1674, 3118
Muscio, I. 1679
muscular Christianity 2082, 2120, 4691
museum studies movement 3127
museums 592, **3125–8**
  and consumption 713, 3126
  cultural tourism 921, 3126
  ecomuseums 921
  interaction studies 2364
  merchandising 3126
  and multimedia 3109
  and visual consumption 769, 771, 3126
music 3128–9
  and Adorno 29

and the charismatic movement 440
classical 2905
consumption of 746–7
and cool 797–8
creolization 817
and cultural capital 891
democratization 3493
digital 739
folk 2905
listening practices 746, 747
and networks of assemblages 2905
and political expression 779
popular music 774, 3128
postmodern 3556, 3557
and protest 3493
regulation 2913–14
rock 2905
science, influence of 4958
and self-construction 746
tools and repertories for action 746
women's music 1675, 3128
and youth culture 774
see also hip-hop; jazz
music and media 3129–34
and Adorno 27
file-sharing networks 3489–90
music and social movements 3134–6
and jazz 3489
Music Television (MTV) 3132
music therapy 747
music videos 914
musical tastes 1361
Musick, K. 1734–7
musicology 3129
Musil, R. 1229
Mussolini, Benito 240, 411, 1644, 1645, 1921,
    3102, 3214
Muste, A. J. 3193
mutual appropriation (labor market closure)
    3286
mutual deviantization 584
Muzzatti, S. L. 2824–7
My Lai 876, 3037
Myers, D. 626, 2177, 3921–6
myopia (organizational dysfunction) 3397
Myrdal, G. 2466, 3422
mysticism
    and asceticism 186–7
    Certeau and 424–5
    charismatic leadership 433
    counterculture and 810
    and cults 885

Islamic 2000
Jewish 268
and magic 2699
myth 261, 2705, 3136–7
alienation of 262
archetypal mythologies 3138
and bricolage 366
cosmogonic mythologies 3138
Frontier Myth 3511–13
and leadership 415
logic and 262
and magic 2699
mythic thinking, cloning and 556
mythmaking process 243
and nationhood 3148
political mythology 2691
and popular religiosity 3523–4
racial myths as propaganda 3673
and ritual 3934
Myth of the American Frontier 3511–13
Myth of Ham 3721
mythogenesis 3137–40
mythopoetic imagination 3511
mythopoetic movement 1873

Nader, Ralph 697, 1115
Naficy, H. 2885–6
Nagata, J. 1692
Nagel, J. 1405, 2280–5
Nagy, Imre 2679
Nahmad, S. 340
Naiad Press 1675, 2603
Naim, B. A. 2001
Naipaul, V. S. 2191
Nakamaki, H. 1400–2
Nakane, C. 238, 2240, 3218, 3992
Nakano, T. 4297–303
Nakayama, I. 2436
Nakayama, M. 2499
Namibia 106
    life expectancy 1864
    prostitution 2161
naming traditions, feminist 2603
Nanda, M. 3612
nanotechnology 691
Naples, N. 1679, 1701–6, 1704, 1710–15, 1712,
    1714, 2848, 4845–6
Napoleon Bonaparte 2230, 2530
Napster 2358, 3133, 3489–90
narcissism 2650, 2698, 2750, 3190,
    3718, 3833
Nardi, P. M. 1804

narrative 3141–2
   and accounts 9, 10
   and autoethnography 231
   and biography 287, 288, 289, 290
   and chronic illness/disability 481, 482
   and collective memory 592
   and feminist research 1702, 1703
   identity, and self-narratives 2217
   illness narrative 2246–8
   mythic narrative 3138
   post-positive interpretive turn 3141
   and self-construction 231, 2246, 4159
   visual narratives 3725
   see also life history
narrative totalization 3557
NASA 1174, 3517
Nash equilibrium (NE) 1822, 1823
Nash, J. 1823
Nathan, M. 697
Nation of Islam 2764, 3203, 4189
nation-state 3142–3
   boundaries 1469, 3020
   and contentious politics 780
   and decolonization 985, 986
   and denationalization 1048–51
   as discursive formations 3148
   economic interdependence 1472
   and economic/military networks 1473
   and ethnic cleansing 1451
   ethnic fragmentation 1472
   and ethnic groups 1457
   and ethnosymbolism 3149, 3151
   and food supplies 722
   imagined communities 618, 628, 1468, 3139,
      3148, 3149
   and immigration 2255, 3012, 3019–20
   and meritocracy 2955
   minzoku 3057
   and monopolization of violence 530, 531
   multiculturalism 1468–9
   nation-building 1468
   nation–state distinction 3142
   and new institutional theory 2352
   Olympics, co-optation of 3263
   pluricultural state 342, 343
   and the public school system 4049
   and public security 2342
   and the public sphere 2908
   self-determination 4166–8
   and separatism 4189
   state-building movements 1466, 1467
   and territoriality 947

   and transnational corporations 5067–8
   and transnationalism 5064–6
nation-state and nationalism 3143–52
   Afrikaner nationalism 162
   and anti–Semitism 156
   boundary making 345
   collective identity 2901
   cultural geography of the nation-state 2901
   Latin America 1925
   minzoku 3057–8
   nation-state interaction 1968
   religious nationalism 507
   school systems 1972
National Academy of Sciences 2850, 3038
National Aeronautics and Space
   Administration 2850
National American Woman Suffrage
   Association (NAWSA) 1673
National Association for the Advancement of
   Colored People (NAACP) 129, 307, 1243
   and Civil Rights Movement 509
   and massive resistance 2831
   and school desegregation 368, 369, 370, 2831
National Association of Colored Women
   (NACW) 307
National Black Feminist Organization (NBFO)
   307, 1676, 3118
National Broadcasting (NBC) 2897, 2898
National Center for Complementary and
   Alternative Medicine 632
National Center for Health Statistics (NCHS)
   1013
national champions 5068
National Coming Out Day 606
National Conference of Charities and
   Corrections (NCCC) 1670
National Congress of American Indians 2283
National Congress of Neighborhood Women's
   (NCNW) college program 1705
National Consumers' League 697
National Council of Negro Women (NCNW)
   307
National Council of Social Welfare (NCSW)
   4537–8
National Crime Victimization Surveys 2870,
   2871
national cultures 933, 957
national defense 2234
National Educational Television (NET) 3704
national health insurance 85, 87
National Health and Nutrition Examination
   Survey 1866

National Health Service (NHS) 2526, 4580–1
National Incident-Based Reporting System
 (NIBRS) 2871–2
National Institute of Mental Health 2933
National Institute for Standards in Technology
 2850
national lottery 1820
National Organization of Men Against Sexism
 (NOMAS) 3379
National Organization for Women (NOW) 307,
 677, 1674–5, 1677, 2602, 3118, 3379
National Science Foundation 2850, 3389, 3390
National Survey of Family Growth (NSFG)
 2320–1
National Tribal Chairmen's Association 2283
National Urban League 509, 2444
National Woman Suffrage Association
 (NWSA) 1673, 2618
National Woman's Party (NWP) 1673
National Women's Service in Chile
 (SERNAM) 1688
nationalism 1477, **3152–8**
 banal nationalism
 and capitalism 517, 3144
 civic model 1486, 1839, 3155
 and communication 2900, 2901, 2902
 and critical theory 874, 876
 and cultural homogeneity 2900
 and cultural imperialism 2900
 cultural nationalism 957, 3058, 3144, 3154,
  3155, 3156, 3219
 and decolonization 985
 definitions 3153
 and diaspora 1153
 diffusion 1473
 economic nationalism 44, 1074, 3155–6
 and empire 1393–4, 2267
 and ethnic cleansing 1451
 ethnic model 1466, 1839, 2755, 3151, 3155
 and ethnicity 1466, 1467
 ethnonationalism 1486–8
 ethnoreligious claims to 3145
 ethnosymbolist explanation 3157
 functionalist explanation 3150
 fundamental nationalism 1474
 homogenizing enterprise 3150, 3153–4
 and ideology 2231
 and imagined communities 2248, 2249
 and immigration 3012
 and industrialism 3150
 instrumentalist explanations 3155
 Islamic 1465, 1467, 2427

 Marxist conception 1838
 media and nationalism 2899–902
 methodological nationalism 1050, 3147
 and modernity 3149–51, 3155
 and music, for consciousness raising 3135
 myths of nationhood 3148
 national identity 745, 926, 957, 1458, 1468,
  1476, 1839, 2248, 2249, 3149, 3156, 3159
 nationalist movements 1465
 nature of nations debate 3147–8
 new nationalisms 1471
 and *nihonjinron* 3218, 3219, 3220
 perennialist explanation 3156–7
 political nationalism 3144, 3150–1, 3153,
  3155, 3159
 and populism 353
 primordial explanation 3156–7
 proto-nationalism 3150
 and racial/ethnic conflict 660, 3013–14
 revival 3157
 and salary men 3993
 secessionist nationalism 3145
 sociobiological explanation 3156
 socioeconomic account 3150
 and sovereignty rights 1465, 1472
 state-building nationalism 1466, 1471
 territorial claims 1466
 transnationalism 1459
 Turkish nationalism 1999–2000
 ultra-nationalism 2802, 2803
 unification nationalism 1466
 see also ethnicity
nationalism, *see also* nation-state and
  nationalism
nationalism and sport 3158–61, 3474
 and national identities 2222
nationalist movements
 and authority 1471
 distinguishing features 1466
 forms of 1465–6
 repression and concession 1470
Native Action 2283
Native American Rights Fund (NARF) 2280,
  2283
Native Americans
 and accommodation 8
 adolescent fertility 1728
 and affirmative action policies 47
 and assimilation 4682
 Boas and 321
 and collective identity 587
 and control of resources 2280

Native Americans (*cont'd*)
  and cultural imperialism 906–7
  and cultural tourism 921
  demography 2282–3
  exogamy 1405
  folk medicine 2079
  and the Frontier Myth 3512
  gaming 2283, 2284
  and genetics 2080
  and genocide 2079, 2421
  graduate education 2013
  grandparents 2020
  healing systems 631
  health problems 276
  identity politics 2284
  intermarriage 2283
  interracial marriage 1405, 2394
  languages 2537
  and manifest destiny doctrine 2755
  and medical experiments 2079
  millenarianism 3048–9
  naming issues 2281
  and political poetry 2421
  population estimates 2282–3
  potlach ritual 1938, 1939
  religion 752
  and reparations 3876
  reservations 137
  rites of passage 4568
  self-determination 2283
  spiritual traditions 2284
  and stigma 584
  totemism 5019
  tribal–federal relationship 2282, 2283
  two-spirit people 4277
nativism 1494, 2260, 2262
NATO 1472
natural disasters 1174
natural experiments 1539
natural rights 652
natural science 871
natural selection theory 292, 1504
naturalism 872, 1481
  and ethnography 1481
naturalistic inquiry 3161–3
nature 3163–6
  biologized nature 4584
  environmental issues 3164, 3165
  humanity–nature relationship 3165
  nature–culture binary 3165
  semi-domestication 4178–9
  and zoos 3500–3

nature environmentalism 2640
nature–nurture debate 257, 1845–6, 2399
  and mental disorder 2695
naturopathy 630, 631, 632
Nayak, A. 2153
Naylor, R. T. 834
Nazif, S. 2001
Nazism
  authoritarianism 1569
  empire 1395
  and ethnic cleansing 1451
  and eugenics 2938
  fascism 152, 1489, 1569, 1646
  frustration–reaction theory 3768–9
  medical experiments 1442
  monopolization of violence 531
  neo-Nazism 1645, 3767
  party organization 3453
  propaganda 877, 1753, 2235–6, 3673
  racial hygiene program 1169, 1489, 1908
  sociological explanation 1805
  totalitarianism 3176
  utopianism 2528
  see also Holocaust
necrophilia 2493
Nederveen Pieterse, J. 1991
Nee, V. 191–6, 1461, 1462, 2257
Needleman, J. 1761, 3202
Neff, K. D. 1797
negation of negation, Hegelian 1148
negative case analysis 134, 135, **3166–70**
negotiated order theory 2961, 2962
negotiations
  clear intentions 2470
  emotions in 1381
  open discussions 2470
Negri, A. 1396, 2268, 3563, 3564, 3565, 3567, 4334
négritude 2984
Neidhart, C. 744
neighborhoods 503
  and access to health care 2079–80
  blue-collar neighborhoods 1278
  broken windows theory of crime 825–6
  businesses 715
  class profiles 619
  and community 637
  crime rates 585, 848, 1614
  deterioration 2074
  dislocation of residents 503
  and drug use 1234
  ethnic neighborhoods 1456

friendship networks 1798
gay 768, 4255
and health outcomes 2072–4
hybridity 2190
interracial neighborhoods 3755
and invasion-succession 2419
and juvenile delinquency 2455
marginalized neighborhoods 2766
neighborhood characteristics and dropping
out of school 1231
and police behavior 3432
and poverty 1614, 5126–7
and redlining 3825–7
and segregation 2197
social disorganization 1081, 4395–7
succession 503
neighbors
reputation 545
and social support 90
Nelkin, D. 2173–4
Nelson, A. C. 1550
Nelson, G. 885
Nelson, H. L. 1682
Nelson, R. R. 3329
Nelson, T. 3110
nenko chingin **3170–2**
neo-asceticism 188
neocapitalism 703
neoclassical economics 1294, 1303–6, 2748,
3366, 3440
and emotions 1384, 1387
equivalence theorem 2777
and exploitation 1543, 1545, 1546
and family migration 1606
and labor–management relations 2512
and markets 2776, 2778, 2779, 2780
and popular culture 3481
neocolonialism *see* colonialism (neocolonialism)
neo-Confucianism 524
neoconservative crime control policies 1122
neoconservatism 681, **3172–5**
cultural doctrine 3174
economic doctrine 3173–4
and ethnic and race relations 661
and neoliberalism 3173–4, 3178
Nietzscheanism 3217
political doctrine 3173
and the republican tradition 3173
Thatcherism 2102
neocorporatism 3435
neo-Darwinian evolutionary theory 292, 293,
2250

neo-fascism 3780
neo-Fordism 1770
neofunctionalism *see* functionalism/
neofunctionalism
neo-institutional theory 3283
neo-institutionalism, and development studies
1296
neo-Kantians 1286
neoliberal capitalism 2814
neoliberal globalization
economic globalization 1960
and global justice movement 1947
resistance to 1947, 1959, 1976
neoliberalism 517, 1069, 2625, **3175–8**
anti-globalist critique 1947
anti-neoliberalist movements 981
anti-poverty strategies 3592–3
and civil society 513
and communitarianism 3177
and conservatism 681, 3177
cultural doctrine 3177–8
and ecological problems 1282
and economic development 1295, 3342
and the global economy 1945
green ideology 1419
ideology 349, 2231
and the Internet 734
and labor markets 2521
and labor–management relations 2512
and laborism 2527
and Latin American economic structures
1567
libertarian element 3177
market fundamentalism 3592
materialist analysis 2838
and neoconservatism 3173–4, 3178
neoliberal urbanism 5147
political doctrine 3177
political rationality of 2008
principles 3176
and the regulatory state 2563
and representative democracy 407
and social accounting 4350–1
and the social market economy 3176, 3178
state role 3177
Washington Consensus 1979, 3178
and the welfare state 1178
and world-system theory 1061
neo-Luddites 962
neo-Malthusianism 3528
neo-Marxism 3178–80, 3195, 4982
anti-imperialism 3179

neo-Marxism (*cont'd*)
  and class struggle 2755
  and consumer culture 744
  critical theory 868
  dependency theory 1068
  and development 1069
  and disability 1170
  and education 2116
  and environmental degradation 1420, 1422
  and ethnic/racial divisions of labor 1463
  and fascism 959
  and feminist anthropology 1690
  Frankfurt School 1805
  and industrialization 2299
  and leisure 2589
  materialist critique 2838
  and the professions 2076, 3663
  regulation theory 2816
  and sport 4696
  underconsumption thesis 3438
  and urban political economy 5122–3
  and worker exploitation 840
  world-system theory 1282
neo-Nazism 1645, 3733
neopaganism 4139
neo-Pentecostalism 439
neophytes
  and socialization 2931
  in sport 2222
neopopulism 413, 3539
neoracism 3750
neorealism 1753
neo-Scholasticism 4975
neoshamanism 631
neo-soul 309
neo-structuralism 1561
neotribalism 2691
  and football hooliganism 1768
  and nationalism 3156
neo-Weberianism 547, 550, 5123–4
Nepal
  capitalist growth 390
  life expectancy 1864
nepotism 2571, 3751
Neruda, Pablo 2550
nest-leaving patterns 2169, 2438, 2570–2, 2573–4
nested event-history models 287
nesting (HML design) 2119
Nestle, J. 2610
Nestorianism 3345, 3346
net reproduction rate (NRR) 1744

Netherlands
  capitalism 396
  cohabitation 566
  complementary and alternative medicine 631
  democracy 1001
  demographic data collection 1012
  elites 1363
  environmental degradation 1424
  euthanasia, decriminlization of 1497
  family migration 1607
  gender poverty ratios 1723
  health care-seeking behavior 2069
  health technology assement 692
  immigration 2258, 2259, 3028
  immigration policies 3020
  industrialization 494
  institutional review boards 2346
  Jewish population 2453
  laicization 4145
  lone parenthood 2665
  medical sociology 2935
  nationalism 1473
  new religious movements 3205
  prostitution 1659
  religious schools 4053
  sex tourism 4201
  social security system 2055
  sports injuries 2093
  technology assessment 689, 690
  teenage motherhood 1728
  wealth inequalities 2312
Netherlands Indies 1492
netizenship 1162
Nettleton, S. 4580–1
network analysis *see* social network analysis
network cities 3113
network exchange theory *see* exchange network theory
network HMOs 2065
network mapping 2742
network megalopolises 2943
network society 3180–2
  actor-network theory and
  see also information society
Network-Episode Model (NEM) 2106
networks 3182–5
  access points 2927
  articulated arrangements 2926–7
  brokers and hubs (nodal points) 2742
  caregivers 2071
  cellular networks 2902
  centrality concept 3183

and civil society 513
coalition formation 3184
and collective action 578
communication networks 3291
and community 620
and conjugal roles 672–4
consolidation 1369
cross–border networks 1050
and cross–sex friendship 878
and cultural trauma, coping with 597
dense networks 672, 673
and digitization 1159, 2910
and divorce adjustment 1209
egalitarian views 673
egocentric networks 4483
elder care networks 1351
exchange network theory 1369
and exchange relations
extension 1369
and family life 2742, 2743
file–sharing networks 1162
flow networks 1356
and friendships 796, 1793, 1794, 1796–7
and gender and friendship 1863
and gift relations 1252
global communication networks 2385
and health 2073
and illness and mortality 1184
immigrants 3012, 3027
industry networks 1313
interfirm networks 1313
and the Internet 2387, 2902
and interpersonal relationships 2392
kinship 1575, 1577, 2471
and knowledge management 2476
low–density networks 673
and management innovations 2741
management networks 2742–4
and markets 2783–4
mathematical approach 2854
media networks 2875, 2902–5
and mesostructure 2961–2
and nation-states 1473
network integration 570–1
networked capitalism 1295
networked cultural production 1160
New Age 3190
outsourcing partnerships 3352
patriarchal views 673
power networks 1354–5, 3461
random and biased nets, theory of 2854
scientific networks 4107–8

small world properties 1312
and social capital 383–4
and social movements 4455–7
social networks 2903
social scientific perspective 2742
and social support 88–9
strong and loose ties 2743
structural traumas 594
structuralism 4858
submerged networks 1679
telecommunications networks 1160
terrorist networks 1167, 1474
tight-knit networks 2742, 2743, 2744
transnational 1152
transnational marriage networks 1665
and trust 1389
urban 637
venture capital syndication network 1313
weak connectivity 2854, 5222–5
Neuman, T. 2848
Neumann, F. 2164
Neumann, J. von 1822
Neurath, O. 3546
neurobiology 291, 1757
neurologically specific theories of crime 823–4
neurology, and decision-making 983
neuropsychology 281
neuroscience 3057
neurosociology 3185–9
biosocial theories of crime and
neuroticism 838
Neustadt, I. 344
neutralization, techniques of 13
Nevarez, L. 5122–5
New Age 3189–92
appropriations of indigenous culture 2284
and complementary and alternative medicine 631
and cults 885
and polyamory 3477
spirituality 752, 4139
New, C. 1683
New Christian Right 507, 1982, 1984
new corporate actors 573
New Deal 317, 2233, 2234, 2288, 2367, 2510, 2519, 2624, 2747, 3179, 3592
New Federalism 2034
New Frontiers 440
new geography 375
New German Cinema 1753
New Giunea 247
new home economics theory 2415

new institutional economics 3433
new institutionalism 2586, 3434, 3461
New Labour 2527
New Left 943, 2806, 3052, **3192–6**
    capitalist critique 2228
    and consciousness-raising 676, 677
    and crime 841
    and feminism 1674
    personal is political concept 3401
new left realism 3196–8
new liberalism 2624, 3176
new managerialism 2929
new media 2876–7
new middle classes in Asia 3198–201
New Nation effect 1001
New Negro 1243
new product development 2734
New Public Management (NPM) 213, 3396–7,
    3664
new religious movements 3201–6, 3855–6,
    3858–9, 4138, 4144
    characteristics 3203
    and charisma 436
    charismatic movement 439–42
    and cults 887, 3874
    deprogramming practice 3203
    fundamentalist NRMs 3204
    New Age religions 3191
    world-accommodating movements 3204
    world-rejecting/world-affirming 3205,
    4144, 4145
new reproductive technologies 337, **3206–7**
    and genomics 2172
    and infertility 2322–3
    reprogenetics 1490
New Right
    and difference 1155
    and millenarianism 3047
New Science 2697
new servant class 685
new social movement theory 780–1, **3208–11**
    animal rights movement 139
    and collective identity 586, 3208, 3209, 3210
    cultural version 3210
    and gay and lesbian movement 1836
    and global justice movements 1977
    local residents' movements 2657–9
    and the new left 3193
    organizational forms 3259
    political version 3210
    politicization of everyday life 3209
    and post-industrial society 3551

postmaterialist values 3209
    and resource mobilization theory 3208, 3209
    and social constructionism 3208
    and the urban revolution 2581
New Social Science 3592
New Taiwanese Cinema 1753
New Thought 3190
new urban sociology 748
new urbanism 504, **3211–12**
New Wave 1753
new work order 2724
New York 821, 865
    crime rates 821
    ethnic enclaves 1454, 1461
    fiscal crisis 2034
    gentrification 1917–18
    ghettos 1938
    global city 1954
    homicide rates 2151
    metropolis 2991
    political machine 3445–6
    zero tolerance policing 825, 826
New York City Radical Cheerleaders 1679
New York Radical Women 677, 3774
New York Radicalesbians 2113
New Zealand
    aging and social policy 86
    child custody and child support 453
    complementary and alternative medicine 62,
    630, 6311
    fertility levels 1738
    gambling 1820
    health care system 2055
    immigration 1457, 2259, 2261
    immigration policy 3022
    indigenous peoples 2280
    internal migration 3017
    labor–management relations 2512
    laborism 2526
    multiracial feminism 3118
    nonmarital births 1587
    political economy and sport 3440
Newell, A. 640
newly industrializing countries (NICs) 1944,
    1961, 2298, 2299
    and political economy 3435
Newman, O. 1427
News Corporation 2873, 2874, 2887, 2898
news production
    depoliticization 348
    hegemonic model 300
    mass medium 2873

news reporting
  content analysis 777
  and cultural production 952
  of deviance 1132
  "hard" and "soft" news 2337
  of public protest 780
  sensationalism 2826
newspapers
  and community and media 628
  and experiential consumption 716
  mass influence 2896–7
  and public opinions 3637–8
  readership, declining 3639
  taxation of 2912
  see also journalism; print media
Newton, E. 1224, 1657, 1658
Newton, Isaac 2836, 4116
Neyman, J. 657
NGO/INGO 1441, **3212–13**, 3340
  Christian 1981
  and civil society 513
  and diasporic relations 1969
  and ecofeminism 1274
  and educational expansion 1974–5
  environmental NGOs/INGOs 1285, 3212
  and global culture 1968–9
  and global justice movements 1977
  and global politics 1951
  GONGOs (government-organized NGOs)
    3212
  human rights INGOs 2182, 2185, 3212
  and middle-class ascendancy 3200
  QUANGOs (quasi-NGOs) 3212
  and social movements 3212
  transnational NHOs 1432
Nguyen, K. 3954–6
Nibert, D. 2177–8
Nicaragua
  civil wars 1473
  electoral processes 1952
  feminist activism 1685, 1686
  gender politics 2214
  revolution 3907, 3909, 3910, 3911
  UN intervention 1952
Niceforo, A. 2015
niche marketing 762, 1851, 3128
niche overlap 1469
niche segregation 1469
Nicholls, B. 2923–8
Nicholls, D. 3424
Nichols, B. 1210, 1212
Nicholson, L. 1438, 3560

Nickelodeons 765
nicknames 2237
Niebrugge, G. 1666–71
Nieburh, H. R. 1051, 4136, 4137
Nielsen, D. A. 1810–13, 4414–16
Nielsen, F. 2293–7
Nienstedt, B. C. 630
Nietzsche, Friedrich 999, **3213–17**
  antiliberalism 3217
  and atheism 197
  and Christianity 477, 3215
  and civilization 516
  and constructionism 1087
  cultural critique 896, 3215, 3217
  and distanciation 1188
  and double consciousness 1220
  elitist individualism 3215
  and Enlightenment rationality 3215
  and existentialism 1520
  and freedom 1520
  genealogical method 896, 1896
  "immoralism" 3216
  Jung on 3213
  modernity, critique of 3213, 3214–15
  and nationalism 3215
  and nihilism 3216, 3563
  perspectivism 2231
  and the Protestant work ethic 3215
  and slave moralities 3214, 3215
  on Spencer 3215
  and subjectivity 4877
  and transgression 5044
  Weber on 3213–14
Niger
  adolescent fertility 1725
  fertility levels 1737
  infant mortality 1726
Nigeria 240
  ancestor worship 3629
  bilingual education 279
  charismatic movement 441
  consumer movements 697
  and federalism 1652
  female genital mutilation 1654
  infertility 2323
Nightingale, C. H. 707
nihilism 1063, 3216, 3563
  epistemological nihilism 1436
nihonjinron 2436, **3217–21**
Nike 352, 730, 739, 1642, 1986, 2883, 3441,
  4701, 4716
Nikolova, N. 3351–4

9/11 *see* World Trade Center, terrorist attack
1984 (Orwell) 3645, 4132
Nippon Steel Corporation 1287
nirvana 372, 3855
Nisbet, R. 1136, 2971
Nishida, K. 1286, 2251
Nishiyama, A. 1332
Nixon, H. L. 1171–4
Nixon, Richard 876, 2421, 2749, 2878, 3173, 3541, 3603
Nixon, S. 736
Nkomo, S. 5287–91
No Child Left behind Act 2001 3274, 3275, 4051
no-fault divorce laws 1207
Nobel, Alfred 3223
Nobel prizes and the scientific elite 3222–3, 4107
Noddings, N. 1438
noise pollution 266, 3476, 3477
Nolan, P. 2287–93, 2297, 3073
Nolasco, M. 340
nomadism 180, 181, 182, 2251, 2459
Nomi, T. 4175–8
nomothetic studies 2134
non-belief
  history of 197
  see also atheism
nonconformist religious groups 1316
nonconsensual sexual intercourse *see* rape
non-family living 2572
nonfoundationalist epistemology 1435
non-human animals 2175–8
  communcation among 2537
  learned helplessness 2567–8
  see also human–nonhuman interaction
nonliterate societies 1597
nonmarital childbearing 1586, 1589, 1621–2, 1734
  adolescent 1735
  and child outcomes 1629
  cohabiting couples 568, 1624, 1736
  and family poverty 1627, 1629, 1721
  and family structure 3223
  increase in 1734, 1735
  measuring 1734
  and non-resident parents 3224
  patterns of 1735
  planned 1737
  racial/ethnic variations 1721
  social attitudes to 1622, 1735, 2792–3
  and urban poverty 5127

and welfare policies 1734–5
  see also fertility: nonmarital; lone-parent families
nonmarital sex *see* extra-marital and premarital sex
non-market societies 517
non-profit organizations 3339, 3340–3
non-renewable resources 3531
non-representationalism 3556
non-resident parents 3223–7
  child custody and child support 451–4, 3225–6
  and childcare 2667
  emotional issues 3224
  non-resident mothers 3224
  parent–child contact 3224–5
  practical issues 3224
  see also lone-parent families
nonviolent direct action 508
Nora, P. 592
Nordenmark, M. 5090–1
norm of reciprocity 3227–9, 3232, 3679, 3680
normal distribution *see* bell curve
normalcy and mormalization
  and disability 1697
  medicalization 1699
Norman, E. H. 2803
normative isomorphism 2351
normative organizations 3310
norms 3229–32
  absolute norms 1440
  aesthetic norms 323
  Asch experiments and 189
  and attitudes and behavior 200
  auditing and 212
  conformity to 1078–9, 3680
  and deference 990
  and deviance 1083, 1116–17
  formal/informal 1093
  and game theory 3232
  gender norms 1872, 3534
  group norms, and institutionalism 2354–5
  and helping behaviors 3680
  human rights norms 2185
  institutionalized norms 2585, 2586
  legal norms 1122
  and power 1079
  prescriptive normalization 1177
  relationality 1177
  scientific norms 4109–11
  social construction of 1079

social Darwinian perspective 3231
statistical deviation from 1122
and Thomas theorem 991
transparent norms 5072
use and abuse of 3230–1
violations of 1077, 1092, 1093, 1100,
    1116, 1117
North American Free Trade Agreement
    (NAFTA) 1115, 1992, 2265, 3020, 3198
North, D. C. 2344
North Korea
    communism 391
    Soviet influence 1295
    stem cell rseearch 2172
Northcliffe, Lord 2873, 2897
Northern Ireland 584
    marginalized groups 2764
    peace processes 3381, 3382
    shuttle diplomacy 3380
Norton, E. H. 307
Norway
    democracy 1001
    demographic data collection 1012
    and earner–carer model 1272
    family leave 1883
    health care system 2055
    immigration 3028
    labor–management relations 2510
    LAT relationships 811
    lone parenthood 2664, 2665
    nonmarital births 2663
    teenage motherhood 1728
Notestein, F. 1034
nouveau riche 2647, 2649
novelty, and consumption 685
Nozick, Robert 3233
    anarcho-capitalism 136
    and distributive justice 3233
    and state legitimacy 3233
nuclear family ideology 811, 939, 1043, 1574,
    1589, 1592, 1597, 1598, 1619, 1630, 2252,
    2469, 2470, 2619, 4765
nuclear freeze frame 1781
nuclear power 688
nuclear power technology, and technology
    assessment 691
nuclear powers 3038–9
nudism 2599, 2683, 3485
nuisance variables 1534, 1535
Null, C. 3675–6
Nunn, S. 960–1
Nuremberg Code 1442, 1447, 2346

Nuremberg Trials (1945–6) 1909, 1912, 2346
nurses and midwives 2077
nursing 3664
    and socialization 2931
nursing and residential care homes 995, 1169
    elder abuse in 1348
    friendship networks 1797
    and late-life sexuality 2540
    nurse:care recipient ratio 403
    placement 402
    utilization 1842
Nussbaum, M. 3419
Nye, F. 1128
Nye, I. 846
Nye, J. 1951

Oakeshott, M. 679
obedience and compliance research 1267
Oberschall, A. 2629, 3066
obesity 326, 336
    in children 1158
    class and 722
    and deviance 1117
    and gender 1865
    health risk behavior 2084
    health-related illnesses 1866
    and McDonaldization 2690
    medicalization of 1110, 1112
    stigma 323, 722
    stigma neutralization 1094
object relation theory 3697
objectification 1088
    of the colonized subject 1396
    and social science methodology 3235
objectivism 2680
    journalistic 3638
    objectivism/subjectivism dilemma 347
    and social science methodology 3235
objectivity 3235–6, 4877
    and empiricism 1682
    scientific 875, 947, 3573, 4095–6
    strong objectivity 1682, 4845–6
    value-free objectivity 2969
oblique rotation 1558–9
obscenity 3540
observable power and prestige order (OPPO)
    1524–5, 1527
observation, participant and
    non-participant 1669, **3236–40**, 4513
    and deviance 1129
    ethical issues 3240
    and ethics in fieldwork 1444

**observation, participant and
non-participant** (*cont'd*)
ethnographic research 1129, 1480, 4513–14
and evaluation 1500
and feminist research 1702
and gangs 2031
gatekeepers 3238–9
learning opportunities, measures of 3273
and medical sociology 2934
and migrant research 1716
and racist movements 3770
and rapport 3790
reactivity 3236, 3238, 3239
role-taking 3237, 3239–40
sampling 3239
sexuality research 4282
and simulation modeling 4106
structured/unstructured observation
3237–8, 3239
trust, building 3240
urban studies 2625–6
see also fieldwork
observational learning 4437–8
obstetric fiistula 1726
occult *see* Satanism; supernaturalism
occupational attainment *see* educational and
occupational attainment
occupational biographies 1142
occupational boundaries 1890
occupational classifications 3241, 3250
occupational communities 617, 1578, 1579–80
occupational crimes 835
occupational cultures 1880
occupational deviance 1084–5
occupational devotion 2599
occupational diversification 3073
occupational group memory 590, 591
occupational mobility 3060, **3240–4**
and career aspirations 1341
class and 533, 549
downward 1400
intergenerational and intragenerational
mobility 2373, 2374
intraorganizational mobility 3286,
3287, 3288
organizational careers 3286
relative mobility 3242
structural mobility 3242
and unemployment 1400
women 3957
see also labor market; professions
occupational prestige 1341–2, 1345, 4751

and ethnicity 1342
and gender 1341
and race 1342
occupational profiles 1341
occupational psychology, and human resource
management 2179
occupational psychosis 379
occupational rewards, inequality in 1809
Occupational Safety and Health Administration
(OSHA) 3304
occupational scaffolding 3249
occupational segregation 1721, 2516,
3244–7, 3957, 5285–6
and affirmative action 41
and breadwinner/homemaker model 1890
and gender 1341, 1892
glass ceiling 3371–2
horizontal segregation 3246
and immigrants 1342
and income differentials 1198
paternalist system 3371–2
perfect segregation 3244
pure discrimination 3245–6
racial segregation 3244–5, 3247
and recruitment practices 1890
sex-based wage gap 4189–91
sex segregation 3244–5, 3246, 3247, 3249
statistical discrimination 3246
and sterotyping 1342
vertical segregation 3246
see also divisions of household labor
occupational specialization 582, 1200
occupational status
class and 533
and intergenerational mobility 3242–3
and social mobility 3060
occupations 3247–50
animal-related occupations 2178
coding 3248, 3249
health professions and occupations 2075–7
legal profession 2583–4
and morbidity and mortality variations 2087
sex/gender-stereotyped occupations 1859,
1894, 2100
status scales 545
see also labor markets; professions
occupations, scaling of 3249, **3250–1**
O'Connell Davidson, J. 3682–5
O'Connor, J. 1420, 1810
O'Connor, P. 1798
Odaka, K. 1287
odds ratios 2369, 2377

O'Donnell, G. 2576
O'Donnell-Trujillo, N. 3292
Odyssey (Homer) 2822
Oedipus complex 302, 1437, 2528, 3697–8
office ladies 3251–4
Office of Technology Assessment (OTA) 688
offshore production processes 2382
Ogbu, J. U. 1327, 1800, 2117
Ogburn, William 443
   cultural lag theory 2486
   and family sociology 1597–8
   and social change 445–7
Ogg, J. 1348
Oguma, E. 3220
Ohashi, I. 3171
Ohlin, L. E. 4781
Ohmae, K. 1958
oikonomnia 1385
oil crisis (1973) 1769, 5247
oil price shocks 3176, 3460
Oldenburg, Claes 2124
older adults, economic well-being of 3254–7
   rural areas 3961–2
older people *see* elderly
oldest old 69, 1904
Oleson, J.C. 836–9
oligarchy and organization 1006, 1009,
   3257–62
   competitive oligarchies 1006
   and democracy 1006
   gradual oligarchization 2996
   "iron law of oligarchy" 1362, 2996, 3258
   tutelary oligarchy 1007
oligopoly 2295, 2776
Oliker, S. 1794, 1798, 1862–4
Oliver, M. L. 2197
Olivera, M. 340
Oliverio, A. 1115
Olivia Records 1675, 2603, 2604
OLS regression techniques 552
Olsen, J. 3307
Olson, A. 1677
Olson, D. 1583
Olson, J. 5047–50
Olson, M. 577, 698, 2629, 3455, 4471
Olympics 2879, 2888, **3262–5**, 3441, 4661–2
   ancient Greece 4690
   Berlin Olympics (1936) 4682
   and drugs/substance use 1239–40
   and economic development 3474
   ethnic protest 4682
   feminist critique 3264

   gender verification 1847–8
   global audience 1987
   and globalization of sport 1988, 3441
   Gramscian accounts 3264
   Marxist critique 3264
   media coverage 2918
   and national identity 3158
   postcolonial critique 3264
   postmodern analysis 3263
   spectacular consumption 4703
   transsexual athletes 4293
   see also Gay Games
Olzak, S. 1465–75
Oman 1724
   female genital mutilation 1654
ombudsman office 5072
Omi, M. 2396
Omolade, B. 1895
Omran, A. 3099
onanism 2833
   see also masturbation
one best way 2746
one drop rule 1405, **3265–7**, 3732
One Inc. 1834
one-worldism 1982
O'Neil, K. M. 750–3
Ong, A. 1691
Ong, W. J. 1213, 3278, 3279
ontogeny 302
ontological authenticity 214
ontological realism, and environmental issues
   1419
ontology
   and organizational culture 949
   quantitative research paradigm 2978
Onwuegbuzie, A. J. 2978–81
Onyx, J. 3340–3
opaque industries 3301
OPEC 1472, 3176
Open University 2101, 2102, 2103
operant conditioning 257, 848, 4438
Operation Phoenix 876
Operation Rescue 3653, 3654
operationalism, and empiricism 1434
operationalization 3115
operations management 3267–71
   hard/soft approaches 3268, 3269, 3270
   manufacturing/service issue 3267–8
   pragmatic perspective 3268, 3269
operations stratgey 3269
opiates 1235
   addiction 134–5

opinion leaders 209, 2564
opinion polling 2407, 3713
　　deliberative polling 3714
　　see also public opinion
opium 1238
Opp, K.-D. 3232
Oppenheimer, F. 1493
Oppenheimer, V. 1734
opportunities for learning 3271–6
　　measuring 3274–5
　　and meritocracy 2955–6
opportunity theory
　　and deviance 1081
　　and school dropout 1231
oppositional consciousness 1713
oppositional culture thesis 1800, 2117, 2118
Optional Protocol to the International
　　Covenant on Civil and Political Rights
　　(ICCPR-OP) 2184
oracles 2699
oral histories
　　and feminist research 1702, 1703
　　and interviewing 2407, 2409
　　and IRB review 2348
　　and life history 2642
　　life stories 288
oral sex 2702, 3276–8
oral tradition 3278
orality 3278–81
　　and African religions 3869
　　and media literacy 2891–2
　　primary 3278, 3279
　　secondary 3278, 3279
O'Rand, A. 73–7, 3899–903
Orbach, S. 326
Orbuch, T. L. 2390–3
Orcutt, J. D. 844–7
ordinary least squares (OLS) linear regression
　　3838, 3839
O'Reilly, B. 2337
Orenstein, D. M. 650–6
organ trade 337, 738
organ transplants 973
organic evolutionary theory 293
organic intellectuals 298, 2228
organic society 581
organic solidarity 1199
organization democracy *see* workers'
　　participation in management (WPM)
organization demography 5288
organization theory 3281–5, 3312
　　behavioral theory of the firm 3281, 3282

Blau on 313–14
and the civilizing process 531
and coercive organizations 3317
Coleman on 570
configuration theory 3282
and entrepreneurship 1410–13
and evolutionary theory 3284
and ideal type 2202
and institutionalism 2355
and management improvisation 2733
and management innovation 2737, 2738
mesostructure in 2962
neo-institutional theory 3283
and network sociology 2744, 3284
and oligarchy 3257–61
and organizational ecology 1290
performance measurement 3396–9
and population ecology 3283
population ecology perspective 2586
and positive psychology 2566
project-based organizations 2744
resource dependence theory 3282–3
resource-based view (RBV) 2476
social worlds perspective 2962
strategic choice theory 3281–2
strategic decisions 4784–9
structural contingency theory 3281,
　　3282, 3283
Taylorism 2828
transaction theory 3282
organizational alliances 355
organizational behavior theory 2566
organizational boundaries 355
organizational branding 355
organizational careers 3286–90
organizational change, structural adaptation to
　　regain fit (SARFIT) 3301
organizational climate 2480
organizational communication 355, 3290–9
　　cooperation 355
　　and diversity 3296
　　feminist perspective 3295, 3296, 3297
　　postmodern analysis 3295–6
　　poststructural analysis 3295–6, 3297
organizational contingencies 3299–302, 3991
organizational contingency theory 3299–302,
　　3313, 3621
organizational culture 934, 949, 1309, 2724,
　　2750, 3337
　　coercive institutions 3315–16
　　and ethics 1439
　　transmission of 2931

organizational democracy 3295
organizational deviance 3303–6
  corporate crime 826–8
  regulatory agencies 3304
organizational differentiation 3073
organizational ecology 1290, 3301
organizational environment
    differentiation–integration typology 3300
    mechanistic–organic typology 3300
organizational failure 3306–7
  and technological disasters 1174
organizational form 3281
organizational founding and failure 2354
organizational goals 2724, 3310
organizational gothic 2717
organizational governance 2724
organizational identity 353, 354, 355, 356, 2477
organizational imprinting 3283
organizational innovation 1309
organizational institutionalism 3461
organizational leadership 3300–1
organizational learning 3307–10, 3330
organizational literature 949
organizational performance 3299
  dysfunctions 3397
  and organizational learning 3307
  performance measurement 3396–9
organizational power 3296
  ethics and 1439
organizational rationality 3295
organizational rationalization 942–3
organizational role theory 3952–3
organizational size 3300
organizational structure 3299–300
  decentralization 3398
  divisional structure 3300
  downsizing 3398
  functional structure 3300
  mechanistic structure 3300
  organic structure 3300
  and outsourcing 3398
organizations 3310–15
  accountability and responsibility 1010
  bureaucratic components 314
  bureaucratic organizations 1893, 2295, 3311
  coercive organizations 3310
  "cold" and "hot" organizations 3316
  corporate forms 2295
  decentralization 1007
  definition 3310
  design–performance relation 641
  and despotism 1010

  differentiation in 314
  emotion management 1383
  emotion work 1382
  emotions, institutionalization of 1387
  and *en* 1401–2
  environmental impact 1440
  and ethics 1440
  facework 1553
  formal/informal 3310, 3311
  functionalist view 3268
  future oriented 1386
  gendered 1892–5
  gendered enterprise 1888–91
  imperfect democracies 1006
  and individualism 2292
  institutional 1007
  and Internet technology 2387
  interorganizational relationships 1387
  interpretive account 2714
  intranets 2387
  and key informants 2457
  and new institutional theory (NIT) 2351–2
  normative organizations 3310
  philanthropy 1440
  postmodern organizations 3313–14, 3563–7
  process view 3268
  recruitment practices 1890
  restrictive practices 3177
  social construction 2714
  social psychological theory 4516
  structural functionalist analysis 3312–13
  taxonomic approaches 2202
  utilitarian organizations 3310
  virtual organizations 2202
  see also bureaucracy
**organizations as coercive institutions
    3315–19**, 3330
  gendered nature 3318
  occupational orientation 3317
  privatization 3319
organizations and sexuality 3319–21
organizations as social structures 3321–6
  interdependency management 3328
  and organizational crime 3303
**organizations and the theory of the firm
    3326–31**
  how theories 3328, 3329, 3330
  knowledge-based theories 3328, 3329
  why theories 3327, 3328, 3330
**organizations as total institutions
    3331–5**
organizations, tradition and 3335–40

organizations, voluntary 3340–3
　chonaikai 471–4
organized skepticism, norm of 3667,
　4110–11
orgasmic sex 3843, 3844, 5270, 5272
Orgaz, R. 2948
Orientalism 399, 1395–6, **3343–5**, 3478
　auto-Orientalism 1494
　colonial discourse 2984
　and Eurocentrism 1492
　and Hinduism 2128
　and Islam 2426–7
　and the Other 1074, 1395
　Said and 603, 1482
　Sarkar and 4007
orientalization, and hybridity 2190
origami 2762
Orlan 325
Orlando 1641
Orser, W. E. 316–18
Orthodoxy 1054, 1056, 1982, **3345–9**
　and American voluntarism 1055
　Jews 2452
　Orthodox Churches 407–8
　ritual 3690
　Russian 4223
orthogonal rotation 1558, 1559
orthopsychiatry 1634
Ortman, J. M. 2258–62
Ortner, S. 1274
Orum, A. M. 5151–4
Orwell, George 3495, 3645, 3673, 4132
Osiel, M. 593
ossification (organizational dysfunction) 3397
Ossowski, S. 545
osteopathic medicine 631
osteopathy 631
Ostrom, E. 1283
O'Sullivan, J. 2755
O'Sullivan, R. G. 3088
Oswald, Lee Harvey 3052
other 231
　black women as 308
　colonized other 1395
　cultural others 3392, 3394
　and difference 1154
　enemy as 876
　ethnography and 1482
　exotic other 4201
　fetishization of 897
　homosexuals as 331
　marginalization 590

orientalized other 1074, 3343
othered bodies 711
　threat of the 260
　woman as 253, 331, 333
　see also generalized other; in-groups and out-
　　groups
other-directed personality 3918, 3919
Otnes, C. C. 753–4
Otter, C. von 2509–14
Otterman, R. 5238–41
Otto, R. 2698, 3403
Ottoman empire 239, 1393, 1461, 1999–2000,
　2001, 2002, 2460, 3145, 3147
Ottomanism 2000
Oudshoorn, N. 1681
Outhwaite, W. 344–5
outliers 2868, **3349–50**
outreach 642
outsider-within 3350–1
　and peer debriefing 3387–8
　see also social exclusion
outsourcing 1344, 1345, 2202, **3351–4**, 3398
　see also supply chains
overdeterminism 125, 1896
overeducation 4031
overfishing 1281, 1285
overload model of family conflict 1581–2
overpopulation, Malthusian model 1040, 1506,
　2706–7, 3071, 3590–1
Oviedo, L. 474–9
Owen, R. 502, 2510, 4549, 4550
Owens, A. 4039–42, 4048–52
Owens, E. 4320–1
Owens, T. J. 4169–72
Oxford School 2290, 2291
OxyContin 1233, 1234
ozone depletion 728, 1285, 1418, 1423

P2P 2904, **3489–90**
　intellectual property issues 2358, 3133
Pacanowsky, M. 3292
Pace, E. 1813–16, 2799–802
Pacific Sociological Association 318
Packard, V. 684, 2647
Padilla, A. 2550
paganism 3477, 3875
Page, F. J. 702, 2431–5
Pahl, J. 3081
Pahl, R. 748
pain 1522
　Buddhist teaching 372
pain relievers 1234

Paine, Thomas 3638
pair bonding 2672
Pakistan 3020
  capitalist growth 390
  child health disparities 1157
  and federalism 1652
  honor killings 2303
  nuclear technology 3038
  power and authority relations 1369–70
Paleo, L. 3496
paleoanthropology 1509
Palerm, A. 342
Palestine 1679, 1814, 3344, 3989
  Israeli occupation 1848
  Israeli–Palestinian dispute 159, 160
  radical movements 2800–1
  refugees 3838
  terrorist activities 4870
Paley, W. 2897
Pallas, A. M. 2358–61
palliative care 973
Palma, E. 222–5
Palmer, C. E. 2176
Pan African Congress (PAC) 163
Pan Asian American Women 1676
pan-Aryanism 3768
pan-Islamism 2000
Pañalosa, F. 2550
Panama, US invasion of 2878
panel studies 2564, 3016, 3760
panhandling 2149, 2150, 2555, 3715
panic peddling 316
panic selling 316
panic sex 3569
panics 1385, 1386
Pankhurst, S. 2841
Pankington, F. 1316
panoptics 1122, 1177, 1178, 1776, 2566,
  4896, 4897
pantheism 3854
papacy 409, 410
"paperless office" 2332
papermaking techniques 3635
Papp, R. 2800, 2801
Papua New Guinea 2987
Paquin, J. 1953–6
Paradeise, C. 3286–90
paradigms 3355–6
  incommensurability of 2969
  linguistic paradigns 2534
  and metatheory 2963
  and naturalistic enquiry 3161, 3162–3

  reflexive use of 3832
  scientific paradigms 2493–6, 2964, 3814–15
  social facts paradigm 2964
  systemic paradigm of social work 4545
Paraguay 390
parallelism 2431, 2434
Paralympics 1171, 1172
paranoia 3005
paranormal beliefs 1140, 1141
paraphilia, exhibitionism 1518–19
parasite singles 2438
parataxis 3278
Pardee, J. W. 2614–15
Paredes, A. 2550
Parekh, B. 1815, 3107
parent–child interactions
  authoritative parenting 3224
  and gender socialization 1668
  intergenerational exchanges 2380, 2381
  and interpersonal relationships 2390
  and intimacy 2413
  and non-resident parenting 3224
  non-resident parents 3224–5
  stepfamilies 4766–72
parental investment 294
**parental involvement in education
  3357–60**
  charter schools 4035
  in desegregated schools 4026
  and educational attainment 1604
  and expectations/aspirations 1529
  and extracurricular activities 1548
  home schooling 4032–4
  homework monitoring 3357
  longitudinal studies 3358
  preschool children 3357
  race and ethnic variations 3358–9
  and school discipline 4110
  social class variations 3358
parental leaves 1272, 1740, 2619
parental separation 3224
parenting 293
  and adoption 2608
  biosociological theory 293
  and caregiving 401
  and fatherhood 1648
  fathers 1602
  and fostering 2608
  gay and lesbian parents 2607
  girls and 725
  life cycle theory 2637
  middle-class 1326

parenting (*cont'd*)
  motivation 4124
  parental responsibility 453–4
  quality of 1736
  and social capital 1326
  stepfamilies 4766–72
  and surrogacy 2608
  surrogate parenting 2019
  time engaged with children 1602
  transition to parenthood 2774
  working-class 1326
  see also childcare; fatherhood; lone-parent
    families; motherhood
parenting, inadequate 450
  see also child abuse; child neglect
Pareto deficient mixed-strategy equilibrium 1823
Pareto efficient cooperation 1822, 3361
Pareto optimality 2777, 2778, 2780, 3361
Pareto, Vilfredo 655, 2015, 2016, 2144,
    3360–2, 3803
  biography 3360–1
  and conflict theory 662
  and elites 1361, 1362, 3102, 3361, 3442
  and emotions 1384, 1386
  and income taxation 2275
  and markets 2784
  and neoclassical economics 1304, 1305, 3360,
    3361
  political party theory 3452
  power analysis 3360
  and scientific knowledge 2475
  and social stratification 547
Paris 765, 3623
  flânerie 1762–3
Paris Commune 591, 592, 4550
parish registers 1045–6
parity-progression functions 1743
Park, Robert E. 319, 320, 1145, 1289, 1996
  and assimilation theory 192, 3025, 3363–4
  and Bernard 271
  biography 3363
  and the Chicago School 443, 443, 445, 714,
    1597, 3362–4
  and immigrant colonies 1454
  and invasion-succession 2418
  and Johnson 2444
  and marginality 2763, 2765
  and Orientalism 3344
  and race relations 129, 1457, 3011
  role theory 3945
  and social change 445–7
  and social groups 2031

and Thomas theorem 991
  urban sociology 443, 501, 1289, 1290, 3466
Park, Robert E. and Burgess, Ernest W.
    3362–5
  and accommodation 7
  and Addams 24
  and Du Bois 131
  social interaction model 7
  urban expansion theory 714–15
  urban sociology 3363–4, 3943–4
Parker, Charlie 797–8
Parker, P. 251–5
Parker, S. 2588
Parkin, F. 663, 664, 1404, 3678
Parkins, W. 1848
Parks, Rosa 508
parliamentary government 1001, 3451
Parmenides 197
parochial realm 3720
parole 803–4, 852, 855
  discretion in 855
Parrillo, Vincent N. 5101–4
parsimony 4989
Parsons, T. 2930
Parsons, Talcott 971, 1322, 1483–4, 2031,
    2344, 2998, **3365–8**
  and the ASA 132
  biography 3365
  and the church 485–6
  and citizenship 2795
  and conflict theory 663
  and cultural production 952
  and deviance 1137
  and Durkheim 582, 1251, 1257
  economic sociology 1320, 1322, 2780, 2782,
    3803, 3804
  and the expressive revolution 325
  and families 1580, 1598, 1619, 1630, 2415,
    2469
  general theory of action 3365, 3366, 3367
  and illness and health-related behavior 2058,
    2105, 2242
  and institution
  medical sociology 479–80, 2245, 2932,
    2933–4, 3374–6
  and Mills 3053
  and money 3079, 3367–8
  and Pareto 3362
  political sociology 3458
  and professions 2075
  and the professions 2075, 3663
  and religion 3861

and role-taking 3949
and scientific facts 1555
and the sick role 479–80, 2245, 2933–4, 3366, 3374–5, 4318
and social change 4362–3
and social order 4487
and social systems 1319, 4532–3
and the societal community 1319
and societal differentiation 1574
sociology of knowledge 2483
and status
structural functionalism 633, 634, 876, 1251, 1252, 1257, 1529, 1598, 1809, 1810–11, 1928, 2031–2, 2309, 2361, 2675, 2832, 2965, 3312, 3366–7, 3374, 3581, 3582, 4524–5, 4852–3, 4915
systems-theoretical approach 2675
and voluntary association 3075–6
part-time work 1400, 1844
female 1721, 1844
partial least squares (PLS) 2969
participation 1922–3
and disabled athletes 1172
extended participation 1924
Germani and 1922–3, 1924
integrated participation 1923
total participation 1924
participatory action research
and action research 16
and evaluation 1500
and feminist methodology 1702, 1704
participatory democracy 3194, 3258, 3259
and social movements 3258, 3259, 4463–6
particularism
and globalization 1957
Japanese 238
national 3152
and science 2860
and utopianism 2528
parties 547, 553
partner choice *see* mate selection
party formation 538
partying 774
Pasko, L. 1857
passing 1484–5, **3368–70**
and agism 58
passion 204
passionate love 2672, 2673
passive entertainment 2598
Passy, F. 578
Pasteur, Louis 2845, 2846
pastiche 3556, 3570

pastoral theism 3870
pastoralism
evolution 2141
and hybridity 2189
pastorate, feminization of 3691
Pastrana, A. 2944–6, 3381
Patch, J. 1917–20
patent law 729, 730
patents 337, 357, 446, 4134, 4135
paternalism 3370–3
and indigenous peoples 341, 2279
and management 2746
and masculinity 1891
paternalistic management 3170
and *shushin koyo* 4312
paternity leave 1649, 2619
Paternoster, R. 385–8
path analysis 313, **3373–4**
path dependency 3433, 4402
and institutional change 2356
path-dependent outcomes 1896
pathological gambling 1817–18
pathways research 1695
patient choice 2246
patient confidentiality 2939
patient safety 2931
Patient Self-Determination Act 1992
patient–physician relationship 480, 2080, **3374–7**
clash of perspectives 2246
communication 2940
democratization 2389
and the expert patient concept 2246
and fear of litigation 2929
Parsonian model 3374–6
patient choice 2246
and the sick role 4318
trust 2389
see also sick role
patients' rights 995
Patil, V. 1871–2
Patillo, M. 709
patriarchal evolutionary theory 1596
patriarchal state 4728
Patriarchate of Constantinople 3345, 3346–7
patriarchy 677, **3377–80**
and the biblical family form 1595
and capitalism 1892, 2841, 2842
and control of female sexuality 336, 1656, 2613, 4801
control of knowledge 1798
and critical qualitative research 869

patriarchy (*cont'd*)
  and cultural feminism 905, 906
  and deviance and crime 1857
  and division of household labor 1687, 3378
  dual systems approach 1711
  and ecofeminism 1275
  and family structure 1615
  and family theory 1633
  and female genital mutilation 1656
  and female migration 1607
  and feminist criminology 1106
  and gender inequalities 2310, 4273
  global pervasiveness 1599–600
  and hegemonic masculinity 1663, 1668, 2101
  and heterosexuality 2601
  institutionalization 2302
  and kinship 2302
  lesbian resistance to 2113, 3775
  and male privilege 639
  networks and 673
  and occupational segregation 3246, 4800–1
  patriarchal households 1844
  patriarchal marriage 2302
  and school curricula 1706
  and sex preferences 1156
  socialist feminist critique 4554
  structuration of 1607
  third world 1600
  urbanization, effects of 1594
patrilinealism 2302
patrilocality 2302
patrimonialism 2858, 3463, 4062
patriotism 1486, 1663
  see also civic nationalism
patron–client networks, and organized crime
  834
patronage 3895
pattern maintenance 1809, 3367
pattern theories 3355–6
Patton, M. 3998–9, 5163
Paul the Apostle 3048, 3348
Paul VI, Pope 441
Paul, A. 1673, 2618
pauper press 3469
pauperization 3593
Pavlich, 986–9
PAVLOV algorithm 641
Pawluch, D. 1091
Paxton, R. O. 1646, 1647
pay equity 1669, 1705
Payne, B. K. 1238–9
peace activism 1166, 1679

  and gender 1874
  nuclear freeze frame 1781
Peace Problems Symposium 2804
peace and reconciliation processes 3380–4
  criteria 3381
  four-phase cycle 3381
  public redress 2141
Peace of Westphalia (1648) 1952, 3380, 4140
peacekeeping operations
  coercive organizations 3316–17
  female peacekeepers 1870
  and manifest destiny doctrine 2755
peacemaking 3384–5
  and criminology 841, 859
Peacock, J. 2642
Pear, T. H. 3777–8
Pearce, D. 1718
Pearson, J. 1859–61
Pearson, K. 426, 805, 1542, 2967
Pearson product-moment correlation
  coefficient 805
Peart, S. J. 3044–7
peasant discontent 664
peasant societies 538, 539, 1577
  class relations 2812
  communal property 3677
  and family and community 1576, 2252
  and *jōmin* 2445, 2446
  marketization 3084–5
  and populism 3537
pedagogy 458
pederasty 2157
pedestrianism 1819
Pedophile Information Exchange (PIE) 3386
pedophilia 2160, 3385–7
  and exhibitionism 1518
  and the Internet 2915
  online 966
  women–boy relationships 3386
  see also child abuse
Pedraza-Baily, S. 2550
peer cultures
  and community colleges 622
  and deviant behavior 1133
  and drug use 1234
  and early childhood 1270
  and friendships 1799–800, 1802
  and gangs 1825, 1827
  and gender socialization 1668
  and the hidden curriculum 2118
  and juvenile delinquency 2454, 2455, 4165
  and nonmarital childbearing 5127

and school climate 4016
and socialization 4567
and youth consumption 773
peer debriefing 3387–8
peer marriages 2303
peer review and quality control in science
2860–1, **3389–91**, 4112
and the Matthew effect 3222–3, 4113
and medical malpractice 2928
and professional deviance 1084–5
Peirce, C. S. 2431, 2536, 3609, 4180–1, 4183–5,
4322
Pelak, C. F. 1845–8, 2395–8
Pelias, R. J. 3391–6
Pellegrin, R. J. 3042
pelvic inflammatory disease 1655
Peña, D. 1275
penal action theory 2
Peñaloza, L. 2548–52
Pence, E. 1711–12
Penley, C. 3498
Penn, William 3692
penny press 3469
pension funds 394
pensions 85, 86–7, 1905, 2053, 2312, 2511,
3900
defined contribution plans 87
pension elites 3900
pension system reforms 1740
private pensions 87, 3900
public pension schemes 86–7
Pentateuch 2450
Pentecostalism 439, 441, 1056, 3689
Catholic Pentecostalism 441
and charisma 3690
global activity 1981
healing systems 631
neo-Pentecostalism 439
people trafficking
cross-border smuggling 3031–3211
see also traffic in women
People's Global Action 1166, 1949, 3259
People's Temple 886, 3047
Pepinsky, H. 859
Pepys, Samuel 3470
Peräkylä, A. 791–4
perception
Asch experiments 191
and management innovation 2739
and neurosociology 3185, 3187
see also impression formation
Perec, G. 2692

performance ethnography **3391–6**
and ritual 3934
performance indicators 213
performance measurement 3396–9
constructivist perspective 3397, 3398
financial indicators 3396
interpretivist perspective 3397–8
and operations management 3269
and organizational failure 3306
performance and performativity
bodily 336
embodied 327
and fandom 1639
and football hooliganism 1768
gender 333
performative consumption 1639
performance-enhancing drugs 1241
performative labor 1187
performative nature of human action 1229
performativity, autoethnographic texts
and 231
performing arts 328
and arts-based research 2972
see also film
period fertility rates 1741
periodicals 3638
permissiveness 680, 3177
Perón, J. D. 413, 1921, 1925
peronism 411, 1925
Perrin, R. D. 1140–2
Perrow, C. 1174–5, 3285, 3332
Perry, N. 242–4, 2821–4, 3331–5
Persell, C. H. 1325
personal communication devices 758, 1107
personal hygiene 2061
personal identities 2217, 2220–1, 2224
personal is political 678, **3399–401**
and liberal feminism 2619
and patriarchy 3379
politicization of everyday life 1502, 3209
and radical feminism 3774
personal space 1117
personalism 205
personality
child development 1269
crime and 838
criminal personality 970, 2602, 2663
cult of personality 259
Freudian theory 837
implicit personality theories 191, 2271
and justice analysis 1195
and leadership theory 2565

personality (*cont'd*)
  and marginality 2763
  personality stereotypes 2271
Peru
  bilingual education 278
  economy 411
  indigenous movements 2278–9
  neopopulism 413
  revolution 3907
  social movements 413
Pesach/Passover 2452
Pescosolido, B. A. 2104–7
Pestello, F. G 199–202
Peter-Zyberk, E. 504
Peters, J. D. 1160
Petersen, A. 2174
Peterson, E. 1666
Peterson, R. A. 952–4, 1361, 3128–9
Peterson, R. R. 1628
petitioning 779, 780
Petrarch, Francesco 2186
Petras, J. 2838
Pettazzoni, R. 2698
Pettigrew, A. 431
Pettigrew, T. F. 220–2, 3751–4
petty bourgeoisie 534, 552, 2227, 3584, 3691
Petty, W. 2087
Peuter, G. de 5192–3
phallocentrism 3698, 3783, 4274, 5271
phantom limb syndrome 2652
Pharaonic circumcision 1654
Pharisees 2450
pharmaceutical companies 1111, 1233, 2172,
    2940, 3335–6
pharmacogenomics 2171
pharmacology 2699
Phelps, H. 131
phenetic fix on society 555
phenomenology 1434, **3401–4**
  and agency 61
  and atheism 197
  and authenticity criteria 214
  and autoethnography 1480
  Barthes and 242
  and biography 287
  Bourdieu and 2045
  and deviance 1137
  first-order constructs 3402
  Hegel and 2098
  and hermeneutics 2108
  of human embodiment 328
  and illness 2059

  and intersubjectivity 2401
  Kurauchi and 2498, 2499–500
  and lifeworld 2651
  of the lived body 326, 335
  Lukács and 2680
  and naturalistic inquiry 3161
  and objectivism 1079
  and reification 3844
  second-order constructs 3403
  and self-fulfilling prophecy 4175
  and sociology of the body 324
  and structuration theory 4860
  transcendental phenomenology 4062, 4063
phenomenology of leisure 2590
phenomenonological sociology 1087
phenotype 1508, 1897, 3731, 3741
pheromones 2672
Philadelphia 2991
philanthropy, corporate 1440
Philippines 441, 3344, 3939, 3940, 4375, 4376
  charismatic movement 441
  colonialism 603
  diaspora 1152
  female migration 1716, 1717
  middleman minorities 3009, 3010
  revolution 3907, 3910
  sex tourism 4201
  transgendered persons 4215
Phillips, K. 3591, 3592
Phillips, M. 2177
Phillipson, C. 1347–9, 1929, 1930, 2632–4
philology 2534
philopedia 2157
philosopher-kings 3545, 3546
philosophes 2186
philosophical anthropology 324
philosophical ecclesiology 483
philosophical parochialism 1838
philosophy, and decision-making 983
phonemics 1372, 1373, 2539
phonetics 1371, 1372, 1373, 2539
phonocentrism 2661
phonograph 3130
phonology 1371
photography **3404–8**
  in anthropological study 247, 2986, 2987
  as art 3406
  birth of 3405
  digital 3407
  ethnographic uses 2866, 3406
  and identity 770–1
  photo-elicitation 770, 2987

semiotics 3406
social documentary photography 3406–7
and visual culture 770, 771, 3406
and visual saturation 756
photojournalism 3406–7
phylogeny 302
physical attractiveness 203–4, 323
physical disability *see* disability
Physical Quality of Life Index 1001
physicality 1878
physics 432, 1532
  and experimentation 1532
  and macro–micro links 2997
  and markets 2776
  wave hypothesis 1556
physiology 1681
Pia, B. 1457–9
Piaget, J. 3679
  developmental theory 876, 3413, 4574–5
  and play 3413
Picasso, Pablo 416
Pickering, A. 2846, 2904, 3548, 3549
Pickering, M. 4773–8
Pico della Mirandola 2697
pidgin languages 817, 1179, 3280
piece rates 2229
Pierce, C. S. 2881–5, 3051
Pierce, D. 1613
Pierce, G. L. 977
Pierce, J. 1894
Piercy, M. 3495
Pieterse, J. N. 2188–91, 2889
Pietism 3408–9, 3692, 3717
Pietz, W. 1746
Pike, K. 1371
pilgrimage 1981, 2130, 3519, 3522
Piliavin, I. M. 846, 1540
Pilkington, A. 3268
Pillemer, K. 1348
pimping 1102
pimps 1659
Pina e Cunha, M. 2733–6
Pinçon, M. 1363–4
Pinçon-Charlot, M. 1364
Pinel, P. 836
pink economy 4255
pink-collar occupations 2620
Pinna, T. 2696–701
Pinochet, Augusto 2575
pioneering 3511–12
Piore, M. J. 2299, 2514, 2829
Piquero, A. R. 830–3

piracy, media 2876–7, 2904
Pirenne, H. 2426
Pitsis, T. S. 2565–7, 2742–4
Piven, F. F. 781, 1166, 1721, 1807
Pixley, J. 1384–9
place 3410–11
place community 617, 1578
place managers 3959
PLACE sampling strategy 2139
place-randomized trials 2404
plagiarism 1084, 1085
Plamenatz, J. 3153
planned communities 5148
planned obsolescence 2582
planned organizational development (OD) 430
Planned Parenthood 3379
plant ecology 447, 1289, 2418
plant propagation 556
Plante, R. F. 4272–5
Plass, P. S. 48–9
plastic sexuality 334, **3411–13**
Plato 173, 534, 1242, 2099, 2609, 2661
  Allegory of the Cave 2924, 3879
  and communism 612
  and the elite nature of science 3222
  and emotions 1374
  and eugenics 1488
  and female sexuality 5268
  and justice 857
  and mediated knowledge 2924
  moral system 1083
  philosopher-kings 3545, 3546
  Republic 5156
  and the role of knowledge in stratification
    2474
  and social stratification 547, 2474
Platt, G. 2930
Platt, J. 366–7, 2969
Platt, M. 2774
Plaut, V. C. 1798
play 3413–17
  children's play 3413, 3414, 3416, 3417
  and early childhood 1270
  and gender socialization 1668
  and leisure 2598
  and postmodernism 3570
  sexual play 1678
play stage 1899, 3415, **3417–18**, 3617, 3948,
    3951, 4563
  and the generalized other 1899, 3417, 3617,
    3949, 3952
  see also game stage

Playboy **3418–19**
  and masculinity and consumerism 1849
Playground Movement 2120
plea bargaining 1128
pleasure principle 837
Plekhanov, G. 1148, 1150, 1409
Plessner, H. 1188
Plessy v. Ferguson 368, 508, 510, 2830, 3369,
    3742, 3747, 4023–4
Pletier, L. 1115
Plummer, K. 462–3, 965–6, 1436–8, 2132–3,
    2157, 2160, 2467–9, 2492–3, 2642, 2643,
    3141, 3568, 3568–9, 3843–4, 4207, 4238–44
Plumwood, V. 1274
plural society 3420–1
pluralism
  and Anglo-conformity 137
  and assimilation 192, 196
  church 483–4
  cosmopolitan 3422
  elite pluralism 3443
  ethnic 1458, 1459
  fragmented 3422
  and industrial relations 2291
  institutionalization 199
  interactive model 3421
  interest group pluralism 3451, 3452
  and the Internet 2387
  and leisure 2588–9
  limited 223, 224
  and media 627
  medical pluralism 630
  methodological pluralism 3425
  political 223, 3423–4
  and political sociology 3459–60
  and power 3597
  religious pluralism 1316, 2530
  sociocultural pluralism, and religious
    denomination 1051
  see also cultural pluralism
pluralism, American 3421–3, 3423, 3811, 4727
  and Du Bois 1245
  and power elites 3602
pluralism, British 3423–4
pluricultural state 342, 343
Podhoretz, N. 3172
Poe, Edgar Allan 1220
POET (Population, Organization, Environment,
    Technology) framework 5110
poetics, social science 3424–6
  investigative poetics 2420–3
poetry 1227

Poggi, G. 1006, 1007
Poggio, A. 4741–6
Poggio, J. 4741–6
pogroms 2453, **3426–8**
  see also Holocaust
Poland
  anti-Jewish violence 3428
  Catholicism 2531
  civil religion 507
  consumer movements 697, 698
  crime rates 582
  cultural tourism 921
  diaspora 1151
  heritage tourism 920
  nationalism 3146
  peasant emigration 1615, 2252, 2637
  social security system 2055
  Solidarity 511
  stratification system 889
Polanyi, Karl 2679, **3428–30**
  biography 3428–9
  and capitalism and civilization 517, 1310
  and disembedded economies 1188,
    3085, 3429
  and economic exchanges 3085
  and embeddedness concept 1188, 3085, 3429,
    4399, 4400–1
  and gift giving 1939
  and industrialization 2298
  and markets 2782, 3429
  and modernity 935, 1309
  and tacit knowledge 1299
Polanyi, M. 4111
police 1107, 1109, 1121, **3430–3**
  and asset forfeiture 1238
  authoritarianism 1176
  coercive institution 3315, 3316, 3317, 3318,
    3430, 3432
  community policing 3431–2
  corruption 3431
  crime-fighting model 3715–6
  discretion 3431
  and football hooliganism 1768
  innovations 3431
  law enforcement 852–3
  minority group representation 3318
  order maintenance model 3715
  recruitment 3315
  riot control 3924
  and suppression of direct action 1166, 1948,
    4475–6, 4478
Polichetti, M. 370–4

politeness theories 1999
political activism 957
political alienation 120
political business cycles 3434
political campaigns 33
  media involvement 2878
political citizenship 497, 498, 499
political contention 779
political correctness 3107
political crime 835–6
political culture 933
political disasters 1174, 1175
political documentaries 1212
political economy 2433–6, 2797, 3440
  classical 1300–3, 3440
  conservative 679–80
  and development 1067–70
  and economic geography 1299
  and environmental degradation 1420
  and health and illness differentials 1186
  and information technology 2333
  liberal 2623
  neoclassical 3440
  political coalition theory 3434
  radical 3440
  spatial theory of voting 3434
  theory of committees 3434
political economy of science 3436–9
political economy and sport 2236, **3440–1,**
  3474
political elites 1002
  coalitions 3714–15
  and populism 3538
political entrepreneurship 3443
political expression, cultural forms 779
political gatherings 880
political generations 1902–3
political ideology 925
political indifference 1008
political leadership 3441–5
  and populism 3538
  see also reputation
political machine 3445–7
political mobilization 3065
political mythology 2691
political objectives 1815
political opportunities 3447–50
  and framing 1783
  political opportunity structures (POS)
    4478
  and social movements 1874, 3455, 3456,
    3457, 4466–9, 4478

political parties 548, **3450–5**
  cadre parties 3452, 3453
  European 2232
  and federalism 1653
  liberal–conservative continuum 2232
  mass parties 3453
  multiple party systems 3453
  single-party systems 3453
  social basis 3451
  two-party systems 3453
  United States 2232, 2233–4
political poetry 2420–3
political power 547, 548, 549–50, 2786
  and deviance 1114
political process theory 3455–8
political representation, women's, and gender
    ideology 1868
political science 3434
political sociology 3458–63
  and alienation 120
  and Arendt 173
  and classical political enquiry, distinguished
    3463
  laborism 2526–7
  and legitimacy 2587
  rational-choice models 3462
  revolutions 3915–16
politics 3463–7
  classical political theory 3717
  trivialization of 2907
politics and media 3467–72
  and the public sphere 2909–10
  and reputation 3886
  see also propaganda; public opinion
politics and sport 3472–6, 4534–5
Poll Tax Riots 881, 1430
Pollard, L. 2849
Polletta, F. 4463–6
Pollock, F. 2163
Pollock, Jackson 218, 797
polluter-pays principle (PPP) 2126
pollution 728, 1418
  air pollution 1418, 2658
  and caste 404
  daily life pollution 967–8
  and environmental racism 2078
  and environmental sociology 1417
  and health 1424
  high-speed transportation pollution 2126–7,
    4855
  and local residents' movements 2657–9
  and neighborhood poverty 1614

pollution (*cont'd*)
soil pollution 2658
and sport events 4680
and urbanization 1423–4
water pollution 1418, 2280, 2658
pollution zones, linear and planar 3476–7
Polonko, K. 448–51
polyamory 303, 3477–9
polyandry 1615, 2789
polyarchy 222
polycentric spatial structure 3115–16
polyethnicity 3479–80
polyfidelity 3478
polygamy 1597, 1615, 2003, 2112, 3534
polygenesis 4114
polygyny 2789, 4277
polyphonics 2409
polytheism 141, 652, 2696, 3477, 3629, 3633
Pontell, H. N. 1123–6
Ponzi finance 2021
Poole, M. S. 3295
pools 1820
Poor Laws (England) 2708, 4491, 4522, 4538
Pop Art 2124
pop music
and cultural production 953
digital aesthetics 1163
and genres 1915
and mass culture concept 2823
and occupational devotion 2599
political economy perspective 2905
and subcultures 1915
techno/rave scene 1523
Popenoe, D. 1582
Popper, Karl 1531, 3176, 3606, 3831, 4084
and falsification 1570–1, 2968, 3577
popular art 2762
popular culture 3480–3
and alienation 3482
and celebrity culture 415–17
and cultural production 952
definition 2596
and elites 1361
entertainment orientation 1108
and genres 1915
highbrow/lowbrow 2123–5
hip-hop 3486–7
and identity formation 730
intellectual property issues 2358
and intertextuality 2402
and leisure 2596–600
and millenarianism 3047

pacification of the proletariat 2236
and patriarchy 3379
and reports on deviance 1107
popular culture forms 3484–503
infotainment 2336–7
popular culture icons 3503–17
mythic icons 3137–8
popular religiosity 3518–25
and animism 141
Catholic 3518–24
folk Hinduism 1764–6
population
bio-politics of 337, 338
city populations 767
classification and 555
regulatory controls 337
population biology 285
population counts *see* censuses
population density 637, 3529
population and development 3525–8
population ecology 2586
and organization theory 3283
**population and economy 1303, 3525–7,
3528–30**
population and the environment 3530–3
and ecological problems 1423
and environmental degradation 1420,
3527
Malthusian theory 1040, 1506, 2706–7, 3071,
3530–1, 3590–1
overpopulation 2706–8
population epidemiology 1433–4
population explosion 972, 1034, 1038
population and gender 3533–7
population genetics 291
population growth 1034
deceleration 1043–4
and economic development 3525–6
and environmental degradation 1420
and fertility levels 1730
and food resources 276, 1040–1, 2706,
2707
and immigration 2263
Malthusian theory 1040, 1506, 2706–7, 3071,
3530–1, 3590–1
nuptiality as regulator of 1047
population explosion 972, 1034, 1038
and poverty 2707–8
and urbanization 1423
zero population growth 3526
population momentum 1029
population parameters 656

population projections and estimates
  cohort-component method 1025–6
  component-based projections 1025–6
  modeling uncertainty 1027–8
  see also demographic data
population pyramids 1029–30
population registers 1011, 1012–13, 3016
population surveys 1011, 1013–14
  cross-sectional 1014
  longitudinal 1014
populism 3537–9
  Latin America 413, 1925
  Marxist perspective 3538
  modernizing perspective 3537–8
  and nationalism 3537
  neopopulism 413
  North American populism 3537
  Russian populism 3537
Porat, M. 2327
pornographication of culture 4243
pornography and erotica 3540–2, 4274
  anti-pornography movement 905, 1115
  and casual leisure 2599
  censorship 3540
  child pornography 960, 1659, 1661, 3542
  childhood eroticism 462
  cyberporn 965
  and cybersexualities 965
  and female oppression/dehumanization 333,
    3419, 3541
  female porn 3540
  and female sex work 1659, 1660, 1661
  gay male porn 3541
  hard-core/soft-core 3540
  health and exploitation issues 3542
  heterosexual 3541
  K/S porn 3498
  lesbian critique 2605
  lesbian erotics 3541
  and misogyny 905
  and obscenity 3540
  online pornography 422, 2541, 2915
  and plastic sexuality 3412
  and *Playboy* 3419
  porn–rape connection 3775, 3786
  same-sex eroticism 1836
  violence 3540
Porpora, D. 873
Port Huron Statement 3194, 3196
Porter, A. C. 3274
Porter, C. O. 3055
Porter, M. 2749

Porter, R. 744
Portes, A. 1461, 1462, 1464, 2254
portfolio theory 3323
portfolio workers 3289
Portugal 393
  capitalism 396
  colonialism 602, 985
  cultural tourism 921
  divorce rates 2664
  health care system 2055
  lone parenthood 2663, 2664, 2665
  prostitution 1659
positional feminist pedagogy 1798
positive deviance 3542–4
positive psychology 2566, 2569–70
positive reinforcement 257
Positive School 1101, 1105, 1118
positive society 652–3
positive thinking 3190
positive-sum games 1822
positivism 259, 2968, **3544–7**
  abstraction 1079
  and attitudes and behavior 199, 201
  Bernard and 270
  Comte and 651, 652–3, 654
  and constructionism 1089
  and criminology 857, 861, 969, 1094
  and critical realism 871
  and dangerousness 969
  and democracy 3545
  and determinism 116, 1101
  and deviance 1079–80, 1081, 1117–21
  and dialectics 1149
  and emotions 1380
  and emotions and economy 1384
  empiricism 1079, 1101, 1118, 1434
  essentialism 1079
  and family migration 1606
  and grounded theory 2024, 2026
  limitations 1712
  logical positivism 3545
  and magic 2697
  materialist positivism 2836
  metatheory 2964
  methodological positivism 1079
  and Mexican sociology 2947, 2949
  objectivism 1079, 1100–1, 1118
  and organizational communication 3293
  positivistic neuroscience 3187
  postpositivism 3577–8
  and research practices 1701
  and science fiction 3497

positivism (*cont'd*)
scientific positivism 1151
social positivism 270
and sociology of knowledge 2757
statistical methods 4747
substantive positivism 1079
positivist criminology 857, 861, 1094, 1426,
1427, 2506
Posocco, S. 1657–8
possession laws 1238
possessive individualism 2712
postcolonial ethnography 2983
postcolonial feminisms 2982, 4996–8
intersectionality 2395, 2398
postcolonialism
and critical qualitative research 869
and cultural anthropology 922
definitions 2981, 2982
Fanon and 1637
and feminist anthropology 1692
and feminist methodology 1703–4, 2892
hybridization 2983
language policies 280
master narratives 2982
and modernity 3070
Nietzscheanism 3217
and the Olympics 3264
and Orientalism 1396
postcolonial methods 2981–5
postcolonial theory 2981
postcolonialism/postmodernism divide 2982
and poststructuralism 2982
and queer theory 2982
and representation 3548
and resistance 1969
postcolonialism and sport 3547–8
post-communist societies
class structures 889
reorientation to capitalist entrepreneurship
596
Poster, M. 2327
post-Fordism *see* Fordism/post-Fordism
postgenomic sciences 2171
posthuman consumption 745
posthumanism 151, 3548–50
and cybersexualities 966
and science fiction 3496
post-industrial cities 767–9, 2297
spatial geometry 1280–1
post-industrial economy 781
post-industrial society 293, 2328, 3550–2
class power perspective 3551

class voting 553
deindustrialization 992–4, 2300
living standards 3551
social dimensions 2334
see also information society
postmaterialism 1429, 2234, 4124
and new social movement theory 3209
Postmes, T. 882
postmodern consumption 744, 3552–6
Comtean heritage 656
conspicuous consumption and 685
and fashion 720
implosion theory 2269
postmodern culture 2821, 3556–8
and intertextuality 2402
and mass culture 2821, 2823
postmodern feminism 937, 1666, 3558–63
and women's inequality 1888–9
postmodern organizations 3324, 3325,
3563–8
postmodern sexualities 3568–9
fetishism 1746
plastic sexuality 3412, 3568
postmodern social theory 3569–72
postmodernism 3559, 3572–6
and advertising 1850
and architecture 3553
and arts-based rseearch 2972
and biography 287
and built environment 375
and charismatic movement 439
and collective memory 589
and community media 628
and conspicuous consumption 685
and criminology 858
and cultural anthropology 922
and cultural criminology 893
and cultural relativism 910
Deleuze and 999, 1000
and difference 1153
and discrimination 1183
and dramaturgy 1229
and Durkheim 1251, 1259
and ethnography 1482
and existential sociology 1523
and family therapy 1636
and femininities/maculinities 1891
and feminist criminology 1695
and feminist methodology 937, 1703–4
and feminist standpoint theory 1713–14
and film 1755
and gender 3699

and gerontology 1930
and global capitalism 3558
and implosion 2692
and information technology 2332, 2336
and intertextuality 2402
and leadership 2566–7
and leisure 2590
and life history research 2643
and lifestyle consumption 2650
and linguistics 2533
and materialist feminisms 2842–3
and metatheory 2965–6
and military theory 3043
and modernity 3069, 3070
and narrative methodology 3141
and the Olympics 3263
and organizations 3313–14
origins 3570
and political sociology 3461
postcolonialism/postmodernism divide 2982
postmodern body 326
postmodern culture 518
postmodern discourses 5297
postmodern epistemology 2534
postmodern interviewing 2407, 2409, 2410
power analyses 1704
and praxis 3613
and reflexivity 3830, 3831
and science fiction 3498
and self-identity 962
postmodernist meta-paradigm 2969
postnationalism 3576–7
Postone, M. 876
post-panoptic society 555
post-partum depression 1112
postpositivism 1435, **3577–8**
and empiricism 1435
Frankfurt School and 865
metatheory 2964
post-self 974
postsocial 3578–80
poststructuralism 301, **3580–4**
anarchist resonances 136
autoethnography and 231
Barthes and 242
and celebrity 416–17
and critical qualitative research 869
Deleuze and 999
Derrida and 244
and dialectics 1149
and digital texts 1164
and disability 1170

and discrimination 1183
and Durkheim 1259
and ethnography 1480, 1482
and fashion 719–20
and fatherhood 1648
and femininities/maculinities 1891
and feminism 937
and film 1755
Foucault and 244
and identity 2212
and ideology 913
and information technology 2333, 2336
Kristeva and 244
linguistic poststructuralism 3580–1
literary poststructuralism 3581
and Marxism 2816
and online identity 962
political economy theory 610
and postcolonialism 2982
and postmodernism 3570
poststructural epistemology 2534
poststructural feminism 1682
and pragmatics 4973
and reflexivity 3830
and sport 1877
and structure-agency debate 2077
and texts/genres 1916
poststructuralist feminism 1888–9
postsuburbia 3113
post-traumatic stress disorder (PTSD) 1111,
1112, 1113, 1194
and learned helplessness 2569
and pedophilia 3387
post-Westphalian global political order 1950,
1952
potlatch ritual 704, 1938, 1939, 1940, 4908, 5220
Potter, S. J. 2165–8
Potter, W. J. 2891–5, 2892
Potts, A. 5268–73
Poulantzas, Nicos 3179, **3584–5**, 3597–8
materialist analysis 2838
and structural functionalism 1810, 3597–8
Poulat, E. 408–11
Pound, Roscoe 2171, **3585–7**
poverty 3587–9
and abortion rates 4
absolute 351, 702, 1718, 1719, 3196, 3587,
3588
and age 1720
and alienation 951
and the caste system 405
Chicago School studies 443

poverty (*cont'd*)

child poverty 450, 1271, 1591, 1614, 1622, 1624, 3587

compensatory consumption 707

and crime 542–3

defeminization 1721

and divorce 1208

and domestic violence 1219

and educational attainment 1338

and ethnicity 1591

family poverty 1612–14

and family status 1719

and family structure 1591, 1612, 1613, 1614, 1626–9

feminization of poverty 1613, 1718–25

and gender 1719, 1720

global poverty 3595

and happiness levels 626

and health 2315

and homelessness 2146–50

idealization as spiritual virtue 2147

and inclusion 901

income poverty 3587, 3588

neighborhood poverty 1614

older adults 3255, 3256

paradigm theory 3356

pathologizing 699

and population growth 2707–8

poverty line, income elasticity of 3588

and race/ethnicity 1719

racial variations 1627, 1628

relative 702, 3196, 3197, 3587

and school dropout 1231

sex poverty ratios 1718, 1723

and social activism 781

and social disorganization theory 585

spatial concentration 2197

stereotyping 952

thresholds 1626

urban poverty 5125–8

World Bank measures 3588

see also feminization of poverty

poverty and disrepute 3589–94

blame culture 707, 3591, 3709

culture of poverty thesis 288, 951–2, 1612, 1613, 1728

and marginalization 699, 700, 2763, 2765–6

the poor as flawed consumers 699, 700

and social exclusion 4411

and stigma 2505, 3593

poverty and free trade 3595–6

Powdermaker, H. 1755, 2704

Powell, B. 1868, 2116–18

Powell, Colin 3175

Powell, J. 1614–18, 3700–3

Powell, J. L. 1926–30, 1930, 3597–8, 3602–3

Powell, W. W. 2351–2, 2714, 2739

power 3597–8

adolescent power 1800

and adult–child sexual relationships 3387

Arendt on 172–3

and *'asabiyya* 182

asymmetrical relations 1445

and authoritarianism 223–4

bio-power 1178, 1776

and the body 326, 335

bureaucratic 377

circulation of 1008

and class 533, 3551

coactive power 2717

coercive power 2717

and collective action 576

and collective memory 589, 593

and collectivities 1079

and colonialism 602, 603

and compliance 229

and conflict theory 662

and consumption 701, 702

and cultural resistance 912

and culture 957

and cyberculture 963

decentralized power 4639

definitions 3597

and democracy 1005

disciplinary power 1177, 1178

and domestic violence 1695

dyadic power-dependence theory 1512

Power, E. 700

power

economic power 602

elite theory 3597

and emotion work 1383, 1389–90

in families 1591

feminist theory 3597

gender-driven differences 3534

global power networks 1987

group process perspective 2028

and language 786

legitimate 229

Marxist theory 3472

media power 2925

medical sociology, and power-domination perspective 2059

mesostructural level 2961, 2962

metapower 2962
organizational power 3296, 3313
pluralist theories 3597
postmodern analyses 1704
power differences, and party formation 538
power and prestige theory 1525, 1527
power-at-a-distance 1353
power/knowledge 786, 787, 2484
premodern forms 3883
punitive-based power 3604
pure power 229
racial and ethnic 661
separation of powers doctrine 2583
sovereign power 1178
state power 3585
and wealth 2311
in the world city 3182
youth culture and 774
see also authority; marital power/resource
    theory
power-balancing processes 3600
power constellations 2443
power-control theory 2818, 2819, 2820
power-dependence theory 2146, **3598–602**
  and bargaining theory 3601
  dyadic relations 1512
  Emerson and 1368, 1512, 2146, 3598–9,
    3600, 3604, 3848, 4409
  and exchange network theory 1512–14, 2146
  and relational cohesion theory 3845
  and social exchange theory 4409
power elite 3597, **3602–3**
  Mills and 3051, 3602–3
  pluralist perspective 3602
  and political leadership 3442
  and political sociology 3459
power equalization arguments 2752
power evangelism 440
power networks 1354–5, 3461
power-oriented theoretical perspectives 869
power relations
  and ethnic/racial boundaries 345
  feminist theory 1633, 2401
  gendered 1841, 1842, 2309, 2310
  and ideological hegemony 2228
  Internet and 732
  intersectionality 1707, 2395
  and intersubjectivity 2401
  in interviews 2401
  Islamic gender relations 2428
  and organizational communication 3292, 3295
  post-September 11 shift 1004

and postcolonialism 3548
sexual politics 4244–7
and sexuality research 4280
sport 3472, 3474
within the household 1844
power resources theory 4813
power sharing 3382
power-status model 1650
power, theories of 3603–6
  bio-power 1776
  class–power relations 4922–3
  and elementary theory 1352–3, 3604
  elite theory 3597
  Emerson and 1368, 1370
  equal power networks 3605
  Foucauldian 1775–6, 3597, 3598
  marital power/resource theories 2770–2
  Marxist theory 3597–8
  and organization theory 3284
  pluralist theories 3597
  and political sociology 3459
  status value theory of power 3605
  strong power structures 3604–5
  Takata and 4922–3
  weak power networks 3605
  see also leadership
Poyago–Theitoky, J. 3031
practical knowledge 3606–7
practice 3607–9
practice theory, agentive turn 290
practitioner research 1444
pragma love 2671
pragmatic racialism 3611
pragmatism 3609–12
  antifoundationalism 3609
  and arts-based research 2972
  Cooley and 798, 801
  criminology, pragmatic value of 859
  and critical realism 872
  culturally contingent pragmatics 3825
  Dewey and 1145
  and dramaturgy 1228
  and epistemology 1435
  and ethnography 1480
  fallibilism 3609
  and grounded theory 2024, 2026
  and humanism 2186, 2187–8
  James and 2431
  meliorism 3609
  and research ethics 1448
  and symbolic interaction 3609, 4913
  and women scholars 3611

Prakash, G. 947, 4074

Prandi, C. 258–62

Pratt, R. 3134

praxis 2680, **3612–13**
  educational praxis 3613
  and feminist methodology 1703, 1704
  Freire and 865–6
  and ideological hegemony 2228
  Marcuse and 2760

pre-industrial societies 548
  characteristics 2327
  family roles and structure 3074

precautionary principle 4082–3

Prechel, H. 1769–71, 4939–40

precision 4989

predestination 1386

predisposition theory, and crowd behavior 882

preferred provider organizations (PPOs) 2065

pregnancy
  and domestic abuse 2315
  ectopic pregnancies 2314
  effect on relationships 2672
  and empowerment 333
  forced pregnancy (slaves) 2621
  intendedness 1626
  and mortality 2314, 2318
  pregnancy-related complications 1726, 2314,
    2315, 2318
  single woman pregnancy 235
  teenage 450, 1617, 2826
  unintended 1609, 1625–6, 1736, 1738, 2315
  see also abortion; childbearing

preimplantation genetic diagnosis (PGD) 1490

Preisendörfer, P. 1281–6, 1284

prejudice 3613–17
  agist 56–9
  anti-Semitism 152–60
  authoritarianism and 221, 3614
  and beliefs 260
  Blumer and 320
  formation 3614–15
  and majorities 2701–2
  psychological and psychoanalytic models 320
  race prejudice 320, 3615
  and racial/ethnic conflict 661
  and sterotyping 3614
  see also bias; discrimination; race (racism);
    segregation

premenstrual syndrome (PMS) 1111, 1112,
  2556

premodern states 3073

prenatal screening and diagnosis 1490, 1699,
  1907, 2173, 3206

prenuptial contracts 2323

prepaid group practices (PGPs) 2065

Presbyterian Church 1051, 1053, 1054

preschool 1269
  oral language development 2654
  preschool literacy 2654–5

preschool ability 1338

preschool programs 2463

Presdee, Michael 246–7

Presley, Elvis 3492

press
  alternative and radical 2905
  press barons 2873, 2897
  press freedom 2912, 2913, 3468
  see also journalism; newspapers

Press, A. 936–42

press counseling 3469
  see also public relations

prestige
  competition for 701, 702, 722
  and consumption 701, 702
  occupational prestige 1341–2, 1461, 3250
  power and prestige theory 1525, 1527
  professional schools 4047
  and social status 1340

prestige differences, and social class 538

prestige scales 545

Preston, S. 1743, 3100

prevalence (of disease) 1433
  cumulative prevalence 1433
  point prevalence 1433

prevention, intervention 3618–20
  intervention studies 2403–6

preventive medicine *see* health lifestyles

Price, D. J. D. S. 276, 4120

price determination 2780

pride/shame component of social integration
  3007

priesthood 476, 652, 2758, 4928

primary groups 3620–2, 4130

Primary Metropolitan Statistical Areas
  (PMSAs) 2992, 2995

primate cities 3622–5
  metropolises 2991

primates and cyborgs 3625–8

primatology 2249, 2250

primitive house church 1523

primitive religion 3629–34, 3854, 3860
  ancestor worship 3629

and magic 2698–9
 Native American 2284
 pantheism 3854
 and popular religiosity 3524
 and the sacred 3973–4
primitivism 2691
 colonial discourse 2984
 and polyamory 3477
primordial sociobehavioral outcomes (PSO)
  1195, 1196
primordialism 1477
 and nationalism 3156
Prince, D. 1661
Prince, V. 5039, 5041
principal–agent problems 573
principal axis methods 1558
principal components analysis 1558, 3121
print capitalism 628
 and linguistic homogeneity 3156
 and nationalism 2900–1
print media 1107, **3634–40**
 corporate ownership 3639
 narcotizing dysfunction 3635
 positive functions 3635
 and the public sphere 876
 regulation 2912, 2913
 see also books; magazines; newspapers;
  periodicals
printing technology 2249, 2294, 2691, 2896,
  3635–6
Prior, L. 1213–16
prison gangs 1825
prison guards 1218
 gendered training 1894
Prisoner's Dilemma (PD) 1266, 1282, 1822–3
 and ethnic mobilization 1469–70
prisoners of war 2183, 3640
 identity change 2205–6
 Japanese 238
prisons 802, 803, 804, 819, 821, 854, **3640–3**
 adaptation to 861
 and drug use 1235
 ex-prisoners and stigma 2505
 Goldman and 2006
 male rape in 2703
 mass imprisonment 1122
 military prisons 3640
 minimum/medium/maximum security
  prisons 3641
 overcrowding 3642
 population composition 3642

privatization 3642
 sexualization 3320
 solitary confinement 3640–1
 and stigma 2505, 2506
 super-maximum prisons 3641–2
 and surveillance 1176–7, 1776
 total institutions 3333
 women prisoners 1857
 see also panoptics
privacy 3643–7
 Arendt and 171
 confidentiality 3644
 decisional privacy 3644
 informational privacy 3644
 and the Internet 734
 and new media concerns 2877
 privacy–publicity continuum 3643
 rights and obligations 3644
 secrecy 3644
 and surveillance 3643, 3644
private law *see* civil law
private sphere 1663, 1763, 1893, 1930, 3720
 museumizing of the 3127
 property rights, protection of 2913
private–centralized institutions 2355
private–decentralized institutions 2354–5
privatization 1069, 2749, **3647–9**
 of coercive institutions 3319
 and the Internet 734
 prisons 3642
 and public housing 3709, 3710
 of religion 4141
 shock privatization 3648
privilege 3649–51
 intergenerational transmission of 1336
 male privilege 3649
pro-choice and pro-life movements 3206,
  3651–6
 and abortion 3, 2234
 political partisanship 2234
 pro-choice ideology 2621
probability
 Bayesian probability theory 2287
 error-based notion of 426
 and statistics 4747
 subjective 425, 426, 1387
 see also chance and probability
probability sampling 3782
probation 854–5
problem-oriented policing 829
problem-solving

problem-solving (*cont.*)
  and decision-making 983
  and social cognition 4381
process analysis 2855–6
process model building 2856
process sociology 1358
processual order 2961
processualists 446
Procter, J. 1403–4
product franchising 1784
product identity 771
product placement 731
Production Code 421, 2874
production and consumption cycles 748
professional class 534
professional deviance 1084–5
professional dominance in medicine 2930,
  2935, **3656–60**
  and complementary and alternative medicine
    630, 631
  countervailing powers 3658–9
  patient–physician relationship 3375–6
  rights and powers 3657
  traditional/new professionalism 3659
professional partnerships 3664
professionalism 3656
professions 3249, **3660–2**
  altruism 3663
  developmental appraoch 3663
  dynamic theory 3663
  entrepreneurial professions 3664
  health professions and occupations 2075–7
  legal profession 2583–4
  liberal professions 3664
  Marxist sociology 3661–2
  neo-Marxist perspective 3663
  neo-Weberian perspective 2076–7
  organizational professions 3664
  power approach to the study of 3661
  professional jurisdiction 2077
  professional schools 4045–8
  professionalization of domains of practice 1542
  professionalization of leadership 1008
  recruitment 1361
  role in modern societies 2583
  socialization 2931
  structural functionalist approach 3663
  symbolic interactionist approach 3661
  systems approach 207
  trait approach 3663
  see also teachers

professions, organized 3662–5
  management consultants 2719–22
professors 3665–9
profit theory 1545
progessivism 2526, 3669–71
programmed change initiatives 2729
progress, idea of 3669–71
  and cultural relativism 908
Progressive Era 250
progressive evolution 1506
Prohibition 115, 118, 820, 954, 1097, 2505
Project Camelot 271, 341
project diaries 2479
project management 3269
proletarianization 704, 2076, 3658
proletariat 1569
proletariat *see* bourgeoisie and proletariat
prominence hierarchy 2225
promiscuity 1856, 2826
Promise Keepers 1665
pronatalism 1740, 3528
propaganda 3671–5
  atrocity propaganda 3672, 3673
  media uses 2879
  wartime 3672, 3673
property
  money surrogate 1759
  private property 1302, 2141, 3676–8
  property holding, state support of
    2627, 4731
  public property 3677
  see also gentrification
property crime 2555, **3675–6**
  and gender 2819
  graffiti vandalism 894
  index crime 2278
  rates of 821, 5190
  robbery 3941–2
property destruction 1166
property, private 1302, **3676–8**
  liberal theory 3677, 3678
  Marxist theory 3677, 3678
  move from communal form to 2141, 3677
property relations, Marx and 245
property rights/relations 396, 397
  communal ownership 538, 1596
  and communism 612–13
  Comte and 652
  and conservatism 679
  intellectual property 729–32
  private ownership 612–13, 614

protection of 2913
and social class 536, 538
property taxes 680
prophetic date-setting 2440
prophetic disconfirmation 2440
prophets, prophecy 434, 439, 2694
proportional hazard models 1018
Cox regression model 1019, 1020
propoxyphene 1235
prosocial behavior 3678–82
bystander intervention studies 3679, 3680
demographic variables 3681
see also altruism; helping behaviors
prosperity gospel 440
Prosser, J. 1658
prostitution 1137, 1597, 2555, **3682–5**
AIDS-related risk 2138
in Asia 4216–17
call girls 1660
as career 1143
child prostitution 3682–3, 4202
definitional problems 3684
and deviance 12, 1856, 1858
entry into 3683
and female sex work 1659, 1660, 1661
feminist abolitionist account 3683
forced prostitution 1886, 1887
illegality 1659
male prostitution 1661, 2160, 3683, 3684,
    4216–17
media portrayal 1109
moral panics 4254
sex tourism 763
sex work feminists, perspective of 3683
and socially disorganized communities 1102
stigma 3682
street prostitution 1660, 3684, 3715
and surveillance 3682
and trafficking in women 1717, 1984, 5031
transgender prostitutes 2161
in war 1887
Protagoras 3813
protectionism 679, 681
proteomics 2171
protest cycles 781, 3456, 3457, 3685
protest, diffusion of 3685–8
and ethnic/nationalist movements 1471, 1472
innovative protest tactics 3686
and political opportunities 3448
and riots 3924–5
typology of protest 780
"protest event" research 780

protest movements *see* social movements
Protestant capitalism 1397
Protestant ethic 391–2, 750, 751, 815, 991,
    1055, 2294, 2516, 3215
and bureaucratic expansion 3311
postmodern alternatives 3567
Weber and 186–7, 750, 815, 1293, 1397,
    2294, 2298, 2768, 2786, 2997, 3631, 3691,
    3692, 3808, 5231–3
women, significance for 2768
Protestant Reformation 391–2, 516–17, 1318,
    3468, 3635, 3689
and *moralpolitik* 3094
and printing technology 2294
Protestantism 652, 654, 671, **3688–94**
and anti-Semitism 153
ascetic Protestantism 188–9, 2699
and capitalism 516–17
charismatic movement 440
conservative Protestantism 1053
and democracy 3692
and denominationalism 1052
ecclesiastical organization 3692
and economics of religion 1316
fundamentalism 1813
and individualism 2285, 2415
ingroup association 795, 1293
and linguistic homogeneity 3156
and national culture 2529
"old"/"modern" Protestantism 3692
and Pietism 3408
and Prohibition 195
proto-nationalism 3150
Protocols of the Elders of Zion 159
Proudhon, P.-J. 136, 197, 1165
Proust, Marcel 216, 3006
Prout, A. 460
provisioning
    mode of provision 748
    systems of provision 748
proxemics 1372, 4627
proximant determinants of fertility 1743
proximity
    and attraction 202–3
    and familiarity 203
Proyas, A. 3497
Prozac 1113, 2953
Pruijt, H. 5115–19
Prus, R. 320, 1126, 1127
pseudo-science 1571
psychiatric disorder *see* mental disorder
psychiatry 1169, 2695

psychiatry (*cont'd*)
  anti-psychiatry movement 248, 3333,
    4117, 4118
  biological psychiatry 2951
  case histories 288
  as communicative activity 248
  and *connaissance/savoir* 1772, 1773
  and emotions 1378
  historic practices 2694
psychic healing 631
psychoactive drugs 1234
psychoanalysis 3694–6, 4542
  and biography 287
  and film 1755
  Frankfurt School and 865
  Freudian 865, 1070–1, 1786, 1897, 2695,
    2698, 2760, 3694, 3696, 4264
  Fromm and 1806
  Gellner and 1838
  and genres 1915
  and hybridity 2189
  and identity formation 295
  Lacan and 2527
  and online identity 962
  and scapegoating 4013
  and Thomas theorem 992
  and visual culture 755
psychoanalytic feminism 1666, **3696–700**
  and cultural feminism 904
  and gender and culture 939
psychobiology 1996
psychodrama 4611
psychohistory 1071, 3495
psycholinguistics 281, 2212, 2536
psychological abuse 1348
psychological behaviorism 1101
psychological determinism 969
psychological linguistics 2535
psychological reductionism 1805, 3148
psychological social psychology 3700–3
  Asch experiments 189–91
  and attitudes and behavior 199
  and emotions 1380
  and group phenomena 3701
  Lewin and 2615
  see also cognitive dissonance theory;
    conformity
psychological theories of crime 836–9
psychological warfare 2879
psychological well-being
  and age identity 50
  and divorce, effects of 1208

psychologically oriented feminist pedagogy 1707
psychology
  animism 141
  classical psychological theory 257
  confidence intervals, use of 658
  and constructionism 1087
  depth psychology 875
  discursive psychology 1181
  and emotions 1378
  evolutionary psychology 292, 635
  personal documents 288
  and Thomas theorem 992
psychometrics 1500, 2660, 2852
psychopathology 65, 846
psychopaths 823, 838, 1081
psychosocial development 1071
psychosocial processes 2073
psychosocial theory 1186
psychosomatic disease 1522, 2694, 4117
psychotherapy
  and constructionism 1087
  psychotherapeutic encounters, structuring
    of 2363
psychoticism 838
psychotropic drugs 995
puberty 773
  and cross-sex friendship 878
public broadcasting 3703–7
  documentaries 1210–13
public–centralized institutions 2355–6
public choice theory 3434
public demonstrations 779, 780, 1165, 1166
Public Engagement with Science and
    Technology (PEST) 4089
public finance 1759
public health
  and applied social psychology 4519
  and McDonaldization 2690
  social epidemiology 1186
public health campaigns 2320
public health sciences, and population
    management 338
public housing 3707–11
  crime in 5108
  funding 3709–10
  housing of last resort 3708
  Section 8 programs 3710
public institutions 2353
  public–centralized institutions 2355–6
  public–decentralized institutions 2353–4
public killing 1178
  see also capital punishment

public opinion 2906, **3711–15**
  and abortion politics 3, 2234
  and agenda setting 63–4
  collective action and opinion shifts 580
  and cultural issues 2234
  industrialization of 2907
  and mass media 3637, 3780–1
  opinion formation 3714
  opinion polling 2407, 3713
  and the political environment 3469
  and ratings 3793
  and socialization 4567
  and technological innovation 3930
  see also propaganda
public order crime 3715–17
public and private 3717–18
  and the body 331, 332
  and division of labor 1840
  Durkheim on 736
  and gender polarities 1668–9, 1862
  and print media 876
  public–private distinction 317, 512, 2909,
    3717
  and urban consumption 766
  see also private sphere; public sphere
public–private dichotomy 317, 512, 2909, 3717
public property 3677
public realm 3718–21
public relations 2907, 3469–71
  party political public relations 3470
  terrorist 3470
Public School Athletic League 2120
public service broadcasting 208, 626, 2874
public sociology 1807, 2838
public space 4627
  and the city 501
  and culture jamming 945
  generation of through film 1753
public sphere 3721–2
  bourgeois public sphere 2908
  cosmopolitan public sphere 3722
  counter-public spheres 3722
  cultural public sphere 2907
  European public sphere 3722
  and everyday life 1502
  evolution of public sphere 915
  Habermas and 628
  interactional dimension 2908
  Internet impacts 2387
  male dominance 1893, 3649
  media and the public sphere 628, 2906–11,
    2913

  and modernity 3722
  national public sphere 2908
  and nationalism 3144
  political public sphere 2907
  public–private distinction 3717
  representational dimension 2907–8
  and secularization 4141
  structural dimension 2907
  transnational public sphere 2909
  and universality 2907
  see also civil society
public understanding of science (PUS) 4089,
    4100–4
publications, scientific 4112
publishing conglomerates 2897, 2898
Puerto Ricans
  clothing styles 715
  and poverty 951
Puerto Rico, economic growth 393
Pugh, A. 699–701
Pugh, D. S. 3281
Pulido, L. 1275
Pulitzer, J. 2873, 2897
Punch, S. 460
punctured equilibrium 1510
punishment
  corporal punishment 4022
  and corporate crime 827
  cruel and unusual punishment 2556
  and deterrence 802, 977
  extralegal punishments 1066–7
  and incapacitation 803
  objective and perceived punishments 1066
  organizational crime 3303
  and power-dependence theory 3601
  punitive-based power 3604
  and rehabilitation 803
  religious 3521–2
  and retribution 802, 804, 977
  school sanctions 4022
  see also capital punishment; prisons
punk rock feminism 3920
punk(s) 298, 324, 330, 719, 2649, 3493
  and cultural resistance 912
puns 2537
purdah 3722–3
pure relationships 1634
Puri, J. 1691
Purim 2452
Puritanism 1114, 1386, 3048, 3691, 3692, 4691
purposive behaviorism 257
Putnam, L. L. 3292

Putnam, R. 512, 618
Pygmalion effect *see* self-fulfilling prophecy
pyramid schemes 2021
Pythagoreans 186

Qatar 1724
Quadagno, Jill 71–3, 131
Quah, S. 2058–61
Quakers 1, 1114, 2768, 3205, 3692
qualitative audience reception studies 210
qualitative comparative analysis (QCA) 2969,
    3908
qualitative computing 3725–6
    focused coding 2025
    and grounded theory 2024–5
    initial coding 2025
qualitative data analysis 14
    quantitative data integration 647
    software 645–9
qualitative interviews 14
qualitative methods 2967–8, 3726–8
    and arts-based research 2971, 2972
    authenticity criteria 213, 214
    computer aided/mediated analysis 645
    and content analysis 776–7, 778
    and conversation analysis 794
    and criminology 861
    and critical qualitative research 867–70
    and evaluation 1500
    and fatherhood 1648
    and fieldwork 1443
    first, second, and third research waves 2978,
        2979
    and grounded theory 234, 2023, 2024–5
    and human resource management 2181
    and identity analysis 2219
    and interviewing 2408
    and journal writing 2447
    mixed methods research 2979–80
    and naturalistic enquiry 3163
    and organizational culture 949–50
    and paradigm theory 3355
    phenomenological perspective 3404
    qualitative research paradigm 2978
    rapport 3789–92
    reconstructive analyses 3822–5
    and sampling 3998–9
    secondary data analysis 4127
    and sociology 1397
    and textual analysis 3777
    Traditional Period for Qualitative Research
        2978

and triangulation 5075–6
and trustworthiness 5083–5
and variables 5176–9
see also qualitative computing
qualitative paradigm 3163
quality controls 1411
quality of life
    and exercise/fitness 1516
    measures 1296–7
    see also health lifestyles
quality management movement 19, 429
Quality Marriage Index (QMI) 2773
quality-of-life view, and euthanasia 1497
QUALRUS QDA program 647
QUANGOs (quasi-NGOs) 3212
quantification revolution in sociology 271, 4096
quantitative methods 2967, 2969, **3726–8**
    bootstrap method 2975
    and content analysis 776, 778
    and conversation analysis 794
    and criminology 852–63
    and cultural criminology 895
    and evaluation studies 1500
    and family migration 1606
    and feminist methodology 1702
    and grounded theory 2023
    and human resource management 2181
    and identity analysis 2218, 2219
    and interviewing 2407, 2408
    and key informants 2457
    and microsociology 3005
    and migrant research 1716
    mixed methods research 2979
    multiple regression 313
    and multivariate analysis 3120–1
    and organizational culture 950
    path analysis 313
    quantitative research paradigm 2978
    and statistical inference 2974
    and variables 5176–9
quantitative revolution 3726
quantum mechanics 1758
Quarrel of the Ancients and Moderns 3068
Quart, A. 359
quasi-experiments 1534
    and network research 2742
Québec 1487, 4188
queer geography 2162
queer movements 303
Queer Nation 1835
queer politics 3729, 4246
Queer, Questioning, and Intersexual (QQI) 2157

queer theory 3728–30, 4246, 4266–7
 and bisexuality 304
 and constructionism 1087
 and critical qualitative research 869
 cyberqueer 965
 and drag king troupes 1223
 and female masculinity 1658
 and femininities/masculinities 1663, 1664
 Foucauldian perspective 1777, 2114, 3728
 and gay and lesbian movement 1837
 gay and lesbian movement and 332
 gendering of sexualities 2612
 and heterosexual–homosexual binary 2155
 heterosexuality critique 2114
 intersectionist approach 2842
 key theorists 2612
 and lesbian feminism 2605
 origins 3728
 performance and peformativity 4258
 and postcolonialism 2982
 poststruturalism 4270
 radical feminist critique 3776
 and sexual identity 4240–1, 4266–7, 4270, 4292
 and the sexualization of organizations 3320
 and social movements 1874
 and transgender 5041
Quetelet, A. 828, 1101, 1118
quinciañera celebrations 2549
Quine, W. V. O. 1571, 1682, 3814, 4070
Quinney, R. 667, 819, 820, 840–1, 848, 859, 3384
quotas, immigration 1453, 2263, 3747
Qur'an 1655, 2003, 2424–5, 2428, 2552, 3723
Qur'an schools 4043

Rabin, Yitzhak 1814
race 3731–4
 and age identity 50
 and aging 69
 and American pluralism 3421–2
 biological thesis 2122, 3479
 Birmingham School studies 297, 299, 300
 and cognitive skills differentials 2654
 cultural definition 1476
 and dialectics 1149
 and diversity 1197, 1198
 and doing gender 1217
 and domestic violence 1220
 and educational attainment 1344
 and feminist standpoint theory 1711
 and gender and consumption 1851
 and health 2078–81
 historical scientific concept of 3013

 and hybridity 2189–90
 and hypersegregation 2196–9
 and intersectionality 2395, 2396
 and intimate union formation and
   dissolution 2415
 and juvenile delinquency 2455
 and literacy differentials 2656
 and melting pot metaphor 2944, 2945
 and occupational prestige 1342
 and partner choice 674
 and passing 3368–70
 and poverty 951, 1719
 and privilege 3649, 3650
 race categories (self-reported) 3757
 social construction 1457, 2078, 2080, 2396,
   2701, 3479, 4686
 and stratification 550, 4815–19
 and victimization 66
race-blindness 3750
race and crime 3734–7
 biological explanation 3735
 class–crime relationship 544
 cultural and structural explanation 3735–6
 slavery, historical impact of 3735
 underclass 3747–8
race and the criminal justice system 3737–40
 arrest decisions, and racial bias 3736, 3738,
   3766
 arrest and incarceration 3766
 capital punishment 386, 977
 incarceration 3733, 3736, 3738, 3739, 3766
race and ethnic consciousness 3740–3
 and Anglo-conformtiy 137
 and creolization 817–18
 and polyethnicity 3480
race and ethnic etiquette 3743–5
 paternalist system 3370–1
race and ethnic politics 3745–9
 and ethnic mobilization 1470
 interracial coalitions 124
 King and 2466–7
race hygiene movements 3683, 4115
race (racism) 1477, **3749–51**
 American Dilemma (Gunnar Myrdal) 128–9
 anti-essentialist understanding of 3014
 anti-Romany racism 3762
 and bio-power 1178
 black feminist resistance 307, 309
 black/white paradigm 3762
 colorblind racism 3615–16
 cultural racism 3014, 4347
 and cultural sociology 926

race (racism) (*cont'd*)
 and cyberculture 963
 and difference 1154
 and discriminatory aggression 1183
 and ecofeminism 1273, 1275
 empirical racisms 3013
 environmental racism 968, 1275, 1421, 2078, 2280, 3533
 and evolutionary theory 3751
 and feminist activism 1677
 and football 4347
 and hate crimes 2050
 and health care 2078, 2080
 and the heterosexual imaginary 2110
 and immigrants 3011
 institutional racism 3650, 3750, 3765–7
 and the Internet 966
 intersectionist approach 2852
 Jim Crow racism 15, 368, 508, 509, 510, 708, 1463, 3369, 3616, 3746
 laissez-faire racism 3616
 macro level perspective 3013
 and manifest destiny doctrine 2755
 and marginalization 2766
 and mind–body dualism 2918
 musical expression 3128
 neoracism 3750
 and occupational segregation 3246
 Orientalist discourse 3343
 and passing 3369–70
 racial conflict 659–62
 "scavenger" aspect 3768
 science fiction critique of 3495
 scientific racism 4113–15
 scriptural justification for racism 260
 and slavery 4337, 4338
 sport and race 4686–90
 and stigma 583–4
 xeno-racism 5299
 see also anti-Semitism (social change); anti-Semitism; apartheid and Nelson Mandela; discrimination; prejudice; segregation
race relations cycle 1457, 3011
race riots 192, 3448, 3686
race and schools 3751–4
 and the hidden curriculum 2117
 kindergarten 2463
 see also school segregation, desegregation
race science 155, 159
race/ethnicity and friendship 3754–6
 adolescent friendships 1800
 child friendships 1801–2

race/ethnicity, health, and mortality 3756–60
 low-mortality populations 1023–4
racial classification 3731, 3732
racial endogamy 1405
racial exclusion 196
racial exogamy 1405
racial gerrymandering 3733
racial hierarchy 3760–4, 3768
 caste system 404–5
 historical legacy of slavery 3761
 Linnaean classification 4114
 racial positionality 3763
 and racial/ethnic conflict 661
racial hygiene program 1169, 1489
racial identity 295, 296, 661, 2222, 3761
racial purity, cult of 2190
 see also one drop rule
racial real estate, blockbusting 316–18
racial relativism 908
racial science 4687
racial supremacism 3767
 see also white supremacists
racialization 345
 and masculinity 735
racialized gender 3764–5
 and doing gender 1218
 and education 1861
 and gender oppression 1872
 and one drop rule 3265–6
racism, structural and institutional 3765–7
 audit study 3766
 direct/indirect 3766
 see also race (racism)
racist movements 3767–71
 anti-Semitic 3767
 competition theory 3769
 frustration–reaction theory 3768–9
 ideologies and agendas 3767–8
 monitoring agencies 3770
 recruitment 3768
 see also Nazism; neo-Nazism; scientific racism; white supremacists
Radcliffe-Brown, Alfred R. 1996, **3771–3**
 and functionalism 1810
 and ritual 2699, 3974
 social anthropology 149, 2704, 2705, 3771–2
 and social structure 314
 structuralist theory of culture 938, 1809
Radek 159
radical behaviorism 257
Radical Caucus 2838

radical feminism 1666, 2610, 2621, **3773–6**
  consciousness raising 677, 3774
  critique of 3776
  and cultural feminism 902, 903, 905
  cultural feminist critique 2603
  and drag subculture 1225
  Goldman and 2004–7
  patriarchal critique 3921
  personal is political 3399–401, 3774
  and prostitution 3683
  self-help and service organizations 3775
  sexuality critique 4265–6
  and sport 1876–7, 4291–2
  theses 3773
  see also Riot Grrrls
radical skepticism 1436
Radicalesbians 2602
radio 2875, **3777–81**
  audiences 208
  and children's consumer culture 694
  community media 618, 627–8, 2905
  and cultural production 953
  ethnic radio stations 3135, 3486
  and experiential consumption 716
  and the home 2922
  mass medium 2874
  music broadcasting 3130, 3131, 3135
  public service broadcasting 2874, 3703
  ratings 3793
  regulation of 2914
  religious broadcasting 3780
  and social movements 3135
  sociology of radio 3777–81
radio advertising 31
radio frequency identification (RFID) 3270
Radway, J. 1915, 2101
Ragin, C. 2969, 3908
ragtime 3488
Rai Sanyo 2498
railway sector 933, 1308
rainbow coalition 3106
Rainwater, L. 1627
Rajan, S. 1691–2
Rajneeshpuram 886
Raley, S. 1030–3
rallies 780
Ramaphosa, C. 47
Rambo movies 877
Ramella, F. 3433–6
Ramirez, F. O. 1971–6
Ramírez, R. G. 1564–8
Ramji, H. 1153–5, 3722–3

Ramos, E. U. 2948
Ramos-Zayas, A. 3135
Rampton, S. 3674
Randolph, A. P. 508
random sample 3782–3, 4899
  and convenience samples 788
  and experimental design 1533, 1534
  and population surveys 1013
  sampling error 1013
  and statistical inference 789
randomized block analysis of variance design
    1536
randomized clinical trials 788
randomized controlled trials 2403, 2404, 2405
randomness 633
Rank, M. R. 1612–14, 1614, 3812–13
Ranke, L. von 143, 599
Rankin, J. 3774
Ransby, B. 309
Rao, H. 698
rap 708, 1050, 3486, 3487, 3557
rape *see* sexual violence and rape
rape crisis centers 3775, 3776
rape culture 3783–7
  backlash theory 3784–5
  feminist theory 3784–5
  victim-blaming 3785
  in war 1885–7
rape-free societies 3787
rape/sexual assault as crime 3787–9
  index crime 2277, 2278
Rapid Action for Process Improvement
    Deployment (RAPID) 2479
Rapoport, A. 2854
rapp, R. 2172, 3206
rapport 3789–92
Rapture, doctrine of the 3049
Rashotte, L. 4426–9
Rastafarianism 719, 1982, 3203, 3510
Rat Pack 3515–16
Rathenau Institute 690
ratings 3792–3
rational capitalism 1318–19, 1319, 2298
rational-choice institutionalism 3461
rational choice Marxism 2816
rational choice theories 3794–9
  and agency 61
  bounded rationality models 3795
  Coleman and 570, 572, 573
  and collective action 3232
  control balance theory 782–4
  and cooperation 3232

rational choice theories (*cont'd*)
  and crowd behavior 882–3
  and decision-making 982
  and ecological problems 1282
  and economics of religion 1315
  and educational segregation 1860
  and emotions and economy 1386, 1387
  and environmental criminology 1427
  and ethnic movements 1469
  explaining values 3797
  and game theory 1557, 3462
  means/ends 3795–8
  measuring values 3796
  and methodological individualism 3794
  and micro–macro links 2997, 3794, 3796
  network exchange approach 3798
  and norms 3232
  and principal–agent problems 573
  and racial/ethnic conflict 661
  revealed preference method 3796
  and secularization 3866–7, 4147–8
  and sexual practices 4249
  see also decision-making
rational choice theory: a crime-related perspective 837, **3799–802**, 3958
rational choice theory (and economic sociology) 3434, **3802–5**
rational expectations 1824
rational instrumentality 3312
rational legal authority 226, 230, **3805–8**
rationalism
  and atheism 197
  Cartesian 650, 1434, 2176
  conservatism and 679
  Deleuze on 999
rationalist epistemology 1434, 1435
rationality
  abstract rationality, alienation of 262
  bounded rationality 2748, 3282, 3287, 3313, 3795–6, 3800, 3802
  bureaucratic rationality 3312
  calculative 935
  communicative rationality 2907
  economic view 1387
  Enlightenment 897, 909, 1839, 2294, 2907, 3213, 3635
  formal 3808
  goal-oriented rationality 3313
  and human relations 935
  hyperrationality 3803
  instrumental rationality 518, 876, 2235, 3233, 3312, 3314

  irrationality of rationality 2690
  Kantian 874
  and liberalism 2623
  organizational rationality 3295
  political 378, 2576
  practical 3808
  and public museums 3126
  "rational" liberalism 2624
  scientific-technical 260
  sociocultural rationality 4077
  substantive 3808, 3809
  theoretical 3808
  and traditions 3338
  Weberian 874, 876
rationalization 3808–10
  capitalist rationalization 3215
  functional rationalization 378
  and litigation, increased 2927
  and McDonaldization 2689, 2690
  McDonaldization 723, 2300, 2689, 2690, 2883, 2965, 3312, 3567
  and modernization 3074, 3075
  organizational rationalization 942
  self-rationalization 378, 3809
  sport 4650
  technology–rationalization relation 3810
Ratzenhofer, Gustav 2038, **3810–12**
Rauh, F. 2040
Rauscher, L. 1892–5
Raven, C. 329
Ravenstein, E. G. 3011
Ravetz, J. 275–6
raw experience 1483
Rawlins, W. K. 247–50, 1788–91
Rawls, A. W. 1250–61
Rawls, John 3812–13
  and rationality 3107
  theory of justice 2954, 3107, 3233, 3812–13
  and value pluralism 3107
Ray, L. 512–13, 1956–60, 4581–3, 5187–8
Ray, N. 218
Raymond, C. 920
re-enchantment of environments 759, 1642
reactivism
  and deviance 1123–6
  moderate reactivism 1125
  strict reactivism 1124
reactivity (observational research)
  pesonal 3236
  procedural 3236
readership as social practice 242

Reagan, Ronald 875, 1676, 2289, 2337, 2420,
2749, 2761, 3516, 3664, 4565
Reaganism 1061
and homophobia 2611
and industrial relations 2512
and millenarianism 3047
and neoconservatism 3172
and privatization 3648
and the pro-life agenda 3654
propaganda 3674
welfare backlash 4494
real estate capital 1919
real estate development, and urban change
3115
real estate speculation and capital formation 389
real virtuality, culture of 3181
realism
analytical realism 3366
and empiricism 1434
metaphysical realism 3235, 3236
new left realism 3196–8
photographic realism 3405
**realism and relativism: truth and
objectivity 3813–16**
Comtean realism 655
and documentaries 1212
and emergent thinking 635
and environmental problems 1422
and interpretivism 1436
reality
figured reality 2432
and intersubjectivity 2400, 2401
micro–macro links 2997, 3003–4
and naturalistic enquiry 3161, 3162
negotiated 2401
social construction 686, 1087, 3400, 3403
reality TV 2827, 3490–2, 4674
audiences 3491
and documentaries 1211
ethics 3491
post-conventional 837
realpolitik 3093
reason, Foucault's problematization of 1773,
1774
reason/emotion duality 1391
reasoning
conventional 837
legal 2584
pre-moral 837
see also decision-making; rational choice
theory
rebellion

and anarchism 136
and anomie 597
and deviance 1103
and sport 1134
and strain theory 1134
rebirth, Buddhist doctrine of 371
recapitulation theory 302
Recaséns, L. 2948
reception studies 3816–18
reception theory 210
recidivism 3818–19
frozen time method of calculation 3818
risk factors for 3819
survival rate analysis 3818
reciprocity
and attraction 203
and friendship 1793
and intergenerational transfers 2367, 2368
population–environment relationship 3531
and rapport 3790
see also social exchange theory
Reckless, Walter C. 443, 846
Reclaim the Streets 981
recognition 3819–22
recommender systems 639, 643
reconciliation *see* peace and reconciliation
processes; Truth and Reconciliation
Commissions
Reconstruction 507
reconstructive analyses 3822–5
Recording Industry Association of America
(RIAA) 3489, 3490
recursive feature elimination (RFE) 2969
recycling 1421, 1425
Red Army Faction 1166
Red Brigades 4332
Red Cross 3339, 4539
Redding, W. C. 3291, 3294
Redfield, R. 320, 443, 1373–4, 1577, 2948
Redhead, S. 760, 1915
redistribution thesis 1939, 4401
Redlich, F. 2933
**redlining 316, 317, 706, 2078, 3733,
3825–8, 4149**
Redmon, D. 980–1
Redstockings 677, 1675, 3773
reduction in maximum flow (RMF) 1513
reductionism 635
economic reductionism 1955, 2648
psychological reductionism 1805, 3138
redundancy (knowledge) 2717
Reed, M. 3664

Reeder, L. 2934
Reefer Madness 1109
Reekie, G. 743
Rees, A. 1503–12, 3625–8, 4073–4
Rees, C. R. 2120–3
reference groups 3828–9, 4321
referenda 3454
reflexive modernization 3829–30
    and uncertainty 5089
reflexivity 287, 348, 3819, **3830–4**
    destabilization 3831–2
    and emotionality 1379
    and family and community 1577
    and feminist methodology 1702–3
    and *flânerie* 1762
    and globalization 1990
    and language usage 2536
    and metatheory 2965
    modern cultural program 524–5
    and modernization 1174
    and narrative 3141
    and the self 2863
    and strong objectivity 4845
Reformation *see* Protestant Reformation
refrigerator mother theory 1573
refugee movements 3834–6
    and immigration policy 2262
    and migration regulation 2256
refugees 3011, 3021, 3022, **3837–8**
    definitions 3834, 3837
    and diaspora 1152
    environmental refugees 3533
    internally displaced persons (IDPs) 3835
    and migration regulation 2256
    see also asylum seekers
Regan, T. 140
Reger, J..1672–81
Regets, M. 3026
regional associations 1472
regional ecologies 3123
regional identity 1476
regionalism 1407, 3123
registers
    parish registers 1045–6
    population registers 1011, 1012–13
regression and regression analysis 3838–9
    and demographic data 1016
    and hierarchical linear models 2119
    and mobility analysis 3063
    multiple regression 3839
    ordinary least squares (OLS) linear
        regression 3838, 3839

path analysis 3373–4
probit regression model 3839
and quantitative methods 3728
regret, politics of 589
regulation theory 1298, **3840–3**
    and Marxism 2816
regulatory science 4636
rehabilitation 337
Reible, H. L. 1762–3
Reich, Wilhelm 3843–4, 3883
    and sexual liberation 2160
Reiche, R. 2159
Reichenbach, H. 4956
Reicher, S. D. 1367
Reid, I. de A. 2466
reification 757, 2691, **3844–5**
    of aging 1929
    and alienation 3845
    capitalist 874
    of cultural systems 1991
    Feuerbach and 1748
    Lukács and 757, 1148, 2679
    Simmel and 2679
    of taste 953
Reiman, J. 820
reincarnation 1400
reinforcement 65
Reinharz, S. 1702
reintegrative shaming theory 1, 2506
Reisman, D. A. 1301, 2822, 3334, 4342–3
Reiss, A. 846, 2340, 2960
Reith, Sir John 2875, 3706
Reitman, B. L. 2006
relational cohesion theory 1369, **3845–8**
relational politics *see* identity politics/relational
        politics
relationship commitment 2673–4
relationship investment 1603
relationships *see* specific kinds e.g sibling ties
relativism
    and absolutism 1436
    aesthetic relativism 3814
    biological relativism 908
    cognitive relativism 3814
    and crime 1092
    cultural relativism 908–9, 1083, 1449,
        1478, 1991
    and deviance 1083, 1092, 2207
    epistemological relativism 908
    ethical relativism 3814
    expedient relativism 4587
    moral relativism 1478

and paradox 3813
philosophical relativism 2474
racial relativism 908
sociocultural relativism 979, 1078, 4585–9
relativity theory 1758, 4116
relaxation, and leisure 2598
reliability 3848–51
and effect sizes 1346
standardized educational tests 4722
reliability generalization 3850–1, **3851–3**
reliability induction 3851
religion 3853–64
and animism 141, 142
asceticism 185–9
and belief 198
club model of 1315
and collective memory 591
competing movements 641–2, 750
and consumption 713, 745, 750–2
counter-cultural religious movements 325
cultural hold of religion 3867–8
and death and dying 974
declining religiosity 4146, 4147
definitions and criteria 3853–4, 3857–63
deinstitutionalization 440
and deviant beliefs 1140
and direct action 1166
and discrimination 1182
economics of 1315–17
etymology 3853, 3854
and Eurocentrism 1982
fundamentalism 507
and globalization 1980–3
group religious practices 1576
and health care 901
and health and well-being 100
and illness and mortality 1184
institutional religion 198, 1980–1
integrative function 1810
interreligious marriages 1198
and magic 2699
Marxist theory 33, 549, 3049, 3524, 4145
and *moralpolitik* 3093–4
non-Christian religions 1493
origins 3629, 3631
outreach 642
para-religion 3861
and partner choice 674, 675
and patriarchy 3379
philosophy of religion 483
pluralism 751
and popular culture 3514

pre-animist theory of 3629–30
quasi-religion 3861
religious belief 258, 475, 1256–7, 1317, 1476, 3858, 3866
religious economies 751
religious identity 198
religious participation 751
Roman religion 174
and science 3865
and sexuality 4275–9
shrine/pilgrimage religion 1054
and socialization 4567
socioconstructionist approach 3862
sport and religion 4690–3
state-subsidized religion 1316
substantive perspective 3864–5
and suicide 4881
and traumatogenic change 595
and women 939, 1053, 1315, 1600, 5265–6
see also animism; asceticism; atheism; church; civil religion; Islam; millenarianism; new religious movements; Orthodoxy; popular religiosity; primitive religion; rite/ritual; sacred; sect; spirituality; theology
Religion of Humanity 650, 652–3
religion, sociology of 485–6, 3858–63, **3864–9**
al-Biruni and 111, 112
and atheism 198
and charisma 434
denominationalism 1051–6
and folk Hinduism 1764–6
functionalist perspective 3865
popular religiosity 3518–24
see also secularization
religions, African 3869–71
religious authority 228
religious broadcasting 3780
religious cults 1141, **3871–6**
social psychological aspects 884–7
see also charismatic movement; millenarianism; specific cults
religious education 3689
see also schools, religious
religious extremism 1315
religious fundamentalism 507, 1473, 1982
and anti-terrorism movements 1297
and class unrest 2816
and deviance 1083
and suicide attacks 2800
religious gatherings 880
religious healing systems 630, 631
religious homogamy 675, 2416

religious identities 198, 2225
religious individualism 3689
religious intermarriage 2416
religious intolerance 1451
religious liberalism 4278
religious nationalism 507
religious orders
    asceticism 186
    female 1874
    see also monasticism
religious persecution 3203, 3348
religious pluralism 1316, 2131
religious rites 730
religious schools 1325, 4052–5
religious skepticism 2296–7
religious vocation 3689
Relman, A. 3658
reluctant suburbs 1551
remarriage
    biosociological theory 293
    blended families 695
    cohabitation and 567, 1585
    and family diversity 1589
    and fatherhood 1649
    and kinship 2471
    and marital quality 2774
Remennick, L. 1151–3, 5064–6
remittances 3081
remorse management 1383
Ren Jiyu 670
Renaissance 493, 718, 722, 1262, 4157
Renan, E. 260, 3146, 3154
Rengo 1414
Renoir, Jean 1753
Renov, M. 1212
rent gap theory 1917, 1919
rent-seeking behavior 1546
rentiers 2034, 2036
Renzulli, L. 4941–5
reparations 3876–7
replicability analyses 3877–9
    and convenience samples 789
replication, and experimental design 1531, 1534
representation 3879–82
    and arts-based methods 2971
    of the body 335
    conceptual 259
    crisis of 231, 3832
    and empiricism 1434
    knowledge representation 3725
    and life history research 2643
    and mixed methods research 2979–80

and performance measurement 3397–8
politics of 300
and postcolonialism 3548
and reality, structuration of 1700
relations of 229
textual 299–300
and transcription 5036–7
and visual sociology 2986–9
representationalist epistemology 3235
repression
    channeling 4476
    coercion 4476
    sexual 5045
    threat model 4477
repression of social movements 4475–8
repressive hypothesis 3882–5
repressive law 581
reproduction
    alternative reproductive strategies 823
    control over 2308
    naturalistic accounts 332
    pathologizing of 332
    selective 2937–8
    see also contraception; fertility
reproduction theories 2116, 2117
reproductive behaviors 1610
reproductive health 4235
reproductive health care 1609, 2620
reproductive labor 1202
    and bifurcated consciousness 274
reproductive liberty 558
reproductive morbidities 1609
reproductive rights 1609, 1907, 1908
reproductive tourism 2172
reproductive tract infections (RTIs) 2320, 2321
reproductivity 1744–5
    gross reproduction rate (GRR) 1744
    net reproduction rate (NRR) 1744
reprogenetics 1490, 1907
Republic of Korea 1728
republicanism 171, **3885–6**
    and the common school system 4040
    and neoconservatism 3173
Republicans 2233, 2234, 3454, 3967
reputation 3886–8
reputation systems 643
Rescher, N. 1819, 2287
research
    institutional review boards and sociological
        research 2345–51
    journal writing 2447–8
    research productivity 3667

with vulnerable populations 2347
see also peer review and quality control in
    science
research and development (R&D) 3438, 3439
researcher role 1444
residence and work permits 2262
residential segregation 370, 2196–7, 2305,
    2306, 3733, **3888–91**, 4149, 4150
    African Americans 2305, 2306, 3707
    see also ethnic enclaves; public housing;
        redlining; social exclusion; steering, racial
        real estate
residues 3361
resistance
    absenteeism as 6
    creative resistance 2397
    and cultural production 953
    culture jamming 946
    language as tool of 2984
    and psychoanalysis 3694
    rituals of resistance 3937
    sport as 4687, 4699–701
Reskin, B. 131, 2516
Resnick, D. 2910
resocialization 3891–3
resource allocation 3366, 3396
resource-based view (RBV) 2476
resource dependence theory 2717, 3282–3, 3301
resource mobilization theory 20, 2559,
    3893–8
    adherents/constituents/bystanders 3894
    and consumer movements 697–8
    cooptation/appropriation 3895
    cultural resources 3896
    and emotions 1390
    and framing 1780, 1783
    and gay and lesbian movement 1835–6
    human resources 3896
    and law–economy relation 2559
    material resources 3896
    moral resources 3895–6
    music as organizing tool 3134–5
    and new social movement theory 3208
    organizational-entrepreneurial branch 3894
    patronage 3895
    and political sociology 3460
    resource aggregation 3895
    and revolutions 3909
    self-production 3895
    social movements 3065, 3066, 3259, 3260,
        3686, 4468, 4479–80
    social organizational resources 3896

resource model of nature 1291
respite care 402
Respondent Driven Sampling 2139
responsibility
    global 1992
    social 2759, 3680
responsibilization of individuals 1178
restaurants 723, 752
    back region staff 1456
    ethnic 768, 1453, 1455–6, 1961
    hybrid menus 2191
Restorationism 440
restorative justice 819
restraint theory *see* self-control theory
restrictive covenants 706, 3748, **3898–9**
    blockbusting and 317
    racially restricted 3898, 3899
retail businesses
    globalized 763
    see also shopping; shopping malls
retaliatory hate crimes 2049
retirement 3899–903
    age and gender 3900
    baby boomers 3902
    and disengagement theory 1928
    and domestic labor responsibilities 1840,
        1841
    and generational change 1901
    and leisure 2593
    and lifestyle migration 3022
    and marital power relations 2547
    and pensions 85
    postponement 1740
    women in 1840
retirement age 1903
retirement communities 3903–6
retirement income 537
retreatism 1103
    and anomie 597
    and sport 1134
retrospective reinterpretation of deviance 2207
revanchism 1920
reverse discrimination 44
reverse racism 44, 46
revolutionary consciousness 2227, 2228
revolutionary feminism 1685, 1686
revolutionary syndicalism 2996
revolutions 535, 785, 1885, **3906–15**, 3940
    actors 3910–11
    anti-colonial revolutionary movements 3907
    Arendt and 170, 171–2
    and class conflict 539

revolutions (*cont'd*)
  and collective action 575
  and cultural resistance 912
  and cultural sociology 923
  failed revolutions 3907, 3910
  Marxist theories 575, 3908, 3915, 3916
  non-violent revolution 4462
  outcomes 3912
  political process theory 3909
  political revolutions 3907
  resource mobilization perspective 3909
  reversed revolutions 3907
  revolutionary class consciousness 540
  Skocpol and 664
  and social order construction 2577
  spontaneity 2687
  and traumatogenic change 594
  workers' revolts 609
revolutions, sociology of 3915–17
Revson, C. 737
reward expectations theory 1525
Rex, J. 344, 3420, 3420–1
Reynolds, L. 2290
Rheingold, H. 962
rhetoric 1227, 1914
  mixed methods research 2979
  and orality 3278–9
  and organizational communication 3292
  and qualitative textual analysis 3777
  quantitative research paradigm 2978
rhizomatics 1000, 3574
Rhodes, C. 1439–42, 2722–5
Ribeiro, D. 342
Ricardo, David
  and commodity relations 607–8
  and markets 2778, 2779, 2837
  and political economy 1300, 1302, 1304, 2797
  theorem of comparative advantage 3595
Riccardo, G. 141–2, 5019–22
Rice, Condoleezza 3175
Rice, J. C. 2659–60
Rich, A. 638, 639, 904, 905, 1679, 2113, 2602, 2604, 3775, 4265
Richards, G. 919, 920
Richardson, D. 2611, 2613
Richardson, J. T. 2440, 2441
Richardson, Samuel 3581
Richie, B. 309
Richmond, M. 4542
Rickert, H. 2484, 2756, 2968
Ricoeur, P. 2109, 2231
  and collective memory 593

Ridgeway, C. L. 1526, 3245, 4756–9
Rieger, J. H. 2457–8
Riegle-Crumb, C. 1859–61
Riesman, David 312, 594, 744, 1807, **3917–20**
  Fromm–Riesman collaboration 1807
Riessman, C. K. 2643
Rigakos, G. S. 1121–3
Rigauer, B. 1751, 2236
Righteous Babe 1677
rights
  of man 170
  workers' rights 2750
  see also animal rights movements; civil rights; human rights
Riker, W. 1651–2
Riley, D. 3450–5
Riley, K. 1424
Riley, Matilda White 131, **1934–5**
Rinder, I. 3009
Riordan, Cornelius 4055–9
Riot Grrrls 726, 1677, **3920–1**
riots 779, **3921–6**
  and crowd behavior 882, 3922–3
  and emergent norm theory 882
  outcomes 3925
  strain and breakdown theories 4480
Risch, N. 1832
risk, risk society, risk behavior, and social problems 333, **3926–32**
  adolescents 1547
  and biomedical science 2173
  and crime 822
  cultural theory 3929
  and decision-theory 3927–8
  and deviance 1128–9
  and disasters 1174, 1175
  and emotions and economy 1386, 1387
  and environmental degradation 1421
  financialization, and risk reward 3325
  and gender 1857, 3535
  and gene therapy 2940
  and genetic engineering 1906
  and global threats 3466
  health risk behavior 2083–4
  and HIV/AIDS 2138
  and individualization 2285
  information-theoretical approach 3927
  and masculinity 1842, 3535
  measurement of 3926, 3929, 4076–9, 4082
  and medical malpractice 2928, 2929
  and participation in sport 2121
  pscyhological risk analysis 3929

and reflexive modernization 3830
risk assessment 3930, 4077–8
risk communication 3929, 3930
risk management 3930
risk reduction 3618
risk and uncertainty 1387
and scientific regulation 4082, 4083
and self-report 1128–9
and sexual behavior 1609
social categorizations of risk 3929
and systems theory 3929–30
and uncertainty 5089
Riska, Elianne 2075–8
Risley, T. 2655
Risse, T. 2185
Rist, R. 4176
Ritchey, F. J. 2928–9
Ritchie, I. 1239–42
rite of passage 3932–3, 3937
and the life course 2631
religious 4146
and socialization 2931, 4568
rite/ritual 3933–6
African religions 3870
ancient Roman 3853
cognitivist theories 3935
definition 3933–4
ecological theories 3935
instrumental/non-instrumental theories 3935
and magic 2696, 2699
popular religiosity 3523
totemic rite 1254
ritual 3936–8
communitas 618, 754
consumption rituals 753–4
Deadhead community 3505
degradation rituals 3892
Durkheim and 1254, 1257, 1376, 1385, 1389, 2032, 2366, 2474, 3146, 3936–7
and facework 1553
and football hooliganism 1768
heterosexual 3729
Hindu 2130
and homosexuality 1078
interaction rituals 3937
order 754
Orthodox church 3690
and political expression 779
potlatch ritual 704, 1938, 1939, 1940, 4908, 5220
and rites of passage 3933
ritual artifacts 753

ritual audience 753–4
ritual performance roles 753
ritual scripts 753
and the sacred 3974
sacrifice 3980–5
and Satanism 4011
sexual rituals 4275–6
and social interaction 1997
and socialization 2931
and solidarity 1389
and sport 1131, 1134, 2236
symbolic components 1389
Taoist 4926
tourism and 763
transformation 754
ritualism
and anomie 597
and deviance 1102–3
Ritzer, George 702, 704, 705, 712–13, 723, 744, 1357–60, 1809, 2125, 2193, 2964–7, 3947
and cathedrals of consumption 734, 752, 2883–4, 3567
credit card analysis 1759, 1761
and glocalization 1994
and grobalization 1963, 1994, 2022
and hyperconsumption 2193
McDonaldization thesis 704, 738, 759, 763, 1187, 2689, 2690, 2883, 2928, 3312, 3567, 3810
and paradigmatic metatheory 2963
and the professions 3663
and secrecy 4133
and spectacular consumption 759
and theming 1642
Ritzer, J. 3506, 3513–15
Riuesch, J. 248
Rivera, J. de 1376
Rivera, S. 1225
Rivero, A. 1004, 1007
Rizal, José 1492, 3938–41
Rizova, P. S. 239–40, 659–62, 3307–10, 4952–5
road rage 3087
Robbers Cave experiments 1540
robbery 3041–2
data 1128
female offenders 4192
UCR definition 2278
Robbins, L. 3176
Robert E. Park, Ernest W. Burgess, and urban social research 3943–5
Róbert, P. 4824–7
Robert, P. 2339–44

Roberts, A. 295–7, 2393–5
Roberts, J. K. 2118–20
Roberts, K. 2588, 2591
Robertson, J. 2516
Robertson, R. 1950, 1957, 1964–70, 1968, 1980, 1990
Robin Hood hypothesis 2276
Robin Wood 1284
Robins, L. 2776
Robinson, C. 3834–6
Robinson, D. T. 35–8
Robinson, J. 1032, 3178, 4712
Robinson, K. S. 3495
Robinson, P. 2468
Robinson, W. S. 2118–19, 3780
Robinson Crusoe metaphor 3486
Robles, B. 2550
Robnett, B. 3776
Rochberg-Halton, E. 742, 743
rock 'n' roll 3132, **3492–4**
    alleged deleterious effect 2826
    and the existential self 1522
    see also individual performers
Rock, Paul 1135–40
rock-climbing 2222
Rockefeller Foundation 1489
Rocker, R. 136
Rodney, W. 2838
Roe, A. 3286
Roe v. *Wade* 1675, 1699, 3652, 3653
Roemer, J. 1544
Rogalin, C. L. 202–4, 2567–70
Rogers, C. 2566
Rogers, E. M. 2738
Rogers, R. G. 4590–3
Rogowski, R. 2675–8
Rohlinger, D. A. 3649–51, 4571–4
Rohypnol 1233
Rojek, C. 312–13, 415–17, 2357–8, 2590, 3489–90, 3515–16
Rokeach, M. 983
role 3945–8
    gender role ideology 1844, 1867, 3535
    and the generalized other 1899
    role conflict in organizations 3342
    self-other roles 3946
    structural analysis 3945, 3946
role conflict 3945, 3953
role differentiation 3074
role discrimination 1183
role diversification 3074
role embracement 2209

role engulfment 2209
role identities 2204, 2205, 2211, 2216, 2224, 2225–6
role-making 2203, 3947, 3949
role models, female, in organizations 1889
role overload 3953
role-sets 3945
role strain 3945, 3953
role-taking 3186, 3228, 3237, 3946, **3948–51**
    Mead and 2862, 3946, 3948
    and observational research 3237, 3239–40
    and self-awareness 3056, 3187
    and semiotics 3056
    and volunteering 3681
role theory 2487–8, **3951–4**
    cognitive role theory 3953
    and consensus 3953
    and constructionism 686
    and disability 1170
    functional role theory 3952
    and gender 1667, 2488
    and gender and friendship 1863
    gender role ideology 1867–8
    Merton and 127, 2486
    organizational role theory 3952–3
    and role conformity 2488
    structural role theory 3952
    symbolic interactionist role theory 3952
Rolling Stones 3493, 3494
Roma people 590, 1152, 3108
    and criminality 2663
    Holocaust 1458, 1489, 1496
Roman civil law 2183
Roman, P. 116–19
Romance of the Rose 1135–6
Romania
    anti-Jewish violence 3428
    bilingual education 280
    nationalism 3145, 3347
    Orthodox Church 3345, 3346, 3347
Romano-Germanic law 2552
Romantic movement 148
    and authorship/originality 730
    conservatism 2758
    and consumer culture 742, 751
    and cultural sociology 923
    and nationalism 3144, 3155
Rome
    Cesarism 411, 412–13
    empire 1392, 3037
    imperial Rome 2990
    republicanism 3885

Römer, L. von 2158
Romo, H. 1269–71
Roof, W. C. 1053
Rook, D. 753, 754
Roos, P. 2516
Roosevelt, Eleanor 307
Roosevelt, F. D. 2233, 2519, 2875
Roosevelt, Theodore 1133
root workers 2079
Rootes, C. 1428–33, 4864–9
Ropp, S. C. 2185
Rorty, R. 2973, 3552, 3832
Rosa, E. A. 1423–6
Rose, A. 2822
Rose, D. 1919
Rose, H. 1682
Rose, N. 1273
Rose, P. 1133
Rosen, H. 1087
Rosenbaum, J. E. 622, 4029–32
Rosenberg, Morris 3954–6
   and self-concept 4161, 4162
Rosenberg, R. 1956
Rosenfeld, Rachel 841, **3956–7**
Rosenkopf, L. 2730
Rosenstock, I. 2105
Rosh Hashanah 2452
Ross, C. 1517
Ross, E. A. 130, 131, 2170, 2171, 3586
Rossi, A. S. 131, 1670, 2960
Rossi, J. S. 1193
Rossi, M. 442
Rossi, P. H. 1192, 1540
Rostow, W. W. 1068, 1566, 1567, 2298, 2490, 2491
Roszak, T. 809
Roth, B. 3776
Roth, J. 479
Roth, P. 2834
Roth, S. 1869–70, 4451–3
Rothbard, M. 136
Rothchild, J. 1843–5
Rothenberg, J. 2421
Rothman, B. K. 3104
Rothschild, M. A. 157
Rothstein, V. 1674
Rotter, J. B. 2063
Rouch, J. 1211
"rough music" 1165
Rousseau, D. M. 1004, 1007
Rousseau, Jean-Jacques 857, 2706
   and civil religion 506

and Durkheim 1251, 1258
and liberty 2186
and materialism 2837
and *moralpolitik* 3093
noble savage 654
and property 613
and social science 2186
sociological theory 4600
Rousseau, Nicole 3368–70
routine activity theory 3957–60
   and crime hot spots 828
   and deviance 1102, 1105
   and environmental criminology 1427
Rove, K. 3471
Rowan, B. 936, 1307, 2351, 2353, 2585, 2714, 3283, 3333
Rowbotham, S. 274
Rowe, D. 4668–77
Rowe, M. 731
Rowlingson, K. 2663–7
Rowntree, S. 1612
Roy, O. 2427
Royal Society 599, 3389, 4089, 4102
Royal Society for the Prevention of Cruelty to Animals (RSPCA) 138
Royce, J. 2861, 3363
Rubin, G. 333, 2114, 2155, 2604, 2841–2, 3775
Rubington, E. 1127
Rubinstein, W. D. 1913
Rucht, D. 1976–80, 2996–7, 3257–62
Ruddick, S. 1438, 1682, 1888, 2848, 3104
Ruef, M. 2756–9
Rueschemeyer, D. 1002
rugby 2222, 2918, 3160
Ruiz, C. 1565
Ruiz, V. 2550
rule breaking 10, 13
ruling relations 3960–1
Rumbaut, R. 2254
Rumbo, J. D. 727–9
Rummel, R. J. 1910
Rumney, P. N. S. 2702–4
rumors 1141
Rumsfeld, Donald 3175
Runciman, W. G. 871, 2627, 3979
running away from home 1858, 4193
Rupp, L. J. 1223–6
rural aging 3961–3
rural cultural tourism 921
rural environmental degradation 1423
rural schools 4042
Rural Sociological Association 133

rural sociology 3963–7
  and elder care 1351
  Japan 4903–4
  population growth 1550
  radio, impact of 3780
  rural and village-based family system 1594
  Sorokin and 4620–1
Rush, B. 836, 3265–6
Rushdie, Salman 2191
Ruskin, John 1165
Russ, J. 3495
Russell, Bertrand 640
Russell, C. T. 2548–9
Russell Sage Foundation 2933
Russia
  AIDS 106
  anti-Semitism 158
  consumer culture 744
  consumer movements 697, 698
  diaspora 1152, 3345
  and federalism 1652
  Jehovah's Witnesses 2439
  Jewish population 2453
  life expectancy 1026
  lifestyle practices 2062
  machine politics 3445
  medical sociology 2935
  Orthodox Church 3345, 3346, 3347, 4223
  pogroms 3427
  populism 3537
  public school system 4051
  religious discrimination 2440
  sexual cultures 4223–6
  World War I 1886
  see also Soviet Union
Russian Civil War 3427
Russian Revolution (1907) 3427
Russian Revolution (1919) 158–9, 594, 615,
    705, 865, 2006, 2014, 2685, 2686, 2687,
    3908, 3909, 3912, 3915, 3916
Rust, P. C. 303, 2041
Rustbelt 3967–9, 5096
Rustin, B. 509
Rutherford, J. F. 2439
Rwandan genocide *see* Burundi and Rwanda
    (Hutu, Tutsi)
Ryan, B. 676–8, 3399–401, 4196–8
Ryan, J. M. 712–13, 734–5, 1357–60, 2022–3,
    2194–6, 3350–1, 3569–72, 4908–9
Ryan, M. T. 701–7, 1199–201, 2580–2
Ryder, N. 1731
Rytina, S. 3247–50

Saada, F. F. 2699
Sabbatian movement 3048
Sabel, C. F. 2299, 2829
Sacerdote, B. 1315
Sacher-Masoch, L. von 3985
Sachs, M. L. 4662–4
Sacks, Harvey 1485, 1995, **3971**
  and conversation analysis 791–2, 1181, 1485,
    2032, 2363, 2537
sacralization 742
  of the body 741
sacred 3972–6
  and animism 142
  beliefs and 262
  magical use of 3976
  and popular religiosity 3523
  sacred–secular relationship 3094
  sacredness of the individual 1447
  and totemism 3972
sacred, eclipse of the 3966–7
sacred and secular law, separation of 2557
sacred sites 2280
sacred/profane 3977–80
  Durkheim and 1257, 3873, 3974, 3977–80
  and health/illness 2081
  and magic 2699
sacrifice 3980–5
  communion 3981
  firstfruit offer 3981
  gift-sacrifice 3981
  martyrdom 2799–801
  sacredness 3972
sacrificial practices 946
Sadducees 2450
Sade, Marquis de 3540, 3569, 3985
sadism 2158, 2493
sadomasochism 303, 330, 1746, **3985–7**,
    4231, 4285
  lesbian community 2603
Sadovnik, A. R. 5112–15
Safavid movement 3048
Safe Motherhood Initiative (SMI) 2317
safer sex 108, 2161, **3987–9**
  cyber sex 3989
  and dissonance theory 564
  and masturbation 2833, 3989
  and oral sex 3278
  telephone sex 3989
Sagarin, E. 2158
Sage, G. H. 3440–1, 4699–702
Sahlin-Andersson, K. 2721
Sahlins, M. 1939

Said, Edward W. 3552, **3989–90**
  and colonial discourse 2984
  Orientalism 603, 1395–6, 1482, 2534, 2981,
    3343–4, 3989–90
Sainsaulieu, Renaud 3990–2
Sainsbury, D. 1272
Saint Onge, J. M. 4590–3
Saint-Simon, H. de 650, 1258, 1542, 2836,
  4549
saints 3520–1, 3522, 3523
Saito, Y. 2097
Sakata, K. 2497
Sala, M. L. R. 2950
"salad bowl" metaphor 25, 2944
Salais, R. 2741
Salamé, G. 2427
salary individualization 2750
salary men 3200, **3992–4**
Salem witch trials 2506
Saletan, W. 3654–5
Salgado, E. 2950
salience hierarchy 2224, 2225
Salkind, N. J. 146–7
saloons 766–7
Salt, H. 150
Saltzman, L. E. 1219
Salvídar, R. 2550
Sambanis, N. 1472
same-sex bonding 2155
same-sex friendship 877
same-sex marriage/civil unions 2162, 2414,
  3995–8
  accommodation and resistance dichotomies
    3996
  and child outcomes 1624
  commitment ceremonies 3997
  and domestic duties 2608
  and domestic violence 1220
  and egalitarianism 3083
  and family units 1575
  Freudian theory 1071
  friendship ethos 2608
  and gay and lesbian movement activism 1835
  legal recognition 1590, 3995, 3996
  money management 3081, 3082, 3083
  and monogamy 2608, 3997
  and parenthood 2608
  and sexual citizenship 4208
  and *The Simpsons* 3514
Sammond, N. 607–12
sampling
  bootstrap method 2974–5

cluster sampling 3782
critical case sampling 3999
extreme or deviant case sampling 3998
homogenous sampling 3999
maximum variation sampling 3999
and mixed methods research 2979
multistage sampling 3782
observational research 3239
probability sampling 3782, 4899
purposive sampling 3998–9
resampling procedures 2974
sampling with replacement method 2975
and sexuality research 4288
stratified random sampling 3782
systematic random sampling 3782
theoretical sampling distribution 2975
typical case sampling 3999
volunteer sampling 3782
  see also random sample
sampling distributions 4744
sampling frame 3782–3
sampling, qualitative (purposive) 3998–9
Sampson, R. J. 830, 831, 2073, 2455
samsara 371, 2130
Samuel, L. 3737–40
Samuelson, P. 2490, 2776, 2778
San Francisco Mime Troupe 1165
San Juan, E. 2551
San people 4209
sanctity-of-life view, and euthanasia 1497
Sanday, P. 2153
Sandefur, M. 2004–7
Sandel, M. J. 1491
Sanders, C. R. 320, 2175–8
Sanders, E. 2420, 2421
Sanders, J. M. 1459–63
Sanders, J. R. 1461, 1498–502
Sanderson, S. K. 263–5, 662–5, 1000–4,
  1002–3, 2140–2, 4083–8, 4247–9
Sandilands, C. 1275
Sandler, S. 1317
Sandoval, C. 1711, 1713, 2551
Sandvoss, C. 761
SANE 1806
Sanford, M. M. 714–16, 1289–91
Sanger, M. 1489, 2841
Sankara, T. 1656
Sanskritization 4000–3
  and folk Hinduism 164, 1764
santana 371
Santana, R. 4354–8
Santayana, G. 3363

Santorno, G. 3488
Sao Paolo 2991
Sapir, E. 909, 2362, 2537, 2866
Sapir-Whorf hypothesis 2537
Sapiro, V. 3419
Sappho 2609
Saraswati, Pandita Ramabai 4003–6
Sarkar, Benoy Kumar 1492, **4006–9**
Sarria, J. 1224
Sarris, A. 218
SARS (severe acute respiratory syndrome)
    2059
Sartain, J. 2830
Sarton, G. 2958–9
Sartre, Jean-Paul 745, 1229, 1775, 3052,
    4009–10
  and atheism 197
  and Beauvoir 252, 254
  and existentialism 1520, 3402
Sassen, S. 1048–51, 1953, 1954, 2305
Sassler, S. L. 565–9
Satanism 1141, **4010–11**
  and child abbuse 1090
  and moral entrepreneurship 3088
  and moral panics 3091
satellite technology 419, 2897
  and diaspora 1153
  and geolinguistic regions 2890
  and visual consumption 771
sati 1692
satisficing model 3795
satyagraha 912, 1165, 1782, 4458–9
Sauceda, L. 1848–52
Saudi Arabia 1724
Sauer, A. 3032
Saunders, Cicely 234
Saunders, P. 748
Saussure, Ferdinand de 4011–12
  and *langue* and *parole* 2537, 2538–9, 4181,
    4328
  semiotics 2661, 3580, 4181–3
  and signs and signifiers 243, 2537
  structural linguistics 1154, 1916, 3581, 4182
Savage, M. 540
savage war theme 3512
Savalescu, J. 2174
Savitch, H. 1175
savoir 1772, 1773, 1774
Sawyer, R. K. 633–6
Say, J.-B. 1300, 1301, 2776
Sayles, J. 1820
Say's law of regulating markets 2776, 2777, 2779

scale, economies of 2828, 2940, 3436
scaled association models 2377–8
scaling 1500
Scambler, G. 2245–6
Scandinavia
  aging and social policy 85–6
  childcare 458
  cities 494, 495
  class conflict 3551
  cultural tourism 921
  divorce 4228
  elder care services 1350
  family planning 4228
  industrial democracy 2750
  industrial relations 2289
  industrialization 494
  labor movements 3551
  labor–management relations 2512
  nonmarital fertility 1587, 1734
  religiosity 1055
  secularization 2529
  sex education 4228
  sexual cultures 4227–9
  sexual permissiveness 4229
  voting behavior 553
  see also Denmark; Finland; Iceland; Norway;
    Sweden
scapegoating 1806, **4012–14**
  and genocide 1911
  Jews 875
  middleman minorities 3008
  and racist movements 3768–9
  and sacrifice 3982
  and stereotyping 4774
scarifiation *see* cicatrization
scatterplots 805
scenario planning 2749
Schaar, J. 1807
Schachter, S. 1379
schadenfreude 1384
Schaffer, S. 786, 1532
Schama, Simon 744
Schatz, T. 1755
Schaub, C. 1259
Schechner, R. 3392
Scheff, T. 990, 1143, 2215, 2695, 3005–8
Scheflen, A. E. 2363
Schegloff, E. 791, 793, 2032, 2363
Scheid, T. L. 2709–10
Schein, E. 335
Schein, L. 1985
Scheler, M. 2482, 2483, 2484, 5169–70

Schellebach, C. 1070–3
schemas 1779, 3714
Schengen Agreement (1995) 3020, 3838
Scherschel, K. 3011–14
Scheurich, J. J. 1771–4
Schiebinger, L. 1684
Schiele, E. 2834
Schieman, S. 4161–3
Schiff, J. 159
Schiffrin, D. 1180
Schijf, H. 1362–4
Schiller, D. 1162
Schiller, F. 896
Schiller, H. 2327
Schiller, K. S. 5022–6
Schimmel, K. S. 4664–5
schizoanalysis 2037
schizophrenia 838, 1635
   double bind theory 248–9
   social schizophrenia 270
Schleicher, A. 1896
Schleiermacher, F. 1747, 2108, 4322
Schlueter, E. 2542–6, 4517–21
Schmid, A. A. 2020–2
Schmidt, L. 1817–18
Schmidt, W. 2698, 3631
Schmitt, C. 229, 3175
Schmitter, P. 2576
Schmoller, G. 2829, 4060
Schnaiberg, A. 1282, 1420
Schnappe D. 3154
Schneerson, R. 3048
Schneider, B. 4354–8
Schneider, C. J. 3129–34
Schneider, D. 2471
Schneider, J. L. 1426–7
Schneider, M. A. 4856–9
Schneidman, E. 974
Schnittker, J. 1868
Schock, K. 4458–63
Schocken, S. 167
Schoen, R. 1021–5
Schoenberg, A. 874, 913
Schofield, M. 2158
Scholastic Aptitude Test (SAT) 4723
Scholasticism 2186, 2536
Scholem, G. 268
Scholz, C. W. 241–2, 5225–6
school choice 4014–16, 5114
   charter schools 4035, 4037
   home schooling 4032–4
   magnet schools 4044

   market approach 4014–15
   and performance outcomes 4015
   religious schools 4052–5
   and school transitions 4028, 4029
   single-sex schools 4057
school climate 4016–19
   and friendship networks 1800, 4017
   and gender bias 1844
   intergenerational climates 4017, 4018
   public schools 4055
   religious schools 4055
   single-sex schools 4056, 4058
   and socialization 4567
school discipline 4019–23
   single-sex schools 4056
school expulsion 4022
school finance litigation 5114
school readiness 2655
school segregation, desegregation 1325–6,
   3733, **4023–7**, 4050
   and affirmative action 39
   Coleman's policy studies 571
   de facto segregation 4026
   de jure segregation 4026
   magnet schools 4043, 4044, 4045
   and massive resistance 2830–1
   and multicultural education 277
   and the public school system 4050–1
   white flight thesis 3753, 4050
   within-school segregation 4024
   see also Brown v. Board of Education
school transitions 4028–9
   and educational attainment 1335
schooling and economic success 4029–32
   credentialism 4030–1
   and globalization of education 1971, 1975
   and literacy levels 2654
   professional school students 4047
   and school dropout 1232
schooling, home 4032–4
schools
   and adolescent social development 1546–7
   and capitalist social arrangements 866
   citizenship schools 866
   and commodity culture 725
   and crime 842–4
   cultural capital in 891–2
   curriculum 1326
   free school movement 866
   laicization 4145
   marketing sites 775
   and multimedia 3109

schools (*cont'd*)
  program and performance auditing 213
  rationalization process 2883
  sex segregation 878
  and stratification 1326
  technology innovations, impact of 2851
schools, charter 4015, **4034–9**
schools, common 1325, **4039–42**, 4050
schools and cultural capital 888, 889
schools, magnet 4042–5
schools, professional 4045–8
schools, public 1324, 4014, **4048–52**, 4054
  black public schools 605
  Catholic schools 571
  and choice initiatives 4015, 4016
  as communities 1146
  desegregation plans 4026
  Dewey and 1146
  dropout rates 571
  funding 4050
  gender bias 1861
  and homophobia 2156
  kindergarten 2464
  magnet schools 4042–5
  and prayer in public schools 2234
  Protestant values 1324–5
  public–religious school distinction 4053
  school climate 4055
schools, religious 4052–5
  Catholic schools 1325, 1326–7
  and high-school dropout 1326–7
  school climate 4055
schools, single-sex 1860, **4055–9**
Schopenhauer, Arthur 2163, 3213
Schor, J. 681–6, 743, 1032, 1033, 2192
Schreiner, O. 1365
Schroeder, J. 351–3, 769–73
Schubert, H.-J. 798–801
Schudson, M. 959, 2600
Schuller, A. 3657
Schulz, J. 2191–4
Schulz, M. S. 27–30, 2163–5
Schumpeter, Joseph A. 2441, 3338, **4059–61**
  and creative destruction 3437
  and economic cycles 2490, 3437
  economic sociology 1300, 1301, 1302,
    1303–4, 1305, 2299, 4060, 4061
  and entrepreneurship 1411, 4060
  and imperialism 2267
  and markets 2775–6, 2777–8, 2780,
    2781, 2782
  and neoclassical economics 1306

  political sociology 3459
  and pure/theoretical economics 2775–6,
    2777–8
  substantive theory 4060
Schur, E. M. 1095–6
Schutt, R. K. 4127–9
Schutte, G. 3401–4
Schütz, Alfred 1484, **4061–4**
  and constructionism 686, 1087
  and ideal type 2201
  and the lifeworld 876, 2651
  phenomenology 274, 2108, 2651, 3402–3,
    4061, 4062–3
  and workplace studies 2364
Schwandt, T. A. 212–13, 1434–6, 3235–6
Schwartz, B. 588–10, 2366
Schwartz, J. 636–8
Schwarzenegger, Arnold 875, 2337
Schwendinger, H. 819
Schwendinger, J. 819
Schwirian, K. 1277–81
science 4064–8
  academic science 4069
  "big science" 916, 3438
  boundary work 2963
  and cultural studies 916
  education, standardization of 1973
  elitism 3222–3
  funding agencies 2852
  gender biases 1681–2
  industrialization of 276
  institutionalization 3038
  "interests" approach 4065, 4066, 4098, 4099
  and magic 2698, 2700
  masculine gaze 947
  metaphysics of 3355
  Nazi science 4109
  objectivity 947
  and politics 276
  professionalization 3223
  public understanding of 2850
  science–industry relations 3437
  speaking truth to power 4635–7
  standardization 4720–1
  strong program 4066
  women in science 5267–8
science, commercialization of 4068–9
science and culture 4069–72
  and anthrozoology 151
science across cultures 4073–4
Science Citation Index 4121
science cities 276

science, ethnographic studies of 4074–6
science fiction 3494–8
  fans 1638, 1639
  literature 3495, 3497
  and television 3516–17
science governance 1908
science and the measurement of risk 3926,
    3929, **4076–9**, 4082–3
science/non-science and boundary work
    4079–82
science and the precautionary principle
    4082–3
science, proof, and law 4083–8
science and public participation: the
    democratization of science 4088–91
  and genetic engineering 1908
  and genomics 2174
science and religion 4091–3
  and evolution 1510
science, social construction of 4093–7
  actor-network theory 20–1
  and chaos and complexity theories 432
  and ecology 1292
  and finalization in science 1757
science and technology studies (STS) 2904,
    2968, 3165, 3549, 4100, 4107
  see also scientometrics
Science Wars 1508, 1509, 1758, 3813, 4089
scientific creationism 1508, 1510
scientific expert witness testimony 1571
scientific knowledge, sociology of 3815, 4065,
    4067–8, 4071, 4085–6, 4089, **4097–100**
  and controversy studies 784–7
  interest model 4096
  and laboratory practice 2524–6
  materiality and scientific practice 2844
  and nature 3165
  and negative case analysis 3167
  and the rational choice paradigm 2475
  see also Kuhn, Thomas and scientific
    paradigms
scientific literacy and public
    understandings of science **4100–4**, 4103
scientific logocentrism 2661
scientific management 364–5, 428, 701, 704,
    1769, 2522, 2710, 2712, 2716
  and management discourse 2724
  and organization theory 3281
  see also Taylorism
scientific method 2286, 2287, 4095
scientific models and simulations 4104–6
scientific naturalism 871

scientific networks and invisible colleges
    4107–8
scientific norms/counternorms 4109–11
scientific positivism 1151
scientific practice, materiality and 2844–6
scientific productivity 3667, 4112–13
  logistic model of scientific growth 4120
  Matthew effect 4113
scientific racialism 3610–11
scientific racism 155, 3013, 4113–15
  and intelligence tests 2359, 2360
  race formalism 4114
scientific revolution 1505, 4116–17
scientific skepticism 786
scientific socialism 1150
scientists as bricoleurs 366
Scientology 630, 631, 4117–19
scientometrics 4119–22
Scimecca, J. 2186–8
Scopes, J. T. 1510
Scopes trial 1510
Scotland 4188
Scotovsky, T. 2192
Scott Brown, D. 2124
Scott, Jerome 2836–9
Scott, Joan 1893
Scott, P. D. 2420, 2421
Scott, R. 3497
Scott, W. R. 2709
Scraton, S. 2588–92
Screen Actors Guild 1098
Scripps, E. W. 2897
scripting theories 4122–3
scripting theory 2162
Scrivern, M. 1499
Sea Organization 4118
Seager, J. 1275, 1276
Seals, B. 1115
Searle, J. 1181, 2031
Sears, J. 2152
seaside resorts 761
Seattle anti-globalization protests (1999) 1062,
    1947, 1948, 1977
secession 1466, 1487, 1488, 4167, 4168
second demographic transition 1037,
    4123–7
  and family demography 1584
  and individualism 1733, 2415
Second Great Awakening 3202
second shift (household labor) 1203, 1248,
    1669, 1881, 2619–20
Second Vatican Council 409, 441

secondary data analysis 778, 1669, **4127–9**
secondary groups 4129–31
secrecy 3644, **4132–5**
  managing secrets 234
  organizational 4178
  racist movements 3768
secret societies 4132
sect 4135–40
  and charisma 436
  Christianity and 476
  church–sect theory 484, 884–5, 3690, 4135,
    4136–9
  cults and 884–5
  and denomination 1051
  and Jehovah's Witnesses 2440
  and new religious movements 3202
  sect–cult distinction 3875, 4118
  sect–demomination distinction 1315
sector model 1279–80
secular ideologies 2296
secular materialism 2000
secular reformist gradualism 1002
secularism, conservatism and 679
secularization 1815, 4092, **4140–8**
  and anticlericalism 2532
  and atheism 197, 199
  and Christianity 478
  and the church 487
  of the clergy 3690–1
  cultural process 2529
  and demographic transition 1043
  and ethnic mobilization 1471
  and functional differentiation 4151
  and fundamentalism 1815
  and industrialization 2299
  internal secularization 4145
  of mind 4147
  and modernization 3074, 3075
  modernization–secularization thesis 3867
  and *moralpolitik* 3094
  and new religious movements 3204
  and nonmarital fertility and cohabitation
    1735
  and the Orthodox Church 3348–9
  and the public/private dichotomy 4141
  and rational choice theory 3866–7
  and sacrality 3979
  sacred–secular relationship 3094
  secularization of knowledge 1922
  Weberian thesis 3867
securities 1387
securities frauds 834, 850

securitization 3324
security
  and information technology 2334, 2335
  privatization of 1387
security economy 2335
  and fear of crime 2342–3
sedatives 1234
Sedek, G. 2569
Sedgwick, E. K. 606, 2155, 2612
segmentalism, bureaucratic 377
segmented assimilation 2254
Segrave, J. O. 3262–5
segregation 3749, **4149–50**
  and civil rights activism 1165
  collective efficacy and crime and 585
  and crime rates, impact on 3735–6
  and cultural pluralism 15
  de facto segregation 370, 4149
  de jure segregation 4149
  and direct action 1166
  and disability 1169
  and disabled athletes 1171
  educational 3742
  ghetto walls 1890
  and the hidden curriculum 2118
  and homicide 544
  horizontal segregation 1890
  hypersegregation 2196–9
  index of dissimilarity 3246
  linguistic 280, 370
  measures of 2197–8
  and passing 3369
  and political disenfranchisement 3746,
    3747
  racial 508, 3746, 3752, 5147
  and racial etiquette 3744
  residential segregation 370, 2196–7, 2305,
    2306, 3732–3, 3748
  and restrictive covenants 3898
  self-segregation 3756
  separate but equal doctrine 368, 369, 370
  size-standard variant measure 3246
  and urbanism 5147
  see also Brown v. Board of Education;
    occupational segregation; residential
    segregation; school segregation,
    desegregation
Seidman, R. 668
Seidman, S. 2157
Seifert, W. 2802–5, 4150–4
Seigfried, C. H. 3611
seikatsu/seikatsusha **4150–4**

Seiyama, K. 4921–4
seken **4154–7**
Sekulic, D. 175–7, 1450–2, 4360–4, 5172–6
Seleucids 2450
self 4157–60
  agentive self 3186, 3187
  animal self 2177
  collectivistic self 598
  deontological view of 3717
  development 1821
  dramaturgical self 1228, 4158
  empirical study of 4159
  evolving self 799
  existential self 1521–2
  and false consciousness 1569
  formation 1996
  functionalist perspective 4158
  and the generalized other 1899
  ideal self 2225
  and identity control theory 2205
  internal dynamics, and behavior 2225
  Internet, transformative impact of 2386
  James's model of 2432–3
  and life history research 2643
  linguistically generated self 3186, 4158
  loss of self 2246
  Mead and 61, 1821, 1899, 1996, 2217, 2224,
    2433, 2862, 2863, 3187, 3228, 3414–15,
    3417, 3617, 3621, 4157, 4563
  narrative reconstruction 231, 2246, 4159
  and neurosociology 3185, 3187, 3188
  ontological definition 4169
  postmodern self 4160
  postsocial self 974, 3579
  presentation of 1930
  preservation of 3332–3
  quest for the self 1582
  and reference groups 3828–9
  reflexivity 2863
  Renaissance concept 4157
  resocialization 3891–3
  second self 333
  self-other roles 3946
  shopping mall selfhood 4310
  social self 799
  symbolic interactionist perspective 4158
  Twenty Statements Test 4158–60
  see also identity theory; looking-glass self
self, genesis of *see* game stage; play stage
self-appraisal 1380, 2433
self-betterment 1329
self-categorization theory 2212

self-concept 4159, **4161–3**
  Aronson and 562
  deviant self-concepts 2502
  formation 4170
  Rosenberg and 3954–5
  and self-esteem 4169–70, 4171
  and significant others 4320
  and stigma 2832
  survey research 4514
self-consciousness 2098, 3056, 3918–19
self-construction, narrative and 231
self-control theory 846, **4163–6**
  control balance theory 782–4
  and deviance 1080, 1102, 1104, 1105,
    1119, 1120
  emotional 1380
  low self-control, crime and 838, 851
  and socialization 4164, 4165
self-defense training 5274
self-definition, black female 306
self-determination 407, **4166–9**
  de Beauvoir and 252
  human right to 2184
  national 1487, 3147
  and nationalist movements 1466
  Native Americans 2283
  and territorial integrity 4168
  uti possidetis doctrine 4167
  see also secession
self-discipline 530
self-efficacy 4161
self-employment
  ethnic 1461–2
  in public housing schemes 3710–11
self-esteem, theories of 2212, 2433–4, **4169–72**
  and dissonance arousal 564
  global self-esteem 4171
  high/low self-esteem 4171
  and identity theory 2212
  James and 2433–4, 4170
  measuring 4161
  "myth" of self-esteem 3136
  Rosenberg Self-Esteem Scale 3955
  and self-concept 4169–70, 4171
  and social identity theory 4419
  social support, effects of 89–90
  and stress reduction 4839
  and success 2434
  survey research 4514
  and symbolic interaction 4170
  and well-being 97
  see also social comparison theory

self-evaluation, and accounts 10
self-evidence 173
self-fulfilling expectations 4172–5
  and cultural stereotypes 4173
  and learned helplessness 2568
self-fulfilling prophecy 4172, 4175–8
  and deviance 1086, 2208, 2506
  and the Great Depression 2021
  and labeling 2117, 2832
  and mental patient strategies 3332–3
  and phenomenology 4175
  Thomas theorem 991, 992, 4172–3, 4175
self-gratification, and leisure 2597–8
self-help manuals 3324
self-identification 296
self-identity 962, 963
self-injurers 2208
self-interest
  compliance and 229
  cooperation and 640
self-knowledge 214
self-made man myth 1329
self-management 2077
self-perception
  balance theory and 562
  Bem and 562
  during later life 97
  trauma, impact of 335
self-presentation 2214
self-rationalization 378
self-reference theory 2676–7
self-regulation
  and censorship 422
  markets 515
self-reported health (SRH) 2085
self-restraint 1359, 1360
self-segregation 3756
self-serving bias 207, 2271
self-structures 2218
Seligman, A. 3070
Seligman, M. E. P. 2566, 2568, 2569–70
Sell, J. 4392–5
Sellin, T. 666, 848
Seltzer, J. A. 2414–18, 3225
Selznick, P. 1146, 2351, 2354, 2355, 2713–14,
  3332
semantics, and reconstructive analyses
  3824–5
semi-adulthood 2570
semi-autonomous work groups 2750, 2753
semi-domestication 4178–9
semilingualism 282

semiology 2539, 4181, 4182
semiotics 2534, 2536, 2537, 2539, **4179–87**
  advertising 32, 300, 703, 758
  anthroposemiotics 2537
  Augustine and 4180
  Barthes and 758, 3581, 3583, 4182
  connotation 1403
  and cultural studies 298
  denotation 1403
  and dramaturgy 1227, 1229
  and genre 1916
  and hermeneutics 2107
  interpretive community 4107
  Locke and 4180
  and logocentrism 2660–1
  and management discourse 2723
  Peirce and 4180–1, 4183–5, 4186
  and photography 3406
  and posthumanism 3549
  and role-taking 3056
  Saussure and 4011–12, 4186
  semiotic democracy 210
  and sense-perception 4180
  social semiology 242
  social semiotics 2723
  and visual consumption 769
  see also signs; simulacra and simulation
semiperipheral development 1061
semiurgy 2691
Sen, A. 1760
Sen, K. 1692
Seneca Falls Women's Rights Convention
  1673, 2618
Senegal, female genital mutilation 1655,
  1656
Senge, P. M. 3269
Senghor, L. 2984
Senior, W. 1300, 1301, 2778
Sennett, M. 1752
Sennett, R. 518, 1582, 2413, 3719
sensationalism 2908
sensitivity analysis 789
sensory stimulation 2598
sentiment 2144
separate but equal doctrine 368, 369, 370
  see also Plessy v. Ferguson
separate spheres ideology 1202, 1510, 1880,
  1881, 3649
  and industrialization 1849
  see also private sphere; public sphere
separation *see* divorce; intimate union formation
  and dissolution

separatism 4187–9
  ethnic separatism 1470
  external 4187–8
  internal 4188
  and racial movements 3767
  and racial/ethnic boundaries 346
Sephardic Jews 2450–1, 2453
September 11, 2003
  and anti-terrorist propaganda 3674
  and collective consciousness 1966
  post-September 11 world situation 1966, 1970
  and US foreign policy 1396
sequestration 2926
Serbia 1451, 1886, 1887
  nationalism 3145, 3347
  Orthodox Church 3345, 3346, 3347
  separatism 4188
serfdom 679
serial commitment 1620
serious leisure 2597–8
Serpe, R. T. 2224
Serrana, M. O. 2946–51
service class 552
service contract 552
service sector 355, 767, 1385
  commercialization 3664
  and deindustrialization 992–3
  female employment 2383
  growth 2383
  and the Industrial Revolution 2295
  and the information society 2330
  and operations management 3267
  and stratification 993
Seton-Watson, H. 3153
Settersten, Jr., Richard A. 49–52
Seventh-Day Adventists 1065, 1981, 2440, 3518, 4144
sewage treatment plants 1425, 3202
Sewell, G. 2566, 3566
Sewell, W. H. 2400
sex
  biologically determined 336, 1591, 1681, 1843, 1847, 1864, 1875, 2307, 4197
  continuum thesis 1846
  cybersex 965–6
  eroticization of 2684
  illicit or risky 1104
  male–defined view 2112
  pedagogization of 464
  sex–gender conflation 1895
  sex–gender distinction 1847, 2111, 2307
  transactional sex 4211

sex-based wage gap and comparable worth 4189–91, 4203
sex categorization 1216
sex-change operations 1109
sex and crime 4191–3
sex discrimination 1675, 1890
sex economy 3843
sex education 4, 450, 2319, 4193–6, 4228
  abstinence-only education 4194–5
  African societies 4211
  and AIDS 108
  childhood 466
  safer sex 3988
sex and gender 4196–8
  doing gender 1216–18
  sex–gender distinction 1847, 2111
sex hormones
  categorization of 1681
  and coronary heart disease risk 1866
sex manuals 3277
sex-negativity climate 2114
sex panics 1097–8, 3090, 3091, 4198–200
  child abuse 3090
  HIV/AIDS 3988
sex preferences 1156, 1158
sex radical lesbian communities 2603, 2610
sex ratios 1029
sex reassignment 5038–9
sex-role socialization 2818, 2819
sex segregation 878
sex testing 1847–8
sex therapy 2468, 3320
sex tourism 763, 1600, 1984, 4200–3
  Asia 4216–17
  female sex tourism 1661
  gay tourism 1985
  Latin America 4220
  and prostitution 3682
  and sexual stereotyping 1665
  US military role in 3118, 5032
sex toys 4243
sex work 3320
  customers 1660–1
  female migrant workers 1717
  female sex work 1659–62
  gendered nature of 1659
  and global capitalism 1984
  indoor sex work 1660
  and international migration 1984
  online sex 1661–2
  public attitude to 1659, 1660–1
  research ethics 2347

sex work (*cont'd*)
 stigma 1660, 1662
 third world 1854
 see also prostitution; sex tourism
sexile 4221
sexism 59, 1667, 2601, 2619, 2702, **4203–5**
 in the academy 1670
 black feminist resistance 306, 307,
  308, 309
 and critical qualitative research 869
 definition 1843
 and football 4347
 in gay groups 1834
 and lesbian feminism 2601, 2602
 materialist analysis 2838
 political system 3400
 and subordination 2100
sexology 2468, 2609
sexual abstinence 4194–5
sexual abuse 1677
 see also child abuse
sexual addiction 1112
sexual assault
 and comfort eating 722
 domestic violence 1219, 1220
 and female criminality 1695
 gender bias 1857
 and health problems 1610
 and HIV infection 109
 in war 1886–7
 see also child abuse; sexual violence
  and rape
sexual behavior 1609
sexual citizenship 2163, **4205–9**
sexual coercion, biosociological theory 293
sexual cultures in Africa 4209–13
sexual cultures in Asia 4213–18
**sexual cultures in Latin America
 4218–23**
sexual cultures in Russia 4223–7
sexual cultures in Scandinavia 4227–30
sexual desire 2612, 2613
sexual deviance 4230–2
 and casual leisure 2598–19
 and dangerousness 969
 exhibitionism 1518–19
 fetishism 1745–6
sexual dysfunction 4237, 4274
 age-related 2541
sexual harassment 677, 1669, 1676, 1677,
 1679, 3320, **4233–4**
 in coercive organizations 3318

 and deviance in sport 1134
 feminist theories 1106, 4233
 and the heterosexual imaginary 2110
 and masculinity 1891
 and occupational deviance 1084
 online 966
 organizational theories 3305, 3320, 4233
 and patriarchy 3378
 same-sex harassment 4233
 in schools 842
 in sport 1878, 4293
 variation in national laws 1099
 verbal 4204
sexual health 4234–8
 late-life sexuality 2539–42
 sexual behavior 1609
 see also safer sex
sexual humor 1891
sexual identities 303, 336, 926, 1437, 2114,
 2793, 3568, 3728–9, **4238–42**
 changes in 2162
 construction 326, 1436–7
 essentialist theories 1437, 1837
 and polyamory 3477
 and postmodern sexualities 3568
sexual intimacy 2411, 2412
sexual liberation 2160, 2606
**sexual markets, commodification, and
 consumption 4242–4**
 see also pornography and erotica;
  prostitution; sex tourism
sexual migration 4220–1
sexual orientation 1592, 4197
 heritability 1830–1
 religious responses to 4277
 scales 303
 and suicide 4883
 see also bisexuality
sexual pleasure 2162
sexual politics 4244–7
 see also queer theory
sexual practices 4247–9
 extramarital affairs 2323–5
 fetishism 1745–6
 oral sex 3276–8
 see also masturbation; sadomasochism
sexual promiscuity 1597
sexual psychopath laws 1098, 1099
sexual repression 3883
sexual revolution 875, 2540, 2541, 3843,
 4125–6
sexual scripting theory 2159, 4122–3

sexual selection 286, 294
sexual violence and rape 2555, 3787–9,
    4249–54
  and abortion 3
  criminalization of African Americans 1664
  cultural feminist account 905
  date rape 4252
  evolutionary/biobehavioral explanations
    3789
  and exhibitionism 1518
  fear of, as social control 2113, 2341
  feminist perspectives 1106, 1695, 3789
  fraternity gang rape 2153
  gender-neutral definition 2556
  and the heterosexual imaginary 2110
  index crime 2277, 2278
  integrative theories 3789
  in Islamic culture 2429
  and male deviance 1856
  male rape 2278, 2702–3
  marital rape 2110, 2303, 3785, 4231
  mass rape 1885–6
  and pornography 905, 3775
  and power relations 332, 3774
  and prostitution 3683
  rape laws 3785, 3788
  rapists, and deviant accounts 12, 13
  and slavery 3786
  and social construction of male sexuality
    2112–13
  sociocultural perspectives 3789
  stigma neutralization 1094
  stranger rape 2309
  in war conditions 1886–7
sexualities, cities and 4254–6
  gay geography 2159
  and homosexuality 2160
  queer geography 2162
sexualities and consumption 4256–60
sexualities and culture wars 4260–3
sexuality 4263–8
  biological explanation 4264, 4272
  childhood 462–6
  constructionist theories 1436–7, 2610
  continuum 4264
  and cultural feminism 904
  and cultural studies 916
  cybersexualities 963, 965–6
  de Beauvoir and 254
  development 1071
  and diversity 1197
  and economics 1984

  essentialist theories 1437
  female 254, 333, 904, 1678, 2611, 2613,
    5268–72
  and female control of 1610
  fixed sexuality 3411
  flexible sexuality 3411
  folk and indigenous models 1985
  Foucault and 332, 335, 1436, 1776, 2114,
    2157, 2158, 2160, 2493, 2609, 3540, 3583,
    3882–4, 4248, 4264, 4290
  Freudian 4264, 4273
  and gender 4265–6
  and globalization 1983–5
  history of 4263–4
  Islamic 2427–30
  and LAT relationships 812
  love-dominated sexuality 2682
  lust-dominated sexuality 2681
  male 904
  masculine regulation of 2115
  masculine sexuality 735, 4272–5
  men's appropriation of women's sexuality
    2114
  plastic sexuality 3411–12
  postmodern sexualities 3568–9
  and privilege 3650
  psychological construction 4264
  regulation of 2110
  social construction 1437
  and trangression 5045
  and visual culture 755
  youth 775
  see also Freud, Sigmund; Kinsey, Alfred;
    queer theory
sexuality education 4195
  see also sex education
sexuality and the law 4268–72
sexuality, masculinity and 4272–5
  and homophobia 1828
  and oral sex 3277
sexuality, religion and 4275–80
  Islamic culture 2428–30
sexuality research: ethics 4280–3
sexuality research: history 4283–7
  see also Ellis, Havelock; Freud, Sigmund;
    Hirschfeld, Magnus; Kinsey, Alfred;
    Krafft-Ebing, Richard von
sexuality research: methods 4287–90
  and the gay gene 1830–3
  Kinsey Institute 2468
sexuality and sport 4290–3
sexualized racialization 4221

exually transmitted infections (STIs) 449, 1609
  in later life 2542
  moral panics 4254
  and pedophilia 3387
  and pornography performers 3542
  school education programs 215
  and sex education 4194
  and sex work 1660
  and sexual/physical abuse 1610
shadow work 2149, 4294–5
Shadow Work (Ivan Illich) 4294–5
Shafiite School 2426
Shahidian, H. 2428–30
Shaker people 1316, 4276–7
Shakespeare, William 1914, 3145, 3581
Shalin, D. 3609
shamanism 630, 2694
shame 1378, 1380, 2502, 2506
  and alienation 3007
  and norm violation 3231–2
Shanas, Ethel 1935
Shandra, J. M. 1423
Shange, N. 306
Shankara 2129
Shapin, S. 786, 1532
Shapiro, E. 2601–6, 3773–6
Shapiro, T. M. 2197
share capital 1945
Shareholder Value (SHV) 2715, 2729
Shariati, Ali 4295–6
Sharpe, E. K. 1380
Sharpeville massacre (1955) 163
Sharpley-Whiting, T. D. 309
Shavit, Y. 1336–40
Shaw, C. S. 443, 828, 1129
Shaw, J. C. 640
Shaw, S. 1895
Shayne, J. 1685–9, 1686
Shea, D. 3255
Sheard, K. 1751
Sheftall, B. G. 309
Shefter, M. 3446
Shehan, C. 2301–4
Sheldon, R. 1856
Shelley, Mary 3495
Shen, B. S. P. 4103
Shenav, Y. 2727
Shepard, B. 2832–5, 3987–9, 4198–200
Shepard, M. 1828
Shepherd, Gary 884–7
Shepherd, Gordon 4569–70
Sherif, C. W. 2338

Sherif, M. 1540, 3828
Sherkat, D. 2081
Sherman, L. 418–19, 828
Sherrill, C. 1171
Sherrod, D. 1804
Shibutani, T. 320, 2961
Shiite Islamism 1814, 2425–6, 2800, 3048
Shils, E. 2365–6, 3156, 3337, 3937
Shinberg, S. S. 5275–9
Shintoism 1980, 2499, 3855, **4297–303**
Shionoya, Y. 4059–61
Shiva, V. 1274, 1275
shock privatization 3648
shoplifting 1856, 3675
  stigma neutralization 1094
shopping 4303–8
  and celebrity culture 421
  and cultural resistance 912
  e-commerce 732, 733
  experiential consumption 717
  flânerie 1762–3
  leisure activity 740
  meaning–making acts 752
  museum merchandising 3126
  online shopping 1851, 2884
  and the public sphere 1850
  reenchanting the experience 752
  rituals 752
  and self-formation 717
  shopping around 717
  shopping for 717
  supermarkets 4888–90
  tourism and 763
  window shopping 766, 769
shopping malls 704, 708, 713, 752, 767, 914,
    4304–5, **4308–11**
  cultural tourism 921
  and the department store 1058
  and *flânerie* 1762–3
  food consumption 764
  and hyperconsumption/overconsumption
    2193
  landscapes of consumption 734–5, 2884
  teenagers in 774
  tourist destinations 763
Short, J. 1128
Shortcake Strategy 695
shotgun weddings 568
Shott, S. 1380
show trials 593
shrine/pilgrimage religion 1054
shushin koyo **4311–14**

Shusterman, R. 327, 336
shuttle diplomacy 3380, 3381
Shuval, J. T. 4833–7
sibling identity 558
sibling relationships during old age
4314–15
sibling ties 1620, **4315–17**
  solidarity 2470
  stepsiblings 4768
sibship
  and educational attainment 1337–8
  and household structure 1625
  and sexual orientation 1831
Sica, A. 4617–9
sick leave 2510–11
sick role 479–80, 1112, **4317–20**
  and deviance 1112
  and help-seeking 2105, 5277
  and illness experience 2245
  Parsons and 479–80, 2245, 2933–4, 3366,
    3374–5, 4318
  and the physician 2075
  see also patient–physician relationship
sickle-cell anemia 1907, 2080
Siddharta Gautama 370
Sidran, B. 797, 798
Siegrist, J. 4840–3
Siemsen, C. 2796–9, 5254–7
Siepmann, C. A. 3778, 3780
Sierra Club 1428, 1429, 3339
Sierra Leone 1654
sign economy 770
sign wars 32
signaling, and collective action 580
significant others 4320–1
  and expectations/aspirations 1530
signified and signifiers 703, 772
  arbitrary signifiers 1159
  and logocentrism 2660–1
  Saussure and 243, 2537, 2539, 4011–12,
    4181–2
  and subcultures 298
  see also semiotics; signs
signology 2539
signs 4321–3
  and advertising 703
  exchange value 703, 704
  political economy of 703
  Saussure and 4012
  signified and signifiers 703
  see also semiotics
Sikes, P. 2642

Sikhism 1980, 2130
  fundamentalism 1813
  international organizations and movements
    1982
Silbey, S. S. 2562
sildenafil *see* Viagra
silent revolution 1900
Silicon Valley 637, 1959, 2737, 3284
Sillars, J. 3159
Sillince, J. 2476–80
Silver, A. 1793
Silver, D. 961–3
Silver, H. 1174–6, 4411–13
Silverman, D. 2714
Silverstein, M. 2366–8, 2380–2, 2633
Simchat Torah 2452
Simiand, F. 1263
similarity 344
  and attraction 203
Simmel, Georg 655, 1749, 1812, 2497, 2767,
    3363, **4323–8**
  and affiliation 1311
  and associations 3075
  biography 4324–5
  and capitalism 390, 516
  and the city 500, 765, 2649, 3164
  and conflict theory 666, 4327
  and conspicuous consumption 719, 741, 934,
    1189, 1190, 1308
  and cultural production 2767
  and distanciation 1188, 1189
  dominance model 7
  and dyads/triads 4326
  and emotions 1384, 1385
  and fashionability 683, 736, 4932
  and formal sociology 2998
  forms, sociology of 2692, 2998, 4325–6
  gender and modernity thesis 2767
  and group interaction 1266, 2030, 4132
  historical materialism 2679
  and interpersonal relationships 2390,
    4484–5
  and the interpretive meta-paradigm 2968
  and Lukács 2679
  and markets 2781, 2783, 2784, 2786
  and modernity 3068–9
  and money 3078, 3079, 3809
  and neurasthenic personalities 312
  rationalization theory 3809
  and reification 2679
  relationist theories 1761
  and religion 3857

Simmel, Georg (*cont'd*)
    secrecy, sociology of 4132, 4133
    and sociability 3415
    and social differentiation 4326
    and social distance 4398
    and social networks 3182, 3184, 3227
    and social structure 315, 1996
    sociology of knowledge 4325–7
    stranger typology 4782–3
    and superordination/subordination 4326–7
    and symbolic interaction 2361
    and triads 3184
    trickle-down theory 719, 744–5, 1189
    and value 5168
Simmons, J. S. 2225
Simmons, L. 216–20
Simon, H. 640, 2144, 2855, 3313, 3323
Simon, J. 3526
Simon, P. 3557
Simon, W. 2112, 2159, 2468, 3568, 4122, 4248
Simonds, W. 2977
Simons, M. 3048
Simpson, B. 3794–9
Simpson, G. E. 2958
Simpson, O. J. 818, 876
Simpsons, The 730, 3513–15
Sims, B 839–42, 841
simulacra and simulation 2691, 2922, 3496,
    3567, 3569, **4328–31**
    and implosion theory 2269
    see also semiotics
simulation modeling 4104–6
simulation and virtuality 4331–4
    cyberculture 961–4
    and digital media 1163
    scientific models and simulations 4104–6
    see also cyberculture
Sinatra, Frank 3515–16
Sinclair, J. 2885–91, 2886
Singapore 4374, 4376
    bilingual education 279
    economic success 1296, 2299
    fantasy cities 1641
    folk religious pracctices 1764, 1765
    Hinduism 1765
    life expectancy 4377
    medical sociology 2935
    migrant domestic workers 1716
    New Confucianism 670
Singer, J. 1379
Singer, P. 140, 150–1, 1490
single- and double-loop learning 3282

single-race classification schemes 295
single-sex schooling 1860, 4055–9
singular value decomposition (SVD) 2969
singularization 742
Sinha, V. 1764–7, 4000–9
Sinti 1489
Siow, A. 1315
Sisters of Perpetual Indulgence 1225
sit-ins 780, 1165, 1166, 1674, 3193
situated knowledges 1682, 1711
situational crime prevention 828
situational identities 2216
situational imperative hypothesis 76
situationalism, Japanese 238
situationists 705, 755, 980–1, 2580, 4329–30,
    4335–6
Six Sigma groups 2753
skateboarding 4653, 4655
skiing 4654
skills
    deskilling thesis 363–4, 366
    portable skills 3289
    spatial-skills mismatch 993
    specialist 378
    specialization 515, 582
    sport, and skill development 2121
    trained incapacity 378–9
skinheads 299
Skinner, B.F.
    and behaviorism 257, 2964
    and language acquisition 258
Sklair, L. 1943–6, 3212–13
Sklar, R. 1755
Skocpol, T. 539, 664, 2133, 2356, 3461, 3908,
    3909, 3911–12, 3916, 4363
Skorupski, J. 2698
Skrla, L. 5036–7
Skvoretz, J. 314, 315, 641
slash fiction 3497–8
Slater, D. 744
slave moralities 3214, 3215
slave plantation system 3420
slave trade 1393
slavery 514, 550, 679, 3369, **4336–9**
    and the American Civil War 2830
    in ancient Greece 1463
    and biracialism 295
    and capitalism 391
    and collective memory 589
    and commodification 706
    and deviance 1114
    and diaspora 1151

and double consciousness 1221
economic benefits 3740, 3745
and economic reparations 3821
and feminism activism 1672–3
forced migration 3011
and forced pregnancy 2621
and interracial marriage 2394
master–slave dialectic 1147
and one drop rule 3265, 3266
paternalism 3370–1, 3650
prohibition on 2183
and racial hierarchy 3761
and rape 3786
rationalization 3744
and reparations 3876–7
slave insurrections 3744
slave-owning societies 613
and traffic in women 3684
Slevin, J. 2384–8, 5009–10
Sloan, M. 307, 3118
slogans 955, 956
Slotkin, R. 3137–40, 3511–13
Slovakia
  anti-Jewish violence 3428
  bilingual education 280
Slovenia 660
  separatism 4188
slum clearance policies 1454–5
slurs (racial/ethnic) 4339–41
Small, Albion W. 24, 130, 3344, 3585–6,
  4341–2
  and the Chicago School 442–3, 3362
  and Orientalism 3344
  and social change 446
small claim courts 814, 853
small group analysis, and emergent norm
  theory 1367
Small, M. L. 3745–9
small world structure 1008, 1312, 1313
Smart, B. 2690
Smeeding, T. 1627
Smelser, N. 1320, 1322, 1388, 1806, 1811,
  1812, 3065, 3909
Smiles, Samuel 1195
Smith, A. D. 1468, 1471, 3057, 3059, 3139,
  3149, 3151, 3153, 3155, 3157, 3394
Smith, Adam 244, 1118, **4342–3**
  and business ethics 1439, 1440
  and capitalism 362, 390, 515, 4601
  and commodity relations 607–8
  on division of labor 515, 1319, 2298
  economic liberalism 2285

and economics of religion 1315, 1316
and emotional appraisal 1376
individualistic thinking 2285
invisible hand principle 613, 2776, 2778,
  2779, 4601
and labor power 2508
and market economy 2776, 2778, 2837,
  3525
and modernization 3071
and political economy 1300, 1301, 2797
and population growth 3525
and prosocial behavior 3679
and social science 2186, 4601
theory of moral sentiments 3227, 3229
and welfare 4522–3
Smith, Andrew 1751
Smith, Anna-Marie 2613
Smith, Anthony 1839
Smith, Barbara 307, 308, 3119
Smith, Beverly 307
Smith, Darren P. 1605–8
Smith, David 876
Smith, Dennis 1751
Smith, Dorothy 1893, 1995, 3959, 4064
  and bifurcated consciousness 274–5
  ethnographic method 1703
  and ethnomethodology 2033
  everyday world sociology 1503, 1711, 1713
  and feminist sociology 1668, 1701, 4064
  and lived experience 1669
  materialist analysis 2838
  and sex categorization 1216
Smith, G. W. H. 1995–9
Smith, I. 3040–3
Smith, J. 5060–4
Smith, L. 1444, 1445, 2983
Smith, M. G. 3420
Smith, M. P. 1955
Smith, M. R. 3550–2
Smith, Melanie 919–21, 1994–5
Smith, N. 1917, 1918, 1919–20
Smith, Paula 3818–19
Smith, Philip 3936–8
Smith, R. 3630
Smith, Stevin Hedake 1820
Smith, Stuart 1751
Smith, T. W. 1902
Smith, W. R. 3981
Smith-Rosenberg, C. 3652
Smithson, J. 3274
Smith Lovin, L. 796
Smock, P. J. 1209, 1380

smoking 1104, 1143, **4343–5**
and absenteeism 5
anti-smoking movement 1115
and disease prevalence 1184, 1185
and dissonance theory 564
and drug use 1233
and health behavior 2060
and health lifestyles 2061
and health locus of control 2064
and health risk behavior 2084
and heart disease 1866
social causes 1185
Smuts, B. 1511
Smyth, M. 1828–30, 3223–7
Snipp, C. M. 2283
Snow, C. P. 2971, 3549
Snow, D. A. 1778–84, 2146–51, 3067, 3456
snowball effect (industry) 2295
snowball method of research 2161
snowboarding 4654–6
Snyder, G. 2421
Snyder, P. 4898–900
soap operas 3498–500
cultural issues 2823
docusoaps 3491
escape mechanism 1850
fans 1638, 1639
Sobel, A. 3419
soccer 4345–50, 4714, 4714–15
American football 2737, 2739
and the civilizing process 1750–1
class perspective 4695–6
and gambling 1133
and globalization 343, 1986, 2236, 3483, 4651
hypercommodification 760
injury risk 2093
Latino soccer leagues 4683
and male stereotyping 2122
and masculine identity 2222
media coverage 2102–3, 2918
and national identities 2222, 3160
racism 4347
sexism 4347
sponsers 4716
and violence 1133
sociability 790, 3415, 4647
sport 4647
social accountability and governance 4350–3
social acts 2862, 2863
social anthropology 1689
social behavior paradigm 2964

social bonding theory 845, 846, 3006, 3007
social capital 383–4, 742, 1321, **4353–4**
Coleman and 572–3, 1326, 4355
and communities 619, 1326–7
and educational attainment 1335
erosion of 3077
ethnicity-based 3529
fan social capital 1640
and friendships 795, 796
and homelessness 2149
hybridity 2189
and intimacy 2413
and knowledge management 2476
and life chances and resources 2627
and management 2715–16
and modernization 3077
and neighborhood poverty 1614
neighborhood social capital and health 2072–3
network-based social capital 4694
networks and 383–4
and parenting 1326
and partner effects 4811
and racial/ethnic consciousness 3742
and sport 4693–4
and voluntary organizations 3342
within families 1326, 1338
social capital and education 4354–8
and dropping out of school 1231
and educational attainment 1338
and extracurricular activities 1546–7
and religious activities 1315
religious schools 4054–5
and school climate 4016
social capital and health 4359–60
and disease prevalence 1184, 1185
social categories 2223
social change 4360–4
Chicago School studies 44–7
and cohort differentiation 95
and collective trauma 593
Cooley and 801
developmental 655
Durkheim and 1261–3, 1506, 4361–2
evolutionary perspective 1261–2, 4361–2
and the existential self 1522–3
and functionalism 1812, 4362
identity-based strategies 1837
and indigenous peoples 2282
and the information and resource processing paradigm 2326
Marxist theory 1506, 4361

and modernization 3071
Parsons and 4362–3
revolutionary 615
and Sanskritization 4000
Spencer and 603, 1258, 1504, 1506,
    1615, 4361
Takata and 4922
and values 5170–1
Weber and 4363
world-systems perspective 1060
see also modernization; revolutions
social change and causal analysis 4364–70
social change: the contributions of S. N.
    Eisenstadt 4370–4
social change, Southeast Asia 1689–92,
    4374–80
social character 3917
social citizenship 497, 498, 499
social class *see* class
social closure theory 664
social cognition 635, **4380–3**
    and impression formation 2270
social comparison theory 4170, **4383–6**
    and attraction 203
social constraints 1359
    Marxist theory 4389
social constructionism
    and abolitionism 1
    and agenda setting 63
    and the body 335, 336, 1847
    and disability 337
    and emotion work 1383
    and the health professions 2077
    and heterosexuality 2112
    Kitsuse and 2471–2
    and lesbianism 2612
    and medical sociology 2935
    and naturalistic enquiry 3161, 3162
    and new social movement theory 3208
    and reflexivity 3831
    and science 4093–6
    and sexual identity 3728–9
    and sexuality research 2160
    and social problems 4500–1
    strong social constructionism 1089
social contract 256, 397, 3589
    Hobbes and 512
social control 2454, **4386–90**
    and accounts 11
    in alliances 121
    by network members 89
    and civil law 2552

community and institution controls 846
and conflict theory 4388
and criminalization of deviance 1099
and delinquency 2454
and deviance 1078, 1079, 1095, 1102, 1104,
    1119, 1120
and deviance processing 1122
and disability sport 1172
and the disciplinary society 1176–8
and family support 846
governmentality and control 2008–11
and the Internet 733, 734
labeling perspective 2952, 4388
mechanical society 581
and medicalization 1112–13
and moral entrepreneurship 3086, 3087
organic society 582
primary group controls 846
riots 3924
and routine activity theory 3959
school discipline 4019–23
and self-control 846
social control theory of crime 844–7
and surveillance 2011
and transcarceration 5034–5
see also governmentality and control
social control agencies 1107
Social Darwinism 291, 1169, 4114, **4390–2**
    and evolutionary biology 1488
    evolutionary theory 1595–7
    and family history 1595–6
    Gumplowicz and 2039
    mores and folkways 3231–2
    Nietzsche and 3215
    and racism 3592
    and social change 1261–2
    Spencer and 1083, 1506
    survivalist ethic 1896, 2121, 4640
social decision schemes 982–3
social democratic parties 553
social determinism 734, 969
social dilemmas 4392–5
    and benefit and victimized zones concept
        266–7
    and daily life pollution 967, 968
    and game theory 1822
    and rational choice sociology 3798
social disorganization theory 846, 848,
    4395–8, 4498
    broken windows theory of crime 825–6, 2341
    collective efficacy and crime and 585
    and deviance 1081, 1102, 1105, 1119, 1136

social disorganization theory (*cont'd*)
   and juvenile delinquency 2455
   and social pathology 4489
social distance 4398–9
social dynamics 651, 1809
social economy 1301, 1304–5, 2442
   see also economic sociology
social embeddedness of economic action
   4399–403
   disembedded economy concept 3429
   distanciation and disembedding 1188–9
   double embeddedness 1412
   and entrepreneurship 1412, 1413
   and the ethnic/informal economy 1459
   and institutions 2345
   markets 2782, 2783, 2784
   and moral economy 3085
social engineering 129, 257, 950, 2617
   see also operant conditioning
social epidemiology 1434, **4403–6**
   diability as a social problem 1168–70
   and disease, prevalence of 1186
social epistemology 4406–8
social evolution 1505–6, 1811
social evolutionism 148–9
   Boas and 322
   Malinowski and 2705
social exchange theory 4408–10
   Blau and 313, 314
   commodity exchange 742
   and decision-making 982, 984
   and dyadic relations 1512
   Emerson and 1370
   and family theory 1630–1
   and helping behaviors 3680
   Homans and 2145
   identity processes and exchange relations 3183
   and power-dependence theory 3598–9
   reciprocity 4401
   and relational cohesion theory 3845–8
   and ritual 3937
   social behavior as exchange 2145
   symbolic exchange 742
   unequal exchange theory 1545
   see also exchange network theory
social exclusion 4411–13
   and absence of community 619
   and the central business district 423
   and drug use 1237
   and homelessness 2146–50
   and marginalization 2765

   and mental disorder 2952
   and poverty 3590
social fact 2964, 2965, **4414–16**
   Durkheim and 1256, 1281, 1417, 1485, 2964,
     3164, 4155–6, 4414
social fitness 292
social fluidity 2368–72, 2377
social gerontology 1927–8
social goods 702
social harmony 651, 652–3
   see also integration
social identity theory 2205, 2211–12, 2216,
   2216–19, 2220, 2224, **4417–20**
social imaginary 406–7, 524
   and utopia 2577
social impact theory 4428
social indicators 4420–6
social inequality
   determinants 264
   and education 2116, 2117
   see also inequality and the city; stratification
     and inequality; stratification and
     inequality, theories of
social influence 228, **4426–9**
social insurance systems 1169, 1809, 2054–5
   see also Social Security
social integration and inclusion 4429–32
   Blau and 314
   Durkheim and 3007–8, 3904, 4429–30
   and mental health 81
social interaction *see* interaction
social intervention *see* prevention, intervention
social issue documentaries 1210
social justice, theories of 3821, **4432–6**
   and autoethnography 231
   and benefit and victimized zones 267
   and black feminism 306
   and black feminists 306
   and disability 480, 481
   Durkheim and 1258–9, 1260
   and environmental movements 1431–2
   and feminist activism 1677
   and global consumption 1963
   King and 2465
   and media messages 2827
   and performance ethnography 3393
   procedural justice 4434–5
   Rawls and 3812–13
   see also distributive justice; global justice as a
     social movement
Social Lamarckism 4391

social learning theory 3505, **4437–40**
  attentional processes 4437
  and deviance 1102, 1119, 1120
  and game theory 1824
  and health locus of control 2063
  and helping behaviors 3680
  and juvenile delinquency 2454
  motor reproduction processes 4438
  reinforcement and motivational processes
    4438
  retention processes 4437–8
  and sexuality 4273
  and socialization 4572
social learning theory of crime 822, 845, 847–9
  and aggressive behavior 65
social market economy 3176
social mobility *see* mobility: intergenerational
  and intragenerational; mobility, horizontal
  and vertical
social modeling 257
social morphology 2047
social movement industry 3894
social movement organizations **4440–3**
  bureaucratization 3259, 4441
  collective action 574–80, 1141
  collective identity 955, 956, 1874
  consumers' leagues 1058
  contentious politics approach 779–82
  counterculture and 809
  culture and 954–6
  deradicalization 3260
  emergence and recruitment 954, 1873
  and emotions 1389–91
  framing processes 1780–3
  gendered 1874
  globalized communication forms 1960
  goals 956, 4468
  identity-oriented 780
  ideology 955
  institutionalization 3258
  internal dynamics 4441
  international 981
  interpretive frames 1874
  life cycle model 3258–9
  mobilization 780, 2847, 3455, 3457
  movement dynamics 955–6
  new social movement theory 780–1, 954
  and NGOs 3212
  in non-democratic states 782
  and political process theory (PPT) 3455–8,
    3460
  and political sociology 3460

  professionalization 3258
  racist movements 3767–71
  strategy-oriented 780
  success 781–2
  tactics 779–82, 1874
  xenophobic movements 1454
  see also Civil Rights Movement; resource
    mobilization theory; social movements
social movement research 1285
social movement sector 3894
social movements **4443–51**
  bisexuals and 303
  Christian 1981
  collective identity and 586–8
  collective trauma and 594
  cross-movement coalitions 124
  deinstitutionalization movement 995–6
  and direct democracy 407
  discontent theories 4444–5
  dynamics 4447–8
  emergence 1390, 4446–7
  and emotions 4446
  ethnic, racial, and nationalist movements
    1465–75
  funding 4444–5
  globalization of 1474
  and group identity 1466, 2224
  and identification 2219
  and institutionalism 2356
  internal dynamics 1390
  Internet presence 2910
  men's movements 1873
  militancy 4449
  moral shock and self-recruitment perspective
    3092–3
  movement demise 1390
  music as organizing tool 3134–6
  and political opportunities 3447–50
  reactive movements 1473, 1474
  recruitment processes 1390
  religious framing 3868
  see also Civil Rights Movement;
    revolutions; women's movements;
    specific movements
social movements, biographical
  consequences of **4451–3**
social movements, leadership in 3261,
  4453–5
social movements, networks and **4455–8**
  collective action 578
  direct network ties 3686
  and environmental movements 1428, 1430

social movements, non-violent **4458–63**
  and direct action 1165–6
  and environmental movements 1428
social movements, participatory
    democracy in 3258, 3260, **4463–6**
  and global justice movement 1949
  and the Internet 2387
social movements, political consequences
    of 4449, **4466–70**
social movements, recruitment to 3067,
    4471–4
  mobilization processes 3066
social movements, relative deprivation
    and **4474–5**
social movements, repression of **4475–9**
social movements, strain and breakdown
    theories of 3065, 3066, **4479–82**
social network analysis 2742, 3182–4, **4482–4**
  and groups 2031
  multivariate analysis 3122
social network theory 2905, **4484–6**
  and economic sociology 1321
  exchange network theory 1512–14
  and small work structure 1312
  weak ties 3754, 4486
social networks 2903, 2905
  and community 620, 637
  Network-Episode Model (NEM) 2106
  online 101–2
  and social support 88–9, 90, 92, 98
  see also networks
social order **4487–9**
  and conservatism 679
  construction through revolution 2577
  Hegel and 2099
  see also civil society
social pacts 2511
social pathology **4489–90**, 4498
  and dangerousness 969–70
social policy, welfare state **4490–5**
  and earner–carer model 1271–2
social problems, concept and perspectives
    4495–502
  agenda-setting 63
  applied sociology 4496
  causes 1597
  claims-making activities 2473
  constructionist perspective 4496–7
  and early childhood 1270
  gambling 1817–18
  problem drug use 1237

social constructionist perspective 1141,
    4500–1
  and social disorganization 4498
  social indicators 4420–6
  and social pathology 4489–90, 4498
  social problems as social harm 4496
  and the social question 4496, 4497
  textbook eclecticism of social
      problems 4496
social problems, politics of **4502–7**
  chidhood disabilities 1572–4
social problems theory 1087
social production 1668
social production function theory 3797
social psychology 2145, 2748, **4508–17**
  altruism 3679
  cognitive and intrapersonal social psychology
      4508–9
  and decision-making 983
  and ethnomethodology 4510
  experimental methods 4514
  and group processes 2027
  and identity control theory 2206
  interaction focus 4514–15
  intergroup relations 4515–16
  interpretive methods 4513–14
  and neuroscience 3186
  organizations and institutions 4516
  prosocial behavior 3679
  and reference groups 3828–9
  structural social psychology 4511–12
  survey and interview methods 4514
  symbolic interactionism 4509–11, 4515
social psychology, applied **4517–21**
social reaction theories 858
social relations of science movement 1542
social reproduction 389
social responsibility
  norm of 2759, 3680
  and rape culture 3785
social rootedness 597
social science 872, 1669–70, 2108, 2400
  aestheticization 2972
  arts/social science overlap 2973
  boundary work 2963
  feminist 2611
  lesbian 2611, 2613
  and linguistics 2534
  and macro–micro links 2997
  and management 2713
  meta-analysis 2963

positivist 2968
research methods and strategies 5076–7
structural turn in social sciences 3069
social science methodology 3235
social scripting 2468
Social Security 1720, 1840, 1842, 1904, 2233, 2288, 2367
and late-life economic inequality 3256
and lone-parent families 2664–5
retirement benefits 3900
social semiology 242
social services 4521–4
and childhood disabilities 1573
social solidarity, Durkheim and 1199, 1256, 1258
social statics 651
social structure 4524–6
Blau on 313, 314–15
Blumer on 319, 320
Germani on 1922
macrostructural theory 313, 314–15
mathematics of social structure 2856
social structure of victims 4526–7
and benefit and victimized zones 267
social structure-social learning (SSSL) theory of crime 849
social studies of science and technology (STS) 1908
social support 4527–31
aging and social support 88–92, 98
availability 90
buffering effects model 89
for caregivers 401, 2070–1
convoy model 90
direct effects model 89, 4528
and health promotion 2080
home-based services 2070
mental health problems 995
and mental well-being 82
neighborhood level 2073
network theory 98
oldest old 2668
positive effects 89
and stress and health 2071, 4832
stress-buffering model 4528
social support and crime 4531–2
social system 4532–3
autopoietic social systems theory 2675–7
and management theory 2714
and voluntary association 3075–6
social systems of production 1411
social theory and sport 2236, 4533–7

social work: history and institutions 4537–41
social work: theory and methods 4541–6
social worlds 4546–9
socialism 4549–54
Castoriadis and 406–7
and communism 614, 616
crisis of 4553
De Beauvoir and 253
democratic socialism 2296, 3585
economic system 2232–3
and Engels 1409
and fascism 1647
Frankfurt School and 865
goals 2296
income redistribution 392
and individualism 614
Jews and 158–60
laborism 2536–7
Luxemburg and 2685
and nationalism 3146
racial/ethnic conflict under 661
revolutionary and proletarian wing 614
revolutionary socialism 158–9, 160, 2296
scientific socialism 245, 1150, 4550
and sport 2236
and the working class 1201
socialist feminism 1711, 4554–5
dual systems approach 1711
and intersectionality 2395
and sport 1877
and women's inequality 1888–9
socialist internationalism 2996
socialist medicine 4555–8
socialization 4558–63
Asian cultures 207
and career mobility 1143
and career readiness 3286, 3287
child socialization 1269, 1270, 1503, 1581, 1594, 1630, 1857, 2020, 2296, 4019, 4321
and the common school system 4039
developmental stages 1071
and education 1336
emotional socialization 1380
Freudian model 4560
gender socialization 1591–2, 1667–8, 1792, 1846, 3698, 4198
grandparent agency 2020
and the lifeworld 2652
mass media and socialization 2824–7, 4561–2, 4573
medical school socialization 2930–1

socialization (*cont'd*)
  and nationalism 3154
  and occupational preferences 3245
  professional 2930–1
  and religion 4147
  resocialization 3891–3
  rites of passage 2931
  and rituals 2931
  and role identities 2224
  and school discipline 4019
  and self-control 4164, 4165
  sex-role socialization 2818
  social learning perspective 4572
  structural functional perspective 4559
  symbolic interactionist perspective 4559,
    4563, 4572, 4574
  through sport 2120, 4708–9
socialization, adult 4564–6
  and resocialization 3891–2
socialization, agents of 4566–8
  medical schools 2930–1
  significant others 4320–1
socialization, anticipatory 4569–70
socialization, gender 4571–4
  and occupational segregation 3245
socialization, primary 4574–5
socialization and sport 1242, **4576–80**
  high school sports 2120
socialized medicine 4580–1
society and biology 4581–5
Society of Equals 614
Society for the Study of Social Problems
  (SSSP) 132, 270
Society for the Study of Symbolic
  Interaction 133
socioanalysis 2748
Socio-Behavioral Model (SBM) 2105
sociobiology 285, 291, 292, 5173
  and the body 331
  and conflict theory 665
  and ethnic and race relations 661
  and evolution 1507, 1510
  feminist sociobiology 1511
  and gender inequalities 2309
  resistance to 4085
sociocultural ecology 2392
sociocultural evolution 293, 1760
sociocultural relativism 979, **4585–90**
  and deviance 1078, 4588–9
socioeconomic assimilation 193
socioeconomic determinism 3075
socioeconomic homogamy 674, 675

socioeconomic life cycle 3062
socioeconomic status, health, and
  mortality 1184, **4590–3**
  and health inequalities 2090
  morbidity and mortality variations 2087
  racial variations 3757, 3759
socioeconomic status (SES)
  black–white income gap 264
  and disease prevalence 1186
  and educational attainment 1335
  and family diversity 1591
  and friendships 1796, 1802
  and health 99–100
  and IQ scores 264
  and models of urban form 1280
  and mortality 99
  parent–child relation 1612
  and partner choice 674
  and psychological distress 2951, 2952, 2953
  status exchange hypothesis 2394
sociohistorical analysis 143, 2760
sociolinguistics 2535, 2536, **4593–6**
  and bilingualism 281, 282
  and conversation 790
  and management discourse 2723
sociological imagination 4596–8
  Fromm and 1807–8
  Mills and 1127, 1245, 2589, 3053, 3400,
    3964, 4596–8, 4604
sociological institutionalism 2353–7
sociological social psychology 228, 2027
Sociologie du travail 1411
sociologism 1520
Sociologists for Women in Society (SWS) 131,
  271, 1670, 1671
sociology 4598–609
  cultural turn 4605
  disciplinarity 4606–7
  global sociology 4606
  institutionalization 4602–6
  origins 4599–602
sociology of health *see* medical sociology
sociology in medicine 4609–11
  see also medical sociology
sociology of scientific knowledge (SSK)
  see scientific knowledge, sociology of
sociometry 1500, 2748, 3182, 4133, **4611–12**
sociopathology 65, 1081, 1136
socio-technical systems (STS) theory 429
sociotheology 4296
Socrates 612, 1114
SOCRATES exchange program 279

sodomy 1096, 2157, 3276
sodomy laws 607, 1834
Soeters, J. 3315–19
soft systems methodology 3268
Sohyo 1414
soil erosion 1423
soil fertility 1425
Soka Gakkai 1982, 3202, 3204
Sokal, A. 1509, 3553
Solar Temple 886, 3047
solicitation 2555
Solidarity 511, 3867
solidarity 4612–15
  bounded 1412, 3530
  collective 1262
  community 1575, 1579
  and community media 628
  cultural 3421
  and cultural reproduction 911
  and deference behaviors 990
  Durkheim and 181, 1199, 1200, 1253, 1256,
    1258, 1262, 1965, 2003, 2560, 3074, 3464,
    3621, 3670, 3918
  emotional 1389
  ethnic 1453, 1457, 1460, 1461, 1462, 1463,
    1465
  family 1618
  fraternal 3524
  gay and lesbian 606
  global 1960
  health care implications 2056
  in-group solidarity 726, 2338, 2750
  of individualism 1940
  internal 1389
  and the Internet 2385, 2387
  intragroup solidarity 2039
  kinship 2469, 2470
  lifestyle effects 2644
  national 3156
  print media function 3635
  racial 1245
  and rituals 1389
  siblings 2470
  social 1258, 1577, 1939, 1965
  trade unions 2289
  worker solidarity 1769, 2288
solidarity, mechanical and organic 1199,
  1200, 3146, **4515–17**
  and collective consciousness 581
  and Durkheim 1254, 1808, 2560, 3074, 3464,
    3621, 3918, 4615–17, 5102, 5104
  and social evolution 1506

Solomon, R. 2567
Solow, R. 3438
Somalia, female genital mutilation 1654, 1655
somaticized illnesses 2067, 2243
somatization 2242
Sombart, Werner 741, 2829, **4617–19**
Song, M. 3760–4
Sonny Bono Copyright Term Extension Act 730
Sony 1642, 2887, 3490
Sorau, O. 2803
Sorensen, A.B. 3301
Sorkin, M. 1642
Sorokin, Pitirim A. 132, 971, 2948, 2958,
  4619–23
  and altruism 3679
  and the Bolshevik revolution 594
  and civiization 4621
  and deviance 3544
  and Merton 2959, 2960
  and occupational mobility 3061
  and rural/urban sociology 4620–1
Souchy, A. 2007
Soul 2434, 2435
  idea of the 3629
  immortality thesis 2439
Soule, S. A. 3685–8, 3687
South Africa
  affirmative action policies 42–4, 45, 47
  AIDS crisis 165
  apartheid 162–5, 404, 511, 660, 3732, 3751,
    3763, 4700
  authoritarian regimes 222
  caste system 404
  charismatic movement 440, 441
  colonial language 2260–1
  cultural tourism 921
  and discriminatory aggression 1183
  drag queens and kings 1224
  electoral processes 1952
  and federalism 1652
  folk religious pracctices 1764
  heritage tourism 920
  interracial marriage 2394
  majorities 2701
  and marginality 2764
  medical sociology 2935
  middleman minorities 3009, 3010
  nuclear technology 3038–9
  peace processes 3381, 3382, 3383
  and plural society 3420
  public school system 4049
  racial conflict 663

South Africa (*cont'd*)
 sporting boycotts 4687
 Truth and Reconciliation Commission 3382,
  5085, 5086, 5087
 UN intervention 1952
South Dakota Hepatitis A-Vaccine Study 2079
South Korea 4376
 democratization 3072
 economic collapse 2022
 economic success 1069, 1073, 2299
 filial piety 2380
 industrialization 2299, 3072
 peripheral state 1395
South Sea Company 2022
South Sea Islands 2867
Southern Christian Leadership Conference
 (SCLC) 509, 1165, 2466
Southerton, D. 748–50
souvenirs 763
sovereignty 4623–6
 'asabiyya 180
 and empire 1393, 1396
 external/international 4624
 and globalizing processes 1952
 Hobbes and 512
 internal/domestic 4623–4
 and liberalism 2623, 3451
 mutual recognition rule 4625
 and nationalist movements 1465, 1466, 1472
 non-intervention rule 4625
 popular sovereignty 2623, 3177
 sustainable development, constraints of 1992
 Westphalian sovereignty 1952
Soviet Union
 collapse of 239, 391, 660, 681, 1471, 1487,
  2625
 and collective trauma 595
 command economy 515, 1384
 communism 391, 615, 616
 conservative statecraft 680
 consumer movements 698
 cultural imperialism 907
 economy 391
 emigration 3020
 empire 1395
 and ethnic cleansing 1451
 global influence 1295
 health care system model 2055, 2056
 and human rights 1952
 industrialization 2298
 inequalities in 664
 life expectancies 3097

 propaganda 1753, 3673
 science and politics 276
 socialist medicine 4555–7
 socialist sports movements 2236
 Soviet anthropology 1839
 see also Russia
Soysal, Y. N. 3576
space 4626–9
 the city and 500, 501
 commercialized leisure space 766
 commodification of social space 703, 705
 and distanciation 1189
 domestic space 3717
 individual space 4627
 priate space 4627
 public spaces 4627
 situated space 4627
"space of flows" 3181
Spain
 anarchism 136
 authoritarian regimes 222
 bilingual education 279
 Catholicism 2530
 centralized control 1488
 cohabitation 567
 colonialism 603, 985, 3940, 4337–8
 cultural tourism 921
 demographic data 1033–4
 divorce rates 2664
 empire 1393
 environmental movements 1430
 ethnic mobilization 1470
 and federalism 1652
 Franquism 411
 health care system 2055
 health technology assessment 692
 immigration 2258, 2263, 3024, 3032
 laicism 2532
 lone parenthood 2663
 marginalized groups 2764
 medical sociology 2935
 nonmarital fertility 1734
 retirement policies 3903
 sport and nationalism 3160
 teenage motherhood 1728
 unions 2289
Spalter-Roth, R. 1705
spam emails 2389
Spangler, D. 3190
Spanier, G. B. 2773
Spanish Civil War 136
Spark, P. 745

Sparxxx, B. 3557
spatial behavior 2363
spatial mismatch hypothesis 2305, **4629–33**
spatial relationships 4633–5
  "space of flows" 3181
  see also public realm
**speaking truth to power: science and
    policy 4635–7**
Spears, Britney 726
Spears, R. 882
special interest unions 1416
Special Olympics 1171
specialists 379
species extinction 1273, 1423
species society 2249, 2251
Species-Being 1748, **4637–8**
speciesism, and ecofeminism 1275
spectacular consumption 755–9
  Debord and 755, 757–8, 2882–3, 3567,
    4329, 4704
  and *flânerie* 1762
  and media culture 2882–3
  and museums 3126
  sport as spectacle 4702–4
  tourism and 763
spectacular society, Debord and 980, 981, 3567
Spectorsky, A. C. 1550, 1551
spectral analysis 5008
speculation, financial 2021
speech act theory 1181
  and management discourse 2723
speech patterns 347
Spence, C. 4350–3
Spence, Donald L. 1936
Spencer, Herbert 1258, 2108, **4638–41**
  and altruism 655
  and attitudes and behavior 199
  dialectical model of social change 4639
  evolutionist sociology 603, 1258, 1504, 1506,
    1615, 4361, 4601, 4638–9
  functionalism 4638–9
  geopolitical theory 4640–1
  Nietzsche on 3215
  and positivism 2186
  social Darwinism 1083, 1506, 1595, 3344, 4640
  and social institutions 2344
  and social systems 4532
Spener, P. J. 3408
Spengler, O. 4363
Sperry, R. 3187
Spice Girls 726
Spielberg, S. 3497, 3881

spiked tire pollution 967–8
Spilerman, S. 3687
Spillman, L. 922–8
spillover 1248
spin-doctoring 2878, 3471
Spinners 3506
Spinoza, Baruch 3006
  rationalist epistemology 1434
Spinsters Ink 2603
spiritual seeking 3868
spiritual warfare doctrine 439, 441
Spiritualism 631
spirituality 751–2, 1981
  dwelling-based spirituality 751
  ecospirituality 752
  feminist spirituality 752
  goddess-focused 2603
  New Age 752
  and polyamory 3477
  practice-based spirituality 751, 752
  seeking-based spirituality 751
  see also new religious movements
spirituality, religion, and aging 4641–3
Spivak, G. 2984, 4790
split labor market theory 664, 1463, 1469, 3012
sponsored mobility systems 5024
sponsors of sport 4716
spontaneity
  and market coordination 2779
  and working-class movements 2687
sport 4643–53
  alternative sports 4701
  amateur sport 2599, 4667
  athletic success, valuing of 570
  character-building ethos 2120, 2122, 4577
  civilizing processes and 1750–1
  college sport 3440
  competition element 4644
  consumption of 760–1
  cruel sports 3473
  dangerous sports 3472, 3473
  democratization 4650–1
  and deviance 1131–5
  disability sport 1171–3
  and drugs/substance use 3473
  elite sport 1135
  embodiment 4643–4
  emotional dialectics 4749
  extreme sports 4652
  and figurational sociology 1749–51
  and gambling 1818–21
  gatherings 880

sport (*cont'd*)
 and gender 1875–9, 4666–7, 4672–3, 4700
 girls and school sport 1548
 globalization 1986–9, 4651, 4711, 4716–17
 goal oriented 4644
 homoerotic potential 4293
 and hybridity 2737
 and identity 2220–3
 and ideology 2235–6
 legitimization 4750
 ludic element 4644–7, 4649
 male identification with 1663
 mass sport 325
 and nationalism 3158–60
 neo-Marxist account 4696
 non-commercialized 768
 and patriarchy 3379
 and play 3416
 political economy of 3440–1
 politics and sport 3472–6, 4534–5
 and postcolonialism 3547–8
 power relations 3472, 3474
 professional sport 2093, 3440, 4684–5,
  4708–9
 quests for excitement 4648–9
 and race/ethnicity 1879
 rationalization 4650
 and ritual 1131
 school sport 1547, 1548
 and sexuality 4290–3
 and sociability 4647
 social theory 4533–7
 and socialization 4576–9
 spectator sports, and experiential
  consumption 716
 sponsors 4716
 structuration 4644
 symbolism 3474
 team sports 1548
 and violence 66, 531, 1133, 4348, 5199–201
 virtual sports 5208–11
 women athletes 1134, 1847, 1879, 2121
 youth sport 5308–11
 see also fans and fan culture; high school
  sports; media and sport
sport, alternative 4653–6
sport, amateur 4656–8
sport and the body 328, **4658–60**
 gendered bodies 1847
 working-class sport 336
sport and capitalism 3440, **4660–2**
sport as catharsis 4662–4

sport and the city 4664–5
sport clubs 761, 767
sport, college 2599, **4665–8**
 violence 1133
sport and culture 4668–77
 and globalization 1988
 and media representation 2918
 and the Olympics 3264
sport culture and subcultures 4677–80
sport and the environment 4680–1
sport ethic 1241
sport and ethnicity 4681–4
 stereotyping 2918
sport, professional 4670, 4677, **4684–6**
 media representation 2918
sport and race 4686–90
 African American stereotyping 2122, 2918
 high school sports 2122
sport and religion 4690–3
sport and social capital 4693–5
sport and social class 4695–9
sport and social resistance 4699–702
sport as spectacle 4702–4
 media representation 2919–20
 sports stadia 4718
sport and the state 4705–8
sport as work 1242, 2093, 3440, 4684–5,
  4708–10
 ancillary occupations 4709
 injury risk 2094
sportification 4650
sporting events and cultural tourism 921
sportization 4710–11
sports diplomacy 3474
sports ethic 2121
sports heroes and celebrities 4711–13
 and deviance 1132
 disabled athletes 1172
sports industry 4713–17
sports injuries 2093–4
sports medicine 4709
sports stadia 4694, **4717–19**
spousal abuse syndrome 2556
spread betting 1820
Springer, Ki. 309
Sprott, W. 1136
Spurlock, M. 356
Sputnik 2850
Squires, G. D. 4762–5
Sri Lanka
 affirmative action policies 45
 Buddhism 371

civil religion 507
ethnic conflict 3383
family planning programs 1738–9
female migration 1716
fundamentalism 1813
mortality decline 3100
riots 3923
self-help movement 1407
Srinivas, M. N. 1764, 4000–1
Srole, L. 145
Staatsnation 3144
staatvolk 3142
Stacey, J. 1671
Stack, C. 1438
Stack, S. 4881–4
Stafford, M. 1065–7, 2341
staged intersections 4548
stagflation 3176
Staggenborg, S. 2604
stakeholders
  and action research 17
  constructivist research 214–15
  organizations 354, 355, 356
  and technology assessment 691
Stalin, Joseph 616, 1150, 1451
Stalinism, and economic determinism 1293
Stalker, G. M. 2738, 3281
stalking 1100, **4719–20**
  cyberstalking 960, 965
Stam, H. 1086, 1087
Stamp Act 1765 2897, 3638
standard deviation 1065
standard error estimation 2974
standard metropolitan area 2991
standardization 4720–1
  demographic technique 1015, 1016
standardized educational tests 4721–5
  intelligence tests 2358–60
standpoint theory *see* feminist standpoint
  theory
Stanfield, J. 2465–7, 3428–30
Stanfield, R. 2493–7
Stanford School 1968, 2353, 2354, 2356
Stanton, Elizabeth Cady 1673, 2308, 2618
Staples, C. L. 1408–10, 1747–9
Star, S. L. 2362
Star Trek 3498, **3516–17**
Star Wars 1638
Starbuck, W. H. 2721, 3309
stare decisis principle 2554
Stark, R. 885, 886, 1315–16, 2146, 2438, 2441,
  3633, 4138

Stark, W. 2483–4
Starke, R. 751
Starks, B. 1568–70, 2564–5
Starr, P. 2167, 2934, 2935, 3657
state 3073, **4725–30**
  authoritarian state 297, 1911, 2576
  and bureaucracy 2356
  capitalist state 663
  class-based models 3462
  coercive organizations 3315–19
  contract state 4728
  corporatist state 4728
  crimes against 835
  despotism 3073–4
  diversification of services 3074
  ecological state 4728
  economic behavior 2355–6
  formation 3461
  green state 4728
  and imagined communities 2249
  and immigration 2255
  and institutionalism 2355–6
  interventionist state 2623, 4727
  Latin American state theory 2575–7
  legitimacy 3233, 4726
  Marx and 663
  and modernization 3974
  nation–state distinction 3142
  neo-Marxist analysis 3179
  neoliberalism and the state role 3177
  oligargic structures 3261
  patriarchal state 4728
  power 3424
  premodern states 3073
  regulatory state 2563
  social problems, and claims-making 4502,
    4503
  and socialization 4567–8
  sport and politics 3473
  sport and the state 4705–8
  state crime 835
  tyranny 3423
  widening of state capacities 3074
  see also nation-state
state constitutions, and criminal law 2554
state courts 812, 813, 853
state criminal codes 2554
state domestic relations laws 2110
state and economy 4730–4
  corporatist model 4732
  liberal model 4731–2
  statist model 4732

state monopoly capitalism 3179
state power 3585
state and private sector employees 4734–7
state regulation and the workplace 4737–41
static sociology 654, 655
statism 136, 3585
    organic 224
statistical estimation 657
statistical hypotheses 1533
statistical inference 657
    randomization and 789
statistical significance testing 4741–6
    and effect sizes 1345–6
    and hypotheses 2199–200
    and replicability analyses 3877–8
statistics 377, **4746–9**
    ANOVA (analysis of variance) technique
        146–7
    bivariate statistics 4748
    and decision-making 983
    descriptive statistics 1064–5, 3727
    general linear model 1897–8
    measures of centrality 2868–9
    multivariate analysis 3120–2
    multivariate statistics 4748–9
    path analysis 3373–4
    probability theory 4747–8
    univariate statistics 3120
    see also regression and regression analysis
status 4749–53
    and ability to forego productive labor 682
    adolescent status hierarchies 1547
    ambiguity 3252, 3253
    attainment 383
    and authority 227–8
    and bilingualism 282–3
    and bodywork 336, 710
    and career development 1143
    and caste 404
    and the civilizing process 721–2
    class and social status 533
    and conspicuous consumption 682, 683, 685,
        742, 816, 1851
    and cultural capital 891
    and cultural consumption 953
    and deference 990
    and education 1345
    emotional expectations and management
        1382, 1384
    employment status changes 1398–400
    employment status classifications 3241
    and extracurricular activities 1547

    and fashion 718
    group process perspective 2028
    and hyperconsumption/overconsumption
        2192
    insecurities 2192
    intergenerational transmission 383
    and labor force participation 699
    master statuses 2205, 2208, 2209, 2832
    and nationalism 3155
    occupational 3245, 4751
    and place 3410–11
    and power/prestige positions 1340, 1525
    and recognition 3821
    resocialization 3892
    and sport 2121
    status emulation, lifestyle as 2647
    teenage status systems 774, 775
    and visual culture 756
    and wealth 2311
    within groups 4751
status attainment 75, **4753–6**
    Blau on 313
    and education 1323, 1344
    and literacy 2654
    Wisconsin model 1529, 1530
status characteristics theory 2028, 4989
status construction theory 4756–9
    and power and prestige theory 1525
status defensiveness 1376
status exchange hypothesis 2394
status goals 1119
status groups 538, 548
    group norms 774
    in schools 774
status honor 2645
status ideology 535–6
status insecurity 1007
status markers 2515
status offenses 2454, 4192–3
status passages 4759–62
status struggles 1750
status symbols 536, 683, 685, 756
status value theory 1356, 3605
Staub-Bernasconi, S. 4541–6
Stauber, J. 3674
Stauth, G. 180–5
Stavenhagen, R. 340
Stavrakis, Y. 2528
Stearns, P. 744
Stebbins, R. A. 2596–601, 2597, 2598, 5000,
        5316–17
Steele, C. M. 562–3

steering, racial real estate 316, 317, 3708, 3733, 3748, **4762–5**
see also redlining
Stefanic, J. 2549
Stehr, N. 2480–2, 3606–7
Stein, A. A. 2338–9, 2604
Stein, E. 1830–3
Stein, R. 1275
Steinberg, R. 1705
Steinmetz, G. 2815–18
stem cell research 738, 2171
Stepan-Norris, J. 2227–30, 4453–5, 5099–101
stepchildren 4766–72
   academic performance 1623
   behavior problems 1623
   stepgrandchildren 2017
   well-being 1623
stepfamilies 4765–8
   and family sociology 1617
   and family structure 1620
   and kinship 2471
   see also stepchildren
stepfathering 1601, **4768–70**
   and childcare 1603
Stephens, S. 460
stepmothering 4770–2
stereotyping and stereotypes 4773–8
   African Americans 1664, 1879, 2918, 3739, 3764
   agist 58
   and anti-Semitism 156
   bisexuals 304
   blackness/whiteness 3737
   of the colonized subject 1396
   cultural stereotypes 2551
   and disabled athletes 1172
   and ethnicity 2702
   fans 1637
   gender stereotyping 1663, 1870, 3764–5
   late-life sexuality 2540
   and majorities 2702
   music and sexual stereotyping 747
   and occupational segregation 1342
   occupations 1859, 3249, 4190
   older workers 104
   personality stereotypes 2271
   and prejudice 3614
   racial 2918
   racist 1984
   and self-fulfilling expectations 4173
   sexual stereotyping 1664, 1665, 1879, 3650, 3764, 4220

sport stereotypes 4688
stepmothers 4772
"third world" women 1692, 1984, 2397
womanhood 308, 1706, 1844, 3786
sterilization 1609, 4115
   as contraception 1738
sterilization policies 1169, 1489, 1496
   and eugenics 1489, 1508, 2938
   forced sterilization 2621
Sterling, B. 3497
Stern, B. 2932
Sternberg, Y. 4370–4
Sterne, J. 963
Sternhell, Z. 1646
steroids 1132, 1134
Steuart, Sir James 3440
Stevens, F. 2052–8
Stevens, G. 1197–9, 2258–62
Stevens, M. L. 4032–4
Stevenson, C. 2220–3, 2222
stewardship, culture of 947
Stewart, A. T. 1057
Stewart, F. 1446
Stiffarm, L. A. 2282
Stigler, G. J. 625
Stiglitz, J. 3592
stigma 4778–9
   agist 58
   and AIDS 109, 711
   alcoholism 583
   apartheid 162
   biracialism 295
   bisexuality 639
   coping strategies 2832
   courtesy stigma 1572, 1573, 2502
   cultural context 323
   and Deadheads 3505
   and deviance 1127, 1140, 2504, 2505, 2506
   disability 323
   and disabled athletes 1172
   and drug use 26
   and football hooliganism 1767
   and genetic information 1907
   homosexuality 324, 583, 639, 1833, 2009, 2159
   and identity politics 2214
   and illness 2246
   and infertility 2322
   and lesbianism 2609
   mental disorder 583, 2505, 2951, 2952
   neutralization 1094
   and norms 1092

stigma (*cont'd*)
  prostitution 3682
  and self-concept 2832
  sex work 1660, 1662
  tattoing 330
  tribal stigma 583–4
Stillman, T. 2689–90
Stimson, J. A. 2233
stimulus sampling theory 2856
stimulus-response theory 209
Stinchcombe, A. 1809, 2960
Sting 3557
Stirner, M. 136
stochastic processes 2855
stock exchanges 394
stock markets 2629, 3323
stock ownership 394
stoicism 1147
Stokes, C. 310
Stokvis, R. 1751
Stone, C. 311
Stone, G. 1379, 2218, 2961
Stone, J. 45–8, 659–62, 1457–9
Stone, L. 1577, 1673
Stone-Sweet, A. 2558
Stonequist, E. 2763
Stoner-Eby, S. 1330, 1331
Stones, R. 873, 4859–64
Stonewall riots (1969) 1225, 1834, 2159
Storey, J. 918–19
storge love 2671
Storper, M. 2741
storytelling 9, 169
Stouffer, S. 2407, 3041
Stowe, Harriet Beecher 3637
strain theories 4779–82
  and anomie 145
  and collective action 575–6
  and conformity 4780
  and delinquency 2819
  and deviance 1102, 1134
  gender role strains 2486, 2487, 2819, 2820
  general strain theory 4781–2
  and relative deprivataion 4474
  and social movements, breakdown of 4479–81
  and social movements, emergence of 954
  and stress 4838
  and suicide 4882
Strange, J.-M. 1381
stranger rape 2309
stranger, the 4782–4
Strasser, S. 743, 5217

strategic choice theory 3281, 3302
strategic decisions 4784–9
  and top management teams 5016–17
strategic essentialism 4789–91
strategic interaction, identity politics and 2214–15
strategic interdependence, and game theory 1822
strategic management (organizations) 4791–6
  performance evaluation 3396
  process approach 4794
  rational approach 4793–4
  strategic decisions 4784–9
strategic niche management, and technology assessment 691
strategy ecology 293
stratification
  age and 74
  American form 534
  and capitalism 390
  caste system 404–5
  and community colleges 621
  and critical realism 872
  and deviance 1137
  economic 535
  and educational outcomes 2463
  and elites 1362
  and family sociology 1599
  and functionalism 1811
  gender stratification 1667, 1668–9
  and the hidden curriculum 2117
  and life chances and resources 2628
  and literacy differentials 2654–6
  racial/ethnic 1895
  and racial/ethnic conflict 661
  and schools 1326
  status groups 535–6
  Weberian approach 664
  and world-systems theory 1060
  see also class
stratification, distinction and 4796–7
  and discourse 1179
stratification: functional and conflict theories 4797–9
stratification, gender and 4799–801
  and occupational segregation 3244–5
stratification and inequality 971
  and disability 1168
  and education 1326, 1339
  and educational attainment 1334–5
  global income inequality 2274–5
  and lifestyle 2645

and meritocracy 2954
in schools 4177
wealth inequality 2310–13
in the workplace 3649
stratification and inequality, theories of 4801–10
class hierarchy 545
class, status, and power 547–51
and cultural capital 888
and income dynamics 98
and justice analysis 1196
and learning opportunities 3272
and life chances and resources 2628, 2629, 2630
meritocratic perspective 2957
and occupations 3248
spiralling processes 2630
see also poverty
stratification: partner effects 4810–12
stratification, politics and 4812–15
stratification, race/ethnicity and 4815–19
and occupational segregation 3244–5
paternalistic relations 3370–1
scientific racism 4113–15
stratification in science 2860
stratification systems: openness 4819–20
stratification: technology and ideology 4820–4
stratification in transition economies 4824–7
stratified reproduction 4827–9
Straus, R. 2067, 2933
Strauss, A. 233, 320, 973, 2023, 2024, 2025, 2026, 2217–18, 2631, 2933, 2934, 2961, 4547
Strauss, D. 896
Strauss, G. 2752–4
Strauss, L. 679, 3173
Strauss, S. 2192
Stravinsky, Igor 1916
Streeck, J. 2363
street crime 820, 1102, 1106, 1121, 2102, 2341, 3197
Street, D. 84–8
street parties 1165
street performance, and political expression 779, 1166
street prostitution 1660, 1661
street theater 1165, 1166
Street Transvestites Action Revolutionaries 1225
street-hawkers 3031
Streib, G. 3903–6

stress
adrenaline response 1866, 1867
economic stress 1614
marital stress 1614
and medical sociology 2935
and poverty 1614
religious coping strategies 2082
self-reported 1867
stress-related illness 1866
stress and health 4829–33
allostatic load 2074
and caregiving 403
coping responses 4831
and divorce 1208
and exercise 1516
life stress paradigm 2069–70
mediators 4831
psychological resources 4831
psychosocial resources 2069, 2070
race/ethnic populations 3759
social resources 4831–2
and social support 2071
stress-related illness 4842
vulnerability factors 4830
stress management programs 2750
stress and migration 4833–7
stress, stress theories 4837–40
and absenteeism 5
children of divorced parents 468
chronic stressors 4837–8
and depression 82
event stressors 4837
and health 100
and life event sequencing 4838
and mental illness 98
occupational pathology 3289
stress exposure 82
stress and work 4840–3
demand-control model 4841
dual-earner couples 1248
effort-reward imbalance 4841–2
stressful life events 4843–5
and child well-being 1622
and mental disorder 2695, 2951
Strickland, A. L. 1495
strikes 780, 1165, 1674, 2288, 2290
strip-mining 1418
stripping, strip clubs 1659, 1661, 1717, 2599
Strobl, R. 4429–32
Strodtbeck, F. 1484
strong objectivity 1682, 4845–6
and feminist methodology 1703

Strong Program 3815, 4065, 4097, **4846–8**
Stroud-Drinkwater, C. 2661
structural adaptation to regain fit (SARFIT) 3301
structural adjustment programs (SAPs) 1724, 2382–3
structural assimilation 1458
structural balance theory 2854, 2856
structural contingency theory 3281, 3282
structural equation modeling 2975, **4848–51**
structural functional theory 4852–5
  and anomie 145
  Chicago School and 448
  critique of 4853–4
  and cybernetics 633
  Davis and 1808–9
  and deviance 1170
  and disability sport 1172
  and division of labor 1199
  and Durkheim 1251, 1254–5, 1259, 1810, 3581, 3582, 4852, 4861
  and expectations/aspirations 1529
  and family theory 1630
  four-function paradigm 3366–7
  and Frankfurt School 876
  and function 1808
  and functionalism 1809–10
  and gender inequalities 2309
  and gender oppression 1871
  and globalization of education 1971
  and identity 2220
  and illness 2059
  and Latin America 1920
  and medical school socialization 2930, 2934
  and Merton 127, 1809, 1810–11
  and Mexican sociology 2949
  and modernization 1600
  and nationalization of education 1972
  Parsons and 633, 634, 876, 1251, 1252, 1257, 1529, 1598, 1809, 1810–11, 1928, 2031–2, 2309, 2361, 2675, 2832, 2965, 3312, 3366–7, 3374, 3581, 3582, 4524–5, 4852–3, 4915
  and social problems concept 4499
structural interactionism, and identity 2218, 2219
structural lag 102
structural social psychology 4511–12
structural strains, successive transition of 4855–6

structuralism 3366, **4856–9**, 4981
  and the Annales School 143
  auteur structuralism 219
  Barthes and 242
  Bourdieu and 347
  and culture 298
  and deviance 2207
  and dramaturgy 1229
  and emotion work 1383
  and ethnography 1480
  and fandom 1640
  and film 1755
  and genres 1916
  and hermeneutics 2107
  historicist structuralism 143
  and ideology 913
  and intertextuality 2402
  and Islam 2427
  and Japanese-style management 2437
  and Latin American economic structures 1567
  new structuralism 3325
  and the state 3458
  see also poststructuralism
structuralist anthropology, and deviance 1137
structuration theory 4859–61
  adaptive structuration theory 3295
structure and agency 4861–4
  agency–structure debate within the social sciences 1074
  and charisma 438
  and intersectionality 2397
  and intersubjectivity 2400
  and intertextuality 2402
  and kin behavior 2470
  structure/agency dilemma 347, 348
structure theorem 561
structured action theory 2818, 2820–1
structured interviewing 2407–8
Strum, S. 3627
strutural cohesion 3846
Stryker, R. 1808–10, 2557–60, 2558, 2559
Stryker, S. 2224, 2225
student cheating stigma neutralization 1094
Student League for Industrial Democracy (SLID) 3194
student movements 509–10, **4864–9**
  mobilization 3067
  and the new left 3193–5
  non-violent protest 3193, 3194
  protest movement 577
Student Non-Violent Coordinating Committee (SNCC) 307, 3194, 4463

student sit-in movement 509
Students for a Democratic Society (SDS) 955,
    3194, 3195
Stufflebeam, D. 1499, 1500
Stulz, R. 1317
Sturdy, A. 2721, 2725–8
Sturgeon, N. 1273–7
Su Dongpo 2498
sub-fecundity *see* infertility
subaltern 2982, 2984, 4790, 4998
    see also third world and postcolonial
        feminisms/subaltern
subcastes 405
subcontracting *see* outsourcing
subcultural capital 1639, 4871
subcultural celebrities 1639
subcultural consensus 950
subculture 931, **4869–72**
    Birmingham School and 297, 299, 301
    and counterculture 809–10
    cross-dressing 1224
    and cultural resistance 912
    and cultural studies 914
    health-related subcultures 2073
    hip-hop 3486–7
    illicit subcultures 894
    indigenous peoples 342
    junkie subculture 797
    and juvenile delinquency 2454
    and pop music 1915
    sexual subcultures 2163
    sport subcultures 4677–9
    and urbanism 5145–6
    youth subcultures 297, 299, 773, 2102, 3089
subcultures, deviant 1129, **4872–7**
    positivist theories 4873–4
subfamilies 1584–5
    related subfamily 1585
    unrelated subfamily 1585
subject
    Cartesian view 2527
    mirror stage 2527–8
    split of the subject 2528
subjective expected utility model 3800
subjectivity 1147, 3820, **4877–8**
    and biography 290
    black radical subjectivity 306
    difference as 1154
    documentaries 1212
    Guattari and 2038
sublimation 2708
subliminal voice accommodation 3186

submarines 3038
submerged networks 1679
suboptimization 3397
subordination
    cultural subordination 1469
    economic subordination 1395
    and empire 1392
    see also patriarchy
subordination of women 1689, 1846, 1874,
    1892, 2100, 2396
    accounting for 2627
    and heterosexuality 2112
subsidiarity 1947
subsistence agriculture 2766
subsistence production 548, 609
subsistence technology 4821
substantive theory 4060
Subud 3204
suburban growth corridors 3113
suburban sprawl 1425
suburbs 102, 501, **4878–81**
    and assimilation 193
    ethnoburbs 1454
    exurbia 1549–50
    and family and community 1576
    and internal migration 3018
    Levittown 2614–15
    mass suburbanization 1920
    and multinucleated metropolitan regions 3113
    and new urbanism 3211
    reluctant suburbs 1551
    space, and interaction patterns 4628
    and urban consumption 767
Suchman, E. A. 1143, 2242
Sudan
    female genital mutilation 1654, 1656
    Mahdi rebellion 3048
    marginalized groups 2764
Sudanese circumcision 1654
sudden infant death syndrome 2314, 3758
Sudnow, D. 1995
Suenens, Cardinal 441
suffering 372
    chronic illness/disability and 481, 482
    and peacemaking 3384
    sociology of 480
suffrage 351, 3469
    female suffrage 902, 2296, 2308, 2687, 3469
    Goldman and 2005
    Luxemburg and 2687
    male suffrage 2296
    mass suffrage 1001

suffrage (*cont'd*)
  political disenfranchisement of blacks 3746,
    3747
  racial issues 3469, 3746
  in totalitarian polities 3076
  universal suffrage 2627, 3076, 3469
suffragist movement 250, 1672, 1673, 1674,
    1686, 2618
  and black feminists 306
  hunger strikes 1848
Sufism 1981, 1982, 2003, 2131
suggestion theory 799
Sugimoto, Y. 2761–3, 3219
Suhomlinova, O. 3299–302
suicide 974, **4881–4**
  active martyrdom 2800
  anomic suicide 144
  copycat suicide 4883
  death instinct 65
  and documentary analysis 1214–15
  Durkheim and 144, 845, 1252, 1254, 1255,
    1256, 2047, 2799, 3008, 3230, 3689,
    4414, 4881
  Durkheim on 144, 845
  and euthanasia 1497
  gender ratio 4883
  media influences 2826
  physician-assisted suicide 1497
  social support, and suicide levels 4527
  and stigma 1497
  suicide attacks 2800–1
Sukkot 2452
Sullivan, D. F. 2096
Sullivan, H. S. 1635
Sullivan method 2096–7
sultanism 2858
Sumner, C. 978
Sumner, William Graham 130, 3592,
    4884–6
  and ethnocentrism 1478
  and family sociology 1615
  and in-group and out-groups 2338
  laissez-faire views 129
  and race relations 129
sumptuary laws 702
Sumter, M. 801–3, 3640–3
Sun Cities 3904
Sun, I. Y. 1942–3, 2199–200, 3430–3
Sunbelt 993, 3114, 3967, **4886–8**, 5096
  ethnic enclaves 1454
Sunday schools 4053
Sundberg, M. 4104–6

Sung, H.-E. 114–16, 1433–4, 5179–80
Sunni Islamism 2425–6, 3048
Super, D. 3286
super-ego 530, 837, 875, 1071, 1786, 2434
super-maximum prisons 3641–2
supermarkets 4888–90
supernaturalism 441, 669, 670, 3862
  and madness 2694
superordination/subordination 4326–7
superstition, and popular religiosity 3524
"superwoman"/"supermom" image 2620
Supplementary Security Income 996
supply chains 1411, 2202, **4890–5**
  international 2741
  management 3269, 3270
supranational organizations 1472
surface acting 1382
surplus-labor extraction 1543–4, 1545
Surrealism 980, 2189, 3406, 4329, 4335
surrogacy 2608, 3104, 3207
surveillance 4895–8
  and academic freedom 2349
  of the body 332, 334
  and deviance processing 1122
  and dyads/tryads 1266
  electronic surveillance 2916
  and fantasy cities 1642
  and Foucault 1122
  and governmentality 2011
  and the information society 2330
  and information technology 2335
  institutional review boards 2346–9
  media regulation 2911–16
  panoptics 1122, 1177, 1178, 1776, 2566,
    4896, 4897
  photographic 3407
  and the post-panoptic society 555
  print media function 3635
  in prisons 1776
  and privacy 3, 366, 2643
  and prostitution 3682
  and racist movements 3770
  self-surveillance 334, 711, 1113
  unlawful state surveillance 835
survey experiments 1540
survey research 1669, 2564, 4514,
    4898–900
  computer-assisted interviewing 1540
  and cultural criminology 895
  illness behavior 2242–3
  Marxist 2816
  and networks 2742

quantitative date collection 3727
  and secondary data analysis 4127
survival analysis 1017
survival of the fittest 1504, 1506, 2121, 4392
Süss-Oppenheimer, J. 157
sustainability 728, 1070, 1285, 1419
  agriculture 1273
  ecology–economy partnership 1292
  environmental 1963
  and global consumption 1963
  social security schemes 1903
sustainable development
  economic development 1563
  and government policies 1285
  tourism and 762
  and western consumption practices 1992
  women's role 1692
Suter, C. 2491
Suter, L. E. 2849–53
Sutherland, Edwin H. 818, 820, 837, 859,
  860, 2472, **4900–3**
  and criminology 856
  and differential association 848, 1103, 1120,
    1133, 3167–8, 4901–2
  and sexual psychopath laws 1097
  and social learning theory 848
  and white-collar crime 543, 850, 851, 4901
Suttles, G. D. 715, 1767–8, 1789
Sutton, J. R. 2354
Suvin, D. 3495
SUVs 728
Suzuki, Eitaro 4903–6
Suzuki, Y. 471–4, 505–6, 4903–6, 5029–30,
  5143–5
Svoboda, D. M. 641
Swaaningen, R. van 1–2
Swann v. *Charlotte-Mecklenbrug Board of*
  Education 369
Swartz, T. 2849
Swatos, W. H., Jr. 686–7, 1051–6, 2050–1,
  3373–4, 3977–80, 4135–40, 4963–5
sweatshops 365, 726, 1679, 1715
  electronic sweatshops 1162
  ethnic 1453, 1454
Swedberg, R. 1321, 1760
Sweden
  aging and social policy 86
  births outside marriage 2663
  child poverty 1627
  cohabitation 566, 1587
  consumer movements 697
  democracy 1001

demographic data collection 1012, 1046
diffusion of protest 3686
divorce rates 2664
  and earner–carer model 1272
eugenic management of the body 325
eugenic sterilization laws 1489
family leave 1883
family migration 1607
gender poverty ratios 1723
health care system 2055
health technology assessment 692
industrial democracy 2750
labor–management relations 2510
LAT relationships 811
lone parenthood 2663, 2664, 2665
marriage, delayed 1587
occupational segregation 3245
operations mangement in 3268
poverty 1723
press freedom 2912
production per worker 1959
retirement policies 3902–3
school system 1324
single motherhood 1723
social class inequalities in mortality 2090
socioeconomic policies 392
teenage motherhood 1728
transnational corporations 1944
wealth inequalities 2312
Sweezy, P. 1395, 2267, 2838, 3039, 3178,
  3179, 3437
Swidler, A. 2484
Swift, Jonathan 4107
Swingewood, A. 2821
swinging 3478
Switzerland
  and balkanization 240
  bilingual education 279
  democracy 1001
  ethnic pluralism 1458
  and federalism 1652
  health technology assement 692
  social security system 2055
  teenage motherhood 1728
  transnational corporations 1944
  welfare policies 4491
swordplay 1819
sylvester theism 3870
symbiosis 3944
  of nature and people 1407
symbolic capital 741, 889, 1639, 3582
symbolic classification 4906–8

symbolic communication 2030
symbolic exchange 705, 1940, **4908–9**
    and gift giving 1940
symbolic interaction 801, 2361, **4909–14**,
    4981, 5000
    and abolitionism 1
    and affect control theory 35, 37
    and agency 61, 4910
    and biracialism 296
    Blumerian 318–21, 1087, 1130, 1436, 1812,
        1996, 2214, 2362, 2997
    and the body 325
    and body modification practices 328, 330
    and computational sociology 644
    and consciousness raising 678
    constructed conditionality 4910–11
    and conversation 790
    Cooley and 319, 847, 858, 1087
    and cross-sex friendship 877
    and crowd behavior 3065
    and cultural criminology 893
    and decision-making 982
    and deviance 1123, 1137, 2502
    and dialectics 4911–12
    and disability studies 1700
    and dramaturgy 1227, 1228, 3680
    emergence 4910
    and emergent norm theory 1367
    and emotions 1379
    and existential sociology 1519
    and facework 1553
    and family theory 1631
    and fatherhood 1648
    and grounded theory 2026
    and helping theories 3680
    and the hidden curriculum 2116, 2117
    and identity 2217, 2218, 2220
    and identity control theory 2203
    and illness 2059
    and interpersonal relationships 2392
    and interpretive interactionism 2362, 2448
    and labeling 2501
    and language 2535–6, 2537
    life course approach 4510–11
    and medical sociology 2930, 2934
    mesostructural analysis 2962
    methodology 4912–13
    process 4910
    and the professions 2075–6, 3661
    and science 4072
    and the self 4158
    and self-esteem 4170

    and sexual scripting theory 4122
    and sexuality 4265
    and slurs 4339–40
    and the social definition paradigm 2964
    and social learning theory 847–8
    social psychology 4509–11
    and social worlds 4546
    Spence and 1936
    Thomas theorem 991, 992
symbolic labor 3565
symbols
    digital 1159
    and dramaturgy 1226–7
    and hermeneutics 2107
    and marginal art 2762
    non-textual symbols 955
    and popular religiosity 3524
    religious 3522
Symonds, John Addington 1365, 2612
sympathy theories of society 3227–9
synagogue tradition 1054
syncretism 818, 2190
syndicated organized crime 833
syndrome defenses 2556
syngenism 2039
synthetic cohort design 4818
system properties 634
system theories 4914–20, 4982
    actor-oriented dynamic systems theories
        4916–17
    autopoietic social systems theory 233, 2675–7
    complex systems theories 4545
    and ecological problems 1282
    and family theory 1632
    and functionalism 1812
    functionalist systems theories 4915
    general systems theory 4544
    Homans and 2144
    and the information and resource processing
        paradigm 2325–6
    and interaction systems 2361
    interdisciplinarity 633
    interstructural relations analysis 4918
    intersystemic linkage 2677
    Luhmann and 1813, 2361
    and management theory 2717, 2748
    and markets 2784–5
    Marxist theory 4916
    and modernization theory 3076
    multidimensionality 4917–18
    and operations management 3267
    organizations as social structures 3322–3

pre-autopoietic systems theory 2677
process orientation 3293
and risk 3929–30
systematic sociology 176
systemic needs 1809
systems implementation 2720
systems rationalism 2724
Szasz, T. 2695, 3333
Szinovacz, M. 2017–20
Sztompka, P. 593–8
Szymanski, A. 664, 2838

"T" groups (basic skills training groups) 2616
table manners 347
Tablighi Jamaat 1982
tabloidization of society 3491
taboo
    Bataille and 246, 5045
    childhood sexuality 462, 464–5
    Freud and 5045
    racial taboos 3744
    and the sacred 3972
    sexual 2682, 2683
Taborites 3048
tactical authenticity 215
tactics
    contentious tactical repertoires 779–82
    insider tactics 780
    outsider tactics 780
    violent tactics 779, 780
Taft-Hartley Act 2520
Tagore, R. 2131
Taiwan 4376
    bilingual education 279
    Confucianism 670
    democratization 3072
    economic success 1069, 1073, 1296, 2299
    family planning programs 1738
    film industry 1753
    industrialization 2299
    legal code 3586
    life expectancies 3097
    migrant domestic workers 1716
    out-migration 1344
    peripheral state 1395
Takahashi, N. 641
Takata, Yasuma 4921–4
Take Back the Night Marches 903
Takebe, T. 2497
"Talented Tenth" 1242–4, 1245
talents 416
Taliban 371, 1315

Talley, H. L. 1696–701
Tamaki, A. 1287
Tamanoi, K. 1407
Tamayo, S. 411–15
Tambiah, S. J. 2698
Tambo, O. 164
Tamil Tigers 2800, 3383
tamkin 2429
Tamla Motown 3492–3
Tanabe, H. 2498
tan'itsu minzoku myth 3058, 3059
Tannen, D. 904, 1779
Tannenbaum, F. 1123, 1124, 2472, 2501
Tansey, M. 3556
Tantra 373, 4278
Tantric sex 4276, 4278
Tanzania
    capitalist growth 390
    migration 1044
    pastoral theism 3870
Taoism 670, 1766, 3855, **4924–30**
Tarantino, Q. 3556–7
Tarde, G. 654, 668, 2002, 2003, 2497, 4933
tariffs 3596
Tarkovsky, A. 218
Tarrow, S. 781, 3448, 3456, 3457, 3909
Tasca, A. 2014
Tashakkori, A. 2979, 2980
task-centered social work 4543
taste, sociology of 4930–5
    class dispositions 541, 710, 723, 1361
    and cultural capital 889
    debasement of 741
    and distinction 1189–91
    elite tastes 34, 685, 889–90
    and fashion 718
    highbrow/lowbrow 2123–5
    and lifestyle 2644, 2645, 2648
    musical tastes 1361
    reification 953
    working class tastes 34–5
    see also aesthetics
tatemae/honne 4155, **4935–8**
tattooing 326, 329, 3543
    and deviance 1078
    fine art tattoing 329
    spectacularization of the body 759
Tausig, M. 2951–4
Tavistock Institute of Human Relations 19,
    429, 2510, 2748, 2753
Tawney, R. H. 3663
tax returns, and demographic data collection 1027

taxation
   and conservatism 680
   and environmental incentives 728
   inheritance taxes 2628
   and marriage 2414
   property taxes 680
   redistributive tax 2558
   state domestic relations laws 2110
   state monopoly on 1750
   tax compliance 625
   wealth taxes 2628
   and welfare spending 4730–1
**taxes: progressive, proportional, and
   regressive 4938–9**
taxonomic linguistics 2535
taxonomies 554
taxonomies of racial difference 3731
taxonomy, and feminist epistemology 1684
Taylor, C. 152, 1177, 3820
Taylor, D. 1275
Taylor, F. W. 428–9, 701, 2745–6, 2828
Taylor, G. 442, 444
Taylor, I. 760, 3197
Taylor, J. R. 3293, 3296
Taylor, M. 709
Taylor, P. 3611
Taylor, S. J. 3950
Taylor, Verta 779–82, 1223–6, 1674, 3776
Taylor, Victor E. 3556–8
Taylor, Y. 4256–60
Taylorism 1870, 2711, 2712, 2746–7, 2828,
   4708, **4939–40**, 5002
   and home-building process 2614
   and knowledge-intensive firms 2524
   and McDonaldization 2746
   and management consulting 2720
   neo-Taylorism 2746
   and operations management 3267
   and political economy of the body 2711, 2713
   principles 2522
   scientific management 105, 325, 364, 701,
      1200, 1769
   Taylorization of family life 458
Taylorist-Fordist model of production 1562
teacher research 1444
teacher–parent relationship 2464
teachers 4940–1
   assaults on 842
   black teachers 605, 866
   critical pedagogy 864–7
   defensive teaching 4357–8
   and expectations/aspirations 1529

   feminist pedagogy 1706–10
   gender hierarchy 4041–2, 4940, 4943
   gender role reinforcement 4573
   and gender-related messages 1844, 2118
   and the hidden curriculum 2117, 2118
   in kindergarten 2464
   math, science, and technology education 2852
   media literacy teaching 2894
   and professional deviance 1085
   and student learning opportunities 3272,
      3273, 3274, 3275
   student–teacher relationship 864, 1707, 2894,
      3273
   student-teachers 866
   teacher-directed discipline 4019, 4021
   unqualified 5113–14
teaching and gender 1895, **4941–5**
   and the hidden curriculum 2118
teamwork 2291, 2387, 2523, 2712, **4945–50**
   cross-cultural virtual teams 2734
   cross-functional teams 2513
   effectiveness 4946–7
   metering problem 3327
   offline (problem solving) teams 2753
   online (semi-autonomous work) teams 2753
   and operations management 3269
   peer control 3566
   processes 4948–9
   productivity 3327
   team composition 4947–8
   team tasks 4947
technical competencies in science 1485
technical experts 377
techno-cultures 965
techno-identities 965
techno/rave scene 1523
technoburbs 2992, 3113
technocracy 1542, 2231, 3550
technocratic media theology 2692
technofuturism 962
technologiam, and cultural production 953
technological change, and cohort
   differentiation 95
technological determinism 689, 734, 1160,
   1386, 2016, 2327, 2328, 2329, 2879, 3075,
   4950–1
   and information technology 2333
   and the Internet 734
   and media technologies 2879
technological disasters 1174, 1421
technological divide 103
technological innovation 1412, **4952–5**

incremental 4953
  radical 4953
  and risk 3926, 3930
  schools, impact on 2851
technological lags 1560
technological modernization 1560
technological reductionism 2195
technological spillovers 1313
technological voluntarism 1160
technologies, Internet-related technologies 2386
technology assessment (TA) 687–93
  project-induced 691
  technology-induced 691
technology forcing programs 691
technology, science, and culture 4092–3,
    4955–60
  actor-network theory 20–1, 22
  and the information society 2326–31
  and older persons 101–3
  and religion 4092–3
technology-based industries 1314
technoscapes 1990
technoscience 2332, 2475, 2532, 4098
Teddlie, C. 2979, 2980
teen magazines 1850, 1851
teenage mothers 1019, 1020
  contraceptive behaviors 1728
  and deviance 1856
  fertility 1019, 1020, 1725–9, 1735–6
  mass media, influences on 2826
  negative outcomes 1736
  peer culture hypothesis 5127
  and poverty 1736
  poverty of relations hypothesis 5127
  and school dropout 1230, 1231
  weathering hypothesis 5127
telecommunications
  convergence with computing power 2332
  and technology assessment 691
telecommunications networks 1160
telecommunities 628
telecommuting 1551, 1895
telemedicine 2388–9
teleneurology 2389
teleology 2968, 2969
  and paradigm theory 3355
teleorthopedics 2389
telephone 4960–3
  mobiles 2905
  and multimedia 3111
  and networks 2905
telephone interviews 2407

telephone sex 1659, 1660, 1661, 3320, 3989
telepsychiatry 2389
televangelism 3874, **4963–5**
television 2825, **4965–9**
  advertising 1233, 2897
  affiliation/avoidance 210
  audiences 208
  and auteurism 219
  and children's consumer culture 694–5
  color technology 2897
  commercial model 2876
  communciation facilitation 210
  community television 627, 628
  competence/dominance 210
  conservatism and 680
  content analysis 777
  cultivation model of influence 2826
  and cultural imperialism 2889
  and cultural production 953
  current affairs programs 2102
  and deviance 1109, 1132
  and deviance as entertainment 1107
  and diffusion of protest 3687
  documentaries 1211, 3491
  domestic effects model 4966–7
  and encoding/decoding 1403
  and experiential consumption 716
  and *flânerie* 1762–3
  and genre 219, 1915
  and global cultural communication 2330
  global effects model 4967
  hegemonic discourse 2102
  and the home 2922
  hours watched weekly 2593
  and ideological hegemony 2229
  media conglomerates 2897–8
  mediated interaction 2921
  motherhood, representation of 940
  and multimedia 3111
  and music broadcasting 3131–2
  ownership and control 1945–6
  privatization 2887
  product placement 731, 3672–3
  public service model 2876
  ratings 3793
  reality television 418, 1211, 3490–2
  regulation of 2914
  relational uses 209
  satellite technology 419
  sensationalism 3491
  and simulation 4331
  soaps 1638, 3498–500

television (*cont'd*)
  social learning 210
  social uses 209–10
  and socialization 4573
  sports coverage 2916–17, 4715
  structural uses 209
  violence 66, 2917
  and visual consumption 769, 770, 771
  and visual saturation 756
  and youth culture 773, 774, 775
temperance movement 905, 1673, 1873
Temple, S. 694
Temporary Aid for Needy Families (TANF) 1884
ten Bos, R. 2730
Ten Commandments 2449
TenHouten, W. 3185
Tennessee Valley Authority (TVA) 2354
Terman, L. 837
Terracini, U. 2014
Terrell, M. C. 306, 307
terricide 705
Terrin, A. N. 3933–6
territorial spirits 440
terrorism 835, 1062, **4969–71**
  and anarchism 4970
  and anti-immigrant sentiments 1153
  cyberterrorism 960
  global 228, 681, 1951
  ideologies 4970
  Islamic 2427
  public relations 3470
  and racist movements 3771
  and secrecy 4132
  student activism 4866
  terrorist disasters 1175
terrorist networks 1167, 1474
Terry, B. 413
test-retest reliability 3850
testosterone 65
  crime and 824
Teubner, G. 2561, 2677
Tevis, T. 620–3
Tewksbury, R. 4229–32
Texas proviso 2265
text
  and genre 1913, 1915
  hermeneutics 2107–9
  intertextuality 918
  and meaning 918–9
text/hypertext 4971–4
  and hypermedia 3110
text retrievers 646

textbase managers 646–7
textile industry 2290, 2294
textual analysis 776
  semiotic theory 300
  and signification 299
textual authority 2643
textual poaching 3497
Thailand 4377
  cultural tourism 921
  educational opportunities 1157
  medical sociology 2935
  self-help movement 1407
  sex tourism 4201
  transgendered persons 4215
  world holidays 740
thalidomide 1573, 1865, 3652
Thanksgiving dinners 753, 754
Tharu, S. 1692
Thatcher, Margaret 2291, 2749, 2897, 3471, 4581
Thatcherism 1061, 2008, 2102, 3664
  and industrial relations 2512
  and privatization 3648
  welfare backlash 4494
theater performance, and political
    expression 779
Theeboom, M. 5308–11
theft 1105
  and deviance 1124
  female thiefs 1858
  and justice analysis 1194
Theil Index 2199
theism 3870
theme parks 713, 914
  and cultural studies 916
  cultural tourism 921
  and Disneyization 1187
  and experiential consumption 716
  and fantasy cities 1641–2
  and hyperreality 2590
  rationalization process 2883
themed entertainment complexes 759
themed environments 768, 2195, 4333, 5142
theocracy 3094
theocratic tact 2441
Theodorus the Atheist 197
Theodosius, Codex of 2696
theological society 651–2
theology 4974–6
  and atheism 198
  Christian 488
  feminist theology 904
theoretical research programs 4976–9

theoretical sampling 234, 2025
theory 1554, **4979–86**
  classical theory 4982, 4983
  closed theories 1758
  contemporary theorizing 4983
  deductive theorizing 1557
  and feminist epistemology 1684
  finalized theories 1757–8
  grounded theory 2023–7
  interpretive theories 1557
  multilevel tehories 3002–3
  post-classical theorizing 4983
  properties 4988–9
  schools 4980–2
  sense making 1556–7
  sociological 655
  see also fact, theory and hypothesis: including
    the history of the scientific fact
theory construction 4987–93
  computational sociology 639–40
  see also metatheory
theory and methods 4993–5
Theory of Reasoned Action 2105
theory triangulation 5076, 5077
theory units 3002
theosis 373
Theosophical Society 3190
therapeutic assumption 1445
therapeutic community 1175, 1421
theravada school of Buddhism 371
Thernborn, G. 2838
Thevenot, Laurent 958
THI Fridays 759
Thiam, A. 1656
Thibaut, John 1512
thick description 947, 1130, 1481, 3292,
    3331, 5084
"think global, act local" 1993
Thio, A. 1092–5
Third Cinema 1753
Third Way in politics 3830, 4488
third world countries, democracy 1001
third world and postcolonial feminisms/
  subaltern 4995–5000
  and feminist anthropology 1691, 1692
  and intersectionality 2395
  Latin American feminism 1685–9
  and multiracial feminism 3117–18
  Orientalist discourse 3344
  and standpoint theory 1711
Thirty Years War 1952
Thoits, P. 2243

Thomas, C. 309
Thomas, D. S. 131, 991, 1670
Thomas, G. M. 1967
Thomas, K. 1583, 2699
Thomas, M. L. 3780
Thomas theorem 991, 992, 4172–3, 4175
Thomas, William I. 131, 1145, 3732, **5000**
  and Addams 24, 25
  assimilation research 192
  and attitudes and behavior 199
  and the Chicago School 442–3, 445–6, 714,
    1129, 1597, 3362
  definition of the situation 2964, 3400, 4325
  documentary method 2407
  and facework 1553
  and life cycle perspective 2637
  and race relations 129
  and the self 2217
  and social change 445–6
  and symbolic interaction 319, 847
  Thomas theorem 991
Thompson, B. 1345–7, 1557–9, 3877–9
Thompson, D. 2466
Thompson, E. E. 2074
Thompson, E. P. 897, 913, 914, 2648, 3052,
    3084, 3192
Thompson, G. 1961
Thompson, J. B. 1640
Thompson, J. D. 3328
Thompson, P. 2716
Thompson, V. 379
Thompson, Warren 1033
Thompson, William 2177
Thomson, R. G. 1697, 1698, 1699, 1700
Thoreau, Henry David 1289
Thorn, Elizabeth 1880–5
Thorne, B. 1671, 2488
Thornton, P. M. 3445–7
Thornton, S. 1639, 3091
Thorpe, Jim 4657
thought communities 2758
Thrasher, F. 443, 447, 1825
threat detection 293
three strikes and you're out policies 1144
thrill crimes 2049, 3801
Throsby, K. 3206–7
Thucydides 186
Thurman, H. 2466
Thurstone measures 1868, 3701
Thye, S. 3603–6
Tiananmen Square protest (1989) 4476, 4868
Tibawi, A. L. 1493

Tibet 4188
  Buddhism 371
Tienda, M. 2550
Tierney, W. G. 2345–51, 2642, 2644
Tilka, B. 2130
Tillich, P. 27
Tillon, G. 2427
Tilly, C. 779, 871, 958, 2133, 3155, 3249, 3448,
    3449, 3455, 3457, 3461
Timberlake, M. 3622–5
time 5001–6
  Aboriginal experience of 3186
  and investigative poetics 2422
  and the life course 2633
  long-wave theory 2740
  residual time, leisure as 2588
  "timeless time" 3181
time crunch 1881
time and motion studies 428
time series 5006–9
time use data collection 1030–3
  time diary methodology 1030–1
Time Warner 2898
time-management skills 2121
time-space 5009–10
time-space compression 759, 1958–9, 1961,
    5005–6, 5010
time/space distanciation 1958
Timmermans, S. 233–5, 3660
Tindall, D. B. 5222–5
Tinker, A. 1348
Tiong Hoa Hwee Koan 670
Tirner, R. H. 1367
Tiryakian, E. 1261–4, 4619–23
Tisak, J. 2543
Tisdell, E. 1708
Title IX 937, 1032, 1675, 1676, 1859,
    1876, 4204
Tittle, C. R. 782–4, 5145–6
tobacco industry 357
tobacco use, legal control of 1098
Tobin Tax 1979
Toby, J. 846
Tocqueville, Alexis de 595, 2647, 2830, 3692,
    5010–11
  and American identity 1968
  Aron on 177
  and civil society 512
  and democracy 170, 1004, 1005–6, 3465
  and the French Revolution 660
  and individualism 2285
  and liberalism 2622

and oligarchy 1006, 1007
  political sociology 3459
  and the public realm 3721
Togliatti, P. 2014
tokenism 1894, 4047
Tokyo 765
  global city 1954, 1955
tolerance 5011–14
Tollison, R. 1316
Tolman, E. C. 257
Tolstoy, Leo 1165, 4224
tomboys 1658
Tomlinson, A. 4695–9
Tomlinson, J. 2889
Tomsen, S. 1829
Tong, C.-K. 4924–30
tongue-splitting 324
Tonkinson, R. 5026–9
Tönnies, Ferdinand 5014–16
  and the city 499
  and communities 620, 1574, 1575, 1576,
    3075, 3227
  on community collapse 594, 3124
  economic sociology 2781, 2784
  and friendships 1798
  Gemeinschaft/Gesellschaft 594, 598, 620, 1576,
    2003, 2031, 2560, 3621, 3964, 4130, 5104
Tooby, J. 1509
top management teams 5016–18
topless dancing, stigma neutralization 1094
topos 237
Torah 2448–9, 2450, 3854
Torigoe, H. 2640–1, 4178–9
Toronto 1955
Toronto Blessing 440
Torr, B. 2570–5
Torr, R. 1797
torture 64, 228, 255, 256, 335, 802, 1115
Toscano, A. 2266–8, 3178–80, 4335–6
total fertility rate (TFR) 1039, 1729–30, 1742
total institutions 2934
  organisations as 3331–5
  and resocialization 3891–2, 4568
total organizations 3332
Total Quality Management (TQM) 213, 2715,
    2729–30, 2753, 2929, 3268
total social phenomenon (TSP) 2041–2
totalitarianism 2624, 5018–19
  Arendt and 167, 168, 169, 175, 1645
  and authoritarianism 222, 223
  and cults 886
  and fascism 1645

Fromm and 1805
and genocide 1910
key features 223
Marcuse and 2760
and media propaganda 2879
Nazi 169, 1805, 3176
Stalinist 169
and suffrage 3076
and total institutions 3334
and utopianism 2528
totemism 608, 3631, 3937, 3981, **5020–1**
and animism 141
Durkheim and 1254, 3344, 3630, 3973
Freudian theory 3972
and the sacred 3972, 3973
Touraine, A. 3070, 3209, 3550
Toure, K. 1785
tourism 2591
beach holidays 3484–5
and consumption 761–4
environmental impacts 762
and experiential consumption 716
global 762, 1963, 1994
and imperialism 1994
and the leisure class 2596
mass tourism 762, 764
reproductive tourism 2172
sights and sightseeing 763
urban tourism 5141–3
and visual consumption 769
visual culture 762–3
see also sex tourism
Townley, B. 3396–9
toxic contamination 1417, 1418, 1421
toxic waste, trading in 1978
Toynbee, A. 1288, 2298, 4363
Toynbee Hall 23
Toyotism 3565
toys
ethnic toys 708
sex toys 1678
Tracey, D. de 2230
tracking 5022–6
career tracking 3252, 3288, 3289
educational 2956, 3272, 4024
and friendship formation 1800
racially stratified tracks 4024
school students 1326, 1800, 5022–6
Tracy, J. 1166, 1167
trade
political barriers to 3596
single-commodity export trade 1853

trade liberalization 2624, 2887
and urbanization 1423
trade name franchising 1784
trade schools 1344
trade secrecy 4134
trademark laws 357, 729, 730
trader communities 1600
trading companies 1393
tradition 5026–9
conservatism and 678, 679
invented traditions 2901
and organizations 3335–40
tradition-directed personality 3917–18
traditional consumption city (Japan) 4905, **5029–30**
traffic in women 677, 1660, **5031–4**
female children 2317
and the Internet 1985
and kinship codes 2155
migrants 3836
and prostitution 3683, 5031
sex workers 1717, 1984
smuggling networks 3836
in war 1885–7
trafficking laws 1238
tragedy of the commons 266, 267, 967, 3532
trained incapacity 378–9
trait approach to occupations 3661
trait theory 2271, 3443
and prosocial behavior 3679
trajectory analysis 829
tranquilizers 1234
trans-science 4636
transaction analysis 4543
transaction cost economics 2355, 3433
transaction cost theory 3282, 3352
transactional sex 4211
transcarceration 5034–6
transcendence theory 4642
Transcendental Meditation (TM) 3067, 4144
transcription 5036–7
transference 3694
transformational grammars 2535
transgender, transvestism, and transsexualism 2160, **5037–43**
and collective identity 588
and drag queens/kings 1223–6
and female masculinity 1657–8, 2161
intersexed conditions 5041
and lesbian feminism 2605
medicalization of 1111, 1113, 5040
radical feminist critique 3776

transgender, transvestism, and transsexualism (*cont'd*)
  self-identification 2162
  sexuality research 2132
  stigmatization 639
  transgender prostitutes 2161
  urban living and consumption 768
  see also cross-dressing
transgression 5043–7
transgression, Bataille and 246–7
transhumanism 1490
transience 636
transition from communism 5047–50
transition economies 5050–4
  stratification in 4824–6
transition from school to work 5054–7
  and employment status changes 1399
  and overeducation 4031
  and school dropout 1231
transnational activism 782
transnational capitalist class (TCC) 1943
  and education nationalization 1972–3
transnational communities 3836
transnational corporations (TNCs) 351, 740,
    820, 1061, 1944–5, 1947, 5098
  control structures 5068–70
  and deindustrialization 994
  and democratic accountability 1947
  and global cities 2305
  and global economy 1943, 1958
  and global politics 1951
  human resource management 2181, 5070
  and industrial development 1560
  and Latin America 1561
  media conglomerates 2884
  media corporations 1945–6, 2887, 2897–8
  national champions 5068
  and NGOs 3212
  and occupational communities 1580
  organizational forms 3260
  ownership and control of 1944
  production relocation 2382, 2383, 3441
  TNC development 1945
  transnational legal order of business
    arbitration 2558
transnational diasporas 1152
**transnational and global feminisms
    5057–60**
  and cultural feminism 905
  and gender mainstreaming 1869–70
  global sisterhood 905
  Latin American feminism 1685–9

  multiracial feminism 3118
transnational movements 5060–4
  and civil society 513
  environmental movements 1428, 1432
  ethnic, racial, and nationalist movements
    1467
  global justice movement 1976–9
  transnational social movements (TSMs)
    1471–2
  see also migration: international; refugee
    movements
transnationalism 1459, 5064–6
  and creolization 818
  and ethnic/racial divisions of labor 1464
  and female labor migration 1715
  and immigration 3012
  and racial/ethnic conflict 661
  and racial/ethnic consciousness 3742
transnationality 3576
transnationals 5066–71
  migrants 2257
transparency and global change 5071–5
  and corruption 808
Transparency International 3259, 5073
transparent industries 3301
transportation
  and diaspora 1152
  and migration 2257
  and older persons 102, 103
transportation advances 761–2, 874
transportation analysis zones (TAZs) 3115, 3116
transsexualism *see* transgender, transvestism,
    and transsexualism
transtextuality 1916
transvestism *see* transgender, transvestism, and
    transsexualism
Trapp, E. 1155–9
trash sport events 4659
traumatic experience
  and embodiment and identity 336
  and self-perception and identity 327
  and selfhood 337
traumatogenic change 593–8
travel writing 2797
Travis, T.-M. C. 137–8
Traweek, S. 2525
treadmill of production model 1420
Treiman, D. 3240–4, 3250
Treitschke, H. von 3146
Trencher, S. R. 5080–1
très longue durée 361
Trevino, A. J. 2557

trials 1383
Triandis, H. 2550
triangulation 778, 1127, 2969, 2978,
    5075–80, 5084
tribal societies, and agency 62
tribal stigma 583–4
tribalism 5080–1
    and *'asabiyya* 180, 181, 184, 2460
    Burundi and Rwanda 380–2
    and dyads/tryads 1264
    gift giving 701
    mana 433
    and millenarianism 3047
    and nation-state formation 2498
    neotribalism 2691
    potlatch ritual 704, 1938, 1939, 1940, 4908
    and ritual 3936–7
    and small world structure 1312–13
    South Africa 163
    and sport 4672
    and symbolic exchange 4908
    tribe–nation distinction 2281
    visual sociology 2986
    see also indigenous peoples
trickle-down theory
    and development 1853
    and education 1333
    of fashion 719, 4932
    of the Internet 733
    and the leisure class 2595, 2596
    of status goods 683, 685, 744–5, 2647
Trilling, L. 2468
Trinh, M. 1692
Trinidad and Tobago
    and accommodation 8
    and women in development 1855
Triplett, N. 3700
Triplett, R. 542–5, 584–6, 847–50, 3734–7,
    4191–3, 4531–2
Trivers, R. L. 292
Trobriand Islands 2699, 2704
Troeltsch, E. 483, 484, 884–5, 1315, 3692,
    4136, 4137
Tromso Heart Study 1866
Tronto, J. 1438
tropical medicine 4073–4
Trotha, T. von 5193–9
Trotsky, L. 159, 2685, 2687, 3908
Troyer, L. 2584–7
truancy 855, 1858, 2826
Trueba, E. 2550
Trujillo, C. 2549

Truman, D. 3460
Truman, Harry S. 3041
trust 5081–3
    cooperation and 641
    and the democratic system 2579
    doctor–patient relationship 2389
    and dramaturgy 1227
    and ethics 1439
    and ethics in fieldwork 1445
    and ethnic groups 1460, 1462
    and exchange relations 1369
    in expert systems 2922
    in experts, loss of 2084
    fiduciary trust 3377
    and globalization 1958
    interpersonal trust 1634
    and interviewing 2408
    and key informants 2458
    and life history research 2643
    and management control 2716
    networks of 1389
    and observational research 3240
    and operations management 3269
    and organizations 1387–8
    in science 4096
    and social capital 4357
    and tolerance 5013
    trust and reputation, and capitalist exchange
        397
    trust-based relationships 2743
    and working relationships 2479–80
trust game 1823
trusteeism 1055
trustworthiness 5083–5
    criteria 213–14, 215
    and scientific truths 786, 787
truth
    Church production of 3572, 3573
    hegemonic truths 919
    postmodernism and 858
    in science 4095
    scientific truths 786
    in sentencing 804
    truth claims, and management theory 2715
truth paradox 3813
**Truth and Reconciliation Commissions
    5085–7**
    and genocide 1912
    and peace processes 3382
Truth, Sojourner 306, 1673, 1845, 2621
Tschannen, O. 4140
Tsiddson, D. 1332

Tsuda, M. 1287, 2436
Tsukuba, H. 1287
Tsurumi, K. 1406–7
Tsurumi, S. 2761, 2762
Tu Wei-ming 670
tuberculosis (TB) 2080, 3099
Tubergen, F. van 4815–19
Tubman, H. 306
Tucker, K. H. 125–7
Tudor, A. 1570–2, 1650, 1651, 2286–7,
    3813–16
Tugan-Baranowsky, M. 245
Tukism 2003
Tulip Mania 2022
Tulloch, J. 1638
Tullock, G. 2276
Tunnell, K. D. 835–6
Turkey
    diaspora 1152
    eugenic management of the body 325
    heritage tourism 920
    honor killings 2303
    industrialization 2299
    laicism 2532
    migrants 661
    population exchange 1451
    revolution 3907
    Turkish identity 2429
    world holidays 740
Turkish nationalism 1999–2000, 2002
Turkle, S. 962
Turnbull, C. 3230
Turner, B. 324–8, 335–8, 948, 2935, 3344,
    4295–6
Turner, C. 3717–18
Turner, F. J. 2944, 3512–13
Turner, J. 1376, 2997–3005, 3186, 3947,
    4638–41
Turner, R. 1324, 2203, 3049, 3065, 3947, 3955,
    4159
Turner, S. 229–30, 425–6, 1541–3, 1554–7,
    3389–91, 4109–11
Turner, V. 754, 923, 2698, 3392, 3933, 3937
Tuskegee syphilis study 1442, 2079, 2347
Tutsis 590
Tuttle, L. 329
Tutu, Desmond 165, 5086
Twaddle, A. C. 4317–20
twins 557–8
    cultural significance of 556
    demographic data 287
    and genetics 1830, 1831, 2359

Twitchell, J. 744
Tylenol 1238
Tyler, P. 1754
Tylor, E. B. 1505, 3872, 3981
Tylor, E. E. 141, 142, 608, 3629
typologies 554
Tyson, W. 3754–6
Tzanelli, R. 1838–40, 1938–40, 3932–3

Ubermenschen 3215, 3216
Uehara, E. S. 3227
Ueno, C. 1401, 1402
Ueno, K. 1803–4
UFOs 1140
Uganda
    adolescent fertility 1725
    aging population 1028
    teenage marriage 1727
Ukraine
    anti-Jewish violence 3428
    electoral processes 1952
    ethnic cleansing 1451
    ethnic mobilization 1470
    Jewish population 2453
    nuclear disarmament 3039
    race and ethnic conflict 1469
    secessionist drive 4168
    UN intervention 1952
ulama 4687
Ullman, E. 1280
Ulmer, G. L. 4971–4
Ulmer, J. T. 2961–3
Ulrichs, K. H. 2132, 2157, 2158, 4285
Ultee, W. 350–1, 547–51, 2275–7, 2626–30,
    3060–2, 3250–1, 4796–7, 4819–20
ultimate attribution error 207
ultimo-geniture 2239
Umesao, T. 1288
umma 2001, 2002, 2003
UN Conference of Environment and
    Development (1992) 1274
UN Conference for Women (1995) 1274
Unani medicine 631
unbelief, atheism 197, 198
uncertainty 5089–90
Uncertainty Principle 3573
uncertainty, training for 2934
the unconscious 1786
    collective unconscious 3540
    Guattari and 2038
    neuroscientific emphasis on 3187–9
    and pornographic obscenity 3540

underclass 264, 537
  anger 1454
  criminality 543
  "genetic underclass" 2172
  immigrant underclass 2306
  mental patients as part of 997
  oppositional culture 4807
  race and 3747
  school drop-out as predictor for 1229
  and unemployment 5093–4
  urban underclass 2306, 4149
underdeterminism 1896
underdevelopment 1069
  and modernization theory 3072
  and monopoly capitalism 3179
  and nationalist umbrage 3145
unemployment 5090–1
  among young people 1399
  and class struggle 548
  definitions 5092
  as determinant of future unemployment 1400
  and development 1852
  and global justice movements 1976
  Great Depression 2021, 5090
  and health problems 1591
  involuntary and problematic leisure 2595
  labor market policies 5094–5
  and labor markets 2515
  and law–economy relation 2559
  long-term unemployment 2516
  mass unemployment 351, 2629
  measures 5092
  neoliberal perspective 3592–3
  and poverty 1612
  and riots 3923
  social indicators 4420
  social and psychological implications 2516
  and spatial mismatch hypothesis 4631
  and status loss 2486
  underemployment 1852
  unemployment scarring 5093
  victim blaming 5094
  and voting behavior 550
unemployment insurance 1720, 2511
unemployment as a social problem 5092–6
  and depression 120
  pathologizing 767
UNESCO 410, 627
  and endogenous development 1407
uneven development 5096–9
  and urban–rural population movements 3018
Unger, R. M. 3462

uni-age behavioral style 1930
UNICEF infant and child health programs 2316–7
UNIFEM 1869
Unification Church 436, 885, 3205, 4144
unification nationalism 1466
Uniform Crime Reports (UCR) 2277, 2278, 3734
unions 118, 351, 5099–101
  anti-union laws 2288
  bureaucracy 377, 2520
  certification elections 4739
  Christian 410
  Coleman and 570
  and collective bargaining 2515
  corporate anti-unionism 2520–1
  and counterhegemony 2229
  craft-based unionism 2519
  and democratic socialism 2296
  and deviance 1114
  elitest characteristics 141
  employee–trade union relations 2179, 2180
  and Fordism 2746
  and global justice movements 1977
  and human resource management 2179, 2180
  Internet presence 2292
  and labor–management relations 2511, 2513
  and law–economy relation 2559
  membership 2511, 2512, 2513, 3550, 5100
  militancy 2512
  political processes 570
  restrictive practices 3177
  solidarity 2289
  special interest unions 1416
  transnational organizing 1948
unipolar depressive disorders 1864
Unitarian Church 1053, 1054
United Arab Emirates 1724
  female genital mutilation 1654
United Church of Christ 1053
United Kingdom 1054
  abortion 3
  absenteeism in 6
  acculturation 16
  aging and social policy 86
  animal rights movement 138–9
  anti-nuclear activism 1273
  anti-trust institutions 2356
  athleticism, cult of 2120
  beach holidays 3484, 3485
  bilingual education 279
  births outside marriage 2663–4

United Kingdom (*cont'd*)
  business schools 2726
  capitalism 396
  centralized control 1488
  child custody and child support 454
  child labor 460
  childcare provision 458
  childhood disabilities 1573
  citizenship 498
  class voting 551, 553
  coal-mining industry 19
  cohabitation 566, 568
  collective bargaining 2512
  colonialism 603, 985, 1394, 3762
  community media 628
  complementary and alternative medicine
    630, 631, 632
  conservatism 678, 680
  criminology and deviance 1093
  cultural tourism 921
  democracy 1001
  demographic data collection 1011, 1012
  devolution 8
  divorce 452, 2664
  drag queens and kings 1224
  drug use 1237
  elder care 1929
  empire 1393
  environmental movements 1430, 1431–2
  extramarital fertility 2793
  football hooliganism 1767
  gambling 1820
  gender poverty ratios 1723
  genomics 2172
  graduate education 2013
  health care delivery system 2056
  health technology assessment 692
  heritage tourism 920
  home schooling 4033
  homicide rates 2151
  homophobia 2611
  household composition 2169–70
  immigration 2258, 3024, 3025, 3028
  imperialism 2981, 4338
  industrial relations 2288, 2289, 2290–1,
    2292
  Jewish population 2453
  labor–management relations 2512
  laborism 2526, 2527
  liberalism 2624
  life course studies 2635
  life expectation 2668

  lone parenthood 2663, 2664, 2665
  marriage rates 2792
  megalopolises 2943
  migration 2264
  military science 3038, 3039
  money management in families 3081–2
  multiracial feminism 3118
  National Health Service (NHS) 2055,
    4580–1
  national identity 3158–9
  nationalism 1473
  Navy 3038
  neoliberalism 3176
  New Left 3192
  New Towns 619
  nonmarital births 1587
  nonmarital fertility 1734
  nuclear technology 3038
  oldest old 2668
  political parties 3453
  political pluralism 3423–4
  privatization 3647–8
  prostitution 1659
  public broadcasting 3703, 3706–7
  public housing 3709–10
  racial accommodation 8
  racial crisis 299
  racism 3762, 3763
  radio and television broadcasting 2875–6,
    2897, 3777–8
  religiosity 1054
  retirement policies 3902
  school system 1324
  secularization 2529
  separatism 4188
  and slavery 4338
  social fluidity 2370
  socialism 614
  sports industry 4713–15
  sports injuries 2093
  sports participation 4697–8
  state school system 4051
  stratification 2628
  Taylorism 2746
  technology assessment 689
  unemployment 2516
  unions 2288, 2291, 2292, 2511, 2628
  war propaganda 3672
  wealth inequalities 2312
  welfare state 1904, 4491
  youth subcultures 809, 2102, 3089, 4870–1
  see also Birmingham School

United Nations 391, 1956
  Convention on the Rights of the Child 455, 456
  cultural imperialism 907
  and decolonization 985
  and ecofeminism 1274
  and endogenous development 1407
  and female status 1339
  human rights discourse 1952
  information society policies 2330
  interventionism 1952
  Millennium Development Goals 2319
  and national censuses 1011
  and NGOs 3212
  and peace processes 3383
  and the Vatican 410
  and women in development (WID) 1853
United Nations Children's Fund (UNICEF) 1974
United Nations Commission on International Trade Law (UNCITRAL) 241
United Nations Decade fpr Human Rights Education 1975
United Nations Development Program (UNDP) 1974
United Nations Educational, Scientific, and Cultural Organization (UNESCO) 1974, 2890
United Nations Environment Program 1292
United Nations Universal Declaration of Human Rights 1083, 1182, 1447, 1910, 1952, 2182, 2183–4, 2509
United States
  abolitionism 1
  abortion politics 3, 4
  acculturation 15, 16
  adolescent childbearing 1727, 1728
  affirmative action policies 39–41, 46, 47–8
  aging and social policy 85, 86
  agism 57, 105
  alcoholism in 114, 115, 117
  American identity 1968
  animal rights movement 138, 139
  anti-nuclear activism 1273
  anti-Semitism 153–4
  anti-trust institutions 2356
  assimilation 192, 193–4, 196, 1458, 3106–7
  baby boom 1030
  bilingual education 277
  births outside marriage 2664
  black feminist thought 305–10
  capital punishment 385–8
  capitalism 396

child abuse 450
child and elder care 1884
child poverty 1627
childcare provision 458
childhood disabilities 1573
citizenship 497, 499
city planning/urban design 503
civil religion 507
class and class conflict 533, 536, 550
class voting 551, 553
cohabitation 566, 1208
collective bargaining 2512
colleges and universities 600
colonialism 603
communism in 1140
community colleges 620–1
community media 627
community–economy relation 624, 625
compensation culture 2562
complementary and alternative medicine 629–30, 631, 632, 2068
consumer culture 743
consumer movements 697
crime in 821, 841, 3675–6, 3734–9
criminal justice system 851–6
criminology and deviance 1093
cultural studies 914, 916
culture industry 897
death and dying in 973
death penalty 977–8
debt liquidation 241
deindustrialization 992–3
democracy 1001
demographic data 1011, 1012, 1013, 1014, 1029, 1033, 1046, 3016
disability in 73
divorce 452, 467, 1206–7, 2417, 2664
domestic violence 1219–20
drug use 1233, 1234, 1235, 1238–9
economic growth 390
economic and political hegemony 1068
education system 1399
educational and occupational attainment 1334–6, 1340–5
educational policies 571
elites 889–90, 1190
empire 1396
environmental movements 1431
ethnic enclaves 1452–6
eugenic sterilization laws 1489
family demography 1585–6
federal court system 812–15

United States (*cont'd*)
  federal government 2354
  and federalism 1652
  female labor force participation 1204
  fertility trends 1588
  gambling 1819–20, 1821
  gay and lesbian community 606
  gay and lesbian movement 1833–7
  gender poverty ratios 1723
  genomics 2172
  global justice groups 1978
  graduate education 2012–13
  health care 72, 2054–5, 2056, 2080, 2709–10
  hegemony 1404
  HIV/AIDS 3099
  homicide 2151
  homophobia 2611
  hospitals 2165–8
  immigration 661, 1198, 1457, 1460, 1464,
    2257, 2259, 2262, 2263–5, 3020,
    3028, 3032
  immigration policies 3022, 3025, 3746
  imperialism 2268, 2755
  income inequality 1943
  industrial relations 2289, 2290
  information society 2328
  institutional review boards 2346–50
  intergenerational mobility 2276–7
  internal migration 3017, 3018, 3028
  interracial marriage 1405, 2394
  Japan–United States relationship 1968
  Jewish community 2452–3
  kindergarten programs 2462, 2463, 2464,
    2465
  labor movement 702, 2518–21
  labor–management relations 2512
  laicism 2532
  learning opportunities 3271–5
  liberalism 2624
  life expectancy 394, 3901
  lone parenthood 2663, 2664, 2665
  management education 2726
  marriage 2414
  media literacy programs 2893–4
  megalopolises 2942–3
  mental health care 994–8
  metropolises 494, 495
  migration 1044
  military sociology 3041
  millenarianism 3048–9
  mortality 69
  multiculturalism 3106, 3107

  neoliberalism 3176
  new left 3192–5
  nonmarital births 1734, 1735
  occupational segregation 3244–5
  older population 898
  political alienation 120
  political economy theory 1929
  political unilateralism 1952
  pollution 967
  population 1044
  population aging 69
  poverty 1718–23
  prison population 804
  public broadcasting 3703, 3704–6
  public housing 3707–9, 3710
  quality of life 1296–7
  racial accommodation strategy 7–8
  racial inequality 661
  racist movements 3768, 3769
  radio and television broadcasting 2897,
    3779–80
  religiosity 751, 1052, 1053, 1054, 1055, 2296,
    2532, 3866
  school drop-out 1229–30
  school system 1324, 1325
  separatism 4188–9
  social stratification 263
  socioeconomic policies 392
  superpower status 1295
  Taylorism 2746
  technology assessment 688, 689, 692
  transnational corporations 1944
  unions 2288, 2511
  wealth inequalities 2312
  welfare systems 952
  workforce 394
  see also black Americans; Native Americans
universal human rights 595, 1952
universalism 1154–5, 4110
  conservatism and 678
  norm of 3667
universities *see* colleges and universities
Unruh, D. 2598
unstructured interviewing 2408–9
Untouchables 404, 405, 1377
Upanishad 2129
uranism 2157, 2158
Urbain, J.-D. 3485
urban 5101–4
  new urbanism 3211
urban apathy 3681
urban branding 1455

urban community studies 5104–7
   chonaikai 471–4
   and gentrification 1917–20
urban conflict 501
urban consumption 765–9
urban crime and violence 5107–9
   and new left realism 3196, 3197
   and poverty 3196
urban cultural parks 5148–9
urban cultural tourism 920–1
urban disasters 1175
urban ecology 1289–90, **5109–12**
   city planning 503
   and invasion-succession 2418–20
   and multinucleated metropolitan regions
      3113–14
   and regional ecologies 3123
   and social disorganization theory 4395–7
   and uneven development 5097
urban economies 637
urban education 5112–15
   kindergarten 2462–5
   and literacy differentials 2654–5
   see also schools, public
urban exclusion 1920
urban folkloristics 2446
Urban League 129
urban malaise 636
urban movements 5115–19
   Latin America 415
urban policy 5119–21
   black urban regime 310–12
   civil minimum 505–6
   urban education and
urban political economy 5122–5
   Fordist cities 3841–2
   and gentrification
   and global cities 2305
   neo-Marxian tradition 5122–3
   neo-Weberian tradition 5123–4
   and political machines 3445
   and urban growth 5129
urban populations 637, 2991
urban poverty 5125–8
   and African Americans 2306, 3968
   biography and 288
   and capitalism 3196
   and homelessness 2146–50
   observation studies 2625–6
   and riots 3923
   Rustbelt cities 3968
urban primacy 3622, 3623

urban regime theory 311, 1455, 2034
   see also black urban regime
urban renewal and redevelopment 501,
      758, 767, **5128–32**
   black urban regime 310–12
   and the central business district 422
   and community 618
   and gentrification 1917–20, 5147–8
   growth machine thesis 2035
   and models of urban form 1280
   new urbanism 3211
   professional design and expertise 3125
   and public housing 3708–9
   and public space 5140
   redlining 3825–7
   slum clearance policies 1454–5
   sport-related construction 4664–5
urban revolution 5132–4
urban riots 660
urban–rural population movements 3965,
      5134–8
   cross-national variations 3018
   demographic transition theory 1037
   patterns of 3017–18
   and young adult living arrangements 2573
urban space 2581, **5138–41**
   built environment 374–6
   capital accumulation and 389
   clustering and scattering 3113
   exurbia 1549–50
   fragmentation, and megalopolis growth 2943
   and global cities 1954
   growth machine thesis 2034
   and hypesegregation 2197
   multinucleated metropolitan regions 3112–17
   and new urbanism 3211
   polycentric spatial structure 3115–16
   racialization 3899
   and segregation 2305
   sexualities and space 4254–6
   and urban hierarchy 2304
urban sprawl 503
urban tourism 5141–3
   fantasy cities 1641–3
urban transition 1036, 1037
urban villages 3113
urban way of life (East Asia) 5143–5
urban–rural continuum 637
urbanism 180
   and globalization 5147
   subcultural theory 637
urbanism, subcultural theory of 5145–6

urbanism/urban culture 5146–51
  Benjamin and 268–9
  chonaikai 471–4
  flâneur and 268–9
  and global cities 1955
  neoliberal urbanism 5147
  new urbanism 3211, 5148
urbanization 5151–4
  black urban regime 310–12
  blockbusting 316–18
  and the central business district 422–3
  and consumption 740
  and cultural sociology 923
  and development 1852
  differential logic 2581
  and economic development 3529
  environment and urbanization 1423–6
  and environmental degradation 1423–4
  and family and community 1597, 1598
  and family demography 1041
  and fertility levels 1727
  and friendships 1798
  and homelessness 2146–50
  hyperurbanization 3624
  indigenous peoples, impact on 2280
  industrialization, effects of 2294, 2298
  and the institution of marriage 674
  Levittown 2614–15
  and organic society 581
  and traumatic change 595
  and weakening of patriarchal authority 1594
  see also suburbs
urning theory 2132
urolagnia 1365
Urry, J. 763, 1959, 2649, 2903, 3164, 3165, 3567
Uruguay
  authoritarian regimes 223, 225
  fertility levels 1730
use-value 261, 702, 703, 709, 757, 762, 1382,
    1515, 2034, 2691, **5155**
uses and gratifications (U&G) tradition 209,
    2877, 2917
Usher, C. L. 2941–2, 4609–11
usury 156
utilitarian bioethics 1490
utilitarian organizations 3310
utilitarianism 1364, 3366
  Cooley and 801
  Jevons and 2441
  and liberalism 2624
utility maximization 3361
utilization review 2066

utopia 522, 2483, **5155–9**
  and anti-authoritarian interest 2576
  anti-rational elements 2758
  communist utopianism 612, 3497
  counterculture and 810
  and cultural convergence 1991
  and distributive justice 3233
  experimental utopias 5157
  feminist 2858, 3495
  Marxist 2815, 3495, 5157
  and millenarianism 3047
  and the New Age 3190, 3191, 3192
  and perfectibility of human society 2706
  political utopianism 2528
  and science fiction 3495, 3496
  and the social imaginary 2577
  utopian belief systems 2756
  utopian imagination, and the new left 3193

Vacha-Haase, T. 3851–3
vagrancy laws 1096–7, 2147
Vaidhyanathan, Siva 731
Vail, D. A. 328–30, 1821–2, 1899–900,
    3417–18
Vajrayana Buddhist tradition 373, 374
Valdivia, A. 2550
Vale, L. 1175
Valencia, E. 340
Valeri, V. 3984
Valhallas 1551
validity
  and legitimacy 2585, 2586, 2980
  mixed methods research 2980
  validity generalization 3851
validity horizon method of analysis 3824–5
validity, qualitative 5161–5
validity, quantitative 5165–7
  standardized educational tests 4722
Valocchi, S. 1833–8
value 5167–8
  labor theory of value 2811, 3179
  value associations 1402
  value neutrality 2968, 3235
  value pluralism 3107
values 5168–72
  anti-globalization value system 1993
  crisis of values 5171
  and decision-making 983–4
  and identity construction 5170
  marginal-utility value theory 1304, 2441
  Marxist value theory 876
  masculine values 2121

materialist–postmaterialist value priorities 2234–5
polytheism of values 3856
and rational choice sociology 3796, 3797
and social change 5170–1
socialization and value systems 2931
values: global 1990–3, **5172–6**
Van Baal, J. 3983
Van Cleef, G. A. 1381
van de Kaa, D. J. 1037, 1733
van de Rijt, A. 1822–5
van de Walle, E. 1045–8
Van den Bergh, O. 1445
Van den Berghe, P. L. 660, 3749–51
Van der Leeuw, G. 3983
Van der Zee, J. 2052–8
Van Gogh, Vincent 518
Vance, C. 3541
vandalism 2826, 3715
Vandecar-Burdin, T. J. 5189–91
Vanhanne, T. 1002
VanLandingham, M. 2136–40
Varcoe, I. 2133–6, 4064–8
Varela, F. J. 232–3
Vares, T. 5268–73
Varese, S. 342
Vargas, V. 1686
variables 5176–9
variables, control 5179–80
variables, dependent 5180–2
  and hypotheses 2109, 2200
variables, independent 5182–4
  and hypotheses 2199
variance 5184–6
variation analysis 1181
Varshney, A. 1470
Vatican 407, 408, 409–10
Veblen, Thorstein 3051, **5186**
  and Addams 24
  and aesthetics 34
  and alienation 609
  and class society 681–2
  and commodity relations 608
  and conspicuous consumption 681–2, 684,
    685, 701, 709, 718, 721, 736, 741, 816,
    934, 1189, 1190, 1308, 1763, 1851, 2192,
    2647, 4619, 4932
  and distinction 1190
  economic sociology 2782
  and fashion 718, 736
  and the leisure class 2594, 2595, 2645
  and neoclassical economics 1304

and symbolic exchange 4908
and trained incapacity 378–9
vector images 1163
Vedic cults 2128–9, 2131
Vedic society 2129
vegetarian movement 956
Vegetarian Society 150
vegetarianism 2690
  Hindu 2130
veiling controversy 1992
veiling practices 1692
Venezuela
  and federalism 1652
  neopopulism 413
Venice 765
Venkatesh, A. 3552–6
venture capital syndication network 1313,
    1314
Venturi, R. 2124, 3556, 3573
verbal aggression 1348
Verbrugge, L. 2095
verificationism 4079, 4084
Verne, Jules 3495, 3497
Verri, Pietro 255, 256
verstehen 4062, **5187–8**
  and hermeneutics 2108, 2535
Vertinsky, P. 1846
Verwoerd, H. 162
Viacom 2898
Viagra 1111, **5188–9**
  Internet medicine 2389
  and late-life sexuality 2541, 2542
Vichy regime 593
Vickery, J. 3136
victimization 5189–91
  child abuse 448–51
  chronic illness/disability and 480
  collective 3715
  crime and 819, 820–1
  criminology and 861
  cybervictims 965
  and deviance 1077
  disaster victims 1175
  domestic violence 1219
  and double consciousness 1221–2
  elder abuse 1348–9
  and environmental criminology 1426
  and exercise 1516
  and fear 1650, 1651, 2341, 2342
  and female deviance and crime 1857
  and feminist criminology 1693–4, 1695
  and gender 66, 5191

victimization (*cont'd*)
  health-damaging consequences 2073
  and heterosexuality 639
  homicide 543
  learned helplessness 67
  male rape 2702–3
  property crime 3676
  and race/ethnicity 66, 3676, 3734, 3788, 5191
  rape and sexual assault 3785, 3788
  and retaliation 66–7
  and routine activity theory 3960
  and scapegoating 4013
  school crime and 842
  and sex workers 1660
  stalking 4719–20
  victim blaming 67
  victim diasporas 1152
  victimization–criminal offending link 1695
victimization surveys 3197, 3716
Victor, J. 1090
Victorian myth of women's ineptitude 1877
Vidal-Ortiz, S. 4218–23
video
  and conversation analysis 791, 793
  and marketing communication 770
  music videos 914
  video letters, and diaspora 2886
  and visual ethnography 1483
  and youth culture 773
video ethnography 1523
video games 2825, 2826, **5192**–3, 5208
  product placement 731
  and visual consumption 769
  and youth culture 773
video nasties 3087
Vidich, A. 1376, 2978
Vienna Circle 3402, 3545, 3546, 4956
Vietnam
  capitalist growth 390
  civil wars 1473
  communism 391
  death penalty 977
  decolonization 985
  nationalism 4375–6
  revolution 3907
Vietnam War 340, 660, 876, 1812, 3216
  anti-war protests 1121, 1165, 2823, 3195, 3460, 3493
  casualties 3319
  and divorce rates 1207
  draft lottery 1539
  media role 2878
  and political poetry 2422
  public opposition to 161, 809, 875, 1086
  US propaganda 3673
Vietnam/Gulf War syndrome 2556
Vietnamese Americans 1664–5
vigilantism 3512
vigils 780
vignette technique 1540
Vincent, G. E. 24, 130, 442, 446
Vineyard movement 440
violence 5193–9
  against immigrants 3012, 3013
  against women 905, 2341, 3419
  animal abuse 2177
  Bataille and 246, 247
  black stereotyping 3739
  and coercive organizations 3316
  collective violence 958
  court monopoly of 1359
  and crowd behavior 881
  culture of violence 66
  and dangerousness 969
  ethnic, racial, and nationalist movements 1466
  and fascism 1645, 1647
  female involvement 2820
  gay bashing 1829–30
  gender-based 3535
  genocidal 1910–11
  glorification of 2826
  homophobic 2156
  hormonal activity 293
  institutional violence 3786
  international 1885–8
  interpersonal 531
  investigative poetics 2420–2
  Islamic male rituals 2429
  learned behavior 843
  martyrdom 2799–801
  nation-state and 530, 531
  pogroms 3426–8
  proletarian 350
  racial violence 661
  sacrificial killing 3984
  and social activism 779, 781
  and sport 531, 1133, 4348, 5199–205
  state violence 1750, 2156, 2279, 2627, 3385
  urban crime and violence 5107–9
  war 1885–6
  see also domestic violence; homicide; rape; revolutions; sadomasochism

violence among athletes 1133, 2092–3,
  5199–202
  and aggression 2093
  sport as catharsis 4663
violence among fans 5202–6
  football hooliganism 1767–8
violent crime 5206–8
  alcohol-related 115
  and child abuse 449
  and the civilizing process 531
  and class 543
  crime rates 3738
  and gender 2819
  hate crimes 2048–50
  index crime 2277, 2278
  juvenile 49
  measuring 820
  see also homicide; rape
Virchow, R. 321, 2067, 2087, 3375
Virgil 174
Virgin Mary 335, 441
Virginia School 3177
virginity 2793
Virilio, P. 2692, 3566, 3570, 4330, 4332
virology 2079
virtual communities 628, 1643, 2333, 2923
virtual consumption 745
virtual organizations 2202, 2750, 3566
Virtual Reality 3110
virtual sex 965, 3569
virtual sports 5208–11
virtuality 4333–4
  see also simulation and virtuality
visa systems 2262
visual consumption 769–72
  and semiotics 769
visual culture 755–6
visual impairment 104
visual narratives 3725
visual sociology 755, 1998, 2971–2, 2986–9
visual studies, and "big science" 916
visualization, guided 631
vital registration systems 1013, 1040
vitamin theory 5090–1
Vitt, L. A. 533–7, 981–4, 1759–62
vocational education 1328, 1399
voice, issues of 3296
voicemail 3279
Volga Germans 1451
Volosinov, V. N. 918
Voltaire, F. M. A. de 155, 857

voluntarism 2680
  technological voluntarism 1160
voluntary association 3075–6
voluntary organizations 3340–3
voluntary simplicity movement 685, 729, 745
volunteer sampling 3782
volunteerism 2593, 2594, 2597
  altruism 3681
  casual volunteering 2598
  sports events 4709
Voss, K. 2518–21
voting behavior
  church interventions 4142
  class differentials 549–50, 551–4, 3451, 4812–13
  and culture wars theory 4262
  learning model 3795
  media influences 3468, 3780
  and the political machine 3445
  social indicators 4420
  sociological perspective 2564
  spatial theory of voting 3434
Voting Rights Act 1965 370, 510, 3747
voyeurism, and cultural tourism 920
Vromen, S. 2047–8
Vryan, K. D. 2216–20

Wachs, F. L. 709–12
Wachtel, P. 2192
Waco siege 886, 3047
Waddell, T. 1134
Waddington, I. 1751, 2091–5
Wafi, Ali Abd al-Wahid 2461
wage
  age-dependent 1929
  gender bias 1844
  immigrants 3025, 3027, 3028, 3029
  minimum wages 2510
  nenko chingin 3170–2
  performance-related 2291
  women with high incomes 1883
wage calculation system 1308
wage gap 1721, 1844, 1859, 5285
  gendered 1724, 2112, 2309, 2310, 2620
  and the heterosexual imaginary 2110
  married men 1882
  and masculine characteristics 2214
  racial/ethnic 3761
  sex-based wage gap and comparable worth
    4189–91, 4203
  single men 1882
  teachers 4952

wage penalty 1882, 1883, 5286
wage restraint 1416
Wagner Act 1935 2288, 2519
Wagner, D. G. 1524–8, 4976–9
Wagner, J. 2986
Wagner, M. W. 2222–5
Wagner, P. 3070
Wagner, Richard 3213
Wagner-Pacifici, R. 959
Wahabism 184
WAIS III intelligence test 2359
Waites, M. 4244–7
Wal-Mart 907, 1059, 1382, 3270, 4306
Walby, S. 1607
Waldby, C. 2172
Waldinger, R. 1460
Waldschmidt, A. 1168–71
Wales 4188
Walker, A. 306, 308, 3088, 3119, 5257
Walker, G. 1311–14
Walker, H. A. 1512–15, 1537–41
Walker, J. 451–5
Walker, L. E. 2569
Walker, Madam C. J. 708
Walker, R. 1553, 1677
Walkerdine, V. 611
Wall, K. 2252–5
Wall Street Crash 2747
Wallace, M. 307, 308
Wallerstein, Immanuel 360–3, 2489–92
    and global exchange structures 1295
    materialist analysis 2838
    and the nation-state 3139
    world-systems theory 144, 351, 1060, 1069,
        1395, 1944, 1961–2, 2135, 2491
Wallis, R. 3205
Walnut Street Jail 802, 3640
Walras, L. 1304–5, 2441, 2776, 2777, 2778,
        3360, 4059–60
Walster, E. 2391, 2672
Walter, J. 3441–5
Walton, J. 947
Walton, R. 2179
Walzer, M. 1177
Walzer, S. 3103–5
Wanamaker, J. 1057
waqf 1317
war 335, **5213–16**
    bilateral wars 1885
    civil wars 1885
    and the civilizing process 531
    and critical theory 874

    demographic consequences 1030
    empire-building wars 1885, 1911
    gendered aspects 1885–8
    and genocide 1910
    and human rights 2183
    and martyrdom 2801
    media role 2878–9
    modernity and 525
    and political long cycles 2491
    post-war trauma 1887
    and reparations 3876
    science and technology 3038
    sexual abuse of women 1885–7
    sporting matches as substitute for 531
    women combatants 1885
    see also revolutions
war crimes tribunals 1048
war criminals 827
war injuries 1169
war invalids 1169
war of maneuver 2228
war of position 2228
War on Poverty 1613, 1679, 2848, 3255,
        3592
War on Terror 228, 681, 1404, 1967, 3383,
        3602, 3913, 4971
    media role 2879
    and millenarianism 3047
    Scientology and 4118
Warbasse, J. 2932
Warburg, M. 159
Ward, Lester Frank 130, 655, 2039, 3227,
        3228–9, **5216**
Wardwell, Walter 630
Warhol, Andy 518, 739, 1361, 2124
warlords 1472
Warman, A. 340
Warner, Amos Griswold 2170
Warner, Andrew 684
Warner, B. D. 4395–8
Warner, J. 3609
Warner, L. 3621
Warner, M. 3728
Warner, S. 2532
Warner, W. Lloyd 535, 545, 971, 1190, 1996
    and the Chicago School 445
    and race relations 129
Warnke, G. 2215
Warren, E. 369
Warren, K. 1274, 1275
warships 3038
Warshow, R. 1755

Washington, Booker T.
  and black education 605
  and Du Bois 1243, 1245
  racial accommodation strategy 7, 9, 129
Washington Consensus 1061, 1295–6, 1945,
  3178
Waskful, D. 965
Wasserman, J. 2067–72, 4533–7
Wasson, L. 432–3, 1378–82, 2214–15, 3136–7,
  3410–11, 4574–5, 4626–9
waste, excess, and second-hand
  consumption 5217–21
Watch Tower Bible and Tract Society 2439,
  2440
water pollution 1418, 3533
Watergate 3037, 3603
Waters, Muddy 3492, 3493
Watson, J. B. 1749, 2187
Watson, J. L. 723
Watson, James 2171
Watson, John B. 256–7
Watsuji, T. 1287
Watts, D. 1312
Watts, R. 1652
wave hypothesis 1556, 5281–2
Way, S. 4019–23
weak ties (strength of) 315, 2903, 5222–5
  and market behaviors 2784
  and networks 2743, 3184
Weakland, J. 248
Weakliem, D. L. 3063–4
wealth 5225–6
  collective wealth 2312
  conservation 1385
  definition 2311
  determinants 2312
  distribution 1302, 1311, 1544, 2356
  economic and material functions 2311
  inherited wealth 1200
  national wealth 2312
  personal wealth 2311, 2312
  short-term manipulation 1385
  wage income–wealth interaction 2312–13
wealth-holding 682
wealth inequalities 745, 1544, 1946, 1959,
  2310–13, 2624
  and global justice movements 1977
  and the information society 2330
  race and 3733
wealth taxes 2628
weapons technology 3037–40
Webb, Beatrice 2289, 2510, 4523, 4551

Webb, G. 1175, 2335
Webb, Sidney 2289, 2510, 4523, 4551
Weber, Alfred 176, 1492–3, 1749, 1805
Weber, Marianne 1252, 1358
  and social change 1234, 2766–9
Weber, Max 655, 661, **5226–35**
  and affinity 1352
  and alienation 609, 664
  and appropriation and property 3678
  Aron and 176
  and asceticism 187
  and authority systems 226, 2585, 2586
  biography 5226–7
  and bureaucracy 313, 376, 377, 378, 428,
    437, 664, 704, 1176, 1441, 2202, 2355,
    2747, 3281, 3287, 3311–12, 3442, 3459,
    3597, 3808–9, 5230–1
  and Calvinism 750
  and capitalism 187, 391–2, 516–17, 1320,
    1352, 2745, 3072, 3075
  and charisma 182, 259, 414, 433–6, 437,
    3049, 3543
  and Chinese religion 668
  and Christianity 477
  and the church 483, 484
  church–sect theory 4136, 4137
  and the city 500, 765
  and the civilizing process 530
  and class 533, 534, 535, 538, 2645
  and class consciousness 540
  comparative historical sociology 2133,
    2134, 3344
  and conflict theory 662, 663
  and Confucianism 3096
  and connubium 674
  and consciousness of kind 2060
  and consumption 1963
  and cults 884
  economic sociology 1318, 2781–2, 2783,
    2785, 2786, 3803, 5228–31
  and economy and culture 932–3
  and education 1323
  and embeddedness concept 4400
  and emotions 1384
  and empiricism 1397
  and ethnicity 1457, 3479
  European city model 493
  and friendships 1798
  historical-comparative methology 2767
  and ideal type concept 2201–2, 2678, 5228
  and industrial capitalism 3550
  and industrialization 2298

Weber, Max (*cont'd*)
  interpretive sociology 2969
  and the labor market 3286
  and law 2583
  and law–economy relationship 2557
  and leadership 2565
  and legitimate authority 229, 3463,
    3464, 4726
  and life chances 2628
  and lifestyles 2061, 2644–5
  and money 3078, 3079
  musicology 3129, 3415
  and nationalism 1457, 3146, 3147, 3154
  and Nietzsche 3213–14
  and Orthodoxy 3349
  and the plantation system 3420
  political party theory 3452
  political sociology 3458–9
  power, typology of 2443, 3597
  and primary patriarchalism 2858
  and Protestant ethic 186–7, 750, 815, 1293,
    1397, 2294, 2298, 2768, 2786, 2997, 3631,
    3691, 3692, 3808, 5231–3
  and rational capitalism 1319
  and rational legal authority 3805–6
  rationalization theory 874, 1148–9, 2133,
    2561, 2758, 2928, 3621, 3803, 3807,
    3808–10, 3866–7
  and religion 2699, 3344, 3524, 3856, 3865,
    3866–7, 3872–3, 3874
  and religious worldviews 1307
  and role of law and state power 2561
  and social change 4363
  social power analysis 2647–8
  sociological vision of history 143
  sociology of science 4109
  status theories 533, 702, 774, 2629, 4750
  stratification theory 535, 2648, 4819–20
  value neutrality 2767
  and *Verstehen* 2535, 2973, 3631, 5187–8
  and written text 1213
Webster, F. 2327
Webster, M. 4987–93
wedding ceremonies 3729
wedding planning 753
Wedgwood, Josiah 743
Weeden, K. 3244–7
Weeks, J. 1033–8, 1364–6, 2157, 2160, 2161,
  2705–8
Weick, K. E. 2733, 3282
Weigert, A. J. 2220

Weiler, B. 147–50, 321–3, 908–10, 2038–40,
  2704–5, 3102–3, 3669–71, 3771–3,
  3810–12, 4390–2, 4884–6
Weinberg, A. 275, 276
Weinberg, D. 63–4, 4386–90, 4720–1
Weinberg, G. 2152, 2154
Weinberg, M. S. 1127, 2159
Weininger, E. B. 887–92
Weinrich, U. 281
Weinstein, R. M. 994–9, 2693–6, 5014–16
Weisburd, D. 1427
Weiss, O. 4680–1
Weitz, T. A. 3651–6
Weitzer, R. 1659–62
Weitzman, E. A. 645–50
Weitzman, L. 1628
Weizsäcker, C. F. von 1758
Wejnert, B. 1003
welfare capitalism 392–3, 2724
welfare dependency and welfare underuse
  5235–8
  and family poverty 1613, 1627
  and lone-parenthood 2664
  and public housing 3708
  social service 4521–4
  and workfare programs 1705
welfare disability programs 995
welfare economics 3361–2
welfare fraud 5238–41
welfare queens 3650, 3748
welfare regimes 5241–2
  Aid to Families with Dependent Children
    (AFDC) 1617, 1884
  conservative regime 4366
  and functional analysis 1809
  liberal regime 4366
  masculine/feminine programs 1720
  social democratic regime 4366
  Temporary Aid for Needy Families (TANF)
    1884
  under deregulation 2513
welfare service delivery, by voluntary
  organizations 3342
welfare state 2296, 4553, 5011, 5090, **5242–6**
  aging and social policy 85
  allocation 5245
  and carework 403
  child support regimes 453–4
  childcare provision 457
  and communities 619
  conservatism 679

and disability 1168, 1169
and the disciplinary society 1177
and elder care 1902, 1903, 1904
and flawed consumers 700
functional alternative to personal wealth 2312
and household economies 1386
and ideology 2231
and immigration 2255–6
and institution of marriage 675
institutionalist approach 4492–3
Keynesian welfare state 1298
and laborism 2526
liberal welfare states 86
macroeconomic efficiency 5246
migration regulation 2256
and neoliberalism 1178
quantitative approach 4492
redistribution 5244–5
and reductions in income inequality 2558
social policy 4490–4
sustainability 1904
welfare reform 1722
welfare socialism 4553
welfare state, retrenchment of 4367, 4494,
    5247–9
and aging and social policies 88
and materialist feminisms 2843
welfare to work strategies 1705
well-being
    age-related changes 97
    forms of 96
    later life 80, 82–3, 96–8
    and social support 89
    subjective well-being 80, 82–3
Welles, Orson 218
Wellman, B. 620, 4482–4
wellness clinics 752
wellness movement 1522
Wells, A. S. 4034–9
Wells, H. G. 1489, 3495, 3497, 3779
Wells, I. B. 2621
Weltanschauung 2757, 2758, 3154
    see also worldviews
Welzel, C. 3071–8, 3075, 3076, 3077
Wernet, C. A. 4938–9
Wernick, A. 1930
Wesley, John 3692
West, B. 3543
West, Candace 1216–17, 2820
West, Carolyn 309
West, Cornel 897, 3611

West, K. 3557
West, M. A. 4945–50
West, T. 309
Westher Underground 1166
Westin Bonaventure Hotel, Los Angeles 759
Westley, W. A. 2159
Westney, F. E. 1968
Weston, K. 2161
Westover, J. H. 1206–10
Westwood, G. 2158
Wheeler, G. C. 2141
Whelan, C. T. 2369
Whewell, W. 1555
Whigs 680
whistle blowing 1440
white Anglo-Saxon Protestants (WASPS) 137,
    2701
White Aryan Resistance 2049
White, C. 952
White, D. M. 1755
white flight 316, 619, 767, 2419, 3733, 3753,
    5139
White, Harrison 1760, 2856
White, Howard 952
White, J. 1630
White, M. J. 5109–12, 5134–8
"white man's burden" 1505, 2267, 2755
white supremacists 777, 2398, 2755, 2838,
    3746, 3767, 3769, 4115
    maternal rhetoric 2848
    and millenarianism 3047
    see also Ku Klux Klan
white-collar crime 543, 820, 3738, 4132, 4901
    cybercrime 960–1
    and deviance 1084, 1102, 1124
    media portrayal 1109
    and organized crime 834
Whitehead, A. N. 640, 2144, 3366
Whitehead, J. T. 818–22
Whitehead, N. L. 2282
whiteness **5249–51**
    and assimilation 195
    deconstruction 1225
    and majorities 2701
    and manifest destiny doctrine 2755
    and Michael Jackson 3508, 3509
    stereotypes 3737
whiteness literature 195
Whittam, F. 2159
Whittier, D. K. 4122–3
Whittier, N. 1872–5, 2604, 3775

whole wage system 3081–2
Wholey, D. R. 2065–6
Whooley, O. 586–8
Whorf, B. L. 2537
Whyte, M. K. 1405
Whyte, W. F. 2411, 2457
Whyte, W. W. 2031
Wicca 3875
Wickham-Crowley, T. 3908, 3909
Wicksell, K. 1304, 1305, 2780
Wicksteed, P. 1304, 2441–2, 2777
widowhood 1037, **5251–3**
  and the oldest old 2668
Wiedenhoft, W. A. 1056–9, 3584–5
Wieder, D. L. 2176–7
Wiener, N. 2325–6
Wieser, F. 1304, 1305, 2776
wife burning 4214
wife-beating *see* domestic violence
Wight, V. 1038–45
Wigstock 1225
Wilcox, M. M. 4275–80
Wildavsky, A. 1283
Wilde, A. W. 1005
Wilde, Oscar 1365
wilderness preservation 1273, 1429, 1431
Wilensky, H. 3287, 3663
Wilkes, R. 2198
Wilkins, L. 1136, 1275, 3543
Wilkins, M. 2171
Wilkinson, J. H. 2831
Wilkinson, R. 1471
Wilkinson, S. 2611
Willaime, J.-P. 3408–9, 3688–94
Willcox, W. 1615
Willems, P. 1733
Willer, D. 1353, 1512, 1537–41, 3604
William of Ockham 1087
William, Prince 415
Williams, Bernard 3541
Williams, Brad 1073–5
Williams, Christine 1848–52
Williams, Christopher R. 665–8
Williams, D. R. 900
Williams, F. P. 255–6, 2662–3
Williams, G. 2246
Williams, G. C. 292
Williams, H. P. 2171
Williams, J. E. 270–3, 2865–8, 3783–7, 4341–2, 4398–9
Williams, M. 1947–50

Williams, Raymond 897, 928, **5253–4**
  and Birmingham School 298, 300, 913, 5253
  and consumer culture 1963
  and elites 1361
  and mass society 2823
  and the new left 3192
  and technological determinism 2879
Williams, Rhys H. 954–7
Williams, Roger 3692
Williams, Rosalind 743
Williams, S. M. 2466
Williams, W. 2152
Williamson, J. 758
Williamson, O. 2344, 2355, 3326, 3352
Williamson, R. 1317
Willie, C. 2837
Willis, Ellen 677
Willis, Evan 630
Willis, L. A. 2078–81
Willis, P. 298, 866, 910, 911, 914, 2117
Willis, S. 611
Willmott, P. 1576, 1578
Wills, J. E. 1966
Wilmoth, J. 67–71
Wilson, B. 1051, 3047, 3204
Wilson, D. C. 2729, 4784–9
Wilson, E. O. 292, 1504, 1507, 1508
Wilson, H. 2290
Wilson, J. Q. 837
Wilson, M. 309
Wilson, N. H. 3915–17
Wilson, William Julius 445, 994, 1613, 1734, 2306
Wilson, Woodrow 3147, 3174, 3672, 4166
Wilterdink, N. 2310–13
Wilton, T. 2609–14, 2611
Wimber, J. 440
Wimmer, A. 345–7
win/lose scenarios 2717
Winant, H. 2396, 5249–51
Winch, P. 2108
Wincup, E. 26–7, 1236–7
Windelband, W. 3363
Windolf, P. 1363
wine tourism 921
Winston, B. 1212
Winter, S. G. 3329
Wirth, Louis 320, 3944
  and the Chicago School 443, 443, 714, 1597
  and the ghetto 1937, 3888
  urban sociology 501, 636, 5151–2

Wisconsin model of status attainment 1337, 1529, 1530
Wiseley, N. 3678–82
Wiseman, J. 320
witch-hunts 1089, 1115, 2696
witchcraft 2699
Withey, S. 625
within-person change 77
Wittfogel, K. 865
Wittgenstein, Ludwig 1251, 1257, 2108, 2539
Wittig, M. 2155
Witz, A. 736
Wohl, R. 2921
Wolf, D. 1129, 1702, 1704
Wolf, K. 3799–802
Wolfe, A. 3232
Wolfe, D. 2770–1
Wolfe, T. 775, 1190
Wolfendden Report 2610
Wolfenstein, M. 1754
Wolff, F.-C. 2633
Wolff, K. 161, 776–9, 902–8, 951–2, 2618–22, 2976–8, 3558–63, 3696–700, 4149–50, 4789–91
Wolfinger, R. 3445
Wolfowitz, P. 3175
Wolfson, M. 1098
Wollstoncraft, Mary 1845, 2618, **5254–7**
  and first wave feminism 1666
  and materialism 2837
Wolmark, J. 3496
womanism 1666, 3119, **5257–9**
  and intersectionality 2395
women
  and adult education 1330
  and agism 58
  in animal rights movement 140
  bifurcated consciousness 274
  biological definitions 905
  commodification 711
  and drug use 26
  economic independence 1207
  and educational attainment 1335
  empowerment 5273–5
  female gangs 1826–7, 1857, 1858, 2820
  and grassroots movements 1429
  health 52–66
  and household consumption 609
  and leisure 2589, 2592, 2593
  marginality 2763
  and marital infidelity 2324, 2325

militarized women 1887
  as Other 253, 331, 333
  and religion 939, 1053, 1315, 1600, 5265–6
  retirement income needs 87
  in science 5267–8
  self-construction 712
  sexuality 254, 333, 904, 1678, 2611, 2613, 5268–72
  status in Southeast Asian society 4378–9
  subjecthood 336, 712
  subordination of 1689, 1846, 1874, 1892, 2100, 2112, 2396, 2627
  see also women in the labor market
Women of All Red Nations (WARN) 2283, 3118
women of color feminism 2621, 3117–20
Women and Development Unit (WAND) 1854–5
women in development (WID) 1852, 1853, 1854, 1869, 4995
women, economy and 5259–62
  law–economy relation 2559
  and the service sector 2383
women, information technology and (Asia) 5262–5
women in the labor market 1202, 1203, 1205, 1207, 1208, 1249, 1272, 1343, 1601, 1648, 1844, 1880, 2516, 3288, 4800
  in Asia 1158
  and conservatism 1868
  and depression 2951
  earning potential 2415, 2416, 2417
  earnings differentials 1343
  economic independence hypothesis 1734
  ethnic minority women 2517
  and family conflict 1581
  and family demography 1588
  and family migration 1606, 1607, 1608
  and family size restriction 1732
  female tied migrant thesis 1606, 1607, 1608
  feminization of the labor force 1399
  and the Industrial Revolution 2296
  and labor market dualism 1249
  lone mothers 2665, 2951
  maternal labor force participation 1601
  migrant women 3032–3, 3536
  occupational segregation 1341
  office ladies (Japan) 3251–4
  part-time work 1844
  pink-collar occupations 2620, 4190
  prestige scores 1341

women in the labor market (*cont'd*)
  and risk of marital dissolution 1208, 2415
  second shift 1203, 1248, 1669, 1881,
    2619–20
  stratified reproduction 4827
  wage penalty 1882, 1883
  and welfare service provision 4368
  and work/family incompatibility 1732
  working mothers 1247, 1341, 1579, 1601,
    1880, 2308, 2463
  see also sex work; wage gap
women, religion and 5265–7
  Judaism 2452
women in science 5267–8
women, sexuality and 5268–73
  late-life sexuality 2540, 2541, 2542
  Victorian ethos 2682
women-identified women 2602
Women-in-Black movement 1848
Women's Christian Temperance Union
  (WCTU)
women's empowerment 5273–5
women's health 5275–9
  experience of illness 1864–5
  and medical sociology 2935
  see also maternal mortality
women's liberation movement 1675, 1693,
  2619, 2620, 2621
  see also feminism, first, second, and third
  waves
women's movements 5279–84
  and collectivities 2029
  consciousness-raising 677
  consumer activism 697
  feminist movements 5280–1
  gender issues 1872–5
  Latin American feminism 1685–9, 1873
  and maternalism 2847
  mobilization 5281
  see also feminism; pro-choice and pro-life
  movements
women's rights branch of feminism 1675
women's studies programs 1675, 1678
Wong, J. 1075
Woo-Cummings, M. 1074, 1075
Wood, E. M. 2268
Wood, H. 2921–3
Wood, R. 507
Wood, S. 363–5
Woods, B. 275–7, 3037–40, 3436–9
Woods, Tiger 4682, 4716
Woodson, C. G. 3265

Wooldredge, J. 861–4
Woolgar, S. 1091, 2525, 2846, 4096
Word of Faith 440
work *see* careers; employment; labor markets
work ability 105
work motivation 2748
work performance
  age-related declines 103–5
  and group dynamics 2747
  measuring 103
  technological change, effects of 103
work satisfaction 2748
work, sociology of 2748, 5284–7
  career development 1142
  dual-earner couples 1247–9
  Fordism/post-Fordism 1769–70
  and the Hawthorne studies 2050–1
  and the professions 2076
  work–leisure–family balance 2591
  and workers' participation in management
    (WPM) 2752–4
work–family balance 811, 1579, 1594, 1880,
  2181, 5286
  immigrant families 2254
work–leisure relationship 2588, 2591
  extension pattern 2588
  neutrality pattern 2588
  opposition pattern 2588
worker consciousness 2746
worker participation 2511
worker productivity 2713
worker solidarity 2288, 2292
worker training 1328
workers' councils 407, 1861, 2753
Workers' Education Association 914
workers' movements 2829
workers' ownership and control (WOC) 2753,
  2754
workers' participation in management (WPM)
  2752–4
  offline (problem solving) teams 2753
  online (semi-autonomous work) teams 2753
workfare programs 1705
workforce flexibility 2749
Workforce Investment Act 19998 (US) 105
workforce mobilization 2750
workforce motivation 2750
workhouses 1169
working class
  Americanization 2649
  and black urban regime 310, 311, 312
  black women 308

bodily efficiency 325
British 1410
and capitalism 394
and class theory 534–5
collective action 1308
and communism 1201
conformist values 3076
and consumption 701, 765–6, 1057, 1851
culture 911, 914, 4807
and the culture industry 897
and democracy 100, 1003
diets 721
embourgeoisement 351
and environmental hazards 1419
exploitation of 538, 663, 840, 841, 1543
false consciousness 1568–9
and fascist aesthetics 325
"feminization" 2649
friendships 1792, 1796
gambling 1819
habitus 2648
heterogeneity 538
homogeneity 539
labor power 609, 703
leisure activities 761
Nazi authoritarianism, acceptance of 1569
politics 914, 2234
poverty 1612
proletariat 1569
resurgence 705
social mobility 911
and social transformation 1201
and socialism 1201
and sport 336, 4706
subcultures 912
values 299
voting behavior 551, 552, 2234
working-class consciousness 539
youth subcultures 719
working hours 1032, 1033, 2513, 2629
working-class movements 614, 2687
workplace
age discrimination 1842
alcoholism in 118
cross-sex friendship in 878, 879
emotional climate 1880
equality in 937
families of workers 1880
gender inequality 2308, 3649
generic descriptions of 1485
interaction studies 2364
new workplace complexity 536

racial discrimination in 41
role-playing 3950
self-direction 1868
sexism in 878, 2702
state regulation 4737–40
worker behavior 1880, 1881
see also glass ceiling
workplace accidents 1169
workplace crime 3305
workplace diversity 5287–91
workplace harassment 1440
workplace policies 1248–9
works councils 4739–40
World Anti-Doping Agency 1239, 1240
World Bank 349, 603, 745, 1294, 1945, 1956
and accountability 1960
and AIDS pandemic 107
anti-poverty policies 3592
cultural imperialism 907
and decolonization 986
development projects 1948
economic globalization strategies 1852
and education initiatives 1974
and female status 1339
Human Development Index (HDI) 1001
loans 1960, 2382
neoclassical economic precepts 1295
and neoliberalism 1948
and NGOs 3212
organizational deviance 3304
poverty measures 3588
protests against 1977, 1978
schooling model 1324
and sustainable development 1419
World Center for Women's Archives 250
world conflict 5291–5
see also war
World Economic Forum 1960, 1978
World Education Forum 1974
World Fertility Survey (WFS) 1013, 1040, 3100
world government 1952
World Health Organization (WHO)
and disability classifications 1168
and female genital mutilation 1653–4
and female status 1339
health, definition of 2078
infant and child health programs 2317
and infertility 2321
nutritional standard 1158
world images 1969
World Indigenous Games 3548
world music 2284

World Social Forum 1949, 1978, 3195, 3212, 3913, 5062
World Trade Center, terrorist attack 1062, 1175, 2888, 4971
  civilian-initiated evacuation 1367
  conservatism and 681
  and global media 2888, 3470
  and neoconservatism 3174
  sexual and religious imagery 4279
World Trade Organization (WTO) 349, 745, 1048, 1115, 1945, 1948–9, 1956, 2890
  anti-war and peace movements and 161
  and democratic accountability 1947
  and global justice movement 1948
  protests against 981, 1115, 1947, 1948, 1977, 1978
  Seattle protests 1977
World War I 874, 1885
  and balkanization 239
  and disability history 1169
  nationalistic cataclysm 3147
  science and technology 3038
  and Taylorism 2712
World War II
  and balkanization 239
  and the life course, effects on 2636
  military science 3038
  and military sociology 3041
World Wide Fund for Nature (WWF) 1284, 1429
World Wide Web
  and adult education 1329
  and digital capitalism 1162
  and information technology 2333
  and visual consumption 771
  see also Internet
world-cultural models 1967
world-economy 360, 361, 363
world-systems theory *see* dependency and world-systems theories
World's Fairs 743, 767
worldviews
  capitalist 2758
  Catholic 3520, 3572, 3573
  competition between 2758
  conservative 2758
  holistic 2757
  pantheistic 3164
  paradigms 3356
  socialist 2758
  utopian 2758
Worsley, P. 2764, 3047
Worth, H. 106–11

Worthen, B. 1498
Wortmann, S. 581–3, 3612–13, 4200–13
Wouters, C. 2681, 2681–5
Wrenn, M. 2493–7
Wright, C. 3609
Wright, D. 3118
Wright, Earl 604–5
Wright, E. O. 536, 2816, 2838, 3179
Wright, J. 3707–11
writing as method 5296–8
  see also author/auteur
writing and speech 1213
Wunder, D. F. 4566–8
Wuthnow, R. 507, 743, 751, 1052
Wykes, A. 1820

X Games 4653–5
xeno-racism 5299
Xenophanon of Colophon 197, 3669
xenophobia 1454, 1487, **5299–300**
  and immigrants 2260
  and refugees 3838
Xerox Corporation 731

Yair, G. 127–8, 2954–8
Yamada, M. 2438
Yamane, D. 506–7
Yamane, H. 237
Yanagita, Kunio 1406, **5301–5**
Yang, G. 1389–92
Yashiv, E. 3028
Yearley, S. 1418
Yeh, Y. 812–15
Yemen 1654
yin and *yang* 4926
Yinger, J. M. 885, 1052, 4137–8
YMCA 1877
yoga 752, 2080
Yom Kippur 2452
Yoneyama, T. 1401
Yoon, S.-Y. 1692
York, R. 1423–6
Yoshida, T. 2325–6
Yoshimura, M. 42–5, 1715–17
Yoshino, K. 1406–7, 3057–60, 3217–21
Young, A. 2777
Young Hegelians 1408, 1748, 2837
Young, J. 2832, 3089, 3197
Young, J. T. 1184–7
Young, K. 220, 2093, 2221, 5199–226
Young, M. 2954, 3937
Young Men's Christian Association 2120

young old 1904
Young Rifai, H. A. 2342
Young, T. R. 3440
Young Turk Revolution 2000
Young Turks 2000, 2001
Youngreen, R. 2615–18
youth/adolescence 5305–8
youth culture
   black American 809
   and the charismatic movement 441
   counterculture 809, 885, 2823
   dating code 2683
   neotribalism 2691
   rituals of resistance 3937
   subcultures 897, 2102, 2103, 5306
youth culture and consumption 694, 773–6
   and the body beautiful 325
   commodification 719
   economic power 773, 774
   girls' consumption 724–7
   proletarianization 704
   working-class subcultures 719
youth mentoring programs 2743
youth movements 1903, 5149
   see also student movements
youth sport 5308–11
youth transitions tradition 5306–7
Yu, J. 620–3
Yugoslav wars 1451, 1458
   ethnic cleansing 3108
   international military operations 3317
   mass killings 1909
   post-war tribunals 1912
Yugoslavia 239, 976
   collapse of 660, 1487
   partitioning 3020
Yuill, R. 3385–7
Yukichi, F. 2802
yuppies 810

Zackodnik, T. 3266
Zafirovski, M. 1300–6, 2441–3, 2775–88
Zaire 3907
Zalay, B. 2756
Zald, M. N. 697
Zambia 1724
Zamiatin, Y. 3495
Zangwell, I. 2944
Zanna, M. P. 562
Zapata, E. 414
Zapatistas 981, 1948, 1949, 1992, 2279, 3911,
   3913, 3914

Zaplin, R. 1857
zaps 2603
Zealots 2800, 3048
Zeiss, R. 687–93, 2844–6, 2845
Zelditch, M. 2856
Zelditch, N. 990
Zelinksy, W. 3018
Zelizer, V. 738, 934, 1309, 1322, 3079, 3080
Zen Buddhism 750, 1286
Zeni, J. 1442–7
Zenteno, R. B. 2950
Zerelli, S. 4558–63
zero population growth 972, 3526
zero tolerance
   policing 825, 826, 2152
   public housing policy tool 3709, 3710
   and school discipline 4021
zero-hour contracts 2514
zero-sum games 1822, 2717, 2753, 3927, 4091
Zerubavel, E. 4134
Zetkin, C. 2687, 2838, 2841
Zetterberg, H. L. 2968
Zettl, H. 2891
Zhou, M. 1453, 1462
Zhu Xi 669
Zimbabwe 106
   human rights abuses 165
   public housing 3710
   revolution 3907
Zimbardo, P. 190, 5313–16
Zimbardo Prison Experiment 5313–16
   and conformity 227
Zimmerman, C. 971
Zimmerman, D. H. 1216–17, 2820
Zimring, F. E. 978
Zinn, H. 2043
Zinn, J. 232–3, 2285–6, 2630–2, 3829–30,
   5089–90
Zinzendorf, Count N. L. von 3409
Zionism 2453, 3427
Zippel, K. 4233–4
Zizek, S. 3880–1, 4333–4
Znaniecki, Florian 447, 2960, **5316–17**
   and analytic deduction 134, 3167, 3168
   and attitudes and behavior 199
   and the Chicago School 1597
   documentary method 2407
   and life cycle perspective 2637
Zola, Émile 743, 1058
Zola, I. K. 481
Zolberg, V. 2905
zoning 504, 2078